# EVERYTHING IS PHOTOGRAPH

Production editor: Yvonne E. Cárdenas
Text designer: Julie Fry
This book was set in Kis and Futura.

10 9 8 7 6 5 4 3 2

 Printed in the United States of America on acid-free paper. For information write to Other Press LLC, 267 Fifth Avenue, 6th Floor, New York, NY 10016. Or visit our Web site: www.otherpress.com

Library of Congress Cataloging-in-Publication Data
Names: Albers, Patricia author
Title: Everything is photograph : a life of André Kertész / Patricia Albers.
Description: New York : Other Press, [2026] | Includes bibliographical references and index.
Identifiers: LCCN 2025025504 (print) | LCCN 2025025505 (ebook) | ISBN 9781590515099 hardcover | ISBN 9781590515105 ebook
Subjects: LCSH: Kertész, André | Photographers—United States—Biography | LCGFT: Biographies
Classification: LCC TR140.K4 A43 2026 (print) | LCC TR140.K4 (ebook) | DDC 770.92/2—dc23/eng/20250902
LC record available at https://lccn.loc.gov/2025025504
LC ebook record available at https://lccn.loc.gov/2025025505

# EVERYTHING IS PHOTOGRAPH

## A LIFE OF ANDRÉ KERTÉSZ

Patricia Albers

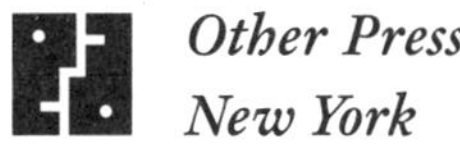

*Other Press*
*New York*

Production editor: Yvonne E. Cárdenas
Text designer: Julie Fry
This book was set in Kis and Futura.

10 9 8 7 6 5 4 3 2 1

 Printed in the United States of America on acid-free paper. For information write to Other Press LLC, 267 Fifth Avenue, 6th Floor, New York, NY 10016. Or visit our Web site: www.otherpress.com

Library of Congress Cataloging-in-Publication Data
Names: Albers, Patricia author
Title: Everything is photograph : a life of André Kertész / Patricia Albers.
Description: New York : Other Press, [2026] | Includes bibliographical references and index.
Identifiers: LCCN 2025025504 (print) | LCCN 2025025505 (ebook) | ISBN 9781590515099 hardcover | ISBN 9781590515105 ebook
Subjects: LCSH: Kertész, André | Photographers—United States—Biography | LCGFT: Biographies
Classification: LCC TR140.K4 A43 2026 (print) | LCC TR140.K4 (ebook) | DDC 770.92/2—dc23/eng/20250902
LC record available at https://lccn.loc.gov/2025025504
LC ebook record available at https://lccn.loc.gov/2025025505

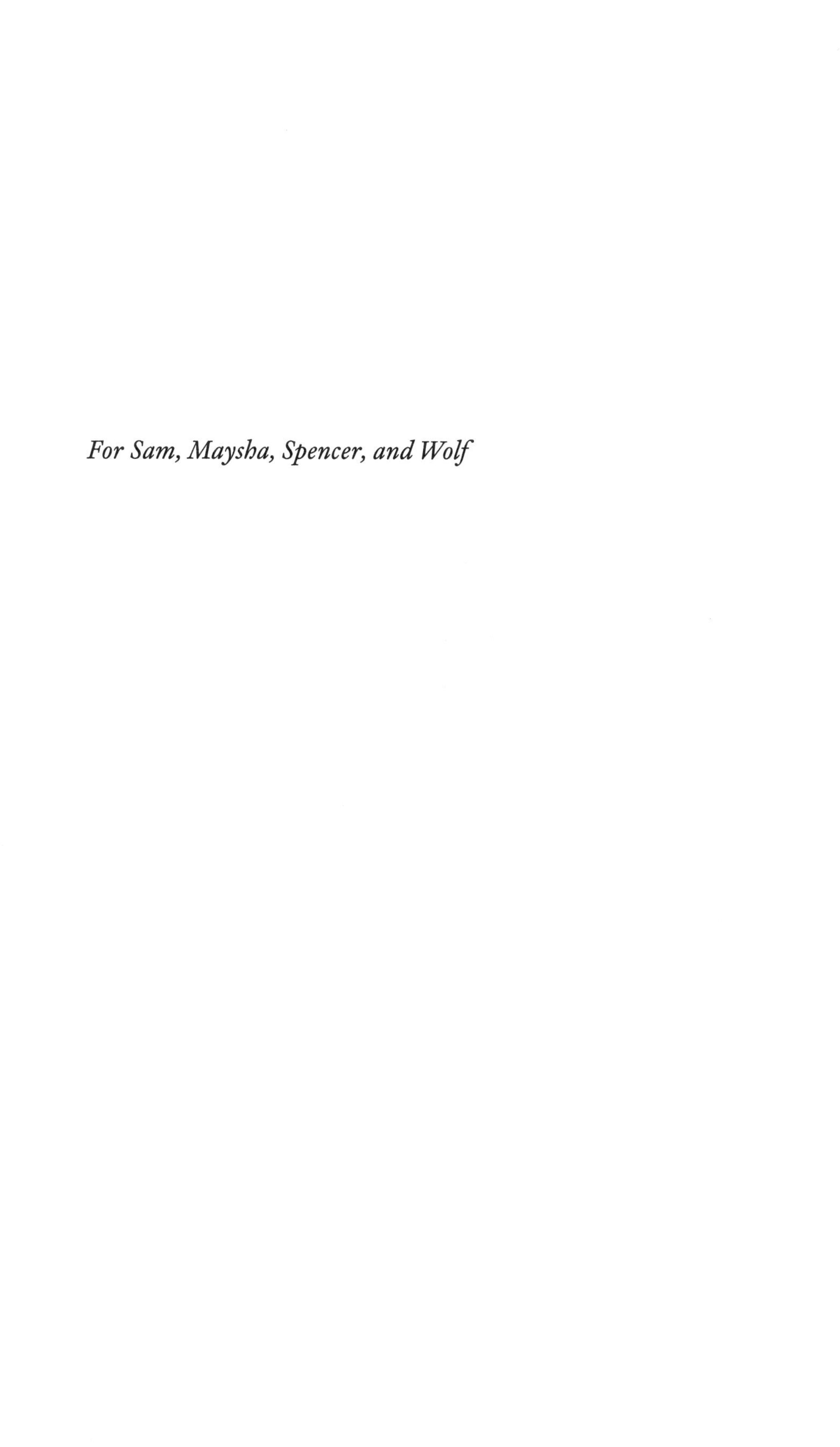

*For Sam, Maysha, Spencer, and Wolf*

This capacity to wonder at trifles no matter the imminent peril, these asides of the spirit, these footnotes in the volume of life are the highest forms of consciousness, and it is in this childishly speculative state of mind, so distant from commonsense and its logic, that we know the world to be good.[1]

—VLADIMIR NABOKOV

We begin to suspect that to grasp Kertész's ungraspable secret would be to grasp the very secret of photography.[2]

—JEAN-CLAUDE LEMAGNY

# CONTENTS

*A Note About the Photographs* xi

Introduction 1

1 Sleeping Boy, 1894–1914 11

2 Forced March to the Front, 1914–1918 45

3 We Lost the War, 1918–1925 77

4 Chez Mondrian, 1925–1927 111

5 Satiric Dancer, 1927–1929 145

6 Clock of the French Academy, 1929–1932 181

7 Elizabeth and I, 1932–1936 213

8 Melancholic Tulip, 1936–1944 247

9 Manhattan Bridge, 1944–1962 283

10 Martinique, 1962–1972 319

11 Flowers for Elizabeth, 1970–1980 357

12 Self-Portrait with Masks, 1979–1985 393

Epilogue 427

*Acknowledgments* 429

*Notes* 433

*Select Bibliography* 499

*Credits* 503

*Index* 505

# A NOTE ABOUT THE PHOTOGRAPHS

**Interpretations of photographs** are always subjective. Context matters. So do the interpreter's experiences, expectations, and inclination, or disinclination, to focus and linger. Like dreams, photographs ultimately deflect description and interpretation. Yet description and interpretation are vital to a biography of one who inhabited his work as fully as André Kertész. I hope that my words will motivate readers to engage with the photographs in their own way.

For each photograph I discuss at length but don't reproduce, I've included an endnote to give information about where readers can find a reproduction. I have prioritized reliable and relatively stable websites. Where none exists at the time of this writing, I have listed a print source.

With few exceptions, Kertész did not title his photographs. Yet curators, editors, and dealers find titles useful in keeping track of a body of work. Thus they often have devised titles. Some photographs have ended up with more than one title. Those taken in quick succession may all bear the same title.

Other photographs are identified by the place and year (or even the exact date) when Kertész took the picture. That was his preferred inventorial method, and he was assiduous about list-making. All the same, he was sometimes wrong about dates, as is revealed by cross-checking primary sources like a weather report or his appointment book. What's more, lists go astray and memories shift. In short, the titles and dates used for his photographs can be inconsistent and confusing.

# EVERYTHING IS PHOTOGRAPH

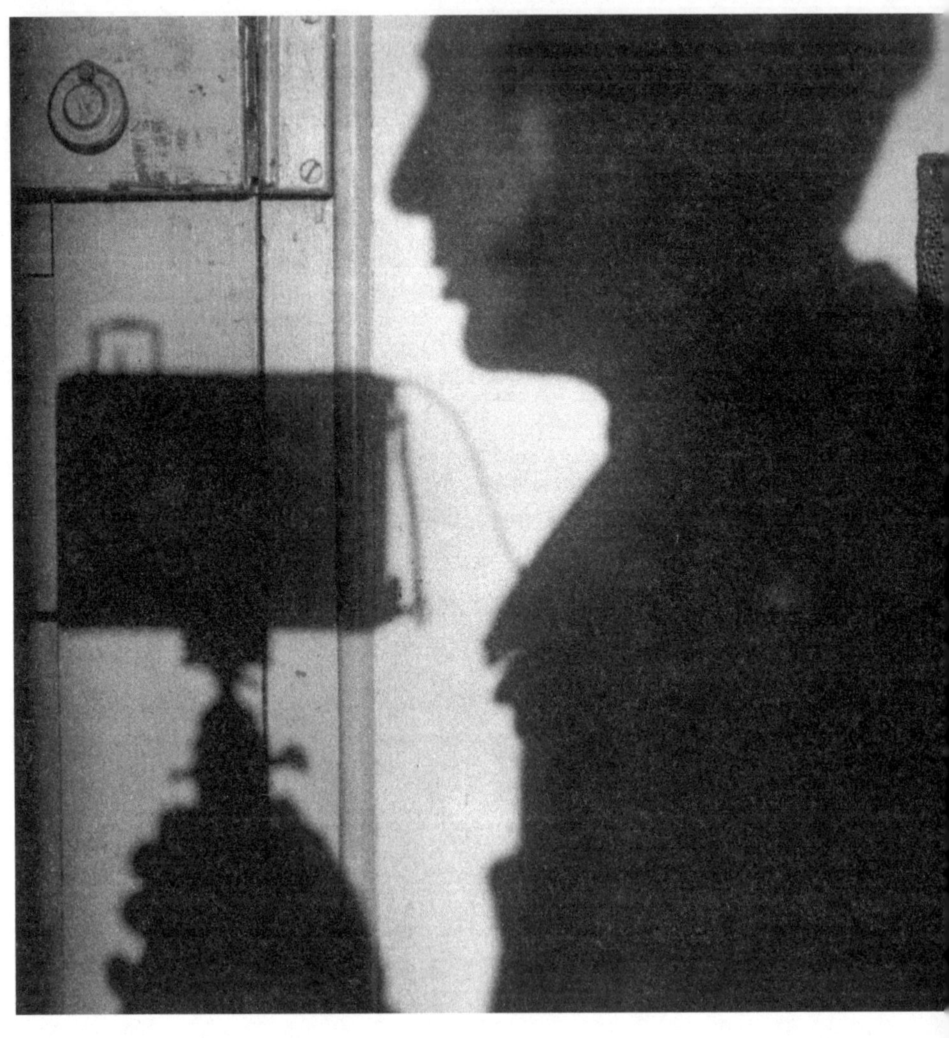

André Kertész, *Self-Portrait, Paris*, 1927

# INTRODUCTION

***Self-Portrait, Paris*** is conjured from practically nothing: parts of a door and a wall, the shadow of the photographer gripping the tripod attached to his camera. A shadow within a shadow, actually, because of the two light sources, one yielding an ordinary profile, the other, an oafish umbra. Tucked into the picture's upper-left corner is the only material object: the box lock on the door. The lock resembles a camera, with its covered keyhole as the lens, complete with focusing ring. What's behind that keyhole? The image offers no clues. *Self-Portrait, Paris* is a scene from a shadow play. A meditation on photography, seeing, and self. A nod to the negative-positive process, described by one of its inventors as "the art of fixing a shadow."[1]

Behind the real camera that winter night in 1927 stood a tall, scrawny, thirty-two-year-old transplant to Paris. André Kertész had arrived from his native Hungary sixteen months earlier on a train ticket purchased with a loan from a cousin. Paris represented his best hope to establish himself as a photographer. Whatever that meant. Photographers made their living from studio portraiture, newspaper work, or commercial jobs like supplying pictures for postcards. All that bored André. He wanted a more direct contact with life. But he did need to eat.

He spoke little French, nor did he believe he could learn. He had no savings. Often he skipped meals or made do with bread, butter, and milk, tallying his purchases each night before bed. A baguette cost the equivalent of a nickel, a bottle of milk and cube of butter, fourteen cents. His eyes were irritated. He couldn't sleep through the night, typically only two or three hours. Come afternoon, he might doze off on a park bench. In letters postmarked Budapest, André's family and friends were pleading with him to forget France and come home. As for his Hungarian girlfriend – if she still *was* his girlfriend – she had ordered him not to come home until he made a success of his life. In the eight years since the Great War ended, he had struggled to square his passion for photography with the pressure he felt to achieve worldly success. Yet he'd left Hungary still "a nobody" in his estimation and hers.[2]

From his first hours in Paris, André had drifted through its parks and streets, brimming with inquisitive wonder about this city he was interpreting with his Goerz Tenax, a favorite camera – his companion, his accomplice, almost his double. Locals tended to scurry by this lost-looking foreigner. But a bevy of friends eased his isolation. Nearly all were Paris-savvy émigré artists centered in Montparnasse, mostly Hungarians. André lingered in their studios, admired their art, showed up at their parties. He would photograph, later giving prints to each of his friends. As they arranged themselves for a group picture – some laughing, some draping an arm on a friend's shoulder, one clutching a violin, another a bottle – André would position his camera on a tripod and set the timer, then dash in to include himself, affable, bright-eyed, and grinning.

Most of his days included a stop at the Hungarian table on the terrace of the Café du Dôme, where every free spirit in Paris landed sooner or later. There his pals introduced him around and started a buzz about his unorthodox portraits, still lifes, and urban scenes, which they passed hand to hand. That had brought André a scattering of commissions. Publicity shots for the string quartet led by his friend Feri Roth. Pictures of the Montmartre villa that the Viennese architect Adolf Loos was building for the Dada poet Tristan Tzara. Portraits of a doctor, a dancer, a bibliophile.

The trickle of income had allowed him to rent the seventh-floor walk-up on the rue de Vanves (today the rue Raymond Losserand) in the fourteenth arrondissement, where he took *Self-Portrait, Paris.* A maid's room the size of a small storage space, it had no kitchen, bathroom, or heat. No one would describe the place as charming, even though André would fix it up with pictures, shelves, and linens sent by his mother. He was installing a darkroom. After sixteen months of lugging his belongings from one threadbare hotel or makeshift bedroom to another, borrowing or improvising workspace, his garret represented a victory. He had a door with a lock and a dormer window. He had an aerie. Almost a home. A *French* home.

**Born in Budapest in 1894,** André began photographing at age eighteen. From the start, he did what others did not. When portraiture meant stiff formal poses, he snapped pictures of Roma children cavorting, his relatives schmoozing, and himself racing, jumping, or swimming with his brothers. When photo reporters were taking head shots of politicians, he—by then, the lead photographer for France's most visually audacious magazine—zeroed in on billboards, marionettes, and a fortune teller reflected in her crystal ball. When razor-sharp prints of grandiose landscapes were winning applause, he concentrated on views of waterfronts, park benches, and vacant lots, all slightly grainy. In a century when the photography world revolved around war, social upheaval, outsize personalities, and fashion, he kept his eyes on the commonplace. All his life, André swam against strong tides, claiming the right to photograph as he pleased.

As well as André's subjects, his ideas about what photographers could do were unorthodox. He conceived of the portrait in absence, a still life selected and arranged to express the animating spirit of the objects' owner. He took some two hundred pictures of female nudes reflected in funhouse mirrors, pictures that so disconcerted even his admirers that the work did not receive a solo exhibition until half a century later. And he was the first major photographer to embrace the Leica, the camera now mythically linked to street photography. The practice of prowling the city in a state of heightened visual sensitivity had been around since the nineteenth century, but it took André and his Leica to make it dynamic and modern.

All the while, photography was radically changing. The improved photomechanical technology of the 1920s allowed the expanding European picture press to deliver images straight to the masses. Shifting the spotlight from the photograph as an object seen by a relative few to the photograph as a reproduction embedded in text and seen by hundreds of thousands transformed the medium into a driving social and cultural force. André was there, pioneering subjective photojournalism and delivering what was arguably the world's first great photo essay.

Insisting that he was an "eternal amateur" (read: he would always work as he pleased), André lived and breathed photography for seventy-three years.[3] Even in old age, he stayed curious and inventive, handling light with nimbleness, skill, and joy.

"Whatever we have done," Henri Cartier-Bresson once declared on behalf of himself and other photographers, "Kertész did first."[4] When the two met, Cartier-Bresson would jokingly fall to his knees, hold out his Leica, and beg for a blessing.[5] He was not alone in following André's lead. André coaxed Brassaï into picking up his first camera and taught him how to shoot pictures at night. Robert Capa owed André an even more elemental debt: The older photographer fed the irrepressible youth, gave him a bed when he couldn't afford a hotel, and tutored him in the basics of photojournalism. The German photographer Marianne Breslauer drew inspiration from André's photographs of pedestrians and shadows, the British Bill Brandt, from his distorted nudes.[6] In the 1940s, the young Robert Frank emulated André's agility with the Leica and even poached one of his favorite subjects: Parisian park chairs.[7] Speaking in 1952, the French photographer Willy Ronis declared himself "open-mouthed with admiration" at André's pictures.[8] Robert Doisneau dubbed him "the Master."[9] In the 1960s, Hiroji Kubota and Sylvia Plachy joined the ranks of his protégés. The list goes on: The currents of modernism delivered the practices of André Kertész to photographers far and wide.

So it's startling that his name, unlike those of some he helped and inspired, has faded from public awareness. During the eleven years I was researching and writing this book, my references to André Kertész to people around me most often drew blank looks or questions about how to pronounce his last name. (It's *Ker*tess.)

Even cultural historians are apt to overlook this photographer's photographer. "Make a list of the major American photographers," proposes Ross Wetzsteon in his intellectual history of Greenwich Village, "and compare it to the list of photographers who have lived in the Village: Mathew Brady, Alfred Stieglitz, Edward Steichen, Jessie Tarbox Beals, Man Ray, Berenice Abbott, Walker Evans, Weegee, Margaret Bourke-White, Robert Frank, and Diane Arbus."[10] Nary a mention of André, a naturalized American. Yet André lived in, loved, and photographed the Village for more than three decades. His lyrical images of a snow-blanketed Washington Square count among his signature works.

A gentle and generous man with an unassuming manner, André was endowed with Old World charm and a roguish sense of humor. Yet he lacked the career-propelling joie de vivre of the photographer Jacques Henri Lartigue, the social instincts of Brassaï, the intellectual sophistication of Walker Evans, and the charisma of Robert Capa. Because he never mastered English or French, conversations with him tended to bog down under his interlocutor's strain to understand what he was saying.

Moreover, outraged and aggrieved by the lack of recognition during his first decades in the United States (he moved to New York in 1936), André never let anyone forget how badly he believed he'd been treated. Even though Americans made him rich and famous in the end, he couldn't get the taste of rejection out of his mouth. "Honors Heap on Bitter André Kertész, Decries Lack of Praise," announced a 1980 United Press International dispatch about the latest shower of awards on the eighty-six-year-old.[11] "Given his accomplishments, one would assume

Kertész would be content," comments the reporter. Kertész was not. He took advantage of that interview, and many others, to spew invective at Americans. "Oh, what an irritating man André Kertész was!" shuddered his friend the *New Yorker* writer Brendan Gill.[12]

A bookworm since childhood and a secular Jew, André may or may not have read the memoirs of the Vienna-born Nazi death camp survivor Jean Améry. If not, he should have. Resentment, writes Améry, "nails every one of us onto the cross of his ruined past."[13]

**I discovered André's photographs** in the late 1960s as he was climbing out of the wreckage of his career in America. One afternoon, I stopped by the Paper Place in Iowa City. Run by grad students and open until midnight, it was the kind of bookshop where nobody cared if you settled in with a title you had no intention of buying. The one that gripped my attention that day was the Czech art historian Anna Fárová's paperback *André Kertész*. I'd never heard of him.

I opened to a vignette from belle epoque Budapest. A couple occupies a leafy bower, the boy leaning in for a kiss. He sports a bow tie; she wears white gloves. I saw bemusement in her porcelain-doll face, ardor in his, and self-consciousness in the gestures that visually knit them together. Elsewhere in Fárová's little book, bodies are in motion. Here, a street acrobat's handstand mirrors the oldfangled chimney pipe on the facing page. There, a flirt pinwheels her legs and arms, mimicking the torqued plaster cast next to the sofa on which she is lounging. The room itself seems to warp. I kept turning pages. Vintage wooden carnival animals. A mysterious man, two distant women, and a broken bench. A flea market's worth of artists' studio clutter.

Until that day, I had never encountered photographs with such emotional resonance. To me, photography meant Kodak cartridges, Instamatic snapshots, and wavy-edged prints, machine-dated and scrapbook ready. It meant amateurish slides shot by my dad, shown with a Kodak Carousel Slide Projector set up on a TV tray and used to narrate stories about family vacations. It meant double-page spreads in *Life* and *Look*, attention-grabbing but seemingly unmediated by anyone's subjective vision. Those by André felt different. Intimate. European. Vaguely melancholic. In gazing at them, I realized—though I didn't word it that way at the time—that photographs could be poetry, not prose.

I bought Fárová's book. It still sits on my desk, dog-eared and loved.

**Picking it up again** some five decades later, I stare at the photograph on page 9, showing an interminable column of foot soldiers snaking across the Ukrainian steppe. André snapped it on July 19, 1915, during World War I. Private André Kertész had been deployed to the Russian front, where the fighting was savage and casualties high. Believing with good reason that he was more likely to die than not, André determined that what mattered most was to "live each of life's moments with pleasure," and, for him, pleasure was synonymous with picture-taking.[14]

From the time he acquired his first camera, he could never imagine himself without one. In later years, his wife would joke that he breakfasted, lunched, and dined photography. The curator and photo historian Jean-Claude Lemagny would dub him *homo photographicus*.[15]

"How did photography influence your life?" a colleague asked the eighty-three-year-old André. He replied: "I would like to turn that question around to ask: how did my life influence my photography."[16]

"How do you decide what to photograph?" This time, it was the cameraman of a PBS crew filming a Kertész documentary who wanted to know. André didn't rule out any subject. "Everything is photograph," he responded.[17]

Between 1912 and 1985 (when he died at age ninety-one, still working), André shot more than a hundred thousand photographs. He treated them, along with his tales about them, as his definitive life story. Ask about a particular image, and he'd launch into the same vague anecdote he'd told dozens of times before. When his words petered out, he would say: "The story is me... is my story."[18]

The diaristic quality of André's work, along with his medium's factuality, lends some weight to his notion that his photographic archive was all the biography anyone needed. Yet André's images, like those of all photographers, are highly selected: what he photographed, which negatives he printed, which prints survive. What's more, photographs never simply reflect how things are. It's tempting to believe that photographers extract fractions of seconds from the flow of life, then serve them up on pieces of paper. In truth, they intervene at each step between reality and the viewer, making choices about camera, lens, aperture, shutter speed, format, framing, focus, and more. Every photograph is both a transcription of the real and an artful construct. It is simultaneously objective and subjective, factual and fictive – not unlike André's stories. Commanding his medium's constructs and codes, he ringmastered an unruly, three-dimensional world into a freshly seen, formally vigorous, emotionally rich, and aesthetically charged visual bounty.

**Over the decades,** legions of curators, photo historians, journalists, and reviewers have scrutinized and interpreted the work of André Kertész. Monographs and catalogs have appeared in Argentina, Britain, France, Germany, Hungary, Israel, Italy, Japan, and the United States. Working within the parameters of their various purposes, interests, and expertise, their authors have tended to privilege one period or another of André's life, whether the Hungarian years (1894–1925), Jazz Age Paris (1925–1936), or mid-twentieth-century New York (1936–1985). Comprehensive works typically involve multiple authors. Scholarly publications include a 147-page analysis of selected contact sheets and a doctoral dissertation about the nude Distortions. There's also a deeply researched study of André's work in Savoy by three historians with roots in that region of France.[19]

As the first full biography of André Kertész, *Everything Is Photograph* takes advantage of this cornucopia of scholarship, along with my own decade of interviews, archival digging, exploration of relevant places and ideas, and immersion in his photographs. Like all interpretations of images, mine are subjective, contextual, and never definitive. I dwell on those I find most revealing of how photography made André who he was and how he construed the medium. Alert to the complexities of the man and his art as he navigated the currents and crosscurrents of twentieth-century photography, politics, literature, and art, *Everything Is Photograph* doubles as a partial history of a vanished world of photography.

**André's window** in the room where he did *Self-Portrait, Paris* commanded a view of the city stretching to a distant Eiffel Tower. Among his many images of the Iron Lady is one he took from that window one day around dawn when Paris was mostly slumbering and grainy with dampness. The medium telephoto lens on André's Voigtländer flattens the scene. Because of his high vantage point, the roofs of nearby buildings block the glint of streetlights. Yet their glow creeps up the facades, brightening the high-ceilinged lower floors where bourgeois families reside. It stops short of the mansard roofs lined with maid's rooms like his. Windows everywhere are shuttered, except for two or three where a brightness behind drawn curtains suggests that someone is stirring. The day ahead, like the sky, is still blank. On the horizon, halfway up the image, flows a pale river of light. From it emerges the Eiffel Tower, piercing the sky like a delicate needle. The picture is a love note to France.

Windows join private life with public space. Congruent with photographs, they frame and shape light. They are metaphors for desire and revelation.

Even as a cameraless fifteen-year-old in Budapest, André lingered at windows. The one in his bedroom afforded a view across the courtyard of the building where he lived to the window of the girl who infatuated him. The shades in his room allowed him to adjust the amount of light filtering in. Just as the hopes of the young-adult André were bound up in Paris, so his adolescent self believed that *she* alone could save him. As he surveys her bedroom window from his, André's story begins.

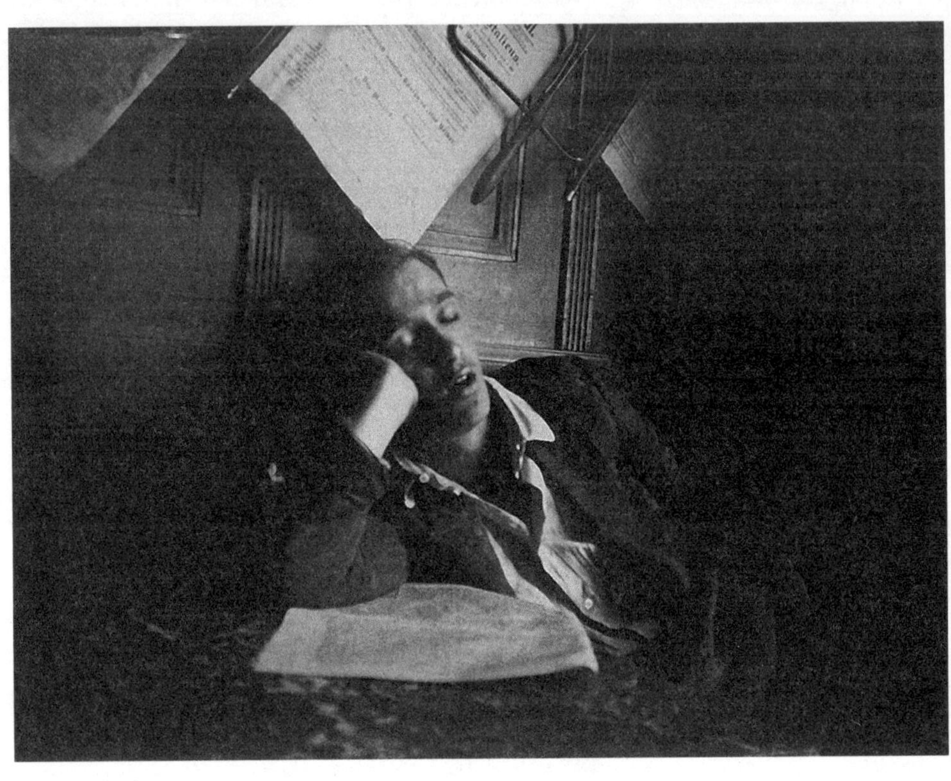

André Kertész, *Sleeping Boy*, 1912

# 1 SLEEPING BOY, 1894–1914

**He fixed his eyes** on the window. Would *she* appear? Jolán Balog was fifteen, one day older than Andor, with slender fingers, an abundance of curls, and a penchant for pretty clothes. For years, he had been smitten. Now he was obsessed. Because of her, he had sequestered himself in his bedroom, willingly leaving only when he stood a chance of running into her or one of her sisters in the courtyard below. Although he had to drag himself to meals and school, he refused to see the doctor, even as he fretted over his insomnia and constipation. The doctor would order him to take daily walks, he figured, and that would interrupt his surveillance.[1]

Hoping to hide his feelings from all but his neighbor herself, Andor took the precaution of burning or hiding the notes that she slipped him. Yet his brothers and uncle were wise to what he was doing. His older brother chided him for unmanly behavior, and the younger one mocked him as a madman who spied on his girlfriend from behind a curtain. One day their uncle strode into Andor's bedroom and pointedly closed the shades, throwing their surroundings into shadow. The boy stayed mute about the peephole he could use when the shades were drawn.

Jolán took Andor's fixation in stride. In one courtyard conversation that escaped his brothers' smirks and her mother's gimlet eye, she told Andor that she loved him and would never have anyone else. Other times she snubbed him. Or so he imagined. Calm down! Jolán urged. But how *could* he? She was driving him wild. Each afternoon at homework time, she stood in her window as they had agreed, while he contemplated her from his. As if his room were a camera, his peephole its viewfinder, and Jolán an image he could mentally possess.

In his first weeks at a commercial academy that fall of 1909, Andor had made sporadic attempts at good grades. When he got his first 4 (the equivalent of a D), he was upset only because Jolán and his classmates would think he was stupid. Then he put grades out of his mind, floating away his worries on daydreams about captivating his beloved and her family with his music. If he could master his shepherd's flute, he felt, the Balogs would accept him. He would play "beautifully, slowly—with feeling," he told his diary. He would put his soul into his melodies. "I would be a beloved boy, and they wouldn't think of me as someone who's not good at anything. It's not my fault that I have this kind of temperament. I really can't help it."[2]

He couldn't help it, he believed, because he was his father's son. Lipót Kertész had died of spinal tuberculosis seven months earlier. A spice and coffee merchant, grain trader, and itinerant bookseller, Lipót had never reliably supported his family. One reason was the poor health he had suffered for the past decade.[3] But also his passion was reading, not achieving worldly success. A gift from his father, Andor's flute would have represented the romantic temperament the boy had inherited. Lipót purchased it as a souvenir at the 1896 Hungarian Millennial Exhibition, celebrating one thousand years of Magyar presence in what is now Hungary. (Magyars are ethnic Hungarians.) The exhibition had occasioned both major public works projects and cultural events like salutes to the woodwind tradition of shepherds on the Hungarian plains. For Andor, playing the flute was a way of imagining a vagabond life like those of the herders, explorers, and Romani he revered, and of mourning his father, the roving bookseller.[4] He kept wanting to cry but felt he should not.[5]

Andor's health problems were also hereditary. When at last he yielded to his family's scolding and consulted a doctor, he found out he had spinal tuberculosis. The doctor prescribed medication and explained that he might develop ulcers or spit up blood. (Apparently, the case proved mild, and that never happened.) His cough and his spinal ailment, the doctor continued, were inherited from his father but dictated by God. Happy to leave the tough choices to God, Andor took a keener interest when the doctor picked up his hand and read in his palm his sadness and pain.

Whether or not Andor ever played his flute for Jolán's family, Mrs. Balog eyed him with suspicion. As for Jolán, Andor alternately reveled in her affection and projected her coldness: "I'm sure she doesn't love me as much as I love her. I know this from her behavior. I'm very scared."[6] Once she asked him to escort her home after an exam. "She's going to be mine," Andor wrote in his diary. "I can't wait. I'll write to her tomorrow. She will be so moved she will cry." But as he walked with her on that occasion, he felt tongue-tied. He realized he was unworthy of a creature "so beautiful...so lovely."[7] Jolán was his reason for living. He decided to kill himself. How could he get a revolver? How could he get morphine? To be Andor Kertész—insecure, self-absorbed, embattled—was exhausting.

Collapsed in a heap or flushed with joy over some favor from Jolán, Andor wrote hackneyed odes to the pleasures of love, flowers, and springtime. Melancholy often prevailed, as in one poem that he set to music and played on his flute: "Die, die, red rose, / ... I myself am dying also. / Because the infidel has left me."[8]

Andor's romantic temperament was not out of place in belle epoque Budapest, where young men felt no obligation to conceal their emotions. His rift with his close friend Jakab Liebermann, nicknamed Jaksay, was a case in point. One day Jaksay confided that he owed someone a large sum of money but couldn't pay. On hearing the story, Andor begged him to take a precious ring that he had inherited from his grandfather. The plan was that Jaksay would pawn the ring, pay the debt, then retrieve the ring using his earnings from work. Instead, he squandered the loan from the pawnshop. Outraged that his friend had broken the code of friendship, Andor vowed to fight a duel with Jaksay. He would never forgive him.

Then Jaksay apologized. At a party a few days later, the two joked about the duel. Later they feuded again.

School, too, felt unbearable. Andor had never been a good or happy student. In the second grade, he had earned acceptable marks: 2s and 3s (B's and C's) in Hungarian, geography, religion, calligraphy, gymnastics, and even German, his hardest subject; and 1s (A's) in behavior and descriptive geometry (a standard class in which pupils learned the theory and practice of representing three-dimensional objects on two-dimensional surfaces).[9] But in the third grade, his marks went into freefall. He failed German and had to repeat the exam.[10] From then on, Andor hovered near the bottom of his classes. The lower his grades, the less he studied. School bored him.

After Lipót died, Andor dropped out. He took an apprenticeship that involved crawling around on a roof and digging a trench in a cemetery. But he soon left that too. Then he got a job at a company that sold windows. Eleven days later, he lied to his boss that an old foot injury was acting up and a doctor had ordered him to stay home and rest. After that, he vanished, not even bothering to pick up his paycheck. He toyed with the idea of training to be an electrician. Why not? He was good at mechanical things. But that urge also faded.

One of his mother's brothers, named Lipót like Andor's father but known as Poldi, intervened by enrolling Andor in a two-year program at the Academy of Commerce on Alkotmány Street. An administrator at the agricultural commodities exchange, Uncle Poldi foresaw a career like his own for his sister's middle son. But Andor was too high-strung for the business world. Once when his mother got sick and he had to fill in at the coffee shop she operated, he ended up in tears because of all he had to suffer from the "ugly people" who were her customers.[11]

At the academy, Andor liked to stare out the window. Other students tried to talk with him or recruit him for their chalk fights. Wrapped up in his own problems, he often ignored them. "I saw a pair of pigeons and a black dog, and I already saw those on my way to school," he recorded of the scene from the classroom window on the first day of school. "The other boys have already noticed my strangeness."[12] Andor was a quiet extrovert and a genial friend when he chose to be but not when faced with the miserable prospect of attending business school.

That first term, Andor earned a 1 (A) in religious studies but mostly 2s and 3s (B's and C's). He again failed German, which was not only his mother's native tongue but also an essential tool for a businessman in the Austro-Hungarian Empire. Blaming herself for his poor grades, Jolán declared that she would no longer distract him from his homework by coming to her window each afternoon. But he begged her not to stop. She relented. Andor attributed his low grades to fate and to *them*: "They kill every desire one has to study."[13] He considered telling his teachers he was sick or half deaf. Or maybe he should pretend to be crazy.

Unable to meet the expectations of Uncle Poldi, his older brother, Imre, and his mother—three paragons of hard steady effort—Andor directed his resentment toward his mother, Ernesztina. Drowsing in bed one morning, he overheard her complaining to the kitchen help that her sons kept urging her to rest but "they don't get up, and they don't help." She was acting the martyr, thought Andor, slaving away, refusing to nap, and never letting her boys forget that she was doing it all for them. Worse, she belittled his father. The couple had been estranged. Lipót had not died at home.

Except for some heavily mortgaged farmland near Budapest that he co-owned with one of his brothers, Lipót had left few assets. Poldi settled his brother-in-law's debts and took over the estate on behalf of his nephews. Ernesztina herself made claims against it: 2,000 korona (about $14,800 in 2024 dollars) in compensation for her dowry, and 1,000 korona for the *hitbér*. (This untranslatable term refers to an ancient transdanubian practice in which a groom pays the bride's father at the time of the wedding or consummation of the marriage, similar to paying a bride price. The *hitbér* was sometimes considered a conjugal fund that a widow could use to sustain herself and her children.)

Lipót had died intestate, and the probate proceedings continued for months. It was no doubt Ernesztina's complaints about Lipót's shortcomings as a breadwinner that led Andor to believe that his father was a bad person. After a talk with Imre, it seems, he realized that was wrong. "Now I know who my father was," he wrote in his diary. "I hate my mother. I despise her. I don't care how big a sin this is. It's true. She deserves it. I'm going to be cold with her. I'm not going to give a damn."[14] But he did.

**Ernesztina Hoffmann Kertész** was born in Tököl, a Swabian village on Csepel Island in the Danube south of Budapest. The Swabians trace their origins to a medieval duchy in southwestern Germany. At the start of the eighteenth century, many Swabians left Germany to accept land in what is now Hungary in exchange for their loyalty to the House of Habsburg. Hungarian Swabians like Ernesztina and her family spoke a German dialect yet felt placidly Hungarian. No more gifted for languages than her middle son, Ernesztina tortured Hungarian in ways that marked her as a Swabian peasant type. One attempt to pen a few sentences in Hungarian left her laughing so hard that she cried, and her glasses slid from her nose.

The Swabian hausfrau, as the stereotype goes, is fanatical about cleaning, dropping to her knees to scour her doorstep, and so tightfisted that she later served as the German chancellor Angela Merkel's poster girl for fiscal responsibility. True to type, young Ernesztina had mastered the housewifely arts of scrubbing, mopping, cooking, laundering, and pinching her korona. At twenty-three, she married Lipót Kohn, who was two years older.[15] Lipót came from Ászár, a village west of Budapest, where his father and grandfather were merchants. Lipót's father, Albert József Kohn, had fought in the Hungarian Revolution of 1848, then married a woman named Leni Berger. The couple had six children. As a young man, Lipót took up the saber too, serving ten years in the Imperial and Royal Hussars (fighters in a light cavalry unit) and two years in the Royal Hungarian Hussars regiment. Many aristocrats of that era wore the hussar's gold-braided uniform and tall leather boots. So when, decades later, Lipót's sons learned from a family friend that their father was possibly the illegitimate son of a count with whom Leni had an affair and that Albert had refused to recognize the boy as his own, the news surprised no one.[16] Lipót had always been more luftmensch than businessman. On hearing the story, Andor, then in his fifties, could have recalled a boyhood conversation in which Lipót had described him as "a noble kind."[17] By then Andor had proved himself the heir to both his mother's drive to make money and his father's indifference to pragmatic matters.

Lipót had brought little of material value to the matrimonial home. Ernesztina's belongings consisted chiefly of clothing and some jewelry, including five gold rings.[18] Their first child, a boy named Andor, was presumably born into poverty. They lost him as a baby. By the time their second son, Imre, arrived, the couple had moved to Budapest. Then came a daughter, Erzsébet, who died of diphtheria before her second birthday. Nine months later, on July 2, 1894, Ernesztina gave birth to another boy they named Andor. The child's first home was an apartment on grimy Bulyovszky Street within spitting distance of the tracks behind Nyugati Station.[19]

In 1898, the Kohns became the Kertészes.[20] Both Lipót's and Ernesztina's families were Jewish, and, in that era, name changes were common for middle-class Budapest Jews. For an oligarchy keenly aware that ethnic Hungarians were a minority, encouraging Magyarization (the process of trading a non-Hungarian name for a typically Hungarian one) was a way to solidify an ethnically diverse nation. For those changing their name, it demonstrated loyalty and consolidated their status as citizens. Indeed, Ernesztina and Lipót's Jewishness was never central to their self-concepts. Culturally assimilated and casually observant, they celebrated both Christian and Jewish holidays. They sent their children to Hebrew school but rarely went to temple.

*Kertész* is a Hungarian version of *Curtis*. A typical Hungarian occupational name, it means "gardener" — a shadow name that would tickle Andor as an adult. So four-year-old Kohn Andor became Kertész Andor, to use Hungarian name order, or, in his name's Western version, its mirrored reflection: Andor Kertész.

The Kertészes' last child, Jenő, was born in 1897. When Jenő was three, thirty-seven-year-old Ernesztina obtained a license to operate as a "lady grocer."[21] Although Lipót's health was already deteriorating, his experience as a spice and coffee merchant would have been invaluable in launching a coffee shop and retail coffee and tea store at 6 Teleki Tér.

Girdled with prayer rooms, bars, and kosher coffee shops like the Kertészes', the square was the site of a swarming outdoor flea market. Through the tall windows of their Teleki Téri Kávémérés (Teleki Tér Coffee Shop), the couple could observe Budapest's other half haggling over used coats, metal bed frames, threadbare rugs, live geese, battered shoes, and a thousand and one other things. Many of the shoppers were caftan- and kerchief-wearing Jews from the shtetls of Poland and Galicia, many of the sellers Orthodox Jews. Every inch of the square was in motion. Peddlers jammed their carts between the stalls. Bicyclists wove through the crowds. Vendors hawked their wares. Ernesztina would have communicated with these Yiddish speakers in countrified German as she served coffee, tea, and sweets like *flódni*, the traditional Jewish pastry with its layers of poppy seeds, apples, walnuts, and plum jam. At home, the Kertészes did not keep kosher, but to do so was vital to business on this square that was Budapest's equivalent of New York's Lower East Side.

Thanks to their income from the coffee shop, the Kertészes could afford to move from Bulyovszky Street to 47 Népszínház (People's Theater) Street. Or at least Ernesztina and the children did. The family's new street sliced through Pest's crowded outer Józsefváros district. Although their apartment was only a five-minute walk from swarming Teleki Tér, the neighborhood was solidly middle class. Home to ambitious craftspeople and merchants with growing families, it smelled of "carters' horses and axle grease, the worn leather interiors of hackney cabs... rotten plums and melon rinds," one writer observed.[22]

A tram line ran up and down Népszínház Street. But when the porte cochere of the Kertészes' building clanged shut, the tram's clatter and screech were muted. In typical Budapest fashion, their courtyard was ringed with wrought-iron walkways on every floor. That made for a small-town atmosphere in the metropolis and lent an air of theater to tenants' comings and goings.[23] The Kertészes lived on the second floor. High-ceilinged, slightly gloomy, and crowded with dark furniture, Oriental rugs, and potted plants, their apartment was typical of turn-of-the-century Budapest. Visiting relatives abounded.

Many were Ernesztina's kin, most of whom had moved to the city. Her sister Leontine lived in Budapest, along with her husband and three children. So did their three unmarried businessmen brothers. Kálmán played cards with his nephews. Józsi, the youngest, was a gentle presence. Poldi came bearing advice and good things to eat. All three liked to pull up to the Kertészes' dining-room table for their sister's home cooking. On Lipót's side, Andor and his brothers had more aunts and uncles, some with multiple children. That made for two dozen cousins. Stir in visits from their Konkoli, Grósz, and Schnur kin; add an appetite for gossip, along with disagreements about loans, repayments, and business dealings; and there was a goulash rich in what Jenő quipped was "sweet family drama."[24]

**A naughty and prankish kid** with distracted parents, Andor grew up ranging over the territory familiar to readers of Ferenc Molnár's classic 1907 novel *The Paul Street Boys*, set in that same Józsefváros district. He and his brothers gallivanted around backstreets where barbers, corset makers, beer brewers, and sausage sellers plied their trades. They hung around Teleki Tér. Once Andor ran away from home, taking his flute, his meager savings, and a few books. His parents described him to the police as a tall skinny eleven-year-old with a lisp and a hankering for adventure. A Budapest newspaper report about the missing boy called him Little Robinson Crusoe, suggesting the lust for exploration, refusal to heed instructions, and stubbornness he shared with Daniel Defoe's protagonist.

As Andor got older, he outgrew his lisp. Yet his other language problems persisted. When he spoke, he was not always able to organize correct word patterns. The rhythm and flow of his speech were affected. Sentences did not always glide off his tongue. Today Andor's condition might be diagnosed as an expressive language disorder.[25] Oral exams were standard in Hungarian schools, so it's no wonder that he struggled academically. Classmates would have mocked him, which could help explain his standoffishness. Andor's language comprehension was fine, and his diary shows him to be a sensitive writer. Yet all his attempts at foreign languages fizzled. His incompetence with German became a sore point at home.

Sports were another matter. The three Kertész boys were lean, coordinated, and wild about all things athletic. Andor grew up running, jumping, wrestling, swimming, bicycling, skating, and horsing around with his brothers and a clatter of cousins.

Other times he retreated to his bedroom and to make-believe worlds animated by treasures like a bronze frog, a toy letterbox, a metal clock dial, and a statuette of a kneeling Atlas shouldering a globe, all of which he squirreled away in biscuit tins and would keep all his life.

Books also quickened Andor's life of the imagination. Like his father and brothers, he read voraciously. He must have known Baroness Orczy's popular tales of fairies, gnomes, and talking animals, along with her novel of romance and adventure, *The Scarlet Pimpernel*. Infatuated with explorers, conquerors, and heroes, he clipped from the newspaper a ballad about Attila, King of the Huns, and cherished his copy of J. W. Tyrrell's *Across the Sub-Arctics of Canada*.[26]

As he moved into adolescence, Andor devoured *Borsszem Jankó* (Tiny Pest), a politically liberal satirical weekly, kin to *Mad* magazine, with a mostly Jewish readership.[27] Among its characters, a shrewd and garrulous Jew named Salamon Seiffensteiner plays the role of Alfred E.

Neuman. *Borsszem Jankó* epitomizes the feisty sophistication, freewheeling attitudes, and improvised jests of Budapest's belle epoque press. This Jewish-inflected Budapest spirit helps explain why Hungary's conservative Catholic and Calvinist hinterlands considered their capital city to be slick, un-Hungarian, and possibly evil. To Andor and his friends, it was vital to their identity.

Before World War I, Budapest was the second-largest Jewish city in Europe, after Warsaw. The 23 percent of its residents who were Jewish comprised a disproportionate number of industrialists, doctors, bankers, journalists, and intellectuals.[28] Jews were kept on the wrong side of an insurmountable social wall and routinely stereotyped, no longer as swarthy peddlers hauling their packs but as potbellied capitalists, their purses bulging with gold. Yet they enjoyed full citizenship, equal legal rights, and growing power. They spoke Hungarian, not Yiddish, and considered Budapest their city. "Why does Cohn [the default Jewish name] want a Jewish state in Palestine?" went a joke making the rounds in those days. The punch line: "So he can be the Jewish ambassador to Budapest."[29]

Small wonder. Tolerant and wealthy, the Hungarian capital was modernizing fast. Its Stock and Commodity Exchange, the largest in Europe, was the beating heart of a metropolis growing faster than Vienna or Paris. Continental Europe's first subway ran under Andrássy Boulevard. Trams crisscrossed thoroughfares newly bejeweled with electric lights. The Danube reflected the majestic neo-Gothic parliament building completed in 1904. The Franz Joseph Bridge linked Pest to Buda.[30] The emperor and king had hammered in the very last rivet himself.

A port, rail terminus, factory city, and mill town, the raw, sprawling Pest—where the Kertészes lived, east of the Danube—laid claim to a large middle class. But it was also home to those who subsisted on the parings of others' prosperity. Servants toiled six and a half days a week for their bed and board. Factory workers slept on filthy mattresses rented by the night.[31] On Sundays, Romani violins sobbed from the bandstands of the leafy Népliget (People's Park), within earshot of the roller coaster where servant girls held their beaux tight.

Across the river lay Buda. Honeycombed with crooked cobblestone streets, dotted with tiny orchards and yellow stucco houses, Buda felt like a collection of villages. On summer evenings, locals lingered in its garden restaurants; on winter mornings, the scent of burning wood wafted through its hills. Buda tarried in the nineteenth century, while Pest, the other half of Hungary's fraternal-twin capital, was hurtling through the twentieth. Both delivered up unforgettable images to an observant boy's mind and heart.

**But that winter,** only Jolán existed. On New Year's Day 1910, fifteen-year-old Andor sat leafing through his diary, revisiting the wilderness of emotions inside him and observing that his feeling for Jolán ("let's call it being in love") had allowed him to survive his father's death.[32] Three weeks later, she gave him a blank volume inscribed "To my dearest Andor from his loving Jolán."[33] He smothered it in kisses and decided to use it to write the story of their love. Then he changed his mind, arranging her notes between its pages, adding some flowers, and stashing it away to show her after they got married.

By spring, Andor was often skipping school—"doing *blicc*" in his now charmingly antiquated Hungarian schoolboy slang—and killing his weekdays in museums and parks. His accomplice was a boy named Lajos Fekete. A great kid, thought Andor, although Fekete (as Andor called him) had the annoying habit of showing up at the Kertészes' apartment at inopportune moments and ruining Andor's chances to sneak out for meetings with Jolán. Fekete aspired to be a man of letters. Andor thought he didn't have the chops. Yet he did recognize his friend's gift for drawing, and he liked posing for Fekete while playing the flute. As for Fekete, he found Andor hard to draw because he lacked dramatic flair. A wiry-bodied boy, he had a lean face, shiny lips, neat brown hair, smooth skin except for two wens near one wing of his nose, and, his best feature, deep-set blue-gray eyes.

That spring, Fekete's graphic skills proved useful not only for portraits but also for absence excuse notes and report cards, both of which required parental signatures. After Andor slipped Fekete a sample of his mother's handwriting, his friend practiced and perfected the forgery. The two skipped school whenever they could get away with it. If they were caught, Andor figured, they could go live abroad.

His brothers were faring better academically. Imre, the older, was conscientious and methodical. Jenő, the younger, acted the clown but applied himself all the same. Curious and inventive, Jenő tinkered with radios, learned to sew, and played the guitar. Jenő also had a speech defect, more serious than Andor's: He stuttered. Ernesztina took him to one speech pathologist after another, but no one could help him overcome his disorder. The boy hid its emotional cost by clowning. By all evidence, the family treated his stutter with sensitivity, as they did Andor's speech problems.

The Kertészes also faced the social handicap of their association with Teleki Tér. To be the son of a Teleki Tér shopkeeper was not a status symbol. The expression "Teleki tér merchandise" meant shoddy goods; to have "Teleki tér manners" was to be boorish.[34] Even though Budapest was a socially dynamic city with a solid middle class, the boys grew up keenly aware of the difficult lives of the poor, the hierarchy of religions, and the unfair privileges of Magyar magnates.

Class differences were even more stark in Hungary's provinces, where a Protestant landed gentry owned large estates worked by serfs. The gentry paid obeisance, too: to Catholic titled aristocrats—the Andrássys, the Károlyis, the Batthyánys, the Esterházys—whose surnames are inextricable from Hungarian history. Under the Dual Monarchy established in the nineteenth century, Hungary had semiautonomous status within the Habsburg Empire. That made it part of a great European power, at the cost, some believed, of its soul.

Operating in tandem with the Catholic emperor and king in Vienna, the aristocrats distractedly ran the internal affairs of the nation. In

Budapest, they greeted each other in French, staged lavish dress balls, and popped corks at the Casino Club. Come summer, they migrated to ancestral castles; in autumn, they converged on their hunting lodges in the Carpathians. Amid such pleasures, one could easily lose track of how Hungary's affairs were progressing or even of how many peasants one had. Pest's modernity notwithstanding, the nation as a whole was politically and culturally stagnant, even semifeudal.

When a German diplomat asked one of the Károlyis why his family did not play music, the count replied: "Why should we play, when the gypsies serve that purpose?" He added: "Just as we keep the gypsies so that they play, we keep the Jews so that they work instead of us."[35]

**Her husband's death** had left Ernesztina with little savings. Yet her coffee shop did a brisk business, Imre had a decent job, and her brother Poldi pitched in. After the probate court gave Ernesztina full custody of her sons, she enlisted her brother as his nephews' legal guardian. A Yul Brynner look-alike with a wayward mustache and kindly smile, Uncle Poldi personified the Swabian dictum, Work, work, to build a house.

He was adamant about their educations. Buckle down to your studies, he urged his nephews. The oldest and youngest one did. But Andor wanted to quit school, wanted to vagabond, wanted he knew not what. "Look, son," Uncle Poldi counseled, gentle yet insistent, "you have to get your school certificate first."[36] Aware that he could never live up to his uncle's expectations, Andor fretted: "What is going to become of me?"[37]

Disapproving of his brother's whimpering and moping, Imre attempted to bribe him with tickets to sporting events, concerts, *anything* to get him away from his bedroom and shake him out of his funk. Sports did prove a balm. So did weekends in and around Szigetbecse, a village at the southern end of Csepel Island in the Danube, where his mother's clan had wide and deep roots.

One traveled to this tidy, introverted village an hour and a half south of Budapest by slow train, then horse cart over rutted roads. Szigetbecse was home to eight hundred souls, mostly Catholics but a few Calvinists and Jews. Virtually all the villagers were Swabians. Ernesztina and her siblings had grown up nearby. Her older sister Rozália had stayed on to marry a man named Jakab Klopfer. The couple had a son named Mihály, called Misi, who was six years older than Andor.[38] Misi had become an affluent vintner and farmer with substantial land holdings on Csepel Island and near Tiszaszalka, a village in far eastern Hungary where his wife, born Margit Grósz, had roots. The Klopfers divided their time between Tiszaszalka and Szigetbecse, where Misi stored and sold prodigious quantities of wine.

His trunk as solid as his bank account and his mustache well trimmed, Misi looked the part of the captain of agriculture that he was. Yet he had a degenerative disease, possibly multiple sclerosis. Now in his thirties, he hobbled around with a cane and made ample use of his carriage and uniformed driver. Misi was a dynamic presence in the village and in the life of his cousin Andor. He and Margit had two daughters, Rozália, called Rózsi, and Lili. Outfitted in pinafores and wearing big hair bows, they were the little sisters Andor never had.

The Klopfers' summer home on Makádi Road on the edge of Szigetbecse was a substantial, two-story stucco structure with decorative elements and vines crawling up the exterior. Its polished-wood furniture, lace curtains, and embroidered tablecloths gave the interior an air of bourgeois prosperity. Yet, unlike in Budapest, there was no electricity, only oil lamps, and a wood-fired clay oven to bake bread. Outside was a large garden, a well, an orchard, and a tree-shaded terrace where the family gathered for breakfast and afternoon coffee, cake, and homegrown fruit. In Budapest, Andor's life moved to the rhythm of school bells and tram schedules; in Szigetbecse, sunrises, sunsets, and seasons served to measure time.

Across the road from the house flowed the Kis-Duna, the Little Danube, a sylvan braid of the river where Andor and his brothers, cousins, and friends shed their clothes, plowed through the rushes, and rowed or fooled around. They fished with basket traps or lines and hooks, sharing the abundance with gray herons, squeaking coots, and great crested grebes.[39] The birds enchanted Andor. The family still teased him about how, as a soft-hearted four- or five-year-old, he had found a baby swallow that had fallen from its nest. Believing that it was dying, Andor was beside himself with anxiety until an adult explained that all was normal, and the mother was still caring for her baby.

Andor delighted in farm animals too, tagging along with the village's young goose tenders and swine herders. Chickens scratched in the dust. Oxcarts lumbered by, their wheels caked with dirt. Evenings brought chirping crickets and pink sunsets, then a sky powdered with stars.

**No such bliss** awaited Andor in Budapest, where he drifted through the academy's two-year baccalaureate program in three years. He graduated in June 1912, shortly before his eighteenth birthday. Uncle Poldi promptly got him a job as a clerk at Giro Bank and Transfers, linked to the Budapest Stock Exchange. (The giro system is an alternate banking system in which money changes hands through direct transfer from one account to another.) Andor hated it no less than school.

After work, he attended soccer, boxing, and rugby matches. He joined a sports club and began lifting weights. He took an interest in art too. But his enjoyment was blunted by discomfort about his lack of critical acumen. After spending the better part of one Sunday with a friend at a museum, Andor lamented in his diary: "Today I could see how useless I am. I believed that I am capable of judging pictures, although I barely am. I judge them too much according to my own personality, which I should not do, as one's personality, unless it is something extraordinary, is usually ignored. I am unable to pass judgment according to the taste of the masses." That was a strength, not a weakness, but Andor saw only his flaws. "I look for the poetic in everything. Criticism requires enormous knowledge and courage. I lack both."[40]

He felt similar inadequacies as a theatergoer. Andor joined his brothers and friends at the great halls of the Hungarian capital, sampling fashionable offerings like Lajos Bíró's *The Robber Knight,* Eduard Knoblauch's *Faun,* Menyhért Lengyel's *The Czarina,* and Pierre Veber and Henri de Gorsse's *The Young Lass,* a four-act "Frenchie." He carefully noted the name, location, and cast members of each play that he attended yet hardly dared formulate an opinion. "The first French comedy I have seen," he reported of *The Young Lass.* "I was pleased by it. I am not able to judge plays yet, but to my greatest joy, lately I am somewhat able to judge objects of art and other solid artistic creations, although only in broad outlines. I cannot penetrate deeply yet." He had no idea how to articulate his responses to works of art. In a statement that sums up what would prove a lifelong problem, he wrote, "I lack the words, even though I have it inside me."[41]

Around the time of his graduation and birthday, Andor purchased, or received as a gift from his mother (perhaps meant to be shared with Jenő), a cheap German-made box camera. It came from a shop owned by a classmate's parents. Andor had been wanting a camera for years, he later claimed. But because he hung back from asking directly, he had grown up getting bicycles and such from his parents. "Whenever I saw something it stayed with me. I said okay, I'll take a picture of it later when I have a camera," he would explain. "Instinctively I started to compose. I learned how to observe the moment."[42]

Andor and Jenő set about plumbing the mysteries of photography. The camera took 4 by 6 centimeter glass plates. It had one preset shutter speed.[43] The novice photographers' first challenge was to determine the proper aperture for each picture they wanted to take. Mostly they guessed. After they made several exposures, a bigger challenge loomed: How to develop the negatives? They pored over an instruction manual, then set up a darkroom in a big armoire. They mixed chemicals, filled their trays, rigged up a safelight. Working at night, they had to whisper so as not to awaken their early-rising mother and brother.

One plate seemed promising. But they ruined it by neglecting to shut tight the armoire door as they were developing. Eventually they did manage a few decent negatives. They then turned to printing, using printing-out paper rather than the developing-out paper that would become standard. With the sheet of paper set in a copy frame, Andor and Jenő brought out the image using exposure to light (as opposed to the chemical development used with developing-out paper). There was no fixed developing time. They just eyeballed the emerging picture. When they decided the print was ready, they submerged it in a water bath, fixed it, washed it again, and air-dried it. It took two days to fumble their way to their first satisfactory picture, a paint-chip-size portrait of Andor by Jenő.

That Sunday morning, they sneaked a picture of Jolán. But Jenő botched the fixing of the negative, and then the plate broke. Jenő then asked for, and was granted, permission to photograph Jolán and her two sisters, who posed in their kitchen doorway. He and Andor hastened to process the image—the best one so far. "I am so happy, there are no words for it," gushed Andor.[44] But he came home from school the next day to discover that standing water on the washbasin had damaged the print. So he and Jenő made two more, one of which was fine. "Tiny picture, but sharp," Andor wrote in his diary. "I can stare at it endlessly, and I am very happy. We gave a copy to [the Balogs] too."[45]

The adults in the Kertész family took no interest in photography except as a means of representing themselves as comfortable middle-class Hungarians. Andor had watched older relatives pull out cameras at family gatherings. One or two of his cousins had snapshot cameras like his. Photography was a popular hobby for boys, who often got cameras for their twelfth or thirteenth birthdays, just as children from a later generation might get a video game console.

Andor was uncommonly observant. He liked looking at pictures and discussing art with friends like Fekete. All the same, his ability to experience certain works of art was limited by tritanopia, a partial color blindness in which blues fade into greens, yellows veer into violets, and tertiary colors can be confusing. Whether or not Andor was aware yet that others perceived colors differently than he did, he did show his fondness for images in which tonal values, rather than hues, dominate. That was the case with both photographs, virtually all black-and-white in that day, and drawings.

Andor would long remember a certain descriptive geometry class. His instructor set up an object, maybe a box, for students to draw. Fascinated by the double shadow caused by the light from the two windows flanking the object, Andor concentrated on that.

"What's this then?" asked the instructor, pointing to the shadows.

"Well, that's what I'm drawing."

"No, there's no need for any of that. You don't need the shadow. I'm only after the form," responded the instructor, failing to recognize his pupil's equally valid interpretation.[46] The use of shadows would become Andor's poetic signature as a photographer. Figuring things out by himself would remain his modus operandi. Everything he would ever do well was self-taught.

From the start, he used his camera for more than special occasions. He took it on rambles with his brothers and friends. He photographed Jenő in the park and Imre by the Danube. He recorded his father's tombstone. During his lunch hour, he lined up office colleagues on a bench and did a group portrait. He also returned the favor of Fekete's drawings with moody photographs of his friend wearing a hat at a rakish angle and viewed in profile against a backdrop of trees. Village scenes enchanted Andor too. He came home from late-winter excursions to the ancient hamlets of Strázsa and Szepesszombat brimming with enthusiasm about returning that summer to take poetic pictures.[47] Another day, he photographed at his mother's coffee shop.

Establishments like Ernesztina's were essential to the cultural fabric of Budapest. Confections of marble, mirrors, and brocaded wallpaper, the great coffeehouses like Café Gerbeaud, New York Café, and Művész Coffeehouse catered to the powerful and the would-be powerful.[48] There deals were hatched, intrigues plotted, love affairs kindled, billiard matches won and lost, and articles penned and delivered to editors.

Meanwhile, hundreds of less glamorous businesses like Ernesztina's Teleki Téri Kávémérés served ordinary folks their coffee and pastries. Cafés doubled as a home away from cramped and chilly apartments. One could meet friends, relax after work, or even, as Andor's picture testifies, catch a wink or two.

His indifferently dressed subject in *Sleeping Boy* probably worked at the Teleki Tér market. Coffee and clatter notwithstanding, the boy has dozed off while scanning a newspaper. His collar open, one elbow planted on the table, his palm on his cheek, his eyes hooded, and his mouth slack, he sleeps. At top center of the photograph a bright triangle of newspaper hanging from a wall rack points to his head. It meets a second triangle, the points of which are the top of his forehead and two corners of the neglected daily. The recessed paneling behind him brackets his face. To his left and right are soft pockets of darkness like sleep closing in. Using light and dark metaphorically, *Sleeping Boy* puts viewers simultaneously inside and outside its subject's mind. It also reveals a beginner's unexpectedly effective use of geometric form. What's more, it nails a gently amusing moment. It's a visual version of the anecdotes of café life that spiced up the columns of the reporters who scoured the city, seeking to witness and interpret its comings and goings.

Andor also created, in effect, a self-portrait as an insomniac, dreamer, and evader of responsibilities. Developing the image may have felt like sizing someone up in a mirror, then abruptly realizing that it's you.

**Andor's relationship with Jolán** grew ever more fraught. Mrs. Balog had long suspected that the son of "the coffee people" was courting her daughter. So the two adolescents would meet at the library or arrange to ride together on the tram. After the library closed its doors and winter set in, they resorted to the ice rink, where Andor begrudgingly shared her with others.

One night, Jolán and her girlfriends went to a dance and didn't come home until dawn. After stewing about this event for two days, Andor sarcastically suggested that she go dancing more often and stay even later. They quarreled. Wedded to romantic notions about women and idealistic expectations of love that he'd absorbed from novels, Andor was a wreck: "I wish I never knew her."[49]

Yet when she wasn't driving him to despair, she was leaving him quaking with happiness. One June morning, she appeared at the Kertészes' apartment wearing a stunning white dress, and Andor fell senseless with joy. Another time, she modeled a black dress she'd acquired because he'd said he wanted to see her in black. He felt "a very soulful connection."[50]

Best of all, Jolán made good on her promise of a picture of herself. After she gave Andor the tiny studio portrait, he raced out to order an enlargement. Then she added a locket for the picture, and his contentment swelled. A portrait of him should go opposite hers in the locket, the young romantic decided. So he made an appointment for a formal studio portrait. He posed in a bow tie with his every hair in place. He surprised Jolán with a small print. When he wore the locket (as some young men did then), there were the two of them, faces touching, close to his heart. Jolán's picture served to poultice the wounds she inflicted. The picture he gave her doubled as a test of her commitment. As they stood talking one day, Andor blurted out, "Where's my picture?" to find out if she was carrying it.[51] She was.

That spring, Jolán discovered a passion for tennis. She favored the courts in the Zugliget, a forested park in the Buda hills, a long tram ride from their homes in Pest. Andor disliked the game and refused to play. But the idea that Jolán would play without him made him sick, even though his interests in art, weight lifting, and sports excluded her. One of her partners was a boy named Révész, whom Andor suspected of playing only as a means of seducing Jolán. Andor begged Jolán to give up tennis, but she refused. Occasionally he did manage to derail her tennis excursions and take her for walks instead. One Saturday in May, the two stood amid the Zugliget's trees expressing their passion with hugs and kisses. Two weeks after that, they smooched on a bench in the park.

Later Andor photographed what must have been that same bench in its woodsy and melancholic setting. Such pictures would have revealed to him that photographs could be more than mechanical likenesses: They could accede to a fuller expressivity.

On a visit to the Museum of Fine Arts (now the Hungarian National Gallery) a few days later, Andor purchased a postcard of Sándor Bihari's 1903 oil *Honeymoon*. Bihari's anecdotal painting depicts two newlyweds in prey to passion. Interrupting their simple meal, they have scraped back their chairs, then collapsed onto a sofa in an ardent embrace. Here was Andor's bench-kissing with Jolán projected into the early days of their marriage. Pinning a postcard to the wall proved easier, however, than pinning down Jolán herself.

In 1910s Hungary, a young woman was supposed to be shy and compliant. Jolán was not living up to that ideal. Irked by her independent streak, Andor spoke to her about the duties of a wife-to-be. She was falling short in other ways too. He was annoyed by her laugh. She wasn't intimate enough. Often he came away from their trysts feeling empty because the "physical urge was stronger than the soul bond. Something is missing."[52] When they crossed paths in the courtyard one day, they had nothing to say to each other and not from too much emotion. Yet for eight years, Andor had worshipped Jolán. When he sensed she was slipping away, he panicked.

As the days turned colder, they traded the bench in the Zugliget for the Kertészes' kitchen, which was mostly deserted when Ernesztina was at work. Even though he and Jolán had found the love nest they had been seeking, the bliss enjoyed by the husband in Bihari's painting continued to elude Andor. When Jolán saw Révész, he agonized; when she did not, he was bored.

Meanwhile, he slogged into the office each weekday. He had no idea how to be anything but a clerk in a city where education and upward mobility were all-important and a successful Jewish man was a doctor, lawyer, intellectual, or businessman. "I do not deserve to be alive," Andor wrote in his diary. "I do not have a drop of ambition in me."[53] Had that been true, he would never have felt so guilty about the shortcomings he perceived in himself.

Andor penned more mawkish poems, attended more plays, and planted himself on other park benches to stare at the trees and brood. On weekends, he and Jenő rowed on the Danube north of Budapest, their hands becoming calloused and their arms bulky and tanned. With friends, they took weekend-long hikes along the river, sleeping outdoors and plunging naked into the Danube before catching a ferryboat home. The girls who went with them skinny-dipped too but at a proper distance.[54] On weekends when they stayed in the city, they headed for Luna Park to play shooting games, sample the rides, and amuse themselves at the funhouses.

The trams clattered up and down Népszínház Street, every noon a cannon boomed from the Citadella atop Gellért Hill, and the Habsburgs would rule Austria-Hungary forever.

**As the former German chancellor** Otto von Bismarck had predicted, it started over "some damned foolish thing in the Balkans."[55] On June 28, 1914, a Serbian nationalist murdered Archduke Franz Ferdinand, the heir apparent to the Austro-Hungarian throne, during his visit to Sarajevo. Seizing upon this opportunity to annex Serbia, Austria-Hungary delivered an ultimatum that it knew would be unacceptable, rejected the Serbian response, and then declared war. Russia leaped to defend its Slavic ally and Germany to meet its treaty obligation to support Austria-Hungary in any conflict with Russia. Diving into the rushing current, France and Britain went to war with the Germans. Festive bellicosity swept Hungary, never mind that the dead archduke had been unpopular and anti-Hungarian. "Serbia, you cur!" scolded the Budapest daily *Az Est*.[56]

Andor turned twenty that summer when the Great War was brewing. Like a poster child for European guilelessness about what was to come, he spent his free days larking around Szigetbecse, camera and tripod in tow. The weather was perfect. Mornings dawned fresh. The meadows were sweet, and the sky eggshell blue. His brother Imre had given him a 9 by 12 centimeter Voigtländer Alpin with a Zeiss Tessar f/6.3 or f/6.8 lens and a triple-extension bellows, making it good for close-ups.[57] Andor loved the camera, even though the weight of the glass plates (he carried up to twelve at a time) and the need for a tripod limited the number of pictures he could take on a single excursion.

He photographed farmhouses, water, trees, fields, reflections, village elders, shepherd boys and their dogs, his brothers, and their relatives. One of his favorite subjects was the draw well. The traditional Hungarian draw well pulls up water in a bucket attached with a chain to a long wooden sweep. It looks like a rustic letter *T* with a bar that tilts up and down. In the nineteenth century, draw wells on the *puszta*, the mythic grassland of eastern Hungary, served as an emblem of national identity and a favorite motif of painters like Károly Lotz and poets like Sándor Petőfi. Draw wells would have appealed to Andor not only as graphic elements against the blank summer sky but also as tokens of a life he romanticized, that of pastoralists living in harmony with Szigetbecse's *kispuszta* (little puszta).

As a beginner, Andor knew nothing about the rules of photography, so he worked under few constraints. What he saw in his viewfinder and pictured in his mind did not always show up on his negative. Yet he kept trying new things. Taking advantage of the Voigtländer's capacity for close-ups, for instance, he sought to capture the details and folds of Margit's lace curtains.[58] In another experiment, he aimed down from the window of a choir loft, excited about framing a scene from above.[59] Another time he took an intentionally semiabstract image of a lily-padded river blotting up the dark clumps of surrounding trees.[60]

Fascinated by the way objects change character when viewed from near or far, in context or isolation, Andor imagined a lens that could glide from one focal length to another. (Focal length measures the distance between the optical center of a lens and its point of focus, that is, the film or glass plate. The greater the focal length, the closer the subject appears and the narrower the angle of view.) If he spotted something photo-worthy in the distance, he fantasized about turning a ring on his lens and seeing that object fly toward his viewfinder.[61]

Back in Budapest, Andor photographed a quartet of gymnasts with shaved heads and farmers' tans. The cast shadow of one hand-standing youth looked intriguingly spiderlike. Pursuing his fascination with shadows, he headed for Buda one evening with Jenő in tow. There they wandered the Tabán, a picturesque section of the city that was another favorite subject of painters. When they saw the ancient stone houses in Bocskay Tér, they halted. In one photograph Andor took, the square's only lamp turns a section of street into a starkly lit stage. A solitary man in an overcoat and hat, his model Jenő, hugs a wall as if in the opening scene of a Gothic melodrama, half merging with his doppelgänger shadow.

Compared to most later types of film, the glass plate Andor used for *Bocskay-tér, Budapest* had little sensitivity to light. He could have compensated for the slowness of the plate and the darkness of parts of the scene by choosing a large aperture. But that would have resulted in a shallow depth of field when he wanted sharpness throughout. (Depth of field denotes the distance between the nearest and the farthest objects that are in focus.) So Andor resorted to six-, eight-, and ten-minute exposures with Jenő posing perfectly still. They did not have a light meter or even know what a light meter was. Andor bracketed his exposures, hoping that one of them was right. (To bracket is to take the same image several times with slightly different exposures.)

In the darkroom, they found themselves mired in another technical issue. One or more of the Bocskay Tér negatives had halation, that is, the spread of the streetlamp's light to other areas of the negative. Halation can result from reflections off the bellows, mist in the atmosphere, or radiation from the silver bromide particles in the emulsion. The problem proved vexing until Andor discovered that he could block out the affected area by applying water-soluble red paint to the back side of the negative.

Such experiments came to an abrupt halt that October when the war rushed in and took possession of his life.

**Conscripted into** the Imperial and Royal Army of the Dual Monarchy of Austria-Hungary, Andor landed in a world of rules, ranks, restrictions, and drills. Wrapping himself in jocular cynicism, he claimed to welcome this "splendid opportunity to escape from this life." That would solve his problems, chief among them a frustrated romance, a job he detested, and a blank future. "I want to be rid of myself, but not through my own hand," he wrote in his diary. "I want to be annihilated."[62] Well, not really. Besides, everyone knew the war would be over by Christmas.

Even after he started basic training in Klagenfurt, Austria, Andor managed to indulge his sweet tooth for photography. Not only did he keep taking pictures but also he found a way to get his plates developed and printed. He sent the results to the family. When they arrived, Uncle Poldi commented that photography was expensive, implying that Andor was wasting his money. As usual, Jenő had a smart reply: Soldiers' mail was exempt from postage, so there was at least that savings. Uncle Kálmán held up the prints, one by one, and let no one distract him from looking. Then he smiled fondly and acknowledged that the pictures were very much Andor's. One of Jolán's sisters was also present. She took her time with the prints, too.

"Nice." Then she picked them up again and announced, "These are not photographs."

"Of course they are not," deadpanned Jenő.

"We have real pictures at home," she replied, meaning conventional soldier's photographs like the ones *her* soldier brother was taking.[63]

Jenő reported it all to Andor.

From Klagenfurt, Andor was ordered to Gorizia in what is now Italy. In Gorizia, he took a self-portrait for his mother, the only type of photograph she really cared about. He mounted his camera on a tripod, then set the crude spring-loaded self-timer he'd had a mechanic build for him in Budapest.[64] (Before Andor left, he and Jenő had batted around ideas about how Andor could take self-portraits without using a mirror. A device that allowed a person to photograph at a distance from the camera, the shutter tripper, as it was then called, had existed for more than a decade but was not yet widely available.)

Flanked by a cannon and a spindly tree, the tall, slender private in Andor's self-portrait stands in the courtyard of his caserne. His mild expression and girlish hands suggest less an Austro-Hungarian fighter in training than a boy playing soldier. He wears the standard Habsburg army pike-gray wool tunic with scalloped pocket flaps and standing collar and a high field cap. His leather belt has cartridge pouches. His breeches taper at the ankle. A quarter-century-old Steyr Mannlicher is slung over his shoulder. Wresting a little joke from his setting, he has positioned himself so that the cannon points straight at him. "Me as a 'Jäger,'" Andor wrote on the back, meaning an Alpine rifleman. But mostly the picture was supposed to say, "See, I'm fine and correctly outfitted." To dress well, no matter what trouble besets you, was a Hungarian thing.

When Andor was training, he shot quick portraits of his fellow soldiers during the rest breaks. When he was off duty, he joined them at a biergarten or pulled out his flute and amused them with parodies of popular songs. Other times he wandered off alone, camera in hand. He photographed a girl in Vertjoba, the cypress-flanked chapel in the Salcano cemetery, and the chapel of the medieval Castello.[65] Gorizia's mild winters, wisteria-hung villas, and corso lined with chestnut trees had earned it the nickname of the Austrian Nice. Now laundry hung from the front gate of the chapel, the buildings looked bruised with age, and the streets lay empty and sad.

That spring, Italy would enter the Great War and capture Gorizia. According to the fictionalized autobiographical account of the American ambulance driver Ernest Hemingway, stationed in Gorizia, some of the town's houses would lose whole sides in the shelling, gardens would be buried in rubble, and the Pannovitz forest, where Andor first trained with live ammunition, would be reduced to charred stumps.[66] Up in the mountains, more than half a million men would die in the twelve-battle bloodbath of the Isonzo. Tens of thousands of others would freeze to death. Andor's photographs of Gorizia are unremarkable. Yet they may be the last ever taken of the town as a dowager winter resort living on time borrowed from the belle epoque.[67]

On Christmas Eve, Andor got orders to lead a four-man patrol around town to keep public order. As they made the rounds of the watering holes, Andor decided that the brothel also needed checking. But when they knocked and informed the madam, she replied that the establishment was closed until after midnight, then slammed the door in their faces. So Andor gave the command to scale a wall and break in. There the men found a warm welcome but not from the madam, who threatened to report their disgraceful behavior. What happened inside?[68] Although Andor loved to tell the story, he never elaborated. That may have been when he lost his virginity. In any case, his Christmas night in a brothel was surely an eye-opener for one whose ideas about women owed much to novels about chivalric romance.

It's unsurprising that Andor got holiday duty. The Czech officer to whom he reported assigned the Hungarians in his unit every undesirable job. Sprawling from Bohemia (in the present-day Czech Republic) to Montenegro, from the Tyrol to Galicia, the Habsburg Empire lumped together Austrian-Germans, Magyars, Czechs, Poles, Croats, Serbs, and half a dozen other peoples. Its diversity was mirrored in its army, except at the highest levels, which were Austrian-German. Aware that his brother's Austrian commanders did not speak Hungarian, Jenő couldn't resist a dig in one of his letters: "How's your German? Is it still *ich sage den* or it is now *ich sage dir*?"[69]

Minority officers with nationalist leanings, like Andor's Czech commander, frequently took out their resentments on Hungarian underlings. Ironically, their anti-Hungarian stance dovetailed with that of the Austrian brass and the imperial family. The murdered Archduke Franz Ferdinand had once told his military chief that he considered the army primarily an instrument against the internal enemy, meaning Jews, Freemasons, Socialists, and Hungarians.[70] Andor labeled himself "a left-winger, like any normal human being, a total left-winger, student, socialist," but not, he added, "the type to strike postures."[71] Had he thought about it, he might have nursed his own resentment that on three counts – Jew, socialist, Hungarian – he was the enemy of the army in which he unwillingly served. Yet, aiming to avoid the most perilous assignments, he had volunteered for the officer training program for which his secondary-school diploma qualified him. He was set to begin after the first of the year.

That New Year's Day, Andor took a portrait of his friend Andor Steiner, one of his cohorts in the assault on the brothel. Steiner was in their barracks, scratching out a letter.

"By any chance are you writing about our adventure on Christmas Eve?"

"Yes, I want my folks at home to know about it."[72]

They burst into laughter.

In Andor's photograph, the self-possessed Steiner applies himself to his task, using a stubby pencil and a sheet of paper. An unlit lamp, sharply focused, hangs in front of his forehead and directly over his pencil, suggesting clarity of thought and expression. All else – the racks stacked with field caps, the knapsacks on hooks, the rows of tightly made iron cots, the piles of clean sheets – is visually soft, as if viewed by one who is mentally AWOL.

The photograph's source of illumination is an unseen window. The pale light it admits falls on the worn edge of the table at which Andor's friend sits. That edge seals off a dark triangle in the picture's lower left corner. Meanwhile the table's far side visually underscores a pipe-smoking cardplayer across the room. A blurry could-be shadow, except for his face, the cardplayer seems alert to what's happening in the room, whereas the letter writer is mentally absent. Snapshots of soldiers writing or reading letters are common in wartime. But Andor's epistolary scene does more than document military life. Its use of selective focus, suggestion of silence, and attention to light turn an everyday occurrence into an archetype.

Andor took the picture using the Ica Bebe that Jenő had purchased and sent him in mid-December. "Just the machine for you," Jenő assured him, and only 120 korona.[73] The camera's main advantage, according to Jenő, was its excellent lens, a Zeiss Tessar so fast (f/5.5) that Andor could photograph even in cloudy or stormy weather. A boxy folding camera with leather bellows, the Ica Bebe came with holders in which to insert glass plates, each 4.5 by 6 centimeters. Because it could house up to seven plates at a time, Andor was able to make several exposures without changing plate holders. The Bebe could be handheld, allowing the photographer to work quickly. It could also be attached to a tripod for greater stability. Those in the know added a light meter. Andor relied on charts and guesses, considering the film speed, lighting conditions, and what he wanted in the print.

Only a week after Andor photographed Steiner, his new camera sat idle. After tumbling into a polluted creek, he had come down with typhoid fever, a life-threatening disease often caused by water contaminated with feces. Typhoid fever brings a high temperature, rashes, headaches, and diarrhea. Andor spent almost three months in a small hillside hospital, where Catholic nuns nursed him back to health. Not until the last weekend in March did he wobble out of the hospital. That Sunday, he drifted through the streets of Gorizia, once again visually decanting the town.[74]

**On June 23rd,** Andor found himself in a train station in Esztergom, Hungary, his unit's home base. His 8th Field Battalion of the 26th Joint Regiment was bound for Galicia (now western Ukraine and southeastern Poland) – the most savage killing ground of the eastern front. On hearing the news, Imre hopped a train from the town of Galgócz, where he was working, to Esztergom. The brothers talked long into the night, Imre attempting to comfort Andor, even though both saw the order as a death warrant. As Imre left the barracks the following morning, he stopped more than once, pivoted, and looked lovingly at his scared younger brother.

By 1:30 on the afternoon their company was to depart, the men thronged the Esztergom station. A military band played a hymn. Then came a song about heroism and mothers' grief that plunged Andor into thoughts of his own mother. Someone wept. A girl gave him a flower. The train steamed up.

Prying themselves from family and friends, the soldiers boarded, then crowded around the half-open windows. Babies were held aloft. Sweethearts and spouses reached out for one last touch. At 1:43, they inched forward. The wailing and goodbyes almost drowned out the sound of the band. Then a shrieking woman darted toward a door of the train, and a sergeant leaped off to embrace her. "But my dear little mommy," he soothed, "don't cry." Squeezed up to a window inside the train, Andor stared hard at this pair acting out his ideas about matrimonial devotion and the hideousness of the war. The sergeant gave his distraught woman another farewell kiss—"a horrible kiss," Andor felt. She clutched at the sergeant. But he tore himself out of her arms, sprinted for the train, and hoisted himself up. She ran after him, her arms flung up as if she expected to be lifted inside. It felt to Andor as if everyone except that one desperate woman had frozen. The train built up speed. As she receded into the distance, he watched, still transfixed. Her head drooped in abject sorrow.[75]

Six hours later, the train crept into Budapest. The men's families had received notice that their journey would include a halt at a suburban station. Jenő, Uncle Poldi, Uncle Józsi, and Andor's cousins Ilonka and Jenő Sommer stood on the platform. Mama and Jolán were absent: Andor was hiding from them the news that he was bound for the front. The family visit had barely begun when the train lurched. At first, Andor thought it was backing up. But it was moving forward, and he had to scramble aboard without properly hugging and kissing each person. Jenő sprinted to the door of Andor's compartment, and the two managed a strong handshake that left Andor limp with emotion. As the train rattled out, he leaned from a window. At first, he could see the family but then only Ilonka's hair in a pool of light.

Settling in for the long journey, the men told stories and sang. Twenty-four hours after they left Budapest, the baking heat of the Hungarian plains gave way to chill as they ascended the Carpathian Mountains dividing Galicia from the rest of the Habsburg Empire. They lumbered through the tunnel at the Łupków Pass, emerging the next morning into a landscape littered with bombed-out bridges, charred houses, and smashed railcars. When they passed a train crammed with the wounded and headed in the opposite direction, Andor observed that its occupants had "already looked death in the eyes."[76]

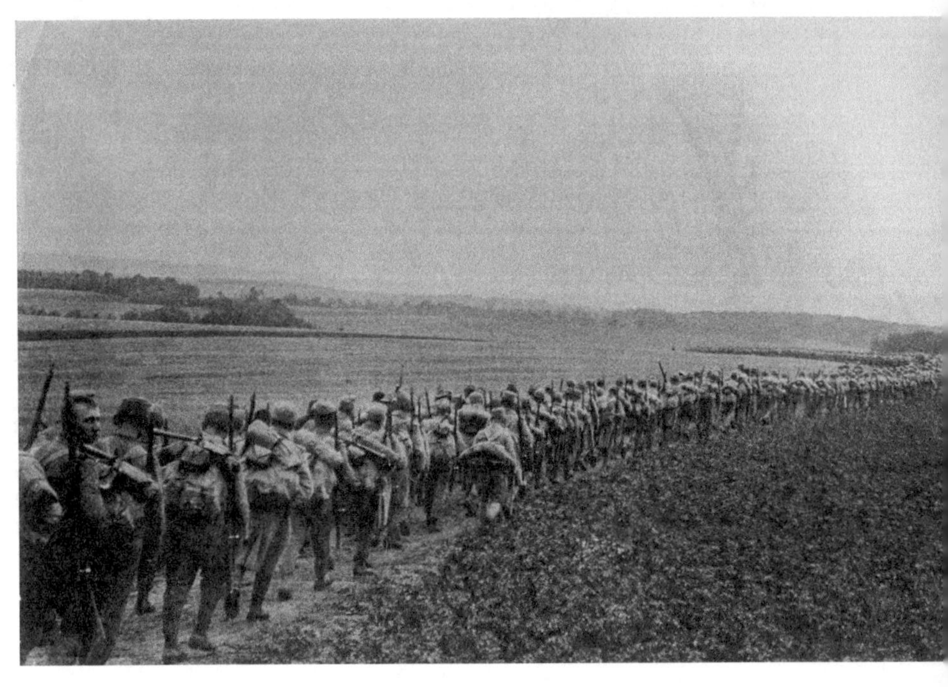

André Kertész, *Forced March to the Front*, 1915

# 2 FORCED MARCH TO THE FRONT, 1914–1918

**As soon as he reached Galicia,** Andor wired Uncle Poldi. Then he wrote to Jolán, revealing that he was bound for the front, begging her forgiveness for keeping his deployment a secret, and bidding her farewell "because there is no hope that I will come out alive."[1]

Andor was arriving at a perilous moment indeed. In the first weeks of the war, the Russians had seized Galicia's capital, Lemberg (today Lviv, Ukraine). That positioned them to cross the Carpathian Mountains and swoop onto the Hungarian plains. The Habsburg high command had responded with three disastrous campaigns in the Carpathians. Hundreds of thousands perished. That March, the Austro-Hungarians took another shattering blow when their garrison at Przemyśl (now in southern Poland) laid down its arms.

Come spring, the Austro-Hungarians' German allies inched forward, raining artillery shells and cannon fire upon the Russians in one deafening attack after another. The Slavic retreat left behind muddy corpses, smoldering rubble, and makeshift signs in Cyrillic. In early June, the Central Powers retook Przemyśl. Three weeks later, they marched into Lemberg. Berlin, Vienna, and Budapest exploded with joy.

Andor's 26th Regiment reached Galicia as the Austro-Hungarians continued to claw their way forward. Decisive battles were brewing. With its professional army decimated by the fiasco in the Carpathians,

Austria-Hungary was depending on raw boys. Many could barely load their rifles or fire properly. Or, as in the case of Andor, had decided to shoot into the air.

Andor was still insisting that his mother not know where he was. So Uncle Poldi, Imre, and Jenő had closed ranks to protect Ernesztina by pretending to write and visit Andor in Esztergom. They assured her that he didn't mind the summer heat up the Danube. They led her to believe they had mailed the box of sour cherries she had lovingly packed for him. Poor Mama, thought Andor. He would die leaving her with little more than three letters, twelve postcards, and some photographs to remember him by.

His unit quickly marched out. One night they bivouacked in a boggy village where Jews had been tortured and robbed. It had escaped Russian torching only because the locals scrawled Eastern Orthodox crosses on every possible surface. Most of Galicia's Ruthenians backed the Russians, their coreligionists and fellow Slavs. But Roman Catholic Polish Galicians remained loyal to the Habsburgs. So did the nine hundred thousand Galician Jews, horror-struck by the czar's pogroms and now brutalized by the Russians.[2]

Andor's diary says little about the treatment of Jews in Galicia, but what it says suggests that he was shaken by the anti-Semitism he observed. It wasn't only the Russians. In Budapest, Jews were generally assumed to be worthy and loyal citizens. But that was not true throughout Hungary. On the way to Galicia, the train carrying Andor's unit had passed the charred remains of a synagogue. A comrade, unaware that Andor was Jewish, had hooted with glee. Andor stayed mute.

Almost two weeks passed between that incident and Andor recording it in his diary. With his days and nights ensnarled, he jotted down what he could when he could. On July 8th, he wrote: "On July 2, I spent my 21st birthday in the unknown in a dirty Polish nest," meaning a hut.[3] One night, he slept in a parked railcar. Once he awoke at 2:00 a.m., agitated by a dream about Jolán and unable to get back to sleep. Pulling out at daybreak that day (or the next or the next), he discerned through the fog what perhaps no one else did: a battalion sleeping on haystacks in the distance. As he trod on, Andor imagined the *civilian* dreams those men were dreaming.[4]

The march was arduous. Heavy rains had swollen the rivers and turned the roads to mud paste and the cornfields to swamps. Battered by sticky heat, Andor's unit pressed on, through rubble-strewn pastures and villages. When finally they got permission to halt, they unstrapped their knapsacks and stretched out next to the road, exhausted. Children popped up, trying to sell things.

Camping on the edge of a forest on July 9th, Andor heard whistling shrapnel, rumbling tanks, and volleys of gunfire. Because his unit had been shifted from one section to another, they had so far escaped combat. Logistics were confused. They were told they would stay near the forest for ten or fourteen days. No, they would split into units of one hundred and head off. That night they ate crispy pork and *palacsinta* (Hungarian crepes), ominously billed as a final dinner. At 5:00 a.m. came the order to move.

The heat grew stifling, the day chaotic. After they made camp late that afternoon, airplanes rumbled out of nowhere and gunfire exploded. Then they were strafed again, not by bullets but by a hard rain that sent them scrambling for cover. As daylight faded, the rain tapered off. The heat had been broken. Andor dreamily watched something moving on the horizon.

He spent the following day in a trench awaiting orders. They arrived by field telephone in late afternoon. It was almost 10:00 p.m. when they entered a pitch-dark forest, where each man had to stay within touching distance and tread in the boot prints of his comrade ahead. After they stopped the next morning in a field glistening from rain, the first mail arrived from Budapest. Everyone feared that his name would not be called. Andor got nothing from Jolán, one letter from Jenő. The men smoked, played cards, or conversed in low voices. Andor caught up on his diary, wondering if that day's entry would be his last.

Nearly so. As he stood in a dugout the next morning, a bullet intended for him whizzed by. He was playing Russian roulette.

**A week later,** Andor's unit fell in for a ten-mile march from Mitulin to Lonie, two villages in what is now western Ukraine.[5] The Central Powers had cleared the Russians out of most of Galicia, and the high command was mulling over the next target. Combat had waned except near the Gnyla Lypa River (today the Hnyla Lypa). There the German Süd Army was hammering the Russians, who were refusing to yield their last strip of Habsburg soil. Andor's 26th Joint Regiment had been ordered to help oust the enemy. One flank of his regiment had been captured and required immediate replacement. So for forty-eight hours, day and night, Andor and his comrades in arms pounded the Galician plain. Occasionally, they halted to unsling their knapsacks, relieve themselves, bolt down some food, maybe catch a catnap. Andor was carrying his gun, sixty rounds of ammunition, a can of rifle grease, a first aid kit, a bedroll, and some clothing – plus his camera, a tripod, a self-timer, eighteen plate holders, a glass cutter, and some glass plates in a metal box.

The camera was a new strut-folding Goerz Tenax, which fit in his pocket when it was folded. The lens was an excellent Dagor f/6.8 75 millimeter lens. Its shutter speeds ranged from one second to 1/250 second. It could focus from six feet to infinity. He used the glass cutter to quarter the plates. That yielded the 4 by 6 centimeter plates he needed. Each was fragile and precious.

At some point during that trek, Andor took a picture. The top half of *Forced March to the Front* is inert sky. Below, a rope of soldiers coils over fenceless fields. Any army's operations rely on subsuming individuals into the corps and reducing them all to sameness. The exception in Andor's picture is one soldier who turns his head, shows his face, and thus reads as an individual. Andor's self-assertion in taking the picture parallels that of the soldier. He too briefly breaks ranks and exits the war machine to act as a seeing and thinking individual. By selecting and recording the scene, he makes it his and not the army's. For the fraction of a second it takes to expose his glass plate, he holds those hundreds of men back from the rush to oblivion.

Every photograph is a memento mori, none more so than one by a soldier-photographer. Even if Andor's glass plate with the latent image of the march was not shattered or lost, would he survive to develop and print it? He tried to record the date of each picture. "July 19, 1915," he wrote of *Forced March to the Front*. At the moment he put pencil to paper, he was alive. He had a pulse, a consciousness, maybe even a future.

Others in Andor's unit probably had cameras too, but no one else was lugging so much equipment or stealing away to the darkest spots at night to cut glass plates. To those who ribbed him, Andor retorted: "If I survive, I'll develop [them]; [if] I don't, I won't."[6] If he did have a life ahead, he felt, it was thanks to his talismanic camera. His love for Jolán had once kept him going; now the Goerz Tenax ballasted his hopes. By photographing, he could be fully present on the front lines but also escape to his old life. He could find purpose in the ludicrous fact of risking death for the ramshackle Habsburg Empire.

In Lonie, Andor experienced trench warfare, with the two armies facing each other over fields cratered by cannonballs and grenades. Yet his photographs reveal little about the tension, fatigue, and grind of facing the enemy twenty-four hours a day; of enduring storms of bullets; of living in ditches, hot and filthy by day, wet and chilly by night. Everything was infested with lice, flies, and rats. A few of Andor's photographs reveal barbed wire and bayoneted rifles. But the muck, the rubble, and the pillars of smoke are mostly absent.

The men's camaraderie *is* very much present. At the end of July, the company rotated back from Lonie to rest, play sports, and celebrate the first anniversary of Austria-Hungary's declaration of war. During that interlude, they boxed and held soccer matches, vying for extra tins of food. A few guys improvised clown costumes and acted the fool. Andor would sidle into the right spot, slip out his camera, and click off a picture. Nobody paid much attention.

The R and R over, Andor's unit maneuvered for an advantageous position in advance of an all-out battle, moving to the uplands near the remains of the livestock-raising village of Gologóry (today Holohory). There, they were pinned down by Russian fire. Surprisingly, they were still getting mail. Hoist this letter as a flag, Jenő joked, and the Russians will flee because my humor is so strong.[7]

During lulls in the fighting, Andor continued to train his lens on his buddies. Once he photographed four men genially seated on the hollow log over their pit latrine. Three have clumps of grass at the ready, and the fourth prepares to use his. After snapping the picture, Andor asked for each man's home address. Then he arranged to get the exposed plates to Jenő via military mail or someone headed for Budapest. He wrote Jenő to ask that he develop the negatives, make prints, and send one to each of the families.

Decades later, the Hungarian British writer George Szirtes would end his poem "Kertész: Latrine" with this couplet:

*Let them dump and move on into the dark plate*
*of the unexposed future, too little and too late.*[8]

Indeed, death was biding its time: One of the four was killed shortly thereafter. Andor told Jenő to mail the print to his widow. It was a hell of a last picture. But there the man was, sutured to paper with rays of light. "Thank you for my sweetheart, my life," she wrote, as Andor would later recount, perhaps embellishing.[9]

The latrine sitters' relatives were not the only ones to receive photos from Andor. He asked Jenő to develop, print, and mail his pictures of others too, either to their families or back to Andor so he could hand them out himself. Jenő should use Andor's savings to pay for supplies and postage. "I thank you in advance, Öcskös [little brother], for your troubles, and I wish that we mutually do a good job to please both of us,"

Andor wrote. "Naturally, the copies do not have to be top quality, just the kind of mass copying. We might have time to make first-class copies together if I may ever get home."[10]

Like his tobacco allotments, which Andor, a nonsmoker, saved up and gave to buddies who'd depleted theirs, his photographs stoked friendships and served as social currency. Andor was no longer a whimpering boy turning his back on his classmates but a generous and socially competent youth. He had gained self-esteem. In taking photographs, getting them developed and printed, and delivering them to their subjects, he engaged with those around him, asserted a self, and registered good times in the midst of war.

Andor's photographs resemble a family album. He captured his comrades eating, fishing, shaving, kneeling in prayer, goofing around, cleaning their straw mattresses, and ladling out soup for the locals. Dinners-to-be caught his eye too: a strung-up suckling pig, a hare someone had shot. He asked his superior officers to pose at the doorstep of their (comparatively) deluxe underground shelter under their handmade sign: "Villa Baba." Sent on a reconnaissance mission, he found himself on a rustic farm that had been spared the storm of combat. There he photographed a fellow soldier smiling and touching the hip of a Galician peasant woman as if to guide her onto the dance floor. That picture would be titled *The Eternal Tender Touch*.[11] Andor could cope with the war only by distancing himself from its horrors.

From time to time, he set up a self-portrait. One baking-hot day when he couldn't stand the trench, with its stench and lice, he decided to combine taking a photograph with "doing *blicc*" from the war. Disobeying orders, he wriggled four or five hundred yards through the dust and yellowed grass to a small stream where Russian shells frequently plumped into the water. There he stripped to his underwear, heaping his uniform on the ground. With his camera on its tripod and his self-timer set, Andor lowered himself to the creek bank and went about pinching lice out of a piece of clothing. The young man in Andor's self-portrait could be a camper dangling his feet in a stream as he attends to a domestic chore. One would never guess he was a soldier in the crosshairs of enemy guns.

After battles, Andor would watch as a government photographer materialized, set up his view camera, and made a panoramic scene worthy of the nineteenth century. Andor and other camera-toting servicemen, for their part, were pioneering the twentieth century by breaking rules about proper subject matter, privileging the private moment over the public event, and shooting on the fly.

World War I was the first conflict in which ordinary soldiers carried cameras. Some photographed weapons and corpses, a practice condoned by the Austro-Hungarian military. Others wanted to cue later stories: *The attack came from over there. This is the type of artillery we used. Here is my buddy who died.* Andor, for one, had no interest in securing bragging rights about his military exploits. Taking for granted that the war was stupid and pointless, he denied its savagery by ignoring it.

As dawn was breaking nine days after Andor photographed himself at the creek, his unit was alerted to what might be an attack. Then he was stunned to see a snowy-haired Moses, propped up by two adolescents, stagger over the crest of a hill. The old man gripped a white flag. Andor heard howls of "*Nicht schießen! Nicht schießen!*" ("Don't shoot!"). Through the early-morning drizzle and fog, he watched as waves of humanity, old men and young boys, poured down the slope. Their faces were yellowed, bloodied, and bruised. Their tattered silky-black caftans dragged in the dirt. They resembled the walking dead of an old Jewish cemetery. All were German-speaking Jews loyal to the Habsburg Empire. Robbed, beaten, and driven from their homes by the Russians, they had been forced to build roads and dig trenches, then driven toward the Hungarian lines. On reaching Andor's unit, some wept, retreated into prayer, or dropped to their knees to kiss the earth.

Later that day, a squad escorted the two hundred and fifty Jews to a village behind the front lines. The oldest and youngest rode on carts.

Five days after that, two hundred more would appear. With a Russian offensive looming, the Hungarian officers' kindness had reached its limit. The second group was driven back to the no-man's-land between the two lines. Later Andor would learn that all had been massacred.[12]

One of Andor's closest friends, a lieutenant and fellow Jew named Frigyes Groszmann, hastened to sound the alarm about this harrowing double event. "These men have suffered just because they are Jewish," he wrote in an article published that fall in Budapest's leading Jewish political weekly. Their expulsion from their homes and persecution resonated with centuries of Jewish history, he continues. Worrying perhaps about the future of Hungary, Groszmann goes on to analyze how anti-Semitism had spread in Russia. He closes with an image of the last Jew disappearing over the hill toward the Russian lines: "My eyes were filled with tears and I sighed painfully to the Lord of the Heavens."[13]

Andor's upbringing had left him ill prepared for such an event, even more shocking because many Galician Jews were wealthy and well educated. He would never forget them. Even so, this was not the turning point in his life that it might have been. His reaction was not to speak out but to look elsewhere, just as he had when his comrade laughed at the charred synagogue. Andor felt he had no power to reset the great wheels of the world. He could only be generous, kind, and curious about the people he met, one by one.

Nor did he train his camera on the wretched, even though his photographs could have been gripping and publishable. Maybe his duties precluded the use of the camera. More to the point, he had no desire to record suffering or document the war. He would stick with the flirtatious tender touch.

And with the comic: He decided to enter his latrine and lice-picking photographs in a contest sponsored by *Borsszem Jankó.* Publishing had been on Andor's mind. Maybe he'd taken the two pictures because he knew that the humor magazine was seeking entries showing the funny side of war. Jenő would handle the developing, printing, and submission.

The young man who had once accused himself of lacking ambition then turned his attention to Budapest's approximately twenty-two newspapers.[14] He instructed Jenő to send out selected enlargements of various pictures, always using a pseudonym. Credit the humorous pictures to "Impostor," Andor directed, and those with serious subjects to "K.A." Sell the simplistic shots to the trashier papers, he continued. Drop no clues about his identity and use a different credit line for each. "Photograph by a volunteer" or some other bland, if not strictly accurate, wording would do.[15]

Andor was also planning to set up a primitive darkroom on the front lines. On August 23, Jenő wrote to say that he was mailing a package containing glass plates, photo paper, chemicals, and gold toner.[16] He would include the portrait of their father that Andor had requested. But if the supplies and the photograph ever reached Andor, he had little or no time to take advantage of them: His sector was abruptly in motion. On the afternoon of the day when Jenő wrote and the second wave of Jews appeared, Royal Hungarian Private First Class Andor Kertész scribbled two brave and kind field postcards and tucked them into his pocket.

One was for his brothers, his uncle Poldi, and his mother, who had learned from a gossip of his transfer to the front. In the postcard, he expresses his gratitude and asks his brothers to love their mother intensely as compensation for his own vanished love. "Live each of life's moments with pleasure," he urges.[17]

Andor addressed the other to "The Honorable Lady Jolán Balog":

> *The outcome of today is uncertain; if this day ever became fatal for me, this little postcard will still be on the way. In that case, take it as my obituary and don't be too saddened because of me. We have gone through so much that it may be better if you then just forget me and my big honest love for you. In that case, I am gone and nowhere to be found, I don't exist anymore, thus any self-torture would be a waste. In that case, my great love shall only be a passing memory along with me; after all, an entire life stands before you. My only request is for you to love and console my*

*Mother so she can more easily handle this blow. You too, my dear Joli, be consoled and have a happy life. This is my wish to you all. Thinking of you with great, honest love, gratefully for your love, Andor.*[18]

Andor survived August 23rd. But at 7:43 on the morning of August 27th, he redated the postcards and put them back in his pocket, along with instructions in case he was killed. The Austro-Hungarians were about to unleash the inferno that would break the Russian lines at Gologóry, pry the enemy from the banks of the Zolota Lypa at Brzezany, and push on. Later, the enemy would retake the river, seize the wooded heights west of the Zolota Lypa, and gain possession of key sections of the railroad. From Zavaloff and Nosoff on the Zolota Lypa to Mariampil on the Dniester, combat would rage.

On August 31st, the press reported "very violent light and heavy artillery fire. The attacks were particularly fierce north of Zloczow."[19] It was there that a Russian bullet bit into Andor's chest as his company pressed up a hill. Eventually treated for his wound, Andor was soon out of mortal danger and transportable. Of the tons of iron hurled by the Russians that day, that was his lucky bullet.

**After Andor vanished** in battle north of Zloczow, his family was frantic for news. When they learned that the Russians had captured his company, they assumed he was a prisoner of war. In fact, he had been wounded earlier in an action for which he would receive a Second Class Silver Medal for Bravery.

Andor had landed in a field hospital. A Russian Jewish writer working in Galicia that summer describes such a place: In one room lay the critically wounded, many of them unconscious and unmovable. Elsewhere, men sprawled, sat, or stood, awaiting surgery amid "piles of blood-soaked gauze. The pungent stench of blood was sickening. The bandaging was done in a separate room on five or six tables. And what ghastly wounds!"[20] Andor himself never spoke of such horrors.

Feeble and ashen, he was then trundled to a hospital in Eperjes (now Prešov, Slovakia). The bullet had passed a quarter of an inch below his heart, and nearly severed the radial nerve in his left arm, paralyzing that arm and hand. As he was stabilizing, he came down with malaria, which can bring a high fever, headache, vomiting, sweating, chills, and sometimes death. Weeks blurred past. Andor got back on his feet. Eventually, he managed a few photographs in the Eperjes hospital, though he needed help manipulating his camera. A self-portrait shows him surveying the town from a window and looking boyish and wistful. The left sleeve of his jacket hangs limp.

When he was strong enough to travel, Andor was packed into a train with thousands of other convalescents for the three-day journey to a Red Cross hospital in Buda. There he learned that he might or might not recover the use of his arm and hand. A doctor performed surgery, then put Andor's arm in a "hideous splint contraption" and ordered physical therapy.[21] However, three or four months of therapy did nothing to bring back sensation. The doctor prepared for a second operation. Then, as Andor was performing his routine in the hydrotherapy pool on the morning of the surgery, he felt twinges in his fingers. He summoned a nurse. She called the surgeon, who canceled the operation. Andor spent that winter in treatment. Come spring, he once again picked up his Goerz Tenax. When he discovered that he was unable to insert a plate using only one hand, he began mulling over how to rig up a device to connect his camera to his wounded arm.[22]

Andor had had time to consider his photography. What had he learned? To work unobtrusively. To be ready to seize the moment by thinking in advance about aperture, shutter speed, distance. Often, he'd had a single chance to get something right. Often, he'd fallen short. He had no light meter, and ISO ratings did not yet exist. (ISO refers to an international standard for measuring the light sensitivity of film.) So he relied on experience and rule of thumb. On bright days, 1/100th of a second was a starting point. But direct sun was one thing and open shade quite another. Under light foliage, he could try 1/50th, while heavy foliage might call for 1/10th of a second.

Most of Andor's images from Galicia are not outstanding for their technical proficiency or aesthetic qualities. Yet few other soldiers endlessly scanned for pictures as he did. Few bothered with self-timers, glass plates, glass cutters, or tripods. Few applied themselves to what was ordinary, not extraordinary, about life at the front.

That winter and spring at Elisabeth Hospital brought more time for reflection and new opportunities for picture-taking. By holding the camera with his right hand and coaxing his left onto the shutter release, Andor could photograph other patients playing cards, kneeling at an outdoor mass, or hanging around with the kitchen crew as they cleaned fish for dinner. Turning silly one day, the men playacted trench warfare, lying on a grassy embankment and pretending their canes were rifles. Six months earlier, Andor had been hunkering down in a grungy trench at risk of death any minute. Now he and other ambulatory patients lunched at a white-clothed table set with china and supplied with a half bottle of wine for each man. Andor's group portrait places him with eight others awaiting the soup that a nun nurse is serving. On another occasion, he picnicked along a stream with two Red Cross volunteers. One plucked flowers and charmed him with her childlike laugh. They became friends, maybe more. Six months later, he would be stunned by news that she had committed suicide using her father's revolver.

Happily, Elisabeth Hospital was only a short walk from the Tabán district, that welter of cobblestoned streets where Andor and Jenő used to muck around before the war. Its whitewashed houses, tiny plum and apricot orchards, and occasional herds of pigs gave the Tabán the air of a timeworn village, albeit one with bordellos, bars, and other features of bohemian urban life. That spring, Andor's best photographs of its crooked streets, dark doorways, and houses with sharply angled roofs subordinate everything else to their compositions. Crisply shadowed and unpeopled, the Tabán photographs connote a place where one could daydream about an idealized past.

Nearly a year after Andor was wounded, orders arrived for him to report to Esztergom, his regiment's home base. The town commands the Danube bend at what is now the Hungarian-Slovakian border. As the seat of the Archbishop of Esztergom-Budapest and the home of King Saint Stephen, Hungary's founder and patron saint, Esztergom is the nation's ecclesiastical center. Its neoclassical basilica sits like a crown jewel atop Castle Hill. The finest land, libraries, and residences, Andor knew, all belonged to the church. Even the best fish went to the Catholic elite: When the locals caught a big pike or carp, they would offer it to the archbishop.

Esztergom's backstreets, however, felt like a different world. There swineherds drove muddy pigs down to the river. Girls hauled yoked water buckets up and down slopes. Country smells wafted through the open-air markets. On sweltering Sunday afternoons, when every shop was padlocked and every house was silent, Esztergom baked in the sun. Come Monday morning, the streets stirred with soldiers cycling in or out of active duty. Veterans abounded, too, many with crutches or canes. They were limping, bandaged, and shell-shocked.

At first, Andor stayed in a military convalescent facility in Párkány (now Štúrovo, Slovakia), across the river. Then he moved to a lawyer's home on Jókai Mór Street in Esztergom, a ten-minute walk from the center near a plane tree–canopied side loop of the Danube. His new duties as a drill instructor and office worker, his group exercise sessions, and his hydrotherapy treatments still left plenty of time to hike, drink with his buddies, see local women, and take photographs. His camera was always at hand. So many subjects caught his attention that the soldiers' handwritten newsletter *Gewehr Heraus!* (Rifle!) joked that the military police had detained him for suspected spying: "As he was found with photographs of the garbage dump and its surroundings, the suspicion seems to have been well founded."[23]

It's a cliché that no one comes back from combat unchanged. Some from the generation of 1914 would stagger from the war cynical and hard-drinking. Andor would exorcise *his* ghosts and master his own narrative, or try to, with photography. Let the generals and politicians tell their lies and play their geopolitical games. He wanted to "live each of life's moments with pleasure," training his attention on moments that made him feel alive. Esztergom, Andor would explain decades later, was "where my vision was shaped and where my view of life was forged."[24]

During the months he was stationed in Esztergom, Andor spent hours tramping the surrounding hills, fields, and roads. When he had the day free, he easily did twelve or fifteen miles between town and old riverine villages like Nyergesújfalu, Dömös, and Visegrád. One Sunday he returned from Bátorkeszi (today Bátorove Kosihy), northwest of Esztergom, with a negative that could illustrate the opening scene of a nineteenth-century novel.[25] There he had met a young notary, pastor, and schoolmaster standing around after church, bandying words and enjoying a smoke. Village men typically donned dark suits on the Sabbath. But those in Andor's picture cut more worldly figures than most with their starched collars, watch chains, and self-possessed airs. The notary makes a graceful hand gesture. Like his offbeat felt hat, it suggests a bureaucrat with a bohemian soul. Andor's picture cocoons him and his friends in an eternal Sunday afternoon, even as the European civilization they represented was shattering all around them.

On another day, Andor was cutting through a cornfield on his way back to town when he spotted an elderly couple in distress. It was September, and the two had been collecting dried stalks to burn that coming winter as fuel. As they strained their overburdened wagon up the slope from field to road, a wheel had come loose, and their nag staggered and fell. Andor got the picture, then hastened to help.

Afterward he asked the man for his name and address.

"Why?" He was taken aback by the question.

Andor wanted to send them a print.

In town, he turned his camera toward street musicians. One was an aging amateur accordionist who had orders to take over a clerical job from a younger man bound for the front. In Andor's image, the man plays as he awaits his paperwork. His head tilts downward. His bespectacled eyes oversee the fingering on the right keyboard. He plays the left keyboard by feel alone. Oblivious to everything but the music, the man pulls at his instrument as if inhaling, using his art to forget hardship, boredom, and pain.

In another photograph, a middle-aged Romani cellist in uniform plays on a bench in a park. He wraps himself around his instrument with the solicitude and sensuality of a lover. Positioned at the man's side, Andor took a picture that speaks of twoness. The paired tree trunks and paired shoots from a young tree behind the man splay out like wayward cello strings. Photographer and subject. Cello and man. Two hands working together, one on the strings, one on the bow.[26]

Like all cameras, Andor's was a literalist, recording the light bouncing off the crack in the wall behind the cellist as faithfully as it did that off the strings of his instrument. All the same, his photographs of both the accordionist and the cellist breach the material world to show how music feels. Are they playing rhapsodies? Or *verbunkos,* the Hungarian folk songs associated with press-ganging men into the army? Or Romani music laced with sweet-sad yearning for the puszta and touching every Magyar's lost Asian soul?

What the two musicians got from their instruments, Andor got from his camera, a box with a bellows like the accordion, all about angles and timing.

Besides taking pictures, Andor was printing his negatives from the front. Working with only one hand was slow. But matters improved after a doctor replaced the arm contraption with a sling. Andor had no enlarger and probably no real darkroom. He did contact prints, placing each glass-plate negative directly on a piece of photographic paper and exposing it to light, resulting in an image of the same size. He started with printing-out paper, which requires sunlight to bring out the images. But the prints tended to be too contrasty (meaning that the differences between the tones were too stark). So, when he could get chemicals, which he had to mix himself, he turned to gaslight paper, a type of developing-out paper that uses chemistry, not sunlight, to bring out the latent image. Made for printing in weak artificial light like that of a gas lamp, gaslight paper is forgiving of amateur photographers unsure about how long to expose their negatives or how long to keep the emerging print in the developing bath. After fixing and washing his pictures, Andor dried them using a blotter or placing them on a piece of glass out in the sun.[27]

When he had a good sampling, Andor showed his pictures to his regiment's higher-ups and proposed that they sponsor a set of ten collotyped photocards. (Collotyping is a photomechanical process akin to lithography.) The postcards would be sold to benefit Red Cross work with war widows and orphans. That was not a novel idea. Postcards were wildly popular during World War I, and small editions of amateur postcards were common. In fact, Andor's regiment had already produced a booklet of detachable postcards. When his officers okayed the plan, he was heartened.

**The war ground on.** In the fall of 1916, Romania seized Transylvania from Hungary, after which the Germans swept in to shove the Romanians back over the Carpathians. The Germans had little help from their demoralized and underequipped Hungarian allies. One German officer reportedly complained: "We are shackled to a corpse."[28] Not only were Hungarian soldiers dropping from exhaustion and hunger, but also their families back home were succumbing to bitterness and despair. The war effort, like the nation, was bankrupt. What were they fighting for anyway? The words of their leaders rang hollow.

Then in November, Emperor of Austria and King of Hungary Franz Joseph died after a reign of sixty-eight years, longer even than Queen Victoria's. Black crepe draped the omnipresent official portrait that had once seemed to guarantee a permanent world order. Even Franz Joseph had lost hope of victory. Worse, he had witnessed the slow-motion death of the Habsburg Empire, established in the thirteenth century. His subjects' affection for their fossilized emperor no longer sufficed to stave off conflict among themselves. Wars were brewing within the war. When Franz Joseph's untested great-nephew inherited the doddering empire, every Austro-Hungarian soldier had to take an oath of allegiance. But things were changing.

In Budapest, there was high-level talk of unyoking Hungary from Austria. Meanwhile, a group of Slovene soldiers mutinied. So did various Serbs, Czechs, and Ruthenians. The army was running on empty. Most enlisted men could barely remember the last time they'd eaten an egg. Yet rumor had it that the imperial-royal household consumed six thousand eggs every day.[29]

Even as Hungarians everywhere experienced deprivations and despair, Budapest's weekly *Az Érdekes Újság* (Interesting News) continued to cheerfully showcase pictures by soldiers. *Az Érdekes Újság* was the only Hungarian newsmagazine to license the rights to rotogravure, a printing process that yielded consistently high-quality images. Even more alluring to readers, its editors had replaced the stiff head-and-shoulders illustrations that were standard in European newspapers with lively photographs and plenty of them. The photography contest for soldiers dated to the early months of the war. What better way to captivate a nation with millions of sons, sweethearts, husbands, and fathers in uniform? Who could be a more authentic witness to war than the fighting man? That first year, some sixteen hundred soldier-photographers had vied for a pot of money. The following year, the publication narrowed its competition to images that gave "witness to our soldiers' invincible spirit... and to the good aspects of war."[30] Contest number three sought visual evidence of the integrity and good nature of Hungarian soldiers. Now, for the fourth competition, *Az Érdekes Újság* was calling simply for photographs of Hungarian subjects. Andor decided to enter.

His earlier submission to *Borsszem Jankó* had met with success. While sitting one day at the bedside of a hospitalized pal, Andor had glanced at the newspaper placed under a glass of water on the nightstand. There he was startled to read that his self-portrait delousing his garment had won ninth place in the *Borsszem Jankó* contest.[31] His prize was something called a shrapnel calendar with drawings by the illustrator Marcel Vertès (a future Academy Award winner for set and costume design and the creator of murals in Café Carlyle in New York).

Andor would again emerge a winner in the *Az Érdekes Újság* competition. On March 25, 1917, his two photographs appeared alongside twenty-one others in a special section. *Village Council* shows five leathery-faced, bowler hat wearing elders in the village of Pomáz. At distant right are cows drinking at the troughs. At near left sit the ruminating men. The empty ground between them suggests a long, eventless Sunday afternoon. Andor had pulled off an audaciously asymmetrical composition, although at the time he had no idea that it was audacious.

The composition of his other winning image, *Fairy Tale*, is more traditional. Three ragamuffins, one with a knee popping out of his pants, sit absorbed in a book. The boy on the left wears hobnail boots; the others are barefoot. They would have reminded Andor of his young self and his brothers as bookworms and of his traveling bookseller father.

How did this photograph come about? In a nation where one in three people was illiterate, how many waifs sat reading together on village streets?[32] How many arranged themselves so charmingly? Surely the scene was a setup. No, Andor would insist decades later to an incredulous friend. "I did not stage this. That's the way I saw them from afar. I sneaked up on them, even stood there for a while before photographing them. I was waiting for the right moment."

"Weren't they aware of you?"

"Oh, yes. They saw me. I even said a couple of words to them, but they were engrossed in the book."[33]

Andor's account may or may not be accurate. The facts are lost to time. But, like many of his stories, it feels simplistic. Andor had a proclivity for bending the truth, for portraying himself as more hero, victim, or lucky guy than he really was. His embellishments would have been fed by tales he devoured as a child, tales in which wishes come true, setbacks don't last, and little boys command the world. Whether poetry or lying, Andor's stories fit with his desire for a more enchanted life. They offered not material gain but internal gratification. Perhaps he got a little high on his own fantasies and didn't think too much about it.

**The contest** in *Az Érdekes Újság* would be his last for several years. The postcard project also ground to a halt. In the fall of 1916, Andor was ordered to return to limited active duty. Although he took the news in stride, the women he'd been seeing did not. The surviving evidence of these relationships is letters from them that he kept all his life. One ladylove calls herself L. Another styles herself Asszonykád (your little woman). A third leaves her letters unsigned. Apparently, each was unaware of the others.

Jolán remained in the picture but perhaps as a figure on a pedestal labeled Future Wife. If so, that pedestal more than once tottered. Even before departing for the eastern front, Andor had entrusted his friend Jaksay with a breakup letter. Later Jaksay handed it back undelivered, along with advice to mend things with Jolán. During Andor's home leave, a month later, she snubbed him on the street. Or so he perceived. They bickered. Both demanded the return of their tokens of affection. A month after that, they made up. Whatever the situation was between them in late 1916, Jolán probably had no idea that her sometime boyfriend was romancing not one but several other women.

Rail thin and sinewy, with clipped brown hair, blue-gray eyes, and olive skin, twenty-two-year-old Andor cut an attractive figure. His uniform and sling marked him as a wounded war hero. He could be sardonic and faultfinding but also flirtatious and gentle.

"My only one, I can't stand it that you're leaving. Maybe this is only an excuse. Don't leave me. I'm very worried about you," fretted Asszonykád in a letter dated early December. "You're not going to go to Pest, are you?"

Six days later, L wrote to him: "My love, I can't stop thinking of you since I got your letter. We don't deserve this fate." Andor must have told her about his call-up to active duty. "Who knows if I will have a chance to say goodbye. It will be the end if I never saw you again. I'm with you every day in my dreams."

A letter from the third woman is dated three days later: "My dear but bad best love, is this what I deserve?"

Andor opened another note from Asszonykád two days before Christmas: "My love, please don't leave. I miss you. I'm yours. Why did you hurt me this afternoon? Tomorrow at 5, I will see you."[34]

But Andor did leave: He'd been assigned to escort fellow soldiers to distant postings. Some of the soldiers he would accompany were disabled or ailing, but it's unclear why others required an escort. He would also courier medical supplies to various outposts and, for a time, help run a prison camp near the Black Sea. For the next two years, he would ricochet around Central and Eastern Europe: Graz, Semmering, Marburg, Wiener Neustadt, and Vienna (Austria); Maribor (present-day Slovenia); Horodok (present-day Ukraine); Orşova, Caransebeş, Timişoara, Craiova, Ploieşti, Brăila, and Bucharest (present-day Romania); Prague and Brno (present-day Czech Republic); Komárno (present-day Slovakia); Čakovec, Rijeka, and Slavonski Brod (present-day Croatia); Perast and Kotor (present-day Montenegro); Belgrade (present-day Serbia); Sarajevo and Mostar (present-day Bosnia and Herzegovina); Shkodër and Durrës (Albania); and all over Hungary. Lags and gaps in his diary make it impossible to track his week-to-week movements.

Andor traveled mostly by military train, which was notoriously slow and unreliable. The different parts of the empire used incompatible rolling stock, so border crossings involved an interminable process of transferring people and goods from one train to another. One time he and his charge ended up in a louvered boxcar crowded with cattle, an episode Andor found hilarious. When the trains were impracticable, he resorted to hitching rides or even walking. Everywhere papers had to be obtained, signed, stamped, approved, and filed. The creakier the Habsburg Empire became, the more its bureaucrats cranked out passes, permits, passports, and other impediments to mobility.

Everything piqued Andor's interest. He photographed farmhouses, a kid smoking a cigar butt, a concert on a ship, trees and streams, a makeshift market set up among ruins, soldiers relieving themselves in a ditch, street cleaners, a sandal maker, and burned-out boxcars. Turks, Russians, Romanians, Germans. Himself. In Albania, he took a self-portrait with a Muslim man and his three sons. Judging from the picture, they were kindred spirits, though it's unlikely that Andor had any language in common with the Albanians. The nationalism that was the root cause of the war was irrelevant.

Along the way, Andor would diligently pull out his little notebook to record the names and addresses of people he encountered, those he befriended, and those he traveled or worked with. When he returned to Esztergom between assignments, he made prints, which he mailed along with letters or postcards. Many people wrote back, greeting him as *Bandi*, the typical nickname for Andor and one his Hungarian friends would use all his life: *Kedves Bandi!* (Dear Bandi!), *Kedves Bandikám!* (My dear Bandi!), and, jokingly, *Kedves Bandi Bátyám!* (Dear Uncle Bandi!).

When photographing was impracticable, Andor would pick up the strands of his diary. The same powers of observation and delight in the odds and ends of everyday life that served him well as a photographer show up in diary entries that read like descriptions of the pictures he never took.

Once, for instance, he had to shepherd a harmless braggart from Esztergom to Romania. Toilworn, malnourished, and ill, the fellow had a drooping mustache and a face like a rotting apple. Their journey included a several-hour layover in Budapest. So Andor took his charge to Mama, who spoiled the fellow with kindness and what food she could scare up. Then the two men caught the 9:10 train. They ended up in a compartment so packed and fetid, Andor observed, that it didn't "smell like people" but rather "like soldiers." He wrested a space next to a junior officer. "He put his head on my shoulder and he's sleeping," Andor recounted, "and I put my head on his shoulder, so we're a pair."[35]

Another time Andor and others were milling around a provincial train station when one soldier pulled out a harmonica and started to play. A second jumped up to dance, clapping his hands and slapping his ankles. Then irritably and inexplicably, that man told the musician to stop. A third objected. A peacemaker then sliced up and doled out chunks of sausage and another shared his gingerbread. Andor held out his hand with the others.

At a more contemplative moment, Andor watched people washing clothes in a flooded river somewhere at dusk. Suddenly a car spun into view, its silhouette twinned in the water's dark shimmer. Fish were jumping, puckering the surface. The car sped off, kicking up gold dust, as the river absorbed its reflection. The incident felt, Andor wrote, like an "infinitely mysterious" kind of beauty "given by God."[36]

Elsewhere God was missing in action. Everyone was suffering, the empire lay in tatters, the world was grimly destroying itself. Travel became more and more arduous. Andor did not always eat. He fueled himself by taking pictures, making friends, and drinking ersatz coffee. In Albania, he slept in a stone farmhouse where his room had no ceiling, and he awoke one night to discover a scorpion on his blanket.[37] All the same, Andor found his life "exciting and colorful."[38] His days were varied and his commanders far distant. Upset though he was by the suffering he saw on all sides, he was thrilled to be vagabonding at last.

Back in Esztergom, Andor's duties and physical therapy left plenty of time for rambles. One took him to a customs tollhouse on the outskirts of town. There the carts of peasants bound for Esztergom's market squares were inspected, and their contents—chickens, vegetables, dairy products, grains—weighed and taxed. In Hungary, too, people had little to eat. Food riots were erupting. Bread, meat, maize, potatoes, and beans were rationed. (Andor's weekly portion had been cut to a hundred grams of bread and three ounces of meat, typically horsemeat, plus a few dried vegetables.[39]) Accusing peasants of hoarding their produce and selling it on the black market, authorities were ransacking farmhouses and digging up courtyards and gardens.[40] Thus the customs tollhouse was a topical subject. Some photographers would have laid in wait for the arrival of a cart. But Andor was less interested in the news of the day than in the rhythms of the millennium. His photographs find abstract form in a telephone pole, toll bar, and rope; the tollhouse itself; the swathe of sky and band of land.

It was also on the outskirts of Esztergom that Andor took pictures in a Romani camp. He had first visited the camp when his unit chanced upon a Romani lean-to as they were conducting drills. When they got a rest period, Andor pulled out his camera and headed over. Some of the children were capering around bare-bottomed, their fright-wig hair as wild as the grasses. Andor took a few exposures and vowed to return.

Six months later, he had an opportunity. Travelers, fortune tellers, and escapees from the strictures of school and work, the Romani felt like kindred free spirits. Andor photographed an elderly woman called Aunt Didi, then turned to a couple tending their cooking pots. A graceful little tree stood behind them. All the while, two toddler siblings were running around naked.

"Do you like your sister?" Andor inquired of one.

"Yes."

"I don't believe you," he teased.[41]

Andor had crept up to the two, low to the ground, awaiting the moment. As their lips met, their bloated bellies kissed too, and he clicked his shutter release.

His portrait of Paprika Horváth catches something more subtle. Andor met the cheeky Romani adolescent, presumably a redhead, at a horse market.[42] Paprika had smooth skin, a cascade of ringlets, and, Andor quickly noticed, a beautiful body. When he asked if he could photograph her seminude, she agreed. But first she wanted a portrait for her fiancé, who was serving at the front.

"Take it only when my eyes are smiling," Paprika commanded.

Andor did as he was told. She taught him that a smile is most beautiful just as it's stealing onto a face because, at that instant, it's a promise open to the beholder's interpretation. "You don't know how many times I used that," Andor would tell a French gallerist decades later, "for the most sophisticated magazines."[43]

*The Swing* also catches a look, this time one of knowing familiarity between sister and brother. Walking to or from the barracks one day, Andor spotted a girl in a pinafore and hobnailed boots minding her toddler brother. The boy had been planted in a swing that was hung in a sunlit doorway. A blanket enveloped his legs. Andor tossed out a greeting, played a bit with the two, and then, when the moment was ripe, pushed his shutter release lever. In the picture, the little boy turns toward big sister as if to catch her expression. She props herself against a door panel in the stance of a chatty showgirl taking a breather.

The titular swing sits perfectly still. But the picture sends the viewer's eye back and forth between exterior and interior, brightness and shadow, texture and form, anecdote and abstraction. Andor was paying attention to geometric form. The doorjamb, the threshold, and the slatted door panel visually bar-clamp the scene. Triangles too – those of the swing's ropes and the sunlit boards on the floor – have their roles. And there's a third triangle, felt but not seen: the gaze from the photographer to sister and brother.[44]

When Andor wasn't photographing or performing his military duties, he was often at the glass-roofed Mala Swimming Pool, either attending his hydrotherapy sessions or swimming for fun. Even there, he kept his Goerz Tenax at the ready. Lounging at the pool one day before lunch, he shifted his attention from guys idling on the steps or plunging into the water to the optical interplay of light, water, and human body. A swimmer was gliding face down under the surface. Reflections flitted about. The stripes on the man's bathing suit suggested a stylized version of the swashing water.

Andor grabbed the shot. His friends scoffed: You're crazy! Why bother with pictures like that?

"Why only girl friends?" Andor retorted, referring to the pictures he took of his pals with their Esztergom sweethearts. "This also exists."[45]

In *Underwater Swimmer*, a man's body registers as stretched, weightless, and nearly headless. Surrendered to the water, he hovers. His arms are wishboned in front of him. Only his feet rise to the surface. Below hangs his water-warped form. He exists in a state of sensory deprivation. He could be in a dream about flying, in which he's both moving and still, out of body, out of time. *Underwater Swimmer* suggests that the self is unstable, and the everyday eerier than people assume.

Andor's photograph would itself become a kind of underwater swimmer. He loaned the negative to someone, perhaps for his postcard project, and that person lost it. Fortunately, Andor had made a print, which he would locate and use in the 1960s to create a copy negative. It was not until then that *Underwater Swimmer* resurfaced (as *Man Diving, Esztergom*) in a widely viewed exhibition and catalog. It won acclaim as the first modern photograph of a swimmer—an iconic image of the twentieth century.

**By 1918,** defeat loomed for Hungary, and the nation was devolving into chaos. More than 660,000 men had perished. Families were shattered. Inflation was skyrocketing. In the absence of able-bodied men and horses, agricultural output had plummeted. Miserable and exhausted, people were scrounging for food and looking for scapegoats.

Among the tensions ripping the nation apart were those between conservative and increasingly politicized Catholic Hungarians and Jewish Hungarians. Some politicians, journalists, and ecclesiastics accused

Jews of being usurers, swindlers, and profiteers. Jews were behind the nation's agony, they asserted. Hungary was a Christian nation, and the morally corrupt Jews were enriching themselves from the war and threatening basic Hungarian values.[46]

Such tensions underpin Andor's exchange with a cassocked priest one day around dusk. Walking along a road in Esztergom, the heart of Catholic Hungary, Andor caught sight of four priests cutting through a flowering orchard. They had emerged from the bishop's residence and were heading to vespers. With his one good hand, Andor pulled his camera from his pocket and plunged into that same orchard, wondering if there was enough light to pull off a decent picture. When he was about seventy feet in, the youngest priest came rushing over.

"You don't have the right to come in. This is private property."

Andor lost it. "You s.o.b.!" he yelled. "I have the right because I am wounded for you." Then, as Andor later told the story, he asserted that God had bestowed beauty on the blossoming orchard and that God-given beauty belonged to him as much as to the church. The priest scurried away, and Andor, an agnostic, got his picture. Organized religion irked him. "And I was in my uniform, and he was in his uniform," Andor would observe of their two social roles.[47]

Andor's final missions took him, now as a noncommissioned officer, from Esztergom to Sarajevo and Shkodër in the Balkans, then to Brăila, a Romanian port and cargo station on the Danube. There he spent four months inventorying equipment and arms. Andor was a tallier and a list maker, and the job suited him, even though it was virtually impossible. As troops surged in and out of the city, Brăila's rail yards and docks filled and emptied helter-skelter with machine parts, tools, lumber, and crates. Supply depots and ammunition dumps stood poorly guarded. Weapons and shells were pilfered by Bolsheviks, ethnic freedom fighters, and petty thieves.

Some of Andor's Brăila pictures allude to going home. In one, a sailor seated on his duffel bag in a supply depot watches a hound attend to her puppy. They could be read as stand-ins for the subject's distant family. In another, a long-suffering horse is loaded by a sling onto the Constantinople-bound *Principessa Cristina*. Andor also trained his lens on horses munching at their feeder boxes aboard the Turkish vessel *Minna Horn*. Straw is scattered around the deck, and sailors sit gabbing as if in a village square. Andor would photograph the port again, deserted after the Turkish debarkation. He took his last Brăila photographs on walks in the woods with a Viennese army clerk named Emmy.

His flirtation with Emmy, if that's what it was, came on the heels of his final break with Jolán. Andor had outgrown the relationship. The war had brought him face-to-face with all kinds of men and women. With Muslims and Christians, Russian and German prisoners of war, anti-Semites. With the suffering, the maimed, and the dying. He had survived typhoid fever, bullets, and malaria. The boy fascinated by tales of exotic travel had matured into a resourceful and well-traveled young man interested in human complexities.

Earlier that summer, Andor asked Jenő to write the long-delayed letter for him, hand it to Jolán, and have her read it in his presence. Why not write Jolán himself? After more than a decade of courtship, did he not owe her that? Maybe the uncertainty of the mail was a factor. Maybe he wanted someone to be with her when she got the news. Why not wait to break up until after his return to Budapest? One charitable explanation is that Andor knew Jolán had other romantic interests and wanted to relieve her of any obligation. Besides, he would have been curious about her reaction.

So Andor trusted Jenő with the task. Indeed, the letter was "very touching," his brother reported, "just like it usually is in novels." It was his heartrending prose, Jenő contended, not Jolán's true feelings, that brought tears to her eyes. "She made a big show of crying," yet "the woman left behind doesn't think of it as tragic."

A second letter from Jenő to Andor suggests that no sooner had Andor learned that the deed was done than he wrote Jenő to say he regretted it. "Oh, why did you make this mistake?" Jenő chastised him. "Did we need this? Anyway, it doesn't matter anymore."[48] It was too late: one of Jolán's sisters had told Jenő that Jolán was engaged. She soon married a mechanic named Ármin Gál. The last tears had been wrung from Andor's thirteen-year romance.

Ármin was a distant cousin of Jolán's, but also, as it turned out, the Kertészes' relative on the Klopfer and Grósz side of the family. At that thought, Jenő's humor burst through. "The Balogs are going to accept the situation," he informed Andor, "but I hope God saves us from the Grósz family."[49]

**Meanwhile** Bolshevik Russia had quit the war, the Central Powers were retreating, and the Austro-Hungarian Empire was coming unglued. Budapest proposed a peace conference. In October, Andor opened a telegram from Jóska Frankl, his best friend in Esztergom:

> *Peace has broken out. Come home immediately. A huge national task is waiting for you. To procreate until the end! A vast amount of material is at your service… We send you comradely hugs and love: in the name of the Hungarian Autonomous Reproductive Committee.*[50]

Five days later, Andor squeezed into a military train or rode with the throng on the roof. He was not headed straight for home, peace, and procreation, however, but for Vienna with a sheaf of official papers. Near the Romanian-Transylvanian border, his train ran out of coal, and the men had to forage for more.[51] After the train finally delivered him to a slate-gray, rain-splattered Budapest, it went out of service. There was no coal in the Hungarian capital. Andor found other arrangements for the papers, then made his way to his base in Esztergom, where he expected to be demobilized. He also expected to retrieve his best war negatives, which he had entrusted to a friend named Antal. It was time to pull that work together and make the postcard book a reality.

Esztergom was blanketed with snow. Arriving at the barracks, Andor was stunned to find the windows shattered, the doors splintered, and the offices in shambles. His regiment had turned into a mob and ravaged the place. No one was there. Not Antal, not Andor's commander, no one. From the rubble on his friend's desk, Andor plucked one and a half glass negatives. The others—his finest pictures, the ones he'd hoped would make his mark—had vanished. Shock. Disbelief. Heartbreak. The war's parting shot.

Several years later, while nosing around one of Budapest's antiquarian bookshops, Andor would stumble upon postcard-format prints of three of the missing pictures.[52] He never found out who had made them or why.

One swallowed one's losses and soldiered on.

Andor returned to Budapest to discover more smashed windows and looted buildings. The streets swarmed with soldiers and deserters—ragged, unshaven, and bitter. Some had covered the Habsburg insignia on their uniforms with rosettes in Hungarian red, white, and green. Some brandished rifles or machine guns. Others rode around in trucks commandeered from the public works department, scuffling with the police over control of banks, bridges, and post offices.[53]

All the while, Romanian and French troops were advancing toward the capital, cutting off supplies of food and coal. Like everyone else, the Kertészes shivered in a gloomy apartment, their cupboards mostly bare. Ernesztina had little to sell at her shop: no coffee, no tea, only burned barley powder. The refugees, widows, and war-wounded who haunted Teleki Tér could ill afford even that. What's more, the Spanish influenza was raging: newspapers were reporting a hundred thousand cases in Budapest alone.[54] Andor's homecoming and those of his cousins and uncles in uniform would have brought the family comfort but scant celebration.

Andor loathed the war. Yet his demobilization thrust him back into a work life that gave him no pleasure. He was lucky to have a job at the

Giro Bank and Transfers. It involved compiling daily statistics for the accounting department. So much for his life of adventure and travel. Arduous though the army had been, he'd seen the world, found his social bearings, discovered photographic possibilities. Now that life slammed shut. Back to drudgery five days a week.

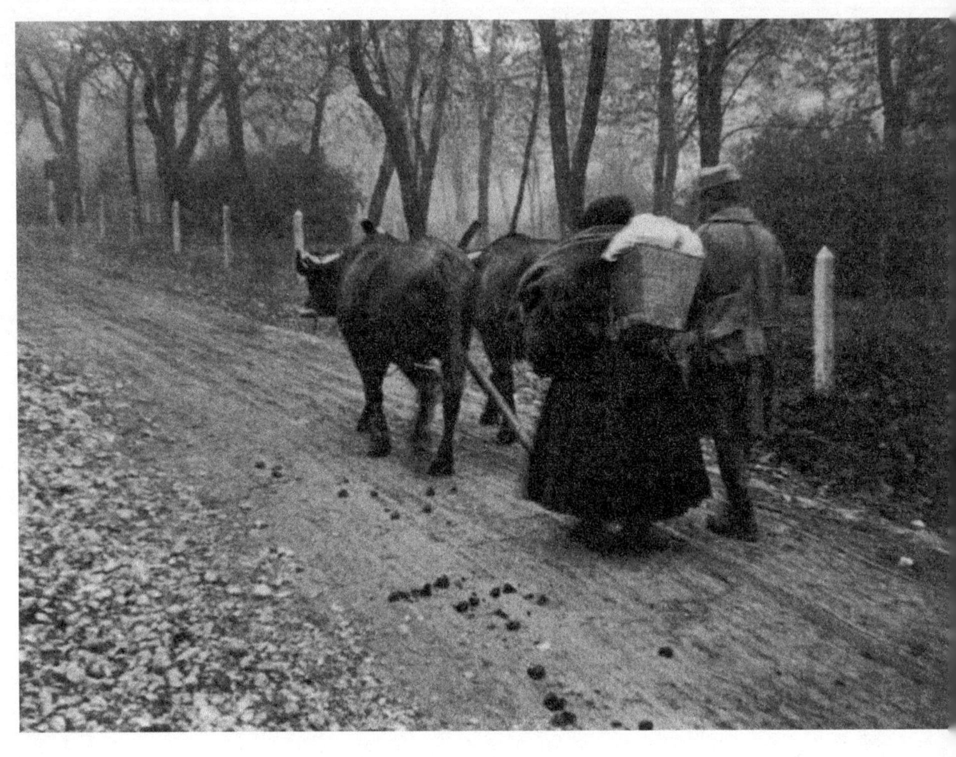

André Kertész, *We Lost the War*, c. 1918

# 3 WE LOST THE WAR, 1918–1925

**A man and a woman,** viewed from the back, plod down a dirt road behind a team of oxen. Although the war has ended, the man wears his uniform because he owns few other clothes. The woman, a beast of burden herself, shoulders a sack and a basket. The two look weary and poor. Yet they have what matters: a home down the road; maybe some land; the oxen, purchased, one imagines, with savings from the man's army pay; and each other. Eventually, Andor's photograph would acquire a title: *We Lost the War*.

That scene of a couple's subdued return to a rural and ancestral way of life bears little resemblance to what Andor was witnessing in Budapest. With the Austro-Hungarian Empire collapsing, the city was consumed by political turmoil. Led by Count Mihály Károlyi, a new National Council scrambled for popular support of a platform that called for a decent peace treaty, democratic reforms, fairness for all ethnic groups, and an independent Hungary. On October 29th, the royal police joined the council. Then factories, shops, and trams shut down, disgorging their employees onto the rain-soaked streets. One by one, other groups threw their weight behind Károlyi's Aster Revolution. Soldiers ripped the imperial buttons from their caps and replaced them with asters. Skirmishes erupted with diehards for the old regime. On October 31st, King Charles IV—who would abdicate two weeks later—named Károlyi prime minister. A democratic order was emerging. Crowds churned through the streets. Shuttered theaters and cinemas reopened. People packed into cafés and restaurants. The First Hungarian Republic was born.

Three months later, the death of a poet once again sent Hungarians reeling. A black ocean of mourners flooded the streets. Schools closed for the funeral. The nation's literary lions gave eulogies next to the catafalque at the national museum.

Endre Ady was no ordinary poet. For years, the publication of each volume of his verse had electrified Andor's generation like the release of a megastar's records in decades to come. Hungary's great poet of the twentieth century embodied the nation's tragedies and aspirations.

Andor had grown up on Ady's poetry. He would turn to it for the rest of his life. Speaking in 1979, with almost seven decades of photography behind him, he would tell an assistant that if the assistant wanted to understand Andor's work, he should read Ady.[1] Was he referring to the cultural values he shared with the poet? To their romantic temperaments? To Ady's launch of literary modernism in Hungary and his own trailblazing of modern photography? Andor didn't explain.

Born in 1877, Endre Ady was a young journalist at a small-town newspaper when he fell in love. The wealthy and sophisticated Adél Brüll embodied the twenty-six-year-old provincial's wildest dreams. The two became lovers. Although Ady met Brüll in Hungary, she and her businessman husband lived in Paris, where Ady promptly followed. His encounter with French culture led the journalist to intensify the attacks he'd been making on Hungary's conservative, self-dealing establishment. Outraged at the backwardness of his own nation, he castigated Hungary for its corruption, its hypocrisy, its decay.

In 1906, Ady published a landmark volume of poetry, *New Verses*. He opens by asking, "Shall I break through beyond Dévény / With new songs for new times?"[2] To break through beyond Dévény, the westernmost village in Hungary, was to smash literary conventions and breathe modernism into the nation's stale traditions. Repudiating what he saw as

Habsburgian Hungary's shallow culture, Ady took inspiration from the popular culture of its Magyar past. Brüll appears in *New Verses* as Léda. In Greek mythology, Zeus transforms himself into a swan and rapes Leda as she sleeps with her husband. She bears the god two children. Ady's children with *his* Leda were the poems that burst from the "sweet, holy torment" of their liaison.[3]

Not until nine agitated years after their first meeting would Ady spill his last bit of ink over his mistress in the poem "Letter of Dismissal." By then, alcoholism, depression, and syphilis were sapping his strength. Resettled in Hungary, he wrote searching and apocalyptic verse about love, God, and moral degeneration. Tragic and pointless in Ady's view, the Great War coincided with the last stages of his illness, driving omens, wraiths, and dead youth into his poems. An angel drummed an alarm. A beehive burst into flame. The world had fallen foul of Christ.[4]

After the war ended and Ady died, his writings continued to illuminate Andor's generation as it struggled to find its bearings. "No one will ever be able to measure his impact on the entire youth of our time," asserts the novelist Zsigmond Móricz. Where Ady's words fell, Móricz raved, "the seeds of new powers were cast in the souls of men."[5]

While the "seeds of new powers" cast in Andor's soul had yet to germinate, the poet's obsession with his mistress Léda resonates with the young man's self-enslavement to an idealized Jolán. Andor, too, was in love with love.

What's more, he would have internalized Ady's tenacity in building a life around creative work and doing it on his own terms. They included a transgressive use of language. Ady warps syntax, invents words, repeats phrases and lines, and piles up adjectives. Conventional language, he believed, could never convey his passions, his dreams, his despair. Young Andor lacked Ady's command of his medium. Yet he too deviated from formulaic practice. He photographed unorthodox subjects like lace curtains and horses copulating. He played with unorthodox angles. He thought about framing and lighting his subjects in unorthodox ways.

Unlike Ady, Andor turned his back on politics; like Ady, he detested Hungary's social stratification. Ady's attacks on class privilege surely made sense to a Jew from a Swabian family, marginalized at birth. When Andor wasn't photographing his family or friends, he might be focusing on a market boy or street sweeper, not as a social case or picturesque element but as a full human being. Like Ady, he judged those sidelined by the establishment to be the soul of the Hungarian nation. Eventually, he would earn the epithet "the great democrat of modern photography."[6]

**The tension between** the Ady that Andor carried inside and the dutiful employee who reported to work five mornings a week could feel unbearable. Andor's mother and uncle stood firm and united against his idea of quitting the bank job to become a photographer. Photography was fine as a hobby, Uncle Poldi maintained, but it was not a career. Andor knew that. "Being a photographer in Budapest was like being zero," he later explained.[7] Photography as *he* practiced it was even less. Could he account for what he was doing—walking around and trawling for pictures? Not really. One imagines Uncle Poldi's kindly voice and hand on the shoulder of his cloud-gazing nephew. It's time to retire your impractical notions and build a solid life for yourself, he counseled. Such discussions would have been haunted by memories of Andor's father, a washout when it came to supporting his family. Andor was fond of his uncle and wanted to meet his expectations. Yet he also wanted to do what he wanted to do: continue the conversation with life that was photography.

To make matters worse, the aftermath of war was straining the family's finances. Andor was diligent about tracking his expenses and saving all he could of his salary and his modest military pension. Casting about for more ways to earn money, he considered moonlighting as a commercial photographer. The idea did not thrill him. Commercial work felt tedious. Hulking professional gear killed all freedom of movement. But the family needed the cash.

Such work required a view camera. While poking around an antique shop one day, Andor chanced on a quaint English camera that took about 3 by 5 inch glass plates. He was smitten. He purchased it with money he knew his mother needed. He then wrangled his first assignment, for which he asked and obtained an audacious fee, recouping his investment in the camera. Next, he photographed the interior of a fancy apartment that belonged to one of his cousins. For that, too, he earned a nice sum.[8] After that, offers dried up, or he simply lost interest.

Like most amateurs, Andor photographed his own family. He would pull out his camera on important occasions like birthdays and his cousin Ilonka's wedding. Atypically, he also took pictures when nothing special was happening: during everyday dinners, walks with his cousins, Ernesztina's klatches with her sisters and sisters-in-law. His fattening stacks of tiny prints and his thinning diary entries confirm that pictures suited him better than words for pinning down what amused him or warmed his heart.

One photograph shows Andor's brothers strolling in sync down a city street. Looking as if they could conquer the world, or at least the stock market, Imre and Jenő flout hard times by cutting fashionable figures. They wear dark overcoats and fedoras, tilted just right and no doubt doffed for the ladies. Andor uses what was becoming a favorite pictorial strategy: two or three subjects face the camera side by side, inviting comparisons, contrasts, and different ideas about who they—and he—might be or become.

In a variation on that approach, *The Circus, Budapest* shows a man and a woman standing together and seen from behind. Andor had been photographing a small traveling circus in the Városliget, Budapest's city park, straining to capture the roustabouts setting up the big top. Then he spotted a couple unwilling or unable to buy tickets.[9] In Andor's photograph, they occupy a strip of hard ground below a band of tent canvas and in front of a wood-plank wall. They press up to that wall, peering through a knothole at the doings inside. Even though the man, probably a veteran, appears to have only one leg, his stance is stable and jaunty.

He and she are a pair. Sealing their complicity, the band of his boater rhymes with the stripe of her headscarf. They read as unsophisticated yet self-sufficient and somehow marvelous. With his lens, another knothole of sorts, Andor has captured their raptness.

*The Circus, Budapest* is simple, rhythmic, and rigorously carpentered. Except for the ribbon of tent canvas, viewers see nothing of the circus, not even the knothole, which is blocked by the couple's heads. They must take on faith that the knothole and the circus exist. Andor's image catapults the imagination into a big top in which the performance will never begin and never end. Who knows what feats are unfolding? As for the two voyeurs, they stare through the knothole as intensely as Andor stared through his lens. He may have intuited the man as himself projected into the future: physically impaired yet emotionally whole, conjoined with his woman, and engrossed in the act of looking.

In the rolling wine country southwest of Buda, Andor took more scenes conjuring the pleasures of photographic vision. One shows a trio of boys piled up – one, two, three, like the cars of a train that's made a too-sudden halt – behind his tripod-mounted Voigtländer. They are wide-eyed at the inverted and reversed image visible on the ground-glass focusing window. (Because light travels in a straight line, all cameras invert and reverse the scene in front of them. Andor's did not correct for this fact.) A fourth child, a girl, her hair flying in the wind, stares at the viewer and at Andor, who is recording the scene with a handheld camera.

Another such picture, this one gently self-mocking, again centers on Andor's camera and tripod, along with a goat who looks to be studying the scene in the viewfinder. A third shows the Voigtländer alone vignetted by foliage and shade. It reads as a metonym for the photographer: I am a camera, the picture asserts.[10]

**A few weeks after** Andor captured Imre and Jenő as boulevardiers, he and his bank colleagues strode down those same central Budapest streets singing "The Internationale" in a massive demonstration. The Hungarian capital was decked out like a Communist bride, its balconies and bridges festooned with red canvas and its classical bronzes adorned with red globes.[11] Marching that May Day was mandatory for all citizens, many less intent on celebrating proletarian solidarity than on consuming the free liquor and food.

President Károlyi's campaign for a fair peace had failed. Even before the new government and republic fully existed, Hungary's ethnic minorities revolted. Intent on humbling the enemy and forcing harsher peace terms, the victorious Allies backed separatist Croat, Serb, Slovak, and Czech insurgents. Then Romania annexed Transylvania. The loss of a region that was vital to their national self-identity left Magyars angry and soul sick. Their country—historic Hungary—was being dismembered even as it was rebirthing itself. The final blow was the French command's order to evacuate the ancestral Magyar lands east of the Tisza River. What remained of southwestern Hungary was wedged between advancing foreign armies. With their nation chewed up, Hungarians were open to the message of the Jewish Communist Béla Kun. When Károlyi's National Council collapsed, the Communists maneuvered their way to power. Kun proclaimed the Hungarian Soviet Republic, a dictatorship of the proletariat.

That spring, Andor hovered around the edges of the city's turmoil. One of his photographs shows two soldiers-turned-communards stripping the stars from a rueful officer's uniform. No more ranks! Everyone was going to be equal. Another picture looks down on armored trucks parked in the courtyard of his office building. Andor's anxiety level was high. The new government was targeting capitalist institutions like the Giro Bank and Transfers. All banks had to close for inventory and reorganization. Andor's boss was reduced to a figurehead. Andor's job, too, was precarious.[12]

With foreign armies bearing down on the city, reservists like Andor received orders to report to a Red Army unit. He recoiled but had to show up. Thankfully, the People's Commissariat for War declared him unfit for duty.

Roving the streets one day, Andor turned his camera on one less fortunate than he. Viewed from behind, a conscripted hussar (light horseman) bids farewell to a frumpy woman, probably his wife. She narrows her eyes as if to memorize his face, ignoring for a moment the squalling child in her arms. The man also seems transfixed. The feeling between them is palpable.

Not only were families being torn apart, but the regime was also carrying out arbitrary arrests and hostage-taking and murdering those it deemed bourgeois obstructionists. In the Red Terror unleashed that spring, people Andor knew were senselessly shot. As weeks passed, the government tightened restrictions. When all coffeehouses were ordered closed, Ernesztina's last trickle of income dried up. But she had savings, and family was close at hand. Andor was probably suspended or unemployed. In any case, he and Jenő spent much of that summer of 1919 with the Klopfers in Szigetbecse.

Curly-haired and jug-eared, twenty-two-year-old Jenő exemplified the red-blooded Hungarian male. He was an athlete, a cutup, a flirt, and a striver. The speech pathologists he had consulted as far away as Vienna had failed to remedy his stuttering. His disability may have sharpened Jenő's determination: He had a near-obsession with professional achievement. As an engineering student at Polytechnic University, he had proved himself a wiz at anything mechanical. Even so, his efforts to find meaningful work had brought only frustration.

With train service disrupted and private use of the telephone banned that summer, Szigetbecse felt far distant from Budapest.[13] Yet parts of rural Hungary also were roiling. Estates were being nationalized, food was requisitioned, and Kun's Lenin Boys rampaged from village to village in search of naysayers. All the same, Andor's photographs give no hint of the political ferment or even the dawn-to-dusk labor of the farmers around him. Instead, they bear witness to young men who have slipped off their obligations to revel in one sunny day after another. To experience mobility and joie de vivre. To skylark and playact in Eden. Andor's awareness of his recovered wholeness must have been acute. It contrasted with his cousin Misi's loss of mobility. By 1923, both of Misi's legs would be paralyzed.[14]

In one of Andor's photographs that summer, Jenő is a pagan nude hoisting a tree seedling. In another, he struts as a pipe-playing Pan. A third, titled *Dancing Faun* (also known as *My Brother as a Scherzo*, meaning a jest, a game, a light and lively composition), again centers on Jenő, now flanked by small trees like rustic stage curtains. He capers against a windswept sky, his backlit body all stylized gesture.

Andor went on to photograph Jenő as Icarus. It's tempting to say that Andor and Jenő identified with this mythical son, who disregards his father's instructions to fly neither so high that the sun melts his wax-and-feather wings nor so low that the wings become waterlogged. Once Icarus is airborne, however, he soars higher and higher. The sun melts the wax, and he plummets into the sea. The Kertész brothers, too, itched to reject their elders' wisdom and fly away—from their precarious jobs, from their country in turmoil—even as they feared self-destruction.

They staged some of the Icarus photographs near a pond where Jenő could gain momentum on high ground, then leap into the water.[15] That was the plan. In fact, he kept landing in sand. But those jumps! His arms thrust upward and his back arched, Jenő outdid himself. Actually, both brothers outdid themselves, Jenő by flinging himself high through the air and Andor by anticipating the eyeblink when Jenő's arc reached its apogee. Later, Andor would return to one of those negatives, reprinting it minus the top half of his brother's body. Jenő's lower torso and legs hang in the sky. What reads as jumping in the full negative reads as flying in the cropped version. Jenő's dark form imprinted on a blank sky becomes a corporal poem about liberation.

The Kertész brothers weren't the only Hungarians enthusiastic about kinesthetic self-expression. The war had left so many broken bodies.

People had suffered so much dehumanizing violence. Many were resorting to body culture as a way of mending themselves and restoring civilization. At Budapest's avant-garde schools of movement, teachers and choreographers were interweaving sports and health with theater and dance. Modern concerns about fitness and authenticity merged with classical Greek thinking about perfect proportion and the unity of body and soul.[16] Even the Kun regime was using body culture to push its messages: The posters plastered on Budapest's walls that spring and summer abounded in brawny, seminude Communist supermen, twisting, mallet-wielding, and tensed like spring-loaded mechanisms. It's no wonder then that an athletic young man and devotee of the performing arts like Andor should turn his attention to bodies in motion. By photographing the cavorting Jenő, and often himself, he was also fulfilling the task Mazdaznan set forth for artists: to provide inspirational models.

A quasi-religion that promises to unlock joy, self-mastery, and full human potential, Mazdaznan was invented by Otoman Zar-Adusht Ha'nish (aka Little Master). He drew from Zoroastrianism, mystical Judaism, and ancient Egyptian beliefs. In the United States, Mazdaznan attracted both rabid devotees and rabid denouncers. The latter chalked up the movement as a La-La Land sunworshipper cult (Ha'nish lived in Los Angeles) and its leader as a degenerate fake. By contrast, many physically and psychologically devastated Europeans saw an effective self-therapy for the wounds inflicted by conflict and hardship. Mazdaznan addresses the body, the mind, the soul, and the spirit. Although followers must master all four, developing a healthy body ranks as the first order of business. That requires breathing routines, a Mazdaznan diet, and nude exercises in the sun.

Seeking new ways to discipline his body and his mind, Jenő was a Mazdaznan believer. For Andor, Mazdaznan was a point of reference but not an active practice.[17] In one of Andor's close-ups that summer, an exhilarated and shirtless Jenő pops up in tall grass like a paragon of Mazdaznan vitality. In another image, he relaxes by the river, along with several nude companions, perhaps after group exercises to rev up the vibrations of the life forces and free their creative powers.

The Kertész brothers' problems defied Mazdaznan solutions, however. One sweltering afternoon they were lounging at a fishing shelter built with brush on an overgrown bank of the Little Danube. Shade was precious. Hours stretched ahead. The two fell into a conversation about their futures. In most families, Jenő observed, at least one person makes a mark in art, science, or public life. Yet their extended family had produced only mediocrities. The brothers laid out their dreams and ambitions. Jenő went on to argue that the two of them were their family's exceptions. Surely, he and Andor were destined for greatness.[18] Andor wasn't so certain. It felt impossible to reconcile his passion for photography with the imperative for financial security. Engineering was useful and respected; photography was not. Besides, how could anyone succeed in a country where people had to dodge armies that were colliding like billiard balls?

The cue ball next struck on August 3rd, when the Romanians occupied Budapest, knocking Kun's Revolutionary Governing Council into exile. Three months later, Rear Admiral Miklós Horthy von Nagybánya swept to power. Arriving in the capital on a glossy white horse, Horthy proclaimed to the mayor: "We shall forgive this criminal city."[19] "Forgive" was code for "punish," and "this criminal city" meant Bolsheviks, intellectuals, industrial workers, and Jews. That winter, Horthy's government executed some five thousand Hungarians and imprisoned seventy thousand others.[20] Because Kun and other leading Reds were Jews, many who had silently opposed the Hungarian Soviet Republic equated anti-Communism with anti-Semitism. Jewish stores were looted, Jewish clubs raided. The century's first anti-Semitic law in Europe limited the number of Jewish students in higher education. Some who did attend universities were beaten or pitched down the stairs. Bloated corpses floated in the Danube. The Budapest of Andor's childhood — a beacon of humanism, education, civil liberties, and the arts — all but vanished.

Faced with the White Terror, Andor's older brother, Imre, converted to Lutheranism. Andor did not, yet he kept cautious. Each weekday, he was back at Giro Bank. Weekends found him hiking and photographing in the hills around Budapest, flapping around in the Tyrolean cape that marked him as an artist and romantic.

Meanwhile, he was picking his way through the paperwork required for emigration, he didn't know where. He wasn't alone. Ever since the start of the Hungarian Soviet Republic, the country had been hemorrhaging creators, intellectuals, and entrepreneurs. Among those who had left (or would soon) were the future filmmakers Alexander Korda and Michael Curtiz, the conductor Eugene Ormandy, the architect and designer Marcel Breuer, the artist László Moholy-Nagy, the mathematician John von Neumann, and the photographer Brassaï.

Jenő, too, wanted out. But their uncle and mother stood firm. Ernesztina argued that hard times demanded that they stick together.

Andor took a portrait that captures his mother's loving yet assessing look. The wedding band Ernesztina wears recalls her widowhood; the safety pin attached to her bodice is the badge of a busy housewife. In printing the image, Andor slightly reframed and tilted it. By accentuating the triangular form of Ernesztina's torso, he evokes her role as the family's stabilizer. In a second print, he radically cropped all but her hands. Veined and arthritic yet graceful, they were constantly mending, cooking, cleaning, or waiting on people. His hardworking, generous, narrow-minded mother. Andor could not break her heart by going abroad. Maybe something decent would materialize in Hungary.

**Andor's print** of Ernesztina's hands was possible thanks to the enlarger he and Jenő had designed, then had a carpenter build, using a bicycle lamp.[21] The contact prints he normally made without an enlarger were too small to allow for singling out a portion of the negative. With the enlarger, Andor was able to make bigger prints in various sizes. That meant he could crop his images. By homing in on Ernesztina's hands (thus changing the format from vertical to horizontal), he gave them a symbolic dimension. Most photographers use cropping to adjust proportions or omit distracting details. Andor realized that it can be a powerful interpretive tool.[22]

That photograph of his mother's hands became one of his favorites. He would have shown it to his new artist friends from the cohort later labeled the Szőnyi Circle. On weekends, he joined them on excursions to the country, the painters toting easels and supplies, Andor his camera and tripod. Jenő sometimes tagged along and modeled. Settled into some bucolic spot, they would picnic, talk, and make pictures.[23] Or they stayed in the city to party and drink with a crew of poets, ceramists, textile artists, and dancers. Andor went home from one gathering with a big-headed caricature of himself captioned "The Prophet of Teleky Square." He wears a bemused look and a silly getup: a military-style jacket, scarf, sandals, and pleated skirt revealing legs so hairy they resemble pincushions.

The painter István Szőnyi was emerging as the group's leading light. As a student at the Academy of Fine Arts, Szőnyi had spearheaded pro-Communist demonstrations during the Hungarian Soviet Republic. When the Reds fled, he was expelled. That same year, he won a spot in the juried winter show at the Palace of Art, a rare honor for a twenty-five-year-old. Then the Ernst Museum exhibited his multifigure pastoral scenes and nudes. While Andor got on well with Szőnyi, his closest artist friend was the painter Vilmos Aba-Novák. A beefy man with a shock of blond hair and a pipe stuck in his mouth, Aba-Novák was studying at the academy and teaching drawing. His shabby apartment, with its potbellied stove and plaster cast of Ady's death mask hanging on the wall, was a favorite party venue.

Academically trained neoclassical painters and sculptors, the artists of the Szőnyi Circle doted on rural Hungary. Most traced their creative lineage to the turn-of-the-century Nagybánya group, the first Hungarian modernists. Let Western artists use the metropolis as the petri dish of modernism. Let them depict urban streets, belching factories, and welters of light. The Nagybánya artists turned their backs on urban Hungary. Corrupt Budapest, they believed, had betrayed Hungary by relinquishing sovereignty to the Habsburgs in exchange for power and wealth. It was Magyar villages and farmsteads that harbored the nation's soul.

The aftermath of the war gave the Szőnyi Circle a new reason to devote themselves to the backcountry. The soon-to-be-signed Treaty of Trianon would strip Hungary of three-fourths of its land and 64 percent of its population. With their homeland isolated, shriveled, disrespected, and poor, the artists sought to reassert Magyar self-worth and presence on the European scene. What was most purely Magyar? Rural life and folk traditions, they believed. Working in plein air, the Szőnyi Circle concentrated on peasants and the arcadian landscapes they tilled.[24]

Not only artists but also composers and dancers were soaking up country traditions. The composer Béla Bartók was collecting the folk songs that would inspire his orchestral suite *Hungarian Pictures.* The avant-garde choreographer Olga Szentpál was incorporating folk-dance movements into her compositions. What Andor experienced of the cultural life around him affirmed that his own poetic images of rural Hungary were not mossbacked but progressive.

To run with the Szőnyi crowd would have been a heady experience for the autodidact. Among Andor's photographs that attest to fresh thinking is a 1919 nude of Jenő reclining among wild grasses. Taking advantage of the soft light, Andor uses shadows to trace the contours of his brother's body and delineate the delicate textures of the grasses. That linear quality recalls images from the early nineteenth century, when photography's coinventor William Henry Fox Talbot conceptualized it as nature's pencil. So does the warm-toned paper Andor chose. But Andor knew little about the history of photography. In taking the photograph, he probably had in mind Aba-Novák's etchings and drypoints of nudes in rustic settings. Like his friend's prints, Andor's photograph testifies to his attention to surfaces, planes, and harmonious proportions. Aba-Novák's work, in turn, owed much to the outdoor bathers of the Postimpressionist Paul Cézanne, whom the artist considered his forebear.

Andor was experimenting with formatting too. He printed that same negative using a cutout that masks all but the oval in which Jenő appears. His use of the oval enhances the vintage charm of the image and takes it beyond the usual conceit of a photograph as a rectangular window on the world. By activating the white area around the printed image, Andor was creating a photographic object. It was an idea to which he would return.[25]

The Szőnyi artists, including Aba-Novák's studio mate Erzsébet Korb, gravitated to double portraiture. Korb's robust figures and compositional strategies owed much to classical and Renaissance art, her visual logic to that of Cézanne. Andor was most impressed, one guesses, by Korb's 1920 oil *Alterego*, depicting a ruminative man in a robe touching foreheads with his nude, gesticulating, irrational other self.

Double portraiture had long amused and intrigued Andor. Conceivably, Korb's paintings led him to pursue that idea in psychologically charged ways, especially in self-portraits involving shadows, mirrors, masks, objects, and other human beings. Photographs manifesting a dual consciousness would have spoken to the conflict he experienced, between a drive for bourgeois success and the wild desires of the child who existed inside him. Korb's *Alterego* may have helped him understand that the self is not a seamless, self-contained entity.

Andor's casual single self-images from this time, viewed together, also suggest the self as a dynamic construct. They show him as a nature lover, athlete, fun seeker, photographer, brother, son, and natty dresser. He is wiry, vigorous, and tanned. Or pale and introspective. His expressions range from melancholic, as befitting a soulful Hungarian, to wryly amused and amusing. The ID picture on his membership card for the Association of Friends of Nature was fodder for silly masquerade: Andor penciled in a mustache.

As other pictures by Andor reveal, the fair sex was charmed. Young women stroll, hike, and picnic with him. One is laughing. One sunbathes at his side. Another dawdles with him in the garden café where they've just shared a meal. Yet another, a snub-nosed art student named Erzsébet Salamon, stands in an apple orchard, looking expectantly at the fellow taking her picture.

Andor had met the olive-skinned young woman at Giro Bank, where she had begun working. Erzsébet had dark-rimmed eyes and a brunette mane pulled back to her nape. Only five feet four to Andor's five feet ten and sixteen years to his twenty-four, she was, he knew, too young for him.[26] Her mother thought so too. So, around her family, he was circumspect. The four mawkish postcards of fairies he sent Erzsébet a few months after they met nodded to her interest in fantasy illustration and to his own cradle robbing. Noting on one that the fairy was a suitable playmate for her, he closed: "With hand kiss. Kertész."[27] Yet Erzsébet's girlishness was part of her charm. So were her pluck and accomplishment. She painted, embroidered, danced, played the piano, and spoke decent German, English, and French. And she liked Andor's pictures.

Born in 1902 in Teszér, a village in northern Hungary (now Hontianske Tesáre, Slovakia), Erzsébet was the seventh child of a railroad worker named Fülöp Salamon.[28] Married by age twenty-five, Fülöp had bounced from one low-level job to another – telegraphist, clerk, traffic controller, manager – all in backwater stations. The Salamons had four children, only two of whom survived infancy. Then Fülöp's wife died, probably in childbirth. He soon remarried. His young bride, Jozefin Klein, nicknamed Pepi, also had deep country roots. Pepi gave birth to three more children: Márta, Zoltán, and, on July 6, 1902, Erzsébet. Sometime during Erzsébet's early childhood, Fülöp and Pepi separated, probably acrimoniously, but they did not divorce. Erzsébet was nine when her father died of typhus at age forty-nine. The family did not participate in his burial.

By the time Erzsébet met Andor, Pepi and her children were living middle-class lives in Budapest. Their apartment was near that of Fülöp's brother Samuel, who held an important job as a head inspector for the railways and probably helped support them. Yet money was tight. Industriousness was expected. Pepi worked as the manager of a guesthouse, Márta as a secretary, Zoltán as a soon-to-be factory technician, and Erzsébet as a helper at Giro Bank.[29]

So Andor and his latest crush had remarkably similar family situations: unreliable fathers lost early in life, strong-willed and capable mothers, prosperous and dependable uncles, and two siblings each. More important, they shared a love of the visual, the artisanal, and the modern. Erzsébet was studying at the prestigious private school of Álmos Jaschik, a graphic artist, illustrator, set designer, and costume designer for Szentpál's modern dance school. Jaschik had synthesized progressive Secessionist ideas, akin to those of Art Nouveau, with Hungarian folk art traditions. He made little distinction between fine art, graphic art, and the art of living. Aiming for a career as a graphic artist, Erzsébet was well on her way, thanks to her celebrated teacher and her own strong work ethic.

During midday breaks from the office, she and Andor would sit talking and lunching on the steps leading down to the Danube near the Parliament Building. After work, their fascination with traditional crafts often took them to the ethnographic galleries of the Hungarian National Museum, where they lingered over handmade toys, kilim dowry rugs, and Transylvanian embroidery. Andor gave Erzsébet a tiny engraving of a Budapest street scene. He introduced her to Szigetbecse and invited her on weekend excursions with friends. Other times, it was just the two of them. Erzsébet's favorite spot was Gellért Hill for its flower-filled slopes and spectacular view of the watery Lágymányos district. She planted her easel on a hillside and painted, while Andor photographed her in flouncy frocks, white stockings, and Mary Jane shoes.

Only a month or two after they met, Andor began taking double portraits that speak of a tender and ardent relationship.[30] One late October day, he set up his camera in a forest clearing. He and Erzsébet positioned their coats to suggest two people sharing a single garment, then posed hand in hand and cheek to cheek, vividly present one to the other. Another photograph, taken in Lágymányos, dates from a few months later. As they strolled at dusk, Andor said, "*Szívecském* (sweetheart), come and let's take a picture of ourselves."[31] He positioned Erzsébet on a spit of land, planted his tripod behind her, cocked his camera's automatic shutter release, then sat down and nestled into her. The photograph shows a smudged strip of sky, some darker buildings and hills, a lustrous but dimming Danube, and a triangular silhouette, the apex of which is Andor's head. Erzsébet's rests on his shoulder. Andor foregrounds and fuses the two of them, using the silhouette to create a private space and manifest the Platonic idea of love as finding one's lost other half.

**Disgruntled and bored** with his job, Andor finagled a transfer to an important agricultural agency, where he continued to clerk, though no more happily than at Giro Bank. A bout of bronchitis gave him an excuse to take six weeks of sick leave.[32] After that, it was back to the office and the realization that his days there were numbered. Hungary's protofascist government had placed a de facto quota on Jewish employees in state-controlled jobs, and he worked for a governmental agency. Stultifying though the job was, he needed the paycheck.

On March 7, 1921, and again the next day, Andor met with Ervin Szűts, a well-connected acquaintance who had offered to help him. A few days later, he walked into an interview at the Hungarian Steel Product Factory, armed with Szűts's letter of recommendation. There he was assaulted with questions, fewer about his qualifications than about his religion. Summoned back two weeks later, he found the managers' "mouths ... touching their ears," a Hungarian expression meaning that they were hypocrites faking kindness.[33] He was not hired. In mid-April, he started a job at Nagy Boconádi, a company that fabricated horizontal beehives. Still, nothing felt settled. Even as he was mulling over whether to join the company's union, his appointments with Szűts continued. Indeed, after a week at Boconádi, Andor was fired. "My being Jewish was the problem," he noted in his diary.[34]

Then a relative suggested farming. Another told him that Hungary's minister of finance was leasing a portion of his family estate in Buda. If they rented it, Andor could live at home while learning to farm. Cousin Misi would have been his role model for a well-heeled farmer. Misi also kept bees: Why not try that? Andor cottoned to the idea of a traditional occupation. Besides, he had a sweet tooth, and those wretched few days at Nagy Boconádi had piqued his interest in apiculture. Yes, he would become a beekeeper.

But how to learn beekeeping? Andor placed a want ad for an apprenticeship in *The Hungarian Bee*.[35] One day after reading an article in that same publication, he grabbed pen and paper and wrote to its author. Ede Papszt lived in Abony, sixty miles southeast of Budapest. May I be your apprentice? Andor inquired. I would welcome you and be happy to train you, Papszt replied, but I cannot afford to pay you. Although Andor's want ad stated his willingness to train at his own expense, he had second thoughts and kept looking.

With his job prospects stalled and his mother and Imre riding him hard about pulling his life together, Andor turned to Erzsébet for consolation. She had demands of her own, however. She wanted to get engaged. Andor would not commit, infuriating her. One day he arrived at the Salamons' apartment to find Erzsébet angry at him and Pepi angry at both him and Erzsébet. Angry at him because he was wrong for her daughter. Angry at Erzsébet because of her tantrums. Break off the relationship, Pepi implored.

For Andor, no less emotionally dependent on Erzsébet than he had been on Julán, that was unthinkable. But how could he marry when he was making a hash of his life? When he was crippled by self-doubt? When he was unemployed and suspected he would hate any job he could get? He could barely stand to be away from Erzsébet for a few hours. Yet he decided to accept Papszt's offer. On May 8th, he left for Abony, an emotional mess.

If Andor expected to be greeted by a crusty old provincial, he was mistaken. Papszt proved a genial thirty-year-old with curly hair and wire-rim spectacles.[36] An orchardist, mechanical engineer, painter, and amateur violinist, he had attended both the Hungarian University of Fine Arts and a British university where he studied engineering. His engineer father had imported the first steam-powered thresher to Hungary. Papszt himself could build, fix, or invent almost anything. After taking up beekeeping to bring in extra cash, he designed a measuring instrument for queen bees and a bee incubation box. He and his pregnant wife had an angelic blond two-year-old daughter nicknamed Csicsó. Papszt's ironworker brother was also part of the household into which they now squeezed the apprentice.

No sooner had Andor arrived than he and Papszt set to work. A drought had diminished the supply of pollen and nectar, leaving the bees famished and crazed. Papszt feared they would be unable to store any honey or even survive. That's me, thought Andor, deprived of what I need and "desperate, like the bees."[37] They fed the survivors sugar syrup and cleaned out the dead, then loaded the hives onto horse-drawn wagons and spent a night creeping along fifteen miles of rutted roads toward the Tisza River, where conditions were better. By early morning, they were setting the hives, dozens of them, along a riverbank canopied with trees and dotted with acacia and rape flowers.

After the bees were installed and the men had pitched their tent in the shade between the hives and the river, they had few pressing tasks. Andor caught up with his diary and photographed avidly. Papszt painted watercolors, including a portrait of Andor, which his companion pronounced "splendid!"[38] They fished, swam, read, and cooked food they bought from nearby farmers. An enamel basin, a small mirror, and a plank nailed to two trees served as a self-barbering setup. Often, they lazed. An ear infection had left Papszt nearly deaf. Yet he was an excellent lip reader and a lively storyteller. Puffing on a cigarette, he would ramble on about his childhood, the social life of bees, the financial ruin of his wife's family during the war, and his ideas about nature.

Among the photographs that Andor took in their camp is one of the two of them in front of the tent. Both cross their arms. Both wear canvas jackets. Papszt sports a newsboy cap, Andor a clownish and beat-up bucket hat. Both fix their eyes on the camera. Simultaneously participant and observer, Andor watches the camera inscribe the image of himself and Papszt, a version of himself as a beekeeper/artist. In years to come, people would gossip that Andor cared above all about women and money, or at least the respect that money can bring. But he would remember these weeks invested in nature, friendship, and taking pictures as the happiest time of his life.

His misery transformed into joy, then into bliss. After he and Papszt returned to town, Andor opened a letter from Erzsébet asking his forgiveness. On June 4th, he rose at 3:00 a.m. to catch a train to Budapest. In a double portrait in a park three days later, Erzsébet cradles his head as if she is about to ravish him with kisses. When he expounded on beekeeping, however, he saw that she was bored. When she pressed him to marry, he demurred.

After Andor returned to Abony, his training continued. The Papszts treated him like family. Among the snapshots he took were two or three in which he wears an arch expression, along with a cloche and patterned dress, an outfit he could have cooked up to amuse little Csicsó, pose for a painting by Papszt, or have fun at a party.

One Sunday morning, Andor took a very different picture. He awoke that day to the sound of a violin just outside the front door. Grabbing his camera, he dashed out to find a blind violinist, a woman, and three barefoot children on dusty Szelei Road. One was Csicsó. Another was an older girl, and the third a boy who was guiding the musician, one hand cupping a few coins. Andor hastened to position himself so that a track left in the dirt by an iron-wheeled cart led the eye to where the man had just set foot. He adjusted his camera's settings, then, as the violinist lifted his bow, clicked his shutter release. A second later, the bow hit a string. The violinist and boy crossed the track in the dirt. The moment had vanished. Andor had no more glass plates.

In *Blind Violinist*, the boy walks in step with the elderly musician in shabby attire. The brim of the man's hat recalls a halo. Eyes closed, face lucent and turned slightly upward, he is no longer a vagabond fiddler seeking alms but a being transported by music. Although straitened and damaged, he is kissed by the gods.

A blind violinist pulls the sublime from a fiddle. A paradise blooms on the banks of the Tisza. A stuttering brother soars, a sweetheart beguiles. Photography allowed Andor to keep a finger on what touched his heart. To reconcile his mother's insistence on hard facts with his father's poetic truths. To "live," as he put it, "each of life's moments with pleasure."[39]

**Probably because of** Erzsébet's lack of enthusiasm, Andor dropped the beekeeping project. But the family kept hammering away at his need for a solid job. He worked for a while for one of his uncles. Then he took a position in a real estate office. The city felt glum. "Life is very sad here in Budapest," one local wrote a compatriot abroad, "unemployment grows almost by the hour, people are naturally sad, the city is desolate in the evenings, and the Winter will be unbearable unless conditions get better in a month or two. The famous good old spirit is gone."[40] More than glum, Budapest could be terrifying: The supposedly banned Association of Awakening Hungarians was organizing anti-Semitic demonstrations and brutalizing Jews.

Days turned to months, months to a year. Andor made sporadic attempts to establish himself as a photographer but met with scant success. His Jewishness would have played a role. He faced other impediments too. The journalistic world was evolving. Andor sometimes submitted pictures to the daily *Pesti Napló*, which published a photo-rich Sunday supplement. Unfortunately, most of its material came from agencies representing foreign photographers. A bit of this, a bit of that—

"a couple of Ziegfeld Girls, a photo of the Greek heir to the throne from ten years ago, a picture of Gloria Swanson," as Imre would describe it, "and the Sunday supplement is ready."[41] Andor also pursued the weekly *Az Érdekes Újság*. No luck there either. Unable to afford professional photographers during the war, Hungarian publications had relied heavily on contests for amateurs, a situation that had served Andor well. But now that the picture press was thriving, competition among photographers had stiffened and amateurs were no longer needed.

Andor kept a close eye on other photographers' work, including Rudolf Balogh's. A staff photographer at *Pesti Napló*, Balogh was the master spirit of the aestheticized Magyar-style photography, an outgrowth of the Pictorialist movement. Sniffing at the vulgarity of the industrial age, the Pictorialists handcrafted self-consciously beautiful landscapes, portraits, and nudes. Using bromoil and other painterly processes, they created pictures with an aura of Old Master or Impressionist art. Although Balogh rejected that painterly look, he too romanticized his subjects. His depictions of Hungarian peasants are pearly and moody orchestrations of shadow and light.

In an interview in the 1980s, the octogenarian Andor would declare his admiration for Balogh's early reportorial work, adding that "unfortunately, even he stepped back later, and illustrated calendars, and joined the camp that affected a folksy style."

"But you also took photographs of folk subjects in those days," rejoined his interviewer.

"Yes but what I did was original. While he accepted the sweetish sham-Hungarianism, I endeavored to show reality."[42]

Andor's jab at Balogh reflects his awareness that some of his Hungarian pictures easily come across as sentimental. *His* work had always been intuitively modern, Andor insisted. Yet he too had a romantic temperament. He too belonged to his time and place, and the aesthetic mood of 1920s Hungary was, in the phrase of the art historian Éva Forgács, one of "past-bound melancholy and nostalgia."[43]

Unlike Balogh, Andor rejected the soft-focus lens. Unlike Balogh, he did not take ethnographic-style pictures of wholesome peasants in traditional dress. Andor's peasants are more likely to have worn-out clothes and dirty feet. All the same, he was smitten with pastoral scenes and good-natured country folk. He turned his lens to bucolic farmsteads, gnarled oldsters enjoying their pipes, and the wholesome-looking daughter of his uncle's farm manager breastfeeding her baby (a "village Madonna," thought Andor[44]). Warm and sweet was his nectar too.

In the decades between the 1920s and the 1980s and the miles between Budapest and New York, modernist ground would shift. What was progressive in post–World War I Hungary was sentimental in Reagan-era America, and the elderly Andor knew it. Speaking around 1980, he would preemptively defend a 1920 image that he took in a mist-gauzed Budapest park and would publish in 1982: "This is not a soft focus picture, as was popular with 'art' photographers."[45] No, this was not Magyar-style work. Its softness was not an aesthetic choice. The day had simply been foggy. To be sure no one missed his point, Andor labeled the picture *Hazy Day, Budapest.*

That was the type of photograph Andor would have submitted to the 1922 juried exhibition of the National Association of Hungarian Amateur Photographers. An influential photography club for well-heeled amateurs, the association allied itself with Pictorialism. Andor had joined because membership was required for participation in their competitions. The judges accepted and hung his work.

Andor may have entered the competition again in 1923. But not until 1924 did he again achieve recognition. He'd submitted three of his most poetic images. Now the association's president wrote to offer him a silver medal on the condition that he reprint all three using bromoil. Yet Andor disdained the velvety look of bromoil and all that the process stood for. To use the Pictorialists' beloved bromoil was to accept the idea that photography had to borrow from painting to be a fully legitimate art form.

Andor had toyed with Pictorialist techniques like toning his prints. But bromoil—no! He refused.

A silver medal from the heavyweights at the National Association of Hungarian Amateur Photographers would have meant national recognition and a cash prize at a time when Andor was feeling despondent and battered. Instead, he took home a certificate of honorable mention. Years later, he would hold forth to young photographers about his principled stand for the integrity of photography. His refusal to shine up to the Pictorialist establishment would become a key early episode in the Kertész saga as Andor told it, whether or not completely accurately. The moral would follow: Always be true to yourself.

Indeed, life was messier than Andor would later care to remember. Happily, he had Jenő. One day the two posed for a double portrait. Both wear suits. Both are stretched out in the grass. Both lean on their elbows. Each fixes his eyes on his brother's face, as if studying himself and his sibling in a mirror: Who am I? Who are you? How do I stack up to you, and you to me? Their bond, his picture implies, transcends that of ordinary biological brotherhood. They read as twins, allies, alter egos.[46]

**Throughout 1924,** Andor's tribulations continued. He was still clerking, now at a stock exchange. The work felt soul-crushing. He watched his friends' careers flourish and their lives move on, while his stagnated. Szőnyi had a second retrospective at the Ernst Museum. He was about to marry and leave Budapest for a village up the Danube, where he would paint scenes of country life. Szőnyi had lost faith in a new Hungary but not in rural Hungarians. Aba-Novák was fresh off two major exhibitions. Imre Zsögödi Nagy was leaving to paint in his native Transylvania. Erzsébet Korb's personal life was in shambles—her husband had left her for her sister—yet she had had her own solo show at the Ernst Museum, and now she was heading to Italy.

One of Andor's photographs that summer reflects feelings of longing and disengagement. There's a hillside, a few saplings, a forest beyond, and a distant thunderhead. Four friends have gathered outside. Erzsébet stretches out with a book. One artist straddles a drawing board. Another paints at his easel. Andor stands hands on waist, contemplating a distant archway, possibly the entrance to a cemetery. Each of the four faces a different direction. Each has shrunk into a different world. They are together and not.[47]

With another photograph, *Wine Cellars at Budafok*, Andor rehearses his escape from Hungary. Casting a bird's-eye view from a hilltop in Budafok (at that time a winemaking village at Budapest's door), he pulls off a composition as narrative-ready as a good stage set. The actors include a solid middle-aged woman, hands on hips, planted in a lot behind a house; a man who strides away from her and toward the road beyond; and one or two others who observe what could be a drama between a mother and the son she is losing. All are tiny figures viewed from afar. The man commands the viewer's attention. He appears at the center of the image, bowling along under an archway. Soon he will disappear behind a stone building, presumably later to emerge and join other walkers farther on.[48]

*Wine Cellars at Budafok* is arguably the most formally sophisticated of Andor's early photographs. It may be indebted to Aba-Novák's spatially dynamic circus and market scenes. Because of his tritanopia, Andor was less than fully sensitive to Aba-Novák's bold use of color. But he would have watched the artist underpaint his canvases in black and white, anchoring complex compositions with juxtapositions of organic and geometric form. In *Wine Cellars at Budafok*, Andor also fixes his attention on shape and space, emphasizing abstract pattern: The road and terrain weave among the geometric shapes of the boxy wine cellars and flat strips of field.

Aba-Novák's canvases play up the intrinsic qualities of paint. *Wine Cellars at Budafok*, for its part, attests to Andor's ability to think in *his* medium's visual language. The elevated vantage point lends itself to semi-abstraction. That day's soft yet bright light allows him to avoid harsh shadows but still articulate the buildings' angles and planes. By omitting the horizon line, he heightens a feeling of enclosure.

Long entranced by Budafok, Andor had often meandered its byways, feeling the landscape around him and observing it photographically. Perhaps he made a mental note to return to this spot, where he must have awaited the *something* that would transform the scene into an image. Indeed, his subjects' positions and gestures suggest a significant relationship among them. Viewed in a biographical context, *Wine Cellars at Budafok* mirrors his own situation. Andor is the observer and, through a surrogate, the observed. Whoever the man and the woman really are, they are also him, adamant that his future lay outside Hungary, and Ernesztina, adamant that the family must stay together.

Then a local opportunity popped up. That summer, the photographer, designer, cinematographer, and theater director Pál Vilmos Funk, known professionally as Angelo, offered Andor an apprenticeship. Angelo had studied with distinguished Pictorialists in Western Europe and worked for the filmmaker Mihály Kertész (not a relative of Andor's), who later became famous as Michael Curtiz, the director of *Casablanca*. Angelo had gone on to establish a Budapest studio. But no sooner had it opened than he, a Jew, had to flee the White Terror. He took refuge in Holland and France. One self-portrait near the Eiffel Tower shows him with his walking stick and raffish jacket nipped at the waist looking like a young Maurice Chevalier. Now back in Budapest, Angelo presided over one of the city's most prestigious photographic establishments, located on swanky Váci Street. There a chorus line of entertainers, literary figures, and fashion plates with cupid's-bow lips and puffy-sleeved gowns posed for portraits. Angelo did art photography, too, mostly landscapes and genre scenes, typically bromoil, that verged on the cloying—the type of images Andor could not stomach. Yet Angelo was celebrated, well connected, and financially comfortable.

Deeply ambivalent about the offer, Andor let a week drift by. His instincts told him not to accept, but his practical side would have ordered him to stop self-sabotaging. Ernesztina, Imre, Uncle Poldi, and Erzsébet were surely pushing him to say yes. Finally he did.

No sooner had he accepted than Angelo postponed the apprenticeship from summer to fall, when his client load would be heavier. All the same, Andor frequented Angelo's studio, helping with the lights during portrait settings, befriending the female retouchers, and learning to be a shopkeeper photographer. He also began handling minor assignments, uncredited, for *Színházi Élet* (Theater Life), at the behest of Angelo, the popular magazine's star photographer.

Once Andor organized a photographic outing to Budafok for Angelo and a dozen or so assistants and hangers-on. Everyone else worked with view cameras and tripods, frowning at Andor's handheld Goerz Tenax. Yet, in Andor's telling, they were all disappointed with their pictures while he was not.[49]

Another time, Andor and Angelo took a day trip up the Danube. "Pictures from Angelo with smarmy dedications," Andor reported to his diary four days later. "I don't like it."[50] He may have been referring to both Angelo's foppish manner and fatuous – so Andor felt – pictures. Yet Angelo was lining his pockets, and Andor was not. Angelo the star was only five months older than Andor the failure.

Two weeks later, Andor picked up the Angelo thread in his diary: "Midday at Angelo's. He received me coldly and purposefully directed the conversation to dissuade me from photography. Then he eased up. Seemingly his vanity is hurt that I did not respond the way he hoped. I am fearful of his reputation. Later he warmed up. I told him that I did not go to him for so long because of the things at home."[51]

Whatever was happening at home, Andor's thirtieth birthday that July 2nd had felt like a fresh bruise. "I am 30 years old and I am a nobody!" he lamented.[52] He had fallen into the habit of taking birthday self-portraits every year, marking his shifting self-interpretations. One self-portrait that year reveals a clean-shaven young man in a white shirt and tie. He looks amiable and introspective. The windows and plants behind him are in focus, Andor himself slightly blurred. Seated at a doorway, he is neither fully inside nor fully outside the house—a metaphor for his situation.

In a photograph taken four days later, on Erzsébet's twenty-second birthday, the two of them cuddle. She drapes one arm around his shoulder, another rests on his leg. His right arm cinches her waist, and he leans into her. Their knees touch. They look like a couple crazy in love.

Erzsébet was consumed by a desire to marry. She had publicly weighed in on one nuptial custom: "Does a good marriage require a dowry?" It was one week's question in "The Curious Photographer," a person-on-the-street feature in *Színházi Élet.* Traditionally, a Hungarian bride brought a dowry of linens and laces. But that would have been a financial strain on the Salamon household. In any case, it was immaterial, Erzsébet asserted: "If it is true that I was created by nature from the missing rib of my future husband, then that marriage should only be a happy one. Two understanding people, if they enter into a lasting contract in the spirit of love, can renounce unfulfilled desires, for which they find compensation in the tranquility of family life."[53] Ironically, Erzsébet's questioner and the photographer for the feature may have been Andor, working on assignment.

Other times, Erzsébet turned sulky, brittle, or furious when the subject of marriage arose. Once when she and Andor were saying goodbye after a quarrel, she fired a parting shot that devastated him: "I am tired of this situation. In the winter of 1924–25 I want to be a bride. Either this will happen, or you go away until you establish an existence, you do not come for me, and we do not even correspond." Erzsébet's frustration is understandable. The two had been together for more than five years. Andor had not launched a career or even secured a steady job. He felt unable to take on the responsibilities of a married man. The ghosts of his father and hers would have lingered.

"I responded with a few bewildered, childish words," Andor recorded. "She walked out on me imperiously. I am having dreadful days. I am so desirous of a little gentleness and I do not get it from her. What will happen to us? There is no promise anywhere. I do not even want to leave any more. I want to feel her next to me but not like this. I suffer terribly."[54]

"Very shaken," he added the next day.[55]

"I think with my heart," he wrote the day after that.[56]

Andor took brooding walks in the country. He consulted a fortune teller, who advised him to follow an elderly gentleman out of Hungary. That would lead him to a beautiful future, she said. As for Angelo, the fortune teller pronounced him a hypocrite who should be ignored.

Yet Andor's situation did not resolve. Another fall. Another winter. Erzsébet did not become a bride. She was keeping her options open. That January 15th, she and her sister attended a carnival ball at the Hotel Gellért, where marriageable young women chatted and danced with junior English, German, American, and Polish diplomats, all potential high-achieving suitors.[57] Andor spent that same evening ensconced at home. He photographed Imre absorbed in a book, and his mother and uncle face-to-face at a white-clothed table. Impeccable in a suit, tie, and white shirt with cuff links, Poldi savors an after-dinner smoke. In another frame, taken perhaps after Poldi departed, Ernesztina rests her head on her hands as if asleep. Andor did a self-portrait too, almost a mirror image of that of his mother. His shirt is rumpled, his hair a mess. His left hand curls over his head, which rests on his right hand as if he were passed out or asleep. A bottle and a half-empty glass sit by his side. A book—or is it his diary?—lies open and abandoned. Next to his right hand is a sharp dinner knife.

It's tempting to interpret Andor's self-portrait as that of a young man acting out his torment about his sweetheart going to a ball by photographing himself in the Romantic tradition of the anguished young lover. But, most likely, Andor's disarray and fatigue are simply those of an unsuspecting office worker on a Thursday evening.

In a practical vein, Andor had obtained a press card. He did not intend to work as a photojournalist. But he was moving toward going abroad, and, if he did emigrate, he would need to show an occupation. Where would he go? What would he do when he got there? He didn't know.

After meeting a Catalan clown in a traveling circus, he reportedly decided on Spain. According to a story he later told a friend, he drained his savings to purchase a train ticket to Barcelona. As a way of breaking the news to his mother, he propped the ticket up on the fireplace mantel. Mistaking it for trash, Ernesztina tossed it into the garbage, leaving Andor both downcast and broke.[58]

His final break with Angelo came when four photographs taken on Váci Street and signed by Angelo appeared in *Színházi Élet*. Andor alleged that the pictures were his.[59] Judging from their appearance, that's likely true. Although Andor never confronted Angelo, he would bear a grudge for the rest of his life. Angelo never publicly told his side of the story.

Then the appearance of one of Andor's pictures in another popular publication broke his chain of misfortunes. On June 26, 1925, a prewar photograph of Jenő in the Tabán district appeared on the cover of *Az Érdekes Újság*. Its aura of nostalgia fit the mood of Horthy-era Hungary. Even if the image was eleven years old, even if *Az Érdekes Újság* had lost some of its luster, there Andor was on the cover.

Ernesztina was coming around to accepting her sons' longing to go abroad. Like Andor, Jenő was demoralized by his inability "to fly with my own wings."[60] He was thinking Brazil. Common sense said Berlin for Andor. The city was a beacon for artists and writers, and, as bad as Andor's German was, it could prove useful. But he had set his sights on Ady's "wondrous, great, holy" Paris.[61] Although he spoke no French, he had been filling a little notebook with the names and addresses of friends of friends who lived in the French capital.

It's impossible to know how he left things with Erzsébet. By one account, he remained under her orders to leave and not even write her until he made something of himself. By another, she begged to go with him, but he dissuaded her because of her age. If all went well, he would send for her. According to a third story, the two got engaged at a favorite meeting spot, the steps of the Parliament Building overlooking the Danube. If so, they kept it quiet. Neither mother was enthusiastic about their relationship.[62] Pepi would have been shaking her head at the thirty-one-year-old loser, while Ernesztina objected to Erzsébet's high-strung personality, which had caused Andor such pain and fueled family gossip over the years.

Given his bent for historical romance and adventure, Andor may have framed his move as a quest. Motivated by love and armed with little but his camera, a young man abandons family and home to embark on an epic adventure. He will face unknown dangers. Only when he rises to the challenge will he be rewarded with the hand of his beloved. Fairy tales aside, Andor brooded over his failure to meet Erzsébet's, his family's, and his own expectations. What would happen in Paris? He must have guessed he would get nowhere, run out of money, and be forced to come home. If so, he might or might not find Erzsébet waiting. She was attending more dances and doing her art. Along with eleven classmates, Erzsébet had spent part of that summer with Álmos Jaschik in a village outside Budapest, where her work was singled out for praise and her desire for a career as a graphic artist probably gained new traction.[63]

That kind of self-confidence eluded Andor. Yet doggedness, curiosity, and excitement about his upcoming adventure did not. He had another advantage: his long self-apprenticeship. In nineteen years of living and breathing photography with no mentor to guide him, Andor had explored everything he could think of. He had made and learned from every possible error. He had photographic interests and values that were distinctly his own.

With the equivalent of $350 shamefacedly borrowed from his cousin Sanyi, Andor purchased a ticket. On October 7th, he stepped onto a train, carrying his Goerz Tenax, his Voigtländer, his flute, the press card, a student passport valid for one year, a three-month French visa, his address book, clothes and such, and his pent-up longing for achievement. A few prints and glass-plate negatives would serve as his photographic calling cards.

His life swung open on the unknown.

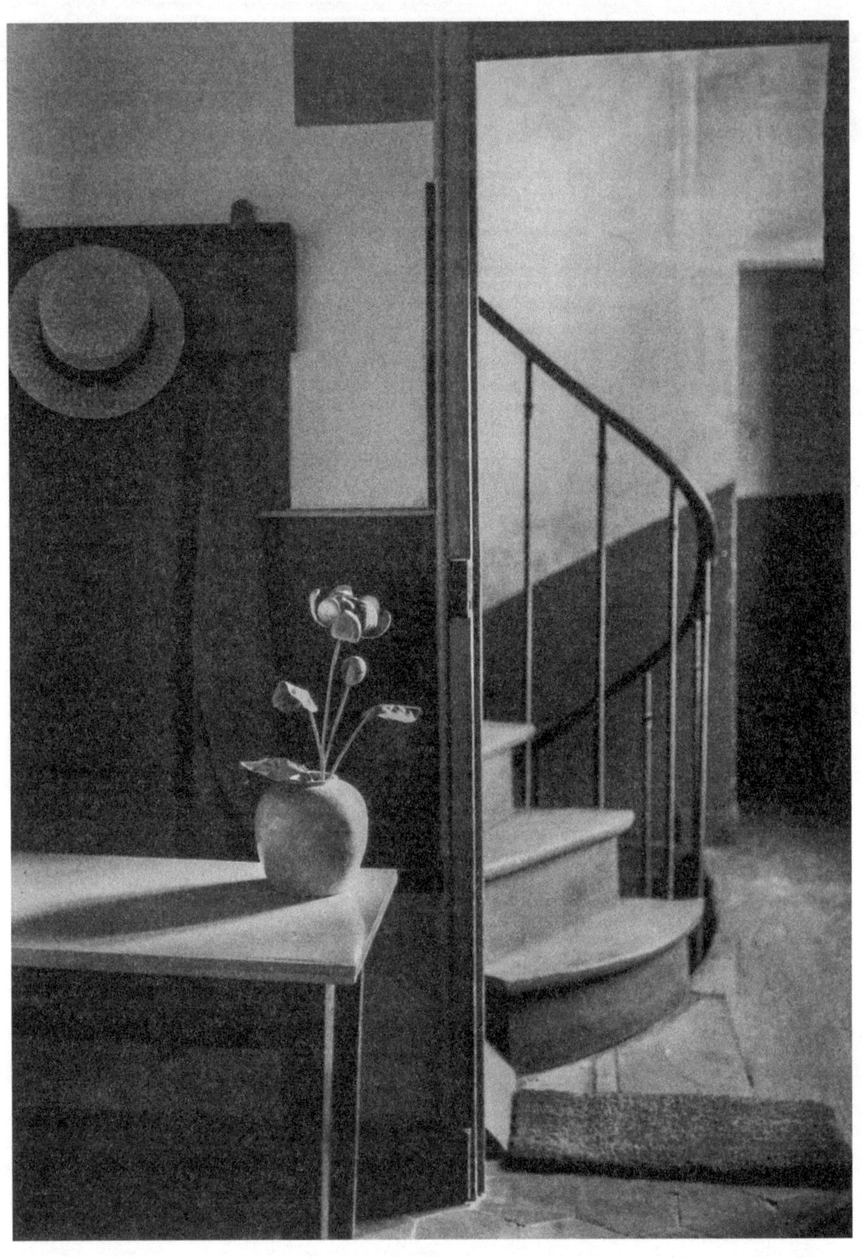

André Kertész, *Chez Mondrian*, 1926

# 4 CHEZ MONDRIAN, 1925–1927

**Café patrons spilled across the sidewalk** of the boulevard du Montparnasse, gossiping, drinking, skimming the newspapers. Tourists who'd "done" the Venus de Milo and the Champs Élysées were unwinding over apéritifs. Neighborhood regulars, among them artists, writers, dancers, and models, packed other tables. Some were French, some émigrés. Many were broke. Theirs was the Café du Dôme of good cheap muscadet, a potbellied stove, and the letter board that foreigners scanned for handwriting from home.

A diffident young Hungarian approached this hub of modernity. Scrawny, neatly combed, and carefully dressed, Andor trained the lens of his Goerz Tenax on the table colonized by his compatriots. He'd probably already met one or two of its occupants, who would have paused and posed, then forgotten the newcomer's camera.

The École des Beaux-Arts student architect Ernő Goldfinger, originally from Budapest, was preparing to depart.[1] Fired up by Le Corbusier's radical rethinking of architecture, Goldfinger had broken with tradition to establish a workshop that championed unadorned concrete construction. A cigarette glued to his lips, he stood exchanging a last word with Marie Vassilieff. Everybody knew the petite Russian painter, if not for her Cubist canvases, then for the soup kitchen for artists that she ran during the war. Once she famously pushed a drunk, pistol-wielding

Modigliani down the stairs and out the door, which Picasso bolted behind him.

Presiding over the Hungarian table was the painter Lajos Tihanyi, flanked by a German dancer and another smart young thing, both wearing their fall suits and cloches. Tihanyi leaned forward, reading the lips of the woman to his right. His eyebrows shot up, he beamed, he pouted, his eyes narrowed to slits, all in a putty face worthy of the actor Bert Lahr.[2] Childhood meningitis had left Tihanyi deaf. His speech was guttural, monotone, and sometimes unintelligible. His teeth were bad. He was scrappy, truculent, and generous.

Tihanyi had arrived from Budapest via Berlin two years before. Once close to Hungary's Nagybánya artists, he had long since absorbed the influences of Cézanne's handling of pictorial space and the Fauvists' expressive palette. His participation in The Eight, a linchpin of Hungarian modernism, had earned him a place in art history. In Paris, he was putting aside the portraits and self-portraits that had made his reputation to explore still life and urban scenes rendered using angled, semiabstract form.

Andor and Tihanyi would quickly become close. Both were uprooted Budapesters, both were Jewish, both had grown up around their parents' cafés, in Tihanyi's case, the sumptuous artistic and literary Café Balaton. The coffeehouse life was in their genes. Neither had money. Not least, both struggled with verbal language, albeit for different reasons, especially in French. Had Andor been fluent, he might have befriended artists like the Japanese-born Tsuguharu Foujita or the Russian-born Chaim Soutine or the American-born Man Ray—Dômiers all, who used French as their lingua franca. But he believed that learning French was impossible. Only at the Hungarians' table did he feel at home. There he idled, nursed a café crème, got to know other expats. His camera was always at hand.

Andor's outsiderness is palpable in his first photographs in France, taken hours after he stepped off the train at the Gare de l'Est. He had shared a room with fellow travelers at a hotel on the rue Vavin. That morning, he stood at its Juliet balcony, gawking at the apartment building across the street. One photograph Andor took frames six of its windows, viewed from above and obliquely. Three are shuttered, and three are not. There's a bouquet of daisies in one window. Another reveals a woman gazing down at the street, the third some patterned curtains.[3] The facade Andor surveyed and the lives he imagined were those of French strangers. The pictures he took manifest his curiosity and anticipation. Paris awaited his interpretation.

But before all else, he had to handle practicalities, starting with a place to live. The Hungarian émigré network soon helped him land in a Hungarian-run rooming house on the rue du Bourg Tibourg near the Hôtel de Ville (city hall). By November, he would be bouncing between that rooming house and two apartments in the suburb of Courbevoie. One belonged to some compatriots who had a darkroom he could use.

He registered with the police as "A. Kertész." He was changing his name to its Gallic equivalent: André. Lajos Tihanyi, known to some as Louis, may have pointed out the advantages of this classic act of self-reinvention. Eventually, Andor would fully settle into André as his self-identity. But for now, it would have exuded an alien Frenchness. To most of his Hungarian pals, he was still Bandi, the typical nickname for Andor.

The police required that he list a profession, so he wrote "photo reporter." On paper, he *was* the Paris correspondent for a Budapest press agency called Continental Photo. But he expected little or nothing from that, and little or nothing would come of it.

Shocked by the high cost of living in Paris, André needed an actual job. Swallowing his pride, he applied at Angelo's Paris studio and was rejected. Then he obtained an auditor's pass for cinematography courses and registered as a film projectionist. That too came to naught. Meanwhile, his brothers coached him by mail. Get in touch with so-and-so, who is *very* influential. Scratch up some cash by photographing children in parks and selling the prints to their parents. Their advice went unheeded.

From Budapest came sad news too. Following surgery for a digestive tract ailment that turned out to be cancer, Uncle Poldi had died of pneumonia. Judging André emotionally fragile, the family waited more than a week to write with the news, by which time Poldi was buried. André grieved alone.

The distribution of their uncle's assets and the family fights it provoked would figure heavily in André's letters to and from his brothers for months to come. Although Poldi left no formal will, he had earmarked pots of money for various relatives, including eleven million korona for André.[4] (Given Hungary's hyperinflation and currency transition from the korona to the pengő at a rate of 12,500:1, the nation's monetary system was in turmoil. It's impossible to get a good fix on how much Poldi intended for his middle Kertész nephew.) In addition, some stocks belonging to the brothers but managed by Poldi would revert to them and could be cashed in. When that would happen, nobody knew.

For now, André was on his own. He knew only a few people in Paris and was reticent about asking for help from those he did know. Without any French, he had few job prospects. So he tried to live on thin air, eating in cheap bistros, getting by on, say, a banana and milk, or skipping meals altogether. He tracked every centime that left his pocket. Undernourished, anxious, and bereft of family and sweetheart, he couldn't sleep either. It didn't help that the weather turned gloomy and wet. Even so, he felt alive to the city around him.

That late fall, a lank figure could be seen ambling along the damp streets. André photographed Paris with a newcomer's heightened visual awareness. Although he followed a tourist's itinerary, he did not view the city with a tourist's eye. Even the Eiffel Tower escaped postcard treatment. One foggy day, Andor visited an architect friend of Goldfinger's who lived in an upper-floor apartment in Passy, across the river from the monument. André's photograph from the friend's window shows a block of apartment buildings and a sky above blank with fog except for the tower's tip hovering like a modernist Christ in ascension.

André came away from the Place de la Concorde with a view of a fountain embellished with a mermaid clutching a sea creature. At the Moulin Rouge, he took a photograph that writes its own caption with electric signage aglow in the night:

*LA REVUE MISTINGUETT*
*MOULIN ROUGE*
*BAL*

That image was among those André took when his insomnia, fascination with electric lights, and search for companionship pushed him out into the streets after dark. Another late night, as he was trekking from the Dôme to a hotel on the rue Saint-Bon, he found the parvis of Notre Dame flanked by spotlights and splotchy with puddles. He halted, screwed his camera into his tripod, and opened the shutter. Then he shivered through a half-hour exposure. He came away with an otherworldly image in which the luminous wet pavement holds the eye longer than the cathedral's facade.

André lingered longest of all along the rain-swollen Seine, where the fishermen caught his attention. Like him, they were casting lines into the unknown and waiting to see what would surface.[5]

**In December,** André opened a package from Jenő to find the developing trays, washer for large glass plates, and camera he had requested. A secondhand Goerz Anschütz, his new camera took 10 by 12.5 centimeter plates. It had a Goerz Dagor 150 millimeter lens, shutter speeds up to 1/1000th of a second, and a top-down viewfinder. By all evidence, it would not prove a favorite. That month's mail also brought bounty from Ernesztina: some pastries, a chunk of goose liver in lard, and three pairs of long stockings. To top off the holidays, Tihanyi blew the cash he'd earned from a few sales to throw a New Year's Eve bash, and 1926 was off to a fine start.

It was probably at Tihanyi's that André met the Hungarian-born French sculptor Joseph Csáky. He and André liked each other immensely.

A master of geometric form, Csáky was known for his prewar Cubist sculptures. He lived in the Left Bank lair known as La Ruche (the Beehive), where his studio neighbored those of Alexander Archipenko, Fernand Léger, and Marc Chagall. André was invited to visit. He photographed his new friend looking professorial in wire-rimmed spectacles and a high-buttoned sweater. Csáky had turned his energies to avant-garde marionettes and decorative furniture. But André most admired, it seems, his bronze and stone sculptures, with their complexes of interlocking masses and planes.

More portraits soon emerged from one of André's ad hoc darkrooms, notably several of Gyula Zilzer. An engineer-turned-artist and onetime classmate of Jenő's in Budapest, Zilzer used to hang around with the Kertész brothers in Budapest and Szitgetbecse. To André, he was almost like family. Zilzer had left Hungary in 1920 for the usual reasons: anti-Semitism and lack of work. He bounced between Trieste and Munich, then back to Budapest, before settling in Paris, where he published anti-Fascist caricatures. He was living mostly on earnings from *Kaleidoscope*, his portfolio of grotesque allegorical lithographs in the spirit of Goya.[6] Taken in Zilzer's hotel room, André's portraits convey the impression of a man who's brainy and brooding. Zilzer clenches his pipe in his mouth. Folk objects sit on his desk. Pen and ink sit at the ready.

André also turned his lens on Tihanyi. In one memorable image, the artist stands in his digs at the Hôtel des Terrasses, the nerve center of bohemian Budapest-by-the-Seine in the thirteenth arrondissement.[7] He wears wool trousers and a wool shirt topped with a stained jacket that could be a bandleader's cast-off. Watchful, affable, and baggy-eyed, Tihanyi faces his portraitist. Smoke from the cigarette he's holding shoots from his lips, does a little dance, and briefly hangs in the air. Although it's rendered with the matter-of-factness of photography, it's also an abstract form and abstract idea: the man's thoughts, the painter's meandering brushstrokes, the deaf person's atonal speech made nimble and graceful.

When the two men traipsed through Paris together, Tihanyi would steer André to places he might want to photograph. One was an atelier where used mannequins were refurbished. A lower-body mannequin caught André's attention. In *Legs, Paris,* it stands upside down on a workbench, its limbs forking toward the window above. The mannequin's waxiness and slender curves stand out in its grungy surroundings. Nearby, rather ominously, hangs a looped rope.[8] Very surreal.

If André knew anything about Surrealism when he took *Legs, Paris,* it would have been from Tihanyi. Launched by the French writer André Breton in 1924, the Surrealist movement mined free association, chance, dreams, anything that flowed from the subconscious. By tapping that inchoate creativity and reconciling it with everyday reality, the Surrealists were attempting to dethrone rationality and liberate humanity. They ferreted out enigmatic objects, fetishized mannequins as objects of erotic fantasy, and legitimized whatever transgressed bourgeois norms, dismembered female bodies included.

Ravaged male bodies also figured in the Surrealist lexicon. Breton's first manifesto speaks of a phrase that came "*knocking at the window*" one evening as the writer was falling asleep: "There is a man cut in two by the window." Those words, Breton writes, were accompanied by "the faint visual image of a man walking cut half way up by a window perpendicular to the axis of his body."[9] Change "man" to "woman" and "window" to "table," and there's André's photograph, taken in Paris the following year.

Another day, André was wandering along the Seine when he chanced upon a trio of canvas-draped hulks stored on the quay. In André's photograph, they suggest a small herd of fantastical beasts grazing next to the river. Beyond stood the Pont de l'Archevêché, its three arches mysteriously reprising the triad.[10]

Like *Legs, Paris,* André's *Behind Notre Dame, Paris* would be labeled Surrealist. It reminded viewers of *The Enigma of Isidore Ducasse,* made in 1920, then remade in 1972, by the Dadaist Man Ray. The artist had wrapped a Singer sewing machine in an army blanket and tied it with twine. Later he photographed this creation inspired by a quote from the nineteenth-century writer and Surrealist idol Isidore Ducasse: "Beautiful as the accidental encounter, on a dissecting table, of a sewing machine and an umbrella."

Stubbornly independent, André would always brush off any link to Surrealism. It's true that he never participated in that or any other artistic movement. He would always be a movement of one, and not even a movement because his work is untheorized and instinctual. One could point out that *Underwater Swimmer*, taken in Esztergom in 1917, before the Surrealist movement existed, demonstrates his natural inclination toward the dreamlike. On the back of one print of *Legs, Paris*, André would write: "Interesting coincidence. They claim it as being surrealist, if it suits people better."[11]

So André kept his distance from Surrealism as an ideology. But he was not immune to Surrealism as a poetic sensibility. Like artists, writers, and photographers in the Surrealist circle, he seized on the irrational side of everyday life, the marvelous inside the mundane. Even though, or because, photography is the most factual of visual mediums, it would emerge—not only in André's work—as arguably the most Surreal and disquieting. In his first manifesto, Breton declares that "what is admirable about the fantastic is that there is no longer anything fantastic: there is only the real."[12]

**"Please send me a picture** of yourself but don't edit it," coaxed André's Szigetbecse cousin Rózsi Klopfer two months after his arrival, "because I want to see how you really look."[13] André complied. He mailed the same picture to the family in Budapest. It showed him looking scrawny and sleep-deprived with irritated eyes. Ernesztina responded that she was happy to get the picture but expected him to look better. As if that wasn't enough Jewish mothering, his brother Imre scolded: "With two or three hours of sleep, one cannot recover from fatigue... I don't have to explain to you that you should take care of yourself... Bandi, this is not a joke.

As I have so often repeated to you, Jewish wisdom culminates in the proverb '*nur gesund*' (only healthy and whole)."[14]

In February, Rózsi herself visited André. Now in her early twenties, she had grown into a well-dressed young woman with hooded eyes, round cheeks, and honeyed skin. By all evidence, Rózsi and André enjoyed each other's company. It's a good guess that she treated him to a few solid meals and that he gave her tips about photography, an interest of hers as well.

On returning to Hungary, Rózsi would have conveyed her impressions to the family. André must have come across as forlorn because Jenő soon wrote from Budapest, pressing him to consider coming home. Did André want him to inquire about jobs at the newspapers? Only two or three weeks later, they had a chance to talk over the future when André's younger brother traveled to Paris, off to make his fortune — so he dreamed — in Brazil. If André didn't want to move back to Hungary, Jenő persisted, why not join him in Latin America? Would Erzsébet be willing? André felt his brother's questions were like a dash of cold water. But Jenő persisted. Even after he left for Amsterdam, he pressed his point: "Take care of yourself. You look very bad," he wrote.[15] And: "You're not the kind of person who should be on his own. Being alone is not for you. You have to belong in some place."[16]

It's true that André was now acutely alone, emotionally, financially, and photographically. Jenő's departure (for Buenos Aires, as it turned out, because he took the first ship he could get) shut the door on their years of working in tandem. No longer could they put their heads together to tinker with a camera or critique a print. No longer could André ask for equipment or supplies and know that Jenő would dispatch them from Budapest. André's "most perfect collaborator" was engaged in his own fierce struggle to gain purchase in the world.[17] His life, like André's, had become unnervingly provisional.

André also fretted about the family back home. Abruptly paralyzed one day by inexplicable anguish, he dashed off a letter to Imre, begging for news. "Tell me what's happening with Mama. What does she do all day? Is she healthy? Is she sick?...Are there any financial problems? In one word, tell me everything because I am going crazy...I can't explain why I'm so anxious. I just know that if I don't receive a reply soon, it's going to be horrible."[18]

Did André share his disquiet in letters to Erzsébet? Did he entreat her to join him? Or did he urge her to stay in Hungary rather than partake of his hardship? Was she still adamant that he pull his life together before she made any commitment? Did she refuse to leave family and friends? A comment by Jenő suggests as much: "Bandi, you know how Bözsi [Erzsébet] would feel if she was taken from her home to Paris. According to your letter, she knows that too."[19] She stayed in Budapest.

Drifting along the streets late one night, André lifted his camera to look through the viewfinder at the facade of a music hall on the rue des Vertus. The word *BAL*, spelled out in lights, was flanked by two glowing arrow-pierced hearts. Another heart blazed from a sign above. Someone had chalked a fourth heart on a wall. Out on the street, a crowd milled around, as if the dance hall had closed for the evening and night owls were figuring out where to go next. André hung back. In one of the photographs he took on that occasion, *Après le Bal*, the pavement stretches between him and the others.[20] If the hearts meant Erzsébet, his distance from the convivial group on the street emphasized his status as an interloper. To the French, he was a fellow who spoke some odd Central European language, wandered around taking pictures of nothing, and couldn't scare up enough cash for a proper night on the town.

Like the clerk he'd been for so many years, André unfailingly listed his daily expenses: a stamp, a cup of coffee, a piece of cake, the Métro, the bus, a loaf of bread. Five francs here, eighty centimes there. His big purchases—a flash, printing paper, a packet of glass plates—were all photographic.

After he found a job as a retoucher at a studio in suburban Boulogne-Billancourt, he had a few extra francs in his pocket. Then someone he met at the Dôme arranged for his first commission: three pictures for the new interior design magazine *Art et Industrie*. It was a start. However, not only did André have to cobble together a living but he also had to invent a new way of life: that of a photographer-poet.

Today the sight of photographers casting about for subjects out on the street is unremarkable. Not in the 1920s. No one else was working the Paris streets like André. Earlier photographers, notably Charles Marville and Eugène Atget, had poetically documented the old Paris using view cameras and tripods. Their photographs imbue the city with a luminous stillness: an ancient tree, a venerable church, a shop front with a wrought-iron sign feel both ephemeral and eternal. André's Paris has a different air: village-like but also mobile and modern.

He was probably still unaware that elsewhere others propelled by the industrial, social, and political transformations of the 1920s were taking photography in novel directions. In Germany, the Hungarian-born Constructivist László Moholy-Nagy was writing the grammar of an inherently photographic visual language for the technological age. Dismissing the traditional idea of photography as a faithful reproducer of scenes, Moholy-Nagy investigated the abilities of a camera and lens to capture and fix pure light. In the Soviet Union, Aleksandr Rodchenko put the medium at the service of the Communist state, dumping what he thought of as "belly-button photography" (conventional photography done with a camera held at waist level) for fresh ways of seeing. His extreme close-ups, tilted horizon lines, and plunging angles defamiliarized the world as a way of advancing a utopian future.

Closer to André—sometimes at a table at the Dôme—was Man Ray, and he too was challenging the status quo. The lone American in Breton's Surrealist fold, Man Ray considered himself primarily a painter but refused to wed himself to a single medium. He also did collages, prints, assemblages, films, and photographs. A sought-after, if reluctant, photographic portraitist, Man Ray published portraits of cultural celebrities in both Surrealist tracts and mainstream magazines like *Vanity Fair*. Many were straightforward. Others played with multiple exposures, unusual angles, or weird props like an unfurled lampshade. For the images he dubbed rayographs, Man Ray needed no camera or sitter. A reinvention of a nineteenth-century process, rayographs involved placing an object on a sheet of light-sensitive paper, exposing it to light, and developing the print. The result (also called a photogram) inverts negative and positive, dislodging the objects from their normal contexts and suspending them in an otherworldly space.

Man Ray was a conceptual thinker, André was not. In contrast to Man Ray, André kept all ideologies at arm's length. He had no interest in rayographs or other darkroom mumbo jumbo, as he would have thought of it. In the mid-1920s, no one else in France, Man Ray included, shared André's simultaneous embrace of the medium's reality and free rein to its interpretive powers. Man Ray always considered painting superior to photography; for André, photography was, and would always be, all.[21]

But how to earn a living? In France, photo-reporting was valued chiefly for its objectivity and usefulness in documenting, say, a building or a politician's face. Considered skilled tradesmen, the relatively few photo-reporters in the French capital typically worked without recognition or credits and earned modest incomes. The agencies that employed them owned their negatives. Their standard equipment was the 9 by 12 centimeter Gaumont with its twelve plate holders.[22] In Germany, photographers for the *Berliner Illustrirte Zeitung* were using the new Ermanox, an innovative miniature camera with a fast lens. The Ermanox allowed them to work dynamically and unobtrusively even under low-light conditions. As a result, candids enlivened the pages of the German weeklies while photographs in the French press remained static and stiff.

Other Parisian photographers ran portrait studios. The renowned rue de Rivoli atelier of Paul Méjat, for one, offered a menu of special effects. Did the client desire a portrait in black and white or an autochrome (an early color process)? A pastel, watercolor, or lithography effect? Perhaps an artistically blurred likeness à la Rembrandt? Studio photography was all about pleasing the client. That typically meant precious and self-consciously arty images—shades of Angelo.

"**During the summer months,** one could see me, here and there in Paris, at the side of a puny little man with a frightened look, who held a camera in his hand or mounted it on a tripod. I piloted this poor fawn from Budapest, who spoke not one word of French, from the Luxembourg Garden to the Pont Marie, from Mondrian's studio to my hotel room, from the Pont des Arts to Montmartre. He wanted to photograph Paris, its squares and its parks."[23] So the Belgian painter, graphic artist, and author Michel Seuphor would write in the 1950s, remembering that summer of 1926 but forgetting that the "puny little man" was nearly six feet tall.

Like Tihanyi, twenty-five-year-old Seuphor lived at the Hôtel des Terrasses. But André met him through their mutual friend Zilzer, who showed up one evening in André's hotel room with Seuphor at his side. Mildly sick, André greeted his visitors from bed. When he pulled out some pictures he'd taken of children, Seuphor dismissed the work as sentimental. So André entertained his guests by playing the flute.[24]

Seuphor had traveled to Paris under the spell of his encounters with the Futurist Filippo Marinetti and the de Stijl artist Theo van Doesburg. He aspired to live the avant-garde life. Accordingly, he scrapped his real name, Louis Ferdinand Berckelaers, for Michel Seuphor, the surname an anagram of the mythological Orpheus. Seuphor was an intellectual who theorized and practiced geometric abstraction, André an intuitive who identified with flute-playing shepherds. They had no common language. Yet they decided to reconnoiter Paris together, André hoping perhaps that Seuphor would commission some pictures or introduce him to someone who would.

"He was hard up, miserable even . . . ," Seuphor later remembered, "and photographed everything I wanted and designated."[25] Why Seuphor "wanted and designated" certain images, he never explained. As for André, he came to despise Seuphor, he once told a friend, partly because the Belgian acted like a smug rich kid. "Seuphor also tried to push his way into my photographs. Often, I interrupted my work, went to him, and told him to go to hell." In what language, he didn't say. "Yet, again and again, he would figure out the moment when I was ready to flash the magnesium and literally jump into the picture before the exposure."[26]

Whether or not Seuphor played the role he claimed in André's choice of subjects, André gained something valuable from their association. Seuphor's championing of geometric formalism helped shape André's vision. More important, on August 19, 1926, Seuphor introduced him to Piet Mondrian. Although the fifty-four-year-old Dutch painter and designer wasn't yet famous, he was widely respected.

André had met Mondrian at the Dôme yet knew little about his art. Seuphor was taking him to the artist's studio because Mondrian had designed the stage set for a Dadaesque play Seuphor had written, and Seuphor "wanted and designated" photographs of the maquettes. So the two headed to 26, rue du Départ, a ramshackle building next to the Montparnasse train station. Its stairwell was typically Parisian: flaking plaster, grimy windows, odors of burned coffee grounds, and a communal toilet. Mondrian's apartment was four flights up.

The man who greeted them at the door had a lean face, broad forehead, and receding hairline. Spectacles completed his schoolmaster look. One might not guess that he loved to listen to jazz and dance the Charleston. The room they entered was spartan. There was a sofa, a table, a narrow iron bed, and little else. Mondrian led his visitors down a passageway rigged up with curtains and past a makeshift kitchen sans electricity or running water. Then a gloomy little staircase took them to an annex abutting that building and linking it to another. They emerged into a different world.

Mondrian's studio was pristine and luminous. The floor was painted black. There was a red rug, a gray rug, and a stove, and nary a speck of dust. Pasteboard rectangles painted in primary colors were arranged on the white walls. Near the center of the longest wall stood a dark easel.

Mondrian painted flat on a table. He used the easel to scrutinize a canvas, to show it to visitors, or, equally important, to act as a matrix of vertical and horizontal lines against the white wall. To balance the easel's dominant verticals with a horizontal, he'd placed a long slat on its lip.[27]

Banishing the incidental, the personal, and the representational from his art and concerning himself with only the universal, Mondrian espoused pure abstraction to convey a spiritual message. The black lines of his canvases map out meticulously calibrated flat planes in primary colors, plus black, white, and gray. Everything is determined by its equivalent opposite. Everything hews to its relationship with everything else.

Mondrian's Neoplasticism, as he called his doctrine, did not stop at the edges of his canvases: He considered painting a surrogate for the universal harmonies of nature and a model for humankind. If everything in his studio was visually weighed against everything else, it was because Mondrian lived his aesthetic.

The studio typically stunned his guests. The Swiss architect Alfred Roth experienced it as "a revelation, a miracle . . . I was seized by a strange elation." The sculptor Alexander Calder would credit his visit to Mondrian's studio with inducing his turn to abstraction.[28] André, too, was dazzled.

As he and Seuphor prepared to leave Mondrian's apartment that day or the next, when they visited again, André was stopped by the view through the open door to the stairwell. So he pushed back the sofa, set up and adjusted his camera, and waited, one guesses, until the light fell as he wanted. Then he released his shutter.

The right side of André's vertically bisected *Chez Mondrian* shows the stairwell landing outside the artist's door. The light from an unseen window falls on the banister, the stairs, the doormat, and the wall across the hall. The darker half of the photograph, to the left, includes Seuphor's boater and a jacket hanging behind a table just inside the apartment. At the table's edge sits a round vase with a painted wooden tulip. André probably moved that too. He knew that its shadow, when it was right, would bring his picture to life.[29]

Seuphor would later weigh in about the vase. "So strongly did [Mondrian] feel the lack of a woman in his daily life that he always kept a flower—an artificial flower suggesting a feminine presence—in the round vase standing on the hall table," he explains. "This was something so strange and unexpected, that in 1926 I had it photographed." Mondrian, estranged from women? Not at all, according to his biographer Hans Janssen. Mondrian enjoyed a rich social life, loved parties, and had many female friends.[30] Whatever Seuphor's contribution to André's photograph or the flower's connection to the artist's relationships with women, *Chez Mondrian* owes much to André's razor-sharp eye and grasp of Mondrian's thinking. Sensing a scene that could embody the artist's ideas, he took pains with pictorial structure, geometric shapes, and the use of equivalent opposition—verticals offsetting horizontals. Like Mondrian, André reconciled inside and out. Mondrian was writing an article in which he argues that the truly evolved individual of the future would achieve harmony by abandoning the idea of the home as a refuge.[31] In an Edenic world, he believed, home and street would be treated as one. Everything would function as a constructive element integrated with everything else, as everything does in André's picture.

*Chez Mondrian* might also be viewed through the lens of the *vanitas* still lifes commissioned by seventeenth-century Dutch merchants. Such paintings depict objects like flowers, skulls, and extinguished candles, sometimes in precarious balance, reminding viewers of the transience of life and inevitability of death. André's photograph centers on a single flower in a vase near the table's edge. Yet that flower is immutably wooden as befits the artist's value system based in the unification of the real and the ideal.

For the fastidious Mondrian, everyday objects had to be positioned just so. "If you lit a cigarette in his atelier and you put the box of matches down in another spot," one visitor observed, "Mondrian would get up to put it back in the original position."[32] *Chez Mondrian* has that same strictness. So does André's *Mondrian's Glasses and Pipe*.[33] Two pairs of the artist's spectacles are artfully arranged near the bowl in which his pipe rests. All are humble objects made iconic and pure. They evoke the artist's gimlet look as he studied, pipe in mouth, this or that pictorial relationship. André shot the photograph at a downward angle, positioning one corner of the table at the top as if to acknowledge the lozenge-shaped canvases the artist was working on at the time.

André would return to Mondrian's studio twice in September and once in November. He took more pictures, including portraits of the Dutch artist. Mondrian's nose bent slightly to one side. He compensated by trimming his toothbrush mustache asymmetrically, just as he would compensate for an off-balance line in a painting. The nose went a bit right. The mustache went a bit left. André noticed that too, and he caught it.

Mondrian's influence on André's work extended beyond the pictures he took in the artist's studio. It became evident, for instance, in the *cartes postales* (postcards) he was creating.[34]

The *carte postale* format involved contact printing his negatives on postcard-size paper. It did not require an enlarger. Happily so, because André could never count on having access to a full darkroom. He did when he was working at the studio in Boulogne-Billancourt or staying in Courbevoie. But after two months he was laid off from his job, and the Courbevoie room wasn't always available.

André's attraction to the postcard format ran deeper than practicalities. It traced back to his childhood postcard collection by way of the thwarted postcard project for his regiment during the war. Postcards could be held in the hand and passed around without fuss, and that kind of easy sharing suited him. What's more, the format lent itself to experimentation.

After trying different papers, André had settled on a sturdy, velvety, yet inexpensive Sédar *carte postale* stock, double weight, with a warm white base and a luster finish.[35] It was made by R. Guilleminot, Bœspflug et Cie, one of the world's oldest manufacturers of photographic paper. André used it judiciously. Working with the precision of a miniaturist, he calibrated the size and format of each *carte postale* to the aesthetics of the image that he was printing.

Technically, the process was simple: André placed the glass-plate negative directly on the postcard paper, exposed it to light, and developed the print. That yielded an image the same size as the negative. He played with the image's placement and cropping, shifting visual relationships and bringing out expressive elements. For one *carte postale* of his Eiffel Tower photograph, made from the 9 by 12 centimeter negative, André even trimmed the paper from standard postcard size down to 7.2 by 4.1 centimeters, a little smaller than a standard business card.

André's Eiffel Tower *carte postale* bleeds to the paper's edges. In printing other negatives, he used whisker-thin margins. For still others, he left a third, a fourth, or more of the paper blank. His favorite format was a vertically oriented postcard that bled to the top edge, or almost, with a big blank space below. He positioned at least one picture diagonally. It's impossible to date each of some two hundred and fifty different *cartes postales* that André created, typically doing multiple prints of each. What can be dated suggests that his formatting started out traditional and became more audacious as he absorbed the abstract art of Csáky, Tihanyi, and especially Mondrian.

By using the blank spaces as active formal elements, André turned the *cartes postales* into photographic objects, underscoring his role as aesthetic decision-maker. Indeed, he finished many of them with a tiny signature and a handwritten "Paris." Those too are compositional elements.

The *cartes postales* hark back to the nineteenth-century concept of photographs as handcrafted and handheld objects. They take as one point of departure the oval vignetted nude of Jenő that André had created in Hungary. Yet they reconceive that approach, replacing the old-fashioned oval with boldly placed rectangular units and the pastoral nude with scenes and personalities from modern urban life.

A case in point is his work for Feri Roth. The Hungarian violinist hired him to take publicity shots for his touring string quartet. At their photo session, André climbed on a piece of furniture to photograph them as they played. He positioned the score on the music stand the four shared so that the score faced not the musicians but the camera. In the darkroom, he made two very different sets of images. The full-framed print was for Roth, the radical version for André. Using the negative as raw material, he created a wide horizontal image with the music score as its compositional hub. The instruments and hands of its interpreters, actively making music, surround it. Their heads and feet have been cropped out. He printed the image at the top of the vertically oriented *carte postale*. The bottom two-thirds are blank. Thus André's version is not about the Roth Quartet as such but about the act of performing classical music.[36]

Even though he was creating postcards, André did not mail them naked. Jenő's and Erzsébet's went off in envelopes with nothing in the blocks for the address and message. André gave others to friends in Paris or passed them around at the Dôme, where people bought them for paltry sums. They became his calling cards. A German doctor, a Mr. Morgan, the artist and art director Vincent Korda, and a ballerina from the Balkans all sat for their *carte postale* portraits. Tihanyi typically brokered the deals, smiling benevolently when they went through.

**Infatuated with the artist's studio** as a privileged, revealing, even quasi-mystical site, André wrangled invitations and took pictures. It would have been Csáky who introduced him to the Belorussian-born sculptor Ossip Zadkine. Working in a rough-hewn space on the rue Rousselet, Zadkine created dramatic wood, stone, and mortar figures in a style indebted to Cubism, along with African and Cycladic object-making traditions.

André took several photographs in Zadkine's studio, most memorably one in which the sculptor is absent.[37] A large, stylized head sits next to a dusty brass lamp, a wine bottle, four glasses on a white cloth, and a Zouave marionette pinned to the wall. (The Zouaves were French light infantrymen in North Africa. They wore Berber-inspired uniforms with fezzes, short jackets, and balloon pants.) The marionette's shadow suggests a multi-limbed dancer, as if it were "acting the Zouave" — meaning, in French, being wild. The bottle, glasses, and lamp also fire the imagination, implying convivial drinking, feverish talking into the night, perhaps yearning for faraway places.

The studio still life was not a new genre. In fact, one of the first photographs ever made, Louis-Jacques-Mandé Daguerre's 1837 *Still Life in Studio*, depicts an assortment of art objects near a window. Daguerre was demonstrating the medium's ability to register materials, among them plaster, wicker, and fabric. Like Daguerre's image, *Chez Ossip Zadkine* directs viewers' attention to the tangible presence of the objects that it depicts. But André was doing more than taking a studio still life. He was using objects meaningful to Zadkine to make a primal connection to the artist himself. One might assume that André stumbled on this miscellany in a corner of the studio. More likely, he chose and arranged it, taking care to get the raking light right. As he exposed his glass plate, the light bounced off this set of objects emblematizing Zadkine, then struck the light-sensitive surface that is the plate, thus creating a material relationship with the sculptor. Zadkine is present in a way that is impossible in a painting. André had invented a photographic genre: the portrait in absence, simultaneously portrait and still life.

He also took traditional portraits, several of which reflect his adoration of women. André typically kept the faces of his female friends soft, saving sharp focus for some detail of their clothing or adornment. What Mondrian's mustache is to his portrait — the arresting detail — the craftswoman Hilda Daus's lace pierrot collar is to hers. With another sitter, it's the ringlet spilling down the middle of her forehead. With the German sculptor Anne-Marie Merkel, it's the piping on her blouse. André would take at least a dozen portraits of Merkel, who became a close friend. He portrayed her as rara avis with porcelain skin, hooded eyes, and a Garboesque air of mystery.[38]

Other sitters included the Dadaist Romanian poet Tristan Tzara, the American photographer Berenice Abbott, and the Norwegian sculptor-turned-painter Gunvor Berg. He depicts Berg not as a creature to be venerated but rather as a working artist. In one portrait, she appears simultaneously in a three-quarter back view, a three-quarter front view (thanks to a mirror), and a full-face painted self-portrait-in-process. Brush in hand, she pauses to consider the canvas.[39]

Infatuated though he was with bohemian circles, André's Paris was wider. He liked nothing better than grabbing his Goerz Tenax and heading to working-class *quartiers*, whose populace appealed to his poetic imagination. He had always gravitated to those who glossed over distinctions between work and play. At a *fête foraine* (fun fair), he photographed two clowns peering from the back of their wagon. In a dance hall, he snapped a white-aproned waiter who'd put down his tray to sway to the music. Dancing with women for a small fee was part of his job.

André also delighted in tree-canopied havens. He found Paris gardens and parks enchanting. Strolling one day near the Medici Fountain in the Luxembourg Garden, he hit upon what would become a signature subject: empty park chairs. The ones he saw on that occasion stood awry, evoking the daydreamers, readers, lovers, and friends who'd come and gone.[40] In that regard, André's *Chairs, Luxembourg Gardens* traces its lineage back to the gently melancholic photograph he'd taken a decade before of a bench in the forest where he once kissed Jolán. Park chairs also are places to be together or idle alone, feeling absence and loss, the émigré's lot.

According to Seuphor, he was at André's side when the photographer spotted those slat-back folding chairs scattered about a shade-dappled walkway. Indeed, Seuphor later claimed that he had stopped André at the sight: "I instructed him to photograph the chairs, only the shadows of the chairs, and he did."[41] No, he was with Tihanyi, André would insist, when he saw the chairs and—equally important—their shadows. Oblique, lozenged, and seemingly stamped on the ground, the shadows cadenced the walkway. As he positioned himself and adjusted his camera, Tihanyi piped up: "You are crazy!"[42]

But when his friend saw the result, André continued, he knew why André had taken the picture. Indeed, his encounter with Mondrian's art had sensitized him to the abstract pattern and geometric structure that informs *Chairs, Luxembourg Gardens.*

**As André well knew,** making the right contacts was key to his future. When he wasn't working, he might be rubbing shoulders at the Dôme. Sometimes his efforts promptly paid off, as when a German editor purchased his photograph of the Dôme's Hungarian table for the magazine *Das Illustrierte Blatt*. More often, André harvested names, addresses, and telephone numbers for his day planner: those of the Austrian architect Adolf Loos, of an editor at *Le Sport Universel Illustré*, of the Hungarian writer Sándor Márai, and many more. Yet it was logistically complicated for someone without a fixed address or dependable access to a telephone to follow up or make arrangements. Better to make himself known at the Dôme. Tihanyi spent evenings working its tables, and André was learning the art. He passed around pictures. It helped that he was picking up a bit of French, which he spoke, a local observed, with "the softness of those peoples of central Europe who have replaced the voice with a sort of music."[43]

The Paris reporter for *Magyar Hírlap* took note of the stir about his compatriot's work. On October 17, 1926, one year after André's arrival, the Budapest daily published a cultural roundup from the French capital. His column flits from one bit of news to another before alighting on "a youth from Pest, who is the sensation of Montparnasse. He is not a painter but a photographer. His name is Andor Székely. What he does is art. We're going to hear a lot about him." The correction appeared eleven days later: "His name is Andor Kertész. He can elicit quite extraordinary results from the camera, he has an original vision, what he does is bordering on art. He gained attention in Paris quickly and we will certainly hear of him more often."[44]

André was sizing up his year, too. Although he believed he had achieved a moral victory, he agonized over his inability to make good money. His financial anxieties ran deep. He felt ashamed that he had not yet repaid the $350 loan from cousin Sanyi to underwrite his move to France. (Eventually, he did settle his debt, using the proceeds from his stocks managed by Uncle Poldi and helped by his mother and brother.) Erzsébet's accusations still stung. His Budapest family kept nagging him about earning more. A Hungarian photographer friend wrote to chide him about not laying a solid foundation for his future and to spell out how he could do so back home. Imre, for his part, acknowledged that André had given Paris a good try. But: "With the fact that you have insurmountable language difficulties, your situation is even more serious... Bandi, come home!"[45] Then Imre switched gears: Maybe André should try the United States. Certainly, André's photographs were better suited to cultivated Paris than to "barbarous" New York. Yet in America, he might hit it big.[46] No wonder Seuphor observed that André "distinguished himself by a very distinctively timid smile which didn't really hide a bitter irony."[47] He was a lump of anxiety. He couldn't sleep. It was unthinkable, or rather too thinkable, that he might flame out in Paris.

Chiming in from Buenos Aires, Jenő reproached his brother for his lack of effort with French, then turned to what mattered to André: "If you had become a stockbroker or if you had a beekeeping operation such that it took seven days to get around to all of your Papszt-type hives, you would be only a rich man." Being a photographer made André a happy man, Jenő recognized, "a Mazdaznan man." Judging from the photographs André had sent him, Jenő saw impressive progress: "It's the photograph of Gunvor Berg that surprised me the most. There, you have something significant, you have a personal style, it is no longer the camera that takes the picture but the lens that draws as you want it to... From a technical point of view, it is perfect, and, as for the composition, I don't even recognize you!"[48]

André hadn't finished what he began with Berg. One day in December 1926 he set up his camera and tripod in the Hungarian Slovakian painter František Reichentál's room at the Hôtel des Terrasses. André wanted to photograph Reichentál with their mutual acquaintance Jean Jaffe, a correspondent for New York's Yiddish-language daily *Der Tog.*[49] Reichentál's wallpaper was patterned with nosegays that resembled peacock eyes, offering an opportunity for gentle Kertészian wit.

Taken in a mirror, André's photograph reveals a fivesome: the doe-eyed Jaffe, Reichentál's painted portrait of Jaffe hanging on the wall, André, his camera, and Reichentál. The artist wears an eye patch. The others' eyes are open wide. So too, for the split second of the shot, is that of André's third eye: his camera. And the wallpaper's pavonine eyes keep staring.

Reichentál's mirror is key to André's picture. Like photographs, mirrors double and frame what is in front of them, turning it into an image. As seen in the mirror, Jaffe is both spectator and reflection, real human being and an image painted on canvas. As for André, he is observer and participant, photographer and subject. This cat's cradle of human and mechanical gazes combines different ways of seeing and representing. The mirrored, the painted, and the photographic intersect.

In the 1920s, full-length mirrors were just becoming common. Finding many in Paris, André used them as photographic playthings. Often he put aside the self-timer that had long been his device for self-portraits and turned instead to the mirror, a favorite tool of painter self-portraitists. He used it to double and fracture his subjects, suggesting dual consciousnesses, multiple selves, objective reality, and subjective states. For his portrait of the actor William Aguet, André strategically positioned his camera and a mirror to capture Aguet twice, once his whole body, once his reflected image bisected vertically by the photographic frame. The result: *One and Half of Actor Aguet.*[50]

It's a witty trick but also more than that. Just as the films in which Aguet acted could be emotionally but not literally true, mirror images are optically but not materially real. That thought would have made sense to Kohn Andor – André's birth name – playing the part of André Kertész.

**Unable to sleep** through the night, André caved in to his fatigue one afternoon on a bench in the Luxembourg Garden. As he was napping, someone slipped a hand into his pocket and stole his beloved Goerz Tenax. That camera and its wondrous Dagor 75 millimeter lens had seen him through the war and all that had followed. The loss broke his heart.

It happened at a time when freelance jobs were accruing. André's old Voigtländer was suited to photographing the architecture of André Lurçat, Ernő Goldfinger, and Adolf Loos or taking portraits like those of Princess Lucien Murat, a woman of letters and a traveler in avant-garde circles. But it was too cumbersome for footloose work on the streets. André couldn't achieve what he desired if he had to stop and set up a tripod for each situation. "Your constant problem, your need for cameras, is still Chinese to me," grumbled Imre in reply to André's venting about his need for better equipment.[51] What was the matter with the Goerz Anschütz that Imre had purchased for André and that Jenő had pronounced excellent? But the Goerz Anschütz was no less ill-matched than the Voigtländer for street photography. The French reporter's camera (probably a Gaumont Reporter) André bought on the cheap after his Goerz Tenax was stolen did little to lesson his problems. A boxy, strut-folding device, it used sheet film fed from a magazine. Although it was intended for reporters, the Gaumont Reporter lacked the lightness, ease of handling, and discretion André would have liked when he locked on to sights like that of a sign painter perched on a ladder.

The ladder and its shadow formed a crisp inverted *V*, with the man on one side and his long shadow self on the other.[52] He was whitewashing the signboard on which his shadow appeared. André looped around, his reporter's camera in hand, feeling out visual relationships and making exposures judiciously. He was after those instants when the painter's brush met the shadow, conveying the illusion that he was putting the finishing touches on his proxy self, a sight worthy of a scene in a two-reeler comedy. André took only four exposures. One advantage of his years of working with glass plate and other cumbersome cameras was that he knew how to concentrate and extract what he wanted with very few shots.

Beyond the gag of the man painting himself, the *Shadow Painter* photographs could be read as metaphors for André's self-creation through photography. Just as a photographic negative is a vestige of the rays of light that have bounced off the photographer's subject, so too does a shadow result from an object's encounter with rays of light. That makes a shadow a proto-photograph.

**That winter** André lamented in a letter to Jenő that the two of them had never been lucky. "Why do you say we haven't had luck?" Jenő shot back. Already they had surpassed their elders in determination and intellectual achievement, he argued. "We don't even need luck. We just need the bad luck to stop... As Mazdaznan says, the present is just the moment, the future is everything."[53]

In fact, André's luck seemed to be turning. For fifteen months, he had ricocheted between Courbevoie and various hotels and rooming houses in central Paris. He was always packing up and hauling around his belongings. As 1927 began, he could finally afford a place of his own. For fifty francs a month, he rented a seventh-floor walk-up maid's room at 5, rue de Vanves, south of the Montparnasse Cemetery. There was no kitchen or bathroom, only a toilet down the hall. But he had electricity, a dormer window with a view of the rooftops, and enough space to set up a tiny darkroom. His mother sent comforters, sheets, pillowcases, and a small tablecloth embroidered with his initials.

Come summer, he would use that tablecloth in what was probably his thirty-third-birthday self-portrait. It covers the table that he's pulled up to the bed where he sits. There's a vase filled with roses and an open book from which a serious André looks up to stare at the camera. He is immaculately groomed and dressed in a dark suit, white shirt, and tie. Portraits of his parents are pinned to the wall behind him, along with his photograph of the Eiffel Tower, affirming his identity as a Parisian. On another wall, his life mask, made by his sculptor friend Frederic Littman, juts out next to a shelf on which he has artfully arranged a few books and letters from home. André's stage-managed image speaks of a measured and self-aware life in which family, books, and photography all have their places. His arrangement follows Mondrian's example. The artist conceived of a room as a structure comprised of the six planes that are its walls, floor, and ceiling. He considered its furnishings to be structural elements too. Accordingly, in André's photograph, the door, table, armoire, and dark section of wall read as planes upon which objects have been artfully placed. André controls his own space, humble though it may be.

His romantic life was a different story. It could be that Erzsébet was involved with somebody else and had informed André. It could be that the two were simply drifting apart. A note from Sándor Márai to André ends with "Give my very best regards to Madame your wife," suggesting either that André was in an intimate relationship that Márai mistook for a marriage or (less likely) that he'd understood Erzsébet to be André's wife.[54] Four months later, Imre gingerly brought up the question of whether André had a girlfriend in Paris, then backed off—"okay, enough said!"[55] By then, André *did*: a twenty-one-year-old Hungarian craftswoman and ex-girlfriend of Csáky's named Éva Révai.[56]

Révai traveled in the same émigré circles as André. She and her mother, the respected photographer Ilka Révai, shared a small atelier apartment filled with folk objects. Hungarian embroideries, French textiles, and Japanese silk scroll paintings counted among Éva's inspirations for the buttons, belt buckles, and silk and organza flowers—fantasy irises, silver bells, lilies—that she created for couturiers like Paul Poiret, Jacques Fath, and Elsa Schiaparelli.[57] Her work turned heads at the prestigious Salon d'Automne. Fashion magazines took note. One of André's photographs, presumably of Éva's bedroom, reveals an artful arrangement of vintage dishes, old-style shelf paper with a decorative edge, and nostalgia-inducing postcards and pictures from home. He would title the picture, discreetly, *A Midinette's Bedroom*. A *midinette* is a young seamstress whose lunch break is so brief that she must *faire dinette* (grab a quick bite) at *midi* (noon) rather than sit down to a proper meal.

André also photographed Éva, her delicate features and pale oval face framed by dark hair. She poses alone, with her mother, and next to friends at the parties that mother and daughter hosted. Their guests typically included the sculptor István Beöthy; Marguerite and Joseph Csáky; the painter Rózsa Klein; the tapestry designer Noémi Ferenczy; the avant-garde puppeteer Géza Blattner and his wife, Helén; the Siberian-born painter Evsa (Evsei) Model; Gyula Zilzer; Lajos Tihanyi; and André. Wine flowed, conversation surged, the Budapest spirit endured.

All the while, André was scurrying to prepare for his first exhibition, originally scheduled to open in February but postponed at his request. The venue was Au Sacre du Printemps, a storefront space on the rue du Cherche-Midi. André had met the gallerist, the Polish pianist Jan Slivinsky, through a German publisher he knew from the Dôme. Tihanyi, who had shown at Au Sacre du Printemps in 1925, probably smoothed the way. It was decided that André's work would hang alongside canvases by the Hungarian geometric abstractionist Ida Thal (also known as Ida Thalhammer). Their opening would inaugurate a series of evenings celebrating the magazine *L'Esprit Nouveau*, an outgrowth of Purism.

Launched in 1918 by the architect Le Corbusier and the artist Amédée Ozenfant, the Purist movement championed a clean, innovative, and universalized art and architecture that embraced industry and the machine. Like Mondrian, the Purists sought to impose order on a chaotic world. Le Corbusier rebuked his colleagues for their inattentional blindness to airplanes, roadsters, grain elevators, and other utilitarian constructions — the quintessential structures of their era. "Our era fixes its style every day," the architect wrote. "It is right before our eyes. Eyes that do not see."[58]

Thus André's photograph of the engineer-designed and -built Eiffel Tower, dematerialized by fog, was featured on the announcement of his exhibition. Next to it appeared the words "*Bergère ô tour Eiffel*" ("Shepherdess O Eiffel Tower"), a quote from Guillaume Apollinaire's urban pastoral poem "Zone," published in 1913. Apollinaire's call for an end to disorder and a search for truth had inspired *L'Esprit Nouveau*. The picture and quote fit André's work too. "Zone" has its narrator "walking in Paris alone inside a crowd."[59] Like André, he despairs of love and waxes nostalgic for the past even as he exalts in the modernity of the monument that was both the symbol of Paris and André's own talisman.

By early March, his show had come together: forty-two photographs – a mix of portraits, street scenes, interiors, and still lifes – printed on semigloss single-weight paper and framed with vellum mats. It was hung, salon-style, on the gallery's three walls, with a dozen of Thal's small paintings interspersed here and there near the top.

At nine on the evening of Saturday, March 12, 1927, André's future arrived. Mondrian showed up for the opening. So did Tzara, Loos, Seuphor, the Dutch photographer Piet Zwart, the Italian Futurist Enrico Prampolini, the German painter and designer Willi Baumeister, Thal's friends, and André's – a group that embodies the omnifarious creativity of 1920s Montparnasse.

The Belgian Dadaist poet Paul Dermée, a torchbearer of *L'Esprit Nouveau*, acted as impresario. Dermée recited "Brother Seeing-Eye," the prose poem he'd written extolling André's achievement. Among its most resonant lines are these:

*To make continuous discoveries in the visual world*
*one need only look with eyes whose retinas, with each blink, become*
*virgin again – film endlessly unwinding.*

His poem ends: "In our home for the blind, Kertész is a 'Brother Seeing-Eye.'"[60] Dermée was alluding to the sighted head monk in a medieval home for the blind who cared for his unsighted brothers.

The end of World War I had ushered in the era of mechanization, a groundbreaking development in human history. Yet, as Le Corbusier asserted, most people glossed over it, oblivious to what stood before them. André did not, Dermée declared. He had eyes that could see. His photographs were not mired in the past; they spoke the truth of their time and did so without artifice: "No rearranging, no posing, no gimmicks, nor fakery. Your technique is as honest, as incorruptible as your vision." From his camera—a machine—came the authentic art of their day.

Others recited Goethe's verse in German, François Villon's in French, and Lajos Kassák's in Hungarian. Attila József, Hungary's proletarian poet, read his own work. Slivinsky played the piano. Food was served. No matter that the festivities—conceived as a convergence of image, word, and music—pivoted around *L'Esprit Nouveau* as much as around André and Thal. André's cloud of no luck had lifted. He'd succeeded on his own terms.

Reviews were few but laudatory. The Paris correspondent for the *Chicago Tribune* praised André as "one of the few talented photographers who recognize that their medium possesses the necessary qualifications for being an independent art." Another reviewer trumpeted: "And here's Kertesz who opens eyes from before the creation of the World. No premeditation. He is curious and smitten... Kertesz doesn't even have the photographer's usual tricks. Thus he makes simple, plain, and true beauty."[61]

In an article prompted by the show, a certain M.S. (Michel Seuphor) asserted that "photographers like Man Ray and Kertész are revealing to us through the darkroom a new domain where fantasy is the twin sister of reality."[62] Seuphor would have been thinking of photographs like André's portrait of Tihanyi smoking, the image of the billboard painter daubing at his own shadow, or an elevated view of a man about to enter a phallic public urinal.

Taken not far from the gallery, that photograph is a jigsaw of storefronts and shadows. The man is the sole human presence. The industrial phallus is both André's little jest and the epitome of Le Corbusier's thinking about the built environment of the modern city. Other than the urinal, there's nothing remarkable about the place. Yet *Man at a Pissoir,*

*Latin Quarter* hints at latent meanings as if the scene existed in a poetic dimension that had awaited revelation. It's a photograph that both a formalist and a Surrealist could love.[63]

So could a shoemaker. One day the neighborhood *cordonnier* walked into the gallery, looked around, and pronounced André's pictures moving. The shoemaker "accepted me too and to show that he said: come eat at our house," as André would long remember.[64] Seventeen months after the Central European just off the train stood gaping at Parisians' windows, he found himself welcome inside a French home. It was no small thing to feel such warmth from a shoemaker, an artisan, the soul of the nation.

Even as André continued to torture the French language, he was inventing a visual language in which the objective and the subjective, seeing and feeling, the real and the fantastic, collapse into each other. He had long since made the essential discovery of his photographic life: that his feelings about what he photographed "*did show up* in the printed images. I knew... that I could project my own feelings and experiences... into the minds of people who'd view them with care."[65] Photographic lenses are indifferent and all-seeing. Yet a poet-photographer could use them to pin down a diaristic vision.

By the time of his exhibition, André had become more self-assured, although he remained deferential to people like Mondrian and the Count and Countess Károlyi. André had met the Károlyis through Tihanyi, who played chess with the count. In Hungary, there was no more ancient, prestigious, and widely known family than that of Mihály Károlyi, unless it was that of the equally pedigreed countess, née Katalin Andrássy. As the president of the Hungarian Republic after the war, Károlyi had attempted to build a constitutional democracy. When Béla Kun's Communists seized power and unleashed the Red Terror, the Károlyis had lost their vast mansions, estates, factories, and mines. The family was forced to flee. Their wanderings in exile had brought them to Paris where the countess was working in a dress shop and moonlighting as a journalist and actress. Tihanyi arranged for André to take portraits of the Károlyis at home, singly and *en famille*, and of the countess in the shop, where she posed with a triple mirror.

Although the Károlyis were now nearly as poor as André, a vast social abyss gaped between photographer and subject. André must have confessed to Imre how intimidated he was at the idea of photographing these luminaries. His brother replied: "You once wrote me, about one of your photographs, that one must never be afraid of one's photographic subject because one has the right to take a picture even of God."[66] Or of demigods like the Károlyis.

More jaw-dropping, the countess proposed to André that they open a photo studio together. *She* was coming to *him*! His ego swelled. However, her offer posed a dilemma. Financially, he was still scraping by, forever scrambling for contacts that might lead to work. Yet he had long spurned the notion of becoming a studio photographer. His feelings had not changed. He also had to consider possible repercussions of such an association should he return to Hungary. André sought counsel from home, and Imre consulted several politically sophisticated acquaintances: Might André jeopardize his own future in Hungary by teaming up with the wife of a deposed president? Most felt that the countess, unlike the count, was uncompromised. Imre believed that the studio idea held commercial promise. André's cousin Sanyi couldn't get over the fact that an aristocratic Károlyi wanted to collaborate with "a little Jew."[67] Yet, in the end, André declined the invitation.

The attention stirred by his exhibition attracted more freelance clients that spring: editors seeking features, individuals wanting portraits, artists and architects needing a record of their work. The avant-garde art community had taken André's measure, found his pictures worthy, and embraced him.

In his photographs at gatherings with friends, everyone clusters at the foot of a staircase, near a fireplace, or around a bistro table. André would set up his camera and timer, then slip into the group. Reciprocating perhaps for the gift of a print after one such soirée, Evsa Model sketched André's portrait. "A lyric poet of light and shadow with the sensitive soul of a photogenic plate," reads the artist's inscription. "Done by my trembling hand on a beautiful March day at the Café du Dôme."[68]

André's poetic disposition coexisted with wry humor and an omnivorous eye. In Hungary, he had photographed people and places he knew by heart. Now his vision was expanding. Less intimate than his Hungarian work, that in France had become more inventive, more formally rigorous, more open to the medium's capacity for arousing dormant meanings in the objects, gestures, and places his camera recorded. Conjured by light, suspended in time, the mysteries of Paris lurk in plain sight.

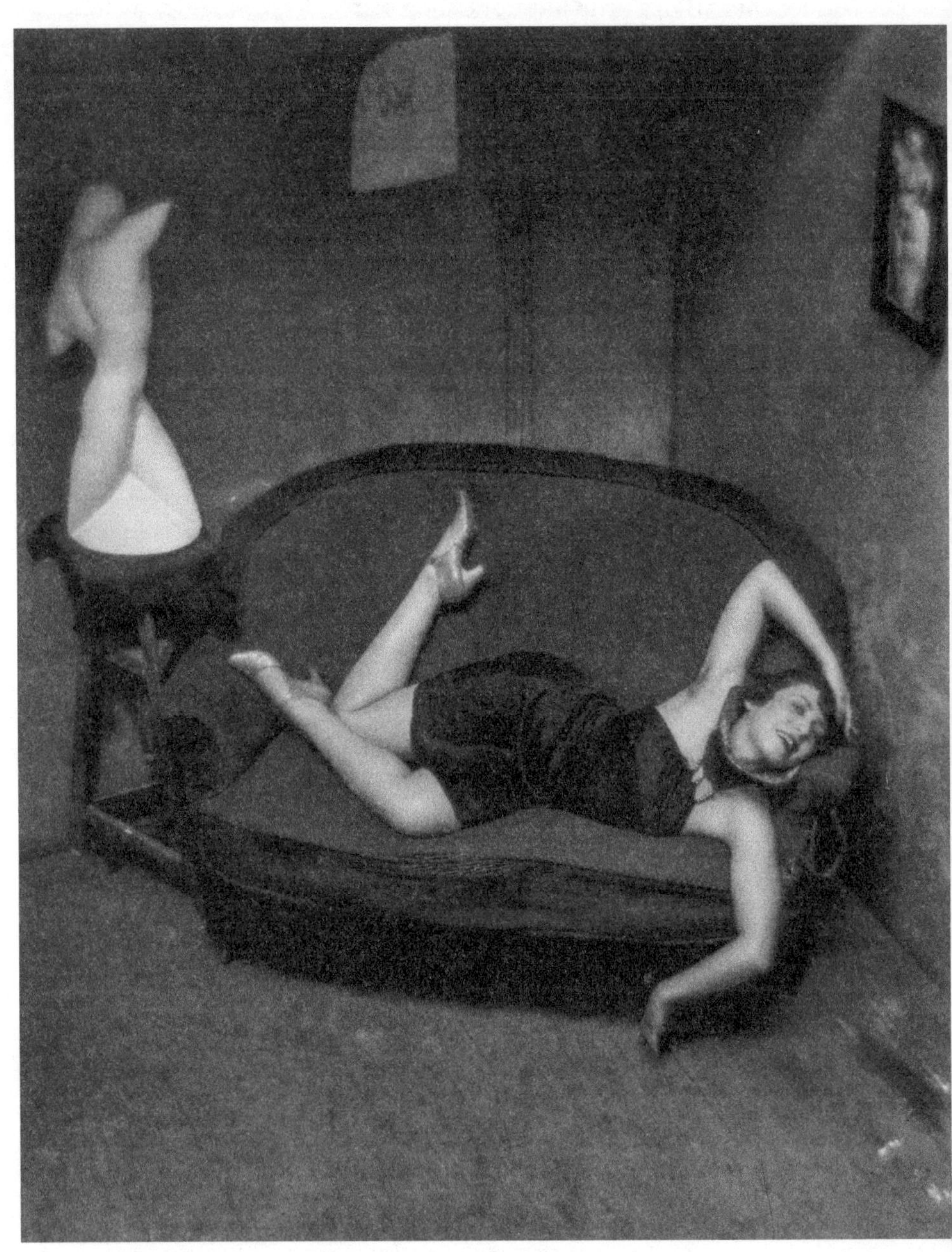

André Kertész, *Satiric Dancer*, 1927

# 5 SATIRIC DANCER, 1927–1929

**Eleven friends** squeezed around a plaid-clothed table to gossip, dine on fruit soup, and sip champagne and beer. The room grew noisy with laughter and talk. The painter Rózsi Klein pulled out her violin and played, perhaps a czardas (a traditional Hungarian folk dance). Then André found a high perch to take a souvenir picture of this latest party at the rue Daguerre studio of the sculptor István Beöthy. His friends would have teased him with the nickname they had borrowed from Dermée's poem, Brother Seeing-Eye (in French, Frère Voyant, a play on the word *clairvoyant*).[1]

That may have been the evening when André met Magda Förstner. The twenty-eight-year-old Hungarian had been dancing in Paris clubs for several weeks. But not until she shared a billing with performers from the Opéra and Comédie Française had her act registered with French dance mavens. The occasion was a matinee at the Sorbonne organized by the minister of education Édouard Herriot to celebrate the arts. Förstner's caricatures—*The Gossip*, *A Slovenian Dance*, and *The Chinese Emperor*—earned loud applause and won over reviewers, among them the composer and critic Jean Marèze.

"Look at Magda Förstner: her eyes vibrate, her mouth tenses, her nostrils quiver, her body knots, folds, opens up; there's one type, there's another, completely different," Marèze raved in *Le Soir*. "Magda Förstner is the whole fantasy, the whole new rhythm, the whole music hall of today with its astonishing verve."[2] Flitting from rhythm to rhythm, gesture to gesture, the dancer frolicked, vamped, and smirked. Her art crackled with the Budapest spirit.

At their first meeting, André struck Förstner as an enthusiastic young man with "a pale, thin, interesting face."[3] He took a few pictures. He was making a living as an artistic photographer, André explained, and he would like to photograph Förstner again. They set a date for a shoot at Beöthy's studio.

She showed up wearing Mary Jane pumps and a short, satiny dog-collar dress. The two chatted. How did she want to pose? They played with an idea or two. André found a perch, possibly some stairs, for a high angle shot of Förstner just inside the open front door. In Beöthy's studio, they shoved a chair or two away from the cabriole couch angled across one corner and may have rotated a sculpture that stood on a nearby table. A stage was set. André readied his tripod and camera. For the next shot, the dancer sank into the sofa, splaying her legs in a limp-puppet move.

Suddenly, as André would later recall, "she had an idea. She threw herself on the couch, and I took it at once," meaning *Satiric Dancer.* "I saw that it was perfect, that there was no need for another take." In a slightly different version of the story, he asked Förstner to throw herself lightly on the couch and do "some funny thing in the spirit" of the sculpture, and that's when she twisted into the pose.[4]

Sprawled on the sofa in *Satiric Dancer*, Förstner mimics Beöthy's *Héros, Action Direct (Torso),* a stylized plaster of a swiveling male torso with no arms or legs. A stool serves as its pedestal; the sofa serves as the dancer's. On the wall above Förstner's head hangs a second Beöthy piece, a female nude bas-relief. The figure's knobby breasts, truncated arms, and exaggerated hips recall those of the pre-Christian fertility figure the Venus of Willendorf (also known as Woman of Willendorf). Her corpulence and immutability contrast with Förstner's litheness and joyful abandon.

*Satiric Dancer* aligns a sculpture, a gesture, and a click of the shutter. Like Förstner, André was a master of mobility and timing. In the decades to follow, his photograph would win acclaim for catching the effervescence of *les années folles* (the Roaring Twenties) when the music hall reigned, liberated women dazzled, and Montparnasse swarmed with artists, writers, and performers. Like all iconic images, it accommodates interpretations beyond those dictated by the circumstances of its creation.

For one thing, *Satiric Dancer* can be seen through the lens of a generation traumatized by war. Although Beöthy's sculpture *Héros, Action Direct (Torso)* has the model torso of a Mazdaznan man, he is also a quadruple amputee. (Beöthy, too, had been gravely wounded.) The dancer's limbs feel like proxies for those the hero is missing. Yet, due to the contrast between Förstner's dark dress and her pale skin, they look disjointed. Her left arm hangs as limp and useless-looking as André's after a bullet pierced it in battle. Madcap though Förstner is, the photograph hints that she also is damaged.[5]

*Satiric Dancer* may betray André's anxieties about women. The sexually vibrant Förstner cavorts on the sofa, windmilling her arms and her legs. She calls to mind the Folies Bergères sensation Josephine Baker, whose zany and provocative *danses sauvages* were spellbinding. Epitomized by Baker, Förstner, and other performers, the New Woman flouted traditional gender roles and freely sought pleasure. All the same, Förstner wears a dog collar. She poses like an articulated marionette, an object to be manipulated by others. As for the figure in the bas-relief hanging on the wall, she is, like Erzsébet, rigid and remote. The situation feels dreamy and irrational. What was André's relationship to the two women? Did he sense himself in Beöthy's energetic yet maimed and vulnerable hero?[6]

*Satiric Dancer* burst from a privileged moment for three modernists reinventing their mediums. Judging from other photographs, André and Förstner saw each other at least twice in the weeks that followed.

Then Förstner departed for Scandinavian stages, Beöthy exhibited *Héros, Action Direct (Torso)*, and André turned his attention elsewhere. He printed *Satiric Dancer* and other Förstner pictures as *cartes postales*, some of which he gave to friends.[7] One print was sold to the German women's magazine *Die Dame*, where it illustrated a jocular story about a cheating wife. After that, André slipped the negatives into glassine envelopes and filed them away.

His fixation on arms and legs did not fade. The ghosts of Galicia's maimed soldiers still lurked, along with André's memories of his cousin Misi's loss of ambulation and of his own wounded arm, which would never be quite the same as before the war. Men with pinned-up sleeves or trousers were everywhere in France. Estimates of the number of disabled veterans vary between seventy thousand and seven million.[8] The shadow of the Great War hung heavy over the City of Light. André enjoyed photographing lively-limbed dancers and acrobats. But just as often he turned to vets with missing appendages, using images of their bodies to express poetically, one suspects, his own remembered damages and those of the people he cared about.

One time a clochard (urban vagabond) steered André to a derelict hotel for the indigent in the light-industrial Batignolles district. There he photographed an old-timer who surely had war stories to tell. The man sits with his peg leg extended, his good leg behind. He's hoisting a glass of red wine, by no means his first. His left eye rivets the camera, but where his right eye should be is a seam. Although André treats his subject as worthy of respect, his sly humor shows through. The man's disfigurement doubles as a wink. And his peg leg is shaped like a wine bottle, with its rubber knob as the cork.[9]

At another shelter, the Hôtel de l'Espérance (Hotel of Hope), André prowled the dormitory area, painted in the institutional manner, light at the top, dark at the bottom. Among the iron-frame cots lined up next to each other, one held his attention. Its lumpy bedding was thrown into relief by the light from a window. A wooden leg lay where one expected a human to be. It was pockmarked and crude with an ungainly hinge at the knee and a leather shoe and cloth stocking.

Abandoned like a forgotten doll, the prosthesis carries a powerful emotional charge in André's portrait in absence, which feels like a scene from a dream. A dream about castration, as Freud would interpret it, in which a man turns into his own artificial leg. Wood and flesh, folk object and body part, inanimate and animate: Boundaries blur. Adding to the oneiric realism, the number 13 is stenciled not once but twice on the wall as if floating above the bed. *Hotel of Hope* hovers between a dreary materiality and the haunting illogic of hypnagogic state. His photographs often seemed "to come more out of a dream than out of reality," André would acknowledge. Perhaps that had to do with his "inexplicable association with the things I see."[10]

**That June 24th,** the police in Villazón, Bolivia, cabled the family via the Bolivian consulate in Paris to inform them that Jenő had gone missing. A letter from Jenő, dated two days after the cable and mailed to Budapest, but addressed to André too, clarified that he had traveled from Buenos Aires to Tarija, in backwater Bolivia, to take a job as a driver.[11] Then Jenő fell silent. Ernesztina knew even less than her sons because Imre had intercepted the cable before she could see it. In a flurry of correspondence, he and André eventually hatched a scheme to shield their mother from the news. André faked a letter from Jenő to the family, explaining that a civil conflict was disrupting the mail.[12] All that summer Imre made frantic, furtive, and unsuccessful attempts to locate their brother. Bad luck had come roaring back.

André's money woes had never departed. His bedtime rituals included the daily tally of income and expenses. The lists of his purchases (bread, Dôme, stamps, cheese) attest to a bare-bones existence. His indulgences were photographic or, rarely, gastronomic. (He *did* love French pastries.) His income was edging upward, yet he continued to live coin by coin.

Tihanyi was in even worse shape. Now that his brother in Hungary had stopped sending checks, the painter was scraping by on money-changing schemes, plus scattered sales. André helped by photographing Tihanyi's art. It was the least he could do for the generous soul whose conviviality was lubricating his career. Tihanyi made contacts, scheduled appointments, and negotiated prices on his behalf, while chiding him for not asking for more: "I understand that your self-esteem is better if you feel you can support yourself, but you have too much to do with both that and what it takes to create your art."[13] Although André's pride got in the way of asking for help, he was gratified to have Tihanyi handle business arrangements so he could be the bohemian.

All that summer, André plied the streets, taking pictures in which urban modernity carries whiffs of Hungarian folk life. He photographed French buskers slapping together a living and Roma circus folks working from lavishly decorated horse-drawn carts. In one shot, a contortionist's kneeling backbend holds a crowd rapt. In another, an acrobat does a handstand atop a pile of blocks. André worshipped these misfits who lived by their wits. However much life beat them up, they were dynamic and marvelous. They muddled through. They brought people joy.

Sometimes he headed for the Quai de Montebello, a haunt of clochards in that era before central Paris was gentrified. Clochards scrounged a living by begging, shining shoes, or selling the cigarette butts they foraged here and there. In summer, they slept under bridges; in winter, they hugged subway grates for the warm air. In the romanticized view that André shared with many, they were street philosophers with colorful pasts, escapees from bourgeois routine, a Parisian folk type. Lounging among them, he would swig from the bottles of rotgut red passing from hand to hand. From time to time, he raised his camera, instructing them to ignore it.[14]

One of his favorite characters was a blind man nicknamed the Gondolier. He appeared twice a day at the Dôme, slicing the air with his cane as if propelling himself through the waters of the Grand Canal.

The Gondolier would crisscross the terrace, silently accepting the coins thrust into his palm. Then he would walk away. Like a businessman heading home from the office, thought André, charmed by the métier the man had invented. Some photographers would have zeroed in on the man's wretched condition. André caught him looking blissful.

In years soon to come, other photographers would portray Paris in that same poetic spirit. But in mid-1920s Paris, there were only André and Man Ray. Brassaï was scraping by mostly as a sportswriter for French and Hungarian papers. The photographer Ilse Bing was in Germany writing her dissertation. A recent transplant from Amsterdam, Germaine Krull was trying her hand at fashion photography. Fourteen-year-old Robert Doisneau was studying to be an engraver-lithographer, and Henri Cartier-Bresson was a schoolboy in knee pants.

**Surprisingly for a penny-pincher,** André left on holiday in early September. Maybe he justified the trip as a chance to range over fresh photographic terrain. Probably his friends paid his way. In any case, Beöthy invited him to a village on a rocky peninsula in Brittany where the sculptor had vacationed before. Beöthy was traveling with the wealthy, free-spirited artist Anna Steiner, with whom he was having an affair. At André's side was *his* lover: Anna's best friend Rózsi Klein.

Twenty-seven-year-old Rózsi could pass for Edith Piaf's Hungarian cousin.[15] For one thing, she shared the Little Sparrow's intensity. Tell Rózsi something she found interesting, and she'd take a drag on her cigarette and demand to know more. She laughed hard. She slammed doors. People found her both fragile and overbearing. Like Piaf, too, Rózsi was more alluring than beautiful. She had thin lips and a slightly roaming left eye. One portrait shows her as a gamine in a frilly blouse, white gloves, and skimmer atop curled bangs. More often, she traipsed around waiflike in shabby shoes and a thirdhand coat that threatened to swallow her up.

Rózsi had not always been poor. She and her three siblings, one her twin sister, were the offspring of a wealthy Budapest eye doctor and a homemaker. They had grown up with a governess. As a child, Rózsi took private violin lessons. Her long hours in violin posture were blamed for the scoliosis that had put her in an iron corset and made her hypersensitive about her body. When Rózsi fell in love with painting after the war, she attended the Hungarian Academy of Fine Arts (now the Hungarian University of Fine Arts). Soon feeling that she had to live in the country of Bonnard, Matisse, and Picasso, she departed for France after the spring semester 1925, a few months before André.

At first, Rózsi rented in the scruffy quartier around the Gare de l'Est, the Paris station where Budapest trains arrive and depart. That choice took inspiration from Endre Ady's love poem to Paris titled "Gare de l'Est." But when she began studying at an art school across town in Montparnasse, she moved to a seventh-floor maid's room at 5, rue de Vanves, the same building and floor as André. By then, the two had long known each other. Had Rózsi found her new place by design or with André's help? In any case, her move drew them into each other's lives. André was often lonely. Rózsi was fun. They spent evenings in bars with Beöthy and Steiner. They would have shared books, talked into the night, and made music together, Rózsi on violin, André on flute.

A letter from Tihanyi to the vacationing André suggests that André was tight-lipped about this new relationship, even with his best friend. "I always feel very open and very honest with you," wrote Tihanyi. "Why haven't you told me what's going on with you?"[16] Maybe André wasn't sure. Maybe he worried that Erzsébet would hear about his romance with Rózsi. Maybe she *did* hear about it. At some point, she took a scissors to seven or eight of André's photographs of the two of them together, cleaving her image from his. André stopped hearing from her. They'd been apart for nearly two years.

Two things are certain: Rózsi was in love with André, and he was happy to be in the French countryside for the first time. The couples stayed at a small hotel near the ocean. They lolled on the beach, visited villages, and strolled through the fields. French peasants turned out to be not so different from Hungarian peasants. And, even though the briny, damp air of Brittany is unlike the dry heat of the Hungarian plain, there was the same chirping of crickets and sweetness of fruit picked off the tree. Back in Paris, he developed and printed his negatives and mailed some of the landscapes to Erzsébet but probably received no reply.[17]

A pattern emerges: despite André's commitment to Erzsébet, he was intimate with other women, just as he'd had flings during the war, even though Jolán had reason to hope he would be faithful to her. Rózsi and Éva Révai were not André's only Paris affairs, all of which he would later attempt to erase, destroying pictures and letters and telling half-truths.

In the 1970s, for instance, André would mention to a New York acquaintance that in Paris he had once taken the photographer Berenice Abbott to get an abortion.[18] Although Abbott was a lesbian, she did end a pregnancy around this time. The curator John Szarkowski, who knew André well, had a different version of this story. According to Szarkowski, André and Abbott shared a girlfriend, who became pregnant, and it was the girlfriend whom André escorted. Abbott was the father, the curator joked.[19]

Then there was André's American flame, Miss Johnson (or Johnston). Shortly after his return from Brittany, he trudged up the last flight of stairs to his room one day to find her sitting outside his door, shrouded with a blanket. André positioned himself and took a picture. Later he would pronounce Miss Johnson "a charming and innocent little girl, a bit stupid."[20] He complained that she and her American pals huddled together at cafés and spoke only English, ignoring the fact that he and his Hungarian pals did the same.[21] In his view, the Americans had traveled to Paris in search of a different life yet were unable to see beyond themselves. By contrast, he mingled with all kinds of people.

He sometimes went trawling for pictures in the city's grubby eastern fringe called the Zone, with its shacks, litter-strewn lots, spindly trees, stray dogs, and ancient leprous buildings. There he photographed Roma caravans, swarms of urchins, and rag sellers at makeshift flea markets, the kind with real fleas. His subjects lived on the margins both geographically and economically. Yet to him, they were vital to what Paris was.

In working-class districts like Belleville and Ménilmontant and at the central market, Les Halles, with its rough-and-ready workers and country smells, André caught the incongruous, the nostalgic, and the amusing. Bodies in motion. Oddities no one else noticed. A worker relights a gas streetlamp after a downpour. Cloth flowers festoon the sides of beef hanging in a butcher's shopwindow. Piles of crates and walls plastered with posters make a visual mosaic. Two oldsters enjoy a chin-wag. As André framed the pair, the billboard behind them features a perky demoiselle wearing a bathing costume circa 1900 and poised to spring from a diving board. Because of the vantage point André has chosen, she looks like she's about to leap over the heads of the talkers. She's a thought bubble, a punch line, a memory from their days as young rakes.

One of André's favorite quartiers was Montmartre, a section that was to Paris as the Tabán was to Budapest: a hilly, cobblestoned village annexed to the capital and beloved by artists, a neighborhood of bordellos, tiny orchards, and hole-in-the-wall bars. André had recently printed an image taken in Montmartre a few months earlier. He had been standing atop one of the staircases leading up and down from the summit crowned by the basilica Sacré Coeur. The shadow of a grilled fence crosshatched the landing and crisscrossed the top flight of stairs. Leafy trees vignetted and shaded the street far below. Fresh from his encounter with Mondrian's art, André had recognized the scene as a play in line, shape, and pattern. The conjuncture of sunlight and shadow felt right. He set up his Voigtländer, then awaited the incident that would complete the scene.[22] When a man pulling a cart appeared at the foot of the stairs, he squeezed the shutter release.

Back in the darkroom, however, André felt less than fully satisfied with his result. Formally and affectively, the picture felt slack. Although his later accounts of what happened next are somewhat confusing, it seems that he returned to that same spot with a new Hugo Meyer Satz Plasmat lens on his camera.

André's second attempt at *The Stairs of Montmartre* resolved the scene into a remarkable image. In this version, a man sits on the bottom step, a woman approaches, and the viewer is left to imagine what will happen between them. They give the image a narrative tension. Formally, André has tightened the composition and, moving down two or three steps, shifted his viewpoint. More subtly, yet powerfully, his choice of lens distinguishes *The Stairs of Montmartre*.

Following his first attempt at the picture, André had disassembled his Voigtländer's lens, then reassembled it in a different configuration. (A camera lens consists of several glass elements, each of which bends light in a particular way.) In Hungary, he and Jenő used to take lenses apart, play with various combinations, and note the slightly different optical effects. Which combination best conveyed what André *felt* about his subject?[23] That question again came to the fore.

In the end, he worked with his new Satz Plasmat. This German-made triple convertible lens would count among the great photographic loves of André's life. Its front and back elements could be used singly or paired with the central element, resulting in five different focal lengths: 9, 11, 13.5, 22, and 28 centimeters.[24] That made it a primitive zoom. Equally important, the Satz Plasmat had optical aberrations, which gave it a distinctive plasticity. No, thought André, they gave it "a soul."[25]

Twenty-first-century lens manufacturers achieve virtually perfect sharpness. Distortion errors are exceedingly rare. That wasn't true in the 1920s. André took pleasure in his lenses' idiosyncrasies, which he turned to expressive advantage. The Satz Plasmat was "optically sharp," he noted, "but not *over* sharp."[26] Just what he wanted. Scalpel sharpness showed off only technique. In *The Stairs of Montmartre*, he wanted atmosphere.

What's more, the Satz Plasmat warps the scene slightly. Although viewers may not consciously register that difference between André's two versions of the staircase, most can sense it. In the second, the pitch of the stairs feels more acute. The cobblestones of the street beyond come up closer. The Satz Plasmat effects a subtly upturned space, conveying a feeling of which today's colder lenses are incapable.

That's analogous to the difference between the sound of a singing voice modified with software to correct for any deviation from a mechanically flawless rendition and the sound of a voice that's subtly and expressively imprecise. The journalist John Colapinto writes of the emotionally powerful music of trained opera singers and African American farmhands, both of whom can flood their listeners with feeling by "edging on or off a pitch, coming in slightly before the beat or slightly after." Colapinto quotes the singer Robert Warsh: It's the "human moment when the voice travels to the note it's seeking" that tugs at the heart.[27] So, too, when the eye travels to the picture's emotional locus. In photography, as in music, impurity can be seductive.

**It could have been** at the Dôme or La Ruche that André's friend Csáky introduced him to the Purist painter Fernand Léger. André jumped at the chance for a picture-taking session at Léger's atelier-apartment. At the last minute, the artist was called away, so André missed out on taking portraits. But he teamed up with Léger's assistant to photograph the studio's contents—canvases, furniture, supplies—as a complex of interlocking forms like those in Léger's art.

The most striking photograph from that session is the portrait in absence, *Corner of Léger's Studio.* It shows a wine bottle, a toy truck, a wall-mounted thermometer, a ball bearing or two, and a cobbler's shoe stretcher. There's also an almanac of the kind that hangs in country kitchens, to be consulted about saints' days and phases of the moon. (Léger came from a family of Norman farmers.) A form built with wooden blocks, both humanoid and machinelike, completes the arrangement. André's picture freights these objects with significance for the artist and his work. As a Purist, Léger wanted to open "eyes which do not see," in the words of Le Corbusier, the movement's cofounder.[28] Léger cared about the social meanings, artistic potential, and beauty of everyday things, including those displayed in the shopwindows of a rapidly commercializing Paris. Indeed, André's photograph recalls a quirky window display, reflecting the artist's interest in bringing the goods on display to people's attention and making them precious. For Léger, a cobbler's shoe stretcher was as worthy of admiration as an artist's oil.[29]

Like Léger, Tihanyi continued to pursue Purist ideas in his semi-abstract still lifes. The pipes and clay chimney pots outside the painter's studio windows had become a favorite subject. Soon they entered André's repertoire too. Their forms and rhythms pleased him. Their anthropomorphic and zoomorphic qualities amused him. They were a secret in plain sight for those who could see.

Not for the first time, André was taking cues from Tihanyi's work, a fact he would later deny. To hear André speak in years to come, no artist had ever influenced him – not Aba-Novák in Hungary; not the Surrealists, Mondrian, Léger, or Tihanyi in France. He claimed to delight in the creative cross-fertilization that made 1920s Paris a seedbed of modernism: "We were like a big family, and each of us borrowed artistic ideas from the other."[30] Yet he griped when colleagues' photographs resembled his and spurned the idea that he took inspiration from the art-making around him. No, no, not him, he would insist, betraying perhaps a baked-in fear of inadequacy. His work had developed independently and "very naturally."[31] So many times André had fallen short of his family's expectations. So many times he had felt the sting of Erzsébet's scolding. So many times he had berated himself for his failures. It was unthinkable that his work should be indebted to anyone else's.

When a journalist asked André how his photography differed from painting, he was tongue-tied. Incapable of theorizing, especially in French, he finally spit out: "Photography should be realistic." By stressing the medium's factuality, he was distancing himself from the Pictorialists' practice of giving their photographs painterly facades and declaring himself a modernist. "Photography is one thing, painting is one thing," André asserted, "but they are not the same thing."[32] A painting springs from the painter's mind and hand; a photographer isolates material things that the camera can register with light.

By 1928, modern photography was gaining traction. That May and June, audiences at the Comédie des Champs-Élysées, a leading theater, discovered unusual photographs hanging in the building's stairwell, a suitably transitional space for convention-busting work. A group of editors and critics had dreamed up this first independent salon of photography, dubbed the Salon de l'Escalier. Scorning the gauzy Pictorialist-style images in the official Salon of Photography, the organizers wanted to shake up people's ideas about the medium and make a case for its status as art. André's photographs hung alongside those of Man Ray, Berenice Abbott, Laure Albin-Guillot, Germaine Krull, and others. Three older photographers positioned as the upstarts' precursors were also represented.

One was the late Eugène Atget. From the turn of the century until his death in 1927, Atget had documented the old-style shopwindows, traditional vendors, and architectural details of Paris. Man Ray introduced Atget's work to the Surrealists, who embraced it as that of a naïf attuned to the latent mysteries of the City of Light. Atget's Paris was quintessential, eternal, and lost.

Atget's inclusion in the Salon de l'Escalier caused a sensation and made him the new darling of the avant-garde. André was ruffled but wisely kept mute. He admired Atget's honesty and sensitivity. Yet he felt jealous. He found the work static, he said. In André's opinion, the difference between the late photographer's images and his own came down to the frontal views that Atget favored versus the oblique views that André preferred. André construed this as the difference between documentation and interpretation. That is debatable: Atget does use oblique angles, and the poetic beauty of his images makes them interpretive. "Look," André would complain, "I was the first to interpret the real Paris. He documented."[33] André took the position that he owned a certain Paris photographically. But Atget had gotten there first.

A more self-assured individual would have left it at that. André headed for the rue de Cléry where Atget once photographed a building that juts out at a corner like the prow of a boat. In Atget's best-known image of that building, the street is deserted. Positioning himself at a similar angle, André waited for some incongruous detail. Eventually, a black cat sauntered up behind a trio of men who stood aligned like bowling pins. André clicked his shutter. *That*, he seemed to say, is interpretation. "I think Atget or Berenice Abbott did this street," he would later comment, disingenuously. "But not with the cat."[34]

André should have had no complaints: While Atget was the most talked-about photographer in the Salon de l'Escalier, the most talked-about photograph was André's *Fork*. A stark composition of shapes and lines, it focuses on the utensil resting upside down on the edge of a plate, along with the two objects' shadows. Some have erroneously claimed that André took *Fork* after a dinner with Léger. The Hungarian musician Paul Arma recalled that André once pulled out his camera after the two consumed a lunch consisting of nothing but hardboiled eggs. Arma's account of a no-frills meal aligns with the picture's spareness. Quite possibly, André did pull out his camera and start playing around. But it's unlikely that he took *Fork* on that occasion: The photograph feels too calibrated to be casual. In another account, Frederic Littman remembered watching André make his first passes at such a picture using a spoon and plate at the Dôme in the first weeks after his arrival in Paris.[35] That sounds right. So does André's memory of buying the utensil he used in *Fork* at the department store Bazar de l'Hôtel de Ville.[36]

Among the formal pleasures of *Fork* are the plate's ovoid crescent shadow, the bent parallelogram of the fork's tines, the tines' split shadow, and the dark line that visually seals the image at top right. *Fork* exemplifies André's concern for abstract shapes intensified by his encounter with Mondrian's art and his commissions from architects like Ernő Goldfinger and André Lurçat. Its clean geometric lines and isolation of an everyday object make it kin to Purist paintings by Léger and Tihanyi.

Can photography be an art? *Fork* figured prominently among the photographs that set that question back in motion. Most critics danced around "yes." One plucked a quote from the nineteenth-century artist Camille Corot, who once observed that a good painting begins with the ability to see. A good photograph, too, the critic ventured. The subject does not determine a photograph's worth. What matters is the photographer's eye. That makes photography art. The critic listed examples, ending with (his emphasis) "*a study with a fork*."[37]

André's subject *was* radically different. Today's Photography 101 instructors typically ask their students to find a common object and interpret it in various ways. But in 1928, it was audacious for a photographer to disrupt expectations about a mundane object or to integrate it into the realm of geometry. Purist painters did that regularly. Why should a photographer not do the same? Is photography inherently any less worthy than painting? People wondered.

A different aspect of André's work intrigued the writer Pierre Mac Orlan. Soon after the Salon de l'Escalier opened, André spent a Saturday with Mac Orlan in tiny Saint-Cyr-sur-Morin, east of Paris. After years of roughing it in sailors' dives and bohemian haunts and scrounging a living as a jack-of-all-literary-trades, Mac Orlan had retreated to a rustic house in the country. From there flowed a torrent of articles, art criticism, poetry, and novels, among them his 1927 *Le Quai des Brumes* (*Port of Shadows*), later to become Marcel Carné's classic film.

A man of the people after André's own heart, Mac Orlan composed and played accordion music, which is as inextricable from Hungarian folk songs as from the French bal musette. Sitting in his garden wearing knickerbockers and dangling a cigarette from his mouth, this man with the body and face of a bulldog pulled poignant music out of his squeezebox that Saturday afternoon. André photographed from an upstairs window. Mac Orlan had his magic box, and André had his.

Spurred by Surrealism and the Salon de l'Escalier, Mac Orlan was publishing a series of essays that developed his concept of the social fantastic. Even though a camera makes mechanical reproductions, he writes, a photograph can uncloak the mysteries of what's in front of its lens. The medium's potential for greatness lies in its ability to freeze time. In so doing, a photograph makes visible what would otherwise succumb to time's flow. In a wink, writes Mac Orlan, the lens "lifts away all the veils that are no more than the result of a few social conventions whose very existence renders our human eyes insensitive."[38] Photography precipitates out of the secret life of all that surrounds us.

Mac Orlan was thinking of images by photographer-poets like Man Ray, Berenice Abbott, Germaine Krull, and André Kertész. In André's pictures, he perceived a Central European anxiety that translates into a "fantastic restlessness of the street." Their "secret elements of shadow and light" pique the novelistic imagination, Mac Orlan felt.[39] He may have been thinking of André's recent exposures from high vantage points showing children walking to school, people conversing, and dogs wandering about. All are foreshortened by the downward angle. Most are seen obliquely. Their shadows shrink, swell, and comingle. André's camera was doing nothing more than mechanically imprinting the scene in front of it. Yet, marveled Mac Orlan, it revealed the mystery that all things possess.

In one photograph from that time, André catches the gesture of a boy playing in the Tuileries Gardens, extracting that sliver of time when the boy's trunk was hidden from view by that of a tree. Only his arms, one leg, and part of his head were visible. He was kicking a ball. In the print, the shadow of the boy's right hand, projected on the wall behind him, appears to touch the ball. The real boy looks to be handing off the ball to his shadow self. Meanwhile, the shadows of his legs stretch across the ground, then head up the wall as if he were a rubber kid on stilts. A straightforward shot, Mac Orlan would say, nothing tricky, yet a portal to another dimension.[40]

**Ten months** after his disappearance, Jenő wrote to the family, lifting his silence and assuaging their anxiety but offering no explanation about what had happened. Curiously, his letter was addressed not to his mother and brothers but to Uncle Poldi, who had been dead for almost two years, as Jenő well knew. "Letters, words, what good does it all do?" he soliloquized. "It is thought shining through infinity that connects us." Jenő's outpouring continued: The chaos, stress, and physical hardship he was experiencing as an immigrant had revealed Poldi's soul to him. Jenő had alternate selves, he explained: an "innocent self, plunged into the vast world, with astonished and wondering eyes" and a worldly self, raised by Uncle Poldi to seek fortune and power.[41]

Jenő's self-description fits André too. And just as his younger brother's identification with Poldi served to externalize himself and express his alienation, so was André's double consciousness that of a photographer observing and recording his surrogates: masks, mirror images, objects, and shadows. Yet André was coping, even flourishing, while Jenő's words suggest traumatic stress from his self-punishing drive to reinvent himself as Eugenio Kertész, alone in a land more than seven thousand miles from home.

**One day that summer** of 1928 found André roaming the Bois de Boulogne, the big park on the western edge of Paris. He scouted locations, coaxed ducks here and there, and approached workers on their wine breaks. He was shooting his first assignment for the new picture weekly *Vu*. It was to illustrate an article conceived as a leisurely ramble through the park's estival pleasures. Ironically, Parisians were flocking to the country for August vacations, the author points out, just as country life was in full swing in the capital's own Bois de Boulogne. Gardeners were haymaking, lumberjacks sawing, and waterfowl swimming, all in the urban park.

André's assignment came from the magazine's founder and editor Lucien Vogel, who had seen and admired his show at Au Sacre du Printemps. It was easy for the two to meet: The affable Vogel conducted much of his business over countless cafés crèmes at the Dôme.[42] André liked this portly, blue-eyed man, equal parts *bürgermeister* and dandy. When Vogel invited him to become a regular contributor to *Vu*, André promptly accepted.

Envisioned as a fast-clipped newsreel in print, *Vu* was delivering features about news, sports, the arts, nature's pleasures (snowflakes, fog), and human quirks (good luck charms, women's smiles). Its tone was that of a blithe and knowing uncle. Layouts were freewheeling, typefaces varied. Playfully shaped, tilted, fanned, or overlapped, photographs romped through its pages. Some involved dramatic angles. Others were extreme close-ups or near-abstractions. The idea was to emulate the hectic rhythms of modern life. Every other French magazine suddenly looked staid by comparison.

Vogel came out of the women's fashion-magazine world. He had launched the classy *La Gazette du Bon Ton*, cofounded *Le Jardin des Modes*, and art-directed French *Vogue*. In presiding over the visual funhouse that was *Vu*, he gave free rein to his curiosity. In those early days of the picture press, magazine editors could operate as they saw fit, and Vogel did so with gusto.

His photographers also enjoyed wide latitude. Vogel valued their personal views of their subjects. He would either sketch out an idea or assign pictures for a finished article. Then he would tell the photographer the number of pages to be filled and cut him or her loose. He did not dictate specific pictures. His only demand was no postcards. Nearly always, he accepted what André submitted as a finished product.

So it was with "The Parisian Forest," published in the August 22, 1928, issue with the words "PHOTOS KERTESZ." To get a photo credit was noteworthy in a culture where press photographers were low-ranking journeymen. *Vu* was enhancing their status. André had just taken a giant step in his career.

Vogel also recruited Germaine Krull, Eli Lotar, and other photographers. All were freelancers. Stock pictures from the agencies, delivered daily by bicycle messenger, took up the slack. Top writers worked for

*Vu* too. Yet for the first time in France, words revolved around pictures, not the reverse. *Vu*'s editorial motto directs its readers' attention to the synergy Vogel was seeking: "The text explains, the photo proves."

For his next *Vu* assignment, André motored to Deauville, the tony resort on the English Channel. Rózsi accompanied him. The writer Jean Gallotti was at the wheel. The point of the story the two men were doing was the defacement of the Norman countryside by newly erected billboards. (To contemporary eyes, they look quaint.) "Here, posters hide a Corot, a weeping willow in a river," chides Gallotti in "The Sacrilegious Signboards." "It is weeping over our contemporaries' vandalism."[43] André concentrated on both the idyllic views and their spoilers. The feature would lead with a photograph that defamiliarizes a billboard by angling in from below and the side. It looks like a giant sail. A fresh vision of an ordinary thing—exactly what Vogel was after.

Deauville was swarming with people of fashion that August, many of whom André knew. No longer was he the timid young man who had crept into the Dôme less than three years ago. He and Rózsi visited with the Hungarian illustrator Marcel Vertès and the Japanese French painter Tsuguharu Foujita and his lover Lucie Badoud, known to their pals as FouFou and Youki. But André and Rózsi could not idle: He had to rush back to Paris to prepare for his departure for Lorraine, where he was traveling as *Vu*'s special envoy.

This new assignment began at the château of Louis-Hubert Lyautey, the marshal of France and a former high-ranking colonial administrator. Received with noblesse oblige, André took exteriors, interiors, and portraits of the old lion himself. Like the Hungarian aristocrats whose privilege stuck in André's craw, Lyautey was a monarchist, elitist, and devout Catholic. André cannot have felt comfortable in that Ali Baba cave of a château. But now he was a special envoy for a leading publication, not a touchy youth cursing at the Catholic priest who tried to shoo him off church property. André swallowed his resentment about social and financial disparities and quietly did his assignment.

After leaving Lyautey's estate, he headed down the Moselle River valley, where he turned his camera to sites beloved to the novelist Maurice Barrès. An inspirational figure to French Fascists, Barrès writes of a mystical link between his native Lorraine and the cultural values he considered exclusively Christian and French. Ironically, the photographer whose images convey that link was Jewish and Hungarian.[44] Vibrant with light, André's photographs of rural Lorraine were among the first of many to reveal his ardor for *la France profonde*, the localist France of rustic beauty and artisanal tradition.

Lyrical photo essays about the regions of France became a specialty. In 1928, the French rarely traveled for pleasure. Most who lived outside Paris had no conception of tourism. However, the expanding automobile industry was about to transform all that.[45] Feature stories about the scenery, customs, and gastronomy of different regions would fast become popular. *Vu* and other publications would dispatch André to Burgundy, Picardy, Normandy, Savoy, the Loire Valley, and Basque country. Corsica's board of tourism would hire him to promote the island. It was physically, logistically, socially, and creatively demanding work but also, André felt, a charmed life. His dream of a life of vagabondage had come true.

A few days after he returned from Lorraine, André got word from Jean Ducrot, a writer colleague at *Vu*, to meet him at the Montparnasse train station. When André arrived, Ducrot handed him a box, instructing him to open it only after he got home. When he did, out hopped several toads. Ducrot had thought up the gag after hearing André reminisce about catching toads in Szigetbecse. André found it hugely funny. Amid peals of laughter, the two later released the toads into the Medici Fountain in the Luxembourg Garden, startling the gardeners. But not before André took pictures that he sold to the *Münchner Illustrierte Presse*.[46] What was better than getting paid for roaming Lorraine if not getting paid for snapping pictures of toads?

**The late 1920s** cemented André's reputation at a time when photographic culture was undergoing a profound transformation. With the emergence of mass-market publications like *Vu*, photographs no longer existed exclusively as handmade objects. Many now emerged into the world as photomechanical reproductions embedded in text and printed in double-page spreads. That meant that photographers' audience was changing. Instead of handfuls of friends and admirers, a vast picture-greedy public was consuming their work. Photo reportage was proving, as Jenő had once advised André, "the only kind of modern photography."

Camera technology was evolving, too. One day André walked into a shop belonging to a colleague who was the exclusive French distributor for the German-made Leica. First introduced to the public in Leipzig in 1925, the camera had only recently come on the market. André walked out of that shop, Leica in hand, deeply in love. The Leica was an indulgence but one he could manage. That June, he would earn 2,476 francs (about $1,700 in 2024 dollars), a decent income in an affordable city. He shelled out 1,800 francs (about $1,300 in 2024 dollars) for his Leica I Model A.[47]

André's camera had a fixed 50 millimeter f/3.5 Elmar lens, faster than those he'd been using. (The faster the lens, the larger the maximum aperture.) That made it easier to get what he wanted in fast-moving situations or low-light conditions. To focus, one estimated the distance from camera to subject, then selected that number on a dial on the camera body. Alternately, one could attach a range finder, which allowed for quicker and more precise measurement. (With a range finder, the photographer selects the subject using a split-image screen viewfinder, then rotates a dial until the two images are superimposed.) As another advantage, André did not have to insert a plate holder, remove the slide, adjust his settings, take the shot, then replace that plate before making the next exposure. Instead, the Leica took 35 millimeter cinema film spooled into a reusable cassette, allowing for thirty-six to forty exposures, one after the other.[48] André could advance the film with a twist of a knob, and—presto!—it was armed and ready to go. His new camera was fast, small, and lightweight, compared to every other device he'd ever used.

Wild with anticipation, André stepped out with his Leica strapped around his neck and no tripod to carry. For him, picture-taking had always been a physical act. Now it could be more so, thanks to the Leica's lightness and compactness. The viewfinder helped too. Rather than peer down to frame his subject through a fold-up device, he could press the peephole viewfinder up to one eye and hit the shutter release. Virtually part of his body, the Leica allowed him to arch his back to point his camera upward, bend over to focus on something below, or alter his viewpoint by tilting or crouching. New technology, André knew, effects new possibilities for camera-seeing. For one of his first shots with the Leica, he crawled under an upturned wagon one day at Les Halles. All angles and shapes, André's image geometrizes a wheel and its skewed shadow. He had long envisioned such an exposure; with the Leica, he could finally take it.

Other Leica negatives show him exploiting the camera's inconspicuousness and capacity for immediacy. He caught a clochard urinating, sandwich-board men pacing, folks clustered around a plein air painter, and children agape at a marionette show. As the first serious photographer in France to purchase a Leica and drift around the city, his device at the ready, André was pioneering what would come to be called street photography. The Leica was always with him: At last he could express much that had felt out of reach.

He continued to shoot judiciously. Although the Leica allowed for quick exposures, one after the other, he did not click off frame after frame. The point was the *right* shots of his subject. "I am ready for the picture before it happens. I feel it coming, but I do not know what or how," he would say, making picture-taking sound orgasmic.[49]

With the Leica came another new tool: the contact sheet. After exposing and developing each roll of film, André would devote a sheet of photographic paper to printing without enlargement all the negatives from that roll. A loupe pressed to his eye, he would study the contact sheet he had made, mulling over individual frames and figuring out cropping and sequencing decisions. Contact sheets became a staging ground for his work.

André stopped making *cartes postales*. Creating them was a slow and deliberate craft. Each required a carefully calibrated contact print from the negative. With the Leica, that wasn't an option. The large-postage-stamp size of the 35 millimeter film frames (24 by 36 millimeters) didn't allow it. Besides, photographs as objects to be held in the hand and examined one by one now felt less relevant.

To say that André delighted in the Leica is not to say that his other cameras began gathering dust. For virtually all of his professional work in the late 1920s and early 1930s, he stuck to a 9 by 12 centimeter camera with sheet film. Aware that medium-format negatives carry more visual information than 35 millimeter frames, most editors dismissed the Leica as a toy even as more photographers began using it. The gold standard for professionals was the Gaumont. When the photographer Gisèle Freund arrived in 1937, Leica in hand, for a job for the French government, she was told to come back with a real camera. Editorial honchos in America also scoffed at the Leica. After *Life* magazine was founded in 1936, its editors instructed photographers not to use the Leica. Only years after André acquired his Leica would it become mythical professional gear for photojournalists, street photographers, and even fashion photographers, in part because of André's groundbreaking use of it.

Unlike most of his colleagues, Vogel deferred to his photographers about camera choice. (He would later acquire a Leica of his own and start shooting.) All the same, André relied on larger cameras—at various times, the Gaumont, the Lorillon, the Linhof, the Zeiss Ideal, the Voigtländer—in his work for hire. Aware that most editors believed that image quality suffered with so-called miniature cameras like the Leica and keen to resell his work whenever he could, André used medium-format cameras even for assignments that would lend themselves to the Leica, like the cover image for the October 3rd issue of *Vu*.

He probably used the Gaumont to shoot that cover. His subject was the actress Blanche Montel rumbling down a road at the wheel of her BNC (Bollack, Netter, et Cie) roadster. A junior member of *Vu*'s art staff named Marcel Ichac had tagged along on the shoot, hoping to pick up a few pointers. He watched as André danced around the roadster in motion, camera at the ready. Suddenly Montel shifted her head to one side as if to peer around an obstacle, and André took an exposure. Ichac did the same. Later they would compare pictures. André's worked, Ichac's did not. In photography, André would explain, "two seconds are a thousand years."[50] He had acted just as Montel's gesture evoked the road ahead. The German master of movement Felix H. Man, another pioneering photojournalist, perceived a dead point in every movement: "And in this dead point you have to shoot."[51] For André, by contrast, that instant—"when something changes into something else"—was intensely alive.[52]

**With André's next assignment,** time slowed and became cyclical. That one led him and his colleague Eli Lotar to La Trappe, a Cistercian abbey in the Norman village of Soligny-la-Trappe. In this strictly observant Benedictine order, most monks took vows of silence broken only during religious services. No other photo reporters had ever been admitted to La Trappe. A curious public had never seen pictures of what went on inside. Probably Vogel had pulled strings.

For some reason, Lotar soon departed. But André stayed on. For two days, he toiled almost around the clock. Using glass-plate cameras, he photographed the monks kneeling at confession, tilling the fields, filing out of mass, and silently lunching as one brother reads aloud. Besides group shots, he took close-ups like one of a sculptor brother putting finishing touches on a statue of Saint Thérèse of the Infant Jesus. Conditions were challenging. The light was dim in many parts of the abbey, and André had to work unobtrusively under a blanket of silence.

In the keystone picture of his photo essay, a lay monk kneels at the feet of a brother who has died. The wooden litter on which the body lies serves as a visual link between the two monks, living and dead. The image is stark. (To that end, André removed a painting and plaque from the wall.) Its angular forms suggest the geometric underpinnings of God's divine plan. Several measures of time converge. For the deceased, earthly time has ended and eternal life has begun. For the brother who attends him, time is meted out in rounds of meditation and prayer. For the photographer, time is about the right fraction of a second.[53]

André promptly delivered his pictures. Yet they would not reach *Vu*'s readers until Ash Wednesday 1930, more than a year and a half after he took them. That's because, upon his return from Soligny-la-Trappe, André quarreled with Vogel.

The editor had long since established *Vu*'s right to sell any photographs the magazine commissioned to other publications. Even so, André, Krull, and Lotar, the weekly's lead photographers, were reselling photographs they took for *Vu* through press agencies or even directly. Indeed, resales were a major source of income for all three. One day that December, they were summoned to *Vu*'s Champs Élysées office to thrash out the issue.

The photographers were at the height of their powers. Thirty-one-year-old Krull had published the masterful *Métal*, a kaleidoscopic and semiabstract vision of the Eiffel Tower and other industrial structures. Her lover and protégé Lotar was about to produce what would become his signature photo essay about the slaughterhouses of suburban La Villette. As for André, he knew that his work at La Trappe was superb. Probably the three went into the meeting assuming they would prevail. But they did not. Vogel ordered a stop to their resales, again stipulating that the magazine owned the rights.

Afterward, the photographers typed up a letter in which they reluctantly agreed to Vogel's demands but only for photographs that appeared in *Vu*, not those that never made it to the magazine's pages. In the case of resale by *Vu*, 50 percent of the price would go to the photographer. A credit line would be mandatory. The exception would be sales to Germany, the most lucrative foreign market. In that case, the photographers would retain all rights.

Vogel read the letter. He wasn't buying.

The photographers had to tread carefully. Remarkable images were the magazine's oxygen, but none of the three had contracts. They were freelancers. In a second joint letter, they attempted to flatter their boss. Yet their aggrievement showed through. How could Vogel take a position that flew in the face of common practice and was inadmissible to "three independent Avant-Garde photographers"?[54]

The editor remained adamant. Even so, André refused to comply. He continued to claim copyright in Germany. His pictures were his. He self-righteously sold the La Trappe photo essay to the Berlin-based publisher Ullstein Verlag. On January 6th, several of them accompanied an article in the weekly *Berliner Illustrierte Zeitung.* Then Ullstein's monthly for Germans on the go, titled *Uhu*, scooped up a few. Shockingly to many, *Uhu* used them for a sensationalized story about a defrocked monk.[55]

Vogel's paternalistic and easygoing management style had reached its limits. He was livid. So was Edmond Wellhoff, the writer who reported the La Trappe piece for *Vu*. Angry words flew. In a letter dated February 4, Wellhoff informed André that the *Uhu* article was causing serious problems between *Vu* and the Catholic authorities.[56] Two weeks later, Wellhoff wrote again to report that certain monasteries in Yugoslavia had filed a complaint with the Vatican against the abbot at La Trappe for allowing access to Jewish photographers. (Lotar was Jewish, too.) André's use of a lavatory to develop his plates was a particular sore point. Wellhoff continued: "The results were immediate: the Father abbot who had received us so graciously is facing a disciplinary action from Rome and will probably be relieved from office. I tell you this not to protest once again against the past, but to demonstrate to you the horrible consequences of your act."[57]

But André did not humble himself with apologies. He wanted the money. The Catholic Church was not his problem. More fundamentally, his photographs, whether done for *Vu* or not, felt inalienably *his*. He continued to resell to the Germans, and he got away with it. Apparently, Vogel weighed the loss of income against the loss of André's work and decided in the photographer's favor. Eventually, the two again warmed up to each other. Wary about offending Catholic readers, Vogel allowed the affair to recede before running the pictures. Thus *Vu* lost, and Ullstein gained, first take on a powerful photo essay.

**Two weeks** after his return from La Trappe—at 9:35 a.m. on October 27, 1928—André Kertész wed Rózsi Klein. Surrounded by friends, the couple took their vows under the chandeliers of the town hall of the fourteenth arrondissement. No photographs or firsthand accounts of their nuptials survive.

By all evidence, Rózsi was deeply in love with her lanky photographer with blue-gray eyes, a warm smile, a sly wit, and a beautiful body. What André felt about Rózsi as he took his vows is unknowable. Witnesses are dead. Photographs and documents have vanished, destroyed by André or lost amid the hardships of Rózsi's life to come.

Eventually, André would pretend that the marriage never happened. By then, it did not fit the self-narrative he had constructed. Ask him about Rózsi and he would turn cagey and act as if he couldn't quite place her. If pressed, he would claim that she had blackmailed him or tricked him into marriage or that she had stood at a window and threatened to jump if he didn't agree.[58]

But there's no reason to trust anything André later said about Rózsi. Most of his few surviving photographs of her show her happily socializing. Another photograph of Rózsi, presumably by André, suggests a different side of their relationship, namely, her vulnerability and his tenderness: Her little foot sticks out from under a duvet as she sleeps. Astringent though she could be, André's new wife was also physically and emotionally fragile – "aggressively anxious to exist," judged a friend.[59]

She became André's assistant. That would have meant aiding in the darkroom and mailing or delivering the finished prints. Rózsi also archived André's negatives and prints, helped manage his photo stock, and handled his correspondence, a task he found irksome. Her French and German were better than his. Like Tihanyi, and Jenő before him, she created the conditions that allowed André to thrive as a photographer. Her contribution was even more vital after Tihanyi left Paris that January to try his luck in America.

Rózsi's painting fell by the wayside. Throughout his life, André would encourage and support the work of women artists. The decision to stop painting must have been Rózsi's. She was eager to share André's life, but also she fell in love with photography. Under his tutelage, she took, developed, and printed her own photographs. One imagines the two working side by side in the red-lamp intimacy of André's makeshift darkroom. On the back of her prints, Rózsi applied his wet stamp. It read "ANDRÉ KERTÉSZ / 5, rue de Vanves / PARIS 14e" – words she prefaced with "Madame" scrawled in black ink.

Three months after they wed, the Kertészes moved from their cramped maid's rooms to an apartment in a classic nineteenth-century building at 75, boulevard du Montparnasse in the heart of bohemian Paris. There Rózsi exhausted herself with housework, hardly her forte but her husband liked order. Work and play mingled. From the mezzanine, probably their bedroom, Rózsi photographed André riveted on the viewfinder of his tripod-mounted camera as he closed in on a portrait of someone's dalmatian.

The two often sauntered through Luna Park, the Coney Island of Paris, cameras in hand. They partied at the Csákys' or at Beöthy's. They met friends in bars. They dropped in at L'Esthétique, the boulevard du Montparnasse bookstore-gallery that belonged to André's painter pal Evsa Model. Evsa would serve them glasses of tea from the samovar that stood in one corner. Then on to the Dôme, where everyone seemed to know the Kertészes.

They also frequented the Arc-en-Ciel (Rainbow) puppet theater. It had been born from their friend Géza Blattner's conviction that, because marionette performances afforded artists more expressive control than any other medium, the puppet theater could steal a march on painting and sculpture. Inspired by Hungarian folklore, the Ballets Russes, Javanese shadow puppetry, and avant-garde art, Blattner was challenging puppetry's every convention. He and his company of forty artists, virtually all Hungarians, designed folding puppets, abstract puppets, and puppets operated by keyboard. They experimented with innovative lighting and nonnarrative scripts and invented a mechanism by which the decor could be changed mid-scene.[60]

For André, the Arc-en-Ciel was accessible in a way the talky Gallic stage was not. Marionettes fascinated him. Like toys, carousel animals, and window displays, they lend themselves to imagining alternate worlds. Like shadows, masks, reflections, and photographs, they recast everyday life. André took dozens of pictures in and around the Arc-en-Ciel. He turned his lens toward individual puppets, scenes in progress, and puppeteers working the wires. Among the productions he and Rózsi attended was *La Rue*, a dawn-to-dusk tale of people interacting on a certain Paris street. Small wonder that André was fascinated, he who loved to photograph the street from upper-floor perches, attending to movement and timing, shadow and light. Puppet photography became another Kertész specialty. Working for *Vu*, *L'Art Vivant*, *Die Dame*, and the *Münchner Illustrierte Presse*, he undertook photo essays about the Guignol theater and gatherings of marionettists in Paris, Lyon, and Liège.

André and Rózsi were close to Blattner, whom both may have known in Budapest, and to his wife, Helén Sulyok. On May Day 1929, the four picnicked, along with the painter and puppeteer Sándor Tóth. André's snapshot conveys the friends' silly mood. They've polished off a bottle or two of wine, and now they're playacting. Rózsi has the role of a marionette threatened by Helén and Sándor, wielding a banana and spoon, and Géza hams it up as their dastardly puppeteer.

The Arc-en-Ciel was in Boulogne-Billancourt just southwest of Paris and about a mile from the Meudon train station, where there was a direct line to Montparnasse.[61] One day that spring, André was wandering in Meudon, probably coming or going from the Arc-en-Ciel. Perhaps he was taking the train and had time to spare. He turned into the rue des Vignes. Lined with decrepit shops, it offered a straight-on view of a nineteenth-century stone viaduct that surmounted a construction site. The scene before him felt like an empty stage set. He stopped and lifted his Leica. When he got the distance and angle right, he clicked the shutter.

Days or weeks passed. Then André returned, perhaps after checking the rail schedule. Once again, the street was deserted. But this time he caught a train speeding across the viaduct. Curiously, wind blew the locomotive's smoke ahead of the engine instead of streaming it behind.[62]

How long André tarried after exposing that frame is anyone's guess. The day was overcast without hard shadows to act as sundials. In any case, when the next train arrived, he was ready. Not only was the train's passage right, but also the street had come alive. In his photograph, three men amble down its slope toward the viaduct. A woman and child trudge along. Others are visible too, notably a bespectacled man wearing a homburg and carrying a mysterious package wrapped in newspaper. He stares straight at the camera. Up on the viaduct, the train steams on, left. Down on the street, the man with the package angles toward the photographer, right. Nothing quite matches, nothing is settled. André corrals a disparate set of facts and makes them a picture. The result, as many have said, recalls the work of Giorgio de Chirico, a metaphysically inclined artist who painted arched viaducts, distant locomotives, and disquieting public spaces during those interwar years.

Decades later, after his photograph *Meudon* became famous, André would maintain that he had discovered the street, made an exposure, heard a train coming, and positioned himself for another. When the train appeared about twenty seconds later, he again hit his shutter release. At just that moment, he added, the stranger with the package walked into view.[63]

Once again, he was twisting the truth. Changes in the construction site show that days, maybe weeks, separate the first image from the two others. What's more, André did know the man with the package, according to the photo historian Hans-Michael Koetzle. He was Willi Baumeister. The German modernist had attended gatherings photographed by André in Mondrian's studio; he was present at André's opening at Au Sacre du Printemps.[64] Although Baumeister lived in Germany, he spent a good deal of time in Paris. A sometime designer of theatrical sets, he could have been accompanying André to the Arc-en-Ciel that day, with drawings to show to Blattner.

Maybe André did not want to own up to this connection because people would assume that the man's appearance was staged. Perhaps it was staged. Better the aura of mystery, as André would have felt.[65] Better the impression that, as with *Satiric Dancer*, he had alighted and created a masterpiece.

**That Pentecost Monday** found André and Rózsi in Brittany, where he photographed the Pardon of the Birds for a feature in *Vu*. The event had its roots in the twelfth century when Saint Maurice founded a Cistercian monastery intended as a haven of silence. The saint was thwarted, however, by the birds' full-throated singing. So, as the story goes, he led them to a distant forest where they would no longer disturb mass and where musicians and dancers now annually marked the event. This bit of rural folklore could have been invented for André, who adored those winged vagabond musicians surveying the world from on high.

After the festival, André and Rózsi traveled by rail and hired car to Quimper, Brest, and the Breton countryside. They explored museums, walked by the water, and sampled local fare.[66] After they washed down one lunch with a bottle of red wine and had cake for dessert, Rózsi fell asleep, or pretended to, her head drooping onto her arms on the oilclothed table. André snapped her picture. Another time, it must have been she who photographed him lying flat on his back on the beach, shoes kicked off and hands cupped in front of his lips as if calling birds.

André had reason to feel self-satisfied. His editorial work was known across Europe. The Germans, in particular, had worked up a big appetite for his photographs. Ullstein's editors would throw out a subject or send him an article that lacked illustrations. If it appealed to him, he'd take the assignment. Or he would shoot a subject of his choice and sell the results. Avant-garde publications like *Der Querschnitt*, women's magazines like *Die Dame*, and dailies like the *Berliner Tageblatt*, plus a dozen illustrated German weeklies, all published his work. The photographer and photo agent Henry Guttmann, who shuttled between Berlin and Paris, dealt chiefly with André in France.[67] The Paris editor of the leftist *Die Weltbühne*, Kurt Tucholsky, was another good client. Best of all, André sold picture after picture to the Hungarian-born Stefan Lorant, who had recently taken the helm of the powerhouse *Münchner Illustrierte Presse*. Like Vogel, Lorant was breaking fresh ground for the picture press and propelling André's reputation forward. Lorant also had come of age as a photography-crazy kid in Pest. When he traveled to Paris, the two socialized. A solid friendship developed.

At age thirty-five, André was riding the crest of modern photography. He had more jobs than he could comfortably manage. His income ballooned. In July 1929, André earned 7,268 francs (about $5,100 in 2024 dollars), nearly six times his monthly earnings that same month only three years before. The average monthly cost of rent for a Parisian that year was the equivalent of $450; food averaged $850 (both in 2024 dollars).[68] As photography achieved higher status, the competition for photographers intensified, and the best earned higher fees. Vogel increased André's rates to 150 francs for the first photograph of a subject and 100 francs for each additional photograph of that same subject.[69] Some of the Germans paid twice that amount.

That March, Gallotti published the third in a series of articles titled "Is Photography an Art?" This one featured André. Although the two were well acquainted, Gallotti presents André as a frustrating interview subject with no gift for explaining his views—indeed, barely able to manage a cogent sentence. "After which," writes Gallotti, "he shows you a set of prints and, as soon as you've seen the first one, you regret that you have lost time in chatting." Gallotti continues: "Indeed, his photos have such personality that they're immediately amazing. Whether it's a village in his country, a view of Paris, or a portrait, one feels such a deliberate choice of time, light, and especially vantage point that the presence of the author is inscribed like an invisible signature."[70]

Three years later, Carlo Rim, then the editor of *Vu*, would take a retrospective look at the photographic scene of the 1920s. He did not name any living photographers, but Krull, Lotar, Isaac Kitrosser, Man Ray, and Kertész—the magazine's stable—would have been on his mind. They had liberated photography as an expressive medium, Rim observed, and made it relevant to modern life: "Photography was invented twice. First by Niépce and Daguerre, about a century ago—and, secondly, by us."[71]

Mac Orlan agreed: "Photography is at the very birth of its glory."[72]

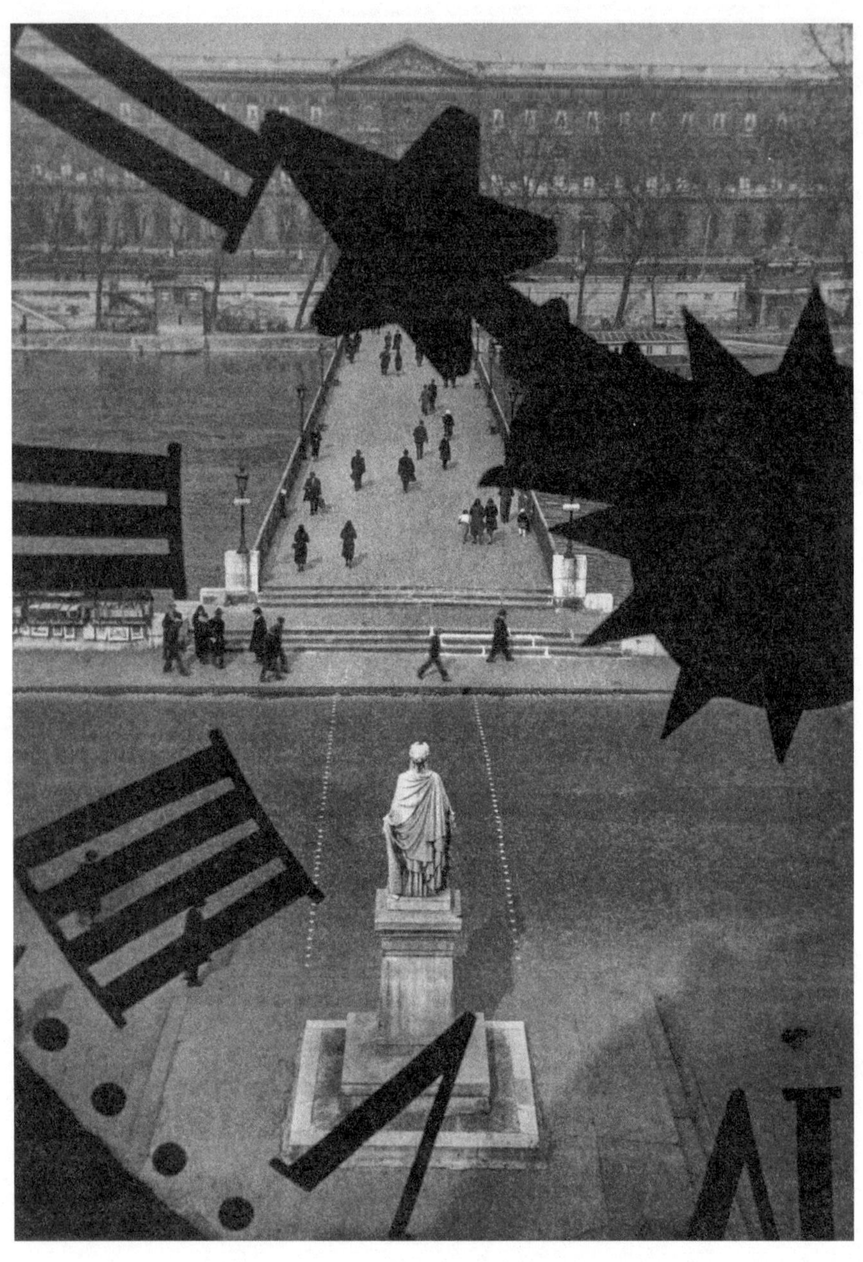

André Kertész, *Clock of the French Academy*, 1929

# 6 CLOCK OF THE FRENCH ACADEMY, 1929–1932

**It began as a routine assignment.** André and a reporter presented their credentials to the secretary-general of the Académie Française, one of five academies that comprise the venerable Institut de France, housed in a seventeenth-century edifice next to the Seine. Credentials accepted. André then tackled his subject: the academy's library. He photographed scholars at work, a cortege of marble busts, a document bearing the seal of Louis XIII, and whatever else caught his eye. Assignment completed. Ever inquisitive and casual about asking permission to photograph, André then ventured up a side staircase, accompanied by an underling, and wandered into a garret.

There he discovered broken statuary, empty wine bottles, old curtains, and graffiti, but not just any graffiti. By tradition, late-nineteenth-century winners of the prestigious Prix de Rome in music had each signed a certain wall, adding a line from a musical score. The lyric opera composer Jules Massenet had tacked on some doodles. Or were those caricatures by a jealous colleague? The markings, inscriptions, and scores overlaid gouges, peeling paint, and centuries of grime.[1] Gleeful about the visual poetry he'd uncovered, André made eight or nine exposures, then continued to forage for pictures.

Further exploration took him to a space behind the glass-faced clock on the pediment of the Institut de France, just under its grandiose dome.

Strewn with broken mannequins, old bed frames, and other debris, it too was an eyesore. Graffiti covered part of a wall so filthy that André couldn't decipher the words. All in the central space of an august cultural institution charged with safeguarding and advancing the arts, sciences, and humanities. André readied his camera. "Naturally, I photographed all that mess right away." Afterward, he hastened to develop his negatives (he was using sheet film), make prints, and offer them to French publications.

But no one in France would touch the story, which seemed likely to cause trouble with the authorities. The Dutch newspaper *De Telegraaf* did express interest. However, fearing that the pictures were fakes, its editors instructed their Paris correspondent to verify them at the source. When the director of the academy set eyes on André's prints, he flew into a rage, denying that such sites existed inside the Institut de France even as he ordered that the walls be painted and the messes tidied up. André railed against that "pompous and stupid French bureaucrat." As for the cleanup: "*C'était tragique*."[2]

The space under the dome had yielded other images, however, ones the director either didn't see or found acceptable. André took the photographs through the glass-faced clock on the building's pediment. He had sometimes idly wondered what was behind that clockface, visible as one approached the institute via the Pont des Arts, a footbridge from the Louvre. Now he knew. At about 1:40 that day, he took two exposures. One showed the entire clock seen from the inside. For the other, he switched to a wide-angle lens and shifted his attention to the clock's lower-left quarter. In that version, the hour hand, the Roman numerals, and the clock's curved edge—all flat, black, and congruent with the picture plane—function as graphic elements. Behind the glass and far below is a view of pedestrians coming and going. An allegorical statue of the French Republic in the institute's front courtyard presides over the scene. Beyond that, the Pont des Arts leads the viewer's eye toward the Louvre. The mismatch in scale, tonal density, and spatial illusion between the clock parts and the outdoor scene may suggest darkroom wiles, yet André's photograph is a straightforward print.

In *Clock of the French Academy*, pedestrians cross the footbridge or move along the sidewalk near the river, the classic metaphor for the passage of time. Compared to the clock, the people look tiny. Visually, they are inside it, although they seem unaware of its presence. Yet the clock is there, evoking celestial time with its sun-and-star motif and meting out mechanical time with its markers for minutes and hours. Beyond the footbridge is the Louvre, a repository of global art dating to pre-antiquity and a keeper of historical time.

Time has its mysteries, André's picture implies, and official Paris is a more disconcerting place than a cursory look reveals. Seen from inside, the clock's Roman numerals are backward, as if the hands were rotating in the wrong direction. They interact enigmatically with elements in the scene beyond. The V doubles as an arrow pointing to the shadow of the statue as if to a piece of evidence. The IIII half-obscures two observers. The III is a barrier along the edge of the Seine. The II acts as a brief resting place for the star hour hand. André takes advantage of the photographer's prerogative of enmeshing near and far by virtue of choices about lens and vantage point.

The Institut de France was not the only iconic structure in André's sights. Another was the Eiffel Tower, the hardest of all to portray in an unhackneyed manner. Over the years, André had photographed the monument casually and often. Sometimes he treated it whimsically. Once he took a picture from a hill in semirural Saint-Cloud that commanded a panoramic view of Paris. Crouched in the grass in just the right spot, André managed a scene of a cow displaying its nether parts to the distant Eiffel Tower. Rustic France trumps the City of Light—the kind of little joke André relished.

Other pictures derived from the monument's form. Standing perhaps at a window one day, André paired the Eiffel Tower, visible on the skyline, with a birdcage placed on the building's roof. The cage's wires and finial mimic the landmark's latticework and spire. Refusing to accord the Eiffel Tower the status of holy shrine, André again inserts it into lived experience. He found a street performer as worthy of attention as a bigwig, a birdcage as alluring as a world-famous attraction.

One spring day in 1929, he gave the Eiffel Tower his undivided attention. The occasion was the Iron Lady's fortieth birthday, and this time the stakes were high. André was on assignment for Stefan Lorant of the *Münchner Illustrierte Presse*. He planned to resell some of the pictures to Vogel. The journalist friend who accompanied him, Gyula Halász, was reporting the story for *Vu*.[3]

A year earlier, *Vu* had published a paean to the Eiffel Tower by Florent Fels, accompanied by three photographs by André's colleague and rival Germaine Krull. Her pictures cast the tower as a complex industrial structure and its "shadow sister," Fels writes, "a sundial's needle" crawling across the ground below.[4] Vogel gave full play to Krull's dizzying images with a dynamic full-page layout.

André and Krull freelanced for the same publications, showed at the same venues, and impressed the same critics and writers. Krull's photographs are more kinetic, less meticulously structured, and less attentive to uncanny detail than André's. But they speak the same visual language involving radical viewpoints and abstracted forms. Both photographers were foreign-born (Krull in Wilda-Poznań, East Prussia), yet together they fostered a distinctly French modern photography that harnessed Surrealist and Constructivist thinking and fused journalism with the avant-garde. Now it was André's turn to step up and address the Eiffel Tower, the supreme symbol of that modernity.

His most memorable photograph that day is a triumph of oblique geometry. Shot from the structure's first platform, *Eiffel Tower, Paris* is anchored pictorially by a section of a latticed iron arch. It curves like a lens around the formal garden below, where people stroll, sit, or prepare to take taxis, oblivious of the camera's eye. They are dwarfed by the late-afternoon shadow of the tower and of their own bodies. By shooting from on high, shearing off a section of the structure, and choosing a lens that compressed near and far, André abstracts the scene. He evokes rather than depicts the Eiffel Tower, shunning the postcard view while expressing the structure's aura. The tower is even more hauntingly present for being mostly absent.

Among the other pictures that André took is one of Halász. His reporter friend sticks his head through the photo-cutout board used by the Eiffel Tower's in-house photographer for jokey tourist souvenirs. The board depicts the body of a man scaling the structure. Halász's insect-like eyes bulge. His eyebrows look like they come from a prop department. His smirk suggests that he's getting a kick from playing a visitor seeing the sights.

A Hungarian from Transylvania, Halász had settled in Paris five years earlier. He arrived via Berlin, where he had studied painting and eked out a living as a stringer for Hungarian newspapers but mostly soaked up the city's bohemian pleasures. Among his closest friends was Lajos Tihanyi, who was living in Berlin at the time. In 1924, Halász followed Tihanyi to Paris. After André arrived the following year, he and Halász struck up a friendship, hanging out at Montparnasse cafés and in bohemian hotel rooms and hoofing around the city together. Halász attended André's opening at Au Sacre du Printemps and his wedding to Rózsi. André wrangled a few jobs for his pal. When Halász's parents visited France, he photographed them *en famille* outside the Transylvanian's studio on the rue Servandoni.

In Paris, Halász continued to scrape by as a journalist, using the pen name Jean d'Erleich. He focused on sports reporting, even though he cared little about sports. He filled in the gaps by copying old articles or making things up. He also freelanced for the German press and for *Vu*, with André or others supplying the pictures. They chuckled their way through assignments like one about a music-hall star that was a monkey named Bubu. Such collaborations confirmed their friendship but did little to relieve Halász's penury. A raconteur with a magnetic personality, he charmed people into buying him dinner. Or he went hungry.

"Well, there were some difficulties in everyday life, certain things happened." Speaking decades later, André picks up the story. "Trouble. No money to pay for the room and such like. One day I said to him, look, what you're doing is madness. Start taking photographs. You can make some money this way, and you won't have any problems, you'll have money for everything, then if you want, you can paint or do sculpture or write." But Halász dismissed the idea, vehemently. "No and no and no."[5] He was a painter. He detested photography. Yet his gigs with André, his stint as an office worker for a Paris-based German photo agency, and his frustration with trying to find pictures for his articles brought him around to the idea of taking his own, if he could afford a camera.

Like the Eiffel Tower, artists' studios were irresistible subjects for André. Working for a periodical, the artist, his own pleasure, or hoping to sell his pictures to an editor, he observed, staged, and interpreted these sites imbued with the mystique of creativity. In the studio of André Lhote, a wood carver-turned-Cubist-painter who was once Rózsi's teacher, André trained his lens on the artist's collections of snow globes and African carvings. In the modernist atelier-home of Jean Lurçat, a close friend, he took a wealth of pictures. A painter, ceramist, and tapestry-maker, Lurçat gravitated to botanical and celestial themes. Among André's most memorable images from chez Lurçat is a scene in the tiny courtyard garden. Shot from an elevated perch, it shows a table and chair, some plants, a cane, and a telescope, along with one of the artist's beloved Afghan hounds.

Even more than André's picture of that corner of Lurçat's world, his close study of a bookshelf in the studio of Polish French painter Moïse Kisling captures the spirit of both artist and man. The shelf houses a few reproductions of canvases by the Italian painter Amedeo Modigliani. Propped next to them is Modigliani's death mask made by Kisling himself in 1920. The two had been close in their youth, carousing, drinking, and womanizing like rowdy brothers. These emblematic objects are flanked by books, the titles on their spines—*Modigliani*, *Fra Angelico*,

Alfred de Musset's *Poésies nouvelles* – presumably revealing of Kisling's creative life. Thumbtacked to the wall below are a dozen snapshots of the artist, his wife, and their two sons on a seaside holiday. High art and high jinks – the type of incongruous juxtaposition André never failed to pick up on.

When André arrived at the studio of Tsuguharu Foujita, he surveyed the premises and tossed out ideas for poses. The Japanese French painter and designer, then at the height of his fame, was in an impish frame of mind. Ignoring André's suggestions, he clambered up on a pedestal, smoked a fat cigar, and wrapped himself in a tatami mat. Moving up to the roof, he pulled out a pistol and aimed it at the heart he'd drawn on the undershirt he was wearing. Once or twice he pretended to follow André's instructions, then wrecked the shots by screwing up his face just as André made the exposures. It was all André could do to tamp down his anger. Yet Foujita's fans loved the pictures when they appeared in *Uhu*.[6]

In a happier frame of mind, André pulled out his camera one spring evening at a party in the Villa Brune studio of the sculptor Alexander Calder, an American friend from the Dôme. He mingled, recording the drinking, dancing, and mirth. Then all subsided as guests gathered around to watch Calder perform his circus. Using wire, wood, string, corks, bottle caps, scraps of fabric, and other detritus, the artist had fashioned dozens of troupers and props for a miniature spectacle. He was both ringmaster and roustabout. His acrobats cavorted on high wires. His trapeze artists flew through the air. His lions strode and pooped. His Wild West riders brandished ten-gallon hats. André thoroughly enjoyed this surrogate world.

Another time, he photographed Calder and his circus one-on-one. In some frames, the artist puzzles out the little world he is twisting, knotting, levering, knitting, and painting into existence amid a cat's cradle of wires and netting. One close-up shows the shadows of this aerial rigging crisscrossing the artist's forehead, evoking the spatial thinking that absorbed him.

André found Calder to be that rare thing, a congenial and unspoiled American. The two cannot have had deep conversations: neither spoke the other's native language, and neither was fluent in French. All the same, their rapport gave birth to a loose yet lifelong friendship. Their connections were also artistic. Both applied their technical expertise to their art. (Calder held a degree in mechanical engineering.) Both delighted in bodies in motion. Both combined playfulness with formal rigor. The French liked to describe Calder as an overgrown boy, reflecting the view that Americans are naïve. That description feels right for one whose art straddled the line between sculpture and toy. Indeed, when Calder put aside his spatial problem-solving, he often looked as tickled as a kid at the circus. So did his portraitist.

While André focused on Calder's version of the greatest show on earth, thirteen of his photographs occupied a world stage four hundred miles to the east. On May 18, 1929, the vast exhibition *Film und Foto*, known as *FiFo*, opened in Stuttgart. It was the brainchild of the Deutscher Werkbund, an association of German craftspeople, architects, designers, and industrialists founded to promote high quality in design. With *FiFo*, the Werkbund was proclaiming the dawn of the optical era. Excited that technology was spawning new creative tools, the group championed photography and film because they gave tangible form to the new age. *FiFo*'s photography section comprised some two hundred images from the realms of art, science, sports, fashion, and advertising. Photographs by French Surrealists, American modernists, and avant-gardists of all stripes shared the exhibition space with X-rays, images from *Vogue*, political reportage, and film stills. The installation felt more like the lively pages of *Vu* than a traditional museum display.

Presiding over this image-fest was the artist and photographer László Moholy-Nagy. This Hungarian-born Constructivist theorized that photography reveals an optical truth of which the human eye is incapable. That's because people interpret what they see based on their individual experiences. Photography can stretch humans' biological limits, Moholy-Nagy believed. Intent on undoing old ways of seeing, he championed photographic practices, including extreme close-ups, aerial shots, photomontages, photograms, and solarizations (photographs using a technique that partially reverses tones). Such work comprised what was coined New Vision photography. Even more radically, Moholy-Nagy argued that a photograph is more than a picture that reproduces reality; it is also the result of light striking a chemically prepared surface – hence its potential for pure abstraction.

Among André's images exhibited at *FiFo* was *Fork*. By isolating, geometrizing, monumentalizing, and idealizing this product of industrial design, he had (unknowingly at the time) drilled to the core of the Werkbund's concerns. The organization's president requested André's permission to use *Fork* in a magazine ad for his silver manufactory. It would also appear in *Foreign Advertising and Industrial Photographs*, a 1931 exhibition at the Art Center in New York City. That exhibition advanced another then-novel idea: that by glamorizing the mundane, photographs could transform advertising.

Gratified though he was to garner international esteem, André continued to claim the freedom to do as he pleased. He was not about to pledge allegiance to the New Vision or any other strand of photographic modernism. In an interview-manifesto published that spring in the newspaper *L'Intransigeant*, he comes across as strong-minded and almost voluble. "I am an amateur, and I intend to remain one my whole life," André informed the journalist. He meant that he would respect his medium's factuality, be spontaneous, pursue any subject that struck his fancy, and reject the "professional virtuosity which could make me betray the rules I have set for myself." Leaning on Pierre Mac Orlan's thinking, André asserted photography's ability to record "the real nature of things, their very soul." That demanded patient observation. But, in the end, life usually dished out what he wanted. He declared his trust in "the inventions and transformations of chance."[7] That's not to say that he didn't stage-manage pictures, *Fork* among them.

After *FiFo* closed in Stuttgart, a smaller version of the exhibition traveled to Zurich, Berlin, Vienna, Danzig, Zagreb, Munich, Tokyo, and Osaka. Concurrently, the Folkwang Museum in Essen sent a group exhibition, including twenty of André's pictures, to Berlin, London, Frankfurt, Dresden, Vienna, and Amsterdam. Espousing the view that certain photographers had earned star status, *Uhu* ran a double-page spread of portraits of eight illustrious Europeans, André included. Each was asked to name a favorite from among their own works. André astutely chose *Fork*. With *FiFo*, the fulcrum had shifted. Photography now owed nothing to painting. Photography owned the world. And for that fleeting moment, *Fork* was its emblem.

Although the *Uhu* feature paired André's portrait with that of Moholy-Nagy, they would not meet until Moholy-Nagy traveled to Paris the following year for a Werkbund exhibition at the Grand Palais. They respected each other's work and enjoyed each other's company (it helped that both were Hungarian Jews). Yet their practices of photography were radically different. Moholy-Nagy was a prophet and André, a poet; Moholy-Nagy, a theorist and André, an intuitive; Moholy-Nagy, an experimenter in multiple mediums and André, a pure photographer. The dispassionate nature of Moholy-Nagy's work sets it even further apart from his compatriot's. While he admired its factuality and its rigor, André found it soulless.

**Calling themselves** "the avant-garde," André, Germaine Krull, Eli Lotar, Berenice Abbott, and the French photographer Maurice Tabard gathered now and again at the café Les Deux Magots. Man Ray would join them or not. "Kertész was the best known," Krull later remembered, "he was Vogel's favorite and we all admired him... We were all penniless but very happy, except perhaps Kertész."[8] Did Krull's reading of André's feelings derive from his Hungarian penchant for sweet melancholy? Or from the state of his marriage? Thirteen months had elapsed since André and Rózsi wed, and their relationship was rocky. Their differences in temperament and style must have grated more now that they were living together and he was leaning heavily on her to get his work out the door.

In fact, André was not penniless. The jobs kept coming. His days blurred past. All that summer and fall, a torrent of pictures poured from his darkroom. Thanks to *Bifur*, *Variétés*, *Jazz*, *Ce Temps-Ci*, and *Vu* (he did four covers that summer) – not to mention a rack of German clients – André's income stream swelled. By October, it would hit 10,400 francs (about $7,300 in 2024 dollars).[9]

That summer, his photographs of the twenty-one-year-old American tap dancer Clayton "Peg Leg" Bates had appeared in Lorant's *Münchner Illustrierte Presse*. After the young Bates lost his leg in a cotton gin accident, an uncle had carved a peg leg for him. Bates then taught himself to dance, using his peg to achieve what able-bodied hoofers could not. He went from the streets of Greenville, South Carolina, where he busked for small change, to Broadway, where he joined the cast of the hit Black musical revue *Blackbirds of 1928*. From the Liberty Theatre, it traveled to the Moulin Rouge. In Paris, too, *Blackbirds* triumphed.

André's session with Bates sounds familiar notes. One image fixes attention on the dancer's crossed hands and splayed legs. Pairing Bates's intact limb with the wooden one central to his artistic persona, André uses the real as a foil for the artificial, as he so often did in pictures of puppets and posters. Another frame from that shoot catches Bates sailing over a stage above his pretzeled shadow, the type of gymnastic feat André happily photographed, his too a corporeal art.

André attached no particular importance to his pictures of Bates. All the same, he must have felt an affinity for this fellow parvenue. Both had achieved the improbable by reinventing their art, making it marvelous, and winning fame in Paris.

Even Sergei Eisenstein was impressed by André's images. The Soviet director and film theorist's masterpiece *Battleship Potemkin* had made its French debut in 1926. En route to Hollywood, where he was to film adaptations of two popular novels (projects that were later aborted),

Eisenstein arrived in Paris that December. He was meeting with filmmakers, artists, writers, and the photographers Krull, Lotar, and André. At ten o'clock one January evening, the two men sat down at the Dôme. There André was flattered to learn that the director famed for harnessing film's capacity for emotional expressivity found *his* work moving. Eisenstein had clipped four Kertész photographs from the pages of *Vu*, he told André, and pasted them into an album.

On a personal level, too, they got along "terribly well" in André's estimation.[10] The two saw each other again at a dinner party, at Eisenstein's hotel, and at André and Rózsi's apartment. There André pulled out his Leica to shoot frames of his guest relaxing on the sofa. Then he switched to a glass-plate camera, and the Russian moved to the floor. Eisenstein leafed through a book before shifting his attention to the camera in front of him. In André's portrait, he leans on a wooden box set at the far end of the Czech folk-art runner on the living-room floor. The rug's repeating motif conjures a strip of film, a witty and elegant visual pun.

**On a bright windless night** a few months later, André attached his camera to a tripod set up on the Pont des Arts, the same pedestrian bridge that appears in his *Clock of the French Academy*. His subject was the *Louise-Catherine*, a coal barge turned floating Salvation Army shelter. It had been renovated by Le Corbusier and anchored near the Louvre. On assignment for *Vu*, André had spent the evening photographing the shelter's dormitories, dining room, and lounge.

At his side was Halász. Although a different journalist was reporting the *Louise-Catherine* story for *Vu*, Halász and André hoped to place an article in a German magazine – the *Münchner Illustrierte Presse*, as it turned out.

Inside the barge, Halász had watched André handling his Leica. He had replaced its fixed Elmar lens with a faster Busche f/2 lens, often used for cinematic work, so he could photograph in low-light conditions at night like those inside the barge yet avoid using a flash. In the darkroom, however, he would discover that his new lens yielded images that he found too soft.[11]

Standing on the Pont des Arts, André switched to a larger-format camera: He wanted a crystalline image of the barge and its surroundings. He would take several exposures. In that era before light meters were widely available, exposure times were a matter of informed guesswork. Relatively slow lenses and slow film speeds meant long exposures for night pictures. André framed an angled bird's-eye view of the *Louise-Catherine* mirrored in the river and opened his shutter, all the while chatting with Halász.

"Well," Halász interjected, "take your picture and let's go."

"It's being taken," replied André, mildly amused. "Wait another fifteen minutes and we'll have it."[12]

That caught Halász's attention. Open a box, stand around in the middle of the night, and half an hour later a picture exists? André used the fifteen minutes to initiate his friend into certain aspects of night photography.

The next day, Halász reportedly purchased the 6.5 by 9 centimeter Voigtländer that André had recommended. That night he placed it on a bench in the Luxembourg Garden, opened the shutter, then cooled his heels for fifteen to thirty minutes.

Halász had realized that photography was anything but the "spiritless and soulless mechanism" he had assumed. "I was trapped by photography," he would later write. "But the bird catcher" – André – "was exceptionally good."[13] He continued to sign his articles with the pen name Jean d'Erleich and his paintings with his real name, Gyula Halász. For his photographs, he chose a name derived from that of his hometown, Brassó (today Braşov, Romania): Brassaï. Ahead lay international fame as the century's most acclaimed night photographer and, in the phrase of the writer Henry Miller, "the eye of Paris."[14]

But in 1930, André was the star. That same spring he was doing highly lucrative work for *Le Jardin des Modes*. Cofounded by Vogel in 1922, the women's fashion magazine now belonged to Condé Nast, though Vogel remained its director. André took an assignment to photograph socialites in motion for an upcoming series about exercise for women for both the magazine and a special 144-page *Jardin des Modes* beauty album.

It was a novel project in an era when socialites typically posed for the camera in gowns or tailored suits, looking as if they were sculpted in marble and modeled with light. The photographer George Hoyningen-Huene's work for French *Vogue* was the exemplar. Now André was to photograph some of the same women wearing sports togs and twisting and leaping, a subject well matched to one for whom photography and athleticism often joyfully mingled.

Vogel was offering André 200 francs for each photograph commissioned by *Le Jardin des Modes* and 100 francs for each one from André's stock. As if wagging his finger at the photographer's transgressions at *Vu*, he added that *Le Jardin des Modes* would retain exclusive reproduction rights for all countries. André agreed to this stipulation about resales but held out for 300 francs for each commissioned photograph and 200 francs each for the others. He got what he wanted.

His first subject was the fashionista Baba d'Erlanger, Princess Jean-Louis de Faucigny-Lucinge. The two approached each other warily. A few months earlier, André had photographed the princess at her villa in Saint-Jean-de-Luz, a fishing town and fashionable resort on the Basque coast. The pictures were commissioned for an ad campaign by the American soft drink company Clicquot Club Company. That project entailed a spate of postponements and last-minute changes, ending with the princess steamed at André because she was never paid for the use of her home (he could do nothing about it), and André steamed at the company's agent because, except for the advance, he was never paid for his work.[15] In the case of the *Jardin des Modes* assignment, no sooner had André wrapped up the shoot than the editorial concept for that section changed, and the pictures had to be redone. Nothing would ever go smoothly between him and Baba d'Erlanger.

Lady Mendl proved only slightly less annoying. Born Elsie de Wolfe in New York City, the interior designer is credited with inventing her profession, from which she reaped a fortune. Celebrated in Europe as a sparkling hostess to the international smart set, Lady Mendl set great store by her daily exercise routine. André photographed her standing on her head, a skill she had mastered at fifty. She followed with a backbend, then changed into pearls and a sequined wrap and smoked a cigarette for his camera. André was unimpressed. The lady's snobbery grated. The main pleasure he took from the assignment was in shooting the panoramic view of the Seine from her window.

For a section of the *Jardin des Modes* album devoted to hand care, André trained his lens on the hands of two of France's most illustrious writers. First, he photographed the Countess Anna de Noailles in the bed that she occupied as if it were both writing desk and throne. Her bejeweled hands and swirling tendrils suit the granddaughter of a Turkish pasha and the daughter of a Romanian prince, who was known for her love affairs as well as her passionate poetry.

André's next subject, another sensualist, was the popular writer Colette. Her semiautobiographical novellas address the pleasures and pains of love and sexuality; her memoirs are poetic accounts of her childhood in rural Burgundy. André had already collaborated with Colette on a feature in *Vu* about Burgundian wine cellars. He found her delightful.

When he arrived at Colette's apartment in the Palais Royal, she greeted him by holding up her bandaged left hand.

"Kertész, look what's happened." She had burned her hand while ironing. She did not want to be photographed.

"Poor little Colette."

He continued: "All right, this has happened. It doesn't bother me. This is everyday life. You are in everyday life too."[16]

Beauty in the flaw, he was thinking. A hand mittened with bandages was just the kind of quirky detail that interested him. It was genuine. The fifty-seven-year-old Colette protested that she wanted to look sexy in *Le*

*Jardin des Modes*. André convinced her that she would, even as he harbored the thought that no other woman would have let him photograph her in that condition.[17]

A table lamp was switched on for their picture-taking session in Colette's dim apartment. André added a floodlight, then mounted his camera on a tripod for the long exposure. In one image, the writer rests her bandaged hand on a glass-topped table and the side of her face on that hand. A canister filled with peony tulips stands in for the gardens she lovingly and sensually describes in her books. Her cat eyes lock on André's lens. She looks watchful, knowing, and real. This was not standard women's magazine fare.

To André, conventionally staged fashion and beauty shots felt like sugar water, pleasant but forgettable. So be it, he once observed, adding "but for myself I wanted wine."[18] Wine or not, the editor of *Le Jardin des Modes* rejected his photographs of both Noailles and Colette.

That late spring of 1930, André was again dispatched to Noailles's and Colette's apartments, this time with explicit instructions to express how the hands of writers differ from those of socialites.[19] He took conventional close-ups. In one, Colette's bandage-less hands linger over a manuscript in progress. André's editor at *Le Jardin des Modes* okayed the new pictures. Soon André was trotting off to photograph the working hands of Coco Chanel—unremarkable images that he knew would be accepted.

Struggling to keep André on schedule, the editor relied on Vogel, who rebuked him for failing to deliver a single proof of the exercise pictures on deadline. A week passed. Still no proofs. Vogel dictated a second letter, even more chastising because exquisitely polite. Eventually, André did deliver. Yet he lagged behind on much else. That October an exceedingly vexed Countess Celani would unexpectedly knock at the door of André's apartment. Three months after their photo session, she was still awaiting her proofs.

In fairness, André was dashing from assignment to assignment, exhibition to exhibition. In May 1930, he contributed twenty-nine prints to

*Das Lichbild*, an offshoot of *FiFo*. In June, he delivered eight more to the Salon de l'Araignée for a three-ring circus of an exhibition organized by the editor Carlo Rim. And *Vu* worked him like crazy that summer. Its July issues featured six stories with images signed "Kertész." He photographed a fencing match, the carousel in the Luxembourg Garden, a collection of lead soldiers, a dance conference, and countless marionettes. His work also appeared in *L'Illustration*, *Art et Décoration*, *Das Illustrierte Blatt*, *Die Dame*, the *Chicago Tribune*, and *Jazz*. Not all the pictures he sold were new ones. But exploiting his photographic stock also required time, effort, and a smooth operation at home.

Was Rózsi able to keep up her rounds of purchasing supplies, retouching negatives, organizing André's archives, and corresponding with his clients? She was doing work of her own as well. In any case, proofs for the Countess Celani, and others, fell by the wayside.

**Whatever else was going on,** André made time to rub shoulders at the Dôme, where he now presided over the Hungarian table, pulled wires for his pals, and networked with potential subjects and clients. Making and keeping contacts was vital to a freelancer's work.

The scene in which he operated was increasingly complex and its participants increasingly mobile. Man Ray was devoting his time to painting and film. Lotar still worked for *Vu*, but he too was gravitating toward filmmaking. Krull was publishing a portfolio of female nudes. Abbott had returned to New York. Her compatriot, the peripatetic James Abbe, dominated *Vu*'s coverage of local stage and screen personalities. Maurice Tabard was wading deeper into surrealism. Emmanuel Sougez, a staffer at *L'Illustration*, was championing color photography. His position was among those emerging in the picture press, where photographers were working in teams alongside art directors, layout artists, and graphic designers. Others were joining agencies. A photo-drunk public was demanding more and more photographs: human interest and reportage but also fashion and advertising. Photography had become a vital element in public life. The ranks of photographers swelled, and André's career was humming.

Montparnasse, by contrast, was not. In October 1929, the US stock market had crashed, sending the dollar plummeting against the franc and forcing many Americans abroad to sail home. Five months later, André wrote Tihanyi, who remained in New York: "I think you will be surprised when you get to see the now-dormant Montparnasse. Life is very sad here nowadays – everything seems to be in a state of suspended animation."[20] While France as a whole continued to prosper, certain Paris jazz clubs went silent, avant-garde magazines folded, and galleries bereft of their American clientele closed their doors.

Meanwhile, France was shifting politically, with both the far right and far left gaining adherents and the center losing ground. That May Day found André on the Champs-Élysées, where thousands of soldiers and police officers were bivouacked in anticipation of Communist violence that never materialized. What held André's attention as he wended his way through the crowd that day had nothing to do with the charged political moment and everything to do with longing and love.

In André's *Muguet Seller*, a street vendor holds out a nosegay in hope of a sale to a chic young woman who is descending into the Métro. French May Day is not only the holiday to celebrate workers and unions but also the occasion to offer little bunches of lilies of the valley (*muguets*) as tokens of affection and springtime. The vendor who caught André's attention is a double-leg amputee with one claw hand. He is probably a veteran. Impervious and imperious, the woman hurries by him. The railing along the Métro stairs diagrams the man's doubt- and desire-filled gaze. In this Chaplinesque scene, he is spurned.[21]

**That fall,** André traveled to Saint-Jean-de-Luz in southwestern France near the Spanish border. He may have been shooting one of his series of advertising photographs for Clicquot Club Company. There he met a man who told him about a wood pigeon hunting expedition planned for the next day. Every fall, flights of pigeons migrate from northern Europe to North Africa, where they stay for the winter. Along the way, they pass over Basque country. Roasted or stewed pigeon, prepared with onions, garlic, red peppers, and wine, is a traditional delicacy. Sensing an interesting subject, André arranged to meet the hunters, who gave him permission to tag along.

The hunts take place in the passes of the Pyrenees. As clouds of birds approach, men stationed in towers at high elevations blow horns, agitate white sheets, and throw battledores to imitate hawk attacks and send the birds diving. Other hunters wait below. André accompanied this second group. Using pulleys, they rigged up nets in the trees, like billowing sails, and poured grain on the ground to attract the birds. Then they settled in to monitor the sky. When at last a flight of pigeons rose over the horizon like a giant gust of leaves, the hunters leaped up, whistling to attract their prey to the bait. The birds approached, sank, hesitated, and then, with a great rustling racket, rushed at the feast like a mob. The men collapsed the nets and set about clubbing the pigeons to death.[22] André would have identified with the trapped and battered birds. To him, they represented the human soul, the creative spirit, freedom, his own very much included.

On that same trip, André spent a night or two in Sare, a village near the Spanish border. A bare-bones guesthouse in Sare may have been the setting for his nude self-portrait. Positioning his camera on an elevated tripod near the foot of his bed, he set up a diagonal composition. André lies on his back with the sheets and bedspread flung off and awry. His hands, as limp wristed as a child's, rest on his chest. One index finger points to his heart. His face lies cheek to pillow. He looks sunk into a dream. Yet the focal point of this singular image is not André's face but his genitals. It's a surprising self-portrait from a leading photo-reporter but not from a photographic diarist and unhappy lover. It expresses vulnerability, longing, and sexual desire.

It was probably that fall that André and Rózsi traveled to Hungary, as reported by the photo historian Sandra Phillips, who interviewed many of the couple's friends. This was André's first visit home since he left for France five years earlier.[23] He had succeeded. He was returning as a leading modernist photographer in the art capital of Europe. He had the clippings, the money, and the comfortable Paris apartment to prove it.

Hollowed out of its liberal and cosmopolitan elements, Budapest was drabber than the city he'd grown up in. The Kertészes' apartment on Népszínház Street was quieter too, and Ernesztina was slowed by cataracts and arthritis. André wanted to spend time with his mother and to meet Rózsi's family. Indeed, photographs survive of Rózsi playfully tugging the ears of a man who may be her father and huddling affectionately with a young man and woman who may be her brother and sister. The pictures belie the calamity about to transpire in slow motion.

With Rózsi distracted by her own family and friends, André almost certainly found an occasion to slip away to see Erzsébet. Had he been planning that visit? Or did he act on impulse? In any case, what he would have discovered was that same schoolgirl-going-on-woman who had seduced him ten years ago. That same round face, olive skin, raven hair, and brown eyes. Although twenty-eight-year-old Erzsébet Salamon held down a job as a clerk, she continued to work as an artist. She had become a heavy smoker and, reportedly, a Catholic, a practical move in a nation with an anti-Semitic government but also a sincere act of faith.

The André that Erzsébet encountered had matured in appearance and manner. With his smiling eyes, wind-ruffled hair, and greatcoat and scarf, he cut an attractive figure. What's more, he had lived up to her demand that he "establish an existence." But he was married.

By all evidence, André once again lost his heart to Erzsébet during that trip but also gained insights into why he'd stopped hearing from her two years before. Reportedly, the Kleins and the Salamons had the same doctor, and, in the waiting room, someone in Rózsi's family had told Erzsébet about his courtship of Rózsi.[24] Perhaps Erzsébet had continued writing, at least for a time. Why had André never received the letters?

His building's concierge would have sorted the mail and deposited her renters' letters on their doorsteps. It's conceivable that, with the right timing, Rózsi intercepted and destroyed those from Erzsébet to André. Yes, that's what happened, André later told a journalist.[25] Judging from later remarks, his anger was boundless that late fall in Budapest, all the more so, one guesses, because he was less than innocent in this situation. Disregarding whatever understanding he'd had with Erzsébet when he left for Paris in 1925, he had, from the start, wooed other women.

That December, André once more pulled out of Budapest's Nyugati Station bound for Paris. It's easier to guess what was in his heart than what was on his mind. He had to figure out his next moves, and strategizing had never been his forte. No doubt he kept quiet about the situation to his devoted wife. As for the mercurial Erzsébet, André's future with her was by no means assured. The fact of his marriage must have infuriated her. She may have set conditions. She may have had romantic involvements of her own. She would not wait forever.

André was returning to a Paris where the Surrealist idea of *l'amour fou* (mad love) was in the air. The irrational power of love gave one permission to sweep away all practical or ethical concerns. He knew what he wanted, but not how to get it. A clipped advertisement found among André's papers suggests that, for insights, he turned to a Madame Paulin at 77, boulevard Magenta. "Are you looking for love? Are you unhappy?" she inquires. "Consult the clairvoyant, your life will be transformed."[26]

Weeks passed. How to bring Erzsébet to Paris? What to do about Rózsi? André didn't know how to end the marriage. Montparnasse was a small community. Rózsi would howl if he left her. Meanwhile, Erzsébet may have been pressuring him in letters, sent perhaps through a mutual friend or a cousin who lived in Paris.[27]

Come spring, Rózsi fell ill. One rare surviving photograph shows her sitting up in an iron-frame single bed. Her hair is tousled and boyishly short, her body is drowning in a white cotton nightgown, and her gums are nicotine stained. She's grinning. Yet her illness was severe enough that she traveled to Budapest to be treated. André, it seems, leaped at the opportunity to unfetter himself. First, he summoned Erzsébet to Paris. She informed her mother that she was going on a trip but either refused to say where or lied about her destination. Pepi still disapproved of André. Only as Erzsébet's train was pulling out of the station did she lean out the window to inform her mother that she was off to Paris to marry the man she loved.[28]

Meanwhile, André must have set about destroying every document and photograph pertaining to his life with Rózsi. Letters vanished. So did negatives and prints in which she appeared. Not one picture of the two of them together—and there must have been many—seems to have survived. Photographs of their wedding, their travels, their home life: gone. Most people cringe at the idea of destroying even anonymous snapshots of strangers. Photographers rarely wipe out their own work. But that's what André did. He missed very few pictures. There should be no evidence that he and Rózsi had ever been happy together. She was to have no place in the starry-eyed tale of his and Erzsébet's love.

The photographic record of André's life resumes a week or two later with almost a dozen frames of him, Erzsébet, and a Hungarian acquaintance talking and drinking side by side in a café, an ordinary event made extraordinary by Erzsébet's presence. The café was not the Dôme or another popular spot on the boulevard du Montparnasse but rather what looks like a modest side-street place. Nor was their companion a close friend. André's usual haunts were Rózsi's too, and their close friends were mutual.

At first, André and Erzsébet would have stayed at the apartment he had shared with Rózsi. That summer, her impending return dictated that they decamp. A job in Savoy came in handy. Better still, it was a job after André's own heart. The novelist and editor in chief of *Les Nouvelles Littéraires*, Frédéric Lefèvre, was researching and writing a novel set in a village in the French Alps, and he had commissioned illustrations from André.

In early July, André and Erzsébet traveled to the region south of Lake Geneva, where they settled into Notre-Dame-du-Pré, a hamlet on a high plateau. There they rented a room above the café and grocery store of a Monsieur Romanet. Each morning, they awoke to the scent of roasting coffee and the sounds of the proprietor bustling around amid shelves packed with jars of candy, blocks of Marseille soap, and tins of sardines and peas.[29] The café occupied a room across the hall from Romanet's store.

A fiction market for photographs was emerging. In fact, André was in negotiations with the detective novelist Georges Simenon, who had proposed that they collaborate on a photo-text featuring Simenon's popular character Inspector Maigret. However, Simenon's first photo-text, undertaken with Krull, would fail to sell, and André's Simenon project imploded.[30]

For now, he had the Lefèvre assignment. The novel, to be titled *Le Sol* (The Soil), takes place in a lightly fictionalized version of Saint-Marcel, a nearby village at a lower elevation. André photographed the area's inhabitants, on whom Lefèvre's characters are based, along with the houses where they lived, the chapel where they attended mass, and the cafés where they bantered, gossiped, and quaffed *limonade* and wine. André's shot of four old-timers gathered around a table in bespattered work clothes belongs to his long string of pictures in which cafés—whether as rustic as Romanet's, as homey as his mother's, or as sophisticated as the Dôme—function as sites of primal human exchange.

When André and Lefèvre were not gathering material in Saint-Marcel or Notre-Dame-du-Pré (where the writer occupied Romanet's other guest room), they were trekking through mountain pastures or following the streams that marble the Tarentaise Valley. André toted a tripod and large-format camera with bellows. The vertiginous terrain allowed him to indulge in the plunging diagonals he favored. Tilting and shifting his lens to keep key elements aligned and in focus, he photographed valleys, slopes, and steep coiling byways. Lefèvre interviewed the locals. Their patois would have stumped André. Yet his photographs exude empathy between photographer and subjects. Their faces etched by light, they eye him with gravitas or good humor while dandling babies, working with tools, or resting weary bones.

*Le Sol* tells the story of a peasant family experiencing the tensions between traditional Savoy, semi-forgotten by the outside world, and an industrializing Savoy, succumbing to the forces of modernity. The elder son is wedded to his native place, while his brother aspires to urban life. Yet events pin the younger one to their plot of land. André, for his part, understood both the desire to rub up against a wider world and the deep love of backwater places.

His photographs confirm his delight in all that was distinctively local and Savoyard. André had, as he liked to explain, "a very, very close relationship with country life."[31] That stands out in his photographs that glorious summer.

For unknown reasons, they never appeared in Lefèvre's book. Perhaps costs had to be cut. Perhaps the two quarreled. All the same, the pictures got lots of mileage. *Vu* used them to illustrate short stories. The magazines *Art et Médecine*, *La France à Table*, and *Marianne* published them. They helped transform the Tarentaise Valley into a tourist destination and, ironically, wipe out the way of life André treasured.

**While André and Erzsébet were in Savoy** quietly celebrating their new life together, Rózsi returned from Budapest to find herself alone in an apartment she could never afford. Presumably, she had been unaware of Erzsébet's presence in Paris. When she realized what was happening, she "almost died out of sorrow."[32] So reports the photographer Lisette Model (at the time Lisette Seybert), whom Rózsi befriended after André deserted her.[33] He had left his wife nearly penniless and in poor health. Rózsi lamented that she had sacrificed her painting for nothing.[34] Her happiness, another friend said, had been so very brief. She and André had a long affair, Rózsi would say with a sigh, but a short marriage.[35] Later André would claim that he had prolonged his time with Rózsi to teach her photography so she could earn her own living.[36] But she had worked with him ever since the two lived on the rue de Vanves, possibly even before they were married.

After returning to the city, André and Erzsébet moved into a luminous apartment at 32 bis, rue du Cotentin, behind the Montparnasse Cemetery. One set of windows overlooked a school playground, another the railroad tracks from the Montparnasse station. They bought sleek blond furniture for their semi-open spaces, added folk rugs, and hung Tihanyi's paintings, André's photographs, and Erzsébet's drawings. Books and curios filled the shelves.

André photographed Erzsébet in their new home. In one image, his lover is sleeping or resting in the nude. In another, she perches on the edge of their bed wearing a wrapper and enjoying a smoke. The pictures evoke intimate moments and slow-starting days.

André's abandonment of Rózsi dictated that he cut ties with many of their mutual friends. His social life shifted. Raucous bohemian soirees with the old crowd receded into the past, often replaced by evenings at home. André was not much of a cook, and Erzsébet even less so. But she tried. Armed with a friend's written instructions, she once set out to make pasta, filling a kettle with water and lighting the stove. When the kettle began singing, she scurried to find André and ask why the water was making that strange noise. That much André knew. Charming Bözsi! he chuckled.

Bözsi was only one of his nicknames for her. Others were Erzsi, Bozska, and Szívecske, Hungarian for "sweetheart." Once he accidently flipped out the word Szivacska (meaning Little Sponge) instead of Szívecske, and the two burst out laughing. So Szivacska she became.[37] With others, she was André's fiancée Elisabeth, which they would later Anglicize to Elizabeth.

She brought her friends in Paris into André's life. One, a former classmate, was Véra Braun, a painter and designer. Braun was the mistress of the electrician-turned-writer Eugène Dabit, whose hugely popular *L'Hôtel du Nord*, published in 1929, had become an instant classic of proletarian literature. Dabit's novel strings together episodes in the lives and loves of working-class misfits who pass through a seedy hotel on the Canal Saint-Martin. André had read it in French. He could relate: He too had haunted the quais along the Canal Saint-Martin, a point of reference in blue-collar Paris.

*L'Hôtel du Nord* was even more timely in 1932 as industrial workers were facing layoffs, shopkeepers were lowering their shutters, and typists and seamstresses were losing their jobs. The Great Depression finally slipped into France, and the ranks of émigré artists were thinning. Yet even as ordinary folks suffered, Parisians with deep pockets or the financial savvy to turn peril into profit kept up their rounds of dinner parties, balls, and jaunts in sleek touring cars. The luxury industries prospered.[38]

Politically, Paris felt chillingly like postwar Budapest. Voices like that of the journalist Albert Flament were growing louder. "A powerful vacuum cleaner seems to have sucked up all the degenerates who used to show off on the hundred meters of sidewalk that stretch from the Dôme to the Pergola," Flament had written of the boulevard du Montparnasse. "Sometimes one has to be thankful for financial disasters."[39] That section of the boulevard was headquarters for the École de Paris, the term for foreign artists working in the French capital, largely Jews from Central Europe, as opposed to the École Française.[40] As it happened, *Art et Médecine* illustrated Flament's series about gardens that spring with photographs by André, who would have ignored Flament's pronouncements, even though he knew from experience where such rhetoric could lead.

His career continued to flourish. In 1932, André published pictures for twenty-three stories in *Vu* and more for the classically stylish *Art et Médecine*. This notable new monthly took as its premise that physicians were humanists who could appreciate and afford life's finer pleasures. Its pages were larded with features about art, food, literature, the theater, design, sports, lifestyle, travel, and medicine. Sometimes André supplied pictures for six or seven articles in a single issue, some of them commissioned, others from his stock. He illustrated at least seven articles about that year's Paris Colonial Exposition, a vast fair that glorified French imperialism. At a center for neonatal medicine, he angled for shots of mothers and babies. In a hospital operating room, he followed a surgeon as he excised a tumor. And he contributed nearly two dozen photographs to a Paris-themed issue that opened with his *Eiffel Tower, Paris*, and featured articles by Jean Cocteau, Francis Carco, and Pierre Mac Orlan. Theirs is largely a romantic vision of concierges, children, dogs, and tranquil little gardens.

At every opportunity, André took self-portraits. Two from that year show him looking carefree as he stands across the street from the chic Hôtel Claridge. He may have been coming or going from the offices of *Vu* on the nearby Champs-Élysées. The thirty-seven-year-old in a suit and tie could pass for a boyish businessman in such high spirits that he could easily break into dance. Life was good. Work was a pleasure. He had money and prestige. Soon he would marry the woman he loved.

**That summer,** André and Elizabeth entertained his brother Imre, who visited with his fiancée, Margit Rosenberg, called Gréti. A stocky divorcée and soon-to-be convert from Judaism to Catholicism, Gréti was the daughter of a wealthy businessman from the minor nobility. Elizabeth's mother visited Paris too. With Elizabeth and André, she sipped tea, picnicked with friends, and shopped on the Champs-Élysées. His snapshots reveal Elizabeth's transformation from a schoolgirlish Budapester to a chic Parisienne in a cloche, light wool suit, and heels. They offer no insights on Pepi's evolving opinion of André.

When it was just the two of them, Elizabeth handled some of the tasks that had once been Rózsi's. She too spoke French, English, and German, the languages vital to André's work life. She would sit primly at the typewriter in their home office taking dictation from André, then edit the letters, mail them, and organize his correspondence in binders.

Their models as coworkers would have been their neighbors in that same apartment building, the Soviets Ilya and Ljuba Ehrenburg. Ljuba, a painter, was her husband's helpmeet. A prolific and widely known writer, Ilya served as the Paris correspondent for *Izvestia* and Joseph Stalin's arranger in France. At the same time, he indulged in the life of a pipe-sucking bohemian and habitué of the Dôme and La Coupole, where he presided over the Soviet table. André photographed the couple in their study. It's easy to picture him lingering to give Ilya tips about handling the Leica the Russian was using for street photographs. Published in 1933, Ehrenburg's *My Paris* takes aim at the disparities between the lives of the wealthy and those of the poor in this bosom of decadent capitalism.

Around that same time, a new arrival from Budapest rented an apartment across the hall from André and Elizabeth: the glass artist and designer Júlia Báthory.[41] Back home, Báthory had reportedly been Elizabeth's confidante during the months when she was plotting her departure for Paris. Now Báthory was preparing her first solo show in the French capital, which André would document. Her friend the ceramist and sculptor Margit Kovács also landed in Paris. A former classmate of Elizabeth's at Álmos Jaschik's school, Kovács was training at the renowned porcelain manufactory in Sèvres, just outside the city. The three women were tight.

As for André's oldest companions in Paris, he turned his back on many. That September, Brassaï wrote his parents: "I haven't seen the photographer Kertész for several months. He divorced his first wife and now lives in seclusion with his new wife."[42]

But André had not divorced Rózsi. He had filed for divorce, and the case *Kertész vs. Kertész née Klein* had been assigned to a court.[43] As the process inched forward, André discovered that extricating himself from the marriage was not a given. Although French law permitted divorce by mutual consent, Rózsi would never consent.[44] So André had to establish grounds for divorce. Rózsi had not committed adultery, beaten him, deserted him, or been convicted of a major crime. He would have to rely on *injures graves* as his motive. This catchall concept referred to insults so grievous that they rendered continued married life impossible.

As French law moved away from a concept of divorce as a sanction for vow-breaking and toward a concept of divorce justified by the collapse of the matrimonial bond, *injures graves* had become the most common grounds. It included everything from failure to consummate the marriage or transmission of a sexual disease to refusal to host one's in-laws.[45]

As the petitioner, André would have hired a lawyer to prepare a summary statement of his grounds for divorce. At the hearing, however, he was required to present that statement to the judge in the presence of Rózsi. One imagines him stammering out a tale of how she had coerced or tricked him into marriage. She would have contested his account and made known her poor health. The judge weighed the testimonies and dismissed the case, likely ordering reconciliation.[46] That left André without a path to divorce.

He pretended otherwise. Word went around that André had divorced. That's what Brassaï heard. So did André's old friend the Hungarian photographer Max Winterstein. Aware that André's mother disliked Rózsi when they met in Budapest and that André had been unhappy in the marriage, Winterstein wrote from Hungary to congratulate him on the divorce that "ended [his] dark period."[47]

André probably told the same story to Elizabeth, who had no way of knowing that the legal break never happened. French courts considered divorce a strictly private matter. Testimony was taken behind the closed doors of the judge's chambers with no reporters present. Newspaper accounts of such litigation were illegal.[48] If Rózsi's account differed from André's, it was her word against his.

Meanwhile, Rózsi had rented a cheap apartment and taken a job developing X-rays in a clinic. After she fell and broke several glass plates, she was fired. Later, she would join the Guttmann Agency, photograph children and dancers, and publish a dozen mediocre pictures in *Vu*. All were signed with her *nom d'artiste* Rogi André.

By one account, André had forbidden her to keep his last name, so she saucily took his first. As for Rogi, it sounds like a childhood nickname or perhaps a pet name from her once lover. In years past, their friend the model and singer Kiki had underscored her intimacy with Man Ray by fusing her name with his: Kiki Man Ray. After she and Man Ray parted ways, Kiki had shed that moniker. But, for the rest of her life, Rózsi would be Rogi André.[49]

The non-divorce would have made André nervous. Rogi knew lots of people. She had a sharp tongue. She hovered on the fringes of his everyday life. Her photographs might pop up in the same magazine or exhibition as his. *She* might pop up at the Dôme or Select. Those who heard her diatribes were shocked that "Kertész, gentle Kertész" had abandoned her.[50]

Around the time his legal proceedings with Rogi dead-ended, a story for *Art et Médecine* took André to the home of Renée Maeterlinck. She and her husband, the Flemish writer and Nobel laureate Maurice Maeterlinck, occupied a fairy-tale estate overlooking the Mediterranean between Nice and Villefranche. Surrounded by rose gardens and cypress and olive groves ending in a rocky trail that descended to the sea, Orlamonde had marble floors, frescoed ceilings, and a light-drenched salon. A borzoi and an uncaged white dove shared the estate.

André enjoyed Maeterlinck's writing. It appealed to his sentimental side and was attuned to the Symbolist strain in André's own art. For Maeterlinck, only indirect, irrational, and sensual language could express the mysteries of existence. Words were to be valued for their associative powers. Unlike language, photography is necessarily fact-based. Yet facts are open to interpretation, and André's photographs make full, if seemingly artless, use of the associative powers of all they depict. And, for Maeterlink, like André, light was revelatory.

Maeterlinck's most famous work was the Symbolist play *The Blue Bird*, a saccharine quest story that had captured the fancy of a generation, traveled around the world, and launched the hackneyed phrase "bluebird of happiness." Nineteen-year-old André had seen the Budapest production in 1913.[51] A porcelain bluebird hung at Orlamonde, he noted approvingly.

In Maeterlinck's play, a fairy disguised as a hag sends two country children, a brother and sister, in pursuit of a bluebird. Its capacity for flight and ascension makes the bird a symbol of the spiritual well-being that derives from seeking and finding the truth. Before the children depart, the fairy gives the boy a cap set with a diamond that will illuminate the souls of the people and things they meet. As the siblings proceed, allegorical places and figures like Luxury, Memory, and Night reveal themselves by the diamond's light. Yet the bluebird remains elusive. They come home empty-handed, to discover that their pet turtledove has turned blue. They give it to a sick child, who is instantly cured. Then the feathered creature streaks off. The play closes with the boy's plea to playgoers to find happiness – the bluebird – in their own lives.

For André, happiness equated with occasions like this second visit on assignment to Orlamonde. The writer was away. So he had the dazzling madame and the storybook estate to himself. Renée was, he fawned, "a figure of the purest poetry."[52] In one of André's portraits, she hugs her borzoi. Her animated stillness, twisting body, and caress of the animal's fur recall Leonardo da Vinci's painting *Lady with an Ermine.* Like the artist, André presents his subject as both an individual and a *belle idéale* of tender womanhood.

A decade would pass. During World War II, the Maeterlincks would be forced to abandon Orlamonde to looters and squatters. Then a Nazi commander occupied the estate. More years hurried by. By 1965, Maeterlinck was dead, the elderly Renée rattling around the recovered château, and André seeking salve for his psychic wounds. That year, he published a portfolio in *Harper's Bazaar*.[53] It brought together his portraits of six legends of interwar Paris: Colette, Magda Förstner, Marie Laurencin, Anna de Noailles, Lady Mendl, and, hugging her borzoi, Renée Maeterlinck. Imbued with, as one writer observed of Maeterlinck's *The Blue Bird*, "an unconquerable longing for what is gone forever . . . the beauty of what was merely a mirage," it seemed to confirm André's romanticized version of his life in France.[54] In photographs, happily, the clock stops ticking.

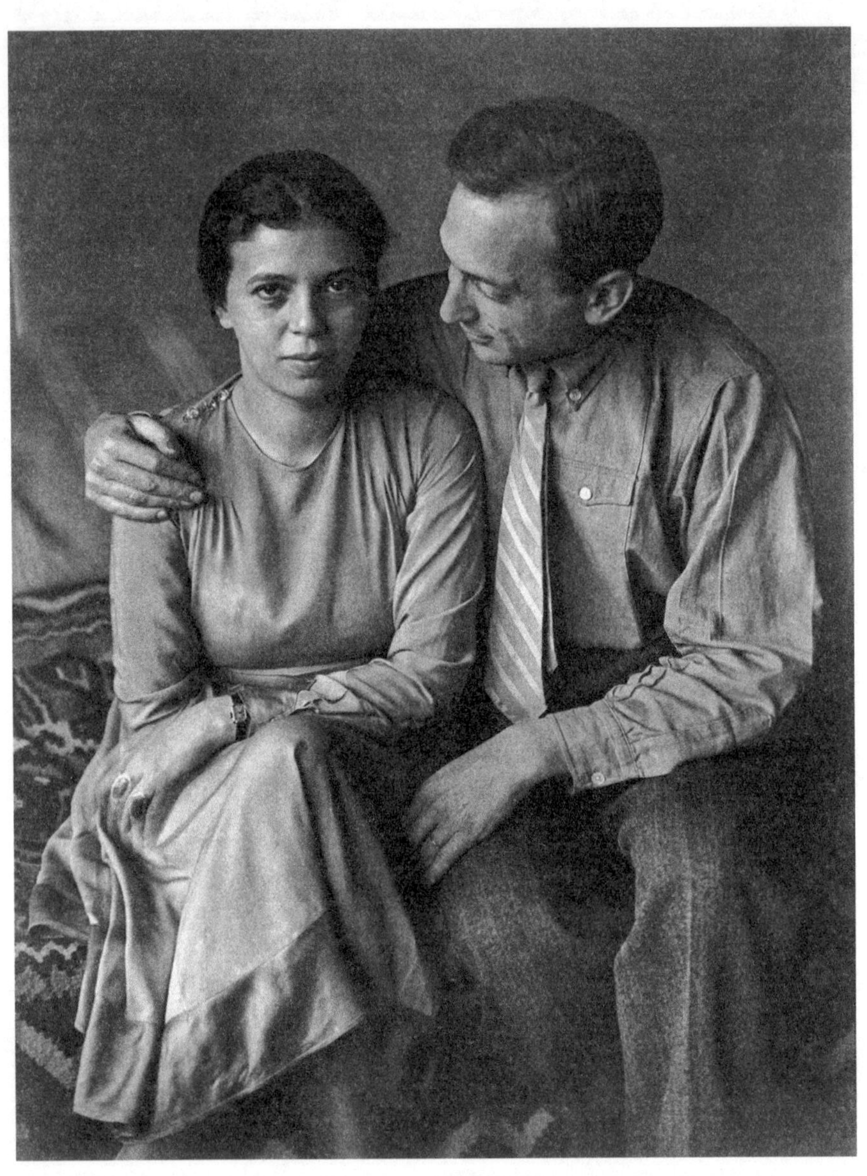

André Kertész, *Elizabeth and I*, 1933

# 7 ELIZABETH AND I, 1932–1936

**It was both an old dream** and a logical career move, and André was poised to achieve it in style. The owner of France's leading type foundry, Charles Peignot, published the magazine *Arts et Métiers Graphiques*, a showcase for innovative design. Now Peignot was proposing a book of André's photographs. However, he was offering only a modest advance. When André fully understood Peignot's terms, he balked: too stingy, unbefitting a photographer of his stature. He didn't know, or refused to believe, that the classy *Arts et Métiers Graphiques* was bleeding money.[1] So the project went nowhere except in the form of André griping to friends.

Among those who heard about the situation was Brassaï, who had been sleeping by day and stalking pictures by night. Seeing an opening for his own work, Brassaï prevailed on an acquaintance to introduce him to Peignot. They cut a book deal. Months passed. Then, in December 1932, Brassaï's *Paris de Nuit* (*Paris by Night*) popped up in display windows around the city. Reviews were glowing. Bookshops sold out. Brassaï achieved instant stardom.

*Paris de Nuit* opens with what look like establishing shots in a film noir set in a louche and desolate city. It goes on to spy out the denizens of circuses, music halls, and *bals*. A has-been cocotte (high-class prostitute) dripping in pearls occupies her usual cabaret table. Members of the smart set glide by in a limousine that is lit like an aquarium. Poor devils paw through the rubbish. Mist slicks empty cobblestones. The city drifts along in a great well of night.

Shortly before the publication of *Paris de Nuit*, André got wind of the book. He reeled. He had taught Brassaï the techniques of night photography, which he and Jenő had learned using trial and error. Now this low blow! Brassaï had vanished for several weeks, André claimed, then reappeared with what was by rights André's. "He came back, and the photos he had taken were absolutely Kertész photographs, in the sense that everything was done as I had done it."[2]

It's easy to imagine André poring over *Paris de Nuit* and pouncing on pictures that resembled his own. One shows an allée in the Luxembourg Garden crosshatched à la Kertész by the shadows of a grille fence. Monuments like the Arc de Triomphe and Notre Dame are angled and viewed in defamiliarizing ways—again, André's approach. Trees overhang quais. Chimney pots, another Kertész signature subject, line up like the pipes of a pan flute. Brassaï had stolen *his* material, André maintained, but also "what I was doing technically and intellectually—what was important, what should be accented."[3] Brassaï presses objects into service to block electric glare, a technique that André would have taught him. Like André, he uses the city's light-scattering dampness to layer objects, play up shapes, and create atmosphere.

Other photographers were doing work not unlike André's. His vision had helped spawn a communal vision. Ilse Bing, for one, photographed park chairs, streetlights, and the gestures of dancers, all favorite Kertész subjects. Like André, Bing used puddles as portals to dream worlds. But she was not André's close Hungarian friend, nor had she published a popular book. In André's view, Brassaï had betrayed their friendship by exploiting his fizzled deal with Peignot, going behind his back, and absconding with subjects and techniques that were rightfully his. After *Paris de Nuit* appeared, Brassaï wrote an article explaining night photography to the readers of *Arts et Métiers Graphiques*. In the article, he declares his debt to filmmakers but never mentions his teacher and friend.[4]

From Brassaï's viewpoint, the thin-skinned André's complaints were absurd. First, it was André, not he, who had vanished. André no longer showed up at parties or prowled the night streets, dusk until dawn, as *Paris de Nuit* had demanded. Where was *he* at 2:00 a.m.? And what did Brassaï have to apologize for? André's deal with Peignot was dead. Besides, André had no lock on the Luxembourg Garden, the quais of the Seine, or any other subject. What's more, night photography dated to the nineteenth century, and standard techniques had long since emerged. There were no real similarities between his work and André's, Brassaï insisted.[5]

The two do have different sensibilities: André's more poetic and distanced, Brassaï's more reportorial and engaged with life's seamy side. To those who saw his photographs as derivative, Brassaï might have countered that he was doing what André did too: soak up anything useful from those around him. Shortly after the book appeared, André confronted Brassaï. In André's telling, the other was unrepentant. "A few weeks later, I had forgotten the whole thing," André later implausibly asserted.[6] In truth, his anger simmered.

**André's ringer box shrilled.** Picking up the earpiece of his telephone, he heard the voice of his Hungarian designer friend Marcel Vertès. "André, you know Querelle, the director of *Le Sourire*. He wants to know if you would agree to do something for his magazine."

The next day, André called Louis Querelle: "Querelle, we know each other. Why didn't you call me yourself?"

"I'll tell you frankly, Kertész, because I wouldn't have liked to hear you tell me no."

Very delicate and very French, thought André.[7]

Querelle assumed that André was too established to accept an assignment to photograph nudes for *Le Sourire* (The Smile), a men's magazine that was naughty in a wink-and-Gallic-shrug kind of way.

"Why would I say no?" André replied. "I like girls, so I like girly too. Of course I accept."[8]

He did so knowing that Querelle was open to his ideas about the feature and seeing an opportunity to play with distorting mirrors. Distortions fascinated André, starting with shadows. So did the effects of light passing through various mediums, whether it was water visually warping a swimmer, crystal-ball glass reflecting the image of a fortune teller, or metal buckling bodies in a carnival mirror. When the writer Carlo Rim took the position as editor in chief of *Vu* in 1930, André introduced him to readers with portraits he took in the funhouse mirrors at Luna Park. The pictures suit Rim's ebullient personality and his sideline as a caricaturist. In one, he looks like a gassed-up blimp ready to lift off.

Nudes were nothing new for André either. In Hungary, friends and artists' models used to pose for him nude or seminude, but most of the glass plates had not survived the chaos after the war.[9] And André knew more than he let on about the shady side of Paris. Always alert to ways to make money, Imre had once pointed out to him that pornography disguised as art was popular in France. Some of André's Parisian photographs would work beautifully in collectors' editions of erotica, Imre continued. Apparently, André never acted on that suggestion and the pictures Imre was referring to evidently did not survive André's later purges.

The *Le Sourire* project moved quickly. Querelle hired the models. Amused by the idea of contrasting old and young, he settled on a middle-aged ex–cabaret dancer and a seventeen- or eighteen-year-old White Russian from a good family named Najinskaya Verackhatz. Spoiled, thought André, yet graceful and lovely.[10] Querelle also provided an apartment and two mirrors from a flea market. Or maybe André found the mirrors. Accounts differ. In any case, one was a convex mirror that André would quickly discard as boring. The other, longer and heavier with an *S* deformation, turned out to be that rarity "an intelligent mirror" with the reflective and refractive qualities André was seeking.[11] As for the camera, he chose a 9 by 12 centimeter Linhof monorail. Used in studio and industrial photography, the monorail camera enables its operator to tilt the front and back independently and thus diminish or intensify distortion.[12]

At times, André pressed his Zeiss Tessar lens into service. But mostly he relied on his Hugo Meyer Satz Plasmat triple convertible lens, which he assembled as a wide angle. Because a wide-angle lens has a short focal length, it swells objects in the foreground, showing them out of proportion to what is more distant. The Satz Plasmat's subtle optical aberrations would add another layer of visual complexity to André's pictures.

Juggling the mirrors, his tripod, his camera, and one or two floodlights, he threw himself into the project he originally called the Grotesques but was later known as the Distortions. Like Alexander Calder cooking up his circus or Géza Blattner reinventing the marionette theater, André straddled the line between work and play. The work side was demanding. Cameras and mirrors are unselective: neither discriminates between what's important and what's not. Controlling the plasticity of his images required technical acumen, a flair for improvisation, and intense concentration. The big mirror was heavy and awkward, so it had to be kept in place.[13] André and his models worked around it. That, too, was tricky. He was relying on the light from a window or two, along with the floods. He had to be careful that his light sources never showed in the mirror—too much glare.

André and the two women improvised one pose after another. He would eyeball what showed up in the mirror, then choose a lens, scrutinize the effect, maybe ask them to turn a bit more or adjust a limb. Next, he would decide between a vertical or horizontal format and pick the camera settings for the effect he was after. Occasionally, he coupled the models with their reflections, but mostly he avoided showing either the flesh-and-blood women or the mirrors as objects. He was photographing reflections.

Taking advantage of the irregularities of his mirror and lenses, André drew out angularities and curves. He mixed blurriness with razor sharpness. Sometimes the results astonished and delighted him. Other times he couldn't get what he wanted. A slight shift and the marvel would vanish. When he had to settle for an image that needed but wouldn't allow for tighter framing, he would crop it in the darkroom, zeroing in on the visual relationships that intrigued him.[14]

Taking up Querelle's idea of contrasting the two models, André photographed Verackhatz's matchstick reflection clasping that of the older woman, who looks as if she has swallowed a rocking horse. Another picture shows a rag-doll Verackhatz wedged against the other woman's rock-solid back. After two sessions and thirtysome negatives, however, André felt he'd exhausted the contrast idea. He thanked the older woman. Then, with Verackhatz alone, he hit his stride.

Working twice a week over the next four weeks, André made some two hundred negatives.[15] He maneuvered, paused, adjusted, approached the model, then stepped back. Shifting his attention from model to mirror to viewfinder, André teased out those instants when—as he once said apropos of *Satiric Dancer*—"something changes into something else."[16]

Indeed, Verackhatz's flesh is swollen, scrunched, taffy-pulled, or puddled. In one shot from a low angle, her body congeals into mounds of flesh topped by a nose that resembles a hilltop shrine. In another, a free-floating leg sprouts feet at both ends. In others, she looks like a victim of elephantiasis. Her shoulders wing out. Her legs sweep behind her like the train of a gown. When a Pinocchio-nosed Verackhatz appears to have sex with her monstrous double, the grotesque becomes the autoerotic. When her legs arc over what looks like a huge phallus, the autoerotic verges on the pornographic.

It must have been exciting for André to team up with a naked young thing. The Distortions might be seen as the expression of otherwise inexpressible sexual fantasies. Yet they don't register as erotic or even flirty. Sometimes they're amusing. Sometimes they suggest wartime mutilation displaced onto the female body. Mostly they bring home André's delight in disporting himself with optics. With light bending and bouncing off surfaces. With a mirror that doubles, deflects, and deforms. With lenses working in concert with light, the mirror, and the model, confounding the corporal and the immaterial, the real and the illusory.

When André showed Verackhatz a few prints, she got upset and protested that that was not her! "Of course, it's you," he replied. "You don't recognize yourself because you've never seen yourself this way, but it's you, my camera cannot lie. You exist like that in the mirror in a very real way."[17]

Mirror images *are* optically, though not literally, real. Like photographs, they have a high truth quotient. Yet they are not the same as reality. Like cameras, they redirect the light bouncing off the piece of the world that's in front of them. Both devices visually double and laterally reverse their subjects (although most modern cameras correct for the lateral reversal). Both conjure a world within a world.

André's Distortions recall the British artist Henry Moore's biomorphic sculptures and Pablo Picasso's female nude paintings from that same era. André may or may not have known Moore's work, but he did attend Picasso's first retrospective at the Galerie Georges Petit in Paris in 1932. That exhibition included the artist's recent canvases inspired by the carnal pleasures of his affair with the young Marie-Thérèse Walter. Picasso stretches and warps Walter's flesh into the ripest of forms. It's easy to imagine André's mind thinking photographically as he scrutinized Picasso's exhibition.

On March 2nd, twelve Distortions appeared in *Le Sourire* without titles or captions.[18] (André assigned each a number.) He felt they expressed a range of emotions, from "excruciatingly comic" to "poignantly tragic." To him, they represented the zenith of his achievement—indeed, "one of the highest artistic forms of photography."[19] Querelle was delighted.

But most critics either stayed silent or groused. One commentator noted affinities with the paintings of Picasso and Modigliani, the sculptures of Constantin Brancusi and Alexander Archipenko, and the circus of a nightmare P. T. Barnum. He wrote of experiencing the same "uneasiness stirred by certain wax casts, the original of which would bring only indifference."[20] Another observer weighed in: "I know some people are amused. As for me, I don't find these games very new: in any case they are unpleasant to see."[21] Posed in a studio, conceived as a group, and focused on the female nude, the Distortions upset people's expectations about the work of André the poet-photographer. The series felt contrived and wrong from one who vowed to reject "professional virtuosity." André might have responded that being an amateur meant, in part, flouting the rules about what he could and could not do, that photography meant freedom from shoulds.

Twelve days after the Distortions were published, word shot through Europe that Stefan Lorant, the innovative Hungarian-born editor of the *Münchner Illustrierte Zeitung*, had been arrested and locked up in Munich. The new German chancellor Adolf Hitler was moving to curtail civil liberties and bridle a freewheeling press. Lorant would be kept behind bars for 196 days but never charged with a crime. In the end, Hungary intervened, and the editor fled Germany. In Berlin, the Jewish owners of Ullstein Verlag, Europe's biggest publishing company, had been forced out too. Like Lorant, Ullstein's editors had long championed André's work. His go-to German contact, Henry Guttmann, also had to decamp. That October's Editors Law would require that everyone in German publishing, photographers included, prove Aryan descent. André's German market slammed shut, cutting him off from five million readers of illustrated weeklies, slashing his income, and leaving him stunned.

Around that same time, he began suffering from bouts of dizziness, frequently enough that he wrote Imre about them. Imre urged him to travel to Budapest to consult a doctor, advice that André shrugged off.

**On Saturday, June 17, 1933,** at the city hall of the fifteenth arrondissement, thirty-eight-year-old André Kertész illegally wed twenty-nine-year-old Elizabeth Salamon. Two city employees acted as witnesses.

In their wedding portrait, taken at home, the bride and groom sit on their folk-coverlet-draped bed.[22] She wears a satiny dress, he a crisply ironed shirt, a striped tie, and light wool slacks. He snuggles up and turns to his bride. His body language declares his adoration. One arm wraps around her like a tendril. That gesture—a pictorial vow to protect her—would become the visual emblem of their relationship. For him, Elizabeth was a *femme-enfant* (woman-child) who needed his safeguarding, even though she was the tougher of the two. André studies Elizabeth's face; she stares at the camera, always the third member of their little family.

Later that summer, they honeymooned in Savoy. They planned to spend the first night or two at a picturesque hotel recommended by a friend. But they arrived to discover that it had been converted into a sanatorium. Stranded in a makeshift lodging until the next morning, they went for a walk. Then a rain squall swept in, sending them scurrying for shelter in what must have been a chilly farm building. Elizabeth hunched on a stool, hand on chin, looking like a child pouting because she's been made to stay in the corner. She was wearing one of her little-girl outfits: a skirt and blouse, rolled down anklets, and Mary Janes. André draped his suit jacket over her shoulders, recalling his gesture in the wedding portrait. Next to her sat a duck. André raised his camera to photograph his beloved.[23]

In reply to a letter in which André proclaimed his joy, his friend Max Winterstein commented: "Erzsike [Elizabeth] surely complements you well as a human being, and I hope that with that you've ended your run of bad luck."[24] How could André blight the moment by admitting that he had failed to wrench himself out of the marriage to Rogi?

Bigamy was a crime. The mechanisms meant to prevent it included posting a notice of each pending marriage on the door of the city hall in the arrondissement where the wedding was to take place. Anyone with information about why it should not was supposed to come forward. In addition, brides- and grooms-to-be had to provide copies of their birth certificates, on which any past marriages and divorces should be recorded. But such mechanisms could be ineffectual. André had wed Rogi in the fourteenth arrondissement, Elizabeth in the fifteenth. Civil records were kept by hand, making irregularities hard to catch.

Few people knew about the aborted divorce proceedings. Nobody had reported the problem. André, of course, knew that his marriage to Elizabeth was legally null and void.[25]

The photo historian Sandra Phillips has suggested that he subconsciously associated Verackhatz, the younger model for the Distortions, with Elizabeth, and the older model with Rogi.[26] (Rogi was two years older than Elizabeth, who looked younger than her age.) Dismissing the older woman and closing ranks with the younger symbolically reprised his situation. If only the break with Rogi had been that neat. Elizabeth probably never knew that the divorce did not go through. Nor could André confide in his friends or his brothers. Imre would have sternly disapproved; Jenő had disappeared into Latin America. André had an ugly secret and no one with whom to share his anxiety and guilt.

In years to come, Rogi would neither dwell on the situation nor conceal it. In a photographic self-portrait from the late 1930s, her wedding band is in plain view. Half a century later, her close friend, the writer Renée Beslon, would report in print that Rogi and André had never divorced. Rogi never remarried. She and André remained legally wed. André had wronged two women. He would have seen no way to fix things and gain forgiveness, so he pretended, perhaps even to himself. Not only did he tell people he had divorced Rogi, but also he would lead people to believe that he had been loyal to Elizabeth since the day they first met.

Eleven days after the wedding, André opened a telegram from Imre: Their mother had died peacefully on her seventieth birthday. André had expected the news. That late spring, he made a short trip home to say goodbye. During his visit, Ernesztina aired her fears about Jenő. It had been more than eight years since his mother or brothers had seen him. The family had learned that he was married and had a son named Imre. Around 1932, Jenő's letters, never frequent, once again stopped arriving. The Chaco War had broken out between Paraguay and Bolivia, consuming the region where Jenő was working and disrupting the mail. At least that's what Imre and André suspected and told their mother. Ernesztina longed to see her youngest son once more and hug her only grandchild. Yet she knew it was never to be.

Laying aside Imre's telegram about their mother's death, André seized pencil and paper to write Jenő. Imre had not always been perfect, André opined, but he had made up for everything by his devotion to Mama in her last months. As for the rest of the family, he and Imre had cut off contact. "With good reason, Öcskös [Little Brother]!" Presumably he meant squabbles over money. "We are now all alone, you understand, and you are the only person who still belongs to us. Write right away, we beg of you, and let there be no more obstacles to our having news about each other."[27]

Silence from Latin America.

From Budapest, by contrast, came a stream of news from Imre and Gréti about Ernesztina's burial (with her brother Poldi, not her husband), the closing of their childhood home, and the divvying up of dishes, silverware, linens, rugs, and money.

André's professional life also was evolving. Political and economic currents were carrying *Vu* away from inquisitive humanism and toward hard news reporting. In 1932, he published fifty-five photographs in *Vu*; in 1933, it was forty-two. His most notable reportage that year, which he may have undertaken on his own and been unable to place, portrayed the painter Marc Chagall and his family. As for *Art et Médecine*, where André had published twenty-six features in 1932, his work still appeared but frequently as reprints. Other photographs, some new, some recycled, showed up in Gaston Gallimard's high-toned weekly *Marianne*, Michel de Brunhoff's French *Vogue*, and *Rails de France*, published by the French State Railways. In July, André's work appeared again in *Le Sourire*, this time soft-porn pictures of rag-doll puppets posed as if engaging in sex acts.

It was not the only project André had going with Querelle. The two had been batting around the idea of a French-German edition of the Distortions. They found a publisher, selected sixty images, and completed a layout. Carlo Rim contributed witty captions. All the while, the implications of Hitler's rule were becoming clearer. Querelle advised forbearance: "Let's be patient, that little man won't last three months."[28] In May, however, German university students seeking to "purify" the fatherland's literature by destroying Jewish and foreign elements burned twenty-five thousand books deemed un-German. There was no longer any point in André knocking himself out to meet his publisher's August deadline. A book of nudes by a Jewish photographer wasn't going anywhere in Hitler's Germany.

André sorely missed his German clients. He wanted assignments. He needed the money. Blame Hitler, blame the Depression, blame the newly minted photographers who were taking the jobs.

He turned to publishing books as a way of monetizing old photographs and rebuilding his income. More than magazine jobs, books gave him control over layout and sequencing. The work fit well with his domestic life. More fundamentally, to create a book was to interpret the world and give full expression to his distinct vision. And to be the son of Lipót Kertész was to love books. André's first would be *Soixante Photographies d'Enfants* (Sixty Photographs of Children).

The subject was apt. André had a gift for working with little ones. They liked him. He knew how to capture their squirming bodies, their clear-eyed expressions, and their earnestness about pretend play. Conveniently, his apartment overlooked a school playground, and he had frequently photographed children from his own windows. André could also avail himself of pictures he'd taken on assignment, notably some charmers for *Vu* of children taking a bath, getting their nails clipped, and sitting on a chamber pot. Then there were friends' offspring and the tots he spotted on the streets or in parks.

This time the advance was decent. André was to pocket 5,000 francs, plus 5 percent royalties.[29] Later correspondence reveals that he received an advance of only 4,000 francs. Even that wasn't bad at a time when France was sunk in a depression, scores of publishing companies had folded, and some booksellers minded their counters for whole days without ringing up a sale.[30] Equally important to André, his publisher, Éditions d'histoire et d'art, was promising a high-quality hardback using Arches vellum paper and photogravure, a printing method that yields long tonal ranges and deliciously sooty blacks.

Chubby and Gallic in their junior berets, lace collars, and hand-knit onesies, the children in *Soixante Photographies* inhabit a now-lost interwar world. Even when they are carrying out adult-dictated activities, André's tots feel like a tribe apart. Sweet gestures abound. A gargling girl appears to air-kiss the ceiling. Boys handle balls and dirt clods like fetish objects. The sturdy and obliging Little Ernest—his name fits—interrupts a classroom art lesson to stand up and pose for monsieur. A lass sleeps with the silky intensity of the very young. Her tousled hair, thicket of lashes, lustrous cheeks, and bee-stung lips suggest that she will someday be a beautiful woman. The French playwright assigned to caption the pictures came up with these words: "Proof of the Existence of God."[31]

Another memorable caption accompanies a picture that centers on X-crossed teeter-totters seen from André's apartment window. The writer's words point to what was happening beyond the schoolyard wall: "The latest news: the ministry has been toppled... The chancellor has delivered an aggressive speech... The dollar is slipping... There is a threat of war in Punjab."[32] In 1933 Europe, there was no escaping world tensions.

André's next book project was obliquely political. In Hungary, the authoritarian Horthy continued to strong-arm his people. Only vestiges of democracy remained. Outraged that his country's rightist regime was co-opting the words of the poet-prophet Endre Ady and thus blunting the edge of Ady's radical politics, the left-liberal writer György Bölöni, once Ady's friend and now André's, had resolved to correct the record.[33] All the same, Bölöni's book *Az Igazi Ady* (The True Ady) would be more anecdotal memoir than political biography. André would provide the pictures. His task was to use the evidentiary force of photography to eternalize the poet's bond with the City of Light. Over the years, Ady had moved back and forth between Budapest and Paris. In Budapest, he had edited the leading progressive journal and provoked scathing denunciations from politicians. In Paris—that "city of marvels"—he found creative and political inspiration and dissolute pleasures.

Late that fall, Bölöni and André ranged over the French capital, ferreting out Ady's belle epoque city amid the rackety modernity of 1933. The idea was to interpret the places Ady had frequented as he would have experienced them. André photographed at the venerable brasserie Chartier, at a stall where Ady used to buy flowers for his mistress Léda, and in a nook in the Luxembourg Garden. Sometimes he enlisted Bölöni as a stand-in for Ady. When he and Bölöni arrived at the rue de Lévis, where Léda had lived, they were tickled to find a horse-drawn carriage, a herd of goats, and the goatherd hawking cheeses and milk, as if the past persisted on that very street. André whipped out his Leica. He was in his element.

André also illustrated one of Ady's best-loved poems. Like many Hungarians of his generation, he could recite by heart the sixteen lines of "The Ghost Got into Paris."[34] It opens with the narrator walking down a stock-still boulevard Saint-Michel one dog day in August. Oddly, his spirit burns with "small, twiggy songs . . . purple and pensive, strange and smoky-hued." With a swirl of "jesting leaves," autumn whispers through the heat. On that boulevard named for the patron saint of the sick and the suffering, death trifles with the poet. He feels what it is to be mortal. Then death vanishes: "She came, but that she came, alone I knew / beneath the moan of the trees."[35]

To take the photograph, André set up his tripod on a stretch of sidewalk that curves outside the Luxembourg Garden along the boulevard Saint-Michel. He timed and staged it so that the shadow of the park's grille fence striates the sidewalk and leads the eye to a lone, distant walker (Bölöni). Except for the shadowed sidewalk with its scatter of leaves, the foreground is empty. "Inspired by Ady's poem, on the corner of Boul' Mich'," reads the caption.

One of André's two portraits in absence of Ady centers on a nightstand in the writer's room at the Hôtel des Balcons in the Latin Quarter. Ady typically spent mornings in bed, reading French and Hungarian newspapers. The artful disarray set up by André evokes the scene after one such morning. There are crocheted table toppers, a tumbler half filled with red wine, an open Protestant Bible (a Calvinist, Ady always kept a Bible close at hand), pages from a Hungarian newspaper, and a copy of the French daily *Le Temps*, folded to show the section heading "Tribune libre" (open forum). Those words alone stir thoughts of the writer hurtling attacks at his morally corrupt homeland and championing a progressive and democratic Hungary. Such polemics were more relevant than ever in 1933, when the autocrat in power in Budapest was courting Hitler.

André's photograph is formally sophisticated and conceptually complex. It bridges fact and fiction, present and past, the poet's inner and outer lives, Hungary and France. Ady's political engagement, emotional turmoil, and feverish dialogue with God are all present. Such visual collaging and multiplicity of references reflect the modern condition of fragmentation, simultaneity, and tumult.

**On February 6, 1934,** only days after André completed the Ady project, forty thousand malcontents, whipped up by right-wing ideologues, converged on the Place de la Concorde. They were protesting high-level corruption in the Stavisky affair. The central figure in this scandal, the Jewish Ukrainian-born swindler Alexandre Stavisky, had enjoyed the protection of prominent politicians. Now he was dead – a suicide. Or, as some claimed, a victim of police officers protecting high-level officials. That day at the Place de la Concorde, objects flew. A bus burst into flames. When a mob threatened to break through police lines sealing off the Pont de la Concorde, the police opened fire to protect the Chamber of Deputies, just across the river. Fifteen people died, and more than a thousand were wounded. The next day, the Radical government toppled, the eleventh to do so since 1930. Bloody strikes followed. France teetered on the edge of civil war.

The Stavisky affair fueled French anti-Semitism, especially toward foreign-born Jews. Among those scapegoating Jews was the writer and diplomat Paul Morand, whose articles André had illustrated. He had briefly collaborated on Morand's 1931 book *La Route Paris Méditerranée*. Distilling the pleasures of automobile travel into the fiction of a trip along National Highway 7, the book begins in predawn Paris and ends with a twilight dip in the Mediterranean. National Highway 7 was equated with freedom, summer happiness, and *la douce France*, as manifested by André's pictures. Yet in a 1933 editorial, that same Morand opined that "every country except ours is killing its vermin... Don't let us leave Hitler to pride himself on being the only person to undertake the moral rehabilitation of the West."[36] So much for freedom, happiness, and *la douce France*. Even though André's photographs helped define Frenchness for the picture press, he was "vermin." Yet he continued to ignore polemics and ideologies: "Politics didn't happen in my everyday life," he later remembered. "It was outside of me."[37]

In the early spring of 1934, André took what would prove to be his last iconic photograph of interwar Paris. One day he spotted a stunningly graphic billboard on one of the boulevards. André's colleague at *Vu*, the artist and designer A. M. Cassandre, had created this first-ever billboard featuring serial images intended to be seen from passing vehicles.

Pasted up with three sets of posters arranged in a step pattern, the billboard advertises Dubonnet, the aromatized wine-based apéritif. One set of posters reads *DUBO*. *Bo* is the homonym of *beau*, meaning "beautiful." Those posters feature a stylized drawing of a man admiring the drink he's about to consume. A second set shows that same man sipping his apéritif. They read *DUBON* (*bon* meaning "good"). In a third set of posters proclaiming *DUBONNET*, the man pours himself another glass. From one poster to the next, the drinker's figure progressively darkens, and the background changes from white to blue to yellow as the Dubonnet warms his insides.

In front of the billboard was a bench with a signboard attached. It advertised the film *Georges et Georgette*. (The French version of a German farce, *Georges et Georgette* would be remade in the United States in 1982 as *Victor/Victoria*.) The film tells the story of a female performer who impersonates a male drag queen. The signboard was crowned by a cutout head-and-shoulders image of the film's top-hatted star. She looked to André's right while the Dubonnet man times three faced left. The setting was right for a picture. André would have positioned his tripod and camera and stood by.

*On the Boulevards, Paris* shows a matron seated on that same bench, probably awaiting a bus. A man walks behind her. Nothing much is happening. Except that everything glances off everything else. The man's panama hat, the woman's cloche, the drinker's bowler, and the film star's topper make a visual glossary of headgear. The real-life bench recasts the drinker's chair in the posters. The woman on the bench could pass for an older and frumpier version of the top-hatted star. The words on the signs – "Georges Georgette," "Ciné Château," "Dubo, Dubon, Dubonnet" – fall somewhere between scat-singing and nursery rhyme. Spatial ambiguities and shifts in scale keep viewers' eyes darting.

Mixing street life with advertisements – the real and the representation – had long figured among André's favorite forms of visual repartee. But *On the Boulevards, Paris* has a darker side too. Everyone is locked in solitude. Neither the man walking by nor the woman on the bench makes eye contact with the photographer or with each other. The Dubonnet man drinks alone. Life lacks the transformational promise glorified by the hawkers of movies and wine.[38]

**One spring day** a month or two later, Maria Giovanna Eisner stood before a photograph hanging in the salon of the chic Art Deco furniture designer Jules Leleu. An Italian-born transplant, Eisner had founded the

Paris photography agency Alliance Photo. She was stopping by the Maison Leleu for the opening of an exhibition sponsored by *Vu* featuring the work of ten luminaries, each represented by ten photographs on a single theme. André was showing the Distortions. The young photographer Pierre Boucher walked up to greet her. Simultaneously, a beanpole of a man bounded up the stairs and into the room.

Boucher introduced her. "I'd like you to meet André Kertész."

Eisner later recalled that she "felt a firm handclasp, a pair of friendly eyes sparkled at me. Then Kertész disappeared, swallowed up by groups of people who all seemed to be waiting for him."

"Not one of the ten of us here is fit to hold a candle to him," Boucher commented. Eisner observed that André was "respected and admired, with almost the veneration that youth is supposed to have for old age." For a younger generation of photographers, he was a foundational figure at age thirty-nine.[39]

Yet the scene was changing in ways André couldn't control. Even the Dôme, the beating heart of his Paris, was no longer the same. The American contingent had long since thinned out. Many French artists and writers had shifted their allegiance to the cafés of Saint-Germain-des-Prés.[40] The Dôme had become a magnet for German Jewish refugees.

André still made it his base of operations. It was there that he met twenty-one-year-old Peter (later Pierre) Gassmann, a transplanted Berliner and self-taught photographer. Eventually, he would launch Pictorial Service, called Picto, the Parisian processing lab used by many of the world's top photographers. But in 1934, Gassmann was a penniless leftist, drunk with joy to be out of Germany. At the Dôme, he learned, "May I sit down?" was code for "Do you have enough money to buy me a coffee?"[41] It was the kind of request to which the reliably kind André usually said yes.

Another left-wing Jew and fledgling photographer had arrived in France. The swarthy twenty-year-old Endre Friedman, a Budapest native, came across as arrogant yet charming. He was living in a two-bit hotel and making the rounds with a portfolio that editors spurned. Even when Friedman did snag jobs, he kept messing up, mouthing off, and getting fired. As for food, he filched it, skipped meals, or, after he and André met, headed for the rue du Cotentin, where Elizabeth cooked for him while they traded gossip. When he couldn't afford the hotel, he slept on André and Elizabeth's couch. Part of André disapproved of Friedman's behavior; all of him found the boy endearing.

What's more, he discerned Friedman's gift for photography and tried to help. When the younger man's camera was in hock, André loaned one of his. He hired Friedman to do some printing (but judged the results lousy).[42] He also introduced him to Vogel, who assigned the novice a feature about a referendum in the Saarland, a region contested by Germany and France.[43] So Friedman chalked up a press card and a publication. "I have shown my latest pictures to André Kertész, who here is truly famous," he wrote his mother, "and he is truly satisfied."[44]

André *was* "truly famous." That March, a writer for the Hungarian-language *Parisi Futár* (Paris Courier) fawned in print over "the uncrowned... Greatest photo-artist, Kertész, whom the French Photo-School declares as the founder of their school."[45] Unfortunately, fame no longer translated into steady work. With his German colleagues in exile vying for the same jobs as André, the market continued to tighten. Editors' needs were shifting too. Preoccupied with the Nazi menace, *Vu*, for one, was turning to foreign correspondents and agencies. The number of agencies circulating photographs to magazine art directors had exploded.[46] Photographers were specializing as reporters, commercial photographers, fashion photographers, or art photographers, categories the free-spirited André had always glossed over. What's more, articles were now more editor driven. The photographer's personal vision was less relevant. "After its golden age with Nadar, Atget, Gerschel, Kertesz, Man Ray and so many others who almost made it an art like the harpsichord and watercolor, photography has become anonymous," observed Carlo Rim.[47] Five years earlier, André was among Europe's most published photographers. Famous though he was, he was now one of many in a Paris swarming with lensmen.

Some jobs he rejected. One day André opened a note from Florent Fels, a veteran editor, the cofounder of the weekly *Voilà*, and a fervent admirer of André's work. "Old man, I thank you very affectionately for the beautiful book you brought me," wrote Fels. "It stirs, once again, my regret that you don't understand how advantageous it would be for you to collaborate with us. If only you could understand that you could be the *maison*'s top reporter and that it's up to you to make that happen. But you remain the poet that you were a few years ago when we did our photographic meandering along the roads of France."[48] André's reasons for turning down the offer are unknown. Fels believed in photo reportage steeped in poetry. Maybe André found the pay too low. Citing his stature in the field, he was refusing to lower his rates. Maybe he disapproved of *Voilà*'s drift toward sensationalism. Yet André had recently resold his most famous photo essay to *Scandale* ("the magazine of criminal affairs"), which hyperbolized it as "La grande Trappe, tomb of the living and the dead."

Most of his income now came from reprints. The gastronomy magazine *La France à Table* was recycling old successes from Savoy, Burgundy, Lyon, and the Pyrenees. *Art et Médecine* milked three more articles from his sessions with the Maeterlincks. The jobs André did snag were varied. For French *Vogue*, he photographed socialites oozing chic as they ice-skated, rode horses, or walked their dogs in the Bois de Boulogne. *Vogue*'s editor, Vogel's brother-in-law Michel de Brunhoff, understood André's gift for capturing fashion as it was lived, a departure from the magazine's more typical studio-based preciousness. Less glamorously, André supplied pictures for a public-service booklet about electricity. As polished and rigorous as ever, his work was also more predictable.

Meanwhile, André turned his attention to a book about Paris. Like *Soixante Photographies d'Enfants*, it would be published by Éditions d'histoire et d'art and distributed by Plon. At 7,000 francs (about $9,800 in

2024 dollars), his advance topped that for *Enfants*. His royalty rate, 10 percent minimum, doubled.

The idea of a subjective view of Paris was hardly original. In novels like Louis Aragon's *Le Paysan de Paris* and André Breton's *Nadja* (illustrated with photographs by Jacques-André Boiffard), the Surrealists fixate on certain streets, parks, and structures that act as magnets for their fantasies and desires. At least six of André's peers had published visual interpretations of the City of Light. André's main reference points were *Atget, Photographe de Paris*; Germaine Krull's *100 x Paris*; and Brassaï's *Paris de Nuit.* Unlike the other titles, André's would point to *his* distinctive vision: *Paris Vu par André Kertész* (Paris Seen by André Kertész).

Its frontispiece suggests that ambition. Taken during André's first days in Paris, it surveys the fishermen who have planted themselves on ramparts along the Seine. Their poles jut over a rain-swollen river. Paris comes across as a tranquil place where folks go fishing for their dinner. The photograph serves as a metaphor for André's method. As one journalist friend put it, André was "a *flâneur* [a stroller attuned to his surroundings] who fishes for photographs. Instead of running to find them, he waits patiently for them to bite."[49] Graphically, the frontispiece is useful too: The rampart's triangular stairways double as arrows pointing to the title page opposite.

André's publisher and editor René Wittmann oversaw the book's layout. But André had a strong voice in the picture selection, arrangement, and sequencing. Each double-page spread is a unit, with one image amplifying another and engaging in a dynamic of form. Atget's, Krull's, and Brassaï's books all feature one image per page with consistent formatting. Taking lessons from *Vu*, André's combines images with various formats and sizes, some of which bleed off the page.

In another innovation, *Paris Vu* unfolds thematically. It's both a suite of short photo essays and a metaphorical narrative about André as a solitary wanderer in the City of Light. More water images follow the frontispiece, some of the Seine and others of rainy-day scenes. Then come hushed corners of the city by night. Clochards sprawl on benches or sidewalks, clutching their bottles. Park chairs cast slatted and looping shadows. Toward the end of the book, Paris becomes a city of stone, iron, and reinforced concrete. Obliques and plunging angles are everywhere. People are rare. When they appear, they're daydreamers and loners.

While the photographs in *Paris Vu* are those of a hawk-eyed outsider, the book's preface and captions are by the consummate insider Pierre Mac Orlan. André himself chose and paid Mac Orlan. Invoking his theory of the social fantastic, the writer perceives a phantasmagorical strangeness in André's images. Manifesting "the disquiet of a street fantastic, more aligned with Central European tastes," they "interpret the secret elements of light and shadow so that others draw novelistic situations from them."[50] With this concept in mind, Mac Orlan's captions treat the images as so many portals to the literary imagination. They allude to a detective novel, a nursery rhyme, the suicide of the nineteenth-century poet Gérard de Nerval, and a tale about Mimi Pinson (a stock fictional character in French operettas and songs) entertaining an equally fictitious "little hunchbacked shoemaker named Gilles."[51]

The critical response to *Paris Vu* was muted, sometimes critical. The author and photographer Marcel Natkin, for one, wrote to André to object that "despite the crisis, Paris is not peopled only by tramps and unemployed workers." A better title, Natkin snorted, would be "misery in Paris."[52] Sales were sluggish. *Paris Vu* was remaindered. By 1934, a poetic interpretation of Paris felt anachronistic.

**André's images** had always been interpretations of his subjective experience. But now, shutting his eyes to his every interest except financial, he did what he had to do to flow with the times and get work: He joined the photographic section of the Association of Revolutionary Writers and Artists (AEAR). Operating under the aegis of the Communist Party, AEAR had mobilized more than five hundred photographers, artists, and writers to manifest their support of proletarian struggle. Everyone belonged: Man Ray, Lotar, Krull, Brassaï, even Rogi. While André was all for working people, he had no itch to participate in proletarian struggle or undertake reporting hard news. In a tactic that made little sense except as an indication that he felt embarrassed about violating his own principles, he signed up as Jean Dupont, the French equivalent of John Doe.[53]

That June, AEAR presented *Documents de la Vie Sociale* at the Galerie de la Pléiade, the city's only gallery devoted exclusively to photography. The exhibition underscored the organization's rejection of avant-garde aesthetics and embrace of politicized practice. It comprised three sections: art photographs co-opted for political purposes (André's among them); documentation of anti-fascist struggles; and an album of photographs of the 1871 populist insurrection known as the Paris Commune. André had unearthed the album at a flea market and loaned it for the occasion.

On the heels of that exhibition came Bastille Day. That morning, French Communists, Socialists, radicals, and trade unionists packed a stadium in Montrouge, just south of Paris. Speakers vowed allegiance to the Popular Front, a coalition of Communists and leftists sanctioned by Moscow and sworn to defend the nation against Fascist aggression. André spent the morning photographing at the stadium and that afternoon on the streets of working-class eastern Paris. There a sea of militants flowed from the Place de la Bastille to the Place de la Nation, fists clenched, red flags and tricolors streaming. They demanded bread, peace, liberty, and a Popular Front platform in the elections scheduled for the following spring. Meanwhile, French Fascists marched along their own *via sacra*, the Champs-Elysées, stiffening their arms in the Nazi salute.

André sold his pictures to publications like *Regards*, a Communist-friendly clone of *Vu*, and for posters for the Popular Front. Many other photographers happily threw themselves into such work. André, for his part, considered such publications "stupidly doctrinaire."[54]

That fall, he accepted a more congenial assignment to photograph the Hungarian thermal baths. He and Elizabeth traveled to Budapest, where they stayed for two months with Imre and Gréti, who were now married. Judging by André's family snapshots, that winter was a respite. He photographed family and friends with a feeling of warmth like in the old days. They sit laughing in cafés or chatting in rooms decorated with Christmas trees, their tables cluttered with cake plates, wineglasses, and cigarette packs. Tihanyi was in Budapest and sometimes joined them.

Back in France that spring, André submitted his first assignment for *Vu* in nine months. It introduced a novel process for printing wallpaper with rollers, hardly the stuff of thrilling reportage. April also marked his final appearance on the cover. *Vu*'s art director was now a debonair twenty-three-year-old from Kiev named Alexander Liberman. His mother was one of Vogel's mistresses.[55] Poised with scissors over his photographers' prints, Liberman was putting together avant-garde photomontages about Germany's Nazification and France's political strife. That April, he used a photograph that André took in his early months in Paris showing two lightning bolts hitting the Eiffel Tower. Liberman added a close-up of a fighter plane and the words "GERMAN AIR STRIKE." What once conveyed excitement now portended terror.

Displeased as he must have been with this use of his photograph, André needed the money. His monthly income was averaging 1,300 francs, minus professional expenses of up to 500 francs.[56] Five years earlier, he had sometimes earned more than 10,000 francs monthly. Now it was only thanks to Elizabeth that the couple could make ends meet.

Elizabeth must have arrived in France hoping for success as an artist. Her closest friends were creating, exhibiting, and selling their work. André had made it in Paris. She was a graduate of the esteemed Álmos Jaschik school with some fifteen years of art-making behind her. Yet she felt discouraged by the brilliance of the art she was seeing in Paris. She was also a practical woman. So she had put aside her paints and easel and taken a job with the cosmetics company Helena Rubinstein.[57] Probably she made the connection through Rubinstein's husband, the American journalist and bookseller Edward Titus, whom André knew from the

Dôme and had photographed. Just temporary, she may have been telling herself and André.

A chagrined André would have remembered his mother, slaving away at the coffee shop to compensate for his father's shortcomings as a breadwinner. André's status as a successful photographer had sealed Elizabeth's commitment to their life together. Not long ago, he'd been "the prince of Paris," as a friend later described him.[58] Now they needed her income, and she was not above wagging her finger. When the two were really pinched, they tapped into André's inheritance from Ernesztina. He had converted the money into ten kilograms (about twenty-two pounds) of gold bars, deposited at a bank in Zurich.[59] He and Elizabeth were "scraping along," he wrote in an August letter to Jenő that received no reply. "Morally I succeed but we better not talk about the material rewards."[60]

Krull had also fallen from grace. Now living in the South of France, she had been mostly unemployed since 1933. Brassaï, however, cut a wide swath. He was publishing in *Vu*, *Vogue*, *Votre Beauté*, *Le Jardin des Modes*, and *Harper's Bazaar*, often pictures of artists and glitterati. It helped that he was an ebullient personality. "Suddenly I was in such demand," Brassaï bragged to his parents in 1935, "that it was as if I were the only reporter in Paris."[61]

Life was also improving for André's protégé Endre Friedman. Under the tutelage of his German-born girlfriend, Gerta Pohorylle, Friedman had cut his unruly mop, started shaving, and sometimes even donned a suit. Such moves earned the approval of André, who understood French snobbery and had never failed to present himself correctly. One day Friedman arrived at the Kertészes' apartment, buoyant even though he had only two francs to his name. He was wildly in love.[62]

He and Pohorylle would soon reinvent themselves as Robert Capa and Gerda Taro. Friedman's pseudonym derived from the name of the American film director Frank Capra and from *cápa*, the Hungarian word for "shark." This name change allowed Taro to sell her boyfriend's pictures as those of the American celebrity photographer Robert Capa—not the Hungarian loser Endre Friedman. Vogel, for one, found the whole business absurd. Once, in Geneva, he watched Friedman photograph the police roughing up a journalist. Not long after that, he was offered those photographs, signed "Robert Capa." The editor snorted: "This is all very interesting about Robert Capa, but please advise the ridiculous boy Friedmann, who goes around shooting pictures in a dirty leather jacket, to report to my office at nine o'clock tomorrow morning."[63] Vogel purchased the pictures.

Jews in Hungary, Hungarians in France, and later Central Europeans in the United States and travelers everywhere, both Capa and André were perennial outsiders who embellished anecdotes about their own lives. Friedman invented a fantasy self named Robert Capa; André embroidered on the facts of his life. Their colleague Burt Glinn used to laugh when he was asked about some Capa episode: "Do you want to know the truth or the Hungarian Empire version?"[64] "Life was so absurd," writes Capa's biographer, "what did it matter if he changed a few details?"[65] By all evidence, André agreed.

**In a crowning event** for photography as modern art, an international exhibition opened in January 1936 at the Musée des Arts Décoratifs, a museum housed in a wing of the Louvre. Photographs by Man Ray, Moholy-Nagy, Brassaï, André, and scores of others—some 1,500 pictures in all—had made it into one of the world's most prestigious art venues. The chief curator, Charles Peignot, had sought work from André early on. But it took two letters to coax him into delivering his prints. Maybe he was still sore about the book deal he'd scrubbed nearly five years earlier because of Peignot's lowball offer. Maybe he was too depressed. André took no remarkable photographs in 1935. In a review of *Paris Vu* in *La Nouvelle Revue Française*, Eugène Dabit lamented that "Today perhaps one pays less attention to his work. That's a real mistake."[66] But so it was.

Then one day André took a call from Alexandre Garai, who headed the Paris office of the Keystone Press Agency. Keystone was the brainchild of Alexandre's brother, a tough little Hungarian named Bernát Garai. Founded in London in 1924, the agency had become a big player in the fiercely competitive world of hard news, operating out of London, Paris, Berlin, and New York. Alexandre inquired: Might André be interested in working for Keystone in New York? He proposed that André handle reportage and fashion. It had not escaped André's attention that celebrity portraiture and fashion photography could be very lucrative. Edward Steichen, who worked for American *Vogue* and *Vanity Fair* and had star billing in Peignot's exhibition, ranked as the world's highest-paid photographer.

Undecided about the offer, André, as usual, sought Imre's advice. His brother reported that Hungarians genuflected at the mention of Keystone. However, Imre cautioned, "I am incapable of assessing the reality of a photo factory like that with all of its commercial brutality and nastiness, and even if I were capable that would in no way change the situation, which is above all and imperatively a question of making money." Imre ventured some alternatives. Don't hide behind modesty, he counseled André. Follow the money. Why not do sequels to *Paris Vu*? Imagine *New York Seen by André Kertész*! Or *Chicago*. Why not contact Charlie Chaplin to see if the actor-director could use André's talents? Why not move to London, where there were "high quality Hungarians"?[67] But André understood better than Imre the distance between "why not" and steady paychecks.

What was certain was that Paris was no longer working. Even André's book projects stalled. Wittmann embraced his idea of doing a book about Chartres Cathedral. But when they arrived in Chartres, they found the building's west portal covered with scaffolding. So André aborted the project. Meanwhile he had reclaimed the rights to the Distortions and was shopping that project around. But it too went nowhere.

The political and social backdrop for André's decision about Keystone's offer was the triumph of the French Popular Front in May's general election. Crowds poured into the streets to celebrate and demand that the new government use its mandate to act on behalf of the working class. Walkouts and sit-ins closed factories. Cafés rolled down their shutters. The government responded by boosting wages, passing labor reforms, and guaranteeing an annual two-week paid vacation. A paid vacation! No one could believe it. Swept up in that summer's holiday spirit, people turned the keys on their doors, packed into jalopies and trains, and took off. Half of France seemed to be frolicking by the sea or fox-trotting in the streets. Yes *but*—prudent voices sounded—we are dancing on a volcano. The rightists were seething, the stock market sank, the rich smuggled their money out of the country.

André's mood matched that summer's weather in Paris, unsettled and gray. Elizabeth hated the New York idea. André dithered. Determined to seal the deal, Bernát Garai's nephew Erney Prince, a commercial photographer who managed Keystone in New York, arrived in Paris and invited André to lunch. As André prepared to leave their apartment, Elizabeth half joked, but only half, that if he accepted Prince's offer, she would divorce him. Yet André had sold and spent nine of the ten kilograms of gold he'd inherited from Ernesztina.[68] Something had to change. As a bonus, the Keystone job would put an ocean between Rogi and him.

André's annual salary was set at $4,000 (about $90,000 in 2024 dollars), plus an 8 percent commission. Those figures agree with André's later recollection that Keystone had paid him $80 to $100 a week or $4,160 to $5,200 annually.[69] That was excellent money at a time when the median annual family income in the United States was $1,070.[70] Yet André judged the contract disadvantageous because it gave the agency exclusive rights to his work. He felt he'd made a Faustian pact, signing away his freedom. Indeed, no sooner had the ink dried than he told Imre and Gréti that his time in America would come to naught.[71] He remembered Tihanyi's dismal experience. He considered Americans vacuous and spoiled.[72] He didn't want to live in New York.

Later André would claim that he'd intended only to take a sabbatical.[73] "There was no reason [to leave Paris]," he lied. "We had everything...

But then I had lunch with Erney Prince and he talked me into coming over for a while. So I said to my wife, 'Look, why don't we go for a year, just to have a change.' It was never my intention to stay."[74] Yet his and Elizabeth's visas, fast-tracked thanks to Keystone's clout, gave them full immigrant status. They could take as much as they wanted without paying customs duties.

Prince followed their meeting with a letter instructing André about how to prepare. He wrote in English because his Hungarian was rusty. "I remind you repeatedly," he told André, "that it is very important that by the time you arrive here, you bubble something in English. Consequently, look at it that you study very seriously until you arrive here."[75] Three weeks later came another letter: "Study, study and again study the English, so that when you arrive, you could bubble already something. Further, study the fashion-photo, page the American *Vogue* and *Harper's Bazaar*... Style is needed here – so you have to concentrate yourself to it."[76] André may have scrutinized the magazines, but he ignored Prince's directive about bubbling English.

**August brought shocking news** of Eugène Dabit's death from scarlet fever during a pilgrimage to the Soviet Union. On September 7, Elizabeth and André would have been among the five thousand mourners at Père Lachaise Cemetery. Disillusioned by what he observed in the supposed workers' paradise and horrified by world events, Dabit had penned a final entry in his diary: "We are hunted, we are lost. Life, in this world, becomes unthinkable."[77] Yet that day at Père Lachaise, French Communist heavyweights speechified about Dabit's "complete moral satisfaction" in the Soviet Union.[78] Their hypocrisy surely deepened André's distaste for the ideologies reordering his life.

The most dramatic struggle was unfolding in Spain. In July, Fascist military units had launched a revolt that became a savage civil war pitting them against the democratically elected Republican government. In August, the self-rebaptized, Leica-slung Bob Capa and Gerda Taro boarded a plane in Toulouse. Vogel, also aboard, was leading *Vu*'s pack of reporters into the conflict. Coming into Barcelona, the plane crash-landed. Vogel was hospitalized, but all survived. Only weeks after that ill-fated flight, Capa would snap a frame of what appears to be a bullet-struck Spanish Loyalist soldier at the split-second of death. Later a controversy would erupt over the authenticity of *The Falling Soldier*. But not until after it became the most famous war photograph of the twentieth century.

Vogel published the image in a special thematic issue of *Vu* that took an editorial stance in support of the Spanish Republicans. That stance enraged the magazine's Swiss shareholders and sent advertising revenues tumbling. *Vu* was already running at a deficit. Vogel—to André, a "boss-comrade" and "protector of photographers"—was ousted.[79]

André's life continued unsettled that early fall. He was trying to collect an old debt from a Hungarian friend to help pay for his visa and moving expenses. He may or may not have succeeded, but he did shore up his finances by supplying baby pictures to Nestlé and illustrating a twelve-page self-promotional volume for Sainrapt et Brice, a manufacturer of glass vats used in the wine industry. When the company first approached him about doing the photographs for *Les Cathédrales du Vin*, they found his fee too steep. Financially hurting or not, André was not about to discount his work. So another photographer got the job. But Sainrapt et Brice was unhappy with the result. So they went back to André, who delivered the elegant images they were after. Grandiose, mysterious, and silent, the wine-aging room André photographed feels like a sanctum. Sainrapt et Brice knew its snobby clientele.

*Les Cathédrales du Vin* couldn't be more different from André's other last-minute publication. Two days in the country yielded enough animal pictures for Wittmann to cobble together *Nos Amies les Bêtes* (Our Friends the Animals). The book would not appear until after André left Paris. When André finally held it in his hands, he judged it overstuffed and poorly laid out.[80] He was right, it's forgettable.

He had much on his mind that September, including thousands of negatives, contact sheets, and prints. Cut into strips of six or so frames and stored in glassine envelopes, the roll-film negatives were lightweight and relatively easy to pack. So were the larger-format film negatives. But the glass-plate negatives were not. At Prince's urging, André selected a few to take to New York in hopes of publication. The rest he entrusted to his French journalist friend Jacqueline Paouillac. They agreed that Paouillac would promote and sell his images, with earnings to be split fifty-fifty. Valid for one year, their contract would automatically renew unless one of them wrote the other to break it.

Domestic tasks pressed too. Before he and Elizabeth dismantled their home, André staged a few pictures. One surveys their usually immaculate living room: rugs bunch up, pillows sag, André's freshly washed black socks dry on a cord like abacus beads. His dress pants and white shirt are draped over a chair, a wrinkled heap as surrogate self. Outside the open window, the city murmurs on. Everything is rendered in the pearly light of Paris, André's raison d'être for the past eleven years, his "*bonne copine*" (girlfriend) as he would call it.[81]

**A few days before** André and Elizabeth departed, a government official showed up at the rue du Cotentin to offer André French citizenship based on his artistic achievement. Or so André later professed, adding that a journalist acquaintance had arranged the matter. The story is suspect. Such an offer from the Popular Front government would have been highly unusual. Probably André was improving on reality. Maybe he misunderstood. He could not imagine a more gratifying offer, he would add, but he had to follow through on his contractual agreement with Keystone.[82] More relevantly, French citizenship would not have fixed his financial woes.

According to another André story, he ran into Man Ray on the day he stopped to say his goodbyes at the Dôme. When André informed the artist that he was moving to New York, Man Ray responded: "Kertész, don't go. I am an American and I can tell you it is not a place for an artist." André replied: "I wish I had spoken to you sooner—now, it's too late."[83] That story rings truer.

As a last-minute treat, André took Elizabeth to dinner at La Tour d'Argent, the restaurant famed for its elegance, pressed duck, and Kertészian views of Notre Dame and the Seine. Then they traveled to Le Havre. On October 9, they embarked on the New York–bound luxury liner the SS *Washington*. "Diplomats Among Many Notables Returning Today on *Washington*," proclaimed the *New York Herald Tribune*. The Americans aboard included the businessman Kermit Roosevelt (the former president's son), the diplomat Prescott Childs, and the Chicago investor and socialite Howard Linn. Yet for the *Herald Tribune*, it was André's presence that merited a subheading: "Photographer Sails to N.Y." The article reads: "André Kertész, Parisian photographer who will sail on the Washington today has been engaged by the Keystone View Company of New York, operating with Prince Studios in New York."[84]

André's Paris dreams had come true, until they had not. America awaited.

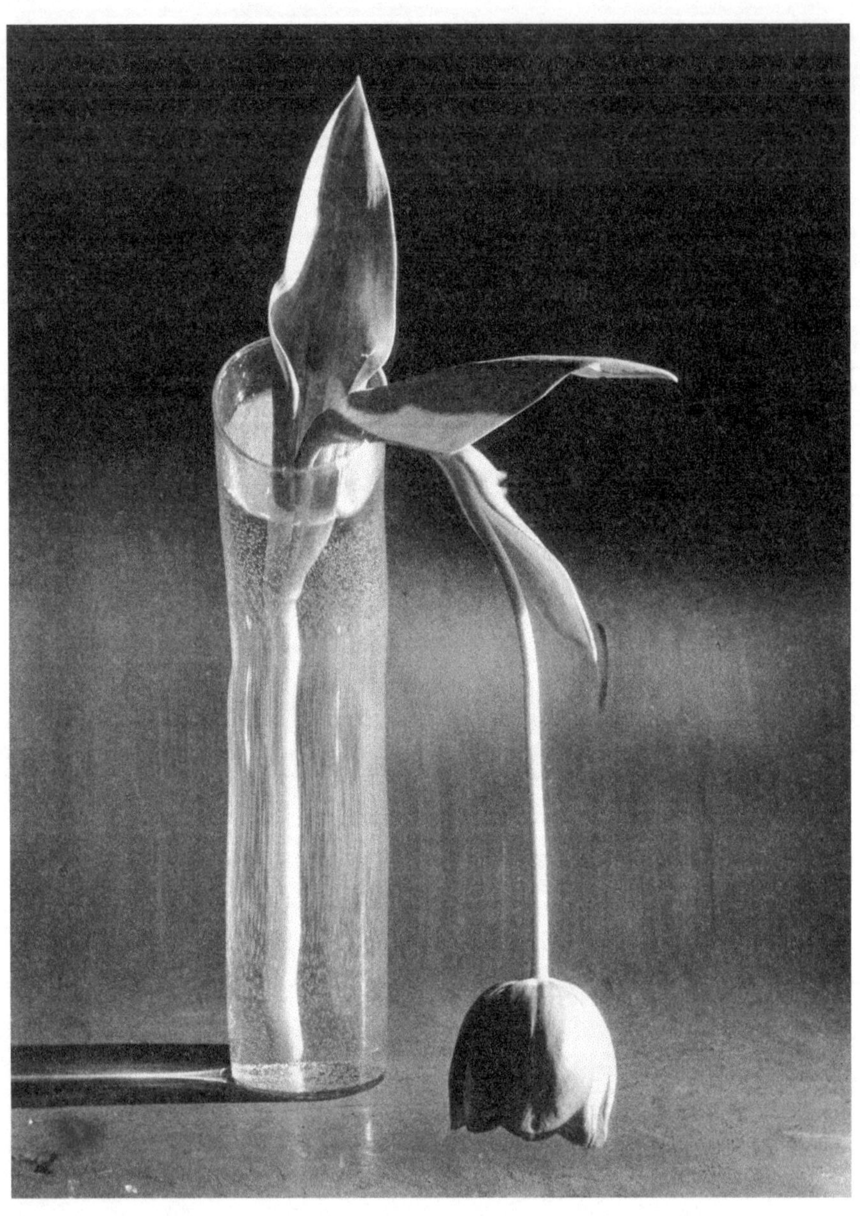

André Kertész, *Melancholic Tulip*, 1939

# 8 MELANCHOLIC TULIP, 1936–1944

**"In the beginning it was,** 'We need you.' I arrive, and find nothing."[1] André stretches the truth. What he found was a trickle of in-studio jobs for swanky retailers like Jay Thorpe, Léron Linens, and Russeks Fifth Avenue.

He was working in the Keystone studio, using a Linhof, the same professional camera he had chosen for the Distortions. That camera appears in his first self-portrait in the United States. The setting is the Kertészes' studio apartment at the Beaux-Arts, a residential hotel on East Forty-Fourth Street, one block from Keystone. Developed by a consortium of architect-investors to foster a Midtown art community, the twin Beaux-Arts buildings boasted brass- and glass-trimmed lobbies and lacquered aluminum elevator cabs in a ritzy Art Deco style. André and Elizabeth's apartment came with a Murphy bed, twice-a-day maid service, and a kitchenette. Tenants were expected to order room service or eat downstairs at the Café Bonaparte.

Preparing to take the self-portrait, André cranked open a window, attached the camera to a tripod, set the self-timer, and assumed a starting-block posture. He gripped the monorail to which the Linhof was attached, like a hunter resting his lance. His sleeves were rolled up, his necktie knotted, his watch buckled on. Visually boxed in by the window frame, a wall, and the curtain, he leans out the window as if assessing the city. Yankees worship success, André knew, and so did he.[2]

André and Elizabeth's first hours in New York had dealt a hard blow. No sooner had the SS *Washington* heaved into dock and they descended the gangplank than customs agents seized their thirty-two ounce gold bar, all that remained of André's inheritance. Their jaws dropped. Their only savings! Before leaving Paris, the couple had registered the bar with the American embassy as merchandise acquired abroad. But they had not understood that the US Gold Reserve Act of 1934 outlawed private possession of monetary gold. Now a Hungarian American contact was guiding them through an appeal.

More happily, or so it seemed, André met with the twenty-eight-year-old Harvard-trained art historian Beaumont Newhall, recently hired as a librarian at the Museum of Modern Art (MoMA), which had been founded in 1929. Newhall was organizing a pioneering historical survey of Western photography, taking cues from the recent exhibition at the Musée des Arts Décoratifs. Newhall wanted five prints from André, including two Distortions, one of which (#157) he purportedly asked André to crop to eliminate the pubic hair.

As a new hire, Newhall would have been wary about displeasing MoMA's trustees, some of whom, it seems, objected to photographs of nudes. The museum was rumored to have an unwritten rule prohibiting photographs that showed pubic hair. Yet Newhall's request shocked André, who knew nothing about American puritanism. In Europe, nudity in photographs met with shrugs; in the United States, it could cause an uproar or even bring police raids. As late as 1946, a New York photography teacher who worked with nude models would be convicted on charges of staging an indecent exhibition. The judge in that case described nude photography as "a filthy, dirty game for the purpose of getting filthy, dirty money from degenerates."[3]

Silently irate over this attack on the integrity of his photograph yet eager to ingratiate himself with MoMA, André hesitated. He rightly felt that cropping the pubic hair ruined the sculptural form of the body.[4] Yet, in the end, he delivered a pared version of #157. He also loaned Newhall his photo album of the Paris Commune and — laughably, given his pidgin French and baby-talk English — offered to help translate a text.

When Newhall's exhibition *Photography 1839–1937* opened five months later, André had an opportunity to take stock of American photography. Newhall had packed more than eight hundred pictures and objects into four floors of MoMA's West Fifty-Third Street townhouse. US- and Paris-based photographers dominated. Recent work occupied most of the wall space, especially straight photography, a purified strain of American modernism. Straight photographers believed that taking full advantage of the medium's capacity for factuality was the only honest manifestation of its nature. They also held that precisely focused imagery could lay bare their subjects' essence and richest emotional meanings.

As André prowled Newhall's exhibition, he would have paused to scrutinize prints like Ansel Adams's *Boards and Thistles* and Edward Weston's *Sand Dunes, Oceano*. Both are pinpoint sharp with finely calibrated tonalities. André agreed with the straight photographers about their medium's singularity. He shared their distaste for darkroom trickery. Yet he recoiled at their cult of technical perfection. For him, Adams and Weston were killing their subjects with irrelevant detail.[5] All that conspicuous craftsmanship but no feeling. "If a little boy learns to write his ABC's perfectly, that is beautiful calligraphy," André fumed, "but it is worthless unless he can express himself well and use technique for his own art."[6] (André may have intended "little boy" as a jab at the assumption that straight photography was manly while pictures that were less than razor-sharp had something feminine, maybe even devious, about them.)

When it came to his own photographs, André tended to apologize for too much technical perfection. Not that he was sloppy. But with a quarter century of picture-taking behind him, he had mastered the technical aspects. What mattered was his feeling for his subject. Humans are always scanning their surroundings for what's emotionally relevant. That absorbs their conscious attention. The rest goes blurry. A frozen world, he believed, is dead.

Thus André did not subscribe to straight photographers' technique of pre-visualization, a practice invented by Adams. To pre-visualize is to fully conceive of the final print before pressing the shutter button. Pre-visualization dictates the photographer's choices involving everything from composition and exposure to development and printing. Nothing should be left to the moment.

Pre-visualization is consistent with the use of a medium- or large-format camera, which allows each image to be considered and processed individually. Here, too, the straight photographers' practice ran counter to André's. Faithful to the Leica for his personal work, he stayed physically and emotionally nimble.

**After five months** at Keystone, André felt chained to the studio. With fewer jobs than he expected, he was earning less than he wanted from commissions. He pulled a long face: "They say, 'Patience, Mr. Kertész, we're preparing things for you.' I don't need preparation, only shooting. Weeks go by and I am confused. Then, they just want commercial things, not reportage."[7] André huffed that he would never have crossed the Atlantic for studio work. Maybe not. Yet his pride demanded he point the finger at Keystone rather than admit that in Paris he and Elizabeth had been surviving on crumbs. He labeled Erney Prince "*un gangster*" who had hired him only to burnish his own tarnished reputation.[8] He claimed he'd been "well and truly hoodwinked."[9]

So when Alexey Brodovitch, the art director at *Harper's Bazaar*, offered André a reportage job, he pounced. A Russian émigré via Paris, Brodovitch knew André's work from *Vu*. In New York, Brodovitch had blown the dust off William Randolph Hearst's once-staid ladies' fashion book. Applying lessons from the French avant-garde, he transformed the look of *Harper's Bazaar*, bleeding pictures to the edge of the pages and using shaped text and white space as active design elements. To keep the magazine fresh, Brodovitch and the editor in chief, Carmel Snow, were always recruiting new writers, illustrators, and photographers. "Astonish me!" Brodovitch would exhort, echoing the ballet impresario Sergei Diaghilev, for whom he had painted sets in Paris.[10]

Among the editorial duo's favorite talents was the Hungarian-born sports-turned-fashion photographer Martin Munkácsi. When Snow first hired Munkácsi for a swimwear feature in 1933, the photographer did something that was unheard-of. He took his model to a Long Island beach where he gestured for her to run while he clicked off frames with his Leica. Munkácsi's snapshot of the model in action, her beach cape streaming behind her, captivated the fashion world. After its publication, Brodovitch and Snow sought other photographers who would grab their minicams (35 millimeter cameras like the Leica), head for the real world, and instruct their models to jump, strut, or gesture. Studio photographs of haughty goddesses sculpted by light still cut a wide swath in women's magazines, especially in *Harper's Bazaar*'s archrival *Vogue*. Yet the fashion photography world was astir. André's visual playfulness and love of expressive gesture felt right for this more dynamic *Harper's Bazaar*.

His project was a feature about the luxury department store Saks Fifth Avenue after hours. As laid out by Brodovitch, "5:30: The Curtain Falls" sets the stage with a shot of Saks's dress-box toting chief executive striding out a front door: "Mr. Adam Gimbel, president, goes home."[11] So do the salespeople and office workers. Then the night owls arrive, and the after-hours toil and fun begin. One of André's shots catches some workmen peeking at price tags. Another shows a dumpy woman sweeping the ultrafashionable hair salon. Yet another zeroes in on a glove stand that looks like it's about to pinch a mannequin's derriere. It's easy to imagine raw material for a lighthearted Broadway musical.

André's photographs appeared in the magazine's April issue, deliberately miscredited to the European Picture Service, an agency to which he had sold a few prints. In fact, André had done the work solely for *Harper's Bazaar*, but that couldn't be stated because he remained under exclusive contract to Keystone.

Then André traveled on the sly to Haverford, Pennsylvania, toting his new 4 by 5 inch Graflex Speed Graphic, the standard reporter's camera. There he photographed Merloyd and Nicholas Ludington, a young sister and brother in their fall outfits, again for *Harper's Bazaar*.[12] Biding his time at that session, André let the children get a little bored. Only after they started exploring, did he set about working in earnest. He was rewarded with pictures like one of four-year-old Nicholas, all awkward grace, trying to wrestle the door handle off the family's limousine.

André relished the jobs for *Harper's Bazaar* and hated the work at Keystone. But if he fell afoul of Prince, he could lose his paycheck and have to face a cutthroat market. He was nervous.

In the mid-1930s, there were about five hundred American magazines, thirty of which had circulations of more than one million.[13] Most used drawings as illustrations. Only a handful—notably those owned by Henry Luce, William Randolph Hearst, and Condé Nast—relied on photographs. Fashion was the most lucrative specialty. At Condé Nast, Edward Steichen was earning an unprecedented annual salary of $35,000 (about $770,000 in 2024 dollars). The British photographer Cecil Beaton, another Condé Nast darling, had signed a two-year contract for $37,000 (about $810,000 in 2024 dollars).[14]

As André knew, he had little knack for, or interest in, the kind of showmanship that makes everything else secondary to the cut of a dress or allure of a hat. He was hooked on subjective reportage. But such jobs were rare, and his name wasn't bankable. Besides, the city teemed with photographers who were armed with excellent credentials, fat address books, and well-honed self-promotional skills. André lacked a network, barely spoke English, and had no gift for self-advertising. And there was no Dôme in New York.

Then what he had feared happened: Keystone got wise to his moonlighting and sued. André hired a Budapest-born Madison Avenue attorney, who filed a countersuit on his behalf, charging that the agency had withheld commissions. While he was at it, André pressured his lawyer to sue *Life* magazine and the movie company RKO. *Life* had published several Distortions-like photographs done with a fish-eye lens. RKO's sin was a scene in its recent release *A Damsel in Distress* in which Fred Astaire and crew prance around funhouse mirrors. Hopeful about the commercial potential of his distorting-mirror technique, André was fiercely possessive. With infinite patience, the attorney explained to his agitated client that he had no grounds for either lawsuit.[15]

So André would have to stake out his own place in America. He turned to the book project his brother Imre had recommended: *New York Seen by André Kertész.*

Ever since his first days in the city, André had been plumbing its mysteries. A left turn from the front door of the Beaux-Arts and a short walk took him to the blackened, foul-smelling Turtle Bay district of piers, slaughterhouses, and suppliers to the meatpacking industry. (The United Nations headquarters now stands in their place.) There he photographed people idling, sheep straggling off to be butchered, and a man peering through a chink in a wall. Parked cars line up behind the man, their bug-eye headlights peering too. Anxious though he was, André hadn't lost his visual twinkle.

A walk west from the Beaux-Arts took him to Third Avenue, where he was intrigued by the El (elevated railway) running north and south from the Bronx to South Ferry. He trained his lens on its steel webwork, shadow patterns on the pavement, and posters for the likes of Allen's Foot-Ease and Dr. Lyon's Tooth Powder. Occasionally, he invested a nickel and rode a local, shooting from the vantage points the El afforded its riders.

More often he walked. On Eighth Street, he watched a workman install a ventilator fan over the door of a coffee shop. The man's right arm emerged between two blades of the fan, like a metallic flower, as he tightened some screws. André tried different angles. One of his frames, cropped in the darkroom, isolates the arm and fan, making this portent of dismemberment darkly witty.[16]

On another ramble, André clapped his eyes on a cotton-ball cloud hovering near one of the towers of Rockefeller Center. Emblematic of capitalism, modernity, and American power, the skyscraper city loomed before him, faceless and cold. André was touched by the little cloud floating in its midst. "Oh, my God," he thought. "This cloud is lost."[17] He knew a metaphor when he saw one.

His photograph, a vertical, visually hews off a section of the tower. Next to it is a smaller section of sky, empty except for that cloud. Anthropomorphized and sentimentalized by its children's book title, *Lost Cloud* is also formally sophisticated and conceptually elegant. Compressing time, place, and feeling, André pins down a state of mind. In Paris, the gatekeepers of the photography world were apt to show up at the Dôme or Select, sipping a café crème at the next table. In New York, they reigned from faceless towers like this one.[18] Where was the creative community he sorely needed? The loss of café culture, vital to his career in France, was daunting.

André kept mining his contacts. His efforts yielded scattered assignments for *Look*, *House & Garden*, and *Town & Country*, which sent him to cover a horse show on Long Island and a collection of marine artifacts owned by a junior Vanderbilt in Newport. It was probably in transit for one such assignment that André found himself at the Poughkeepsie railroad station. Standing on the overpass and looking down at the platform, he took a photograph that's a tour de force of rigorous construction and poetic suggestion.

*Poughkeepsie* frames travelers awaiting their train in the shadow of stairs zigzagging down to the tracks. Some stand together. Yet no one interacts with anyone else. Among them is a man in white. Thanks to the optics of André's beloved Hugo Meyer Satz Plasmat lens, the man appears to be hanging on to the platform like a carnival-goer on the side of a Gravitron ride. The tracks evoke the staccato rhythms of the train ride to come; the man's stance anticipates its speed and its force. The travelers' solitude could be André's own but also perhaps the anticipation.[19] Maybe *Lost Cloud* was not the whole story.

**That August,** a grieving Robert Capa arrived in New York. Only weeks earlier, Gerda Taro had been fatally hit by a tank in Spain. Now Capa was finalizing plans for a book dedicated to the woman he loved. Published by Covici-Friede, it would marry his and Taro's most powerful photographs of the Spanish Civil War, plus those of their friend David Seymour (known as Chim). Holed up at the Hotel Bedford on East Fortieth Street, Capa struggled with the captions. He appealed to André to handle the layout and final image selection. For days, the two huddled over the coffee table in Capa's hotel room, prints strewn everywhere.[20]

Once again, André came through for his protégé, knitting picture to picture. Attentive to placement, sequencing, and shifts in scale, he treated each double-page spread as a scene. Published in 1938, *Death in the Making* would become the iconic photo book of the Spanish Civil War and seal Capa's reputation as the era's leading war photographer.

Moreover, *Life* magazine was giving Capa a contract based on his work in Spain. His first assignment was a feature about Stillman's Gym, a gloomy Eighth Avenue spot reeking of sweat and cigar smoke, famous as a training ground for prizefighters. But Capa blew the job because he'd never mastered the flash. So once again he ran to André, who accompanied him back to Stillman's and taught him what to do. *Life* accepted but did not publish his second submission.[21] Then Capa left for China to cover the Sino-Japanese War.

André had no such high-flying assignments. He and Elizabeth had depleted their savings. The gold bar had been melted, the metal sold, and a check for $1,078 delivered to the couple and spent. At the end of July 1937, André had $605 in the bank. Two months later, his balance had sunk to $25. He was paying his attorney's $100 retainer in installments. On October 21, his bank book read $1.00.[22] Combing the streets for pictures, André had seen plenty of hardscrabble living, shockingly at odds with the doings of the flossy set showcased in the magazines for which he freelanced. Being poor in Paris made you a poet; being poor in New York made you a loser.

Unable to afford the Café Bonaparte, André and Elizabeth ate, sparingly, in Third Avenue diners and coffee shops. New Yorkers would have perceived two correctly dressed middle-aged foreigners. Elizabeth was a "quaint-looking girl" who could pass for the British actress Elsa Lanchester, one observed.[23] André was skinny and fit, six inches taller than she. Those who overheard them ordering dinner would have found her English accented yet decent, his woolly and barely comprehensible. With each other, they spoke a strange tongue, as Americans perceived it, in conversations interrupted by the rattling of dishes and shriek of metal on metal each time a train passed on the El. Money—always money—lay heavy on their minds.

It was probably Alexey Brodovitch who introduced André to Robert L. Leslie, the owner of an innovative typesetting shop. Leslie's clients—art directors, designers, production staffers, and other insiders in the print and advertising worlds—were the very people André needed to know and impress. His meeting with Leslie went well, yielding plans for an exhibition in an area off his shop that Leslie dignified as the PM Galleries.

Thus it was that one evening that early December, André stood in the makeshift gallery, smiling as he greeted visitors in his soft, lilting voice. Elizabeth hovered beside him, while Leslie worked the room. On its walls hung sixty photographs mounted on rag board and arranged salon style. There were fashion shots, product work, landscapes, portraits, and still lifes. Some of the labels (like *For Town & Country*) drew attention to André's credentials as a magazine photographer. The nude he had cropped for MoMA, *Distortion #157*, hung nearby, the model's pubic hair restored. Determined to promote his distortion technique as a tool for admen, André had included two close-ups of warped packs of Camels.

His gambit proved modestly successful. CBS ordered photographs of bees on flowers for a brochure. *House & Garden* wanted babies' nurseries and artisanal workshops. *Vogue*'s art director, Mehemed Fehmy Agha, hired André to photograph luggage, scenes from plays, and Social Register types at leisure.

The Agha connection, especially, held promise. Like Brodovitch, the monocled Ukrainian-born Turk had swept away his magazine's prim, album-like ways and set pictures and type in motion. Agha conceived of each feature as a creative unit with photographs, not text, at its core. *Harper's Bazaar* whipped up more graphic excitement and commanded more attention by folding literary fiction into its froth. But when it came to glamour and ad revenue, *Vogue* reigned.

Two weeks after André's show closed, *Vogue* announced that its lead photographer, Edward Steichen, was quitting and heading to Connecticut to grow delphiniums. Agha turned to Cecil Beaton, George Hoyningen-Huene, Horst P. Horst, and Toni Frissell for the magazine's splashiest features. André's jobs multiplied too. But some were uncredited, and many were tedious. Even faithful readers of *Vogue* could easily miss the evidence that André Kertész existed. All the same, he handled his new assignments with quiet authority. As *Vogue*'s features editor would later observe: "He never underlines, he never puts anything in italics or adds exclamation points."[24] She might have added that underlining, italics, and exclamation points sell magazines. When it came to the commercial world, the artless look of André's work did not serve him well.

Unlike in France, André now had to take one kind of photograph to make a living and a different kind to please himself. Few people showed interest in the images that meant the most to him. But then he met Arnold Gingrich, the editor of *Coronet*. Their connection was brokered by a friend of André's from the old days at the Dôme, the saucy-tongued American writer, photographer, and once-expat Manuel Komroff.

The hand-size *Coronet* presented itself as a mass-market treasury of opinion, history, entertainment, short stories, and art. Its publisher, David A. Smart, also owned the men's monthly *Esquire*. That magazine was proving so lucrative that Smart had risked starting *Coronet*. As Gingrich explained, *Coronet* was meant "to give the public what it ought to like, whether it liked it or not, and if it didn't make money that was all right too."[25] As it turned out, the public did like it: *Coronet* was raking in a big readership and a big profit.

The twin tent poles of *Coronet*'s art coverage were modern photographs and Old Master paintings. Finding reproductions of paintings was easy, but Smart and Gingrich knew little about photography. Then someone told them that the best camera art came from Budapest. So Smart dispatched Gingrich to Hungary. He returned with stacks of prints by so-called Hungarian-style photographers, who dwelt on an aestheticized and nostalgic version of Magyar identity. In issue after issue, *Coronet* trotted out their pictures. "And perhaps mention should be made, if only defensively, of the perennial pastorals by Hungarian photographers, because we do seem to run to quantity in them," Gingrich editorialized. "But can we help it if the best photographs [are] by Hungarians?"[26]

For once, André's Hungarianness proved useful. He debuted in *Coronet* in May 1938 with half a dozen pictures, mostly from Paris. Gingrich wanted more. So André gave him ninety-eight prints. The editor kept almost half.

*Coronet* paid poorly. The quality of the reproductions was mediocre. Gingrich leaned toward the saccharine. He was slow to mete out André's pictures. Yet André was gratified that his real work was wanted. When a picture did appear, *Coronet* served it up alone on a page to a robust national audience.

Meanwhile, André was campaigning to get the Distortions published and exhibited and to commercialize the process. One tactic was to seek the blessing of the septuagenarian photographer and gallerist Alfred Stieglitz. André considered the American a photographer in the most profound sense – the first American, in his view, with "the photographic feeling."[27] Like André, Stieglitz understood that photographs can communicate their maker's inner states and that quality does not depend on subject matter. Inspired by classical music, Stieglitz had photographed clouds as surrogates for his feelings. (That analogy with music may have prompted André's description of the Distortions as "a symphony of mirrors."[28]) Surely Stieglitz would appreciate and promote the Distortions. So André leaned on Gyula Zilzer, his artist friend from Budapest and Paris, who was now working as a Hollywood set designer and knew the famous photographer.

At their meeting, Stieglitz looked through André's prints, then, speaking in French, advised him: Show them once, then put them away. People will imitate you. Then the fad will pass.[29] André explained that the Distortions were a high form of art that required great skill. To his enormous disappointment, Stieglitz dismissed them as a novelty.

While Stieglitz was the faded paterfamilias of American fine-art photography, the monthly *Popular Photography* showed the medium's hobbyist face. That March, the magazine published a feature about the Distortions. Its author, Gray Strider, would have seen the PM Galleries show. Keeping in mind his mostly male readership, Strider flags the series' "startlingly aphrodisiac" effect and raves about how André had long "kept Europe excited with his exotic pictures" – apparently intending "exotic" as in "exotic dancer." He goes on to report that the Distortions had sold briskly in Europe, an inaccuracy that probably came from André. But the writer was on his own when he wrongly asserted that André's "weird studies" had introduced Surrealism into photography.[30]

Americans' understanding of Surrealism was different from that of the French. André Breton's Surrealist circle in Paris believed that to eroticize and fetishize the female body was to liberate the creative potential of the unconscious. A Surrealist could see the Distortions as exemplary of Breton's tenet that the external world of facts and the internal world of feeling are "communicating vessels." In the United States, however, the movement's ideology barely registered, except perhaps as a fun version of Freudian psychology. A wildly popular 1936–1937 exhibition at MoMA titled *Fantastic Art, Dada, Surrealism* had crystallized the idea of Surrealism as zany entertainment with the painter Salvador Dalí as its greatest star. One *New York Times* critic pronounced the exhibition "perhaps the most incredibly mad divertissement the town has ever seen." *The Literary Digest* dubbed the Surrealists the "Marx Brothers of the art world."[31]

In speaking with Strider, André went along with the writer's view of Surrealism, dismissing it as "any craziness in art."[32] Indifferent to Surrealist ideology, he was driving for the commercialization of his distortion technique – the ticket, he hoped, to big earnings.

M. F. Agha concurred that Surrealist practices had marketing and editorial potential. In a speech to the Advertising Club of New York, he likened Surrealism's penchant for "eye-catching, story-telling, bewildering devices" to those of "many a sound advertising campaign."[33] André took Agha's opinion as an invitation to wangle *Vogue* assignments. Riding on Dalí's coattails, he photographed a distorting-mirror reflection of an alarm clock, his version of the melting watches in Dalí's painting *The Persistence of Memory*. Agha used the picture for the "Vogue's-Eye View" teaser page of its May 1938 issue with time as its theme.[34]

With the cognoscenti, André took a more benevolent view of perceptions of his work as Surrealist. His Surrealism came naturally, he would say, not out of allegiance to any group or ideology. But even such mild statements did André no favors with art photographers and critics who curled their lips at the European avant-garde. In a 1932 review of a group show of modern European photography (André's included) at Julien Levy's Madison Avenue gallery, a *New York Times* critic had spelled out what many took as gospel. The critic noted American photographers' proclivity for "a minimum of distortion, 'arrangement,' and subjective expression." Europeans, by contrast, relied on "tricks of the conjurer" like photomontage, double exposure, symbolic abstraction, and unconventional camera angles.[35] The foreigners, the critic insinuated, were manipulative.

The influential Ansel Adams also swatted at European work, contrasting his own photographs, devoid of "the least smell of trickery," with "the shallow fashions of surface-contemporaneous thought."[36] Adams described the work of László Moholy-Nagy—the epitome of European experimentalism—as "the greatest perversion of serious photography that has ever come to my attention."[37]

Indeed, Americans tended to treat the Atlantic Ocean as a cultural barricade. Such isolationism could "flourish because the number of gifted photographers was so large, their work so distinguished, and their pictures so omnipresent that the atmosphere of an American renaissance militated against heterodoxy," explains the cultural historian John Raeburn.[38] Native photography *was* often dazzling. So much so that it blinded many to foreign-accented photographs like André's. Even the foreign-born Agha shared the inclination to acclaim American singularity. Photography might just be "this elusive thing—A Real American Native Art," he mused. The nation's ebullient popular culture was spawning "bigger and better photographers," Agha believed, their work "a monument to the American Supremacy in the field of Modern Photography."[39] Adams agreed: "America has brought forth superior photography, photography is, in fact, a decisive American art."[40]

Among leading US photographers, Walker Evans won André's approval. That October, André saw *American Photographs*, an exhibition at MoMA that elevated Evans to the first rank of observers of the American scene. Unlike André, Evans fixed a cold hard stare on the world. Unlike André, he opted for frontality, spatial clarity, and vivid detail. Yet their interests overlapped. Movie posters, Coney Island, barbershops, and rural Alabama figure in the American's repertoire; street posters, Luna Park, popular cafés, and rural Europe in the Hungarian's. The two shared a fascination with vernacular objects and ordinary lives. Evans's *American Photographs* locates the most vital repositories of American culture outside its cities. That would have made sense to André, who had come up as a photographer in a milieu that equated Hungarianness with rural culture and whose images of "*la France profonde*" (deep France) converge on the fundamentals of Gallic identity.

**Elizabeth, for her part,** had teamed up with a thirty-five-year-old chemist of Hungarian, French, and German descent and former colleague at Helena Rubinstein in Paris. Frank Tamás was lured to New York by a firm that intended to hire him. When that deal fell through, Tamás established Cosmia Laboratories to create and package fragrances under others' brand names. Elizabeth's business savvy, knowledge of cosmetics, and facility with languages made her the right partner. Yet few people were buying perfume during the Depression. Her attempts to secure investors foundered. Probably she was working other jobs here and there. In any case, she was bringing in little money.

After Tamás exhausted his savings, he sometimes stayed with the Kertészes, adding to André's financial and emotional stress. Besides paying rent at the Beaux-Arts, André was shelling out for a darkroom, office, and studio that he shared with D. Richard Statile, a photographer he'd met at Keystone. Statile's space was on West Forty-Fourth Street near Sixth Avenue, a location well suited to the professional image André wanted to project.

It was there that he developed and printed. Or tried to: He had been experiencing debilitating episodes of dizziness, most intensely in the darkroom. With his trays set up and the odor of acetic acid wafting through the air, he would click on the red safelight and flip off the light. Then the room would start spinning. André was diagnosed with Ménière's disease, a progressive disorder of the inner ear that can bring vertigo, tinnitus, nausea, trouble with balance, and hearing loss.[41] Stress is believed to contribute to its onset. Indeed, André's first bouts of dizziness dated to 1933, the year he lost the German market and consequently much of his income. The disorder itself can fuel more upset, setting up a spiral of anxiety and depression.[42]

Now a doctor ordered André to stay out of the darkroom. But he ignored the instruction and hid his condition from all but Elizabeth.[43] What if word got out? What if he became dizzy while on assignment?

Art directors might shun him. Disaster! His episodes of vertigo and nausea multiplied.

It didn't help that he and Elizabeth couldn't always afford enough food. Already thin, André lost weight. He slept little. He was anemic. He was getting liver injections, possibly to treat a vitamin B12 deficiency. Someone reported to Imre that his brother and sister-in-law had been "starving for months" and "deteriorating to the extremes."[44]

It was in that state that André roamed New York, photographing as much with his nerves as with his heart. Other foreigners were awed by the city's skyscrapers, amused by its Automats, and wowed by its up-to-date plumbing. André was not. At a Chinese market on Fourteenth Street, he aimed his lens at plucked geese heaped on a barrel. At a gritty railroad siding, he recorded billowing smoke and a sinister figure staring him down.

Desperate for a way out, André and Elizabeth chewed over the idea of returning to France or even of André freelancing in Spain. Maybe he could pick up with the Spanish Civil War where he'd left off in World War I.[45] That a forty-four-year-old in poor health would consider traveling to war-torn Spain speaks of the intensity of André's desire to escape New York and find meaningful work. That a Jew would consider moving from the United States to Europe in 1938 suggests a willful disregard for political realities.

Slowly, those realities did register. André learned that Imre had lost his job because of Hungary's new laws curtailing Jewish participation in commercial life. Imre's Lutheran faith didn't matter; the Hungarian government was defining Judaism in racial terms. Required to prove that he was not "foreign seepage" to retain his Hungarian passport, André's brother was scouring family records for obscure and probably nonexistent documents like their grandfathers' tax receipts. All he could do in this tragicomic situation, Imre confided, was keep his "soul...in great balance."[46]

On September 30, 1938, the Western European powers agreed to cede Czechoslovakia's Sudetenland to the Reich. Hitler's war machine was gearing up. A few days later, Bob Capa's younger brother, Cornell, who lived in New York, reported to Bob, who remained in China: "The Kertészes are struggling, but considering the situation in Europe, they are relatively well. At the moment even Szivacs [Elizabeth] is glad to be over here, which is saying a lot."[47]

A letter from Imre confirmed the wisdom of staying in America: "Human existences are reduced to zero on this contemptible, vile continent, smeared with the thin veneer of culture. I don't know what tomorrow will bring, and I don't know if there will be a tomorrow here at all."[48] It brought Kristallnacht, a spasm of anti-Semitic violence orchestrated by the Nazis as a pretext for sending tens of thousands of German Jews to concentration camps. Imre marveled at "how right it was for the two of you to leave Europe." France too, he pointed out, had experienced "tremendous convulsions and anxieties."[49] Now, he pressed, get your citizenship. André and Elizabeth had applied for naturalization a year after arriving in the United States but never followed up. Even with Imre's prodding, they stalled.

Their immediate problem was money. André had always been one to accept invitations, drop by to say hello, give people prints. Someone would introduce him to someone else, friendships would develop, jobs would materialize. In New York, he'd met many people. Yet he felt that his relationships with Americans rarely went beyond hollow jocularity.[50] His only real American friends were Statile and a Swiss-born photographer and naturalized citizen named Rudolf Hoffmann (no relation to André's family on his mother's side), with whom he spoke French. Tellingly, he was taking very few portraits.

Then a colleague introduced him to a go-getter agent named Wick Miller. For a 50 percent cut, Miller proposed to rev up André's commercial career. André said okay, and Miller delivered. André's favorite and most frequent new client was Isadora Bennett, a leading publicity agent for modern dance. His first subjects for Bennett were Martha Graham Dance Company and the Ballet Theatre (today the American Ballet Theatre), whose first season lay just ahead.

That fall the dancers were keeping hectic rehearsal schedules that left little time for photo shoots. André pulled off several quick sessions on the roof of Radio City Music Hall. Then some members of the Ballet Theatre did a benefit performance in the rooftop playground of a children's aid society in Hell's Kitchen, a shabby neighborhood on the West Side.[51] André's most memorable image from that event eternalizes four leaping tulle-skirted ballerinas, their bat-like shadows imprinting the roof. Behind them is a grungy wall made charming by its 1920s picture book–style mural depicting a family at the seashore. Most children who lived in Hell's Kitchen could only imagine a day by the sea. Yet they had their tar-beach roof and, for an hour or two, the fairy-princess ballerinas. In André's picture, the children bunch up stage left, their body language speaking of adoration and awe. André delighted in the mix of "art, glamour and reality" that he had captured.[52]

Another day, he claimed, he was arranging his beat-up lights in a theater or rehearsal space when he heard a man shout: "Stop, you have no right to put any lights here. You are not in the union." The two went back and forth until André hurled: "This is my daily work, my daily bread. You eat, I want to eat, too." But he lost the dispute.[53] So went André's impossible-to-verify story, likely a self-pitying mistelling of some real exchange.

Over the next three years, André took hundreds of pictures of dancers, work that more often roused his good spirits. Meanwhile, Miller was prospecting corporations, including Goodyear Tire and Rubber, Scott Paper, and the Hartford Steam Boiler and Inspection Company. Aware that most people drew a blank at his client's name, the agent churned out information sheets, branding André a storyteller who interpreted subjects with what "we lump under the term feeling." André was bored with his work in America, Miller explained, "as his line is much more to look into the social aspects of things... than just photographing nice things."[54] But the agent's efforts reaped only jobs involving "nice things," many of them in the upper Midwest. Like traveling salesmen, he and Miller lugged cases of film and equipment back and forth by train to Michigan, Illinois, and Ohio.

André's New York book still waited in the wings. When time allowed, he made the rounds of publishers, dummy in hand. Surely there was room in America for a photographic free spirit. Yet he came away with rejection after rejection. One editor objected to his feeling for the sweetness of life: "You are too human, Kertész, sorry, make it brutal."[55] That story, perhaps not quite true, also became part of his well-practiced repertoire.

André's proclivity for bending the truth had become more pronounced as he suffered setback after setback. It meets the definition of the psychiatric syndrome called pseudologia fantastica. People with this condition tell stories that interweave fact and fantasy. Plausible, consistent, and often colorful, such stories have no obvious purpose. They bring their tellers few objective benefits. Pseudologues are emotionally needy, not calculating. By casting themselves as victims or heroes, they stand to rouse listeners' sympathy or admiration and thus soothe their own egos. Psychiatrists distinguish pseudologia fantastica from false memory, delusion, and basic lying. (Some equate it with mythomania.) Pseudologues may or may not believe everything they themselves say, one psychiatric study reports, but they do not lose touch with reality.[56]

After two and a half years in New York, André felt betrayed, depressed, and humiliated. Exaggerating stories about Americans' failings would have salved his emotional wounds. So would self-mythologizing and taking photographs as poetic expressions of what he wouldn't or couldn't say outright.

**On February 10, 1939,** a wet and gloomy Friday, André contemplated a drooping Darwin hybrid tulip. Forcing that variety into colorful early tokens of spring was a fad in the 1930s.[57] André's subject may have been partly inspired by his distaste for the dull close-ups of flowers in *House & Garden*, a magazine he freelanced for but found unimpressive. His photograph also demonstrated, once again, the expressive potential of the distortion technique.

André placed the tulip in a glass bud vase filled with water and positioned it in front of seamless background paper. He then set up a photoflood, giving the blossom some glamour. Peering into his camera's ground-glass viewfinder, he framed not the flower but its distorted reflection. The stem visually undulated in the water, it too bending light. André chose a large aperture to achieve a shallow depth of field. Lastly, he fine-tuned his camera's position vis-à-vis the mirror, adjusting the framing, orchestrating verticals and horizontals, sharpness and blur. Thanks to the mirror's diffuse reflections, he managed contrasting viewing angles at the top and bottom of the vase as if in a Cubist still life. He pressed his shutter release. He would title the work *Melancholic Tulip*.[58]

The slumping blossom is André's surrogate self. Tulips figure prominently in Hungarian folk culture. Taking the picture would have stirred memories of tulips in the handicraft of his youth: tulips carved into Magyar trunks, baked into Magyar tiles, embroidered on Magyar tablecloths. And flowers are classic memento mori, symbolic reminders of the transient nature of all earthly things. André's youth had vanished. That year, he would turn forty-five.

That spring Alexander King, an editorial assistant at *Life*, wrote a brief but impassioned argument for André's greatness. Titled "Are Editors Vandals?" the article appeared in the popular monthly *Minicam* (later *Modern Photography*). King laments that André had never been able to publish any of his serious work in the United States. Why not? In King's view, American picture editors worshipped at the shrine of Hollywood-style glamour. Put more crudely: "American editors suffer from 'Glamoroids.'" As evidence of the fineness of André's work, King reproduced five photographs from his Trappist monastery series. Even "the uninitiated must be instantly stirred by the unearthly somberness of these prints," he insisted.[59] As André knew, King was no run-of-the-mill

*Life* staffer. Born Alexander Koenig in Vienna, he was an amusing bow-tied raconteur who spoke fluent Hungarian.

Among André's other contacts at *Life*, some belonged to a club called the Circle of Confusion. (Its name refers to the optical spot that shows up when the light rays from a lens are imperfectly focused.) The Circle of Confusion brought together expert users of the minicam, especially the Leica. Conventional wisdom still held that small-format cameras were unsuited for professional work because 35 millimeter negatives could not yield high-quality prints. The circle's members disputed that view. At their meetings, they kicked around ideas about the minicam and its developing technology, in which some of them were playing vital roles. André had been voted in thanks to his friend, the cofounder Manuel Komroff. Besides photo-lab owners and industry professionals from Leitz, Kodak, DuPont, and Bell Labs, his fellow members, all male, included Peter Stackpole and Alfred Eisenstaedt, both well-known staff photographers at *Life*.

Willard Morgan belonged too. A photographer, writer, and editor, and the publisher of *Leica Manual*, Morgan had been *Life*'s first contributions editor. In that role, he supplemented staff photographs with work by amateurs and freelancers. Thanks to Morgan, André had visited *Life*'s offices. The two were friendly. Morgan admired and would have published André's work. But *Life* paid outside contributors only six to eight dollars per picture. So André shunned that route to publication. He was angling for, and believed he deserved, a full-scale photo essay. Indeed, Miller had been sending out Kertész information sheets blemished by the false statement (a misunderstanding? a fib?) "Oh, By the Way, LIFE has 4 of his series—bought and paid for, which will come out soon too."[60]

André had expected *Life* to recruit him. As he knew, *Life* was modeled after *Vu*, and he had been *Vu*'s star photographer. The connection between the two was clear from *Life*'s inception. In 1931, a *Vanity Fair* editor named Clare Boothe urged her boss, Condé Nast, to create a weekly newsmagazine. Its angle, Boothe explained, would be journalism that took full advantage of photographs interpreted editorially. To get an idea of how that would work, Nast should leaf through *Vu*.[61] Condé Nast expressed interest but never committed. Three years later, Boothe met Nast's fellow mogul Henry Luce. The publisher was fishing for ideas for new publications. One of his employees had written to *Vu* to inquire about using some of its photographs.[62] Boothe's pitch to Luce proved a dual success. By 1935, she was Mrs. Henry Luce, and the newsmagazine she envisioned was speeding toward launch day. *Vu*'s influence was such that, at the height of *Life*'s glory, Henry Luce would write: "Without *Vu*, *Life* would never have seen the light of day."[63]

*Life* had first appeared on the newsstands five weeks after André's arrival in the United States. He pored over each issue. Although he saw more "humanity, warmth, intellectual depth, and literary dimension" in *Vu*, *Life* had the numbers.[64] Its circulation zoomed past a million. By 1939, *Life* was fat and self-satisfied. Each issue weighed nearly a pound.

That summer, André finally snagged an assignment. Like all freelancers, he would have begun by meeting with the picture editor, who supplied a list of shots the editors wanted and gave instructions to overshoot. André had always believed that taking few pictures, the *right* pictures, was the mark of a skilled photo reporter. But *Life* editors thought in terms of "picture supply."[65] Okay, they wanted overshooting. So André would overshoot. Equally important, he would slant his work in *Life*'s direction. The magazine demanded pictures with impact. André would do his best to override his subtle and interpretive manner and think "educate" and "entertain."

His topic was tugboat life in New York harbor. André approached the harbor as a vast machine kept in motion by the seven hundred tugs churning its waters. Turning for help to his friend and darkroom-mate Statile, an aerial and industrial photographer and freelancer at *Life*, André took five flights over the harbor that August. Working before 10:00 a.m., when the haze started thickening, he shot from a Piper Cub and, once or twice, a dirigible.

It wasn't easy to make visual sense of a heavily trafficked estuarial complex with six hundred and fifty miles of docks, shipyards, railyards, and warehouses. Wielding his Speed Graphic with a 135 millimeter Zeiss Tessar lens and an Aero 2 filter and photographing at an altitude of 1,500 to 1,800 feet, André recorded the docks and berths of the great ocean liners. On the ground, he picked his way through the salt marshes of Weehawken, New Jersey, using their rotting pilings and half-collapsed piers to carpenter semiabstractions. On the New York waterfront, he moved in on three workhorse boats thrusting their weight against the listing Italian liner SS *Rex*. Tugboats come across as vital players in a global port but also as little worlds, almost villages, unto themselves. One of André's pictures spotlights three crew members about to dig into a hearty breakfast served by a tug's cook. Another focuses on an old-timer sitting on deck, stroking a tabby and enjoying a smoke as he waits for boiler water to be loaded. Yet another shows two cabinmates winding down the day in their bunks. Newspapers litter the floor. On a stool sits a recent issue of *Life* with a swimsuit-clad actress on its cover—very André.[66]

Along the way, he took a self-portrait. Speed Graphic in hand, André lounges on the deck of a Moran diesel-powered tug, looking athletic and self-assured. One would never guess that he had been grappling with vertigo and depression. His juices were flowing. *This* was the kind of reportage that brought him alive. At the end of August, he delivered to *Life* one hundred and twenty-five pictures. The curator Weston Naef has rightly characterized the submission as "one of the most accomplished essays in the early history of American photojournalism."[67]

Five days later, America awoke to news of the Nazi invasion of Poland. Britain and France then declared war on Germany. As Europe feverishly prepared for combat, US liners rounded up citizens abroad and rushed them home, zigzagging across the Atlantic lanes to avoid capture by Nazi warships. On the New York docks, vessels belonging to belligerent nations awaited instructions from their governments or sailed home with their portholes painted gray and their lights half extinguished.

At that time of tension and disarray, it would have been tone-deaf to publish a photo essay about the routine workings of New York harbor. *Life* bombarded its readers with war-related material. André's story was killed.[68]

New York "can destroy an individual, or it can fulfill him, depending a good deal on luck," the writer E. B. White once reflected. "No one should come to New York to live unless he is willing to be lucky."[69] Was André still willing? Over the past three years, he'd made every effort, only to be mired in failure. Now he attempted to bounce back by submitting a set of ballet pictures to *Life*. It was a smart move: *Life* was interspersing lighter material among the war stories. But the ballet pictures also were rejected, on grounds that the editors couldn't figure out how to place them.

In truth, André and *Life* were a poor fit. The magazine's notoriously cold-blooded executive editor Wilson Hicks once asked rhetorically: Should *Life* impose photography on the journalist or journalism on the photographer? "To impose journalism on the photographer was the only alternative," he argued. Luce's executives thought of photographs as the nuts and bolts they needed to build "the ultimate product."[70] The "word men" – not the "picture men" – ruled.[71] That sat badly with André, who believed that photographers should take the lead in creating picture stories: "In Paris, we did not do it this way. In the *real* reportage style, you read the article and go out with your personality. Not everybody two-centing."[72]

Around that same time, the great social documentarian photographer Lewis Hine, who was also hurting financially, made his own bid to work for *Life*. The answer was no: "too much of a nonconformist."[73] As a *Life* editor once told André: "You are talking too much in your pictures."[74]

André would later try again with *Life*, submitting his reportage about the French Trappist monastery in 1942 and a witty series about New York City chimneys in 1949. Rejected and rejected.

On November 18, 1939, two months after *Life* returned his harbor essay, André donned a suit and a tie and indulged in some melodramatic self-portraiture. In the photograph he took that day, he slumps over a table. His gaze is downcast and interiorized. One hand props up a cheek, the other fingers an empty shot glass. There's a second shot glass, not that André has a drinking companion but that he has abandoned himself to alcohol and rumination. The contrast between this self-image and the one on the tug couldn't be starker. Sunlight has ceded to stage lighting, the air of spontaneity to the carefully crafted persona, the ace photographer to the lugubrious has-been.[75]

He had no choice but to keep plugging away. He sold the New York harbor pictures piecemeal and collaborated with Statile on aerial shots of timely subjects, like a navy destroyer (for *Collier's*) and the Goodyear blimp (for the stockholders' magazine of Standard Oil of New Jersey). *Town & Country* used him for odds and ends. *Vogue* kept him handy for day-in-the-life stories and children's fashions.

From time to time, he would drop in on King, *Life*'s eccentric in residence, to bellyache about how badly he was treated.[76] King was finagling to get fired, so he could draw severance pay. When *Life* cooperated, he jumped to a position as managing editor of the magazine *Stage*. The driving force behind *Stage* was a Hungarian who had modeled the monthly after *Színházi Élet*, the performing-arts magazine he had founded in turn-of-the-century Budapest. André knew him, of course, from his Angelo days when he sometimes worked for *Színházi Élet*. With King running *Stage*, André was published in every issue. But King lasted only a year.

Thanks to Miller, André was still putting his shoulder to dull industrial assignments and feature stories, like one for *The American Magazine* about the Cleveland Play House. It could have been handled by any competent lensman.[77] The job didn't even fatten his bank account. The magazine paid $400. After deducting expenses, including the cost of two weeks in Cleveland and Miller's commission, André took home only $110 (about $2,500 in 2024 dollars).[78]

He supplemented his income by selling pictures to a stock agency, which licensed them for use in textbooks and such, and by photographing artworks for museums and collectors, demeaning and low-paying work for a master photographer.

As February approached, André pulled the Beaux-Arts' manager aside one day to let him know that his rent, due in a week, would be late. It was probably not the first time. Possibly he and Elizabeth were already in arrears. That same evening, the two came home around eleven to find their door padlocked. Panicky and embarrassed, they retreated to the sidewalk outside. André felt queasy. His ears started ringing. Then the pavement listed, his legs buckled, and the street spun away from him. He collapsed, hitting his head. Elizabeth pleaded for help from two or three passersby, but they scurried past. Not until midnight was André lucid enough to talk about how they would make it to morning. Exactly what happened next is unknown, except that they left the Beaux-Arts and moved to a place in Rye, a town north of New York on Long Island Sound.

That June, *Vogue* published a fulsomely self-congratulatory photography issue praising its own editors for being "among the first to see [the medium's] potentialities, to foresee its future."[79] *Vogue* was showcasing sixteen photographers matured by their work for Condé Nast. Not a word about André. That Steichen got star treatment was unsurprising. All the same, it's easy to imagine André fulminating. He considered Steichen to be a slick showman. Not to mention others like George Karger. A German-born ex-banker and semiprofessional magician, Karger infused his shots of handbags and hats with the same theatricality as his magic acts.

Everywhere, fashion photographers ruled. At *Harper's Bazaar*, the big winner was Martin Munkácsi. André's compatriot was reportedly earning more than $100,000 a year for his photographs flaunting the active American woman. Munkácsi had built a Gatsby-style mansion on Long Island. "A picture isn't worth a thousand words," he quipped, "it's worth a thousand bucks!"[80]

André was not a fashion photographer, celebrity chaser, or newshound. Yet he had invented a visual vocabulary, won wide acclaim, and secured — or so he believed — a place in photography's gallery of greats. But American editors didn't know or care. They found his work too poetic, too measured, too European. It rewarded slow looking. What was a circulation- and deadline-whipped editor supposed to do with *that*?

Even *Coronet* snubbed him. Their fifth anniversary issue reprised what the editors deemed the best of the more than 1,800 photographs the magazine had published. Twenty-three forgettable images, none by André. He should have been pleased to be spared. But rejection after rejection had gutted him. That omission too stung.

**On December 7, 1941,** a cold and clear Sunday, radios blared the heart-pounding news that Japan had bombed Pearl Harbor. The United States declared war on Japan and, three days later, on Germany and Italy. Aligned with the Axis, Hungary cut diplomatic relations with the United States.

In New York, the police had already sent André into a tailspin by stopping him once or twice for questioning. That spring was "a tense, jittery time all over the world no less so in New York," the journalist Merwin Dembling would write of André's wartime experiences. "Grim suspicion greeted everyone who ventured outdoors with a camera — particularly if that everyone was a suave, foreign-looking slender man with an indeterminate accent and a strange curiosity about the picture possibilities of everything."[81] Adding to André's upset, the Smith Act of 1940 required that noncitizen residents register and be fingerprinted. André and Elizabeth complied, then reactivated their applications for citizenship.

Hungary's break with the United States did not make André an "alien enemy," as he claimed. That category was reserved for nationals of Japan, Germany, and Italy. Citizens of Hungary and other Axis-allied nations living in the United States were classified as "aliens of enemy nationality."

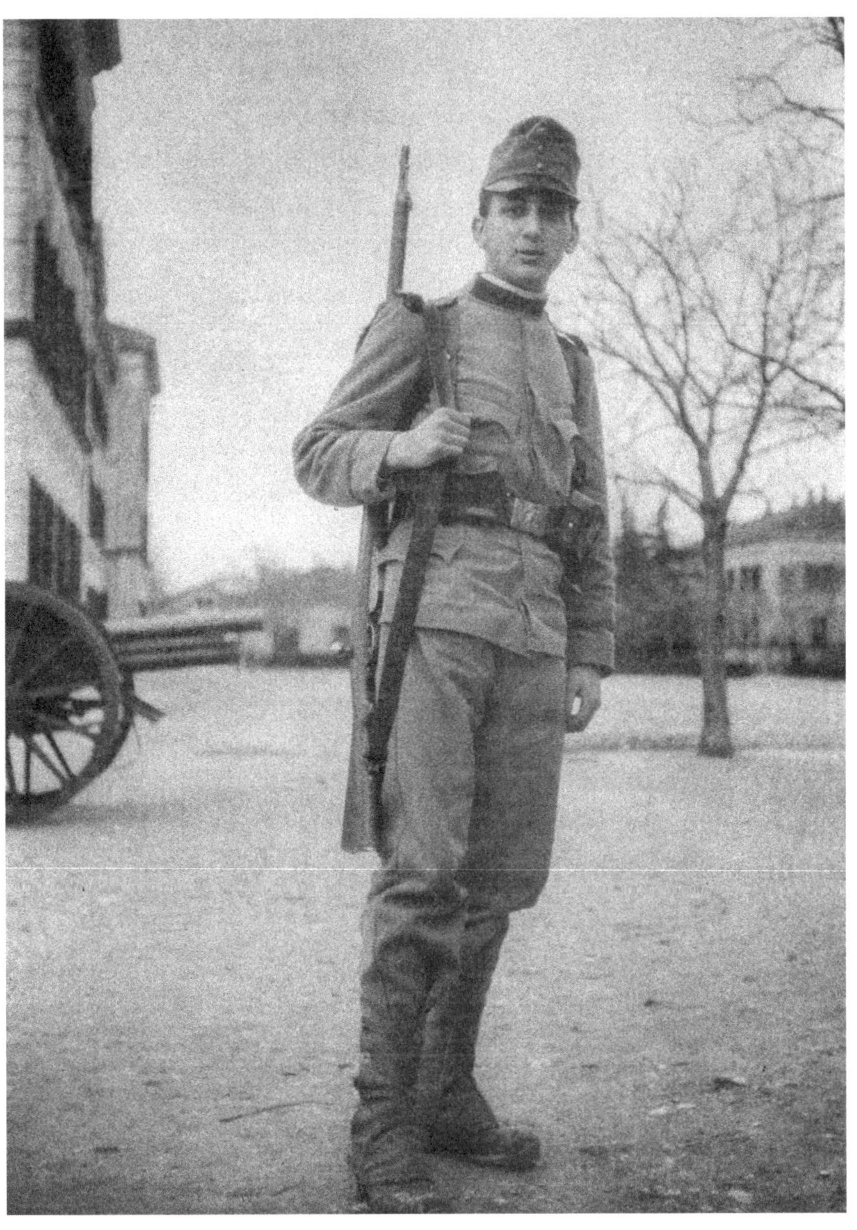

**1.** André as a rifleman in basic training at the start of World War I

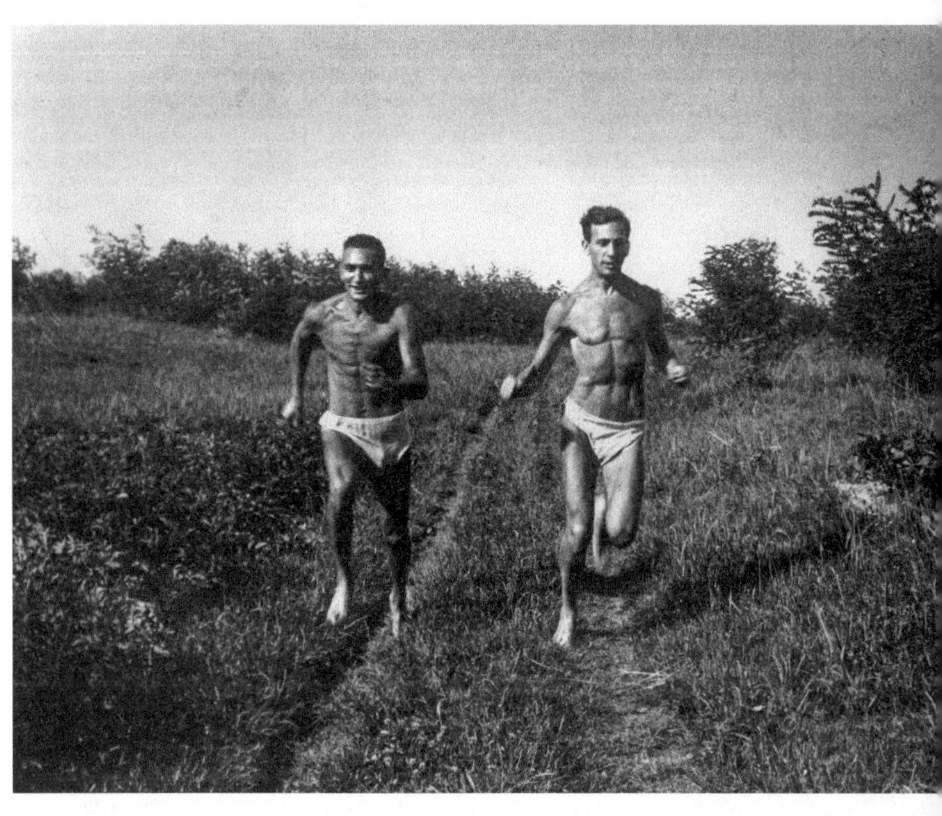

**2.** André competing with Jenő after the war

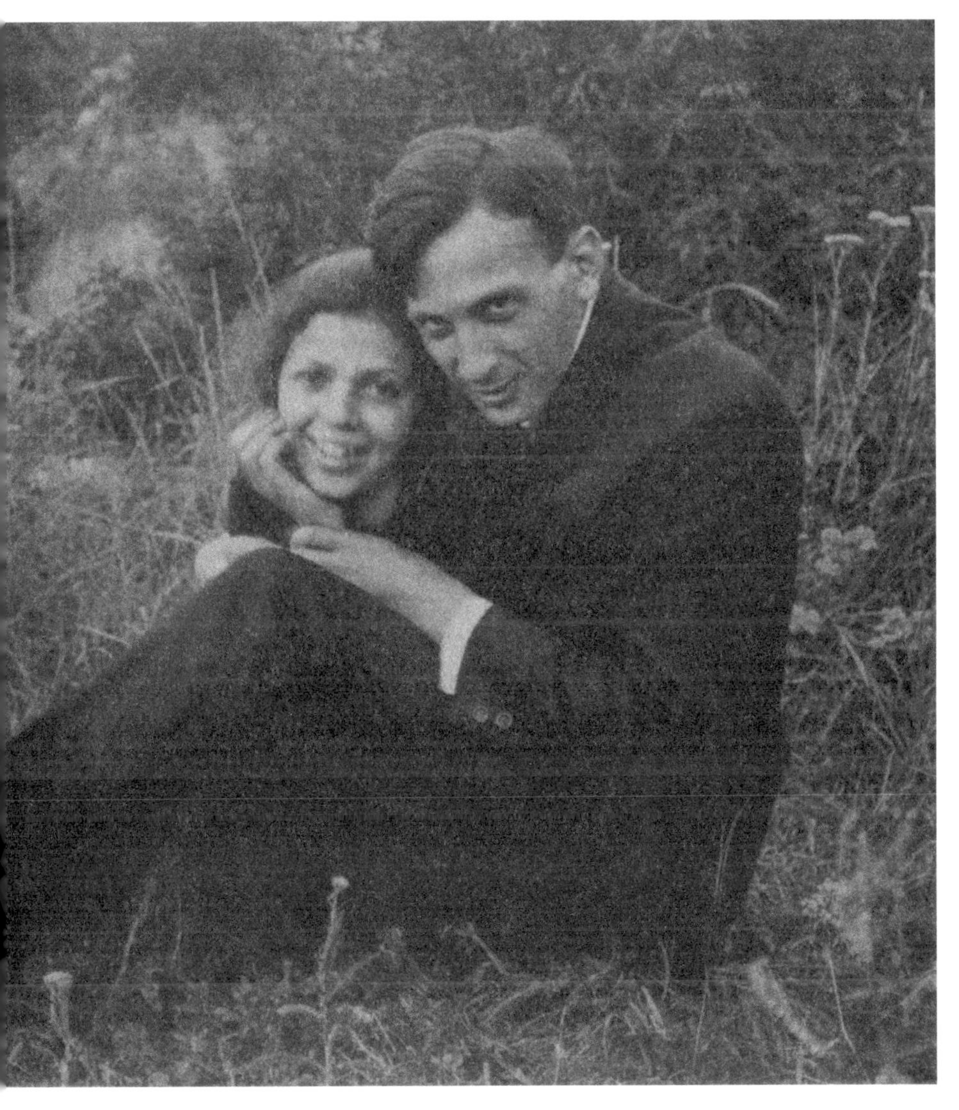

**3.** André and Elizabeth beaming, 1921

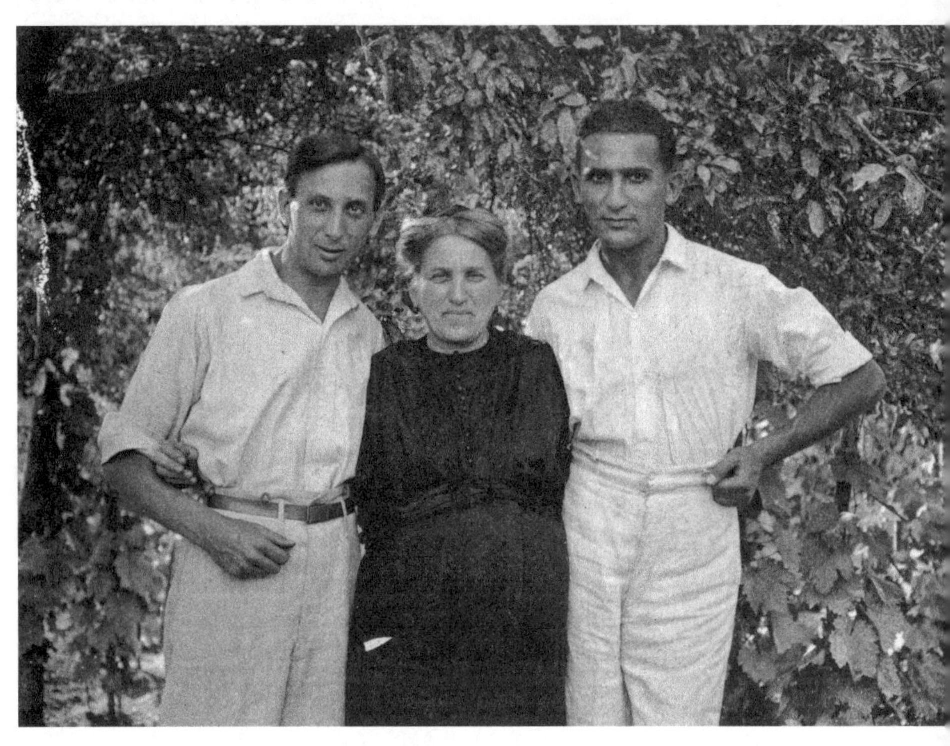

**4.** André and Jenő flank their mother, Ernesztina, during a stay in the country

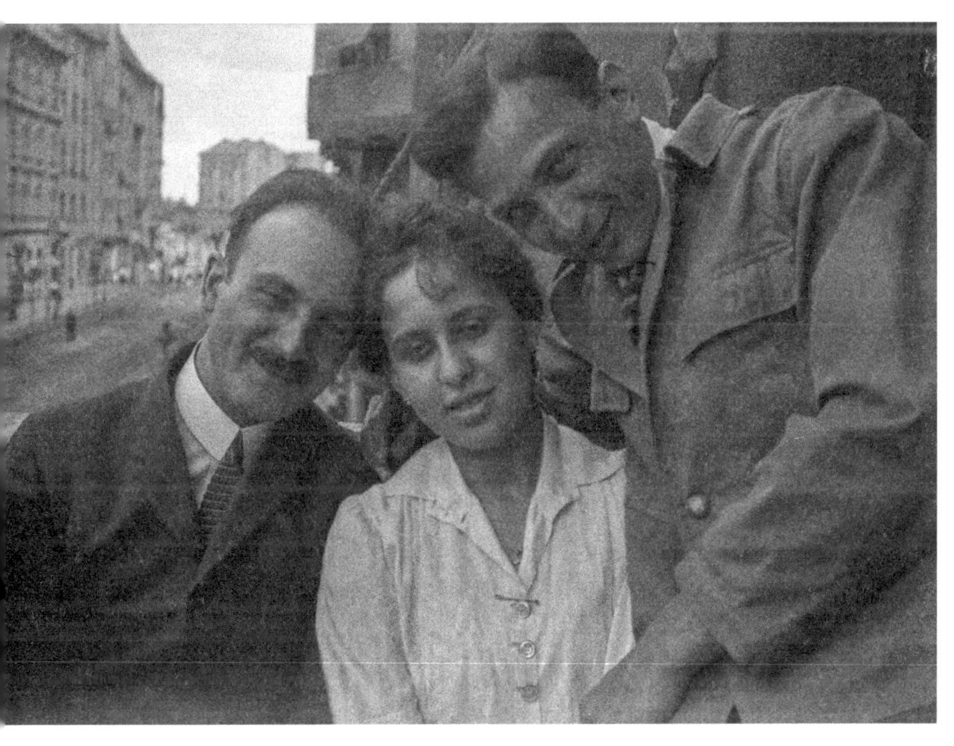

**5.** Imre and André with their cousin Rózsi Klopfer on the balcony of the Kertészes' Budapest apartment, c. 1921

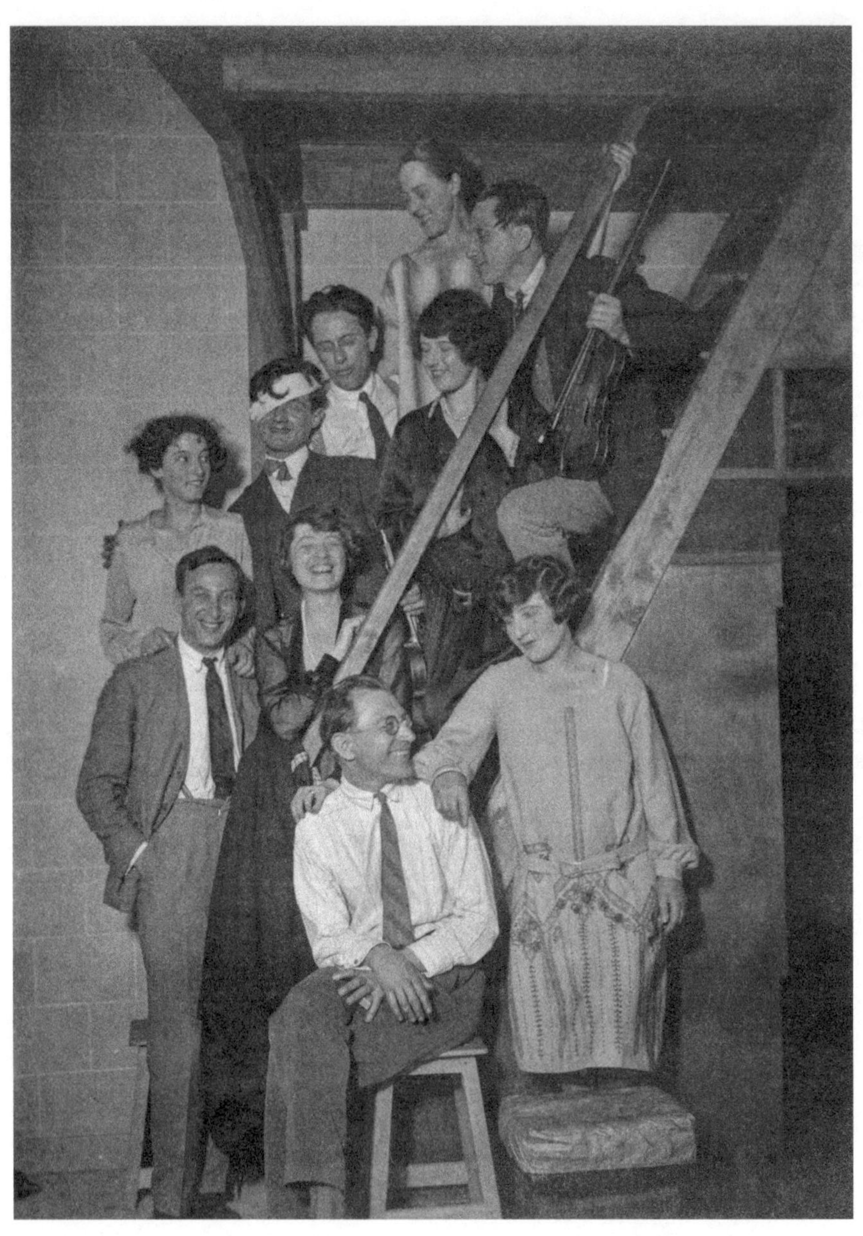

**6.** Partying at the artist Joseph Csáky's studio in Paris, 1927

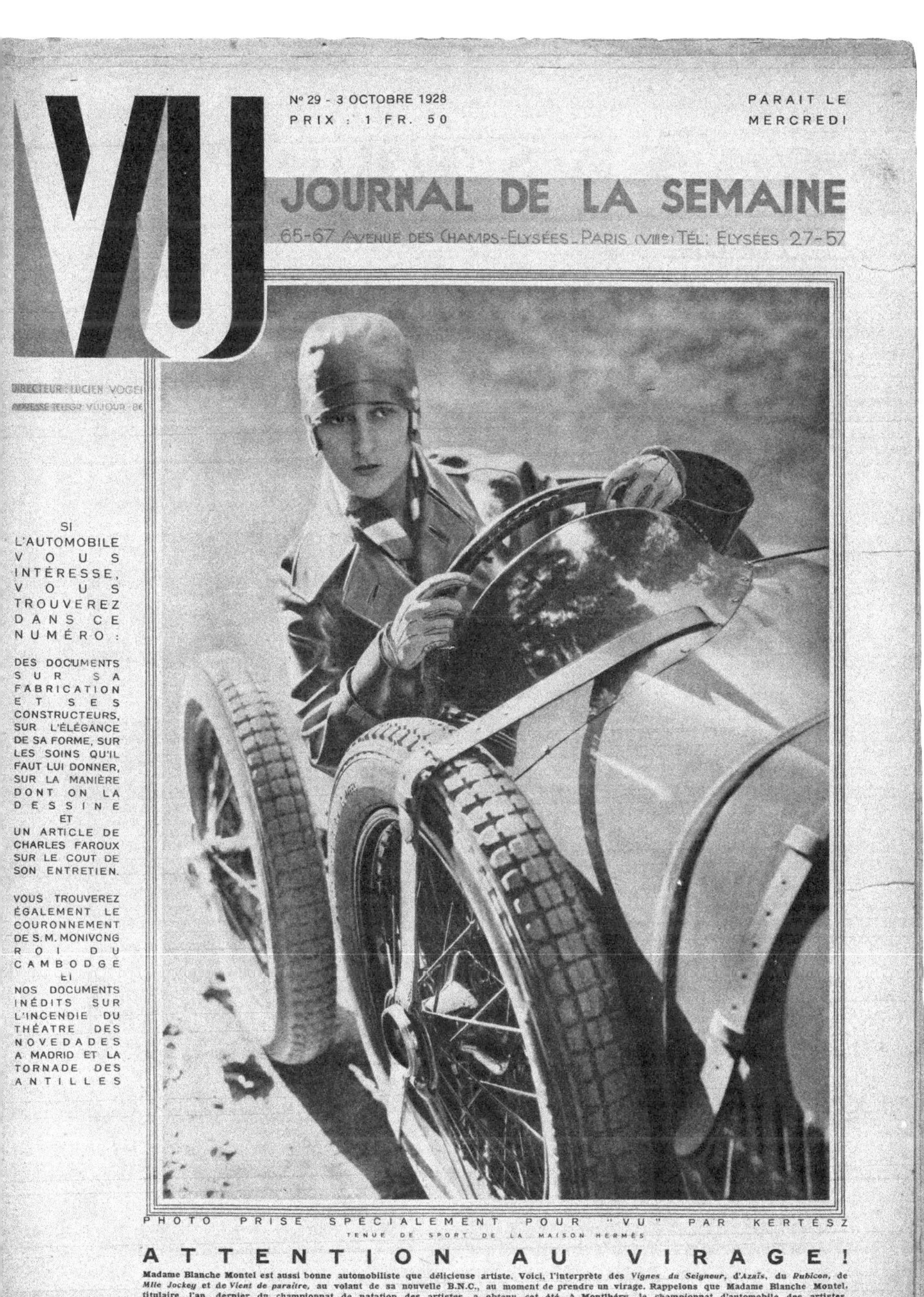

VU

Nº 29 - 3 OCTOBRE 1928
PRIX : 1 FR. 50

PARAIT LE MERCREDI

JOURNAL DE LA SEMAINE

65-67 AVENUE DES CHAMPS-ELYSÉES_PARIS (VIIIe) TÉL: ELYSÉES 27-57

DIRECTEUR: LUCIEN VOGEL
ADRESSE TELEGR: VUJOUR 86

SI L'AUTOMOBILE VOUS INTÉRESSE, VOUS TROUVEREZ DANS CE NUMÉRO :

DES DOCUMENTS SUR SA FABRICATION ET SES CONSTRUCTEURS, SUR L'ÉLÉGANCE DE SA FORME, SUR LES SOINS QU'IL FAUT LUI DONNER, SUR LA MANIÈRE DONT ON LA DESSINE ET UN ARTICLE DE CHARLES FAROUX SUR LE COUT DE SON ENTRETIEN.

VOUS TROUVEREZ ÉGALEMENT LE COURONNEMENT DE S.M. MONIVONG ROI DU CAMBODGE ET NOS DOCUMENTS INÉDITS SUR L'INCENDIE DU THÉATRE DES NOVEDADES A MADRID ET LA TORNADE DES ANTILLES

PHOTO PRISE SPÉCIALEMENT POUR "VU" PAR KERTÉSZ

TENUE DE SPORT DE LA MAISON HERMÈS

ATTENTION AU VIRAGE!

Madame Blanche Montel est aussi bonne automobiliste que délicieuse artiste. Voici, l'interprète des *Vignes du Seigneur*, d'*Azaïs*, du *Rubicon*, de *Mlle Jockey* et de *Vient de paraître*, au volant de sa nouvelle B.N.C., au moment de prendre un virage. Rappelons que Madame Blanche Montel, titulaire l'an dernier du championnat de natation des artistes, a obtenu cet été, à Montlhéry, le championnat d'automobile des artistes.

NUMÉRO SPÉCIAL DU SALON DE L'AUTOMOBILE

**7.** The October 3, 1928, cover of *Vu* with André's shot of the actress Blanche Montel at the wheel of her BNC roadster

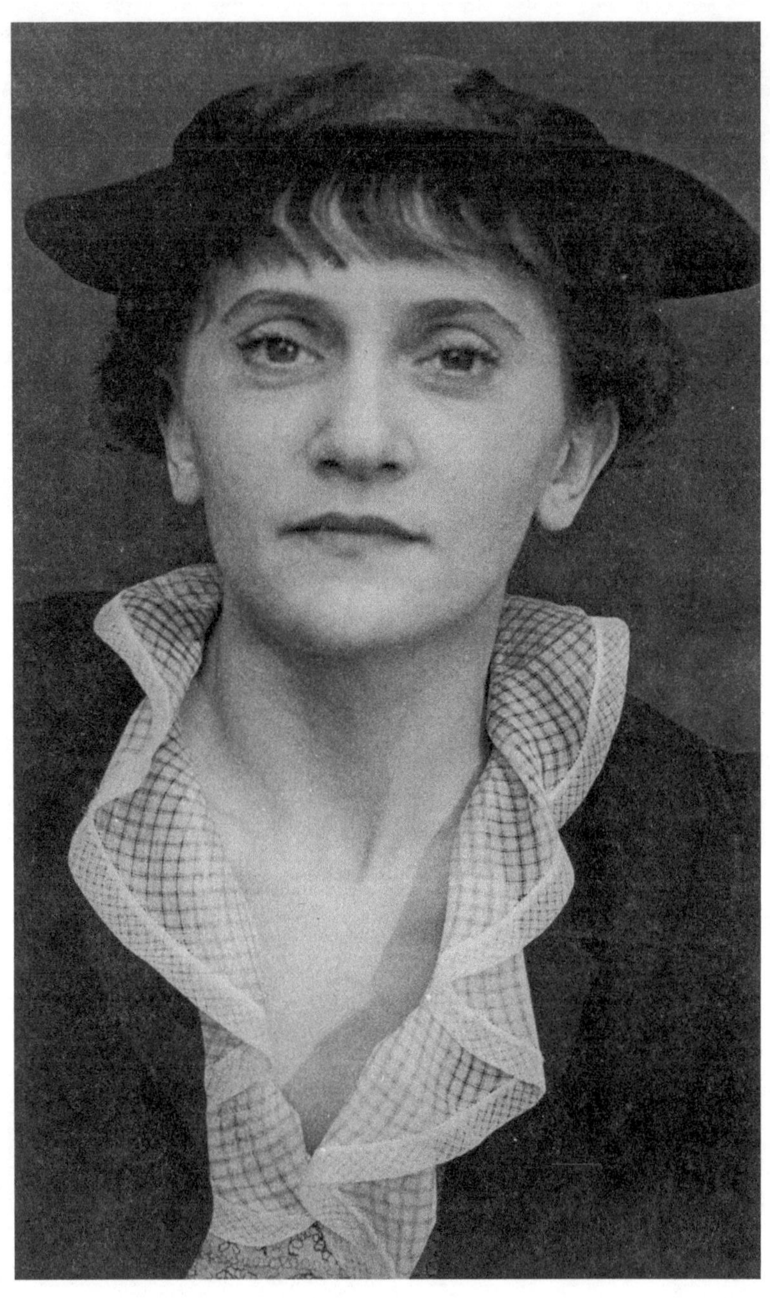

**8.** Rogi André's presumed self-portrait from during her time with André

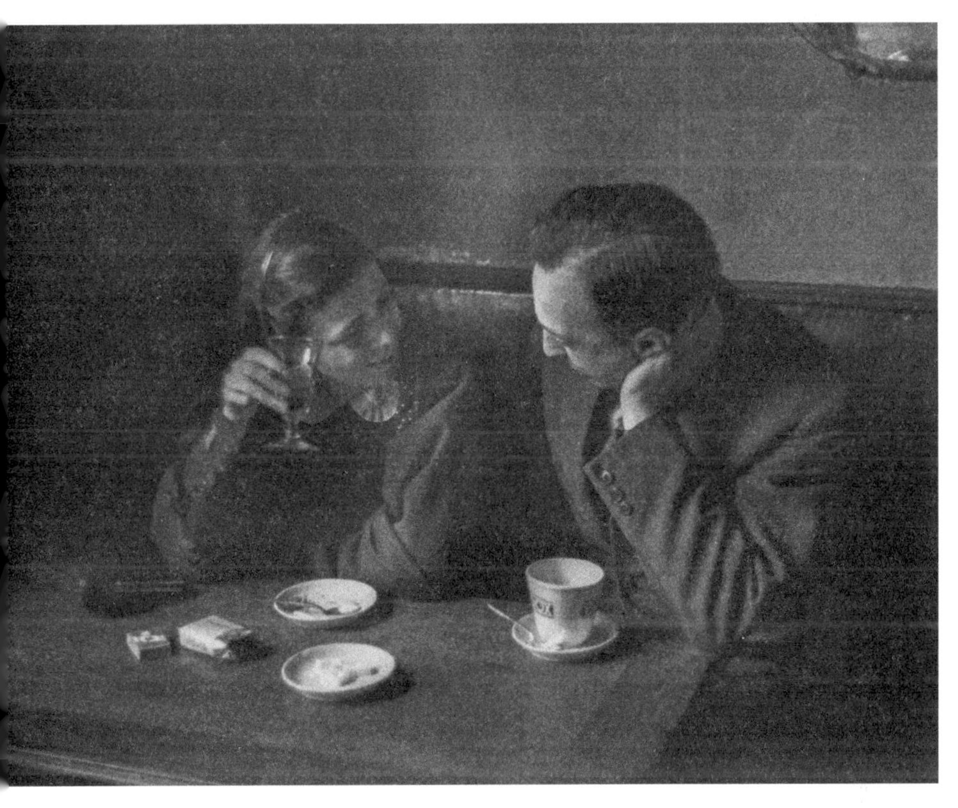

**9.** Elizabeth and André reunited in Paris, 1931

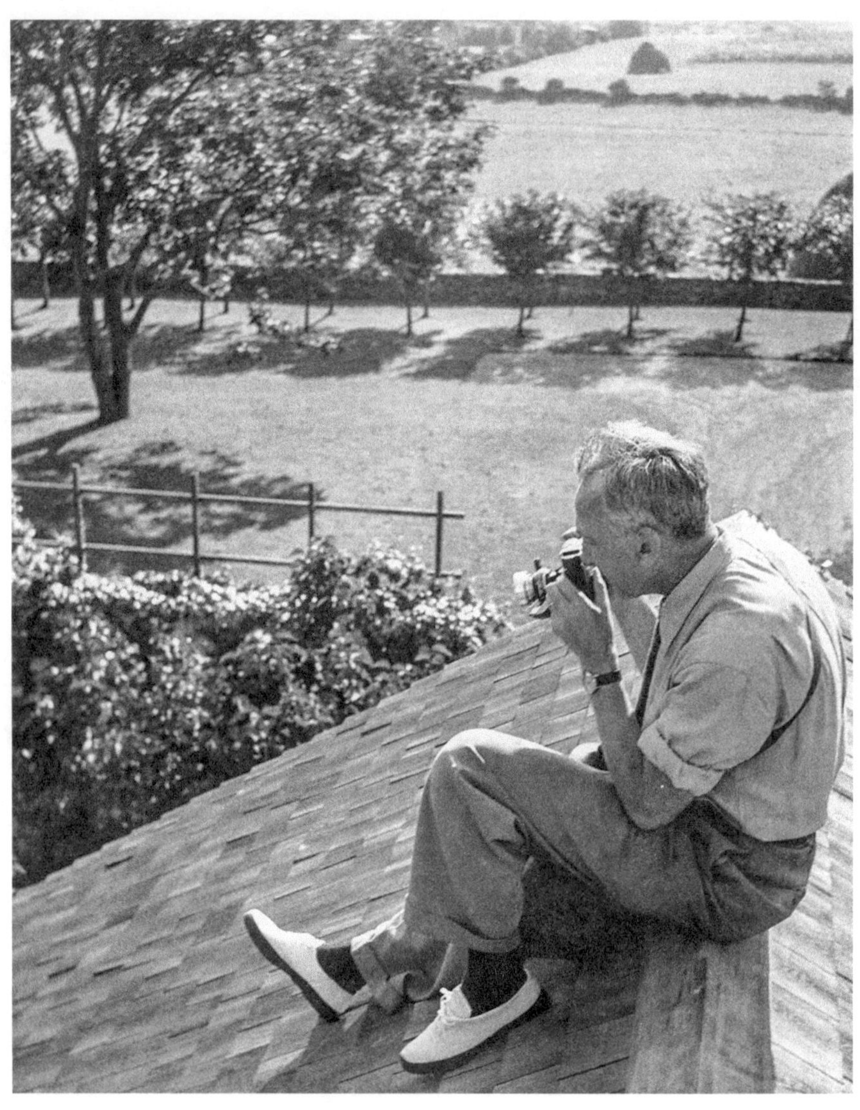

**10.** André's self-portrait set up by him and taken by John Platt as André worked on a feature story for *House & Garden*, 1946

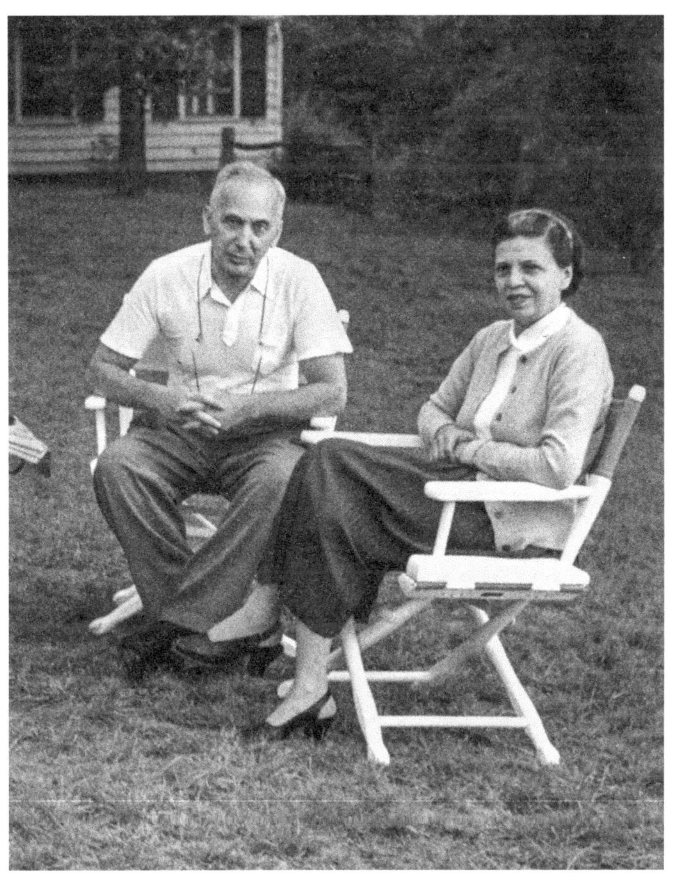

**11.** André and Elizabeth relax at their weekend home in Newtown, Connecticut, c. 1955

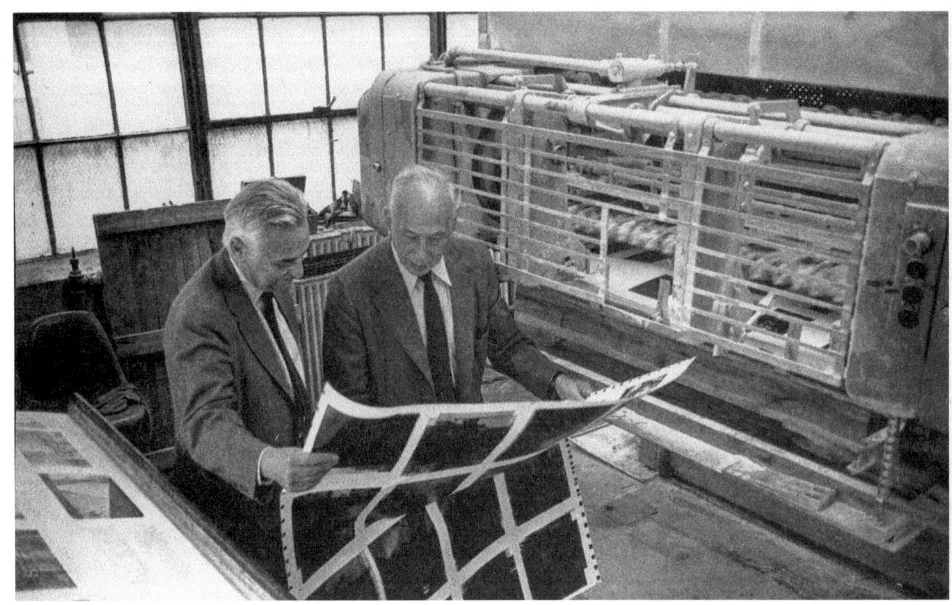

**12.** André and his friend the literary agent Frank Dobo review proofs of André's book *J'aime Paris*

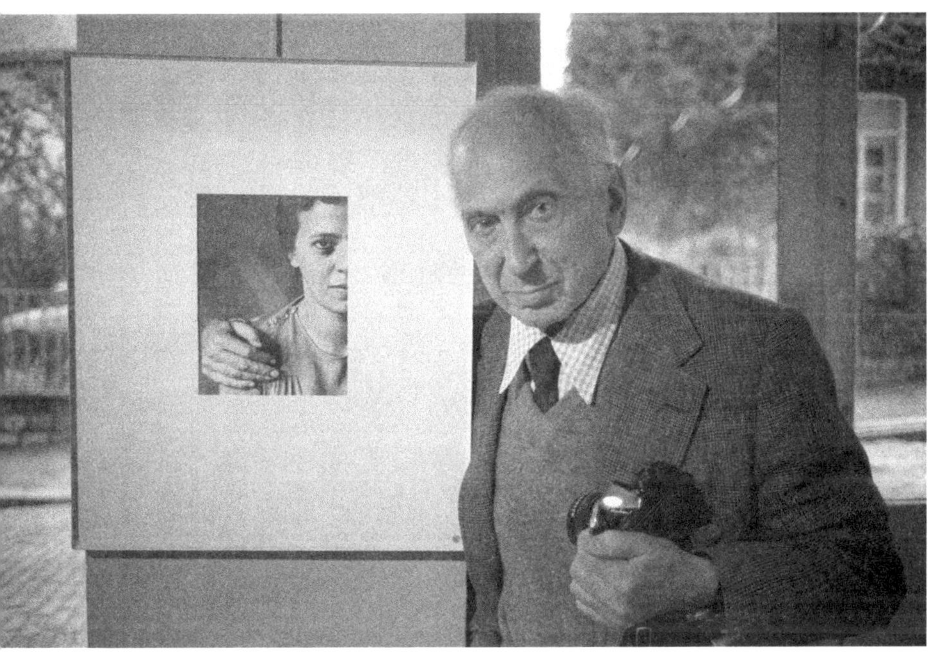

**13.** Martine Franck's poignant portrait of the widowed André with his cropped wedding picture of Elizabeth, 1980

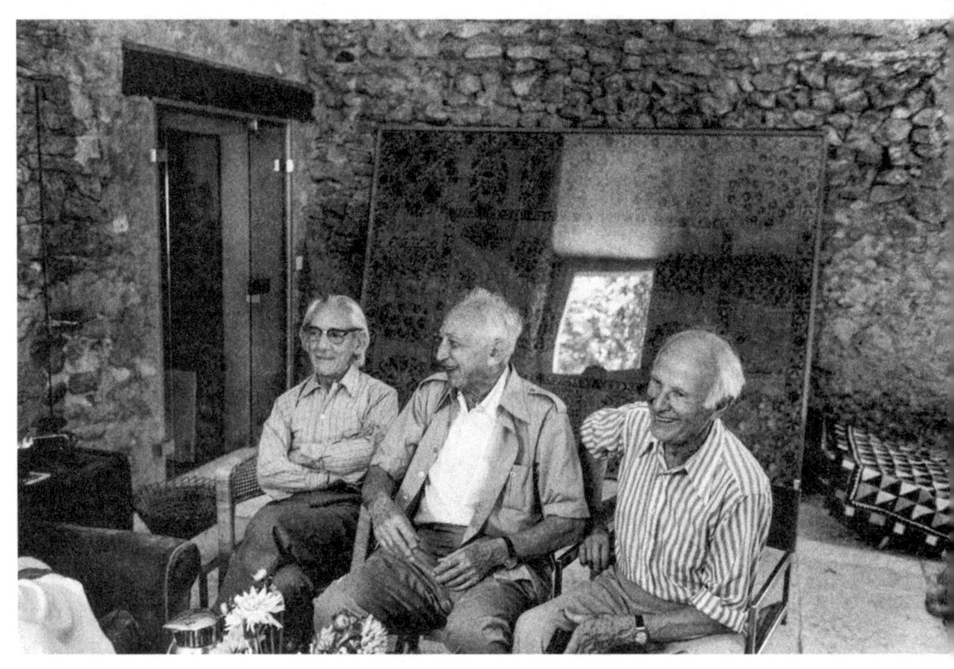

**14.** Photographic legends Manual Álvarez Bravo, André Kertész, and Henri Cartier-Bresson at the Rencontres d'Arles, 1979

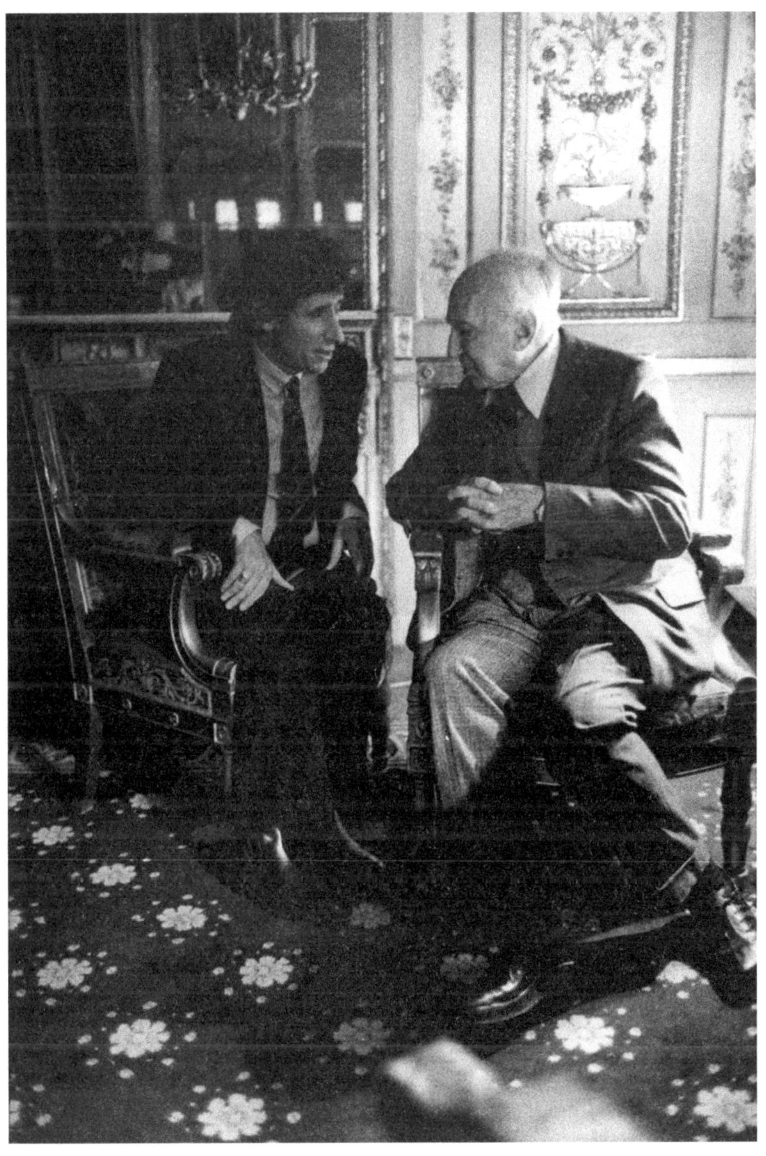

**15.** André with the French minister of culture Jack Lang, March 1984

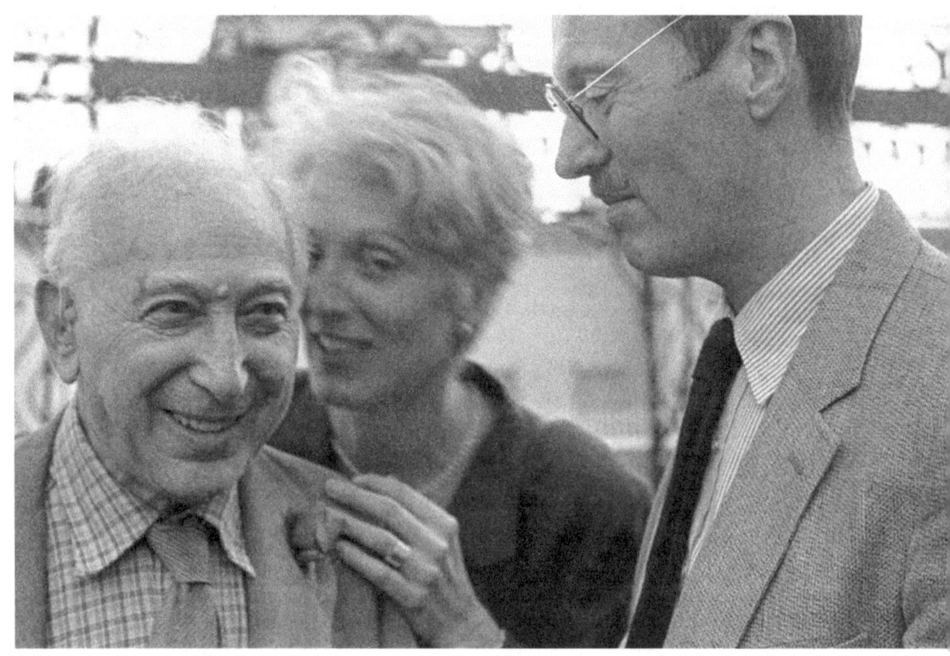

**16.** Celebrating his ninetieth birthday with the editor Carole Kismaric and the curator Weston Naef

For photographers, that was a vital if subtle distinction. In early January, the Department of Justice decreed that alien enemies had to surrender their cameras. André then requested a license to use photographic equipment. After learning that he was Hungarian, the local US attorney's office informed him that restrictions on cameras did not apply to him.[82] On February 5, 1942, the Department of Justice issued new regulations. Except for those who took pictures as their "regular and customary mode of earning a livelihood," aliens of enemy nationality *were* forbidden to photograph. But that edict was swiftly reversed. Five days later, the attorney general announced that aliens of enemy nationality did *not* have to surrender their cameras. He added that most people in that category were "believers in democracy and loyal to the United States."[83] So, like a US citizen, André could photograph anything except military subjects and could travel freely to do so. Yet André's story was set: "They took my fingerprints and I wasn't allowed to use a camera except between four walls."[84] *They* had forbidden a street photographer to work on the streets: "In street with camera, I was spy."[85] The Americans had deprived him of oxygen.

Maybe he misunderstood the rules, maybe not. Five years of stress, social isolation, and blows to his self-esteem had left André traumatized. His work had not entered the bloodstream of American photography. Once again, he was a nobody. He had lost his fight for recognition, a fight he'd believed he had won long ago.

André coped by lashing out at the flaws he perceived in Americans' character and behavior. A self-image as a victim of cheating and exploitation became central to his understanding of his American years. He misinterpreted people's actions, misread benign comments as hostile, and suspected slights where none were intended. You could joke around and have a good time with Americans, André felt, yet relationships were always transactional. His American friends were all *business* friends, he asserted.[86] Wisely—he still needed work—he was circumspect about airing his resentments.

To blame America for his every disappointment and setback was to ignore his own responsibility for the situation: his poor English, his rigidity about the type of work he was willing to do, his predilection for distrust, self-pity, and melancholy.

**By the time of the attack** on Pearl Harbor, André and Elizabeth were back in Manhattan. They had rented a furnished room on the top floor of a shabby boardinghouse on West Twentieth Street. The kitchen and bathroom were shared with other tenants. Rent was due weekly.

The building's only attraction was its roof, where they liked to relax on Sunday afternoons. It overlooked a neighborhood of Civil War–era brownstones gutted by mom-and-pop manufacturers, most of which had failed during the Depression. Now the brownstones stood half empty. The streets were dirty and charmless. But the roof commanded a wide view of the metropolis spilling out in all directions. When the light waned and the sparkle left the water at sunset, New York would erase itself. Thousands of streetlights were blacked out that year, obscuring major arteries and diminishing the shore-glow that made ships vulnerable to U-boats.

Ironically, André, who felt so unfree in America, had two prints in an exhibition titled *Image of Freedom* at MoMA that fall and winter. Even before Pearl Harbor, the museum had oriented its programming to the cause of democracy. Participation was required of every department, hence the photography department's juried exhibition. *Image of Freedom* comprised photographs by the sixty-four amateurs and professionals whose submissions best answered the question "What to you most deeply signifies America?" The concept was to express and affirm the American way and remind New Yorkers about all there is to love outside the five boroughs. André *had* discovered a few things to love, like the tiny old church, reportedly in Westchester County, that was the subject of one of his winning prints.

Beyond the two images chosen for *Image of Freedom*, however, André's work barely existed for MoMA's photo department.[87] Its establishment in

1940, the first such department in a major American museum, had positioned MoMA as photography's arbiter of quality. Beaumont Newhall was the founding curator. Under the sway of the department's cofounder, Ansel Adams, Newhall was now rejecting the more inclusive view of photographic merit that had informed his 1937 survey and hewing more closely to Adams's ideas. Straight photography ruled. Surrealism was anathema. Pictures taken for social, commercial, scientific, or political purposes were ignored. So narrow were Newhall and Adams's selections for one exhibition that when MoMA's director stopped by during the installation, he asked, a propos of the aestheticized Western landscapes, "Why do great photographers like to photograph bushes?"[88]

Shortly after *Image of Freedom* closed, André came away from a conversation with Newhall convinced that the curator had promised to find him a job. Called up for military duty, Newhall was preparing to leave for basic training before joining a photo reconnaissance unit of the Army Air Force. His wife, Nancy Newhall, would serve as MoMA's curator during his absence.

One day that August, André popped into her office, intent on continuing the job discussion. He planned to work at whatever the Newhalls came up with pending the arrival of his citizenship papers, then join the army as an aerial photographer. Or maybe he could land a job as a photographer for a government agency or corporation. "If only his English weren't almost as bad as my French, he would probably get something quite good," Nancy told her husband. "I said I would do what I could."[89] Beaumont responded that he'd never promised to find André a job, only to offer suggestions. No job materialized.

At Condé Nast too, André was trying to work the angles. Happily, his old "boss-comrade" from *Vu*, Lucien Vogel, was riding out the war in New York. After fleeing the Nazi invasion of Paris, Vogel had installed his family on Sutton Place South and himself at Condé Nast's Madison Avenue headquarters. There this longtime ally of Condé Nast and living legend in the magazine world held court for his many admirers.

André would have seen him as a conduit to *Vogue*'s upper echelon. As weeks passed, however, Vogel's prestige faded. Condé Nast rejected his redesign of *Glamour*, the brand's up-and-coming glossy for young working women. What's more, Vogel's baggy tweeds and old-school affability embarrassed sleek fashionistas. *Vogue*'s editor in chief Edna Chase took one look at Vogel's protruding eyes and chin buried in his collar and pronounced him a "dandified frog."[90] Like André, he seemed to belong to the European past, not the American present.

Devastating though it was, the fall of Paris to the Nazis in June 1940 presented an opportunity for André to revive his coffee-table book about the City of Light. Yet his meetings with editors brought only frustration. His proposal for a book of Distortions was eliciting another chorus of noes. Production costs were too high, there was a risk of obscenity charges, the images displeased the powers that be.[91] André sought out John Rewald, a Berlin-born art historian who ran the gallery E. Weyhe, a pillar of modern art on Lexington Avenue. Rewald found the Distortions interesting and began planning to show them. But then he got wind of an impending Surrealist exhibition elsewhere and changed his mind.

Over the summer of 1943, André snagged a job or two for *Look*, then shot the October cover of *The Bride's Magazine*. Both publications were lackluster clients, and André disliked the work. But it was what he could get.

His many contacts among European exiles would seem likely to lead to jobs. André had participated in a group show at the International Study Center on Park Avenue, a nerve center for refugee intellectuals and frequent venue for classical concerts. *First Photographic Exhibition* comprised prints by twenty foreign-born photographers, as one of a string of shows intended to help New Yorkers view these new arrivals as assets, not liabilities. Its organizer, the artist and librarian Kate Steinitz, originally from Poland, was well connected. Nor was André a stranger to the three Germans who had transplanted the Black Star agency from Berlin. Or to the German whose European Picture Service had been a New York player for more than a decade. Or to the Hungarian-born

Charles Rado, who ran Rapho Guillumette Pictures. André and Rado no doubt met in the 1920s, when Rado worked for the German publisher Ullstein Verlag, and André was among Ullstein's favorite photographers. With the Nazis' rise to power, Rado fled Berlin for Paris, where he launched the photo agency Rapho. In 1941, he had to restart again, cofounding Rapho Guillumette on Fifth Avenue. The agency favored humanist work and Hungarian-born photographers, and André and Rado had a firm friendship. From time to time, they worked together. Yet André's income stayed distressfully inadequate.

That autumn, he fell behind on his share of the phone bill at the darkroom and office he shared with Statile. It took him two months to scrape together the overdue $12.77.[92] He then ended the arrangement with Statile. In any case, his vertigo had made darkroom work almost impossible. When he needed to get film developed or prints made, André used Leco, a respected lab on West Forty-Second Street.[93] He struggled to pay Leco's bills too. Without telling Elizabeth, he pawned a tripod and a favorite old camera. He was taking few pictures. It's a fair guess that he retreated into reading, walking, listening to music, and brooding.

New Year's Eve 1943 brought an unexpected stab of joy when John Adam Knight, the *New York Post*'s photography critic, devoted his column to heaping praise on André's artistry. Over the years, André had been courting heavyweights like Knight with holiday cards, each one an original print. That year's was a photograph of a bistro in Paris. It had arrived at Knight's home in the same batch of mail as a publication that reproduced André's 1941 portrait of the writer Ève Curie for *Town & Country*. "Kertész has the gift of photographing the soul of his sitter," Knight marvels, "as well as the physical being." He continues: "It was a great day for American photography when André Kertész landed on our shores – a greater day than many editors, critics and museum curators realize as yet. Not having a flair for self-advertising, he is being 'discovered' but slowly."[94]

André got ahold of eight copies of Knight's column. He pasted several on heavy paper and underlined Knight's words of praise. Apparently, he never met Knight. He would have been unaware that John Adam Knight was the pseudonym of a French writer and chef named Pierre de Rohan. Scratch a champion of André's work in the 1940s, and there's a European.

**Following their mother's death** in 1933, André had stopped hearing from Jenő. A few weeks before quitting Paris for New York, André had written, lamenting that the past three and a half years had brought "no news, none at all" of his little brother.[95] Later that fall, Jenő did answer. He had achieved financial and domestic stability. Jenő described his Bolivian-born wife, his children, and his job as the superintendent of an oil field for Standard Oil of Argentina. He even sent pictures. Aware that André was then working for Keystone, he assumed that his brother also was happy and well, living as he did in "the only country where you can cash in on ambition."[96]

After that, each wrote sporadically. Ashamed to admit worldly failure, André would have said little about his misfortunes. Toward the end of 1942, however, Jenő learned from Imre that André and Elizabeth were struggling even to buy food. So he dispatched a small money order. When André received it, he choked up with anger. Help from Jenő must have felt like a blow to his vanity. Jenő had a nice house and a well-paying job; André did not. He fired back a reply that hit his brother "like boiling water."[97] Their correspondence went silent for nearly a year. Not until André and Elizabeth sent Christmas greetings that December did Jenő respond with an apology, disparaging Imre for exaggerating (although he had not) and imploring André to move to Argentina. Curiously, he wrote in Spanish, a language that neither André nor Elizabeth spoke.

Jenő had another reason to be angry at Imre. Their older brother had never responded to his pleas to mail the birth certificate Jenő needed to apply for Argentine citizenship. By the time Jenő hired someone to obtain the document, Argentina, a neutral country, had stopped extending the residency permits of citizens of belligerent nations. Jenő feared deportation. "He may be our brother," he complained to André of Imre, "but sincerely, our shared blood doesn't attract me to him."

It's impossible to know why Imre didn't respond to his brother's supplications or if he ever received them. In Hungary, the Nazi menace hung heavy. The nation's quasi-Fascist government agreed with Hitler that Jews were poisoning the blood of a "pure Aryan race." Businesses had been Aryanized, and Jews subjected to punishing anti-Semitic regulations. Most Hungarian Jews felt physically safe, however, until March 1944, when the Führer ordered Hungary occupied. His deputy Adolf Eichmann arrived to organize a campaign of extermination.

Three months later, some 220,000 Budapest Jews were forced into about 2,000 so-called yellow-star houses in preparation for their deportation. Six months after that, the Hungarian Fascist group Arrow Cross drove many into a ghetto around the main synagogue. Food soon ran low. The streets stank of garbage, feces, dead rats, and corpses. The Arrow Cross Party went on murderous sprees, roping Jews together in twos or threes, dragging them to the edge of the Danube, and shooting them into its icy chop. Others were driven like animals to the Austrian border, where the strongest were enslaved, and the rest left to die of starvation, disease, and exposure. On Teleki Tér, where Ernesztina had once poured coffee and spread cheer, Jewish resisters were slaughtered.

What was happening to Imre and Gréti? To Elizabeth's mother and siblings? To other relatives and friends? The devoutly Catholic Elizabeth would have prayed for their safety, then reached for another cigarette. André could only worry and be thankful, though he'd never admit it, that he and Elizabeth were safe in New York.

His citizenship had come through that February, Elizabeth's two weeks before. For him, citizenship was an expedient, not a transformation. The rolling disaster that was Europe was one thing, André's feelings about the United States quite another. He never saw the United States as a land of opportunity. He never bought into the American dream. By anchoring his self-identity to a romanticized version of Paris and believing in the myth of a lost wholeness, he tempered his powerlessness to regain what he had lost. He would never be Andrew Kertész, always *André.*

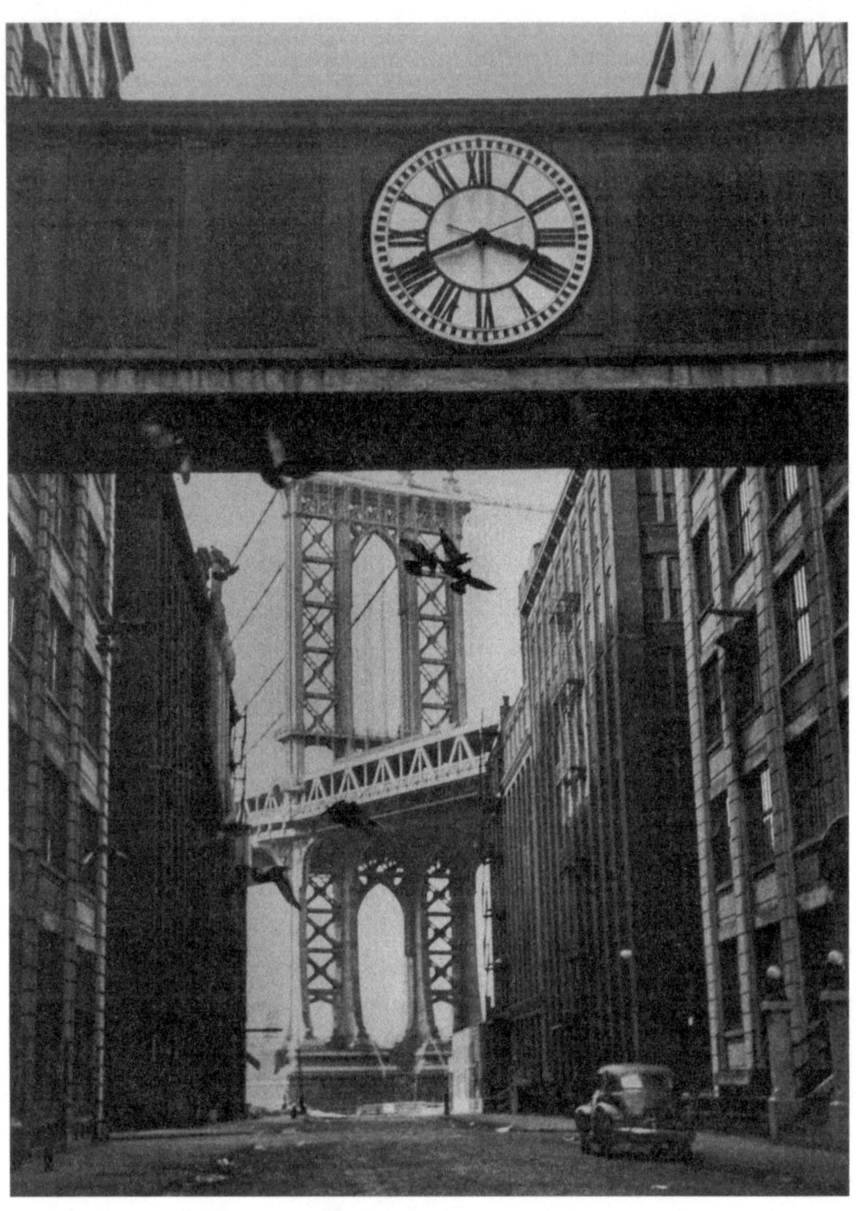

André Kertész, *Manhattan Bridge, New York*, 1947

# 9 MANHATTAN BRIDGE, 1944–1962

**On April 19, 1944,** André checked into the Mayflower, *the* hotel in Akron, Ohio. Ladened with cameras, a tripod, lights, and other gear, plus bags full of film, he had three days of shooting ahead. Time Inc. was footing the bill.

The Depression had hit Akron hard, then the war cut off the rubber supply essential to the corporations that made the city the world's tire capital. Goodyear, Firestone, Goodrich, and General Tire had all diversified or converted to military production. Now, with the invasion of Europe imminent, Akron's Big Four were flexing their muscles for a postwar consumerist boom. Natural rubber would once again be available; synthetic rubber production had expanded.

The article André was illustrating for *Fortune* addressed Firestone's retooling for peacetime. He did day-on-the-job shots of workers on the factory floor, a portrait of the chairman in his office, and panoramas of Plants I and II, their stacks bellowing rubber-flavored smoke. Beyond Firestone's walls, he photographed kids killing time along a polluted canal, thus reflecting *Fortune*'s concern for a socially responsible capitalism and evoking the stagnancy and promise of Rubber City.[1]

The American Viscose Corporation had hired him too. They needed photographs of workers at a plant in Marcus Hook, Pennsylvania, for a twenty-eight-page educational brochure. American Viscose was the world's top producer of viscose rayon, a strategic war material that was turning heads in the fashion world yet was still unfamiliar to ordinary consumers.

André had a gift for industrial photography, and such work paid handsomely. Only a month before traveling to Akron, he had pawned a tripod for a desperately needed ten dollars. Now he pocketed nearly $1,500 (about $26,700 in 2024 dollars) from Time and American Viscose.

Elizabeth's income was also ballooning. Her naturalization papers list her as a housewife. Yet each weekday morning she made a beeline to Cosmia's office or factory. During the war, the company had achieved modest success with replicas of French fragrances that were unavailable in the United States. After the invasion of Europe got underway that June, the advertising industry roared back to life and, with it, Americans' pent-up desire for luxury goods. Elizabeth was determined to cash in. Cosmia created and bottled an expanding number of scents and creams sold under other brand names. (Cosmia was "the cosmetics companies' cosmetic company," as *Harper's Bazaar* once described it.[2])

Thanks to their revved-up careers, André and Elizabeth were able to leave the boardinghouse they'd been chagrined to call home for three years for a modest yet cozy apartment on East Twelfth Street. Its proximity to Greenwich Village pleased them. André enjoyed poking around the outdoor art fairs in Washington Square and the literary treasure houses along Book Row, otherwise known as Fourth Avenue. Elizabeth's University Place office was almost around the corner.

Four blocks north was André's new fifth-floor office on Union Square West. There he was building and equipping a darkroom, buying lumber, a sink, an enlarger, steel trays, and supplies, as he could afford them. Never fully satisfied with the results from any lab, he intended to develop and print his own negatives again. His vertigo had tapered off, so "I try cheating the doctor…Go in the darkroom and try and try and try."[3]

André's actions and words speak of a man moving forward. All the same, that fall's shorter days and more transient light brought diaristic photographs that suggest a dispirited soul. The money was a relief. Yet André yearned for more. "All I wanted was to live *my* way," he would later explain, "artist way, *human* way."[4]

At twilight on October 8, he trained his lens on a man and woman lingering at a parapet in Riverside Park near 153rd Street. Automobiles slipped along the parkway below, their headlights flicking on. Beyond lay the river, crawling with seafaring vessels and spanned, farther up, by a ghostly George Washington Bridge. *Hudson River Parkway* recalls a picture he took in Budapest after World War I. In that long-ago double portrait, André and Elizabeth cling to each other as they gaze upon the darkening Danube. In this one, the Danube is supplanted by the Hudson, the young sweethearts by two middle-aged strangers, and love and longing by nostalgia and loss.[5]

Six days later, André took the oneiric *Homing Ship*. It had been raining off and on that Saturday morning. Central Park was quiet.[6] By the time André reached Conservatory Water, a model-boat pond across from East Seventy-Fourth Street, the rain had let up. The sky was overcast yet bright, the foliage dripping and clean. He halted, blocked by a big puddle.

That puddle occupies the lower half of his photograph. The trunk of the tree it reflects points to four benches that line the sidewalk beyond. A favorite subject since his beginnings as a photographer, André's benches are, like his park chairs, imbued with loneliness, pleasure, and yearning. That mix of feelings that can't be explained, only impressed into pictures. The benches in *Homing Ship* lead the eye to the sole human presence: a tyke who trots along beyond that ocean of a puddle, carrying a toy schooner. Part child, part talismanic boat, he feels like a hybrid creature from folklore. For an adult, the puddle may be an inconvenience, for a photographer, an inverting pool of light. For a child, it can be the membrane of a kingdom upside down and yonder.

The cultural historian Annette Kuhn writes of drawing on the past as "a way of reaching for myth, for the story that is deep enough to express the profound feelings we have in the present."[7] As André took *Homing Ship*, he surely felt his exile from childhood and the places he most loved: "Very touching... The little ship arrives safely home."[8] New York had failed him. His real life had been in Europe. His vital experiences lay "on the other side."[9]

*Homing Ship* may have been among the pictures André planned to send to *Minicam*. The Cincinnati-based monthly had offered to pay him, albeit modestly, to shoot whatever he wanted for one week, then send them the results. The editors would publish their favorites. "We have never worked with a photographer like this before," observed *Minicam*'s business manager, "but, on the other hand, we have never met André Kertész before."[10]

André's contact at *Minicam* could have been his compatriot and colleague László Moholy-Nagy, who was living in Chicago and serving as one of the magazine's editorial associates.[11] More likely, it was Maria Eisner, the Italian-born photo editor and journalist who knew André from Paris. Eisner had published an affectionate and admiring profile of him in that June's issue of *Minicam*. André was not some musty historical figure, Eisner informed readers, but a great photographer, very much alive, whose work should be rediscovered.

Launched in 1937 as the shutterbug's guide to good picture-taking, *Minicam* approached small-format photography from a technical angle, instructing readers in the dos and don'ts of exposure meters, backlighting, shutter speeds, and the like. By 1944, the editors had broadened its scope, featuring images by photographers whose ideas and methods might prod readers to consider the medium as art. André's were ideal because their snapshot look and reliance on everyday subjects made them less daunting than other master photographers' aestheticized prints.

Even though the *Minicam* project promised him a large and appreciative audience, André procrastinated. Maybe his darkroom project delayed him. Maybe he was paralyzed by that summer's news from Europe. Relief organizations had revealed that four hundred thousand

Hungarian Jews had been deported to extermination camps at Auschwitz and Birkenau. About 30 percent were known to have perished.[12] André and Elizabeth probably had no word about their families and friends. Budapest remained in the hands of the Nazis.

André took a different gut punch that November when *Harper's Bazaar* published a twelve-page survey of the history of photography.[13] The author was M. F. Agha, who had left *Vogue* and was working as a consultant. According to Agha, all photographers descend from one of the medium's key inventors, William Henry Fox Talbot ("art photography") or Jacques-Louis-Mandé Daguerre ("straight photography"). Agha shoehorns five dozen photographers, including lots of *Vogue* talent, into this dual lineage. Once again, André is missing. Yet his work easily fits in more than one place. *Fork,* for instance, qualifies as a photograph that removes an object from the flow of life and makes it meaningful, one category that Agha establishes. *Lost Cloud* meets Agha's definition of a snapshot.

Agha had known André's work since the 1920s, when he did a stint as art director at Paris *Vogue*. Over the years that André had lived in New York, the two had collaborated now and again. Yet Agha had never given André major assignments, nor had André's best work ever circulated meaningfully in the United States, as Eisner pointed out. Clearly, she had hoped her *Minicam* article would buoy his career.

André sent the *Minicam* pictures at the end of the year. Which ones and how many is anyone's guess. It's known only that the magazine's business manager responded with a deferential yet crushing three-page rejection.

"So, Mr. Kertész," the manager concluded, "I return these pictures to you, and I don't know what to say... I feel if you took the pictures they must be good, and if I can't see value in them it is just lack of seeing on my part."

The letter reproduces verbatim a conversation between two *Minicam* editors after the first summoned the second to eyeball André's prints spread out on his desk.

| | |
|---|---|
| SECOND EDITOR | *This man must be an artist (points to pictures A and B) but what is it you want me to see about these pictures?* |
| FIRST EDITOR | *What do you think of them?* |
| SECOND EDITOR | *I don't understand them.*[14] |

He seemed to speak for all of America. Erased from photography's history by *Harper's Bazaar*, André was denied a role in its present by *Minicam*.

**All fall and winter,** André's emotional life was roiled by events overseas. Squadrons of American B-17 Flying Fortresses were pounding Hungarian rail lines and bridges as Soviet troops smashed in from the east. By Christmas, the Red Army had encircled Nazi-occupied Budapest. Hitler ordered the city defended to the last soldier. The siege of Budapest would drag on until mid-February 1945, when the Germans surrendered at last.

Not until October would André and Elizabeth get news of his brother Imre and sister-in-law Gréti via a message column in New York's Hungarian daily *Magyar Jövő*: "Totally looted but somehow we survive. Send me a message about the Jancsis [Jenő and his family]...We telegraphed three times to your old address. We hug you with love."[15] The two had spent the final months of the Nazi occupation hiding in a rat-infested cellar. After the Soviets gained control of Budapest, they shuffled out to the street, dazed by the light and half dead from starvation. Spotting the frozen corpses of horses, they used picks and axes to hack out chunks, then sank their teeth into the flesh.[16]

What of the rest of André's and Elizabeth's sprawling families? Hungary lay in shambles. The postal system was half functional. In some cases, official confirmation of deaths in the camps would not come until 1948. Eventually, André and Elizabeth learned that Elizabeth's mother, sister, and brother had survived. (Most Budapest Jews remained alive only because of a Nazi decision to exterminate provincial Jews first.) But they lost at least thirteen other relatives, most at Auschwitz. On Elizabeth's side, the dead included an aunt, an uncle, and two cousins. Seven of André's cousins perished at Auschwitz or Dachau. Four other relatives, two of Elizabeth's cousins and two of André's, disappeared into Soviet prison camps.[17] Years later, *The Times* (London) would report, perhaps accurately, that André had lost twenty-two relatives in the Holocaust.[18]

Most devastating was the loss of his cousin Rózsi Klopfer, André's beloved companion in the old days at Szigetbecse. She had married a pharmacist named Lajos Szilágyi and moved to Kisvárda, a town in northeastern Hungary. The couple owned the pharmacy, along with vast vineyards and farmland. By the standards of 1940s Hungary, they were very wealthy, until the vineyards and land were confiscated in 1942. Two years later, they and their teenage daughter were among seven thousand Jews forced into the Kisvárda ghetto. They included the sister and brother-in-law of André's friend the New York photo agent Charles Rado, who was originally from Kisvárda. Both Rado's brother-in-law and Rózsi's husband were elected to Kisvárda's Jewish Council. (Each ghetto was forced to form such a council. Members had the agonizing and impossible task of enforcing Nazi orders in the Jewish community.) In February, the Nazis deported Rado's relatives to Auschwitz, where his sister was killed. That May, it was Rózsi and her family. Transferred from one camp to another, Rózsi's daughter would survive. But Lajos did not. Nor did Rózsi: She was gassed on May 31, 1944, the day she arrived at the death camp. She was forty years old.

Despite such shattering news, André would never publicly discuss his loss, nor utter a word about the Holocaust. You can't change the course of the world, he believed. You internalize. You bury your pain. You keep your head down.

But Paris! After August 25, 1944, Paris breathed free. On that day, Charles de Gaulle stood on the steps of the Hôtel de Ville to proclaim the city martyrized but liberated. American *Vogue* had covered the liberation, reprinting a jubilant cable from the British *Vogue* war correspondent in Paris, the photographer Lee Miller, and illustrating the feature with a photo by André. Its setting is the Cantine La Marseillaise, a Free French rendezvous on Second Avenue in New York, where a mobile by Alexander Calder in the colors of the French flag—*bleu, blanc, rouge*—swayed above the dance floor. André homes in on the *cantine*'s founder, the translator Maria Jolas, belting out the nostalgic "La Madelon" as revelers sway to the sounds of the accordion and the harmonica.[19]

The unshackling of the city he adored prompted André to reprise his rounds of publishers with the proposal for a book about Paris. This time, he garnered twenty-five rejections. He vented his frustration to Alexey Brodovitch.

The friendship between the brilliant but arrogant Russian and the amicable but aggrieved Hungarian had continued. It drew, in part, on their mutual love of dance and their mutual belief in what André called "talking pictures." His phrase was a slap at *Life*, where an editor had accused him of "talking too much" with his work.[20] Brodovitch shared André's faith in expressive photographs. That fall, he was wrapping up his own limited-edition book of dance photographs taken between 1935 and 1937. Brodovitch had used a handheld 35 millimeter Contax, available light, and slow shutter speeds to effect blurred, grainy, and high-contrast images. Glued picture-to-picture in his layout, they gleefully broke every rule of good photography, the better to convey how ballet *feels*.

Admiring of André's Paris work, Brodovitch pitched his friend's project to J. J. Augustin, his Manhattan-based publisher. He said yes. Johannes Jakob Augustin was the scion of a Jewish German family of printers whose firm dated to the seventeenth century. Once again, it was a European who stepped up for André. He signed.

Brodovitch and a curator colleague would handle the layout with input from André. For captions, they tapped George Davis, a bourbon-swilling literary editor at *Mademoiselle* and former expat in Paris. Davis suggested a three-part structure – morning, afternoon, evening – thus the book's title, *Day of Paris*.[21] Brodovitch's sequencing and Davis's captions impose a loose narrative: Over the course of a day, a solitary wanderer, understood as male, observes the city's intimate gestures as he might observe those of a woman, marveling at her mysteries. The icons of Paris appear – Notre Dame, Sacré Coeur, the Eiffel Tower – but woven into everyday living, not singled out as ooh-aah tourist attractions. Most of the 102 photographs were making their American debut.[22]

*Day of Paris* hit the stores just after VE Day. Because the US Army had helmed the liberation of Paris, André's book seemed to confirm that the mythic City of Light was America's gift to the world. During the years of defeat, occupation, and Vichy collaboration, the French soul had hung by a thread. *Day of Paris*, some felt, stitched it up. The journalist and novelist Elliot Paul said as much in an article in *Saturday Review*, calling it a "balm to throbbing nerves" of war-battered humanity. "There is nothing civil or military in its pages. It is purely philosophic."[23]

The book garnered dream reviews from a then-robust critical community. Some dwelt on the city itself. The captions were superfluous for anyone smitten with Paris, according to *The Christian Science Monitor*. A reviewer for the *Sunday Call-Chronicle* in Allentown, Pennsylvania, noted that "the camera of Kertész has caught spirit as well as actuality." Others raved about André's know-how. "'To serious photographers . . . [*Day of Paris*] is an absolute must," advised an editor at *Popular Photography*.[24]

Still buoyed by such reviews months later, André took advantage of a job on Chicago's North Shore to call on the curator Carl O. Schniewind at the Art Institute of Chicago.

"Oh, are you the famous André Kertész?" Schniewind greeted him, peering from behind horn-rimmed glasses.

"Yes, yes, I'm the famous Kertész." André's expression turned glum. "Only nobody knows it."[25]

Schniewind had lived in Europe during André's glory days, and he knew it. The two proceeded to sketch out an exhibition wrapped around

*Day of Paris*. Eventually, André persuaded Schniewind to include his 1918 *Underwater Swimmer* and a few other Hungarian photographs as a way of adding weight to his status as an early modernist innovator. He pitched the Distortions too, but the curator demurred because the public was likely to react to nudes "in the most curious sort of way."[26]

*Photographs by André Kertész* opened at the Art Institute of Chicago on June 7, 1946. André rejoiced to read of its "total success" in a letter from Schniewind.[27] He replied with a request for the press clippings, which he planned to use to generate more heat for his work. Perhaps a New York version of the exhibition? Silence from Schniewind. Two months later, André opened a second letter to learn that there were no clippings, only a mention in a sloppily edited omnibus column in the *Chicago Tribune*.[28] Schniewind attributed the lack of coverage to the sorry state of art criticism in Chicago. But André was hurt: "I felt like I was buried alive."[29]

He promoted *Day of Paris* as best he could. One copy went to Chicago's pioneering curator of modern art, Katharine Kuh. "You have never sent a gift to a more appreciative friend," Kuh assured him.[30] André also talked up his book to the writer Struthers Burt as the two traveled together in Mississippi for a *Ladies' Home Journal* feature. Back in New York, Burt took *Day of Paris* to Maxwell Perkins, Scribner's editor in chief, who liked the idea of a *Day of* series. Perkins scheduled a meeting with André. But the project came to naught.

It was Brodovitch who showed the book to Robert Frank soon after the young Swiss-born photographer arrived in New York in 1947. Moved by the photographs, Frank began patterning his practice after André's. Roaming the streets with his Leica, he bobbed and darted, catching slight yet resonant gestures and nabbing the crude poetry of the everyday. When Frank traveled to Paris in 1949, he hung around the Tuileries and Luxembourg Garden, taking dozens of photographs of park chairs inspired by André's but more comedic and anthropomorphized. (Several would be published in *Life*.)[31]

Less sophisticated viewers failed to grasp André's achievement.

Some mistook the *Day of Paris* photographs for documents—simply the way Paris *was*—as if he were only a button-pusher. Despite its critical triumph, the book sold only 1,500 copies before it went out of print.[32] *Day of Paris* would have one last turn in the spotlight in 1955, when it showed up in *The New York Times Magazine* as a prop in an ad for Rite-Form girdles.[33]

The liberation of Europe meant that André and Elizabeth could pack up and return to France. But they did not. André would dance around an explanation: "We were up in the air. And I was not young anymore. I had no idea what had happened with my reputation in Paris." A pause. "Yes, I was afraid that I was too old."[34] (He was fifty when the city was liberated.) He said nothing about other possible reasons. André's legal wife, Rogi, had survived the war and was living in Paris. Keeping the marriage secret was easier 3,600 miles away. Besides, it must have seemed foolish to abandon a city astir with financial opportunity for one where residents had to endure long lines to buy rationed baguettes. After a decade of poverty, André and Elizabeth shared Americans' appetite for prosperity, and then some. They continued to fetishize Paris. André had come to New York on a one- or two-year sabbatical, he insisted. After the Keystone debacle, he would have returned to France if only US customs had not confiscated the gold bar he needed to pay for the boat tickets. That statement is false: The gold bar had been melted and sold and a check sent to the Kertészes by the time Keystone sued him.

Some have inaccurately framed André's move to the United States in 1936 as that of a Jew escaping the Nazis. They hitch his story to those of the Surrealist artists and writers who fled France and rode out the war in New York. As a Jew, André must have been grateful to America for harboring him. But no. "I'd rather be dead in Paris than live over what happened to me here," he said.[35] André knew that tens of thousands of Jews, French and foreign, had been rounded up in France, interned in the Paris suburb of Drancy, then packed into trains headed for extermination camps. As an assimilationist Hungarian Jew living abroad, he enjoyed the luxury of refusing to carry that baggage.[36] "Jewish doesn't exist," he asserted, speaking of his self-identity. He described himself as "*cosmopolitan*."[37]

**In the magazine photography world** of those heady days, the men and women behind the camera were emerging as public personalities. *Vogue* published a first-person account of the wartime experiences of the photographer Irving Penn. A feature about the home of Cecil Beaton was in the works.[38] *Harper's Bazaar* presented personal work like Bill Brandt's series about the denizens of a London pub and Brassaï's about Parisian cats. Another article in *Harper's Bazaar* confirmed Brassaï's fame with a subtitle that marked him as a personality in his own right: "Picasso and His Studio: Photographed by Brassai."[39]

Buried in the product-promotion column (Shopping Bazaar) of that same issue was this: "André Kertész . . . will come to your home by appointment to photograph your child . . . His prices are average for top-notch photographers and you can reach him for an appointment at 31 Union Square, or by calling GRamercy 3-2564."[40] But when a Chicago reader tried to schedule a portrait session with her toddler, André bristled. The item was not an advertisement, he insisted, but simply "a token of enthusiasm of the editor."[41] Should André find himself in Chicago, he would photograph the child, but he did *reportage*. His humiliation at the contrast between the splashy feature by Brassaï, *photographe extraordinaire*, and the mention of André, kiddie photographer, is palpable.

Other photographers — Edward Steichen, Alma Lavenson, Berenice Abbott, Ansel Adams, Harry Callahan — were burnishing their reputations by writing articles for *Minicam* or *U.S. Camera* or publishing their credos in *The American Annual of Photography*. André, however, did not believe in public pronouncements, written or spoken. "You don't talk photography," he insisted to *Popular Photography* editor Jacob Deschin, "you do it."[42]

His relationships with colleagues were pleasant yet limited. The

Circle of Confusion met every other Monday evening at a family-style Italian place on MacDougal Street. Dinner at Mike's, wine included, cost only $1.10. (After Mike's closed, they went to Mona Lisa, also on MacDougal.) Yet the club's single rule – "You paid for your own dinner" – had limited André's attendance over the years, even though he benefited more than once from help from "the boys."[43] When he did attend meetings, his participation in the verbal free-for-alls was stymied by his hearing loss and poor English. Americans got impatient with the word soup he ladled out. At home, Elizabeth shook her head at his refusal to work on his English: "André just won't try."[44]

Colleagues threw parties. In May 1946, André attended one at the home of Beaumont and Nancy Newhall, where he mingled with fellow photographers Paul Strand, Helen Levitt, Minor White, Berenice Abbott, and Dorothy Norman. Once or twice, Evsa and Lisette Model hosted him at their apartment on Riverside Drive, along with Brodovitch, Ralph Steiner, and Abbott. André's once close friend Evsa Model had married Rogi's confidante Lisette Seybert, now Lisette Model. In 1938, the couple had moved to New York. André and Evsa's reconnection did not prove enduring. The Models could not forgive André for his treatment of Rogi.[45] As for Abbott, she considered André "a prick" for the same reason, even though she admired his work, which she included in a juried show she organized at the New School.[46]

Such gatherings tended to bring André down. Back home, he would grumble to Elizabeth: Why were *they* more famous than he was?[47]

**As 1946 drew to a close,** André unexpectedly found himself wanted, at Condé Nast, no less. "Please, André, we have to work together, we're old friends, you have to help me at the start of this work."[48] Alexander Liberman's pencil mustache, slicked-back hair, and polished manner gave him the air of a Continental gallant. By André's account, he was begging.

In only five years in New York, André's colleague at *Vu* had come far. Not long after Liberman's arrival, Lucien Vogel had prevailed on Condé

Nast to try the young man in *Vogue*'s art department. Thus Liberman became an assistant to M. F. Agha. Unbeknownst to Nast, Agha had already hired and fired him. For two years, Liberman again worked for Agha, now at Nast's behest. When the friction between the two grew unbearable, Agha issued a me-or-him ultimatum. Nast chose Liberman. At age thirty, Liberman had clinched a top job as *Vogue*'s art director. Aiming to make the magazine less starry-eyed and more journalistic – more modern – he ratcheted up photography at the expense of illustration.[49] By 1946, Liberman was art directing *Glamour* and *House & Garden* too, still ousting Agha's people and hiring his own.[50]

André freelanced for all three Condé Nast publications. Liberman would have been impressed by pictures like those he took for a *House & Garden* feature about the summer home of June and Joseph Platt in Little Compton, Rhode Island. Both Platts were *House & Garden* editors. Joseph moonlighted as a Hollywood set designer. With the same flair as in Joseph's interiors of Manderley in *Rebecca* and Tara in *Gone with the Wind*, the Platts made ample use of folk objects in their own home: a cherub from a circus cart, a figurehead from a French frigate, a painted watchmaker's sign the size of a wagon wheel. André's photographs show off such objects in the context of the couple's stylish living. Images that merely illustrated design ideas did not interest André. He wanted to convey the feeling of life unfolding in the spaces he photographed.

During his shoot at the Platts', André donned canvas shoes, rolled up his sleeves, and, despite his vertigo, hoisted himself up to the roof where he craned to take some exposures of the garden below. Maybe it was that climb that prompted Joseph to inquire about André's specialty. "Everything in photography is my specialty," the photographer replied breezily.[51]

Everything. According to André, he refused Liberman's offer of a contract, insisting on his identity as a photo reporter. He was tempted, however. He liked Liberman. They shared Paris and the old days at *Vu*. Condé Nast was Francophile and prestigious. Besides, when André surveyed the crowded magazine field, he saw few other places where he might land. He was neither a fashion photographer nor a hard-news photojournalist. The new travel monthly *Holiday* hadn't yet found its footing. *Look* was filled with mediocre staff work supplemented by stock pictures from commercial agencies. *Life* didn't want him. Then there was *Fortune*. Henry Luce's monthly incorporated features about the arts into its coverage of business. The magazine's concept of the humanist businessman paralleled *Art et Médecine*'s concept of the humanist doctor, and André had once been happy freelancing for *Art et Médecine*.[52] His work would have fit at *Fortune*. Unfortunately for André, the magazine had just hired Walker Evans as staff photographer.

All the while, he would have been watching the plummeting star of his compatriot Martin Munkácsi. Owing to Munkácsi's incapacitating heart attack and his aversion to color photography, *Ladies' Home Journal* had canceled his lucrative contract. *Harper's Bazaar* was also about to drop him. Munkácsi's was a cautionary tale about seizing the occasion. He was fifty; André, fifty-two. André signed with Liberman.

"I promise you," said Liberman—again, in André's version of the exchange—"that, once we're on the right track, you'll be able to work as you did in Paris."[53] Yet both men should have known that the freedom André had enjoyed in the salad days of European picture magazines was impossible in a postwar American publishing empire. André would later claim that Liberman assured him of steady assignments for *Vogue*. His contract did not specify work for any one magazine. Condé Nast publications shared their talent. Yet Liberman's biographers Dodie Kazanjian and Calvin Tomkins lend credence to André's claim. The *Vogue* plan was scuttled, they explain, when Liberman realized that André was ill-suited for fashion. The art director's fallback was to make him the lead photographer at *House & Garden*.[54] So André wound up with glamorous *Vogue*'s plain sister. *House & Garden* was "horrible," he complained to Liberman.[55] You can help change it, the art director replied. Liberman felt "slightly guilty about Kertész," report his biographers. "'It was the first time in history,' he once said, 'that a great artist had been asked to photograph interiors.'"[56]

Effective January 1, 1947, and valid for one year, André's contract stipulated that he work exclusively for Condé Nast. He would earn between $150 and $175 per page for black-and-white pictures and $200 for color. At a time when Americans' median annual income was just over $3,000 (about $43,000 in 2024 dollars), he was guaranteed a minimum of $10,000 (about $143,000 in 2024 dollars). After years of poverty, the prospect of a steady and substantial paycheck would have relieved him and put him in Elizabeth's good graces.

André wasn't the only émigré photographer who had to adjust to American realities. The Russian-born Roman Vishniac had opened a portrait studio. László Moholy-Nagy founded a school. Lisette Model combined magazine work with teaching. But André couldn't let go of the idea that he should be well compensated for taking pictures as he pleased. He would speak of it like a recalcitrant child: "I wanted to do what I wanted, the way I did in Europe."[57] Practicalities dictated otherwise. To anyone who would listen, he complained.

**With home construction booming,** the economy firing on all cylinders, and postwar America obsessed with domesticity, *House & Garden* was poised to rake in subscriptions and advertising dollars. Its editors scurried to reposition the magazine for the new era. Photographs got bigger, layouts airier, pages more colorful. Prim dining rooms ceded space to open-plan kitchens. Articles that read like home economics textbooks thinned out. *House & Garden* was going to be "the *Vogue* of architecture and house furnishing," as one staffer put it.[58] Just as *Vogue*'s editors had shifted their thinking from clothing as such to the lifestyle of the active woman, so *House & Garden*'s editors looked beyond home decor and gardens, urging readers to "live as well as you look."[59] The magazine's scope widened to include topics like entertaining and buying at auction. The socialite Brooke Marshall (later Brooke Astor) was hired to sweet-talk her rich friends into allowing *House & Garden* photographers inside their homes.[60] André was dispatched to shoot the Newport cottage of Mr. and Mrs. Persifor Frazer III, the Connecticut farm of the investment banker Dewees Dilworth, and the wooden-Indian collection of the artist Charles Green Shaw, an heir to the Woolworth fortune.

André threw himself into the task of waking up *House & Garden*. He traveled incessantly, usually with an editor or writer. Colleagues found him good-natured, likable, and utterly professional. They respected his perfectionism even when it tried their patience. A single image might require hours of preparation. Furniture had to be moved, dishes rearranged, bushes trimmed. André would fuss over the angle of a door, the placement of a bouquet, or the position of a book left open on a table or chair – his signature touch – as if its reader had just stepped away. He made ample use of the oblique, leading the eye from one object or space to another and implying the way a person might move through a garden or room. His goal was to convey the feeling of each place that he photographed: to reveal the essence of, say, a den or a rose garden and underscore its relevant details. He might take advantage of a cast shadow to articulate space or use a sun pattern from a multipaned window to make a nook feel cozy. Some of the pictures were quietly stunning.

Photographing buildings is technically challenging. Verticals must come out vertical, and horizontals, horizontal. Depth of field is important. Orchestrating light and shadow can be tricky. André coordinated natural and artificial light. He avoided stray reflections and distracting shadows. When a dim interior and bright exterior appeared in the same image, he captured details in both. If the *House & Garden* team arrived at someone's home in the late afternoon and the light was wrong, he would insist on returning the next morning, despite an always tight schedule.[61] He had to get everything right the first time. He did not enjoy the luxury of redos.

André relied heavily on both his Linhof and a 4 by 5 inch Stegemann view camera. Occasionally, he switched to a medium-format camera, either a Rolleiflex f/3.5 twin reflex or a Zeiss Super Ikonta. His favorite black-and-white film was the Eastman Kodak Super XX panchromatic, rated about ISO 250 by today's standards. When Kodak retired Super XX in 1954, he would opt for the photojournalist's workhorse, Tri-X (ISO 400).[62]

André's color photographs were mostly 4 by 5 inch Kodachrome transparencies. Liberman was pushing color. Although he considered black-and-white "the probity of all photography," the art director was aware that color was its future.[63] A good color photograph, Liberman decreed, relies on a dominant hue to bind it together. André complied, despite his tritanopia (blue-yellow color blindness). He had been doing color work for hire since the late 1930s. But he too believed that black-and-white was intrinsic to what photography was. André considered color photography unrealistic. That seems counterintuitive. He meant that color flaunts its hypernaturalism at the expense of the emotional authenticity of black-and-white, and even in magazine work, André sought authenticity.

Happily, he was not studio-bound. His assignments took him to some of America's most beautiful homes and gardens. They played to his fascination with objects. So the amateur became a professional. The individualist worked with a team. The Leica devotee deployed tripod-mounted large-format cameras. Within the parameters set for him, André pursued his interpretive vision. He completed each job with integrity and forbearance. Marshall, who often accompanied him on assignments, watched as he "rejoiced in whatever his camera could catch."[64]

The photographs André was taking for himself convey little rejoicing. Their settings are not those frequented by the design-savvy rich. Nor are their subjects the family, friends, and street characters who once piqued his desire to pull his camera to his eye. André's Hungarian images reveal his joy at being alive, face-to-face, side by side, with family and friends. His French images spring from curiosity about the hive of creativity that was interwar Paris, his lively social life, and a burgeoning confidence in his own vision. His New York pictures speak of estrangement.

André saw a city devoid of the intimate public spaces that so pleased him in Europe. He did not perceive individuals on the streets, only the masses.[65] The chemistry he had with Budapest, Paris, and villages everywhere was lacking. The city was crushing his soul with consumerism and competition. As a secular Jew, André had always worked with other secular Jews in informal yet effective networks. New York's vibrant Jewish presence notwithstanding, his photographs recall the stereotype of the Jew as marginalized and alienated.

One overcast Saturday found him on Washington Street in Gairville, a run-down waterfront section of Brooklyn, today gentrified and rebaptized DUMBO. Littered and desolate and lined with turn-of-the-century factories, Washington Street stopped just short of the East River. There loomed one tower of the Manhattan Bridge, linking Brooklyn to Lower Manhattan. Except for a parked car, the street showed no sign of human activity. Its outstanding feature was a clock embedded in an overpass between factories on opposite sides of the street. So stagnant is the atmosphere in the photograph André took that afternoon that the clock's hands, reading 3:42, feel cemented in place.[66]

Yet something *is* stirring: birds, maybe pigeons, swooping and flapping around. André has framed the image to visually cage the birds, using the overpass, the facades, the pavement, and the bridge trusses. His short telephoto lens flattens the scene, enhancing the locked-in effect. *Manhattan Bridge* is a record of observed reality but also a mindscape in which André's birds once again embody nature, freedom, and the creative spirit.

Another time-stilled image, taken in Carl Schurz Park near the East River, dates from a steely cold January day. A man in an overcoat and homburg stands in the frozen slush, observing a passing tug. His face is not visible. A second loner has drifted past, staring in the opposite direction. Alienated, bourgeois, and anonymous, such men wander through André's work during these years. Although they sometimes turn up in his European pictures too, in New York, they come into their own. In *River Walk of Carl Schurz Park*, there are only people alone, plus a long row of empty benches curving along the river walk as evenly spaced as markers on the face of a clock. They stretch into the distance or, metaphorically, into the future.[67]

In September 1948, André had an opportunity to reckon with the past when Condé Nast dispatched him first to Britain to photograph country houses, then to Paris. Elizabeth accompanied him. Only hours after landing in France, André launched into a packed schedule that took him to the homes of the designer Elsa Schiaparelli and the couturier Marcel Rochas, among dozens of others. He had a second assignment from the French embassy to photograph monuments and country scenes. Not until he took a few days off could André fully register Paris: *his* Paris but not. Coffee was rationed. Lajos Tihanyi was dead. The Dôme was passé.

From France, the couple traveled to Hungary, André's first visit in fourteen years. Budapest was a hull of the city where he had grown up. Neighborhoods had been pulverized by Allied bombs, bridges lay smashed in the Danube, the gilded cafés had vanished. People in threadbare overcoats trudged along once lively Váci Street, past shopwindows displaying fashions that no one could afford. Trucks blaring military music crept down the boulevards of what was now the capital of the Hungarian People's Republic.

André saw a lot of his brother Imre. One day, the two headed for the funfair at the city park, where they stopped at a vintage swing ride. Its seats encircled a fake *Mitteleuropa*-style castle, an absurd Habsburgian anachronism in Soviet-controlled Hungary. That comic-opera setting spoke of the old Budapest. Imre lowered himself onto the platform, and André raised his camera. Like the empty park benches André photographed, the empty swing seats in his portrait evoke primal thoughts of the missing. Everything that was beautiful in our life here is gone, thought André.[68]

A survivor of the Budapest ghetto, Imre wore a suit that hung rather too loosely. André's frame was spare too. At age fifty-four, he weighed

154 pounds, eleven pounds less than when he sailed into New York in 1936. His face had thinned. His hair had grayed. His gentle manner and exuberant smile were intact, yet Hungarians would have been startled to see him – the lucky one, the American! – looking faded and gaunt.

Elizabeth was forty-six, though she claimed to be forty-two. Her scraped-back hair, dark-circled eyes, and tailored suits suggested a woman who brooked little frivolity. The couple's American experience had brought out the sharp edges in her personality. Elizabeth was "not dainty," observed one acquaintance. "She looked like she could do a job."[69] Her entrepreneurial spirit, financial acumen, and hard work had paid off. Elizabeth's latest move had been to purchase a forty-two-unit apartment building in the Bronx as an investment. For Christmas, she would give André a $305 Patek Philippe watch from Tiffany, a gift that he cherished.

From Budapest, the couple traveled to the third cardinal point in André's existence: Szigetbecse. The village was physically intact yet morally devastated. Some locals had been Nazi sympathizers or active participants in the Nazi cause. Some had joined the German military. The rest had prayed that the war would end with occupation by the Allies and not the dreaded Red Army. Yet it was the Soviets who rolled into town. They stripped the "traitor" Swabians – "traitor" because of their German ancestry – of their possessions and deported them to Germany or to labor camps in the east.

André arrived in Szigetbecse carrying copies of *Nos Amies les Bêtes* (Our Friends the Animals), his 1936 book dedicated to the village. Szigetbecse had long embodied the rootedness and community lacking in New York. Yet events from the past decade told a different story. André's view of the village was as antiquated as the vintage swing ride.

**He would spend the next thirteen years** crisscrossing the United States for Condé Nast: Chicago, Raleigh, San Antonio, Baltimore, Los Angeles, Pittsburgh, Boston, Washington, Massachusetts, Virginia, Connecticut,

New Jersey. He flew. He drove. He took the train. He slept in hotels, motels, and guest rooms.

One typical assignment took him and his favorite colleague, the architectural editor Katherine Morrow Ford, to Dallas and Fort Worth, where André shot twenty-four locales. In her thank-you note after the pair departed, the Dallas journalist Patsy Swank remarked that her husband, the architect Arch Swank, was still getting up in the morning and muttering "Poor André."[70] He was thinking of the photographer's endless checklists and of the rainstorms he'd dodged all that week.

André's Dallas and Fort Worth tasks did not end when he returned to New York. Many whose homes got the *House & Garden* treatment wanted prints for themselves. After André's images ran in the magazine, Ford would approve most such requests, pull the negatives, and grant permissions. Up to his ears in orders and constantly traveling, André lagged with the printing and billing. Payments went directly to him. His bank account fattened. So did his files, with letters like one from the prominent Dallas landscape architect Marie Berger. Berger's gardens had won wide admiration for their play of sunlight and shade, an effect one *House & Garden* editor dubbed "Texas chiaroscuro." Berger gushed to André: "This message carries the highest praise and gratitude to you for those beautiful photographs in the Feb. issue of H&G. They were singingly handsome and are the best garden photographs I have ever seen."[71] André would have felt simultaneously gratified and galled.

More kudos, plus an order for one hundred prints, came from Gerald M. Loeb, an art collector, hobbyist photographer, and partner at the New York stock brokerage firm E. F. Hutton. Meaning to be collegial and kind, Loeb cultivated André. His attentions would have felt like noblesse oblige. Once André and Elizabeth spent a day at Loeb's Connecticut farm, with its bowling alley and CinemaScope projection room. As if André wasn't already up to his eyeballs in the worldly goods of the rich. On another occasion, Loeb invited him, along with the designer Norman

Bel Geddes, the architects Philip Johnson, I. M. Pei, and Marcel Breuer, and other creative giants, to a luncheon at the Waldorf Astoria. The occasion would have been salve for his ego. But what was one luncheon when he was spiritually starving?

**Clouds swam** through the sky. Rain pearled the glass. As the light dimmed that afternoon, André and Elizabeth's first at 2 Fifth Avenue, André faced a window in the dining alcove. On its sill stood a metal weathercock he'd unearthed at an antique shop in Connecticut. It would have reminded him of Magyar folktales and Magyar folk art but also of the Gallic rooster symbolic of the French nation. In André's photograph, the weathercock is silhouetted against the skyline of Lower Manhattan. Just across Washington Square stands Judson Memorial Church, its bell tower topped with a cross. It's one of a jumble of buildings optically flattened like paper cutouts by the telephoto lens he was using. The photograph projects the serenity of watching from a place of glassed-in comfort as rain soaks a vast and impersonal metropolis.[72] Once again, André was photographing from a window to mark a new phase in his life.

He had spotted 2 Fifth Avenue when the white glazed-brick building was under construction. It appealed to him for its location on Washington Square. As early comers, he and Elizabeth had their pick of almost four hundred apartments on twenty floors. So André roved from floor to floor, apartment to apartment, assessing the photographic potential of each. The twelfth floor, he observed, was neither so high that the scenes below lacked detail nor so low as to hinder the possibilities of abstraction. Situated at the building's southwest corner, the luminous apartment 12J offered a 160 degree panorama. It had an eight by ten foot balcony with nothing directly above.[73] They could easily afford the $360 rent.[74] Perfect. In fall 1952, they moved in.

Twenty years earlier, André and Elizabeth had opted for modernist decor in their Paris apartment. Now their perspective was different. Considering 12J a sanctuary from life in the United States, they wanted an Old World feeling. Elizabeth fussed over the eggshell hue for the walls. She purchased Directoire chairs, a tea table, and, from the Parke-Bernet Galleries auction house, armchairs and a Steinway piano. Rejecting what they saw as the ostentatious display yet cultural impoverishment of many American homes, they hung paintings by Elizabeth and their artist friends. Books abounded. So did curios, statuettes, handmade toys, and fine china. As for the flute André inherited from his father, it was wrapped and tucked away on a shelf by the kitchen door, its melodies—those of the vagabond, the shepherd, the dreamer—now fallen silent.

The move anchored the couple. Life settled into a routine. The 1950s brought pleasant interludes. They vacationed in Mexico and the Bahamas. They weekended in Connecticut and in Lenox, Massachusetts, the home of the Hungarian-born editor Stefan Lorant, with whom they attended concerts at Tanglewood.[75]

In New York, André's most loyal friends were also Francophile Hungarian Jews. He was close to the Budapest-born Edie Capa, Cornell's wife, a skilled organizer and generous soul. André's bonds with Charles Rado, the photographer Camilla Koffler (known professionally as Ylla), and the literary agent and Bach devotee Ferenc "Frank" Dobo, all old friends from Paris, proved enduring.

André's friendship with the beret-wearing, Budapest-born painter Tivadar Fried, called Ted, also traced to Paris. There André had done portraits of him moonlighting as a marionettist and had taught him photography. André's lessons probably saved Fried's life. Stuck in Nazi-occupied Toulouse during the war, Fried had supported himself as a studio photographer—some of his clients were German—while making fake documents for the Resistance. After the artist reached New York, André could often be found at Fried's studio on West Twenty-Third Street.[76]

Among André's younger Hungarian-born friends, the photographer Suzanne Szasz was a central figure. Following a postwar stint in Washington, DC, with her diplomat husband, Szasz divorced, moved to New York, and remarried. André and Elizabeth attended the parties she hosted in New York and Westhampton, where Szasz and her second husband had a home. Unlike some of his colleagues who sniffed at Szasz's subject matter, André esteemed her photographs of children, published in *Life*, *Look*, *McCall's*, and *Ladies' Home Journal*. He also shared her love of cats and her penchant for flirting.

Every December, Condé Nast's business manager sent André the same contractual agreement. Every December, he signed and went on.

From time to time, he tried to broaden his reputation. In 1952, he submitted one of the Distortions to the *World Exhibition of Photography* organized in Switzerland by the photo historian Helmut Gernsheim. It was rejected. Then he courted the European art publisher Skira. Nothing came of that either. Closer to home, he contacted the Gentry Galleries through his old friend, the writer and former expat Meyer Levin. André wanted a show. Housed in a Broadway hotel, the Gentry Galleries was hardly a hotbed of the avant-garde. "Unfortunately, Gentry said 'No,'" Levin reported to André. "Too modern or something. They're all crazy."[77]

One more belly flop.

**In his spare time,** André strolled through the Village, alone or with friends, or dallied in Washington Square, camera in hand, attentive to body language and little human interactions. What read as a semiabstract pattern twelve stories up came into focus as dog walkers, children, sketch artists, chess players, and buskers. André paid attention to what most people unthinkingly filter out as unimportant. Two bespectacled readers leaning against the same tree. Some amateurish watercolors of cats lined up for sale next to a live feline. Couples kissing.

In the late fall and winter, when foliage did not block the view, he liked to plant himself on his balcony with a tripod-mounted camera. Typically up early, André took pleasure in the first hours after a snowfall, when the footprints below were sparse and distinct. Sometimes tire tracks scored the road that cut under the arch and circled a snow-padded fountain. Their graphic possibilities thrilled him.

It was on one such early morning in 1954 that André took what became the most beloved of his hibernal photographs: *Washington Square, Winter*.[78] The day dawned overcast yet bright. In André's picture, the naked tree branches interlace like organic filigree. Fences and rows of benches wind through the park, empty except for two tiny figures. A man strides along an elliptical path. A woman, more distant, presses in the opposite direction. Theirs is an existential passing. Yet the photograph's poetic beauty, not unlike that of the slow movement of a sonata, overcomes any feeling of sadness. Like most of André's Washington Square pictures taken from on high, *Washington Square, Winter* evokes a classic European urban garden walled off from the hubbub and din of the city.

One day four months later, André withdrew at dusk, not to his balcony but to the roof of 2 Fifth Avenue. The sky was lowering. Lights flicked on to the west. Hours earlier had come news that forty-year-old Robert Capa had been killed when he stepped on a land mine in Thai Binh, Vietnam, while reporting for *Life*. As the world paid homage to a courageous war correspondent, André stood on the roof observing the gathering night and grieving for his "little child."[79]

With Capa based in Paris after the war and traveling widely, the two had seen each other only rarely in recent years. Often their visits took place around Christmas, when Capa would blow into New York to spend time with his family. One mutual friend had observed the "special look" that came over Capa's face when he announced that he was off to see André.[80] As for André, he spoke of "that boy" with warmth and affection: "that boy" who shared his memories of Budapest and his devotion to Paris, who used to sleep on his couch, who wore his courage so lightly.

Capa's fame had long since eclipsed André's. Yet the younger photographer still sometimes leaned on his elder. In 1950, Capa had asked André to do the layout for *Report on Israel*, his book with writer Irwin Shaw about the birth of the nation. In a letter, Capa pronounced the layout "really the best thing in the book," adding: "I thank you again for your guidance and help, during all those long years."[81]

With Bob Capa's death, his younger brother, Cornell, now a *Life* photographer, felt that he had inherited Bob's debt. He sent André a book about Bob, along with a note pointing out that to read it would be "pure anguish, full of recollections almost better forgotten... However, this is just what life is, and with all that bitter, there are many sweet things to recall," especially about the young Robert "who you have so befriended."[82]

Like André, the Capas were humanists. In 1947, Bob had photographed farm families in the American Midwest and the Soviet Union for the *Ladies' Home Journal* series "People Are People the World Over." That feature about human commonalities reportedly inspired Edward Steichen when he curated the 1955 exhibition *The Family of Man*. Organized at the Museum of Modern Art and eventually viewed by more than ten million people worldwide, *The Family of Man* would become the most popular photography exhibition of all time.

Steichen had long since outmaneuvered Beaumont Newhall for the position of head of MoMA's photo department. He espoused a broader view of the medium than his predecessor. For Steichen, photography was a kind of visual Esperanto that could bond humanity together. With *The Family of Man*, he used it to countervail Cold War propaganda by communicating people's essential sameness. In organizing the exhibition, Steichen and his assistants combed through two million photographs, from which they extracted five hundred and three. These they categorized by themes like children, music, and couples. Scores of photographers, both amateur and professional, were represented, among them Brassaï, Robert Capa, Robert Frank, and Ansel Adams. André's work was a natural. Yet it was absent. André had never kept secret his opinion of Steichen as a showman. Steichen was no fan of André's either. As a curator at MoMA, he shunned André's work even for modest group shows. So André remained on the outs with America's leading venue for photography.

It was not only André's erasure from the photography world that made the mid-1950s a difficult time. In Budapest, Elizabeth's mother died of a heart attack. Then a nationalist uprising was crushed by the Soviets after only twelve days. The Hungarian Revolution left twenty-five hundred people dead and two hundred thousand homeless. Among them was Elizabeth's sister Márta, now a stateless refugee evacuated to the United States thanks to the military's Operation Safe Haven. Márta (who was accompanied or soon joined by her daughter Veronika) arrived in January 1957, a time when Elizabeth was hard taxed by Cosmia: Her partner, Frank Tamás, was going blind. Although he still came to the office, responsibilities fell heavily on Elizabeth's shoulders.

Meanwhile, André was struggling with his own health problems. He suffered from erysipelas, an acute bacterial skin infection also known as Saint Anthony's fire after the martyred saint. Erysipelas brings shiny and painfully swollen red plaques and often a fever. All the while, the dizzy spells caused by Ménière's disease came and went, probably intensified by the stress of his job. One day, André walked up Fifth Avenue to Cornell and Edie Capa's apartment. To Edie, he poured out his heart about the miseries of his job and his life in America.[83] Only weeks later, André's brother Imre died at age sixty-six.

André did what he did when life felt grim: He turned to nature.

**In August 1955,** the Kertészes purchased a house on Parmalee Hill Road in Newtown, Connecticut.[84] The road hooks off the main route from town, climbing and plunging past meadows, dairy farms, and fields that had reverted to hardwood and hemlock. To the east flows the Housatonic. An undistinguished yet pleasant Cape Cod, André and Elizabeth's weekend retreat had a fireplace and a decorative pool. But its glory lay in its surroundings. Only ten minutes from downtown, it felt buried in the country.

Sometimes they invited weekend guests, but often it was just the two of them. When the weather was pleasant, they read on the portico or pulled lawn chairs to the front yard to have a drink and gaze at the trees and the clouds. For the first time in years, Elizabeth set up her easel and painted. André combed the meadows and woods, his Leica slung from his neck.

In one picture redolent of summer sweetness, birds freckle the sky and cattle flank a lone tree. In another, taken on a foggy September day, a man who may be a houseguest sits reading off in the distance. Like some of the trees towering above, he is ghosted by mist. That visual dissolve could be read as a metaphor for the man's mental remoteness. Transported by the book, he is oblivious to all that surrounds him.

André's Newtown landscapes evince a primitive pleasure in light. So does his interior *Chez Moi, Newtown*. That image centers on a drawing easel positioned against a multipaned window curtained in voile. The fabric's folds and shadows turn the light-splashed tree branches outside into a joyful distortion. On the easel sits an open book, one page of which refuses to lie flat. The imagination takes flight, one might think. Next to it sits a ceramic bird, its beak pointing like an arrow to the book. For once, André's bird isn't swooping or darting or milling around but nesting.[85]

Elsewhere, too, André sought out nature. Once he clipped a *New York Times* article titled "Going for a Walk" that surveyed scenic hiking trails accessible from the city.[86] On a Saturday just after Christmas four months later, he positioned that clipping on a light-washed wall in his Union Square office, then overlapped it with an envelope and a clear plastic triangle and skewered everything with a pushpin. The envelope bore an arty rubber-stamp image of a hand holding a business card–like rectangle in which the sender had penned André's name and address. As André had positioned the envelope, the index finger pointed toward a window covered by venetian blinds.

One of the pleasures of *Going for a Walk* is its wit: André's photograph could be read as a sophisticated Gone Fishin' sign. Another is his nod to Synthetic Cubism, invented by Pablo Picasso and Georges Braque in the first years of the twentieth century. Maybe André was reminded of Cubism by the exhibition *Picasso: 75th Anniversary*, which he had probably seen at MoMA the previous summer. That exhibition included more than a dozen Synthetic Cubist artworks using ink, pencil, oil, and pasted papers and cloth. In any case, *Going for a Walk* evokes Synthetic Cubism in its use of everyday objects, its collage-like sensibility, its concern for planar surface, and its synergistic play between visual and verbal languages.

*Going for a Walk* could also be read as an image about photography as André practiced it. The triangle evokes his formal rigor. The finger printed on the envelope points toward the light from an unseen window—the medium's lifeblood. And the name that appears in the center of the image is his own: "André Kertész," photographer going for a walk, Leica in hand.

For the larger photography community, André the pioneering modernist barely existed. One day, Lisette Model stumbled on a group of André's early photographs. Although she had long known some of his work, her main frame of reference for André was his desertion of Rogi. After discovering the earlier pictures, she told the photographer, writer, and teacher David Vestal, a major player in the photography world, about her find. André's work was "wonderful," Model reported. It was André who had opened up photographic modernism! Vestal was startled. "She was much impressed," he later remembered, "which wasn't like Lisette." Vestal had noted André's credit line under pictures of posh houses in Condé Nast publications. But he too had no idea that André was "also a real photographer. Hardly anyone knew it."[87]

**Brassaï did.**

How are you? he inquired.

"I'm dead! You're seeing a dead man."[88]

André's words tumbled out amid the hubbub at Pier 89 on the morning of April 8, 1957. His old friend and rival Brassaï, just debarked from the SS *Liberté*, was glad-handing greeters. Some were staffers from

*Holiday*, the monthly that was sponsoring Brassaï's three-month stay in the United States.

André's answer to Brassaï's question alludes to a poem known to virtually every Hungarian of their generation: Endre Ady's autobiographical "Gare de l'Est." The setting for Ady's poem is a compartment in an evening train about to depart Paris for Budapest. The narrator sits dreading his awakening the next morning in "the sunless East!" As the train twitches into motion and Paris blurs by, faster and faster, Ady hears the "City of marvels, holy treasure" singing to him. Ahead await only "songless hearts [that] my heart do kill." He continues: "Joy never shall I know. / I sprawl here, cold, so stupidly." The poem ends with the words "the monster of iron / With on it a dead man."[89]

Brassaï, by contrast, was thriving. He had become a cultural icon. People were fascinated with the noir Paris of brothels, bars, and dimly lit cobblestone streets in his pictures. Along with Picasso and the Surrealists, Brassaï embodied the prestige and glamour of the prewar avant-garde. His solo exhibition of Parisian graffiti at MoMA had been last fall's New York sensation. Brassaï had conquered the magazine world too. At *Harper's Bazaar*, Carmel Snow gave him wide latitude in choosing his subjects. He covered Sweden at Christmastime, the perfume town of Grasse, and all things Parisian—the kind of roaming reportage that André once owned and still coveted. Now *Holiday* was allowing Brassaï carte blanche to photograph in New York and Louisiana. "I'm the opposite of Christopher Columbus," Brassaï would crow. "This time it's America who has just discovered me."[90]

"Let me tell you what has happened to me in this damn country." That day at the dock, André hastened to explain why he had washed up at *House & Garden*. His contract dictated that he work for *Vogue*, he claimed. (It did not.) "Liberman tricked me," he groused. "I've become his slave."[91] Yoked to *House & Garden*, André was fed lists of subjects that bored him, as Brassaï would have heard. That spring it was breakfast nooks and cleverly organized kitchens.

With changes at Condé Nast in the early 1960s, André's unhappiness grew. Liberman had once operated from the premise that magazines should hew to classic aesthetic standards. Then he fell hard for pop culture. He began dictating more audacious layouts and outré pictures, especially in *Vogue*. "I came to believe in the unexpected, in chance," he would explain, "in doing things that hadn't been done before and didn't conform to any established design principles."[92] Liberman so admired the high-octane style of the *New York Post* that he thumbtacked copies of the tabloid on *Vogue*'s layout room walls.[93] He was betting on brash photographers like William Klein for his flagship publication. At *House & Garden*, the focus shifted from architecturally distinctive homes that expressed their owners' personalities to generic interiors where middle-class readers could imagine their families. Liberman wanted shots with a bright suburban feeling. "Make your living room a place where in equal comfort you can enjoy listening to music, reading, dining, writing letters or pursuing a hobby," one article urged.[94]

Regarding photography itself, Liberman's views were self-contradictory. Although he denied that photographs were art, he penned an article for *Vogue* lavishing praise on Steichen as the preeminent practitioner of the "major art form" that is photography.[95] (Liberman was also an ambitious photographer. His article about Steichen appeared two months before the opening of *The Artist in His Studio: Photographs by Alexander Liberman*, organized by Steichen at MoMA.) *Vogue* published another feature extoling Irving Penn's photography as "extraordinarily brilliant work in the arts."[96] Liberman had a warmly collaborative relationship with his new wunderkind Penn, whose poetic vision now singularized Condé Nast's pages.

That was not the case for the other poet-photographer Liberman employed. The art director let it be known that he no longer considered André either a great artist or a great photographer—too "sentimental," out of step with the times.[97] Nor did André consider Liberman a great art director. He chalked up *House & Garden*'s shortcomings to Liberman's choice to be “an American, not an artist,” meaning a crass worshipper of the almighty dollar.[98]

Each man found the other prickly and difficult. Nicknamed the Silver Fox, Liberman enjoyed a reputation as a high-powered charmer who moved in glittering circles. But Condé Nast staffers knew other sides of him. “He could be contrary and capricious, and even devious at times,” write his biographers. “You couldn't be sure where you stood with Alex, whose opinions were subject to instant revision, and whose ironic courtliness masked a relentlessly critical mind.”[99] André was among those who heard the art director address him in honeyed tones one minute – “dear friend” – and felt the sting of his icy glare the next.[100]

Among André's assignments that fell afoul of the art director was a 1957 feature for *Vogue*. He shot it at the Williamstown, Massachusetts, estate of Cole Porter. Porter's adored late wife, Linda, had transformed their carriage house into a studio for the composer and lyricist. After her death, Porter could no longer face the main house, imbued as it was with her spirit. So he had it demolished, then moved into the studio and added a wing. André was to photograph the results. When he heard the story, he was touched by the songwriter's devotion to his wife's memory. During the shoot, he banished his *House & Garden* colleagues to other parts of the estate, the better to concentrate on details that revealed what Linda had meant to Porter. He spent two days on the job.

But when he showed the pictures to Liberman, his boss responded: “It's marvelous, it's excellent, but, look, forget all this feeling, don't think about the composition, re-do it for me, something ordinary, don't be sentimental.”

André recoiled.

“But why are you asking me to do it?”[101]

Anyone could do the slicker piece Liberman was demanding, André stewed. He was furious. But he did as he was told.

**In September 1961,** André was hospitalized at Mount Sinai, apparently to repair a hernia. Lying in bed, he took stock. He was in his late sixties. His health was fraying. Liberman had cut back on his assignments, and those he got felt joyless. Nearly fifteen years at *House & Garden* had shot his reputation. His life had resolved into failure.

"I think over my American existence, and I decided I don't want to give in, even if I have nothing to eat," he said. "Is more important with this son of a bitch life to hold on and do what *I* want, honestly, humanly, artistically. In cents and dollars, I have a difficult life, not making the big money a la Avedon and company."[102] André was galled by Richard Avedon, whose photographs he dismissed as flashy and derivative of those of Martin Munkácsi. At the time, Avedon was earning a quarter million dollars a year, mostly from advertising work.[103]

André's contract still specified a minimum of $10,000 annually. He had never had a raise in his base salary. All the same, his statement about potential starvation is hyperbole. Cosmia kept expanding. Elizabeth was earning excellent money and investing it shrewdly. André had built up his own savings. And the two had banked a modest profit from the sale of their Newtown home in advance of the construction of an interstate highway that threatened to blunt its pleasures. All the same, Elizabeth opposed André's departure from Condé Nast because he would have no steady income. She pleaded with him to stay. He refused.

What had André accomplished at *House & Garden*? The magazine published more than three thousand Kertész photographs between 1945 and 1962. According to the curator Weston Naef, André's was the largest body of work ever to appear in a single publication by a major twentieth-century photographer.[104] He shared the magazine's pages with others, notably the architectural photographer Ezra Stoller and *Vogue* stalwarts Irving Penn and Horst P. Horst. But for a decade and a half, he was *House & Garden*'s go-to photographer. Penn and Cecil Beaton applauded his brilliant work. So did many whose homes, gardens, and institutions he photographed. He deserves a central place in the annals of interior and garden photography. However, André himself dismissed his contributions to Condé Nast publications as "worthless hackwork."[105]

That October, he took a leave of absence, never to return. He was feeling so marginalized that he wondered if anyone at Condé Nast even noticed he was gone.[106] André claimed that he quit, while Liberman's biographers write that "*House & Garden* decided that he was 'too difficult' to work with" and was let go.[107]

"As I give up the slave work, I start again where I stopped before I stepped onto this sacred land," he sneered to his sister-in-law, Imre's widow, Gréti.[108] At sixty-seven, André would reinvent himself. No longer would he kowtow to Liberman or anyone else, no longer would he be a professional—but once more an amateur.

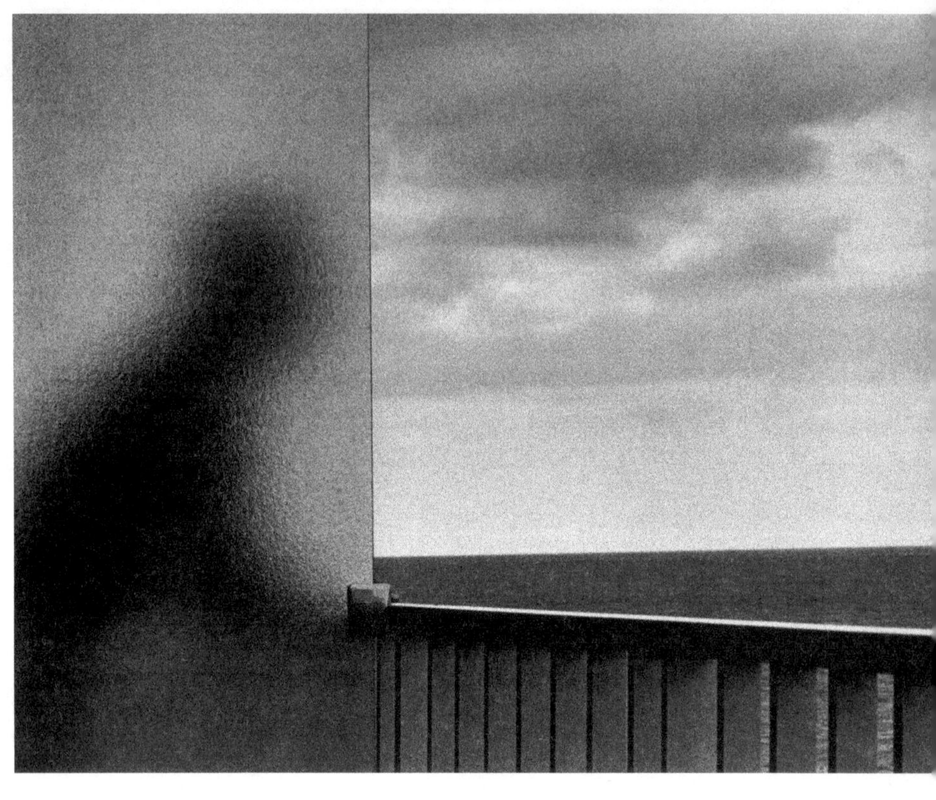

André Kertész, *Martinique*, 1972

# 10 MARTINIQUE, 1962–1972

**For the first time** in thirty-six years, André heard his brother's voice. Jenő. Eugenio, as he had renamed himself. Öcskös, as André liked to call him. In 1962, overseas telephone calls had to go through an operator. A call between New York and Buenos Aires was an event, and this one was extraordinary.

There was no reason to believe that America would now accept André. Year after year, he had languished at Condé Nast. Surely more failure was brewing. Yet this was his last chance. How much time did he have left? He wanted his brother's presence and counsel. Jenő had once believed in him when no one else had. The two made plans for André to travel to Buenos Aires that summer.

Shifting his mindset from working mostly for hire to steering his own career, from photographing for mass reproduction to handcrafting prints, André had begun combing through years' worth of negatives and contact sheets. Contact sheets map out a photographer's picture-taking experiences, material and emotional. Each sequence is intact, each change of position or variance in light still on the record. As André sorted, ghosts appeared, inscribed in silver salts and suspended in time. He marked frames that he wanted to print. He made lists. He rediscovered people and places. Driven by anger and ambition, he intended to show that he had created modern photography, even as certain imitators had become rich and famous.

Already he had created a portfolio and put it into the hands of Monroe Wheeler, MoMA's genial head of exhibitions and publications. André had been courting Wheeler since the early 1940s. From time to time, he'd helped Wheeler by supplying photographs of artists or artworks. Their relationship had always been cordial. Now André nursed hopes that Wheeler would make things happen for him at MoMA.

When he wasn't renewing his contacts or wrestling old pictures into order, André was prospecting for new ones. A subject from his French days reclaimed his attention. In New York, as in Paris, chimney pots inhabit realms that most people ignore. Tall or short, topped with conical hats or bulbous knobs, elbowed or not, André's come across as folk objects, modernist marionettes, stylized owls, rooftop Rockettes. They are also, as the photo historian Michel Frizot rightly observes, André's doubles, "scanning the terraces and the rooftops in search of other souls in sorrow."[1]

One incentive for André's return to pictures of chimney pots was his infatuation with the zoom lens. The zoom was the latest must-have, first for movie cameras and projectors, then for single-lens reflex 35 millimeter cameras. A zoom offers different focal lengths in a single lens. Its fields of view range from wide (with relatively little magnification) to narrow (with more magnification and visual compression). The lens moves, in effect; the photographer doesn't have to. André had long dreamed of such a lens. Now he tried different brands, then purchased a Schneider and an Angénieux.

"I *love* zoom," he gushed. Friends wondered if a zoom wasn't too heavy for him (it can weigh four or five pounds). But he pooh-poohed their concern. "Zoom was *made* for me. Like the Leica was *made* for me."[2] Others viewed André's new signature tool as a crutch for an aging street photographer. He remained a vigorous walker. But he also kept a zoom-lensed camera mounted on a tripod and positioned at a window or on his balcony. When he wasn't using a zoom, he sometimes took things even further with an ultra-magnifying telephoto lens.

Thanks to the zoom, André could pore over his surroundings from on high. Looking south, he watched corporate towers emerge from the demolition of old New York. His favorite perches were on his apartment's west side, where an older New York still existed. There he could survey MacDougal Alley, a nineteenth-century mews lined with artists' studios, and, beyond that, Eighth Street with its mom-and-pop stores and modest dwellings. He thought of those as his Paris views.

Peering into his viewfinder, André would visually roam the roofscapes: chimney pots, water tanks, ventilation hardware, laundry hung to dry. He watched shadows creep across rooftops. He ferreted out sunbathers, readers, and solitude-seekers. Someone sprawled in a lawn chair. Someone staring from a window onto an airshaft. With a twist of his wrist, he could send them whizzing toward him, extracting them from their surroundings. With the zoom, he could "penetrate into people's private lives."[3]

The 50 millimeter lens has about the same angle of view as human vision. Because of this perspectival relationship, it's considered the normal lens. Thus it is assumed to hold the "promise of shared perspective and common understanding," argues the multimedia designer Allain Daigle.[4] By contrast, a zoom lens used in telephoto mode, say 200 or 400 millimeter, implies a private, even voyeuristic vision. The classic example is James Stewart's wheelchair-bound character in Alfred Hitchcock's *Rear Window*, who uses his 400 millimeter telephoto lens to spy on goings-on in his neighbors' apartments. After a quarter century in New York, André still felt like a stranger.

Similarly, the photographs of the city André took on walks are formally sophisticated yet emotionally remote. His New York was a metropolis of brick walls, modernist facades, and vacant spaces slabbed in concrete and steel. Space is compressed and abstracted. A stray dog, a pigeon, or a tree branch appears here or there. Passersby tend to be marginalized or even visually headless or legless because of the framing. Light, shadows, and reflective surfaces sometimes coax out a more congenial side of the city. Yet the wit and curiosity evident in his pictures from other times are mostly absent.

As for André's relationship with Elizabeth, it's hard to know how things stood between them. He claimed to adore her, yet rumors circulated about their fierce fights. The two "had a very fractious relationship," says one observer. "He pretended." "There may have been difficulties in the relationship, but at the same time there was a basic pull—he really did love her," insists another.[5]

As André must have been aware, many of his friends viewed Elizabeth differently than he did. They disliked her. If they happened to be visiting André when she returned from work, Elizabeth would nod politely but curtly, decline an invitation to join them, and head straight for her bedroom. (Elizabeth and André each had their own room. André's was his study, where he slept on the daybed.) Elizabeth was "a cold fish," reports one friend, "a bossy lady." "Very stern," in the view of another. "Shell-shocked," says a third.[6]

Whatever else was going on, she was overworked and exhausted. Sales were up at Cosmia, and the company was about to launch its first product line under its own name. An ad agency had been hired and a logo created for Bleu de Mer bath and shower toiletries. Elizabeth was running operations, distribution, and marketing. Frank Tamás still came to work every day, but, now legally blind, he had to be escorted.

Although André was circumspect in speaking publicly about Elizabeth's business partner, friends sensed his resentment and jealousy. He griped that Tamás was irresponsible and intrusive. Elizabeth may have shared that opinion, yet she reportedly gave Tamás money. Vexed though he was about that, André couldn't object. They were her earnings, not his.[7] Elizabeth was astute about managing money but also spent freely, while André's spending habits were shaped by past penury and perhaps some regret about quitting a well-paying job. When the owner of a local hardware store arrived to install an air conditioner in their apartment, André offered to pay him in photographic prints. (The installer refused.)[8]

André's 1962 photograph *Broken Bench* alludes to his domestic situation. Its setting is the grounds of a mental institution on Long Island. He was there because of a troubled young woman Elizabeth had befriended in her ballet class. The friend's mother had died. Her father drank. She was emotionally unstable. The Kertészes had treated her kindly, even inviting her to spend weekends with them in the country. On one occasion, their guest flew into an uncontrollable rage, and a doctor had to be summoned. She was institutionalized. After she stabilized, André and Elizabeth agreed to sponsor the woman's release. On the day André took *Broken Bench*, they were handling the formalities. Tamás had come along.

In the picture's lower right is a bench, its back slats missing or askew. One slat sends the eye in the direction of two women seated on a more distant bench. André's wide-angle lens accentuates that distance. One woman is the patient, the other Elizabeth. Much closer to the camera, on the left, stands a man with his back to the viewer. He belongs to that race of anonymous men in overcoats who drift in and out of André's photographs over the years. In fact, he is Tamás. Ironically, the blind man appears to be scoping out the women on the bench. There's an implied fourth presence too: the photographer. As in every photograph, it's congruent with the camera's position, and thus the viewer's. The effect is powerful in this most Hitchcockian of André's images.[9] It's unclear if things are normal or not. The photographer is watching the man who's staring at the women. Is he a voyeur? A menace? What event is unfolding?

"We had a tragic situation at home," André would explain. "I saw this scene with the broken bench. Symbolically everything was together. I felt it and took it."[10] By "tragic," is André referring to the young woman? To the blind Tamás, whose wealthy sister refused to help him and whose problems weighed heavily on them? To his relationship with Elizabeth? It's tempting to read the exaggerated distance between André's camera and Elizabeth as a sign of her emotional inaccessibility. It's tempting too to view Tamás as simultaneously André's rival for Elizabeth's attention and a surrogate for André himself. As in a dream, people irrationally merge.

**That spring,** André's sorting of negatives and contact sheets gained immediacy with the visit of Romeo Martinez, the Paris-based editor in chief of *Camera*. The Swiss monthly was among the magazines that were taking up orbits around creators and viewers of photography as a creative art. Shunning the how-to features that filled hobbyist publications, *Camera* spotlighted portfolios by individual photographers. *Aperture* in the United States and *Creative Camera* in Britain shared that approach. *Camera* distinguished itself by its high-quality printing and its internationalism. Each issue appeared in separate French, English, and German editions.

As for Martinez, he was a humanist who espoused *photographie d'auteur*, that is, photography as a subjective art imbued with the photographer's inner life. Martinez never published anyone's portfolio before getting to know that person and taking his or her measure. A French citizen born of a Spanish father and Mexican mother, he had probing eyes, a bald head, and a mustache that curtained his mouth. Martinez's idiosyncratic mind and wicked sense of humor won people over. The photographer Henri Cartier-Bresson considered him a "father confessor."[11]

Martinez and André had met a few years earlier through Alex Liberman. Now the French editor arrived in New York with an offer for André: He wanted to publish a Kertész portfolio as a cover story in *Camera*. Huddled at André's apartment, the two set about choosing the pictures. Shuffling prints and contact sheets, they devoted the better part of four days to thrashing out a checklist. André saw that Martinez deeply understood his work.

Then the editor stunned him with a second announcement: He planned to feature André's photographs at the next Venice Photography Biennale scheduled for May 1963. The biennial was an invitation-only event showcasing photography as an expressive art. It complemented the

Venice Biennale, with which it alternated years. (In that era, the Venice Biennale did not include photographs.) Martinez was its driving force. He left New York that June with 119 Kertész works: prints, glass plates, and 35 millimeter negatives.[12]

No sooner had Martinez departed than André convinced himself that something would go wrong. Because it always did. Before traveling to Buenos Aires, he conveyed his anxieties to Martinez, who replied to Elizabeth in André's absence: Tell him "above all to calm down."[13] Nothing had changed.

In Argentina, meanwhile, André and Jenő were experiencing the shock and joy of being together for the first time since 1926, when both had been struggling and eager. Now sixty-five, Jenő was presumably satisfied with his life. Not so André. Jenő would have heard plenty. André had been victimized, humiliated, cheated. Tricked by Keystone, enslaved by Condé Nast, ignored by the American powers that be.

As the brothers mulled over André's eleventh-hour attempt to win back the success he believed he deserved, it must have emerged that some Americans *had* tried to be helpful. One was Nathan Resnick, a photographer, member of the Circle of Confusion, and administrator at the Brooklyn campus of Long Island University. André had a long-standing invitation from Resnick to exhibit at the university. Probably at Jenő's urging, André sent a postcard to Resnick accepting the offer. After three weeks in Buenos Aires, he flew home with one of his brother's pithy observations in mind: "You are still André Kertész. You can still be the world's greatest photographer."[14]

So André set to work on his first retrospective. It would occupy a room on the eleventh floor of Metcalfe Hall, a movie palace and office building that the school was transforming into multipurpose spaces. What the venue lacked in prestige and amenities, André tried to make up for with artfulness. He arranged his books in display cases, next to vintage prints he'd retrieved from Jenő. More recent photographs were thumbtacked to walls that had been painted in regrettable colors.[15]

The show was a modest success. Writing to Imre's widow, Gréti, shortly before it closed, André lied that he never before wanted to exhibit in a country where people worked "with elbows and knives," a skill that he didn't possess.[16] But André *had* exhibited, notably at the Art Institute of Chicago in 1946, and he had tried hard for other shows. His latest failure was MoMA. Wheeler had kept his portfolio for three months, then turned him down.

There was more than one door into MoMA, however. André got wind that Edward Steichen was about to retire as the museum's director of photography. Excellent news for André. Someone named John Szarkowski was to take Steichen's place. Szarkowski turned out to be a thirty-six-year-old Wisconsin-born photographer, teacher, and raconteur in horn-rimmed glasses.

Shortly after his arrival that July 1, Szarkowski set a policy that anyone could drop off a portfolio on a Wednesday and pick it up the next day, knowing that the curator had examined it but most likely left no comments. So it was that one Wednesday, André joined a parade of hopefuls riding the elevator to the museum's fourth floor. He was toting two shopping bags bulging with the boxes that photo paper was sold in, yellow for Kodak, black-and-white for Ilford. The elevator doors opened onto a hall lined with framed stills from classic films. André walked down that hall, turned left, passed the film library, then entered the photography department. Flat drawers, filing cabinets, and bookshelves lined the walls.[17] He approached the reception desk. Most photographers submitted about fifty prints to Szarkowski. André was bringing five hundred. He signed his name on the sheet at the desk, nudged the bags toward the receptionist, and headed off.

No sooner had the door shut behind him than Szarkowski emerged from an office on the far side of the room. He had been watching this stooped-shoulder relic who reminded him of Willy Loman, the beat-down, self-deceptive protagonist of Arthur Miller's drama *Death of a Salesman.* Like Loman, the man was lugging his sample cases, still chasing success.

"Who was that?"

The receptionist scanned the sign-in sheet, then fumbled the pronunciation: "André Kertész."

Szarkowski's jaw dropped. Of course he knew the work of André Kertész. But Kertész had dropped out of sight ages ago. Wasn't he *dead*?

As Szarkowski riffled through the photographs André had left, he found some ho-hum, some indifferently printed, but many wonderful and some absolute knockouts. When André returned the next day, he was ushered into Szarkowski's office to discuss a solo exhibition.[18]

**André was not the only photographer** whose work caught Szarkowski's attention. Another was the French amateur Jacques Henri Lartigue.

Like André, Lartigue was born in 1894, but into one of France's wealthiest families. He began taking pictures at age six or seven. Using a handheld camera, the boy captured the antics of his fun-loving family, along with anything else that amused him.

Not until 1962 did Lartigue first travel to the United States. In New York, he showed his vintage prints and albums to Charles Rado. Rado then phoned Szarkowski and urged him to take a look. Szarkowski acquired forty-two photographs for the museum and scheduled an exhibition. The unknown Lartigue had waltzed in and grabbed a prize that André had, for so many years, sweated and ached for.

Many people viewed Lartigue's pictures as glimpses into a mythic belle epoque. But Szarkowski was using a different lens. He saw "fresh perceptions, poetically sensed and graphically fixed." The curator noted Lartigue's sensitivity to "the momentary, never to be repeated images created by the accidents of overlapping shapes, and by shapes interrupted by the picture edge. This is the essence of modern photographic seeing: to see not objects but their projected images."[19] That Lartigue had photographed brilliantly as a child underscored Szarkowski's argument that his pictures owed nothing to fancy equipment or aesthetic theory and much to an instinct for the medium's syntactical structure.

Even before he touched a camera, Lartigue had told Szarkowski, his five-year-old self was snapping pictures: "By opening and shutting my eyes in a 'certain fashion' I had found the way of capturing all the images that pleased me!... I caught it all! the colors! the sounds, the true measure of things!"[20]

André would have heard Lartigue's story from Szarkowski and Rado. Probably he had it in mind when he sat down with the journalist Carol Schwalberg that late fall. She was writing an article about André for *U.S. Camera*. During that interview, André fished out a memory he'd never previously publicly mentioned: He too had discovered photography as a child and had taken imaginary pictures. The story would assume a key place in André's self-narrative. From then on, he would trot it out over and over again.

When he was six, André would begin, he had traveled with his family to his relatives' home in Szigetbecse. At that time, the Klopfers owned some twenty acres of vineyards in the area.[21] The grape harvest was at hand, and everyone had come to help with the crush. One day, André wandered up to the attic. There he discovered stacks of old newspapers and magazines, among them the German-language weekly *Die Gartenlaube* (The Garden Arbor). Popular with the German diaspora, it featured reportage, historical sketches, travel articles, and fiction illustrated mostly with woodcuts and lithographs. Many of them vignetted adoring parents and innocent children living and working in picturesque settings, domestic bliss, and harmony with nature. They were to the German peasantry what Norman Rockwell's illustrations would later be to the American middle class.[22] As André's eyes lingered on them, he said, he was flooded with the desire to take photographs. "So for a time, whenever I saw something, it stayed with me, I said okay, I'll take a picture of it later, when I have a camera. Instinctively I started to compose. I learned how to observe the moment."[23]

The photo historian and curator Sarah Greenough observes that twelve years separate that experience in the attic from André's first mention of photography in his diary. More than sixty years separate it from Schwalberg's interview. So the tale "is, perhaps, a later construction," as Greenough delicately puts it. She also notes that his conversation with Schwalberg marks the first time André had ever asserted that, as a child, he photographed in his mind's eye.[24]

Although many artists create a persona and every immigrant must invent a new self, Greenberg and her coauthor Robert Gurbo write, André was a particularly skilled manipulator of the truth. His belief in his own greatness, drive for recognition, and envy of his better-known colleagues led him to misrepresent his own past. To ignore the ways in which others tutored and helped him was to play up his self-image as an instinctive modernist from the time he first picked up a camera, far from the nerve centers of the avant-garde.[25]

André may have been improving on some dimly remembered incident. Cognitive neuroscientists explain that remembering is not a matter of retrieving memories like documents from a safe-deposit box but of actively and creatively reconstituting a situation. Memories were once erroneously believed to be stable. In fact, they are subject to reconsolidation. Their contents and meanings evolve. Both André's situation with MoMA and the fuss over Lartigue now made it desirable that he too be a child genius of modern photography.

André's recent liberation from Condé Nast would have helped clear the way for the tale of the attic. He intended to become that child again. "Here in America, photographers do what they are dictated to do," he griped to Schwalberg. "The photographers get exact instructions—do this, do that."[26] By contrast, he was a freewheeling amateur. The little boy took pictures in his mind. The old man "still stalks the streets after a snowfall, still pokes into artists' haunts, still conducts experiments," writes Schwalberg.

Why was André's secular annunciation precipitated by the illustrations in *Die Gartenlaube*? He explained that he enjoyed their sentimental atmosphere. The life they depicted resembled that of his family. That sounds more like an old man's nostalgia than the reality of a disobedient six-year-old whose relatives quarreled and whose parents were semi-estranged. All the same, many of André's early photographs are imbued with a sweet domesticity. Even decades later, as Schwalberg points out, nobody ever seems cross or conflicted in a Kertész photograph: André was "overwhelmingly kind. His photographs never mock the subject, nor do they show people at less than their best."[27]

**It was to Brassaï** that Martinez had entrusted the task of writing the text to accompany André's three dozen pictures in *Camera.* What emerged after some editorial skirmishing between writer and editor was a warm, if slightly reserved, tribute titled "My Friend André Kertész." Brassaï lauded André for two qualities essential to a great photographer but rarely found in the same person: "an insatiable curiosity" and "a precise sense of form."[28] It was André who revealed the seductively photographic strangeness of Paris, writes Brassaï.

The *Camera* article had been postponed to coincide with the Venice Photography Biennale, originally scheduled for May but delayed by financial and organizational issues. On September 8, André and Elizabeth finally flew to Italy. Ensconced at the Gritti Palace in Venice, they toured the city and mingled with heavyweights in the photography world. André's exhibition, one of five, occupied the Ala Napoleonica in Piazza San Marco. He won that year's prestigious gold medal.

From Venice, they traveled to Zagreb to visit Elizabeth's half brother, Géza, and from there to Vienna and Budapest, then Paris. They flew into Orly on a rainy Monday, André clicking off pictures through a window. Three days later, Elizabeth departed for London. There she was meeting Tamás on Cosmia business, while André shouldered the task of bringing his show to Paris. The idea had surfaced in a conversation in Venice with Bertrand Girod de l'Ain, a journalist from *Le Monde*. The story Girod de l'Ain had filed asked why Paris should not present the work of this vital yet forgotten precursor to so many photographers and filmmakers. He prodded Parisian museum officials to put aside "their cool indifference to photography."[29]

It was anything but certain that André could negotiate a Paris venue. His first stop was Romeo Martinez's rue de Seine apartment, a rendezvous for the European photography world. There photographers, writers, curators, and other members of the tribe gathered at an octagonal table cluttered with coffee cups, liquor bottles, and brimming ashtrays. Speaking French, English, Spanish, or German, they discussed various photographers' latest and took stock of the state of their medium. André buttonholed André Jammes, a dealer in antiquarian books and world-class collector of nineteenth-century photographs. They arranged to talk again the next day. Their second meeting took André to the nearby Librairie Paul Jammes, the bookshop opened by Jammes's father in 1925. Its lace curtains, leather-spined volumes, and old-paper aroma would have reconfirmed to André *this* city as his emotional home.

Jammes presented André with a copy of a book he had recently published about the nineteenth-century photographer Charles Nègre. Nègre's subjects included artists, writers, and working-class Parisians. His images fuse rigor with poetry in a way not unlike André's. Yet Jammes's book did not get the enthusiastic response its author expected. André couldn't concentrate on much except the writer of the preface, Jean Adhémar, who headed the prints department at the Bibliothèque Nationale, the prestigious national library where André aspired to show.[30]

In 1963, there were no photography galleries in France. Photography as art? Cultural mandarins sniffed at the idea. When museums presented photographs, it was as historical documentation or, rarely, paragons of Frenchness. In 1955, the Musée des Arts Décoratifs organized an Henri Cartier-Bresson retrospective. More recently, Adhémar had exhibited Brassaï.

Indeed, the Bibliothèque Nationale did not have a photography department or even a space dedicated to photography. Still, Adhémar was among the few who considered the medium as worthy of aesthetic contemplation as the etchings and lithographs his print department collected and showed. Jammes agreed to speak to Adhémar after the weekend: "On Monday he will try to place the Biennale material at the BN," André jotted in his datebook that evening.[31]

Adhémar said yes. Six days later, he and André sat down to iron out the details. The curator wanted thirty more pictures, mostly American work. Elizabeth would send them from New York, where she was traveling five days later, but not before André dashed to London to kiss her goodbye.

Jammes also reconnected André with René Wittmann, the publisher of his three books in the 1930s. André proposed to Wittmann that they do a book of the photographs he had been shooting since his arrival. It could be titled *Paris Automne* (Paris Autumn). Wittmann agreed and did André one better. How about a reissue of André's 1933 *Soixante Photographies d'Enfants*? Such a book had excellent sales potential in a country in the midst of a baby boom.

On mornings when he had no appointments, André would set off, toting two Leicas, one loaded with Tri-X and the other with Kodachrome, plus a panoply of filters and lenses. He most often worked with a telephoto lens. In earlier years, he would have let instinct guide his wanderings. Now, with limited time, he mapped out the city like a magazine photographer on assignment, devoting a day or two to each quartier of historic Paris. France was enjoying an economic expansion that later would be dubbed the Thirty Glorious Years. The eleven-story Esso Tower anchored a new business district. A Gallic version of the American drugstore was doing a brisk business in the shadow of the Arc de Triomphe. France belonged to the nuclear club. But André ignored Paris as the capital city of a robust commercial and political power. He was there for the poetry, not for the prose.

"Worked in Montmartre and after that as if in a trance," he noted one evening.[32] He aimed his lens at couples kissing, youngsters cavorting, and people gathered around café tables. Half-bare trees, piles of leaves, and folded park chairs, all seductively melancholic, caught his eye. The pictures are those of an old hand, less inquisitive than the wide-eyed outsider he'd once been but no less enchanted with the City of Light. He tramped and worked energetically, exposing forty-six rolls of film and three hundred color slides.

When André wasn't taking pictures or making the rounds, he was fretting. Problems were accruing with the exhibition that Adhémar hoped to pull together fast. The crates hadn't shown up from Italy, and attempts to track them brought only frustration. The opening was postponed to November 15, then November 21. Had André's pattern of making a move and getting his hopes up, then being crushed, pursued him to France? His bouts of vertigo multiplied. Adding to the pressure, Elizabeth wrote from New York: "Andris, Andris darling, take care of yourself and do something so I can return to Paris... Go and see everyone – try to make a new career in Paris and then we will go over and live there."[33]

Abruptly, the crates did arrive, and the installation was happening. André shot a telegram to Elizabeth. Although they had planned for her to fly over for the opening, she telegrammed back: "I really wanted to be there. Write everything."[34] The mailed announcement arrived in New York the next day. "I was upset. I cried myself sick," she told André. Still, she did not rush out to buy a plane ticket. "You were so uncertain writing about the day of the opening and I had so little trust in the fact that the Venice pictures would show up that this is almost the main reason why I didn't go over."[35] The main reason was Cosmia.

The exhibition catalog was modest and the installation staid. Yet André's reviews were superb. "The Kertész Exhibition at the Nationale. When the Eye Has Genius," read the title of an article in *Les Nouvelles Littéraires.* The city for which André carried a torch had come through. Yet, as always, there were complications. Twenty-four hours after André's opening, President John F. Kennedy was assassinated in Dallas, and all of France reeled. That weekend saw stunned Parisians milling around, their noses in newspapers with enormous headlines. In New York, Elizabeth stewed that Kennedy's death would keep viewers away from the show. She needled André about publicity, even dispatching a PR list she'd compiled. Why not keep traveling the work after Paris? Contact the right people, she pressed. "Learn from me."[36]

André *was* rubbing shoulders. He saw Man Ray. He dined chez Jammes. He spent long hours with Wittmann. He socialized with Cartier-Bresson, Martinez, and Szarkowski, who happened to be honeymooning in France.[37] André saw other old pals at Picto, the city's premier photo lab, where he had his films developed. When Pierre Gassmann, the owner of Picto and André's friend of three decades, threw a party to celebrate the lab's move to the rue Delambre, just behind the Dôme, André was there, chatting with friends and clicking off frames as the event's self-appointed photo reporter.[38]

Tamping down any negative feelings, André also caught up with Brassaï.[39] One of André's beefs with Brassaï was his Transmutations. In the mid-1930s, Brassaï had scratched drawings on glass-plate negatives of nudes, which he printed photographically at various intervals. Inspired by Picasso and the Surrealists, the Transmutations are more graphic than photographic. No one would mistake them for the Distortions. Yet, for André, the series was part of Brassaï's pattern of copying him. As Jammes noted, the very mention of the Transmutations made André livid.[40]

All the same, the two went way back, and Brassaï had come through for him with the article in *Camera*. One day when they were together, André took a witty portrait of Brassaï as they waited for the Métro in the Denfert-Rochereau station. Brassaï sits in front of a billboard with a giant hand holding what could be a piece of candy between the index finger and thumb, a gesture that seems to be saying: Yes, he's okay.

**Another matter** was claiming André's attention. In October, he'd received a phone call from Girod de l'Ain, who informed him that a letter from Jacqueline Paouillac had arrived at *Le Monde*. Paouillac had read Girod de l'Ain's article about André and was responding to his mention that André was searching for the negatives he'd left in France before the war. After speaking with Girod de l'Ain, André rang Paouillac at the number she'd left. The photojournalist confirmed that she had the negatives, "not in very good order I think, but...fully at your disposal."[41] It was to Paouillac that André had entrusted his glass plates, too heavy and fragile to take with him to New York in 1936. In speaking with Girod de l'Ain in Venice, André had implied that the negatives' whereabouts were a mystery. In truth, he knew full well that Paouillac had them.

The two had seen each other during André's 1948 trip to Paris, when he had learned how Paouillac protected his work during the war. In 1938, as the German military machine was rumbling louder, she had packed the plates in a trunk stashed in the cellar of her building in Paris. After France declared war on Germany, she began transferring them to suitcases, which she carried, one or two at a time, to southwestern France. Friends there had agreed to store them. Moving more than two hundred fragile, heavy glass plates was a slow and arduous task. Yet keeping them out of Nazi hands meant safeguarding not only the negatives but also herself. If the Germans invaded, it would be dangerous to get caught with a Jewish photographer's work. Most of the negatives were Distortions. What could be more "degenerate"—to use the Nazis' description of modern art—than semiabstract nudes by a Jewish photographer?

In 1940, France split into the Nazi-occupied zone and the puppet state Vichy France. One day that July, two Vichy policemen had stopped Paouillac in a train station, demanding to search her bag for black market goods. While she was stalling, one snapped open a latch and stuck his hand in. He pulled out a nightgown and some feminine hygiene products packed on top of the plates. That ended the search.

When André and Paouillac met during André's 1948 trip to France, they had agreed that he would arrange to retrieve the negatives. Still waiting three years after that, Paouillac had written to prod him. He did nothing. Then she moved to an old estate in La Réunion, a village in southwestern France. There she repacked the negatives in a trunk and had it lowered into an abandoned root cellar overgrown with grasses and ivy.

Two weeks after his opening at the Bibliothèque Nationale, André arrived at La Réunion for the unearthing. The trunk was carried up, its lid lifted, a layer of yellowed magazines laid aside. His negatives! But as he picked them up to inspect them, he realized that more were broken than not. Or so he once asserted. No, the trunk's contents were intact, he would later report: Some plates broke later, when they were shipped to New York, improperly packed.[42]

Before recovering the trunk, André liked to imply that most of his French work was irrecoverable. In leaving for America in 1936, he had wedged a few packets of contact prints into his bags, he would explain, some for sentimental reasons, others almost haphazardly. Marie Eisner had summarized the situation in her 1944 article for *Minicam*: "These little pictures, a few negatives among them, some albums filled with beautiful enlargements and his book on Paris, are all he saved from two world wars."[43] Yet André had traveled to the United States with immigrant status, thanks to Keystone, and could bring as much luggage as he wanted without paying customs duties.[44] He probably arrived with virtually all the acetate-based negatives made with the Leica and other 35 millimeter cameras, plus copy prints (made by rephotographing existing prints) of the Distortions and other images.

Never one to let dry facts spoil a juicy story, André would sometimes claim that Paouillac had vanished during the war and that for years he'd searched for her.[45] She did not vanish, and André did not search for her, although he did misplace her address. But the tale was irresistible: a lost treasure, a flight from evil, a man spurred to action, a remote castle, the recovery—"miraculously"—of a buried trove.[46] The only missing element is the damsel needing rescue, but it was the damsel who pulled off the brave deeds.

The trunk's full contents are unknown. Not only the Distortions but also other long-unseen photographs, some from glass-plate negatives, resurfaced during this period. André was rounding up his negatives and prints. He had returned from Argentina with prints that he had long ago sent to Jenő and that Jenő had safeguarded. André asked a Hungarian-born friend traveling to Budapest to retrieve fifty negatives stored there. He may have picked up others during his stop in Budapest after the Biennale.

The real reason André had long ignored the trunk was because nobody wanted its contents. Americans had proved indifferent to his European work. Publishers were ill-disposed to, and curators skittish about, the Distortions.[47] Now things had changed. With his coming retrospective at MoMA, staking a claim to the status of modernist innovator took on an urgency. He needed the goods.

**André returned from Europe** riding the crest of success yet feeling each bump. "I hope for an end to your miseries," Paouillac wrote that March as they were drawing up plans for shipping the plates.[48] Some of the miseries were personal. All that spring, Elizabeth was sick with the flu. André caught it too. And their twenty-eight-year-old niece Veronika, the daughter of Elizabeth's sister, Márta, was diagnosed with cancer. Although the sisters were semi-estranged, Elizabeth and André felt compelled to offer their support, emotional, practical, and maybe also financial.

André's professional life fared no better. That winter had brought plaudits to other photographic lions. *Vogue* published a fawning feature about Steichen's post-MoMA life. Reviewers of Nancy Newhall's biography of Ansel Adams were rhapsodizing over his work. In the afterglow of his show at MoMA and a feature in *Life*, Lartigue was photography's twinkly-eyed darling. As for André, he was again making the rounds of publishers with a mock-up of the New York book he'd been pitching since the 1930s and again getting nowhere. *Paris Automne* stalled too. After he selected fifty-nine images and completed the dummy, Wittmann started pushing for an American copublisher. An editor at Knopf was mulling it over. Late that spring, however, Wittmann stopped writing.

Not until July did a letter arrive from the publisher, explaining that his distributor had terminated their contract, forcing him to drop both *Paris Automne* and *Enfants.* Then a "no" from Knopf scuttled the American version. Meanwhile, the trunk arrived from France. Close examination revealed that many plates were not only broken but also damaged by oxidative deterioration. Another disaster.

A different turn of the lens shows 1964 to be an excellent year for André. His reputation as an essential modernist was taking root on both sides of the Atlantic. Events in Europe were one reason why. Another was Szarkowski's *The Photographer's Eye*. Following a five-month closure for remodeling and expansion, MoMA had reopened with a VIP gala, surge of publicity, and suite of exhibitions showcasing the museum's permanent collection. Szarkowski's landmark contribution, along with the catalog that accompanied it, served as the curator's credo about the nature of photographic vision. Photography had seldom been theorized, especially in the United States. With *The Photographer's Eye*, Szarkowski did just that, effecting a paradigm shift toward a formalist view of the medium.

Photography distinguishes itself in five ways, Szarkowski argues. First, a photographic subject is necessarily something tangible and real. Photographers cannot invent. They can only show "a simpler, more permanent, more clearly visible version of the plain fact."[49] Second, photographers rely on significant detail, as opposed to narration, and significant detail tends to read as symbol. Third, the act of framing—determining a picture's edges—is key to photographic seeing. By visually isolating selected things, photographers establish connections among them, even if they have no obvious affinity. Fourth, the medium's relationship with time is also singular, Szarkowski continues. Unlike, say, painters, photographers must work with the present. Finally, photographers can approach their subjects from unexpected vantage points, thus refreshing our vision and revealing the world to be stranger than people assume.

Of the two hundred images in *The Photographer's Eye*, nine were André's. That was more than any other photographer save the Civil War–

era photographer Mathew Brady. For Szarkowski, André's plunging view of the Poughkeepsie railroad station, for instance, exemplified the photographic act of selection, forcing viewers to pay attention to the picture's edges and the shapes they help create. *Underwater Swimmer* demonstrated another inherent and defining characteristic: the medium's ability to reveal what's in plain sight yet seemingly invisible until a camera puts it before people's "astonished and protesting eyes."[50]

Three months after *The Photographer's Eye* closed, the exhibition *André Kertész* opened. On the Tuesday evening before Thanksgiving, André and Elizabeth walked through MoMA's glass doors and into his retrospective. What was never going to happen was happening. André was seventy. He and Elizabeth were an affluent, poised, and polished couple. Though plumper and grayer, Elizabeth was still an attractive woman. She wore suits from luxury stores like Henri Bendel and styled her hair in classic updos. André's uniform for such occasions was gray flannel slacks, a fine cotton shirt, and a J. Press wool herringbone sport coat. He favored a subtly lemony cologne by Cosmia.[51] With shiny-lipped smiles and slate-blue eyes turned down at the corners, he would have been greeting friends, colleagues, and admirers with hugs, handshakes, and a lilting "Charming! Charming!"

The gallery to the right of the entrance displayed eleven prints from André's Hungarian youth. The hallway ahead grouped still lifes from artists' studios and other Paris images. At its end, André's portrait of Sergei Eisenstein beckoned visitors to a larger gallery, installed with both French and American work. Many of the seventy-one pictures in this rigorously edited retrospective had been shown abroad but never in the United States. As David Vestal made the rounds that evening, he was startled: "It was the first opening night I ever saw where, for an hour or more at the start, more people were looking at pictures than socializing. They really looked. Phenomenal."[52]

The photographs had been printed by a MoMA staffer working under André's direction. Many were cropped to bring out their formal and abstract qualities, suggesting André's sensitivity to Szarkowski's thinking. For the 1912 *Sleeping Boy*, for instance, André had lopped off the darker areas that bookend the sleeper. In so doing, he changed the format from horizontal to vertical and made the picture less a vignette of café life and more a play of forms.

Indeed, Szarkowski's descriptions of André's photographs in his catalog essay amount to a checklist of the medium's inherent qualities. Even sweeter to André's ears, the curator declared that André's work, "perhaps more than that of any other photographer, defined the direction in which modern European photography developed." And the recent pictures? "The work of a master."[53]

"Let me say only that it is great what you have accomplished and what is happening to you now. There is no more that... one can achieve in a life."[54] So Elizabeth had written André before his opening at the Bibliothèque Nationale. For thirty years, she had sidelined her art to support him financially, emotionally, and materially. Now André had the satisfaction of knowing that he had come through.

But he wanted her to enjoy her own opportunities. Viewing the two of them as artistic soulmates, he urged Elizabeth to quit the life of a businesswoman and return to making art. She was "a very talented artist," he insisted, "*very* talented."[55] All the same, he shrank from doing what he needed to do to free her from the office. The question of how André would earn an income now that he'd left Condé Nast had yet to be resolved. He rationalized that knuckling down to practicalities might corrupt his photography. There was a "determined helplessness" about him, one friend observed. "He didn't want to deal with the ugliness" of business dealings.[56]

Cosmia had kept Elizabeth in New York while he traveled to Argentina. Cosmia had sent her to London and New York while André spent the autumn in Paris. Cosmia had taken precedence over André's opening at the Bibliothèque Nationale. But Cosmia had also enabled him to quit Condé Nast and live in comfort.

"Elizabeth was rich and Kertész was poor," Jammes noted.[57] Few photographers had it so good. When Lynn Davis shot a portrait of André for a never-published feature for *Esquire* about elderly photographers, she was struck by the gap between his situation and those of other historic figures. James Van Der Zee lived in a shambolic apartment in Harlem. Lisette Model made do with a Seventh Avenue basement. Berenice Abbott occupied a log cabin in Maine.[58]

**John Szarkowski** powered up André's American career; Cornell Capa kept it going. Robert Capa's brother was a wily and big-hearted charmer with rascally eyes and untamable hair. After Bob's death in 1954, Cornell had quit his job as a *Life* photojournalist and devoted himself to preserving and extending his brother's legacy. Grateful to André for all he'd done for Bob, awed by his brilliant pictures, and fond of "those lovely, quintessential Kertész stories," Cornell set about making things happen for the older photographer.[59]

For one thing, he plugged André's work to the French-born Czech art historian Anna Fárová. In an era when art historians paid scant attention to photography as an expressive medium, Fárová was championing it. Her current project was a series of paperback monographs for Paragraphic Books, an imprint of Grossman Publishers. Fárová needed no persuading to undertake one about André. His portfolio in *Camera* had felt to her like "a shock and a new adventure... in the history of photography."[60] Unlike Szarkowski, who considered the single image the epitome of photographic art, Fárová premised her book's layout and sequencing on her conviction that pictures amplify, complicate, and distill the meanings of others around them.[61]

Capa also pitched a Kertész show to the Smithsonian (it never happened) and brought him into the photographic cooperative Magnum. Founded in 1947 by Robert Capa, Henri Cartier-Bresson, and others, Magnum sprang from the idea that photographers could be free agents. Magnum photographers pursued their own projects, tackling stories that needed telling but didn't fit the agenda of mainstream publications. The photographers, not the publications, retained the rights to the negatives. Glamorous, semi-dysfunctional, and perennially broke, Magnum set a high standard for photojournalism. In the early days, Bob's charisma had held it together. Now Cornell served as president. It was Cornell who invented the status of honorary associate member so that Magnum could benefit from the counsel of old hands like Dorothea Lange, Philippe Halsman, and André Kertész.

Cornell attempted to drum up sales for André's commercially dormant early photographs. Magnum was a press agency. It was not in the business of selling prints. But here was a way for André to earn money, and Cornell didn't mind bending rules.[62] They also agreed that André could function as a Magnum photographer. The agency announced his availability for freelance work. Yet only a few jobs materialized. After meeting the editor Robert E. Hood, he would freelance occasionally for the Boy Scouts' monthly *Boys' Life*, contributing photo essays in color about subjects that included kite flying, Louisiana, and a scout ranch in New Mexico.

As for black-and-white, André was hard-pressed to achieve anything in the darkroom. As his Ménière's disease progressed, the bouts of vertigo had become so incapacitating that he'd given up his Union Square workspace. Sometimes he used a darkroom at Cosmia. He also tried different printers, yet none could coax exactly what he wanted from his negatives.

Once again Capa helped, introducing André to his own printer, Igor Bakht. Born in Tbilisi, Georgia, and raised in Teheran, Bakht (who now uses his original name, Igor Bakhtamian) had learned darkroom skills from his father, an official photographer to Iran's royal family. After working for years in professional labs in New York, Bakht had set up his own business on West Fifty-Seventh Street. André immediately liked this Old World–style man with an unlit pipe stuck in a corner of his mouth and a way of getting straight to the point.[63] He gave Bakht a few negatives to print. Always careful with money, he ordered sparingly.

What he got back was right: rich prints but not too rich, nothing arty or dramatic, a long gray scale. Bakht used Ilford Multigrade Glossy paper, double weight, for André's photographs, along with the standard developer, Dektol. They began working together.

**André and Bakht** had little trouble communicating, visually or verbally, but that wasn't the case with every English speaker André encountered. He bungled tenses. His phrasing and timing could be disconcerting. French words bobbed up like flotsam and jetsam. Even his simple statements could snarl conversations. People joked that André spoke Kertészian. More than once, the journalist Carol Schwalberg reports, he had interrupted their interview to ask, hopefully: "You speak Hungarian?" Even his Hungarian was faulty. "My English is bad. My French is bad. Photography is my only language," André acknowledged.[64]

Indeed, even his Hungarian was laced with syntactical errors and quaint turns of phrase. All the same, André communicated most effectively in his native tongue. When one American photo editor read a translation of André's conversations with a Hungarian-born friend, the editor finally understood certain things the photographer had long been saying: "It was as if I had been looking through a steamed-up window and suddenly it was wiped clean so that I could see in clear detail what was on the other side."[65]

Unsurprisingly, André cottoned to visitors from Hungary. One day when he was out walking, he overheard a conversation. Approaching the speakers, he asked: "Are you Hungarians too?" Yes, and not only that, they were jugglers and acrobats performing with the Ringling Bros. and Barnum & Bailey Circus at Madison Square Garden. André was delighted. The entertainers found him kind, outgoing, and "infinitely humble." He came away from that encounter with a ticket to the circus, where he had so much fun that the troupe got him a pass for the duration and made him an honorary member. He photographed them backstage, in rehearsal, and during performances; hosted them at MoMA for an interlude of art; and gave them photographs.[66] That was André, generous and helpful. If someone he liked admired a picture, he would likely slip them a print: "Oh, you must take it!"[67] If someone needed a jacket, he'd donate that too.

Yet "beneath his affability," reports the photographer Duane Michals, "André was a closet curmudgeon." Michals was a thirty-two-year-old freelancer for *Show* magazine in 1964, the year he met André. When *Show* published a Kertész portfolio, Michals was startled to see two photographs dated 1960. Like Szarkowski, he had assumed that Kertész was dead. He then got André's contact information, phoned him, and discovered that they were neighbors. André invited him over. The better Michals got to know André, the more he liked him. But he learned not to ask, "André, how are you?" Inevitably, the answer would be: "How *am* I? Terrible!"[68] Something had always just gone wrong or was about to. Americans needed to acknowledge his grievances, sympathize with him, feel remorseful, André insisted.

André frequently entertained visitors while Elizabeth was working. Dressed in a nice shirt, maybe a cardigan, and gray flannel slacks, he would sit behind his desk in the study, showing his latest prints and conversing. Other times, he would pad around in stocking feet, making phone calls, and editing his work. Lunch would be bread slathered with cream cheese and jam (preferably apricot jam from Mrs. Herbst's Hungarian bakery uptown), washed down with tea. After Elizabeth came home, she would cook dinner. Or they would head for their favorite neighborhood restaurant, the Knickerbocker Bar and Grill on University Place. Elizabeth attended evening classes. André went to openings. Both enjoyed classical concerts. At home they read, listened to music, and watched TV. Around midnight, the phone sometimes rang. It would be Alexey Brodovitch: "André, I'm so lonely."[69] So André would get dressed and walk over to Brodovitch's place on East Sixteenth Street. Fired from *Harper's Bazaar* in 1958 when his drinking got out of hand, then widowed, Brodovitch indulged in the self-pity that kept him reaching for a bottle as the two old friends unburdened themselves into the small hours.

On days when André went to Bakht's to order or pick up prints, he liked to drop in at Magnum's offices on West Forty-Fifth Street. He would coax the Belgian-born picture editor Jimmy Fox to a coffee shop across the street, where they gabbed in French. Or André and Cornell would chew over ideas for Capa's obsession: the Fund for Concerned Photography.

Television, as Capa was acutely aware, was sucking the air from the news magazines that had long been the primary vehicle for photojournalists' work. Museums rarely collected photographs. Those that did acquired and showed only a fraction of any photographer's work. The audience for monographs was tiny. How then to keep his brother's legacy alive? How to get vital images in front of a distracted public? How to use photography as a tool for political awareness and social justice? Capa was planning an exhibition to leverage the money and attention required to build an organization that would champion his cause.

*The Concerned Photographer* opened on October 1, 1967, at the Riverside Museum. Housed in an Art Deco apartment building on Riverside Drive at 103rd Street, the museum was a two-person operation, modest but it would do. The building's first three floors had been designed for performances and exhibitions. There Cornell and his cohorts installed work by six photojournalists: Robert Capa, Werner Bischof, David "Chim" Seymour, and Dan Weiner, all of whom had died on assignment, plus the young Leonard Freed and the elderly André Kertész.

The photojournalist, as Bob Capa had invented the persona, was a hard-driving, danger-courting maverick. A Leica-wielding witness to war, famine, and social injustice. A gambler and heartbreaker in his off hours. That sounds little like André. All the same, Cornell Capa considered him the father of photojournalism for his pioneering subjective reportage and candid picture-taking with a small camera. Capa shoehorned André into *The Concerned Photographer* by quoting the socially concerned photographer Lewis Hine: "There were two things I wanted to do. I wanted to show the things that had to be corrected." And—André's forte—"I wanted to show the things that had to be appreciated."[70] One hundred Kertész photographs hung, salon style, in the Riverside Museum's main gallery. On opening day, two thousand people pressed in. Thirty-five thousand others would follow. Nearly half a million American troops were fighting in Vietnam that year. Three weeks after the opening, more than one hundred thousand protesters marched on the Pentagon. War was on people's minds.

Its popularity notwithstanding, *The Concerned Photographer* ran a deficit. In an unconventional move, Cornell decided to sell prints to pay it off. The most popular, André's *Chez Mondrian*, topped the price list at $200, later increased to $300. That image alone—the epitome of balance and serenity—pulled in half of the $4,700 raised by print sales, enough to make up the shortfall and seed the Fund for Concerned Photography.

One might guess that André and Cornell Capa were close, and they were, yet their friendship was rocky. They teamed up, squabbled, reconciled, gossiped, laughed, squabbled again. Once Capa lost one of André's negatives, and their falling out lasted for months until Bakht persuaded them to make up.[71] André was nursing a deeper rancor. The psychological trauma he had experienced made him quick to suspect dirty tricks and cast blame. When Capa kept several prints that André believed he had loaned, not donated, for the exhibition, André felt betrayed. Other times, he complained about earning no royalties from the catalog that Capa published in advance of the exhibition's international tour, a catalog in which Capa effused about André's contribution. In fact, he had signed, but never bothered to read, an agreement assigning all royalties to the Fund for Concerned Photography. Capa was a phony, a lightweight, another fast-talking New Yorker, André groused, except when he was a dear friend.[72]

In August 1968, André traveled to Tokyo with Cornell and his wife, Edie. The Matsuya department store was hosting *The Concerned*

*Photographer*. Working side by side with the photographer Hiroshi Hamaya, Capa and André hustled together the installation, finishing at 3:00 a.m. on the morning of opening day. Only a few hours later, they greeted dignitaries streaming up the red carpet. The US ambassador to Japan arrived. So did Kikuko, Princess Takamatsu, and her entourage. People bowed. The speakers heaped praise on the photojournalists. A tea ceremony followed. Then the princess cut the ribbon, and crowds poured in.

Thirty thousand people would view the exhibition in Tokyo, and many more during its six-month tour of Japan. André's section kicked off with a mural-size print of his World War I image *Forced March to the Front*. His work again proved a winner. Japanese viewers valued the exhibition's humanism, of which André seemed the living representative. They responded to his poetic vision, respected his age, and appreciated his gentle manner. Long lines formed to get his autograph.[73] André's takeaway was that the Japanese immediately accepted him while the Americans had immediately shunned him. Never mind that 1936 America and 1968 Japan were vastly different places. In Japan, he was a rock star.

André was rooming with the twenty-nine-year-old photographer Hiroji Kubota, who could have been his grandson. Yet the young photographer felt as if they were brothers. He found André kind, attentive, and active. Thinning hair and liver spots notwithstanding, the seventy-four-year-old exuded the energy of a younger man. When Kubota awoke in the morning, he would find André at a window of their hotel room, observing and taking pictures. When André hit the streets, he would crouch down for one shot, clamber up a wall for another.

After the Capas flew out, André stayed on, traveling to Kyoto, Osaka, and Nara. In Nara, his guide was a Buddhist priest. One afternoon, the priest led André to a wooden storage building where sixteen statues of deities stood in rows facing each other. The building's windows were shuttered. André strained to make out his surroundings. Suddenly sunlight streamed through a gap in one of the shutters. André hastened to position his tripod and camera and make some exposures. Two minutes. Four minutes. Then six, then eight. His subject was the illuminated hand and sleeve of a Buddha. After his film was processed and a few frames were printed, he showed one print to the depository's director. In *Nara (Oct. 8, 1968)*, the Buddha's hand and sleeve float in a tenebrous eternity. To André's deep satisfaction, the director pronounced the image a reflection of "the purest Japanese religious spirit."[74] There was something divine about that hand and that light.

**The idea of photography** as a fine art was again gaining traction. In 1969, André okayed a request from a Parisian bookstore employee named Agathe Gaillard to use *Satiric Dancer* for her Masterpieces of Photography postcard project. Gaillard was proposing to publish five sets of ten postcards, each with a stellar image by a different photographer. The idea that postcards could be art derived from the cultural politics of the French mass protests of May 1968, even if Gaillard was using the elitist term *masterpieces*. The postcards proved a hit. All the same, people asked, *Really? Is there such a thing as a masterpiece in photography?*[75]

In New York, Inge Bondi thought there was. Bondi had quit her job at Magnum to sell fine-art prints to collectors, another unorthodox venture. Inspired by the popularity of André's prints at the Riverside Museum show, she opened Photography House, a by appointment only gallery on Second Avenue devoted to the work of four photographers, André among them. Bondi commissioned a limited edition of *Melancholic Tulip*. Each print was signed, dated, numbered, and priced at $250. After the edition of 150 prints sold out, Bondi told collectors, the negative would be permanently retired, per her agreement with André. They had rented a safe-deposit box and locked up the plate. But then family plans dictated that Bondi move to Europe. With many prints still unsold, she handed André her key, and that ended that. *Melancholic Tulip* would emerge from the safe-deposit box to become one of André's most collected images.[76]

Gratified though he was by the growing interest in his prints, André most loved doing books. One day he realized that he had always photographed people reading. Hungarian urchins. Kyoto commuters. Carnival folks. Knobby-kneed schoolgirls. A distingué Frenchman. All absorbed in the written word. André had never thought of his pictures of people reading as a coherent body of work, but they were. He approached Grossman about doing a book. The publisher said yes.

*On Reading* does not identify the distingué Frenchman or anyone else. It is implicitly egalitarian. It doesn't matter if you are the director of the Bibliothèque Nationale (the Frenchman) or a destitute soul on the Bowery scanning a tabloid pulled from the trash, you are experiencing the private rapture that André called the "*miracle du livre*" (miracle of the book).[77] His book implies that reading—that delightful form of mental vagabondage—is a ubiquitous act.[78]

According to conventional wisdom, dramatic images do best as crowd-pleasers. Yet people warmed to this book in which the drama is wholly interiorized. *On Reading* garnered a large and enthusiastic audience. In the age of digital distraction, it would become a cult classic. Even though it has no text (except a list of places and dates), there are Spanish, British, French, and Japanese editions.

There's also a companion project by the journalist Steve McCurry. Years after McCurry purchased *On Reading,* he registered that he too had scores of pictures of readers. McCurry's 2016 *On Reading* is as richly hued as André's is richly black-and-white. In McCurry's version, people from across the globe soak up words while sprawled on the hood of a car, ensconced in a baronial library, or propped against an elephant. McCurry dedicated his book to André for "his talent, his influence, his genius." Doing the project felt, he says, like a way to "touch the hem of his garment."[79]

The success of *On Reading* led Richard Grossman to move forward with a Kertész monograph. However, Grossman quarreled with Elizabeth, who took the reins from André in discussions of contracts, contents, and sometimes even design and choice of pictures. Grossman then turned the project over to Nicolas Ducrot, a French editor at Viking, which had acquired Grossman Publishers. Ducrot's father, Jean Ducrot, a freelancer for *Vu*, had been André's chum in the 1920s, and André knew Nicolas's photographer brother. Nicolas felt almost like family. André's new editor had his own differences with Elizabeth, a "tough little woman."[80] If he appealed to André, the response was usually that Elizabeth wanted it that way. Such was their relationship. "Elizabeth ruled everything," remembers Ducrot's then-assistant.[81] Yet they pulled off the book.

Among the three photographs of Elizabeth in the front matter is a radically cropped version of André's wedding double portrait from their early days together in Paris. André had always related that picture to the Hungarian word *feleség,* meaning both *wife* and *half,* akin to the expression "my better half."[82] He had printed one version that eliminates all but their heads and shoulders. Another zeroes in on his sideward and downward look at Elizabeth and her gaze into the camera lens. In preparing for the MoMA retrospective, André again picked up his experiments with *Elizabeth and I.* He wanted to assert himself as a formalist but also to pry out the photograph's deepest meanings. The print that hung on MoMA's wall and that opened *Sixty Years of Photography, 1912–1972* — the definitive version, André decided — shows only one half of Elizabeth's face, along with her right shoulder and his hand molded to it. It uses no more than one-fourteenth of the negative. For André, it embodied the essential: her steady look, his protective hand. All the same, a viewer can't help but note that Elizabeth attends to the camera, not to André, and, except for his hand, André has cropped himself out.

*Sixty Years* hit the bookstores shortly before Christmas 1972. Skillfully sequenced and well printed using photogravure, it's a 224-page visual cornucopia. No sooner was it published than a chorus of critics rose in praise. Reviewing the book for *The New York Times,* Sanford Schwartz rhapsodized about André's "witty and ironic vision" and "sophisticated knowingness." This was "easily the most extraordinary photography book of the year," he proclaimed, and André among "the most original and inventive of all modern still photographers." Ainslie Ellis agreed. His article for the *British Journal of Photography* pronounced that there was no living photographer "of greater importance... to the history and the future of photography." When a French edition of *Sixty Years* came out that same year, it won the prestigious Prix Nadar by unanimous vote of the jury. *Le Monde* deemed André the "Picasso of photography." Like the artist, he had "attempted everything, looked at everything, grasped everything."[83] The veteran reporter Jacob Deschin couldn't recall such an effusive outpouring for any other photographer's work. The writer Nancy Stevens agreed, writing that the critical adulation was "almost embarrassing."[84] Sales were brisk.

No voice touched André more than that of Cartier-Bresson. After viewing the dummy for the French edition, André's colleague put pen to paper: "I want to tell you... that your way of seeing and feeling puts you in the firmament of photography. Your rigor, your depth, your simplicity kindle such joy that one wants to get to work... With all my admiration and affectionate friendship."[85] Cartier-Bresson's letter reached André that August in East Hampton, where he and Elizabeth had rented a cottage on Further Lane.

The weather was glorious. André and Elizabeth took long walks by the water. He photographed her laughing and drying her hair in the sun. Now he set about fashioning a photographic reply to Cartier-Bresson. First, he tacked the letter and envelope to a wooden door of their restored eighteenth-century cottage. Below that he chalked, in a French grade-school-style hand: "Aug. 17 1972 / *Mon ami Henri* / *Merci André*." The antique lock and skeleton key would be the photograph's visual fulcrum. Setting the door slightly ajar, André then positioned himself outside, his eyes riveted on something far distant. He clicked the cable release or had Elizabeth take the picture.[86]

André had met Cartier-Bresson years earlier, probably through Brodovitch or the Newhalls. In the 1920s, the French schoolboy used to spot the famous photographer in cafés along the boulevard du Montparnasse.[87] He studied André's reportages for *Vu*, admiring his "tenderness, his simple and honest approach, his sense of form."[88]

In 1931, Cartier-Bresson acquired a Leica and began photographing under the spell of André's work and that of Martin Munkácsi. Fixed on geometry of form and infatuated with Surrealism, Cartier-Bresson drew upon his sharp-eyed intuition, powers of concentration, and knack for making himself inconspicuous. His images won wide admiration. After the war, however, Bob Capa cautioned him about being stuck with the label "little surrealist photographer." Stay in touch with the world, Capa advised. Continue to do what you are doing "but with the label of photojournalist, and keep the rest deep in your heart."[89] Cartier-Bresson heeded his friend's advice, cofounding Magnum and becoming the master spirit of its Paris office.

For Cartier-Bresson, photography meant "prowl[ing] the streets all day, feeling very strung-up and ready to pounce, determined to 'trap' life."[90] Seeking to catch dynamic situations in ways that laid bare their essential meanings, he would whip his Leica up to his eye and hit the shutter release, sometimes before his subject knew what had happened. André had trailblazed that way of working. (He described it more blandly: "You have only a thousandth of a second to discover and do the thing. You must be prepared mentally."[91]) Yet André had never worked in that way alone, and aging had made it harder. Both men will always be remembered as masters of the Leica. However, André's bag held other cameras too, along with zoom lenses, while Cartier-Bresson was wedded to the Leica with a 50 or 35 millimeter lens.

Both photographers fused a poetic sensibility with formal rigor. Both shuddered at the falsity of the picture story à la *Life*, although Cartier-Bresson freelanced for the magazine and André aspired to. At bottom, said Cartier-Bresson, he was interested only in "*la vérité des petits faits* (the truth of small facts)."[92] For André, photography was about "little happenings, that's all."[93] Yet their sensibilities differ. André's pictures are wittier and more poetic, Cartier-Bresson's more filmic and broadly humanist. André used negatives as raw material to be interpreted by cropping. For Cartier-Bresson, a picture had to be grasped and registered all at once – no after-adjustments, ever.

Even after Cartier-Bresson became arguably the world's best-known photographer, he "never ceased to pay homage to André Kertész," writes his biographer.[94] Speaking with a journalist from *Le Monde*, he declared: "Seeing a good photograph makes me want to photograph, first and foremost, [a photograph] by Kertész, my 'poetic wellspring.'"[95]

**The Kertészes' sojourn** in East Hampton followed months of medical problems. Smoking, stress, and fatigue were taxing Elizabeth's health. She had been seeing doctors. She made a will.

One day Kubota arrived for a visit, and André pulled out some recent prints. Kubota looked, hesitated, then ventured: "André, you have blurred photographs." André acknowledged that he did. He had developed a tremor in his hands. "I am worried about my health," he told Kubota. "My arms are weak now, and I am unable to support the camera fast. This is because of son of bitch America."[96] Deep rest was in order. In late December, André and Elizabeth flew out of a sleeting New York for a vacation at a beach hotel at Les Trois-Îlets on the French Caribbean island of Martinique.

At first, the room next to theirs was vacant. On the third day, a French family with children arrived. André kept watching their soft shadows on the frosted pebbled glass that separated the two balconies. Whenever he could, he stationed himself in a chair, camera at the ready. On New Year's Day, the family breakfasted on their balcony. Then the woman and two of the children went inside. The man and the third child did not. They kept moving about and talking. André made an exposure with two silhouettes. After that, the father and son disappeared. When the father returned alone and stood behind the partition, André got what he wanted.

*Martinique* shows a hard, flat sea wedged between a cloud-softened sky and a slatted balcony. The balcony railing slices across the image, underscoring the triangle of water. To the left, the figure behind the partition leans forward, as enigmatic, velvety, and silent as one in a Conté crayon drawing by the Postimpressionist Georges Seurat. The posture suggests a seeker and seer.

The figure also recalls André's own in his 1936 self-portrait leaning out a window of the Beaux-Arts. That older photograph checks all the boxes of careerist aspiration: the camera, the watch, the rolled-up shirt-sleeves, the steady gaze, the city to be conquered. In *Martinique*, taken when André was seventy-seven and feeling his mortality, temporal concerns have fallen away. What remains is existential: shadow, sky, and sea. Stillness and light. The power of *Martinique* derives from its economy of language. It's photography as haiku.

Arguably, it's also photography about photography. André foregrounds a photographer's essential act of isolating some part of the world and saying: This is meaningful. In *Martinique*, he frames what most would consider two separate scenes, each resonant with the other and with photography itself. On the left, there's the shadow, its forward tilt implying hard looking, its grainy quality recalling an unfocused image. Like a photograph, a shadow is a trace of something real. Then there's the scene on the right, with its razor-sharp triangle of sea. A piece of a world, indifferent yet gleaming, with photography's potential for everythingness.

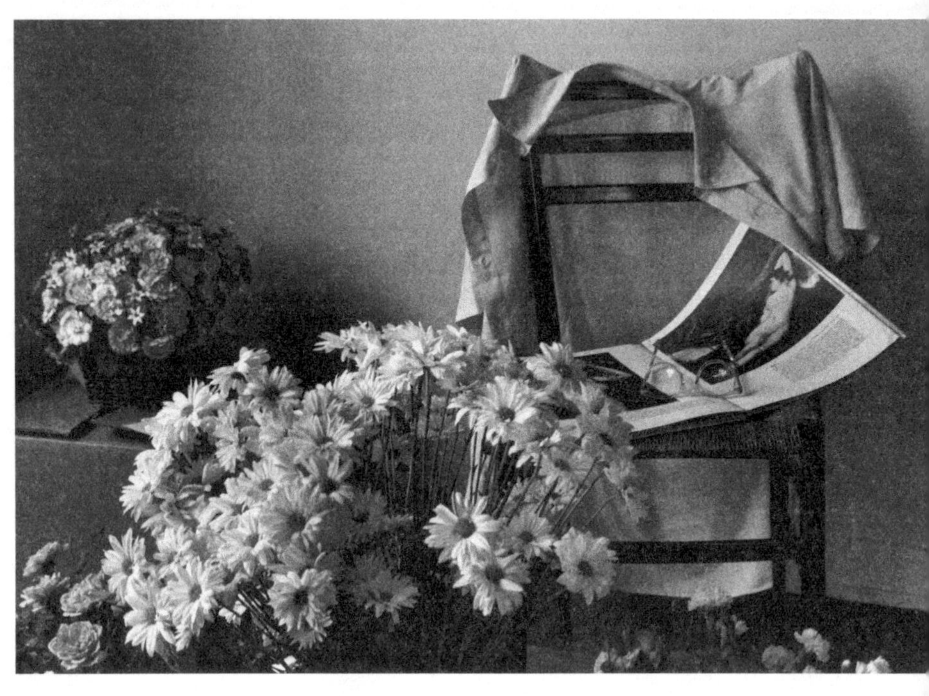

André Kertész, *Flowers for Elizabeth*, 1977

# 11 FLOWERS FOR ELIZABETH, 1970–1980

**In 1969,** the editor and photographer Lee Witkin quit his job, rented a space on East Sixtieth Street, and poured his life savings into a quixotic crusade: selling photographic prints. Two years later, Marjorie Neikrug shifted the focus of her Sixth-Eighth Street gallery from pre-Columbian art to photography. Then Light Gallery opened its doors. Its founders, the intellectual property lawyer Tennyson Schad and the former *Life* picture editor Fern Schad, were gambling even bigger than their colleagues. Unlike the others, Light would deal exclusively in the work of living photographers, although no viable market existed.

New York had seen other photography galleries: Alfred Stieglitz's, starting in 1905; Julien Levy's in the 1930s; the Greenwich Village café gallery Limelight at mid-century. After Limelight went dark, enthusiasts sought out photographs at street fairs, co-op galleries, or little shops on shoestring budgets. They would rifle through bins, pay as little as twenty-five cents for a print, and then go home and thumbtack their finds to a wall.

At Light, photographs were handled with white gloves, matted, stored in flat drawers, and meticulously framed and hung. They sold at three-digit prices. The gallery's location at 1018 Madison Avenue in Upper East Side art gallery terrain underscored the idea of photographs as fine art. Was that going to fly? Skeptics abounded.

Light got rolling with a roster of thirteen photographers. Some, like Aaron Siskind and Harry Callahan, were well known, others not at all. Each signed a contract for exclusive representation. It spelled out that Light would stock and sell their prints, work with publishers on their behalf, and otherwise advance their careers. The gallery took a 40 percent commission, 45 percent on sales over $2,000.

Harold Jones, the gallery's thirty-two-year-old director, typically signed new photographers. In courting André, however, the older and more urbane Tennyson Schad took the lead. André and Elizabeth quickly warmed to Schad, and the feeling was mutual. All the same, negotiations were fraught. When Schad presented the offer of representation, the couple expressed interest but insisted that the standard terms wouldn't do. André had prints for sale at Witkin and elsewhere, and he refused to cut relationships he'd already built. Besides, he'd always sold prints directly. He was a free man. No exclusivity.

Certainly, Schad responded, he could accommodate that. Yet, he explained, André stood to reap substantial benefits from representation by Light. The gallery could place an exhibition in a museum to coincide with the release of André's *Sixty Years*. (He was speaking with the Kertészes five months before the book's publication.) Light could handle sales sparked by *Sixty Years*. They could organize a Kertész show. André agreed to a show in September 1973. But no contract materialized. For one thing, he and Elizabeth were holding out for 66.66 percent of the sales price as opposed to the usual 60 percent for the photographer. That would be unfair to others that Light represented, the dealer replied.[1]

Schad floated a second proposal. He understood that potential buyers, unsure about both photography's legitimacy as art and their own judgment, hesitated to invest in individual prints. What if they chose the wrong one? The gallery's tactic for tamping down people's qualms and boosting its revenues was to package photographs to resemble that traditional collectible, the rare book. Buyers could hedge their bets by acquiring a set of ten. Portfolios by four photographers were underway.

In André's case, Schad was proposing two limited-edition sets of masterworks spanning his career. Igor Bakht would print. The photographs would be signed by André, dry-mounted on acid-free board, and housed in an archival slipcase. The price would be $2,000 (about $14,700 in 2024 dollars). Photographer and gallery would split the income, minus the gallery's costs of production. André could expect to earn about $37,000 (about $277,000 in 2024 dollars).[2]

Discussions continued all summer. Elizabeth pored over the fine print and haggled over the numbers. Decades of fending for themselves had left her and André determined to wring all they could from his new status. The lawyer cajoled, reasoned, amended, rephrased. Eventually they reached an agreement on the portfolio deal. But the matter of representation bogged down in objections and misunderstandings. Photographers come out ahead when their affairs are professionally managed, Schad kept insisting. Case in point: the Hallmark show.

A few months earlier, the greeting card company had proposed a modest presentation of André's work at its Hallmark Gallery on Fifth Avenue. Schad was happy to facilitate. André and Elizabeth couldn't leave it at that, however. In side talks with Hallmark, they agreed to transform a small display of landscapes and pictures of children and animals into a 204-image extravaganza, including dozens of previously unexhibited and unpublished prints. By August, Schad was judging the upcoming show "a nightmare, with the only winner a greeting card company." It's nice that Hallmark is bringing attention to your work, he told André, but that's of little financial benefit to you if people don't know where to buy it. What's more, the exhibition that was being planned at Light Gallery would position him as an innovative modernist. If many of the same photographs had just been exhibited, the show would generate little heat. "The point will have been lost," Schad argued. "Light will look plain silly." But from André's point of view, Hallmark wanted him, and he wanted to be wanted. Schad could only hammer away at the argument he'd been making: By not acting strategically, André was letting others take advantage.

Late that summer, the dealer laid out two options. Option one: Light would be André's dealer. The gallery would bow to his demand that Witkin and others be grandfathered in, though Schad still cautioned against it: "I can't think of any living artist who has his work spread around in many galleries. And for many good reasons."[3] Under that option, Light would present André's work, handle sales, manage exhibitions, and cultivate the right people and institutions on his behalf. They would guarantee him an income larger than his current income from gallery and direct sales combined. Option two: Light would sell whatever prints André supplied. One September morning, Schad sat down with André and Elizabeth, expecting negativity—to his surprise, they opted for exclusivity. On October 5, André signed an eighteen-month contract.

The Hallmark show proved a sensation. The gallery teemed with viewers. Many critics also were wowed by the photographs, less so by the installation. The *New York Times* reviewer A. D. Coleman urged readers to see the show because André was "one of the greatest of all photographers, quite literally in a league by himself." Yet their pleasure would be diluted, he cautioned, by the poor lighting, glib labels, and chockablock installation. When the exhibition at Light rolled around seven months later, Coleman would write, as Schad had predicted, that there was little point to yet another overview of André's work (as opposed to a thematic exhibition).[4] André's response: "The dogs bark, but the caravan moves on."[5]

Besides the triumph of *Sixty Years*, André could boast of solo shows at museums in Budapest and Stockholm in 1971 and Helsinki in 1972. In a letter to Inge Bondi, Elizabeth reeled off more accomplishments:

> *A is still very much in 'Vogue.' Can you imagine, 45,000 people, that's the minimum count, have visited his exhibition at the Hallmark. He was repeated on TV* [André had been on the program *In and Out of Focus*]*; CBS, NBC, Channels 9 and 31 in Toronto, and now they want to do a ½-hour film in London. The FAN-MAIL is touching. And—a new book is in the making. With Grossman of course.*

*Oh, and the book '60 Years'... won the Nadar-award in France.*

She ended with André's favorite slur: "Still, s.o.b. America is going on and it's just as well."[6]

As André sized up his life in the United States, the years from 1936 to 1972, when *Sixty Years* appeared, were "an absolute tragedy. No one understood me."[7]

History abounds in examples of artists who were misunderstood, at first anyway, because they bucked the rules. William Blake and Hilma af Klint come to mind. So do the photographers Julia Margaret Cameron and Alfred Stieglitz. André had arrived in a United States where photojournalists bowed to the dictates of editorial teams. Swallowed up by the commercial world, André had "devoted himself primarily to work which might have been adequately executed by a score of talented mechanics," John Szarkowski wrote in 1964 of André's years at *House & Garden*. "The time and the conditions were not propitious," Szarkowski continues. "Still, might not an artist like Kertész prevail over the system, create his own opportunities, slowly bend the situation to his own advantage?"[8] Incapable of work that was anything but "centrifugal, unpredictable, and romantic"—as Szarkowski describes it—André had not.

The American experience of this "Picasso of photography" begs comparison to the French experience of Pablo Picasso. The moneyless Spaniard first arrived in a xenophobic France in 1900, determined to "get his bearings... impose himself, overthrow the avant-garde," writes his biographer, the cultural historian Annie Cohen-Solal. "But how do you penetrate a territory when you don't know its topography, its language, or its codes?"[9] It took Picasso only five years to upend the rules of art and penetrate the territory ruled by old-guard artists under the banner of French good taste.

André had no less drive, creative resourcefulness, or conviction about the worth of his work. He did have a less forceful personality, a very different territory to conquer, a medium with other demands, and a fixation on his own victimization. Rather than "bend the situation to his own advantage," he had insisted that Americans do the bending.[10] Now that they did admire his work, he couldn't stop picking over the bones of their long refusal to recognize his genius. He spewed the phrase "God damn son of a bitch" – pronounced *sonofbeech* – "America!," or some variation thereof, at the slightest contretemps or even for no obvious reason. Szarkowski, for one, had heard it ad nauseam. The curator fantasized that André's morning rituals included disgorging a list of his enemies, virtually everyone in the American photography world, in a tirade that powered his day.[11]

Many found André's rants tiresome, especially from someone with a well-padded bank account, desirable apartment, and growing fame. The gallerist Helen Gee pronounced him "an insufferable bore."[12] The French writer and photographer François-Marie Banier agreed: André was "the most boring man on earth, but... the greatest [of photographers], overwhelmingly sensitive."[13]

André was rarely confrontational. He unloaded to Harold Jones about Tennyson Schad and to Schad about Jones. Szarkowski, he grumped to Schad, was a phony. Foreigners also drew his accusations. Schad heard from André about Romeo Martinez, who had allegedly "conned him" into sending 149 color slides for a guidebook project and never returned them.[14] Fritz Gruber, the German founder of the European photographic trade fair Photokina, was hoarding prints *he* was supposed to return, according to André. Yet André appeared to have amiable relationships with these men, and all of them had advanced his career.

Friends knew to avoid above all any mention of Beaumont Newhall or Alex Liberman. They topped the list of those who had supposedly humiliated and robbed him of recognition for all those long years. Now that his status gave André a sturdy platform, he seized every opportunity to let people know. "The more successful he became," Duane Michals noticed, "the meaner he got."[15]

Another user, according to André, was the British artist David Hockney. André believed that Hockney had copied the 1972 *Portrait of an*

*Artist (Pool with Two Figures)* from his own 1917 *Underwater Swimmer.* The first truly modern image of a swimmer, André's photograph had appeared in his MoMA show and again in *Sixty Years*. Around that same time, Hockney photographed a friend frog-legged in a rippling pool, and the snapshot served as a study for his painting.

Fascinated by the problem of representing water with paint, Hockney had been depicting swimming pools for nearly a decade. In *Portrait of an Artist*, he treats the water in a way that recalls André's photograph. Indeed, Hockney has acknowledged his debt to *Underwater Swimmer*.[16] But his work is a colorful, 7 by 10 foot acrylic with a Pop Art sensibility; André's is a proto-Surrealist black-and-white from a 1.8 by 2.4 inch negative. A sophisticated artist, Hockney assimilates multiple art-historical sources. *Portrait of an Artist* is no copy. Yet André believed that Hockney had pilfered it.

One day André ran into Michals in the waiting room at Bakht's studio. Like André, Michals relied on Bakht for printing. As they chatted, Michals noticed that Bakht's sofa resembled the sofa in Hockney's 1969 double portrait *Henry Geldzahler and Christopher Scott*. Like the sofa in the painting, it sat in front of a window. Michals proposed they do a parody. "No!...David Hockney ripped me off." Michals replied: "We're going to rip Hockney off."

So Michals set up *Self-Portrait with André Kertész in the Manner of David Hockney*. André was the Henry Geldzahler in Hockney's painting, and Michals the Christopher Scott. Bakht hit the shutter release. Did André feel that settled his score with Hockney? Surely not, although Michals came away believing that he had "pulled the splinter from [André's] paw."[17]

Such incidents notwithstanding, André professed to be easygoing, an idea many would find laughable. "If someone is unhappy, he is the cause of it," he told the Hungarian Canadian photographer Denes Devenyi. "It is amazing how easily people can convince themselves that they should be unhappy. Yet there is no reason for it. Unhappiness is an attitude we choose."

"So optimism is the basic tenor of André Kertész."

"Well, I put myself in the flow of events. There are many things that are not nice or pleasant. But how many can I really change? Not too many. So why worry about those?"[18] The important thing, André believed, was to engage with life, stay curious, keep a healthy perspective.

Indeed, those who didn't experience André as a thicket of complaints, and some who did, fell under the spell of his lively charm and puckish sense of humor. He was "a warm, outgoing person, completely natural and modest to a fault," one writer observed.[19] When he got testy, friends humored him as one humors a cranky yet beloved grandfather. He got on especially well with young women with creative lives of their own. He took their art seriously, listened to their problems, and served them soup or tea and toast with jam and sour cream spooned over the top. When Elizabeth came home from work to find one of "those little girls who [were] always hovering around André," she would pull a long face.[20] But so it was.

He was closest to the Budapest-born Sylvia Plachy, whose family had fled Hungary for Austria after the 1956 revolution. The thirteen-year-old rode part of the way hidden under a pile of corn husks in a farm cart, her suitcase and teddy bear at her side. After two years in a refugee camp, the family landed in New Jersey, where Plachy attended high school. She went on to the Pratt Institute, where she weighed a career in photography. An instructor advised her to try to meet some photographers. One was André.

Soon he was affectionately calling her *taknyos*, meaning "snot nose," a Hungarian version of "you little brat." At his urging, she considered him her honorary grandfather. She shared her photographs, her problems, and her dreams. One would come true only a few years after she graduated: In 1974, Plachy was hired as a staff photographer with *The Village Voice*. André had long insisted that she could find a way to do what she really wanted to do. Look at him, he smiled, the world's most egotistical photographer.

Plachy viewed André's bitterness and backbiting as a cultural habit, Hungarian Weltschmerz. "*Sírva vigad a magyar*" goes the saying: Hungarians are happy when they are miserable. That attitude stems from the nation's experience as a perennial loser in Europe's power struggles. Bent to the will of the Ottomans, the Habsburgs, the Allies, the Nazis, and the Soviets, Hungarians are sometimes said to harbor a mélange of self-pity and superiority.[21] Hungarian Jews, it goes without saying, have experienced humanity's worst.

The aggrieved André and the endearing André coexist in *Perfidy*, his 1970 self-portrait in absence. The photograph centers on the life mask made for him in Paris in 1926 by his friend Frederic Littman. André had used it before in still lifes that mix self-revelation, self-concealment, and self-mythology. In *Perfidy*, it's flanked by statuettes: a jester on one side and two owls and a cat on the other. The animals guard a blocky object pierced with holes of various sizes. It may be an antiquated factory device. It suggests an aperture chart. In conflating a found object with a camera, André is up to his old game of visual substitution.

He plays another round with a second flea market–type object, a convex mirror framed by a heavy circular object. It sits atop the aperture chart–like object. The mirror reflects his own image as he is taking the picture. It resembles a lens. Thus the reflected image of André photographing is juxtaposed with whimsical versions of parts of the camera he's using.

Yet, as its title conveys, not all is playful in *Perfidy*. Behind the objects is a shelf full of books that act as an autobiographical device and mingle references to joy and pain. Among them is János Hock's *Virágmesék: Felnőttek Számára* (Flower Tales for Adults), published in 1931. "How many beautiful things are in this world," writes Hock, "and what happiness it is to feel them!" Hock's tales were born, the author explains, of his desire to "tie Hungarian flowers into a bouquet with a Hungarian heart." Words that must have touched André's soul.[22]

There's also a history of American quilt-making, alluding to his love of folk art. Paris is represented by Alice B. Toklas's memoir of her years with Gertrude Stein and by Richard Le Gallienne's of his bohemian life on the Left Bank. The textbook *Modern Culture and the Arts* speaks to André's role in modern photography. (Among the illustrations are four of his pictures.) As if cracking a little joke, André adds *The Handy Encyclopedia of Useful Information* and a volume of bestsellers from Reader's Digest Condensed Books. Here is a handy encyclopedia, he seems to say—or a condensed book, if you will—about *me*.

Startlingly, this self-portrait in absence flags André's Judaism. André was Jewish because he was born Jewish. He never hid that fact, but neither did he consider it a hallmark of his identity. He called himself a nonbeliever and a citizen of the world. Yet three books with Holocaust or post-Holocaust themes appear in this photograph, which takes its title, *Perfidy*, from one of the three, writ large on its spine.

Among the books is Ladislav Fuks's tragicomic novel *Mr. Theodore Mundstock*, set in 1942 Nazi-occupied Prague. Readers follow the elderly protagonist's bleak life with a pigeon and his own shadow—Mundstock calls him Mon—as his closest companions. Person by person, family by family, Mundstock's fellow Jews vanish. Realizing that the dreaded knock will come to his door too, he steels himself for the terrors ahead by living as if in a concentration camp. Ironically, it's through his creative, sometimes comic, preparations for hell on earth that he finds purpose in life.

The other two books are nonfiction. Itzhak Gurion's *Triumph on the Gallows* recounts the heroism and martyrdom of Israeli fighters during the last days of British rule of pre-Israel Palestine. Finally, the writer and director Ben Hecht's *Perfidy* is a damning version of the postwar trial of Rudolf Kastner, a Hungarian-born lawyer accused of betraying Budapest's Jews. Kastner helped handpicked Jews escape the Nazis yet allegedly benefited financially and colluded with the occupiers. Hecht uses court transcripts but enhances them with a screenwriter's Hollywoodian arts. (Some historians and journalists have contested Hecht's account of Kastner's actions. Kastner remains a controversial figure.)

In framing the still life he had created, André lined up *Triumph on the Gallows* on the left edge, side by side with Hecht's *Perfidy*. Why foreground Holocaust and post-Holocaust books in a self-portrait in absence from 1970 America? Ceremonies took place in New York that year to mark the twenty-fifth anniversary of the liberation of Auschwitz and other death camps. One can speculate that they rekindled the grief, horror, and outrage André must have felt yet never publicly revealed. Perversely, he would have also intended an analogy between his treatment in the United States and the martyrdom of European Jews. *Perfidy* is the self-image of a man who claimed that he would rather be murdered in Paris than cut dead by the American photography world.[23]

**That April,** sixty-nine-year-old Rogi André died in Paris. She had been living in a third-floor walkup in a derelict building on the Left Bank. Besides André's name, Rogi had taken from her marriage a creative practice as a portrait photographer. In the decade after he left her, she could be seen lugging around her battered and outmoded equipment: a tripod, lights, boxes of glass plates, and a Voigtländer Bergheil or Voigtländer Alpin circa 1912. The latter she had borrowed from André and never returned. Rogi made portraits of Marcel Duchamp, Colette, Henri Matisse, Piet Mondrian, Dora Maar, Alberto Giacometti, Django Reinhardt, Peggy Guggenheim, and scores of others—a cultural pantheon of interwar France. Picasso reportedly deemed her "the very great Rogi André."[24] How she convinced such luminaries to surrender to what the painter Fernand Léger described as her "chamber for spontaneous confessions," no one knows.[25] Rogi's process was distinctly her own. Flouting the modernist concern for medium purity, she slipped painting into photography. Subtly brushing out or heightening certain details on her negatives, she effected a tenuous strangeness. Few people noticed. If someone did, she'd respond, "It's better that way."[26]

As the Nazis approached Paris in 1940, Rogi had fled to the unoccupied zone. Later she returned to the capital to accept a gallerist friend's offer of a room in a little house set back from the street, where she, a Jew, could keep to herself. Yet she reportedly picked up some cash by taking portraits of German soldiers. After the war, she did little photography—nobody wanted her pictures, she ranted—but continued to paint. She became frail and wraithlike with wispy hair crimped 1930s style and thin lips painted dark red. She seemed profoundly alone.

André had news of Rogi over the years. One conduit was his old friend Pierre Gassmann, the owner of Picto. When the two got together in New York or Paris, André would slip Gassmann some cash for his legal wife. Romeo Martinez was another go-between. Still unhappy that Rogi had kept his Voigtländer Alpin, André reportedly leaned on Martinez to recover it for him. That never happened. Now Martinez was attempting to raise money to buy Rogi a tombstone. Fearing that his name would be associated with hers, André refused to contribute.[27]

Over the years, the cost of André's secret would have been less financial than psychological. He implied that he had devoted himself exclusively to Elizabeth from the day they met, and he pretended that his marriage to Rogi never happened. Elizabeth probably never found out that André had not divorced. He would have lived nearly four decades with a need for self-justification and a low-level yet persistent fear that the facts would surface. Rogi's death must have left him hoping that he could put all that behind him.

Rogi left no will and no known heirs. Her belongings were hauled to the sidewalk for garbage collection. Her photographs, however, went to an auction house where the Bibliothèque Nationale curator of prints and photography Jean-Claude Lemagny purchased them for the institution.[28] Lemagny had begun assembling a world-class collection of contemporary photographs and was preparing to launch the Bibliothèque Nationale's first photography gallery.

**In the United States,** the fine-art photography world was evolving faster. At Light Gallery, eyebrow-raising pictures by then-unknowns Stephen Shore, Bea Nettles, and Robert Mapplethorpe shared the walls with pictures by established photographers like Paul Strand and Arnold Newman. Openings were heady affairs where shaggy kids with cameras around their necks mingled with collectors and connoisseurs. The doors would swing open, and in would walk the curator Sam Wagstaff, the actress Diane Keaton, the writer Janet Malcolm, or the architect and philanthropist Phyllis Lambert. Cornell Capa came to everything. Photographic legends like Ansel Adams showed up on occasion. André was viewed as a living legend, too, and a "big deal" — albeit a tetchy one.[29]

One day in the spring of 1973 found him especially so. When Tennyson Schad handed him a check for $820, his first-quarter earnings from Light, André paused and stared at it for a moment. His hands trembled. "Something must be wrong. I thought it would be much higher."

Schad explained that the gallery had sold considerably more work than that check represented. Everything had been billed, but many purchasers hadn't yet paid.

André replied that *he* always required payment at the time of the sale. Why was he selling through a gallery? He could have done better himself. And what about his portfolios? Sales had been sluggish, Schad admitted, but Light intended to market the portfolios more aggressively.[30]

Over the months that followed, André's portfolio sales did pick up, and sales of his single prints skyrocketed. *Satiric Dancer* hit the sweet spot. Priced at $250 each (later $450), prints flew out the door. The photorealist artist Chuck Close bought one. So did the photography critic Andy Grundberg.[31] For those who mythologized *les années folles*, *Satiric Dancer* put a finger on a moment of "Shalimar perfume and champagne and Paris nights with no mornings," thought the Light staffer Irene Borger.[32] Others saw not bohemian glamour but female empowerment. The women's movement was gaining momentum, and the human body had become a favored site for creative experimentation, variously labeled body art, performance art, or feminist art. Magda Förstner's unshaved underarms, bobbed hair, decorum-flouting minidress, and look of joyful abandon made her a feminist sister.

André's mostly unloved photographs of female bodies, the Distortions, were also about to come to the fore. After his ballyhooed glass negatives from the trunk arrived in New York in 1964, André had realized the full extent of their damage. Many were broken, and most badly oxidized. André had contacted Kodak and other experts to inquire about restoration, but no one could guarantee that their process would not cause further damage. Besides, restoration would cost thousands of dollars. Finding no practical solution, André put the negatives aside, his fairy-tale account of recovered treasure missing its happily ever after.

From time to time, he fulminated about the situation. Brendan Gill was among those who listened. A writer for *The New Yorker*, Gill was a consummate urbanite and journalistic lion. He and André had developed a friendship after Nicolas Ducrot hired Gill to write an introduction to André's *Washington Square*. Gill was both amused and annoyed by André's moaning about "the perpetually rising sea of troubles that daily—or hourly, or even from one moment to the next—threatened to engulf him." The writer suggested a solution to the restoration problem. Why not apply for a Guggenheim Fellowship? André could use the money to restore the negatives.

That would be useless, André flung back. The Guggenheim people would laugh at him. "Do something nice for a man in his eighties? Forget it! That's how life is. Yunnerstan?"

Not necessarily, thought Gill. So he and Ducrot wrote the application and persuaded the naysayer to sign. For letters of recommendation, they turned to John Szarkowski and *New York Times* chief art critic Hilton Kramer, who had reviewed André's Hallmark show and proclaimed him a genius.

"Months passed and André squeezed the last drop of sour pleasure out of the silence that had ensued," Gill reports. "What had he told me? Hadn't I known that money doesn't grow on trees?"

Then a letter arrived: André had a Guggenheim. He would get $15,000. "The first time, yunnerstan?"[33]

André's bent for gloom notwithstanding, the sun kept shining on the restoration project, thanks to his neighbor Wolf von dem Bussche. The German-born photographer lived with his wife and son two floors above the Kertészes. Von dem Bussche had been an art history student at Columbia until André persuaded him to ditch the scholarly life and devote himself to photography. André taught his neighbor how to use a camera and urged him to concentrate on his immediate surroundings. He too would take classic photographs of Washington Square.

Von dem Bussche now introduced André to Gerd Sander, the grandson of the early twentieth-century German photographic portraitist August Sander. Gerd had developed techniques for restoring his grandfather's glass-plate negatives. He agreed to do the same for André's and make backups using Kodak SO-015 film.

With that process underway, Ducrot turned to nettling, begging, and arguing with Elizabeth, who took a dim view of the Distortions and was balking at the idea of a book. But Ducrot stood firm, and so did André. Elizabeth eventually relented. So it was settled: Kramer would write the introduction, and Knopf would publish. Sander in his darkroom in Maryland, then Bakht in his darkroom in Manhattan, were exhorted to hurry. André's excitement was palpable.[34]

Not every plate in the trunk was a Distortion. Soon after the shipment arrived in 1964, André had pulled out a negative with an unremarkable view of Paris rooftops. He took it in 1929 to test a Telepeconar lens, a primitive zoom. By the time it arrived in New York, the plate had a hole in it, as if it had been pierced by a pebble but somehow not shattered. Cracks projected from the hole like the rays in a child's drawing of the sun. A mediocre picture, a cracked plate: Most people would have tossed it. But André and Bakht stabilized the plate by taping the edges, then sandwiching it between two sheets of glass, and made a print.[35]

At a careless first glance, *Broken Plate* looks like a picture of a broken window. But no: The inside of the hole is pitch-black. The window never existed. André uses his damaged negative to pull off a Wizard of

Oz moment, drawing back the curtain on the illusion that a photograph is a window on the world.

In looking at any photograph, viewers tacitly agree to certain conventions. If the photograph is a cityscape like this one by André, they see depth, even though they know they are looking at a flat sheet of paper. In *Broken Plate*, the blackness inside the hole keeps the viewer's eyes on that flat surface, undermining the pictorial illusion of an urban scene. André's photograph reads as both a camera-made view of buildings (the illusion) and a sheet of photographic paper that's been placed under cracked glass and exposed to light in an enlarger (the material reality).

Considered symbolically, it recalls André's loss of Paris and all it represented. The hole suggests a stray bullet. That life had been shattered, leaving only a void. "*Mon Paris*," André kept sighing.[36]

**Twenty months after** André agreed to exclusivity with Light Gallery, the matter of renewal pressed. But André kept resisting. One June day, he and Schad sat down to resolve their differences.

André began. "So I have been a bad boy?"

Light's staff had discovered that he was in talks with the Carleton Gallery in Ottawa about showing his color work. That violated his lapsed contract.

"Yes."

"Tell me about it."

Schad said that André had hurt everyone's feelings by going behind their backs. He'd acted unfairly.

André listened patiently for a time, then boiled over. He had *never* been unfair! The Carleton Gallery had inquired about exhibiting his color photographs, in which Light had never shown the slightest interest. André had not said yes. (The show never happened.)

"So am I a bad boy?"

His real issue, it emerged, was Schad's failure to promote, place, and sell his work as André thought fitting. As the two spoke, André's pictures hung at both MoMA (in a three-person exhibition with the photographic giants Aleksandr Rodchenko and László Moholy-Nagy) and the New York Historical Society (in *Manhattan Now*, a group show that moved the *New York Times* architecture critic Ada Louise Huxtable to laud André's "special genius" and describe him as a photographer who had "mastered all of the difficult insights and responses that add up to recognition of the city's soul."[37]). Not bad. Yet, in André's view, Schad had never capitalized on his prestige.

"Is it possible that the Ansel Adams show at the Metropolitan has his goat?" Schad wondered.[38] The Met's exhibition of one hundred and fifty-six Adams photographs was drawing adoring crowds and consuming critical attention.

Schad reached over to touch André's hand, expecting a warm response. Instead, he saw the sweetness drain from the photographer's face. André spoke faster and louder, berating Light for not using "publicity gimmicks." He had in mind "The Greatest People in Town," a feature in *New York* magazine naming him one of the city's treasures. The illustration, a composite portrait of eighty-nine New Yorkers, showed him next to the baseball legend Willie Mays.[39] That feature thrilled André because it showed that he belonged, that he was respected, that he stood "at the top of his profession." Yet Schad had done nothing with it, and that rankled. No wonder he wasn't selling more. Light was the wrong place for his work.

It was the dealer's turn to get angry. The feature in *New York* had nothing to do with selling photographs, he riposted. The general public didn't buy photographs. Collectors and museums did. Cultivating them was an art. André looked tired, Schad noted. He kept repeating himself.

Over lunch, their conversation shifted to Schad's interest in making a bulk purchase of André's work. Earlier that spring, he and Fern had met with André and Elizabeth to sketch out a plan that would guarantee the Kertészes an income for life and keep André's images safe and visible long into the future. No sooner were the words out of Tennyson's mouth than Elizabeth interrupted: "We don't need the money."[40]

But they did need a plan, she agreed. Now Schad brought up the idea again. André listened, then requested more specifics. He too had been pondering the future. He spoke of doing a definitive print of each important image before it was too late. Light might be able to fund such a project, Schad replied. They left it at that, with André still wrought up about gimmicks.

Two weeks later, Schad supplied the details. He was putting together a syndicate to buy photographs from the world's greatest photographers, he confided. The photographs would be held for at least five years, then made available for purchase by museums, universities, and selected other collectors. In André's case, he proposed to acquire five thousand photographs – ten prints each of five hundred negatives – with payments to extend over several years, giving André an annual income and lightening the tax burden of a figure "well in excess of $100,000." Such an arrangement would not only bring in good money for both André and Light Gallery but also preserve André's work for generations. André could, of course, continue selling his pictures as usual.[41]

So things stood three weeks later when André and Elizabeth departed for Asia. How would André's work be preserved after his death? Where would it be stored? Who would manage it and work to extend his legacy? The questions remained unanswered. André and Elizabeth had no children to pick up the burden.

**Their trip to Asia** was a prearranged tour booked by Elizabeth. At seventy-two, she shared André's intensified awareness of mortality. This pause in her professional life would last five weeks in all.

Following a few days in San Francisco, they flew to Japan, then traveled to Hong Kong, Thailand, Singapore, Bali, Australia, Fiji, Tahiti, and Hawaii. Their accommodations were high-end, yet most left much to be desired. Or so Elizabeth thought. Only one hotel, near the dormant volcano Mauna Kea on the Big Island of Hawaii, earned her undiluted approval. It was there that André photographed her on their balcony.

Elizabeth wore a kimono-style wrap as she sat writing. Her right hand held a pen; her left shielded her eyes from the sun but also from André's lens. He angled around, questing for images that would meld feeling and form. It's easy to imagine Elizabeth shooting him an exasperated look and a half-laughing command ("Stop it, Bandi") as she did when he danced too much attendance upon her.[42]

Sensitive about aging (witness her lies about her birth year), Elizabeth disliked being photographed, a trait André claimed to find charming. He did photograph her but took care to shoot from a distance or, as in *Mauna Kea* (also known as *Mauna Kea #7*), make sure that her face was obscured. For viewers of his photographs in future years, he would gallantly keep her forever young.[43]

To take *Mauna Kea,* André positioned himself above and slightly to the side of Elizabeth with the bright sun behind him.[44] That canted view draws attention to her distancing gesture, emphasized by the crosshatching shadow of the balcony's railing. On the blank wall beyond are their shadows, André's recognizably that of a photographer with camera in hand. A shadow-puppet play seems about to unfold. Yet *Mauna Kea* does not tell a story. Whatever insight it offers about the couple's relationship is by contrast. André is literally absent yet emotionally present; Elizabeth is physically present yet emotionally elsewhere.

Back in New York, André had his film developed and his negatives printed. On the back of one print, he penciled the words "*Mauna Kea . . . Kamuela, August 4–1974.*" Imposed by curators and publishers, titles like *Mauna Kea* are more practical than the place and date information that André preferred. It aligns with his metaphor for his work: "a visual diary."[45] André explained: "A writer makes a note with a pen, but if I see something and want to make a note, I do it with a camera. It's no different, with a pen or a camera — it's absolutely the same."[46]

His diary had blank pages. He no longer photographed every day. A roll of film might sit in his camera for weeks. It was okay to miss potentially wonderful photographs, André felt, as long as he fully lived the moment. Undistracted emotional receptivity was vital. "The intense feeling is primary; to record it (with photography, in my case) is secondary," he told one interviewer. "Seeing things will help you to feel things. But it is our emotional response that makes the world a rich place for us."[47] Even when the moment is bittersweet.

**In the 1970s,** André was commonly called a genius. "Kertész is, of course, a genius whose artistry appears deceptively simple," remarks the *Chicago Tribune* critic Alan Artner in his review of a three-person show at the Center for Photographic Arts in Chicago. Artner brushes aside the two younger Light photographers whose work hung next to André's. Put the thirtysomething "young lions" in the arena with the "eighty-year-old master," Artner opines, and the master easily triumphs.[48]

In New York, Gill observed that André was "a sort of tutelary god" for young Greenwich Village photographers.[49] Indeed, photographers everywhere were taking cues from André. His penchant for roaming the city, Leica in hand. His rejection of the cult of blade-sharp perfection. His attentiveness to the photographic frame, point of view, and other aspects of camera vision. His determination to photograph what he, not photography's gatekeepers, found meaningful. The unpretentiousness of his pictures.

In the early 1960s, a New York art director named Joel Meyerowitz had quit his job the same day that he watched Robert Frank at work with his Leica. Frank's fluid movements and faultless timing caught his subject's every small yet meaningful gesture. The first photograph to exert a powerful impact on Meyerowitz was by André. It taught him, he said, that obscurity and clarity could coexist.[50] Meyerowitz prowled the streets, his Leica looped around his wrist, responding to the emotional immediacy of random encounters and the evasiveness of things clearly shown.

Another photographer who paid close attention to André's pictures was the social landscapist Lee Friedlander. Enlisting shadows, signs, and reflections in plate-glass windows, Friedlander collaged himself onto the world. His pictures are temperamentally cooler and more brittle than André's. But like André's, they are witty, formally nimble, and involved with everyday living. "I love his work," Friedlander avowed, speaking of André half a century later. Did it influence his own? Yes, André was "right up there."[51]

In Europe, his admirers were legion. That July, he and Elizabeth traveled to southern France, where André was participating in the 1975 Rencontres d'Arles (then known as the Rencontres Internationales de la Photographie d'Arles). The annual photography festival had debuted five years earlier in what felt like the dark ages of French photography. Now Arles was showcasing the medium's emergence as a vital form of art. Enthusiasts huddled at portfolio reviews, thronged after-dark slide shows, and lingered at cafés on the Place du Forum, drinking pastis and talking pictures. André was that year's guest of honor, along with Robert Doisneau, Yousuf Karsh, and W. Eugene Smith, all pillars of modern photography.

From the moment he emerged from the Hôtel L'Arlatan into the morning sunshine, André was besieged. He held court at his exhibition, accepted a medal from the mayor, and fielded questions at a panel discussion. He renewed his acquaintance with the curator Jean-Claude Lemagny, the photographer Doisneau, and the photographer and photographic impresario Fritz Gruber. Youngsters mobbed him. Elizabeth hovered, fending off those who would monopolize him. He reveled in his star status, even as it flustered him a bit.

Following Arles, the couple visited Budapest, then returned home, where André prepared for a spate of fall exhibitions, along with BBC and German TV documentaries. The proofs for *Of New York* arrived: The book André had been pitching for decades was about to be published by Knopf. Meanwhile, Bakht was printing *Chez Mondrian*, *Satiric Dancer*, *Meudon*, and *Martinique* over and over. André's sales at Light Gallery were brisk. His prices sailed upward.

All the same, André was telling people seeking to purchase his work to bypass the gallery and come directly to him. Schad was still trying to lure him back into exclusivity, and he was still refusing. Light Gallery was fine for younger photographers, André conceded, but ill-suited for a grand old man of photography. His meetings with Schad and Jones had resumed. André's responses to their prodding about representation were alternately cordial and heated but always firm. "I've learned the hard way," he declared. "The party is over."

He was keen, however, on the idea of Light buying his prints in bulk. Jones suggested a price of $75,000 (about $440,000 in 2024 dollars), a figure that André rebuffed. Schad explained that the offer could go higher or lower depending on how the deal was structured. If they could pay André over several years and get exclusivity, the amount would increase. That conversation soured too. Schad suspected that the real problem was André's hurt feelings about Light's lack of attentiveness. Someone from Light should visit him once every two weeks, he and Jones decided, take him to lunch, flatter his ego. More than money, André craved the love and respect that money represented.[52]

Meanwhile, André was flirting with others. The old-line gallery Marlborough Fine Art was poised to sweep into the photography market with a show of one hundred portraits by Richard Avedon. According to a letter from Elizabeth to friends, Marlborough had wanted to launch its photography program with a Kertész exhibition, but André refused. Other sources speak of different sets of negotiations. Schad heard from Paul Katz, Marlborough's curator of photography, that Katz had approached André—or was it the other way around? Schad was uncertain—about handling André's work. Katz remembers contacting André about some prints from the 1920s that someone was offering Marlborough. Coached by Ducrot, André reportedly proposed that the gallery purchase a full set of his vintage work (older photographs he had printed around the time that he took them) for $225,000 (almost $1.5 million in 2024 dollars). Marlborough's directors considered the offer. They would have taken into account multiple factors. André's reputation for crankiness weighed against him. Marlborough said no.[53]

André also met with the Romanian American gallerist Ileana Sonnabend, who had declared herself "passionate" about his work. Sonnabend championed Post-minimalist and performance art at her gallery in Soho. When she showed photographs, they tended to be conceptual, like Hilla and Bernd Becher's grids of industrial structures, or artist-made, like David Hockney's photocollages. André's, in contrast, were rooted in distinctively photographic concerns. Even so, Sonnabend was thinking of showing them at both her New York and Paris galleries. Yet, after digging into André's relationship with Light Gallery, she backed out. The French wanted to do a portfolio, André replied. Perhaps Sonnabend could collaborate? That idea also went nowhere.[54]

As such moves by art gallerists suggest, photography had secured a wider purchase in the culture. By mid-decade, more than thirty New York City dealers were showing primarily photography. The magazine *Artforum* was publishing articles parsing photography as art. In *The New York Review of Books*, the public intellectual Susan Sontag was publishing essays about the medium's social dynamics. Sontag laid out an adversarial case, stressing the predatory nature of the photographic act and spurring fierce debate. Meanwhile, museums were giving photography close attention, creating curatorial positions, building collections, and showcasing the work. The dizzying rise in the medium's status also led to the creation of photography departments at universities. At auction houses, like Swann and Sotheby Parke Bernet, gallerists, curators, and collector-investors vied for important nineteenth- and early twentieth-century images. The status distinction between vintage photographs and contemporary prints widened. So did the price gap.

There's usually no way of knowing how many vintage prints exist from a single negative. Often there are few, because, until the photography market emerged in the 1970s, photographers lacked incentives to make masses of prints. Instead, they printed as needed. By the mid-1970s, the rarity of vintage photographs was leading auctioneers and dealers to drive up prices and collectors to splurge. A vintage Kertész sold for between $1,500 and $4,000.[55] At the same time, André was typically charging between $300 and $350 for a print of that same negative by Bakht. André earned nothing from sales on the secondary market. The infatuation with vintage prints? "A collectors' mania," he fussed.[56]

Yet there was more to the vintage phenomenon than shrewd investing. Often printed on paper coated with an emulsion high in silver content, vintage prints can be ravishingly beautiful. They carry the mystique of other times and places. When the German journalist and art historian Wilfred Wiegand acquired a *carte postale* of *Satiric Dancer*, it struck him as "a message in a bottle from a long-ago bohemian world." The image barely exceeded 4 by 3 inches, plus a band of white space below. "I was holding the Mona Lisa of photography in my hands," Wiegand recounts, "and it was only the size of a postcard."

At first, he was disappointed. "But it rapidly became clear to me that its delicate nature made it all the more exquisite. This print was not meant to decorate a wall; it was meant to be a precious little toy for the viewer's fantasy." He was holding an image made with a machine and chemically fixed on a piece of paper but "also a magical plaything that could intoxicate you, transport you, arouse your latent desires."[57]

**In January 1976,** Elizabeth was hospitalized. Three weeks later, she had surgery, possibly a partial colectomy. A few weeks after that, doctors performed a second operation, for complications from a colonic abscess. Then André developed gout, leading to the painful inflammation of a vein in his leg and provoking a dangerous blood clot. That sent him to Doctors Hospital for one week in March. He recovered, then had to be hospitalized again with another clot.

Back at home that spring and summer, Elizabeth languished with flu-like symptoms. She had trouble breathing. Ignoring any link between Elizabeth's decades of heavy smoking and her lung problems, André blamed New York City's dirty air.[58] She was in and out of doctors' offices and hospitals. When her medical team's provisional diagnosis proved incorrect, he fulminated against the ineptitude of American doctors. Finally, Ducrot, acting on André's behalf, got Elizabeth transferred to a different set of doctors in a different institution. They determined that she had synchronous lung and colon cancers. More surgery followed.

André's professional life continued that year in stop-and-go fashion. In October, he attended the cocktail party and dinner for the preview of Alexander Calder's exhibition at the Whitney Museum. Calder had delighted André by popping into his opening at Light Gallery. Now André returned the favor. *Women's Wear Daily* ran a picture of him schmoozing over drinks with the architect Marcel Breuer and the playwright Arthur Miller. "I accept very few invitations these days," André informed the reporter, "but I've known Sandy for more than 40 years."[59] A month later, Calder was dead from a heart attack.

That November, at the Cultural Services of the French Embassy on Fifth Avenue, Elizabeth watched a dignitary award André the medallion of the Order of Arts and Letters. André reveled in this recognition of his contribution to French culture. A prestigious exhibition was in the works too. The youthful curator and photographer Pierre de Fenoÿl had been jetting over from France every few months to mine the lode of images in André's archive. De Fenoÿl was overseeing the inaugural photography offerings at the much-anticipated Centre Pompidou, a museum of modern and contemporary art under construction in Paris. A Kertész retrospective would occupy center stage.

Recognition from France meant everything to André. But so did Elizabeth's approving presence. That December, she was still typing letters and making business calls, yet feeling "bitter, depressed and very much frightened." She was not expected to survive.[60] In January, Elizabeth returned to the hospital. As weeks passed and her suffering intensified, she let go of André's career along with her own. Shuttling between their apartment and her hospital bed, André was distressed, overwhelmed, and exhausted. For once, he had to make decisions for her instead of the other way around.

He was leaning heavily on Ducrot. André had done well by his young editor. After Ducrot's employer, Grossman, was acquired by Viking, he had shepherded André's *Washington Square* and *J'aime Paris: Photographs Since the Twenties* through Viking's Grossman division. Then Penguin purchased Viking, and Ducrot jumped to E. P. Dutton. When Dutton also was acquired, by a Dutch publisher, Ducrot's department was cut. That layoff freed him to spend more time and energy on André's affairs. He managed direct sales of prints, filled in for André at business meetings, interceded with doctors on his behalf, and handled the contractual and financial matters that André found distasteful.

Like Schad and others, Ducrot feared for André's health. The older man remained a vigorous walker. He thought nothing of dashing for a subway door. Once when Paul Katz came by his apartment, André answered the doorbell stark naked. Katz saw that he still had a beautiful body.[61] Yet André would turn eighty-three that summer. He had gout and Ménière's disease. His hands trembled.

Ducrot prodded him about estate planning and even met with an official from the Guggenheim Foundation to ask for advice. The proposal Ducrot put together after that meeting urged that André's archive be moved from his apartment to a secure art-storage facility. Only André, Elizabeth, Ducrot, and his wife would have access. Ducrot signed the note pressing for that cozy arrangement as "your son of the heart."[62]

André did have a paternal feeling for Ducrot. The younger man had proved his unassailable belief in André's work and his willingness to take on whatever André threw at him. The two were like-minded about book design. That Ducrot was French and the son of André's pal from *Vu* sealed their relationship. André gave Ducrot free rein to rummage around in his study—surely a first—and pull out negatives and prints for future projects.

But more demands were piling up and more ideas tumbling through Ducrot's mind than he could productively track. Besides handling André's affairs, he was struggling to build the book-packaging business that he and a friend had started. Master juggler though he was, Ducrot was on the verge of losing control. "I was the one running after him, catching all the balls," his then-assistant recalls.[63]

**Come mid-summer 1977,** André found reason to believe that Elizabeth would leave the hospital and they would resume normal life. He decided to have their apartment repainted as a welcome-home surprise. But even as he clung to a vision of life as it had been, part of André seemed to know that it wasn't to be. On July 6—Elizabeth's seventy-fifth birthday—he took advantage of the disruption caused by the painting project to create *Flowers for Elizabeth*, an image-poem that emblematizes anticipatory grief.

In André's photograph, floral arrangements are scattered about, probably friends' birthday gifts awaiting transport to the hospital. A bouquet of daisies dwarfs the others. That one was surely from André. Flowers in still life traditionally symbolize both sensuality and the brevity of life. Daisies were Elizabeth's favorite. He had used them in other still lifes, notably the 1973 *Chez Moi*, a photograph that evokes domesticity. It combines a newspaper folded to show an advertisement for his appearance at Rizzoli, an ashtray holding one of Elizabeth's half-smoked cigarettes, and a glassful of daisies on the sill of a rain-splattered window.[64]

In *Chez Moi*, André's home life is in order; in *Flowers for Elizabeth*, it is not. Everything is provisional and awry. Behind the daisies sits a folding chair. One of André's shirts is skewed over its back, a surrogate for the photographer. On its seat is an art catalog opened to a painting of an odalisque. André has positioned this image within an image so that his shirt drapes over one corner. That protective gesture reprises his own in the wedding portrait he'd taken in Paris so many years ago. But now the flesh-and-blood Elizabeth and André are both missing. André's reading glasses rest atop the catalog, suggesting that, for once, he can't bear to look. That he has taken them off to remember or cry.

Elizabeth died on October 21, 1977. André photographed her as she lay dying and after she died. Following her funeral and the interment of her ashes, he reserved his Saturdays for excursions by train to the cemetery in Westchester County. Sitting close to the crypt, he would unburden himself to Elizabeth, falling silent now and again to ruminate or wander around, taking pictures of tombstones, flowers, and clouds.

Other days he stayed home, flattened by vertigo and shattered by the existential shock of Elizabeth's nonbeing. He read books about medical malpractice, death, and grief. He turned Elizabeth's canopy bed into a shrine, arranging her dresses and bathrobe across the frilly satin spread and setting out her slippers just so, then taking pictures. Thanks to his sister-in-law, Márta Ács, all was dustless. Elizabeth's older sister came regularly to keep house, help André with paperwork, and prepare the Hungarian cold fruit soups he enjoyed. She set up a desk in Elizabeth's bedroom. André wasn't especially fond of his matronly sister-in-law, but he tolerated (and paid) her.

Others stepped up too, calling or coming by, bringing food, and helping with practical tasks. The photographers Charles Harbutt and Joan Liftin, close friends of his who lived across the street, invited him to dinner. Their sixteenth-floor apartment had views like André's. One time, he walked in to find that, as a prank, Harbutt had put a sign in each window overlooking lower Manhattan. It read "© André Kertész." That brought a wan smile.[65]

Yet his mind was elsewhere. Rumor had it that he hung up on important curators. When Light's associate director Peter MacGill sold a stack of Kertész prints to a St. Louis collector, André's share came to a fat $18,000 (about $81,300 in 2024 dollars). MacGill hand-delivered the check. He watched André open the envelope, glance at its contents, then toss it aside. "This is nothing," he scoffed. "She is not here."[66]

"I can't hear the birds sing," André lamented. He meant it literally but perhaps metaphorically too.[67]

Even though Elizabeth had smoked heavily for decades, she had considered herself "a victim of a horrible malpractice."[68] André blamed American doctors for her death. He told his friend Carol Brower that a surgeon had left an instrument inside Elizabeth, causing an infection. The photographer Eva Rubinstein heard André contend that she had contracted cancer during her first hospitalization, as if cancer were the flu. Rubinstein couldn't convince him otherwise.[69] "It is beyond description what Elizabeth went through and through her sufferings also myself," André bared his bitterness and pain in a letter to an Australian curator. "Had I ever believed in a god or in any higher powers, I have every reason to deny it. One is helpless at the ignorance of the medical profession here, the goal of which is only to make money. What happened to Elizabeth, never would happen in Australia or France, the way she lost her life and how my life became totally ruined."[70]

Besides maligning her doctors for Elizabeth's death, André lashed out at gallerists, curators, even the counterman at his neighborhood deli. He had been cheated, abused, misunderstood. Why had he stayed in the United States, a lair of gangsters and crooks? "So many rot-talking scoundrels I cannot imagine."[71] The Almighty too came in for chastisement: "Son of a bitch God!"[72] As if to validate his fury, André was mugged in his own neighborhood. A half-deaf old man with expensive equipment proved an easy target.

So much for New York. He stopped photographing in the streets. But France was different. Seven weeks after Elizabeth's death, André flew to Paris, where the Kertész retrospective of two hundred and fifty images at the Centre Pompidou opened to raves. He would spend a few days in the French capital, then photograph in the cathedral town of Chartres.

"One would like to speak of André Kertész without saying: he's the greatest photographer of the century," wrote *Le Monde*'s photography critic. "There's something lacking in the superlative. One would like to speak of the very simple emotion one felt in front of this or that photo. One would like just to transcribe one's raw feeling. One can't help but have a direct relationship with these photographs, like Kertész had a direct relationship with life."[73]

On the title wall, André's wedding portrait of Elizabeth hung like a solitaire jewel. Underneath was a message, painted at the photographer's request: "*Merci.* A.K."

**Months passed.** One day, André opened his door to the San Francisco gallerist Simon Lowinsky. At Lowinsky's side stood Graham and Susan Nash. They were in town for the No Nukes concert at Madison Square Garden, organized by Nash and his fellow musician Jackson Browne, among others. The megastar was also a photographer and collector who owned four Distortions. During their visit, he gave André a Polaroid SX-70 and twenty film packs. The four talked, fooled around with the camera, and had fun.

At one point, Susan Nash turned to André: "Have you ever done a nude of a pregnant woman?"

"Where would I get such a woman?" André's eyes twinkled. Nash was seven months pregnant.

They agreed that she would return the next morning.

After his guest arrived, André gave her a tour of his apartment. Nash oohed over this and that, especially Elizabeth's fine china on display in a breakfront. Then they did the shoot. André could not coordinate his movements that day. Maybe it was because of his tremors and balance problems, maybe because of his infatuation with the twenty-seven-year-old blonde. He struggled to attach his camera to the tripod. The tripod tipped over. He fumbled with the lens cap. No sooner had he started shooting than he paused. "I have an idea." He vanished, soon returning with a distorting mirror dug out of a closet.

After they finished the session, Nash retreated to another room to get dressed. She emerged to discover that André had rearranged the card table he had preset for tea. The Melmac dishes were gone. So was the nondescript table cover. Now Nash was looking at Elizabeth's china and silver laid out on a hand-embroidered cloth. A tea towel draped over his arm, André pulled out a chair for Nash and then, like a Hungarian waiter of old, served pastries and tea. She experienced "the most endearing – oh my God! – great movie moment of my life!"[74]

As for the Polaroid SX-70 from Graham Nash, André already had one, a gift from MacGill in 1974. Before Elizabeth fell ill, he'd pottered around with his toy, then tucked it away.[75]

First sold in 1972, the SX-70 was *the* photographic novelty of the decade. At parties, people would cluster around as it propelled out milky-blue self-developing images. Although black-and-white Polaroid film existed, color prevailed. Everyone from the photographer William Eggleston to the Pop Art god Andy Warhol was giving the SX-70 a whirl. Ansel Adams served as consultant and spokesman for the brand. Polaroid and the Polaroid Foundation established programs to provide artists, André included, with cameras and film.

Color photography had long been controversial. Only in 1976 did MoMA first show color photographs as art. Conventional wisdom held that color was for amateurs, advertisers, and the picture press. A generational gap had opened between younger photographers excited by color and elders who agreed with the venerable Paul Strand that "higher emotions could not be communicated in color."[76] André too was deeply attached to black-and-white. Yet he couldn't help but scratch the itch to explore the interpretive potential of Polaroid color. He began using his Polaroids to photograph the objects that spoke of his life with Elizabeth and filled their curio-cabinet apartment.

In years past, André had taken thousands of Kodachrome transparencies for Condé Nast and others and nearly as many on his own. But Kodachrome's colors were naturalistic and dependable, Polaroid's showy and inconsistent. André would try two shots of the same blue object in the same light, and the blues would come out differently. His partial color blindness didn't help. He had other issues with the Polaroid. High tones tended to white out. The darken/lighten control was rudimentary.

Contrast was a problem. Prints lacked definition. He did test after test to tease out the camera's abilities. "Nothing comes out the way you want... You can't treat the film the way you want; it does exactly what *it* wants," he said with a sigh. "If I open the lens a little more, everything is bad. And with this *ridicule* thing I tried expressing myself."[77]

All the same, the Polaroid SX-70 had its advantages, like its good depth of field and capacity for close focusing. It was self-focusing, an especially helpful feature for someone like André whose eyesight was declining.[78] The prints' small size, not much larger than the images in his *cartes postales* of the 1920s, suited his purposes. So did the immediacy of the process.

With the Polaroids, he didn't have to wait to finish a roll of film, then schlep the exposed film to a lab and the processed film to Bakht. Holed up at home, he could scrutinize an image as soon as it developed, then adjust the setup, reposition himself, take advantage of a shift in the light, try a new version.

A routine emerged. Soon after dawn, André would create a still life, pick up a camera, and start taking pictures. He propped up the prints he liked best on Elizabeth's piano. As morning sagged into midday and the light flattened, he would turn to other matters. Yet the Polaroids kept pulling him back for another look. By the time the late-afternoon light was setting his apartment aflame, André was selecting, juxtaposing, and rearranging more objects. The apartment was strewn with Polaroids. Taking them was a way of holding on to Elizabeth but also of letting her go.

"I began shooting slowly, slowly, slowly, but soon, going crazy," André would later recall. "I worked mornings and late afternoons... I would come out in the morning and begin shooting, shooting, shooting; no time to eat. I discover the time has gone, and no breakfast. The same in the afternoon... I forget my medicine. Suddenly, I'm losing myself, losing pain, losing hunger, and, yes, losing the sadness."

In setting up a still life, André was apt to reach for one of the glass knickknacks he and Elizabeth collected: a bird, a moon, or especially a heart. *Szívecske* ("little heart" in Hungarian) was among his pet names for her, hence the many hearts he'd ferreted out in shops and brought home as gifts over the years.

Now a semiabstract, smoky blue bust joined his glass collection. The bust had jolted him when he spotted it in the window of a neighborhood shop. Its sloping shoulders and long neck curving into a tilted head were *hers*. André entered, looked, hesitated, then decided: "Don't buy."[79] But he kept passing that shop, halting, walking on. One murky March day, André found himself once more riveted by the bust in the window. The wind was biting, the street deserted. He entered and put down his money. The purchase set his heart racing.

Back home, he placed the bust on a windowsill. It looked graceful yet forlorn against the dimming sky and the vast loneliness of the metropolis. He garlanded it with flowers. He approached it from different distances and angles. Another day, he pushed it close to a pane beaded with raindrops, surrogates for tears. He took advantage of its distorting, refractive, and light-transmitting properties. At times, it swallowed the city and sky, inverting, abstracting, polishing, and miniaturizing them. "Look how the face of the bust is always changing," he marveled of his Elizabeth transmuted into gesture and light, "a shadow, which is the shadow of the curtain, then a passing cloud."[80]

After André bought a second, identical bust—an understudy for himself—he and Elizabeth became a couple again, albeit a spectral one. He photographed the two of them with their heads together, the space between their bodies vaguely heart- or tear-shaped. "Play, you see?" he told a writer friend. "I'm playing around. That's all."[81] He *was* engaging in theatrical play, not unlike Calder dreaming up his circus or Géza Blattner inventing scenes for his marionettes. The Polaroids occupy a liminal space between presence and absence, the material and immaterial worlds, his being and hers.

Mixing playfulness with poignancy, André placed one bust atop an hourglass, turning the hourglass into a curvaceous female body. He paired it with a wire tchotchke of a photographer at work. He did setups using a flower, a plastic Venus, even a roll of paper towels. Sometimes he arranged objects by a window with a view of the campanile of the Judson Memorial Church. Its cross reminded him of Elizabeth's faith. Beyond stood the World Trade Center towers, one appearing to be slightly taller than the other with only a ribbon of light in between, not unlike a couple.

André's shadow played a role too. Like the fictional Mr. Theodore Mundstock, he heeded its doings. At times he photographed it when the late-afternoon light turned his walls tawny and shadows grotesque. In one ambered Polaroid, the distended silhouette of his hand swims toward a doorknob as if the octogenarian were reaching for the exit beyond which might await his beloved.

As month followed month, André's subject matter grew more varied. Once he waggishly placed a souvenir Eiffel Tower atop a toy block with the letter *A*, then used a ballpoint pen to write *ndré* on the print. He purchased more objects to use in the Polaroids. At a Seventh Avenue bead shop, he lucked upon some prisms from crystal chandeliers. In Bethlehem, Israel, where he spent a day in November 1980 roaming the streets after his opening at the Israel Museum in Jerusalem, André bought a crown of thorns from a street vendor.

Back in New York, he placed it on a print of his wedding portrait of Elizabeth and pulled out his camera. The Bible tells of Christ's captors placing a crown of thorns on his head as an act of persecution as he made his way along the Via Dolorosa. In the late stages of her cancer, Elizabeth had suffered terribly. To André, the crown of thorns would have embodied her martyrdom: her painful death at the hands of American doctors (so he believed) but also the hardships of the 1930s and 1940s, the surrender of her art career, and the crushing demands of her business. His images with the crown of thorns came and went on the piano as elements in an ever-changing patchwork of Polaroids—the photographic equivalent of the mourning quilt made by the bereaved from scraps of the beloved's clothing.

With André's passing, his and Elizabeth's belongings would scatter. The microculture of their life together would disappear. She would die a second death. Except that André was pulling objects out of obscurity, putting them on a little stage, shining a spotlight, giving them meaning. He – not death – would have the last word.

Endre Ady was again on André's mind. A recent edition of an Ady biography stood on his bookshelf, along with a volume of Ady's poems. The writer who had quickened André's pulse when he was young still mattered. Both were romantics and French-mangling Francophiles. Both had flouted convention to make work that was radically new. Both held up mirrors to their own subjectivity and equated seeing with feeling. Both wrapped their lives around a deeply loved woman.

André's retrospective state of mind would have sent him to lines like these from Ady's "Alone with the Sea":

*She is gone and comes again no more. She is gone and comes again no more.*
*She has left a flower in her place,*
*On the shabby couch which I embrace, On the shabby couch which I embrace.*[82]

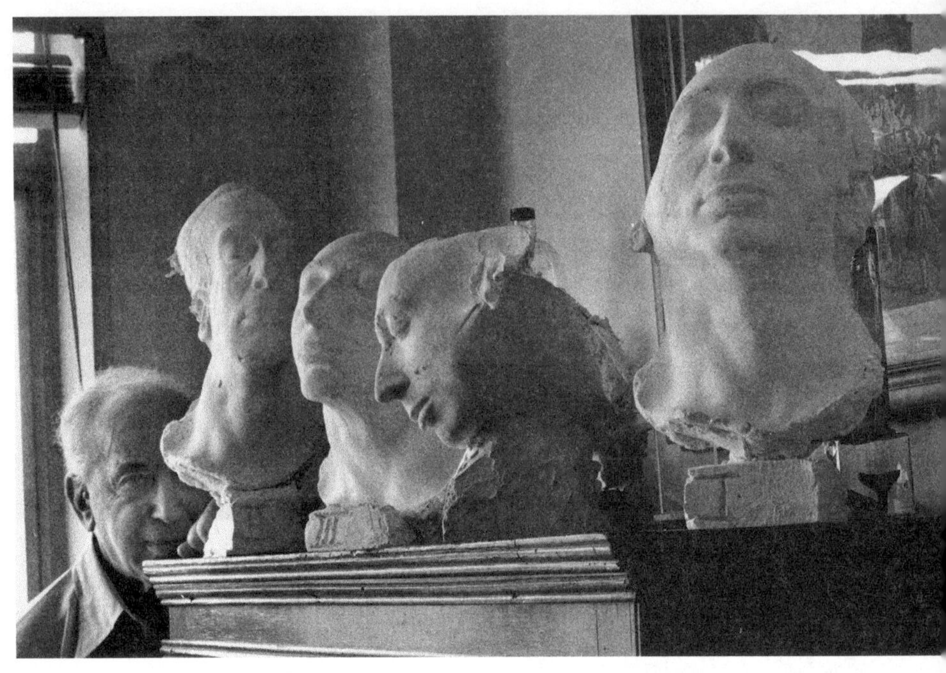

André Kertész, *Self-Portrait with Masks*, 1976

# 12 SELF-PORTRAIT WITH MASKS, 1979–1985

**In July 1979,** André charmed and clicked his way through another Rencontres d'Arles in southern France. The roll call of legendary photographers at that summer's festival comprised Aaron Siskind, Gisèle Freund, Henri Cartier-Bresson, Eikoh Hosoe, Jacques Henri Lartigue, and the Mexican photographer Manuel Álvarez Bravo. People marveled at how well André and Álvarez Bravo got along. The two breakfasted together, posed for snapshots, and acted like old chums, even though they had no language in common, photography excepted. André's French was no less Kertészian than his English. His outdoor slide lecture one night had people rolling their eyes at what the photographer Ralph Gibson describes as his "desperado French."[1] But everybody loved the pictures.

André enjoyed himself. When the actor slated to play the role of a corpse in an art film shot in Arles that summer failed to show up, André replaced him. His hours of lying on a marble slab, barefoot and stripped to the waist, were a rehearsal, he joked, for his own future as a corpse. It didn't hurt that the star of *Les suaires de Véronique* (The Shrouds of Veronica) was the German artist and supermodel Verushka, described by Richard Avedon as "the most beautiful woman in the world."[2] Recognizing André's love of women was vital to understanding the man, as Romeo Martinez had always contended. So too, Martinez added, was André's love of money.[3]

Eight months later, André sat in his New York living room with one of his favorite women, his French dealer Agathe Gaillard. He called her *A-ga-ta.* They may have been sipping Lillet, André's favorite apéritif, as he spouted old war stories from his seven decades of photography. His face was animated, his mood blithe. With her sleeveless sheath and cascade of honey-blond waves, Gaillard was the picture of artless French chic. André wore a short-sleeved shirt and trousers pulled high at the waist. Gaillard was gathering material for her uncritical account of André's life for a French publisher's series about iconic photographers. The French journalist and editor Françoise Ayxendri was present too. The buzzer sounded. Gaillard switched off her tape recorder as two friends joined them. They chatted, joked, and snapped pictures. The buzzer again. Susan Harder.

André and Harder had met in the early 1970s when Harder was working for Light Gallery. She traveled for the gallery, visiting museums, spreading the gospel of photography, and promoting work from Light's stable. After leaving that job, Harder had proposed to André that she become his adviser. Not his agent. André stood firm that he sold his own prints, arranged his own shows, and handled his own reproduction rights. But he no longer had Elizabeth to read the fine print, ask the right questions, and keep things on track.

Harder was "icy and smiling," reports Gaillard of their first encounter that day, "with a competent look, pretty and well made up behind her efficient nurse-secretary style glasses." She seemed bewildered to find André surrounded by Parisiennes. As Gaillard tells the story, André responded with a little lesson: "Susan, until you go to Paris, you will not truly be a woman."

"We laugh about everything, we take nothing seriously," Gaillard explained, "or rather we are so deeply serious that we don't need to look that way."[4] Harder politely acquiesced. André loved it when people fought over him. Women especially.

Like Gaillard, Harder was proving vital to André's career at a time when the photography world was fast evolving. The 1980s began with a deep recession and overcrowded market. Photographs were well established as solid investments. Museums had photography departments. Corporations were projecting a humanistic image by funding photography programs and building the collections they used as marketing tools. Yet the dazzle of the 1970s had dimmed. Prices and sales had tapered off. Deep-pocket collectors and top-tier museums were less interested in buying contemporary prints than in securing the finest vintage work. The price gap between vintage and contemporary photographs had widened, with vintage prints selling for up to thirty to forty times the price of later prints from the same negative.[5]

Operating from a prestigious address on Fifth Avenue near Fifty-Seventh Street, Light Gallery still had a presence, although it was no longer a central player. The gallery's financial situation had clouded. All the same, Tennyson Schad kept hatching plans, albeit less grandiose, to purchase André's pictures in bulk. Five or six sets each of the best, a total of three or four hundred pictures, he told Peter MacGill, Light's latest director. "We would underwrite the entire project. The sale of the prints to the donors would be handled by André directly so that he need not feel he was being 'ripped off' by the gallery." Light's fee would be one set of prints, plus one set for sale on consignment by André. The stumbling block, MacGill pointed out, was that Light owed André $38,000 for past sales. Another $21,000 was due to him soon.[6]

Light had done well by André's classic black-and-whites. To own a Kertész was to own a piece of photographic history, and an Igor Bakht print was many times cheaper than a vintage. In 1980, an 8 by 10 of *Chez Mondrian* printed by Bakht fetched $1,000 at Light.[7] By 1992, that same Bakht print might go for $2,500. A vintage of *Chez Mondrian* printed by André in 1926 would sell that same year for $250,000.[8]

*Chez Mondrian* was among the world's most purchased photographs but also among the trickiest Kertész negatives to print.[9] Many of André's old glass plates were poorly exposed or overdeveloped, or both, with blocked highlights or shadows. *Chez Mondrian* was overdeveloped, making the staircase too dark. So Bakht had to burn in the stairs (give them alone extra exposure) and do so precisely enough to avoid a dark halo on the print. That's what he did, over and over.

Besides Light, a handful of galleries in other cities, American and foreign, regularly exhibited and sold André's work. In 1980, his biggest sale, brokered by his friend, colleague, and neighbor Charles Harbutt, was four hundred prints to a trust in Manchester, England. Established by a local construction company and its CEO, the trust intended to donate the prints to its home city for permanent display. The Manchester Collection would debut at Salford 80, a cash-poor but high-energy festival aimed at vitalizing art photography in the Midlands and kickstarting a photography program at the nearby University of Salford. André's exhibition was one of twenty on view in the two cities when he arrived in early July.

Prince Philip, Duke of Edinburgh, the chancellor of the University of Salford, presided over the opening. At the luncheon that day, the prince was flanked by André and the other honoree, the Texan Russell Lee, best known for his photographs for the Farm Security Administration during the Depression. The three exchanged niceties over poached fillet of sole and sauvignon blanc. Then His Royal Highness presented awards to André and Lee, expressing his deep admiration.

Other luminaries also had descended on Salford: gallerists, critics, curators, editors, and photographers, American and European. The organizers put André up in a delightful old house, along with the New York dealer Lee Witkin, Witkin's assistant, and Harbutt, Joan Liftin, and their family. The housemates ranged in age from sixteen (one of Harbutt and Liftin's children) to eighty-six (André). Between official engagements, they were a gang of rowdies who couldn't stop joking and laughing.

When the schedule allowed, the festival's cigar-chomping organizer piled his guests into two twelve-seater vans and toured them around. In Liverpool, they lunched at a revolving skyscraper restaurant. At a country pub, they talked Pre-Raphaelite art as they watched the sun set. Late one afternoon they zoomed out of Salford, destination unknown to the passengers. After a while, the drivers pulled over, and their assistants hopped out. When they reappeared, one was carrying a box packed with fish and chips, each portion wrapped in newspaper and "piping hot, the oil and vinegar oozing through and the odor mouthwatering," as Witkin later remembered. The other handed out sodas and beer. André devoured his first meal of fish and chips.

By the time they reached Blackpool that evening, Britain's Coney Island was a kaleidoscopic blaze of shops and amusement piers. André wiped the last grease off his fingers, grabbed his tripod and equipment bag, and plunged into the crowd. But the highlight of the day was the feast. When hunger gnawed on other road trips, André would amuse his companions by stomping his feet and chanting "Fish and *chips*! Fish and *chips*!"[10]

He glumly insisted that it was all too late, that none of it mattered. But he showed up and had fun.

**By 1980,** André was ready to publish the Polaroids. However, a rupture with Ducrot had left him with no clear path. Around the time of Elizabeth's death, Ducrot had proposed they do four thematic paperbacks, each priced at two or three dollars, about the same as a roll of film, so that young people could afford them. Ducrot's own start-ups, Visual Books and Mayflower Books, would publish and distribute. André was amenable. So Ducrot proceeded. André was picturing four little gems dedicated to Elizabeth.

But that's not what he got. Strapped for cash and beset by personal problems, Ducrot was "flying by the seat of his pants," recalls his then-assistant.[11] He scrimped on paper and printing and never showed André the proofs. Paralyzed with grief, André let that slip, even though he had always been deeply and uncompromisingly involved in planning and designing his books.[12] When *Landscapes*, *Birds*, *Portraits*, and *Americana* came out in 1979, he was staggered by their mediocrity. Instead of gems, he got eyesores. When he spotted the words "For E.K." amid the clutter of their copyright pages, he became livid. If asked to sign one of the books, he refused.

Sales were weak. The press snubbed the books too. André was horrified to spot them in remaindered bins, marked down to fifty cents each. Another betrayal, this time by a surrogate son. André cut Ducrot out of his life.

Then he heard from an editor at the New York Graphic Society/Little, Brown. Floyd Yearout was contacting André on the advice of John Szarkowski. When Yearout and the graphic designer Katy Homans visited apartment 12J, Homans found the "desperated" man (as he described himself) endearing for his "lovely manners, romantic accent and graceful stoop... He was widowed, and sad. Was that really a crown of thorns on his wedding portrait of Elizabeth?"[13] Yes, it was, and a Polaroid of the photograph with the crown of thorns would appear on the dedication page of *From My Window*.

*From My Window* was not the book that Yearout had intended to publish. He wanted to do a survey of André's early Hungarian work. But André had stood firm. Aware that he might not otherwise find a publisher, fearful that someone would steal his concept, and intent on publishing *From My Window* to coincide with an exhibition of the same work at MoMA (which never happened), he insisted on doing the Polaroids first, then *Hungarian Memories*. Yearout acquiesced.

*Hungarian Memories* would be printed in Switzerland. Before traveling to Lausanne to oversee the job, Yearout went by André's apartment to pick up some additional images. He was astounded to watch the photographer open a desk drawer, rummage around, pull out a few tiny prints, and reach for an empty hard eyeglasses case. After inserting the prints, André passed it to Yearout. But before the editor hand-carried it overseas, his bosses at Little, Brown insisted that its contents be insured. For $3 million.[14]

Another visitor at 2 Fifth Avenue was a doctoral student at City University of New York. Sandra Phillips was conducting research for her dissertation about his French period, the first scholarly study of André's work. Earlier accounts had not "cleared the air of the romantic mists" that enveloped it, Phillips noted.[15] She would attempt to do that. Meanwhile, André was generating more mist.

Take what happened in London, where he traveled in February 1980 for the opening of his exhibition at the Serpentine Gallery. One day, André and the director, Sue Grayson Ford, were discussing his 1928 *Meudon*. Ford remarked that the inscrutable man with a package resembled her father, a Hungarian-born artist who lived in Paris in the 1920s. André generously gave Ford a print. But when she showed it to her mother, the older woman said that the man was *not* her late husband. Ford so informed André. But the story was too good for him to relinquish. Instead, he embellished. According to André's version, Ford's mother saw the photograph, then "turned to her daughter with great bewilderment and tears in her eyes. Imagine! The man in the photograph, the one crossing the street, was her late husband!"[16]

As André approached his nineties, he seemed determined to lock in selected stories for posterity. Well-practiced yet vague, they were typically exaggerated or misleading versions of actual events, not downright lies. André's eyes would light up as he pattered on about his years in Paris. He gave listeners the impression that he had been close to Mondrian, Chagall, and Léger.[17] As for Colette: "And she can't drink, poor girl, two glasses, and finished." Then he would laugh, as if he and the French writer used to barhop together.[18]

What about Rogi André? After Phillips turned up information about André's marriage, she inquired. André's eyes clouded over. He feigned semi-ignorance: "I think she was a photographer in Paris."

When Phillips persisted, André turned indignant and frosty. Rogi was *not* part of his biography! She had been "bossy and difficult and neurotic." Not only that: She was "very ugly . . . I didn't really marry her."[19]

Phillips assured him that Rogi would be only a footnote in her dissertation. André appeared to be mollified. But not really. For days, he raged about Phillips to anyone who would listen.[20]

André also drew a curtain over the financial desperation that had sent him to America in 1936. He let people assume he was fleeing the Nazis, or he explained that he had intended only a sabbatical. He and Elizabeth were forced to stay in New York, he sometimes added, because it took years to get compensation for the gold they brought into the country, and, by then, war was consuming Europe. In fact, the matter had been resolved within months. "Everything bad that happened to me in life happened in America," André ranted. "I was cheated. My work was not accepted. I was fingerprinted and accused of being a spy. It got worse and worse. I never hurt anyone. I wanted to keep on creating what I was creating, but I was pushed down. America was responsible for this."[21]

Could he be more specific? Robert Hayes wanted to know. Quizzing the photographer for a feature in *Interview*, Hayes tried to pin down exactly what had happened in those first decades in New York. But he got nowhere. In the end, the journalist wrote that events were "obfuscated with time and the frailty of memory." He continued: "Broken promises, stolen pictures and a general ignorance of the man's brilliance summarize the problems that still stir his rage, and narrow his protruding milky eyes."[22]

Again and again, André trotted out the story of his 1936 meeting with Beaumont Newhall. When Witkin's assistant Jain Kelly asked him to contribute to her book *Nude: Theory*, André rode that story hard. Kelly reproduces *Distortion #157*, the picture Newhall reportedly asked André to crop for MoMA's 1937 survey of photography. According to André's version of what happened, Newhall had said that with the model's pubic hair showing, the picture was pornography, but without the pubic hair it was art. André replied: "Mr. Newhall! How do you like if somebody cutting on the top of your head and the finger and your leg? You are mutilated. *Mais, non! Mais, non!*"

André reluctantly complied with Newhall's request, he sometimes explained, because the curator represented MoMA and André was a newcomer eager to make his mark. "This was my welcome to America," he griped to Kelly.[23]

André's interviews with Kelly refueled his old grievance. One day he propped up a print of *Distortion #157* behind a kitschy plastic statuette of the Last Supper, then snapped a picture. It creates the impression that the model is gazing at the scene in which Christ reveals that one of his disciples will betray him. Gazing with sadness, André lamented, because *someone* — André's own Judas — had amputated her private parts.

He ran into that *someone* in April 1982, when the Art Institute of Chicago opened its renovated photography galleries. Both André and Newhall, then a professor at the University of New Mexico, attended the reception. When Newhall walked up with his hand extended, André ignored him.

"André, it's Beaumont."

André responded by slapping Newhall's hand aside. "Shame on you!"[24]

Newhall must have looked blank. Questioned about the incident in an interview fifteen months later, he responded that he had no recollection whatsoever of "mutilating" André's photograph, adding that virtually all photographers object to other people cropping their work.[25]

As for *Distortion #157*, André was trying to sell it. "Look," he told one writer, "I have the original print that was exhibited in the Museum of Modern Art," meaning the cropped version. "I am selling it for one million along with the story!"[26]

**In 1981,** Harder launched an André-centric gallery in Bakht's former waiting room. Open four afternoons a week, the Susan Harder Gallery occasionally featured work by photographers in André's entourage, like Sylvia Plachy, or group shows like *Images of Water*. But mostly it showcased André.

Once again, Harder proved an ace marketer. The gallery's first major show, *Vintage Photographs of Hungary, 1912–25*, was timed to coincide with the publication of *Hungarian Memories*. She also embarked on a portfolio project. Bakht contact-printed ten negatives on Ilford Galerie paper, then selenium-toned the prints. They were mounted on handmade Dieu Donné mattes and housed in a cloth box with a leather spine. The sets sold for $20,000 each (about $65,000 in 2024 dollars). Turning to the Polaroids, Harder faced a roadblock: Each is necessarily one of a kind. She got around that by ordering Cibachrome (color print) versions and getting André to sign and declare the color quality better than in the Polaroids. She marketed them in editions of twenty-five or fifty.

At openings and award ceremonies, Harder was the scarlet-lipped thirtysomething blonde at the side of the tottering, wispy-haired octogenarian. Unlike Gaillard, Harder's assistant Liza Macrae saw her boss as "a kick in the pants," all vitality. She treated André "like royalty," Macrae observed. Harder handled the paperwork and other professional tasks that André found tedious, posed nude for him, accompanied him on out-of-town trips, and hosted him one summer at her rental in Wainscott on Long Island.[27]

All the while, Bakht was printing André's classics—*Chez Mondrian, Satiric Dancer, Melancholic Tulip, Martinique*—in batches of fifty or a hundred. André did much of the selling. Harder would set things up for him at the gallery, then absent herself while he met with potential buyers. People gossiped that Harder made André a millionaire in his own right. Some buyers later resold. Indeed, so many prints of *Chez Mondrian* and *Satiric Dancer* landed at auction houses that staffers would raise their eyebrows at the arrival of yet another. André bristled at the very existence of the secondary market: He earned nothing from those sales. He did not need the money. He needed the psychological satisfaction triggered by sales. With people who genuinely loved the work, he remained the generous soul he'd always been, giving away prints on impulse and waiving reproduction fees for those who couldn't afford them.

He was equally willing to offer advice. Whether at the gallery or at home, André liked holding court with younger photographers who wanted a critique or simply a brush with his greatness. He was easy to meet, easy to be with, and forthright yet kind in assessing their work. One day, the writer and photographer Peter C. Jones was amused to walk into the Susan Harder Gallery to find André installed behind the desk with four admirers, including the photographer Joel Meyerowitz, kneeling on the floor around him "like good Catholic boys awaiting communion at the altar rail."[28]

André urged his acolytes to learn to photograph everything. Don't be afraid of making mistakes, he counseled. Use mistakes to acquire new skills. Always remember that liking something isn't enough: "You can reach your subject only if you truly feel it, if you are in love with it." Seeing is superficial and passive. Looking is affective and active. Thinking can be an impediment. "You don't *think*. You *feel*. And you do."[29]

That kind of emotional connection is impossible with the motor drives that were becoming standard on 35 millimeter cameras. By automatically winding the film and arming the shutter after each click, motor drives enable photographers to shoot several frames a second. "The simplicity of photography lies in the fact that it is very easy to make a picture," John Szarkowski once wrote. "The staggering complexity of it lies in the fact that a thousand other pictures of the same subject would have been equally easy."[30] André expressed a similar idea in a folksier way, invoking a Hungarian proverb about blind barnyard chickens. "You get a little chicken—*peek, peek, peek* a thousand times; they're blind, they pick stones and one time grain. Ah, that is the system. You make a roll, six rolls, for two pictures... People don't concentrate—just shoot, shoot, shoot—maybe one or two or three real ones."[31] He might have added that some of his great early works, like *Blind Violinist* and *Cellars at Budafok*, resulted from a single snap of his shutter.

Writing in a popular 1981 compendium of great living photographers, the editor and photojournalist Bryn Campbell noted that it had become a cliché to call André Kertész "the father of modern photography."[32] André had regained his stature. His work was back in the canon. But, as always, photography was shape-shifting.

Raised on television, films, magazines, and advertising, the post–World War II generation had grown up in a world vastly different from that André had once known. American artists like Cindy Sherman and Richard Prince were using photographic images to expose the social construction of gender, race, and class in the mass media. Ed Ruscha put photography in the service of conceptual art. Drawing on clichéd and appropriated visuals, such artists made work that discredited the idea of photographs as subjective interpretations of the world. Photography's distinctive traditions and craft did not concern them. "It's a playground, is all it is. Photography's just a playground for me," avowed Ruscha, who self-published books with deadpan pictures of subjects like gas stations and buildings on the Sunset Strip. "I'm not a photographer at all."[33]

Not only conceptual art but also the culture wars, the AIDs crisis, identity politics, and accelerating globalization conspired to relegate André's work to a more innocent, if not illusory, time. His romantic individualism, concern for primary experience, and belief in pure photography marked him as old school at a time rife with ironic detachment, mediatized imagery, and a view of photography as simply one tool in an artist's tool kit. André photographed dogs, cats, and children. More than once, he staged emotive self-portraits. Certain Kertész titles, like *Melancholic Tulip* and *Lost Cloud*, indulged in pathetic fallacy. He steered clear of the ugly, the cynical, and the mean. He adored gardens, birds, and old stones.

"I guess I am romantic," André acknowledged to an interviewer. "I am sentimental."[34] *Sentimental* implies shallow and excessive, while *romantic* suggests more depth and complexity. But André didn't make that distinction. For him, both meant feasting on the richness of life. His interlocutor expressed her amazement at the gentleness of his worldview given all he'd endured. Well, life was an emotional tangle: "You have different feelings with each happening — good ones and bad ones: a killer can be an artistic person; wars are fought in beautiful landscapes."[35] Losses pile up no matter what. Why not attend to the beauty? It helps you carry on. Now in his late eighties, André stayed alive to everyday pleasures. He took witty black-and-whites of the reflection of his barber holding up a mirror to show him the back of his haircut. He did a study of objects in the shopwindow of a violin maker. He photographed his boxes of vitamins and pills. He set up more poignant still lifes. André found truth "in silence, contemplation, the flight of a pigeon," observed Hervé Guibert, the young photography critic for *Le Monde* after spending an afternoon in New York with his photographic hero.[36]

André had acquired a Canon FT QL in the early 1970s. He liked its behind-the-lens light metering as well as the feeling of direct contact with his subjects that it allowed. Then, in 1972, the Olympus OM-1 came out and stole his affection. Compact, lightweight, and inventively simple, the OM-1 has a large viewfinder, excellent optics, and manual controls. The photographer, not the camera, selects the exposure and focus.

Both the Canon and the Olympus are single-lens reflex (SLR) cameras as opposed to the range finder Leica. SLR cameras have a mirror that reflects the image into the viewfinder, then flips out of the way when the photographer hits the shutter release. The image in the viewfinder and the image from the lens are identical. With a rangefinder, however, the two are slightly different, and that difference must be compensated for.

Observing André's manner with his camera, younger photographers marveled that his trembling hands seemed to still when he was homing in on an image. They showed "a confidence that only a lifetime of camera-handling can produce," as Ralph Gibson put it.[37]

Gibson frequently visited apartment 12J. So did Joan Liftin, who would walk across the street to have lunch with André, then sometimes stay on to watch tennis with him on cable. Weston Naef, a curator at the Metropolitan Museum, showed up once a week with André's favorite blintzes from a certain Russian deli, and the two chatted over dinner. Collectors, dealers, photo historians, and journalists came and went. Friends who had once hesitated to stop by because of Elizabeth's coolness now felt more at ease. André would make tea or break out a bottle of Lillet, pull out some photographs, and begin telling stories, stretching their visits into the twilight hours.

Besides Harder, Peter MacGill squired André around. When André needed clothes, MacGill helped him pick out herringbone jackets and flannel pants at J. Press. When he received an honorary doctorate from Bard College, MacGill drove him up to Dutchess County in his Volkswagen Beetle, top down. When Jenő and his wife, Olga, visited from Buenos Aires, MacGill hosted them all for brunch at his Prince Street apartment. People sensed the competitiveness between him and Harder.

MacGill had left Light Gallery, earned an MFA in photography, and worked as a curator before returning to the gallery as its director. Then in 1983, Pace Gallery stepped into the photography arena, establishing Pace/MacGill Gallery, which specialized in modern and contemporary work and was run by MacGill. Offered the inaugural exhibition of his choice, André leaped at the opportunity for the first solo exhibition of the Distortions, half a century after their creation. Pace/MacGill opened its doors on Fifty-Seventh Street that November. Three iterations of selected Distortions hung on walls that were painted dusty rose. The idea was to highlight André's use of cropping as an interpretive tool. The three versions – in each case, a vintage print by André from the 1930s, a later contact print with André's crop marks, and a recent version by Bakht – invited comparisons.

Despite efforts by MacGill, Harder, and others to organize André, his professional life kept fraying. His dogged independence, on-again, off-again grudges, poor hearing, mangled English, and spotty attention to business made him essentially unmanageable. On top of that, he presided over a vast archive: tens of thousands of negatives, plus contact sheets and prints. The apartment was packed. Things got misplaced, half forgotten in boxes, too casually loaned, or – people whispered – filched. Everyone wanted a piece of him. "Too little too late," André groused, "and now they are stealing my life's work." Well, he sighed, rather enjoying the situation, it was the price he had to pay to stay in the game.[38]

**Twice a year,** André would duck out of New York to spend a few weeks in Paris. He most often stayed at the Hôtel Esmeralda, where old stone and red velvet abounded, and the stairways were narrow and steep. The trumpeter Chet Baker was a sometime guest at the Esmeralda. So was the actress-singer Jane Birkin. Only steps from the hotel's front door stood the Romanesque church Saint-Julien-le-Pauvre. The Esmeralda felt like a holdover from a bohemian Paris where clochards were poets, a waiter put down his tray to dance a *java,* and a photographer might round a corner to find goats roaming the street where Ady once romanced his mistress.

One snowy morning, André paused breakfast in his room to record the moment.[39] *Paris Breakfast No. 30, Jan. 3, 1982* conveys the same wistfulness the photographer Michael Somoroff sensed when he met André for coffee and picture-taking around that same time. "He seemed lonely and frail, having lost his wife," Somoroff later recalled. "He reflected on how much he missed her."[40]

In *Paris Breakfast No. 30*, André's tray sits near a frosty window. Around it is what he will need to get through the day: his eyeglasses, a lens filter, stacks of letters and notes, and a snapshot of a mirthful Elizabeth. That radiant August day in East Hampton—so remote from this snowy morning in Paris. Elizabeth would not see him accept the 1982 French National Grand Prize in Photography or, in 1983, be named a Chevalier of the Legion of Honor, a prestigious award. André was negotiating with the Ministry of Culture about leaving his work to France, and the French were gilding the deal.

Negotiations had begun in 1980 during the first Mois de la Photo, held every other November in photography-crazed Paris. Fifty-two exhibitions drew tens of thousands of people that inaugural year. The Galerie Agathe Gaillard was showing Kertész. André had practically moved into the gallery, where he was mobbed by fans.

During his stay in Paris, André learned that Jacques Henri Lartigue had recently donated his body of work to the French state, the first living photographer to do so. The idea of such donations stemmed from conversations between two photographers, Michel Delaborde, who occupied a key position at the Ministry of Culture, and Gisèle Freund. In exchange for the gift, the state would preserve and archive the materials, organize and circulate exhibitions, and manage reproduction rights. In the case of Lartigue, that involved tens of thousands of negatives and some one hundred photo albums.

That fall of 1980, André visited *Bonjour Monsieur Lartigue*, an exhibition of 152 photographs and eight paintings in a wing of the prestigious Grand Palais. It was curated by the photo historian and bookseller Isabelle Jammes, the daughter of André's old friend André Jammes, on behalf of the Association des Amis de Jacques Henri Lartigue, a group of cultural officials and other notables established to manage the gift. André was deeply impressed. He reportedly met with Lartigue, who waxed enthusiastic.

At dinner one evening not long afterward, André announced to Gaillard that he too wanted to donate his life's work to the French people. After years of dithering over estate planning, he seemed decided. So Gaillard contacted officials at the Ministry of Culture. She and André launched discussions with Delaborde and others.

The election of François Mitterrand as president six months later brought a new cast of interlocutors and propelled the project forward. Aiming to promote cultural democracy and modernize the nation's stuffy national identity, Jack Lang, Mitterrand's minister of culture, was reconceptualizing, reactivating, and reinterpreting the nation's cultural heritage. Popular and folk arts like the circus, comic books, the bal musette (a lowbrow style of dance and accordion music), and photography came to the fore. The acquisition of photographic archives and estates took on fresh importance. None fit the spirit of the moment better than that of the Francophile photographer of everyday life André Kertész.

In August 1981, Gaillard put together the Association des Amis d'André Kertész to move the project forward. Henri Cartier-Bresson agreed to serve as president; Gaillard became vice president. The photographers Robert Doisneau, Martine Franck, Gilles Walusinski, and Marc Riboud, among others, came on board.

In another happy development, a director of the French publisher Flammarion had invited André to do a book about a subject of his choice. Was it Lartigue's lighthearted pictures that gave André the idea for *On S'amuse* (Having fun)? He conceived of one hundred playful paired images taken in France. Back in New York, he huddled with Harder to assemble and sequence the volume. Later, however, the director who had asked him to do the book left Flammarion, and his successor killed the project. After that, the only amusement had from it was that of those who heard the photographer venting. His "Flammarion *shit*!" came out "Flammarion *sheet*!," tickling listeners but spoiling the invective.[41]

Continuing his estate planning, André was advised by his tax attorney and his accountant to set up an artist-endowed private foundation as a tax strategy. So on January 13, 1982, he filed papers for the André and Elizabeth Kertész Foundation, naming himself president and the attorney and accountant as vice president and treasurer, respectively. The two had earned their reputations working with the garment and fashion industries, Cosmia included. They knew little about the photography world. Regardless, André wanted them. They accepted.

An artist-endowed foundation is required to own the artist's work and copyrights and to use them for educational and charitable activities benefiting the public. André's prints would be divided between the foundation and the trust he set up to manage the work. He envisioned sales and savvy institutional gifts of his prints, along with traveling exhibitions and grants to deserving younger photographers. Allegedly, the issue of copyright was never addressed. Did André fully understand the terms and implications of what he was signing? Did he get solid advice about how his foundation and trust would dovetail with his intended gift to the French? Probably not.

Toward the end of 1982, André formalized his decision to donate his work to the French state. In exchange, he wanted an apartment in Paris. The negotiations were rocky at times. The head of the Mission pour la Photographie, the group of officials charged with working out the accord, rubbed André the wrong way. "If it's him, I'm not donating," André announced after their first encounter.[42] But the association persisted. By early 1984, the terms of the agreement had been nailed down. Notified that the papers were ready to sign, André departed New York for Paris via Hungary.

Although he framed the visit to his homeland as one last prowl around old haunts, it took on the trappings of an official tour. In Budapest, he was honored in parliament, wined and dined by the minister of culture, awarded the prestigious Order of the Banner, and celebrated with exhibitions, interviews, roundtables, publications, and a TV documentary. In Szigetbecse, the mayor escorted him through a traditional Swabian house slated to become the André Kertész Museum. Colleagues found him jovial, relaxed, and articulate. A "grandfather of folk tales," thought one.[43] A dean of photography on a victory lap. A legend. A giant.

All the while, a Paris-born, New York–raised former producer of art and culture programming for French TV named Teri Wehn-Damisch was shooting footage for a sixty-minute documentary for the French channel TF1. Underwritten by the Ministry of Culture, her film would eventually appear in the PBS series American Masters. She was calling it *André dans les Villes (André Kertész of the Cities)*, after Wim Wenders's quirky road movie *Alice in the Cities*. André does come across as a free spirit. "I am an ordinary and egotistical photographer," he announces. "I do what I want, that's all."[44] When Wehn-Damisch uses her hands in lieu of a clapper board, André catches one and kisses it, his eyes crinkling into a smile. He laughs and clicks off a picture.

In Esztergom, his unit's base in World War I, André was joined by his friend the Hungarian-born French painter Robert Solyom. Viewers of Wehn-Damisch's film follow the two as they seek out the settings for André's *The Swing* and *Underwater Swimmer*. When they chance upon four elderly women idling on a bench, André snaps a shot or two, then pulls out one of his books. The pictures make the women ooh, aah, and giggle. As they examine his wedding portrait with Elizabeth, André offends one by airily denouncing God as "that son of a bitch!" for robbing him of the love of his life.[45]

The filming paused while André took a road trip with Solyom and his family, then resumed after he flew to France, devoting his time in the air to grousing about New York to his seatmate.[46] In Paris, Wehn-Damisch proposed that he undertake a new series of Distortions for the film. André made his acceptance conditional on finding the right model and an "intelligent" mirror. No sooner did the dark-haired beauty Danielle Schirman (later a respected writer and director) walk into the room than André pronounced her perfect. Digging up the mirror proved harder. Visits to shops and flea markets elicited only noes. André refused to compromise. Then someone hit on the idea of Mylar, the material used for helium-filled balloons. That elicited a yes. A frame was built, and Mylar stretched over it.

The filming took place at the Hôtel Esmeralda. An assistant pressed the Mylar this way and that as André murmured directions to his model. "*Oh, c'est bien, très bien, très bien, excellent. Merci... Ça, c'est beau aussi. Tournez, tournez, tournez, plus... attendez, restez... Oui, oui, oui.*" From time to time, he adjusted the position of his tripod-mounted Olympus or fingered its focusing ring (he was using a 35-to-70 millimeter zoom) before squeezing the plunger of the shutter release cable. Directed by Wehn-Damisch, the cameraman captured their movements. Five skilled players were engrossed in a game with multiple moving parts.

So engrossed that, on March 30, André caused a brief panic by leaving late for the Galerie Agathe Gaillard. He and Gaillard were due at the Ministry of Culture, where they would rendezvous with the members of the association, then meet with Jack Lang, the minister of culture. André was to sign his deed of gift in the minister's presence. Some 97,800 negatives and 15,000 color transparencies, along with his contact sheets and documents dating to his youth—the "entire body of work of André Kertész"—would go to the French state after his death.[47] He put no restrictions on their use. The document's single paragraph that addressed copyright was deficient in Cartier-Bresson's view. But so it was.[48] The gift was assessed at 5 million francs (about $1,900,000 in 2024 dollars).[49]

André got his apartment in Paris, a modest yet pleasant place on the fourth floor directly above Gaillard's gallery. The location, on the rue du Pont Louis-Philippe near the Seine, was ideal. Solyom's studio was nearby, and Lucien Vogel's elder daughter, the journalist and human rights activist Marie-Claude Vaillant-Couturier, lived two doors down. André had always been fond of his old boss's daughter, to whom he had taught photography half a century earlier. And if André needed something, Gaillard was downstairs. "I am your grandfather, and you are my mother," he quipped to his dealer.[50] After he moved in, mornings found him ambling around the *quartier*, a bucket hat planted on his head, the Olympus slung around his neck, his pockets lumpy with filters and lenses.

In one scene in Wehn-Damisch's film, André sits near a window of his pied-à-terre. Below is a nursery-school playground. The view recalls the one from the apartment on the rue du Cotentin where he and Elizabeth had been happy. Its windows had overlooked a school, too. André gazes once more at his wedding portrait, reproduced in the open book in his lap. Then he whispers to Elizabeth, his pleasure clouded with sadness: "Now we're finally home together in Paris."

**Late one afternoon** in early July, André sat with Solyom near that same window. They were nibbling on cherries and amusing themselves with a pastime invented by André: He would create hand shadows, and Solyom would photograph them with his Minox. A knock at the door. It was Gaillard. She had closed the gallery early to deliver some news.

"André, Brassaï died."

"Ah."

An awkward pause. He was unmoved.

"I wanted to resolve things with him," André began. "I wanted to say to him 'You're a bastard,' but in the way one says that to a friend."[51]

Tensions between the two had intensified. In 1973, Brassaï had written to announce his arrival in New York for his solo exhibition at Witkin. (He had a show at the Corcoran Gallery of Art in Washington, DC, that same summer.) André may or may not have replied. When Brassaï phoned from Manhattan, Elizabeth told him that André was hospitalized following minor surgery but would be happy to see him. She gave Brassaï the phone number. According to André, Brassaï did not visit or call.

"The book was in his hand," André later explained, "and he saw what he'd said in it, how things had been served up, and to disappear, to not show himself, was the simplest thing."[52] He meant the Brassaï portfolio that Witkin had published. In his foreword, Brassaï asserts that he took up photography out of a desire to express nocturnal Paris. He implies that he was self-taught. There's no mention of André. "Because he could well imagine that if he came up to see me, that I would already know [what he had written]," André continued, "and I would say, 'How could you do that? You are a son of a bitch.' The easiest solution was not to come."

Eventually, Brassaï did phone. When André asked if he was happy with everything, Brassaï was blandly positive. That was too much for his thin-skinned listener. By the time they hung up, André was finished with Brassaï. Such behavior, he felt, fit with Brassaï's old pattern of taking unfair advantage. "I wouldn't have cared if we'd had no contact," André clarified. "We were supposedly friends."[53] Friendship required reciprocity, and Brassaï had betrayed him. His resentment over Brassaï stealing his photographic identity welled up again.

That was André's version. Brassaï would recall the episode differently. He told the editor Stefan Lorant that Elizabeth had blocked his visit to the hospital. "Brassaï was really upset," Lorant would report. "I tried to make peace between them, but it wasn't Bandi's [André's] fault. It was the two women, the females."[54] (Brassaï's wife accompanied him to New York.)

From then on, André stonewalled Brassaï. In the fall of 1976, Marlborough—the gallery that had just rejected André's vintage prints—showed Brassaï's *Secret Paris of the 1930s.* André ignored repeated invitations to the opening. Brassaï phoned the next morning: "Hello André, this is Brassaï. *Comment tu vas*?"

In reply, André unleashed about the Witkin portfolio and more, ending with this: "Excuse me, if one of us was a friend, it was me, not you. Farewell."[55] Brassaï was bewildered, then irate.

In the years that followed, each man did acknowledge the other's greatness. Yet, in shifting stories, Brassaï would downplay, and André exaggerate, Brassaï's debt to André. Brassaï misreported that he used to ask André to supply pictures for the articles he was writing. But it was André the star photographer who introduced Brassaï the impoverished journalist to the right editorial people.[56] Brassaï also magnified the role his article for *Camera* had played in revitalizing André's career. "Instead of being grateful to me for having resuscitated the self-professed 'dead man,' Kertész succumbed to an odd jealousy," Brassaï contended. "I cannot get over this behavior of Kertész's, which I regard as a sign either of immense stupidity or of some kind of betrayal, but which, above all, has been a disappointment to me."[57]

"In fact he was a stinking rascal," André sniped back. "Everything that I showed to him, he pretended to have created."[58] Presumably aware that it didn't behoove him to trash a widely admired colleague, André sometimes backpedaled: Brassaï was also "an absolute artist with a wonderful talent."[59]

Six days before Brassaï died, André turned ninety. Accolades rolled in. In England the National Museum of Photography, Film, and Television celebrated with a retrospective and 185-page publication intermixing tributes with pictures. The Olympus Gallery in London organized *Paris Revisited.* The fine-art publisher Abbeville Press was preparing *Kertész on Kertész: A Self-Portrait,* featuring excerpts from André's BBC interviews. The Maine Photographic Workshop honored his lifetime achievement.

After returning home, André redid his will, setting up regular payments to Elizabeth's sister Márta and directing that the income from his trust go to Jenő and eventually Jenő's family. Most significantly, he bequeathed to the André and Elizabeth Kertész Foundation "all of the negatives, representing my work in photography and all my correspondence," except for family pictures and papers.[60] The stage was set for a trans-Atlantic conflict.

**Six months later,** André received the inaugural Master of Photography Lifetime Achievement Award from the International Center of Photography (ICP). Cornell Capa's devotion to the cause of concerned photography had culminated in his launch of the ICP, which he ran with his usual effusion and fervor. New York City's first museum devoted solely to photography, the ICP occupied a neo-Georgian building on Fifth Avenue at East Ninety-Fourth Street. It carried weight in American cultural life. Capa's view of photography as a tool for dynamic social engagement, as seen at the ICP, contrasted with Szarkowski's, as seen at MoMA. For Szarkowski, photographic content and form are inseparable, from which one could conclude that photographs are fundamentally about the medium itself. André was pleased to be claimed by both camps.

Most who saw André and Capa together rightly assumed a family-like connection. They had in common the old days in Budapest, Paris, and New York, along with lost loved ones: Elizabeth, Capa's mother, Bob. Capa viewed André's life as "part fairytale, part Hungarian tragicomedy."[61] André had been so generous with Bob. Cornell indulged his crotchety friend. André, on the other hand, railed behind his back that Cornell was "rotten at the core." That Cornell was riding on his brother's reputation. That Cornell couldn't wait for him to die because that would boost the value of the Kertész prints he owned.[62] One hopes, perhaps unrealistically, that he expressed some gratitude for the prestigious award.

The black-tie ceremony took place on April 23, 1985, in the Starlight Room of the Waldorf Astoria. After dinner, a packed crowd heard Capa laud André as the father of photojournalism, then call him up to the stage. Thunderous applause erupted. André set off from the back of the room. After two or three minutes, the applause subsided, then picked up again. André shuffled along. Eventually, people tired of clapping. The room quieted. André continued to baby-step forward. The audience's enthusiasm turned to embarrassment.

At ninety, André was suffering from advanced Ménière's disease, causing hearing loss, ear congestion, and balance problems. He had been diagnosed with Parkinson's disease. His arthritis had worsened. Still affected by his old war wound, his left shoulder was hurting again.[63] Such health issues would have convinced many that the time was right to pack it in. Why don't you quit? one friend inquired.

"I am still hungry," André replied.[64]

Seeing no reason to live if he couldn't work, André ignored his doctors' orders to slow down. He continued to travel, packing a few things into a bag and lugging his tripod onto planes. "I should have been an angel," he joked, "I feel better at over 5000 feet."[65] In Florida for his opening at the Jacksonville Art Museum (now MOCA Jacksonville), he plunged into the Atlantic for a swim. His hands trembled, but his handshake was firm. If he faltered, he took it in stride. One day he fell outside Bakht's studio, injuring his wrist, banging up his forehead, and getting a black eye. After he was treated, André pulled out a Polaroid and asked someone to snap the picture.[66]

Ten days after the ICP event, André flew to Chicago for his openings at the Edwynn Houk Gallery and the Art Institute. Based on Sandra Phillips's doctoral research, the museum's partial retrospective (up to the 1950s) had started as a collaboration between Phillips and David Travis, the Art Institute's curator of photography. Then Weston Naef joined the project for the Metropolitan Museum of Art in New York. The three sleuthed out vintage prints, some in odd corners of Europe, others in odd corners of André's apartment. *Cartes postales* turned up in drawers or in shoeboxes tucked in a closet. One much sought-after print was doing double duty as a bookmark. After four years of research, the curators believed they had ferreted out every vintage print in André's possession. But then he would lay his hands on a few more. Naef likens the project to an archaeological dig.[67]

André transferred some of the *cartes postales* to an envelope, which he brandished at the curators. "A million dollars! A million dollars!" Get one of their museums to buy![68] He was at it again.

Waving around the coveted prints was a way to needle the curators. *He* could treat the vintages cavalierly. For decades, André had sweated to please American gatekeepers, and they had ignored him. Now they were clamoring for his work. Let them pay. Besides, it was his turn to profit from the older work. "My tragedy," he hyperbolized, "is that the dealers all bought up my old vintage photographs in Europe. They made a pile, and I didn't make a bean."[69]

Poised to leave the Met to helm a new photography department at the J. Paul Getty Museum, Naef wanted to purchase the lot for the Los Angeles museum. The timing seemed perfect. Flush with cash, the Getty was assembling a superlative photography collection from the ground up. The gallerist Daniel Wolf was quietly acquiring major private collections from around the globe on the museum's behalf. Among the twenty-five thousand photographs Wolf secured for $20 to $30 million were many by André. In that context, the administration declined to splash out another million. Meanwhile, the Met purchased a hundred of his vintage New York prints.

As for the Art Institute, a million was not in the departmental budget. However, Travis negotiated an arrangement by which the Hyatt Hotels magnate and philanthropist Nicholas Pritzker would purchase the prints with the understanding that he would eventually donate them to the museum. André gave the nod to that plan.

The opening of *André Kertész: Of Paris and New York* at the Art Institute of Chicago on May 9, 1985, was "a hugely festive affair," Phillips remembers. "The whole institution pulled out all the stops."[70] Pritzker put André up in a fancy suite at the Park Hyatt, where the photographer chuckled to discover a telephone in every room, even the bathroom. Just being in Chicago put André in a good mood. His retrospective had been slated to debut at the Met, but administrative complications and museum politics dictated a last-minute switch, which André applauded. He still begrudged the Met its 1978 blockbuster Avedon exhibition.[71] Besides, he had a warm spot in his heart for the Art Institute because they had exhibited his work in 1946, when no one else would. André never overlooked a slight, Travis observed, but neither did he forget a favor.

In Chicago, André's schedule was wonderfully hectic. He lunched, he dined, he took pictures, he gave interviews, he counseled photographers. People found him jaunty and delightful. On opening night, he signed copies of the catalog and chatted with each of its buyers. The wait time was forty-five minutes. When Travis suggested he might want a break, André briskly dismissed that idea: "In Hungary, I signed eight hundred books." After glancing at the line as if wondering if he could beat his own record, André got back to business. Turning to the young woman who stood before him, he inquired, slightly flirtatiously, "What is *your* name?"[72]

Everywhere, André brightened in the presence of women. His female friends enjoyed his courtly manners, thoughtful gestures, and elfin appeal. Each felt that her relationship with him was special. He kissed women's hands. At home, he had long talks with them in his study, André behind his desk and his visitor in the creaky rocker. At restaurants, he might spoon-feed them bites of dessert. On birthdays, he would pull out a little gift and a card signed "Uncle André." He persuaded some to pose nude for him, with or without his distorting mirror. But he did not come across as a dirty old man.

Carol Brower had met André when she joined the staff at Light Gallery in 1974. She remembers him as "a lamb to me. He didn't know how to put on a coat of armor to protect himself."[73] On their walks around the Village, he would point out "a magical sunbeam, a newly budding violet, two chairs conversing without occupants."[74] Not everyone felt such sunshine. Brendan Gill, for one. "The weather of his soul was charged with gloom," Gill observed of André, "and he was determined to share that gloom with all the rest of us."[75]

**Perched on his balcony,** André would gaze at the birds in Washington Square. They helped him, he felt, by embodying freedom, physical vitality, and the creative spirit. Peering through his telephoto lens, he could mentally command them to fly into a scene when he needed them for the composition. So he claimed. André identified most closely with pigeons, pecking at seeds and bugs, ignored or shooed away by New Yorkers, yet subtly beautiful and able to glide on rising air currents.[76] Doris Schwerin's memoir *Diary of a Pigeon Watcher* stood on his bookshelf. Keeping tabs on the nesting pigeons on her neighbor's ledge had helped Schwerin come to terms with a difficult past. André could relate.

Pressing on with his work, he collaborated with Harder, Capa, Kubota, and the *Esquire* film critic Hal Hinson on a sumptuous new monograph. Meanwhile, his assistant Robert Gurbo was building a wall-storage unit in the apartment to house André's reorganized negatives, for which Gurbo would print new contact sheets.

In the evening, André read, watched TV, perused old letters and pictures, or puttered around, tired and achy. The underwater photographer Douglas Faulkner, a neighbor, came by regularly to check on him. Sylvia Plachy remembers arriving one evening to find André absorbed in wrestling shows on TV. "Watch!" he would urge her. "You can learn from anything." (He was also partial to the artist Francis Bacon's tortured and vaguely Distortion-like paintings of wrestlers.)[77]

In July, André and Harder flew to Osaka for the opening of *André Kertész: A Portrait at Ninety*, organized by the ICP. André exhausted himself with interviews, events, and signings, then made an excursion to his beloved city of Nara with Kubota and Kubota's young son.

Five weeks later, André departed for New Mexico for a gallery show. A month after that, he was in Buenos Aires, where the Museo Nacional de

Bellas Artes was presenting a Kertész retrospective. One section brought together photographs selected by André for their special meaning to him and Jenő. André had imagined the two of them lingering and reminiscing. But that didn't happen. Jenő would never see the exhibition because he was hospitalized following a stroke and making little progress.

André visited Jenő daily. At the hospital, too, he was thwarted. Jenő's speech was halting and slurred, and even though André kept bending closer and adjusting his hearing aids, he couldn't catch most of what his brother was saying. So they resigned themselves to holding hands and gazing into each other's eyes. In a tour de force of the linguistic mash-up known as Kertészian, André told one Argentine interviewer: "My best *amigo, c'est mon frère*."[78] He must have known they were spending their last hours together.

A bad cold was exacerbating André's exhaustion and dejection. One day he had to cut short his time with Jenő to return to his hotel and take a hot bath. Yet he soldiered on. On André's final day in Buenos Aires, he and Gaillard, who had flown over from Paris, went to the Consejo Argentino de Fotografía. André's friend Ralph Gibson, another mainstay of Gaillard's gallery, was exhibiting there. André took installation shots for Gibson. En route to the airport the following day, he looked haggard and spent. For once, the ever-gallant André let Gaillard carry his bag.[79]

Back in his New York apartment, André got out of bed late one night to turn off the hallway light. He tripped and fell. Feeble and feverish, he struggled to stand. In the end, he drifted off on the floor. Bestirring himself at dawn, André thought: "How strange... what lovely light... such interesting angles... where am I?"[80]

That day, he went to his doctor, who diagnosed borderline pneumonia and hospitalized him at Beth Israel for observation and rest. Yet André chafed to be released so he could prepare to fly to Montreal for his show there. When the photographer Béla Ugrin called and heard him outline his travel plans in a hollow rasp, he begged, "André, please don't go."[81]

The morning after leaving the hospital, André awoke to news that one of the strongest hurricanes on record was churning toward New York City. Schools were closing. Cranes were secured. Store windows were x'd with tape. Newscasters hyped the Storm of the Century. Yet when Hurricane Gloria made landfall near JFK airport two days later, it was weaker than anticipated. Nothing is known of André's activities that day except that he set his apartment door ajar before lying down on the daybed in his study.

The following morning—Saturday, September 28, 1985—Kubota arrived for a visit. He knocked. Getting no answer and finding the door cracked open, he walked in to find André lifeless. Kubota phoned Cornell Capa, who rushed over. More calls ensued. The police. Márta. Plachy. Capa had to leave a message for Harder. By the time she arrived, a policewoman and police photographer were present, and a doctor was signing the declaration of death. Gibson had already heard the news and phoned Robert Frank. "So," Frank recapped, "Hurricane Gloria took the old man up."[82]

An era ended. With his death, André surrendered the status of photography's preeminent living legend, as the writer and art critic Alexandra Anderson would attest in *Artforum*. His peers Ansel Adams, Brassaï, Walker Evans, Lewis Hine, Germaine Krull, Dorothea Lange, László Moholy-Nagy, Man Ray, W. Eugene Smith, and Edward Weston were gone. Photography had existed for 146 years: for half of them, André had been working.[83] He had started in the glass-plate and gaslight paper era and ended at the dawn of the digital age.

The opening of *André Kertész: Of Paris and New York* at the Met that December gave New York critics the opportunity to escort him into the history books. Reviewing the exhibition for *The New York Times*, Andy Grundberg judged it the year's best. It served to "measure, for the first time, the extent of his impact on 20th-century photography," Grundberg wrote. Surely it would bring "a re-evaluation of Kertesz's place in history—especially now that he is no longer able to supply his own 'official' version."[84]

Tributes flooded in, especially from France. Gisèle Freund described him as the greatest photographer of their time. The portraitist and fashion photographer Jeanloup Sieff concurred: André "did everything before everyone. We are all his children." An emotional Henri Cartier-Bresson underscored Sieff's point: "Kertész is us... If he was truly a father for us, as for other Hungarians, that's linked to a period that he carried single-handedly and to the intelligence in his photographs. He's someone who never cheated, never."[85]

André's standing-room-only memorial service took place at the upscale Frank E. Campbell Funeral Chapel on Madison Avenue. Then he was cremated, and his ashes buried with Elizabeth's. Jenő's son Imre, who represented the Argentine family, flew home with personal pictures and mementos.

Besides wreathing André with praise, the French were girding for battle. The Association des Amis d'André Kertész "will have its hands full," editorialized *Libération*, "given what one knows about American lawyers and dealers, who, as soon as Kertész's passing was announced, sent telegrams intended to block the sale of art prints, which they want to control. The vultures are in place."[86]

As the artistic director responsible for the Kertész donation, Isabelle Jammes hastened to New York. She was tasked with inventorying the negatives and arranging to ship them to Paris, along with André's papers, which Phillips was hired to catalog. But André's executors blocked the shipment. Contending that his 1984 will superseded his agreement with the French state, they too laid claim to his negatives and papers.

A year and a half after André's death, the Americans would finally take a step back, relinquishing their claim and shipping the negatives and papers to Paris. André's prints remained in New York, where Harder agreed to serve as the foundation's curator and exclusive agent. She would sell the work as she had during André's lifetime, consigning modern prints to selected galleries and giving priority for the remaining vintage work to museums. That arrangement lasted until the executors made a deal with a Canadian gallery, which later consigned thirty-seven vintage prints for auction at Christie's. They fetched $1.36 million. A *carte postale* of *Mondrian's Glasses and Pipe*, printed by an impoverished André in 1926, sold for $376,500, the second-highest price ever paid for a single photograph at auction.[87] Speaking to a reporter years later, Harder slammed André's executors: "By accident, his estate had been assigned to his accountants" and they "treated his photographs like zippers."[88]

The copyright issue continued to fester. Both the French state and the André and Elizabeth Kertész Foundation claimed exclusive authority to manage and sell André's reproduction rights. Six years after his death, one of his executors fired off a comment to *New York* magazine meant to be heard across the Atlantic: "What André gave them was the negatives and nothing else. André didn't give anything of commercial value to the French people. Now they are saying, 'We have the negatives, and therefore we have the rights.' They are completely wrong."[89]

His mention of "commercial value" is telling. American and French copyright laws derive from different philosophies about creative work, and that difference aggravated the dispute. American copyright law centers on the creator's economic interests; French copyright law is broader. It manifests the creator's moral rights, a type of civil right whereby the work is an inviolable and untransferable extension of its creator's very being. From the French point of view, the Association des Amis d'André Kertész existed, in part, to represent and defend André's moral rights after his death.

That makes it startling that, in 1994, the French governmental agency charged with managing photographic donations and acquisitions violated André's moral rights.[90] Late that year, an exhibition marking the tenth anniversary of André's death opened in the Pavillon des Arts, a non-collecting museum situated in the mall that had replaced Les Halles, the once central market of Paris. The exhibition included new prints made by a French photographer from André's negatives and color transparencies that André himself had never exhibited or published. Nobody had consulted the Association des Amis d'André Kertész.

Photographers howled foul play. Posthumous prints are often viewed as a betrayal because there is no unequivocal way to distinguish between the negatives their creators might have printed but never did and those their creators would never have printed, whether for personal, practical, or aesthetic reasons. Nor is it possible to know how their creators would have printed the work. André had always been adamant about how his work should be printed and cropped. Now his closest photographer friends lambasted the quality of the black-and-white prints—too dark and contrasty—and decried the inclusion of color work. Tempers flared. At least one French photographer announced that he would never donate his life's work to an agency that would do *whatever*. Cartier-Bresson dissolved the Association des Amis d'André Kertész and took steps to establish a private foundation to preserve his own work and ensure his legacy.[91]

For its organizers, the exhibition addressed a major problem: The ministry did not own any Kertész photographs. As one commentator pointed out, a negative is only "the promise of a work," and one cannot exhibit promises.[92] As for the color prints, they pointed out that André's fifteen thousand color images constituted some 15 percent of his life's work and argued that the agency had a duty to share it with the public.[93]

The curmudgeon in André would have found much to deplore in these posthumous quarrels, even as he would have relished the attention to his work. The romantic in him might have remembered a custom of the Austro-Hungarian Dual Monarchy into which he was born. The bodies of its Habsburg rulers were interred in the imperial crypt in Vienna. But the rulers' hearts went to the places they held most dear. In 2011, the last Habsburg crown prince, Otto von Habsburg, was buried in Vienna. All but his heart. Sheathed in a silver urn, it was transported to an abbey in rural Hungary, where he had studied as a youth and for which he felt deep affection. Similarly, André's earthly remains stayed in New York, while his negatives—his heart, one might say—went to Paris, the city that spoke to his soul. Like Otto von Habsburg, he died a remnant of a fabled era.

**One day in 1976,** André banged or dropped the life mask that Frederic Littman made for him half a century earlier. It broke. André told Nicolas Ducrot, at the time still in his good graces, and Ducrot offered to have it repaired. He contacted the sculptor Mihail Simeonov, who agreed to do the job. As Ducrot was en route to Simeonov's studio, he lit on the idea of asking the sculptor to create warped versions of the mask, using the original as a mold. What more amusing way to mark the publication of *Distortions*?[94] Simeonov mounted the original on a base for stability and fashioned three new masks, each contorted and, like the repaired original, attached to a base inscribed with a Roman numeral.

Ducrot's gift tickled André, who lined up the masks atop the armoire in his study. When his camera was set and the light was right, he half hid behind the armoire, so that its fluted cornice would lead viewers' eyes to him, a lurking fifth presence. Assuming a steady gaze and the half smile of a deft mischief-maker, he had Ducrot's wife, who was visiting that day, snap the picture.

The creator of any photographic self-portrait is simultaneously set designer, director, and actor. A viewer of André's *Self-Portrait with Masks* might gaze at the busts' closed eyes and shifting positions and decide that André is presenting himself as a restless sleeper caught up in his dreams. Another might read the busts as salvaged faux antiquities depicting the immortals, with André claiming a place among them. A third might draw on the fractured self-identities inherent in the modern condition. A fourth might note the way André leans on the play between object and human, artificial and real, double and self. Simultaneously self-disclosive and self-concealing, the image implies the ultimate unknowability of any photographic subject. Is André's real face any less a mask than the plaster copies? Any less a mask than the faces everyone dons for posed photographs? Such questions hang in the air.

So does the issue of photography and reality. The idea that a photograph is "a transcription of the real," writes the scholar Mary Price, makes it a "mask concealing what is behind it and thwarting confrontation with the real" — a practice to which André was no stranger. "Perception is imperfect," Price contends, "we *always* envision as we see."[95]

Like photographs, life masks have a physical connection to their subject. To make such a mask, an artist coats the subject's face with molding paste, then covers it with plaster gauze. The result (a negative) serves as a mold for the plaster from which the mask (a positive) is produced. Analogously, a darkroom photographer exposes film to create a negative, it too a matrix. That negative yields a positive. Both a life mask and a photographic print result from material contact with their subjects, using molding paste for the mask, light rays for the picture. Both are imprints, faithful to every curve, bump, and wrinkle. Both appear to attest to their own infallibility. And yet: "Of Kertész," rightly observes the writer Brigitte Ollier of this creator of a vast archive of such imprints, "we know everything and nothing."[96]

Early in life, André married his sense of self to photography. "I always have my cameras," he once remarked. "It is impossible to imagine myself without them."[97] In the mid-1970s, the Manhattan bookseller Burt Britton asked André, among dozens of others, to draw a self-portrait for Britton's *Self-Portrait: Book People Picture Themselves*. Sandwiched between Richard Avedon's smudgy rendering of his own face and Berenice Abbott's scribbled version of hers, André's drawing appears on a page torn from his desk calendar. He has circled 12:30, then sketched a tripod-mounted Leica with a viewfinder, shutter release, rewinding knob, and flirtatious eye signaling his evergreen romance with his art. "I am the Camera," he wrote.[98]

# EPILOGUE

**André favored** the oblique, the slyly witty, the distanced yet intimate view, and less than finicky focus. That said, he had no signature style, subject, genre, or light-bulb phrase like Henri Cartier-Bresson's "decisive moment." His work ranged from still life to landscape, from interiors to reportage. He took portraits, portraits in absence, and self-portraits in absence, using objects as surrogates and transforming his own interiority into representations of facts. He toyed with collage. He borrowed from the Szőnyi Circle, from Piet Mondrian, from the Cubists, the Surrealists, the Symbolists, and the Purists, then kept moving on. Aesthetic ideologies mattered to him no more than political ones. He let each image dictate its own terms. Sometimes he seized the instant as nimbly as the acrobats he loved to photograph. Other times, he awaited that something he needed or rearranged a setting to his liking. He cropped. Or not. He commanded the view camera, the Leica, the Linhof, the Olympus, the Polaroid. Any camera, really, would do, although not any lens. If he were younger, the nonagenarian told an acquaintance, he would try video.[1] It's hard to find toeholds for generalizing about the work of André Kertész. What his pictures do share, asserts the photo historian Jean-Claude Lemagny, is "the strange and precise particularity of being among the most beautiful that ever were and yet belonging to a temperate, coherent, and sensible visual universe."[2]

André insisted that everyday living gave him all he needed: "Look—you see that pigeon over there—look, now he just left. You see his shadow, how beautiful it was? You see? That's how I make photography; you do nothing and it comes."[3] What came to him was often ordinary: a kid brother, a swimmer, a fork, the sea, the light in the trees. "Everything is photograph," André explained, meaning everything that flushed out his feelings. To photograph was to give "a reason to everything and to every happening around me."[4]

The writer and photographer David Vestal once observed that André's photographs never proclaim, "'Look at me, how sensitive I am!' They just say 'Look!'"[5] André saw smoke speak (*Lajos Tihanyi*). Viewed the Louvre from inside a timepiece (*Clock of the French Academy*). Watched a man put finishing touches on his own shadow (*Shadow Painter*). Caught sight of a toy boat hoofing through Central Park (*Homing Ship*). He had only to pay attention, camera at the ready, for reality to catch up with his dreams.

Often it did.

# ACKNOWLEDGMENTS

**My deep appreciation** goes to the Hungarian speakers who translated texts, supplied documents, and helped me better understand Hungarian history and culture. They include Melinda Borbély, Kinga Dobos, Béla and Klári Kurucz, Julia Michael, Csaba Mórocz, Erika Pollák, Maryll I. Telegdy, Gergely Tóth, Eszter Wainwright-Déri, and especially György Németh, whose research skills, tenacity, and generosity are jaw-dropping. His contributions have made my book immeasurably better.

I am also grateful to Péter Baki and Balázs Zoltán Tóth, who guided my research at the Hungarian Museum of Photography, and to Janka Szakonyi, who worked with me at the Hungarian Jewish Museum and Archive.

Many of André's colleagues and friends shared their memories and insights. My thanks to Igor Bakhtamian, Nina Barrett, Yvette E. Benedek, Dorothy Bohm, Inge Bondi, Irene Borger, Trudy Lee Cohen, Lynn Davis, Louis Dienes, Michael Dobo, Nicolas Ducrot, Milton Ellenbogen, Oriole Horch Farb Feshbach, Jimmy Fox, Lee Friedlander, Agathe Gaillard, Ralph Gibson, Robert Gurbo, Susan Harder, Marvin Heiferman, Katy Homans, Jean-François Jaeger, Muriel Jaeger, André Jammes, Paul Katz, Dorothy Koppelman, Hiroji Kubota, Merloyd Ludington Lawrence, Mikael Levin, Joan Liftin, Nicholas Ludington, Peter MacGill, Liza Macrae, Lajos Magasitz, Jacqueline Martinez, Steve McCurry,

Duane Michals, Voja Mitrovic, Weston Naef, Graham Nash, Susan Nash, Sandra Phillips, Sylvia Plachy, Jill Quasha, Gerd Sander, Fern Schad, Robert Solyom, Michael Somoroff, Linda Swenson, Susan May Tell, David Travis, David Turnley, Peter Turnley, JoAnn Verburg, Nicolas von dem Bussche, Gilles Walusinski, Teri Wehn-Damisch, Carol Brower Wilhelm, Anna Winand, Emese Wood, and Floyd Yearout.

Librarians and archivists stepped up each time I asked. Évelyne Cohen, Florence Ertaud, and especially Matthieu Rivallin at the Médiathèque du patrimoine et de la photographie, Ministère de la Culture, Charenton-le-Pont, France, and the staff of the Getty Research Center, Los Angeles, were gracious and knowledgeable. The Archives de Paris, Archives of American Art, Smithsonian Institution, Bibliothèque Kandinsky, Bibliothèque Nationale de France (Dominique Versavel), C. H. Booth Library (Andy Forsyth), Center for Creative Photography (Emily Una Weirich), Frick Art Research Library, International Center of Photography (Cynthia Young), Long Island University Library (Constance Woo), Musée Nicéphore Niépce (Émilie Bernard), Musée Zadkine (Laurence Goux), Museum of Modern Art Library, New York Public Library, Palo Alto City Library (Rebecca Kohn), Robert Crown Law Library, Stanford University (Sergio Stone), Sherwin Miller Museum of Jewish Art (Mickel Yantz), Time-Life Archive, New York Historical Society (Bill Hooper and Ted O'Reilly), and Thomas J. Watson Library, Metropolitan Museum of Art also provided valuable information and expertise, as did Robert Gurbo of the André and Elizabeth Kertész Foundation.

For support and kindnesses of many sorts, I am grateful to Joseph Bartscherer, Csaba Benedek, France Bequette, Sandy Blin, Monica Bohm-Duchen, Oliver A. I. Botar, Frish Brandt, Meutia Chaerani, Wendy Cook, Dan Cruson, Michel Delaborde, Julie DeStefano, Katherine Dever, Gianfranco Ellero, Meredith Flerlage, Colin Ford, Michel Frizot, Pamela Glintenkamp, Todd Gustavson (George Eastman Museum), Chantal Hourcade, April Johnson, Patricia Kertész, Károly Kincses, Richard

Lehfeldt, Laurence Miller, John G. Morris, Ellen Odoner, Brigitte Ollier, Mark Osterman (George Eastman Museum), Bill Oudegeest, Barbara Pollitt (Sari Dienes Foundation), John Raeburn, Norberto L. Rivera, Leo Rubinfein, Andra Samelson, Livia Sibalin, Jeffrey Steinman, Judy Stoffman, and Julia Van Haaften. Mary Wyler took heroic measures to return my lost briefcase. Jean Boulanger of the Red Rock kept me caffeinated. Stephan Chodorov kindly allowed me to borrow from the title of the 1978 documentary that he wrote and John Musilli directed: *Everything Is Photograph: A Profile of André Kertész.*

I am beholden to the Robert B. Silvers Foundation and the San Jose State University Emeritus and Retired Faculty Association for their financial support and to the UCross Foundation for the gift of tranquility and time.

Richard Bram, William Hackman, Sandra Phillips, and Carol Sklenicka generously read and improved my manuscript. My writers group – Carol Goldfield, Linda Gray Sexton, Celia Stahr, and Wendy Tokunaga – helped me gain momentum by commenting on early drafts. At the Stephen Bulger Gallery, Stephen Bulger, Robyn Zolnai, and Owen Zilles worked with me on the images.

In addition, I am profoundly indebted to my publisher, Judith Gurewich, for her encouragement, enthusiasm, and patience. My deep thanks also go to my skilled editor, Alexandra Poreda, and my copyeditor, Karla Eoff. I extend my gratitude to the entire staff of Other Press, including Yvonne Cárdenas, Gage Desser, Janice Goldklang, Jessica Greer, Lauren Shekari, and Iisha Stevens.

To my agent extraordinaire and dear friend, Laurie Fox, a profound thank you.

Benjamin McKendall began this journey with me and remains with me always in spirit.

# NOTES

Translations from French are my own except where otherwise noted. Translators from Hungarian are identified.

### ABBREVIATIONS — INDIVIDUALS

| | | | |
|---|---|---|---|
| AK | André Kertész | IK | Imre Kertész |
| EK | Elizabeth Kertész | JK | Jenő Kertész |
| GK | Gréti Kertész | OK | Olga Kertész |

### ABBREVIATIONS — ARCHIVES

**CCP** Center for Creative Photography, University of Arizona, Tucson, Arizona

**GRI** André Kertész, Selected Papers, Photocopies, 1899–1985, Getty Research Institute, Los Angeles

**MPP** André Kertész Archive, Médiathèque du patrimoine et de la photographie, Charenton-le-Pont, France

For foreign conversions and inflation calculations, I used the following:

- https://canvasresources-prod.le.unimelb.edu.au/projects/CURRENCY_CALC/
- https://www.geshergalicia.org/about-galicia/historical-austro-hungarian-empire-exchange-rates/
- United States Department of Labor Bureau of Labor Statistics, "CPI Inflation Calculator," Bureau of Labor Statistics, www.bls.gov/data/inflation_calculator.htm

**EPIGRAPH**

1. Vladimir Nabokov, *Think, Write, Speak: Uncollected Essays, Reviews, Interviews, and Letters to the Editor*, edited by Brian Boyd and Anastasia Tolstoy (Knopf, 2019), 194.

2. Jean-Claude Lemagny, "André Kertész, maître de la mesure," in Pierre Bonhomme et al., *André Kertész: Ma France* (La Manufacture/Ministère de la Culture, 1990), 110.

**INTRODUCTION**

1. William Henry Fox Talbot used that phrase to describe what he had created.

2. AK quoted in Kati Marton, *The Great Escape: Nine Jews Who Fled Hitler and Changed the World* (Simon & Schuster, 2006), 51.

3. AK quoted in Jacob Deschin, "André Kertész: Rebirth of an Eternal Amateur," *Popular Photography* 55, no. 6 (December 1964): 42.

4. Henri Cartier-Bresson quoted in Debbie Lawson, "Go Buy," *The Guardian*, April 28, 2001.

5. Hervé Guibert, "Les tendres malices d'André Kertész," *Le Monde*, October 1, 1985.

6. Anne Grobot-Dreyfus, "L'École de Paris à travers le parcours de trois 'artistes-femmes': Chana Orloff, Alice Halicka, Marianne Breslauer," paper presented at "Les leçons de l'École de Paris," Musée d'art et d'histoire du Judaïsme, Paris, June 17–18, 2021: 20; Paul Delany, *Bill Brandt: A Life* (Stanford University Press, 2004), 298n6.

7. Richard Whelan, *Double Take: A Comparative Look at Photographs* (Clarkson N. Potter, 1981), 158; "Speaking of Pictures: A Photographer in Paris Finds Chairs Everywhere," *Life* (May 21, 1951): 26–28.

8. Julie Smith, "Willy Ronis," *Modern Photography* (April 1952): 58.

9. Robert Doisneau quoted by Peter Turnley, interview by author, July 28, 2014.

10. Ross Wetzsteon, *Republic of Dreams: Greenwich Village: The American Bohemia, 1910–1960* (Simon & Schuster, 2002), xiv.

11. Frederick H. Marks, "Honors Heap on Bitter André Kertész, Decries Lack of Praise," October 19, 1980, https://www.upi.com/Archives/1980/10/19/Honors-heap-on-bitter-Andre-Kertesz-Decries-lack-of-praise/3278340776000/.

12. Brendan Gill, "Outrageous Fortune: Memories of André Kertész," *Architectural Digest* 47 (September 1990): 33.

13. Jean Améry, *At the Mind's Limits: Contemplations by a Survivor on Auschwitz and Its Realities*, translated by Sidney Rosenfeld and Stella P. Rosenfeld (Indiana University Press, 2009), ebook, 32.

14. MPP, postcard from AK to Ernesztina Kertész, IK, JK, and Lipót Hoffmann, August 23, 1915, translated by Katalin Szabolcs-Perry.

15. Carol Schwalberg, "André Kertész: Unsung Pioneer," *U.S. Camera* 26, no. 1 (January 1963): 65; Jean-Claude Lemagny, "André Kertész, maître de la mesure," in Pierre Bonhomme et al., *André Kertész: Ma France* (La Manufacture/Ministère de la Culture, 1990), 112.

16. Denes Devenyi, "Kertesz: Denes Devenyi Interviews the 'Father of 35mm Vision,'" *Photo Life* (January 1978): 11.

17. *Everything Is Photograph: A Profile of André Kertész*, written by Stephan Chodorov, directed by John Musilli, Creative Arts Television, 1978.

18. Robert Gurbo, *André Kertész: New York State of Mind* (Stephen Daiter Gallery, 2001), 7.

19. Évelyne Rogniat, *André Kertész: Le photographe à l'oeuvre* (Presses universitaires de Lyon, 1997); Sandy Blin, "La série des Distorsions de 1933: Une parenthèse dans l'oeuvre d'André Kertész?," PhD dissertation, University of Lyon, 2012; Jean Nicolas, Renée Nicolas, and Pascal Lemaître, *La Savoie d'André Kertész* (Fontaine de Siloé, 2004).

## CHAPTER ONE

1. GRI, AK diary, December 20, 1909.

2. Ibid., September 27, 1909.

3. Budapest City Archives, Documents of the Orphans Office of Budapest Székesfőváros, HU BFL-IV.1411.b-1910-0387-Kertész, https://www.hungaricana.hu/en/databases/archives/.

4. The Hungarian Romani (or Romany) are alternately known as Gypsies, *cigányok* (singular: *cigány*), and *zigeuner* (singular: *zigeuner*), terms now considered pejorative and/or outdated. *Zigeuner* is a German word used by the Nazis but also by some Hungarian Romani. Although the word *Romani* was not current among other Hungarians in Andor's day, I use it here.

5. GRI, AK diary, November 30, 1909.

6. Ibid., November 22, 1909.

7. Ibid., December 28, 1909.

8. Ibid., "The Rose-Bush Is Opening," translated by Márta Ács.

9. Károly Kincses and Magdolna Kolta, *Pictures from Home: Photo Diary. André Kertész and Hungarians* (Mai Manó House, 2005), 21.

10. Ibid., 21–22.

11. GRI, AK diary, September 28, 1913.

12. Ibid., September 8, 1909.

13. Ibid., December 28, 1909.

14. Ibid., November 27, 1909.

15. Census record for 1869, Ászár, Hungary, Komárom County, Latter-Day Saints microfilm 2201135#2.

16. MPP, letter from IK and GK to AK and EK, May 8, 1946.

17. GRI, AK diary, January 24, 1910.

18. Lipót Kohn and Ernesztina Hoffmann marriage contract, trans. Rebecca Maria Dominici. https://archives.hungaricana.hu/en/lear/Kozjegyzoi/269689/view/?pg=1&bbox=-593%2C-4424%2C6190%2C-9.

19. Bulyovszky Street is now Rippl-Rónai Street.

20. Case No. 53062, June 27, 1898, National Archives of Hungary, courtesy of Hungarian Jewish Archives Family Research Center. The families of the Hungarian writer Imre Kertész and the conductor István Kertész (neither related to Andor) also took the name Kertész. The director Michael Curtiz of *Casablanca* fame, a Budapest native, was born Manó Kaminer. He later became Mihály Kertész.

21. Record 177052, Budapest Főváros Levéltára Központi Kereső.

22. Gyula Krúdy, *Krúdy's Chronicles: Turn-of-the-Century Hungary in Gyula Krúdy's Journalism*, edited and translated by John Bátki (Central European University Press, 2000), 197.

23. The building no longer exists. My description is based on a photograph in Kertész's collage *Some Souvenirs from 1913 to 1923* and on entries in his diary. For more general information, see Péter Hanák, *The Garden and the Workshop: Essays on the Cultural History of Vienna and Budapest* (Princeton University Press, 1998), 21–30.

24. GRI, letter from JK to AK, November 17, 1914.

25. My thanks to the Stanford Children's Hospital speech-language pathologist April Johnson for speaking with me about Kertész's speech problems.

26. GRI, Károly Kós, "The Death of Attila," *Budapesti Hírlap*, November 18, 1909.

27. Mary Gluck, *The Invisible Jewish Budapest: Metropolitan Culture at the Fin de Siècle* (University of Wisconsin Press, 2016), 37.

28. Less than 5 percent of Hungarians were Jewish. See Mary Gluck, "The Budapest Flâneur: Urban Modernity, Popular Culture, and the 'Jewish Question' in Fin-de-Siècle Hungary," *Jewish Social Studies* 10 (Spring/Summer 2004): 3. Gluck's source is Judit Kubinszky's *Politikai anti-szemitizmus Magyarországon.*

29. Mary Gluck, *Georg Lukács and His Generation, 1900–1918* (Harvard University Press, 1985), 48.

30. This bridge was later renamed the Liberty Bridge (Szabadság híd).

31. John Lukacs, *Budapest 1900: A Historical Portrait of a City and Its Culture* (Weidenfeld & Nicolson, 1988), 98.

32. GRI, AK diary, January 1, 1910.

33. Ibid., January 24, 1910.

34. Kinga Frojimovics, Géza Komoróczy, Viktória Pusztai, and Andrea Strbik, *Jewish Budapest: Monuments, Rites, History*, edited by Géza Komoróczy (Central European University Press, 1999), 348.

35. Raphael Patai, *The Jews of Hungary: History, Culture, Psychology* (Wayne State University Press, 1996), 360.

36. Lipót Hoffmann quoted in Károly Kincses, "A Belated Interview with André Kertész," *The Hungarian Quarterly* 47, no. 181 (Spring 2006): 97. Kincses's fictitious interview is compiled from real interviews that AK gave to eight Hungarian writers between 1981 and 1985, plus AK's 1981 letter to the Hungarian photographer András Balla. See Kincses's sources on page 97.

37. GRI, AK diary, February 4, 1910.

38. Misi's full name was Móricz Mihály Klopfer. My thanks to György Németh for tracking down Mihály and Margit's marriage document as well as much of the genealogical information in this chapter and those that follow. AK sometimes referred to Mihály and Margit as his uncle and aunt, presumably because of their age differences, and thus they are erroneously identified. See, for instance, https://capacenter.hu/en/kiallitasok/andre-kertesz-his-photographs-donated-to-szigetbecse/.

39. My thanks to Kókay Szabolcs for information about bird life on Csepel Island.

40. AK diary, January 28, 1912, "Chronology, 1894–1985," in Sarah Greenough, Robert Gurbo, and Sarah Kennel, *André Kertész*, translated by Bulcsú Veress (National Gallery of Art/Princeton University Press, 2005), 246.

41. Ibid., AK diary, April 15, 1912, 246.

42. AK quoted in Krisztina Passuth, "Conversation in Paris with André Kertész," October 15, 1982, 1, Károly Kincses and Magdolna Kolta, *Pictures from Home: Photo Diary. André Kertész and Hungarians* (Mai Manó House, 2005), 20. My thanks to Julia Michael for her translation.

43. Jain Kelly, *Nude: Theory* (Lustrum, 1979), 118.

44. GRI, AK diary, June 23, 1912.

45. Ibid., June 24, 1912.

46. AK quoted in Kincses, "A Belated Interview with André Kertész," 97.

47. AK diary, February 25, 1912, "Chronology, 1894–1985," 246. Strázsa is today Strázsa-hegy, Hungary, and Szepesszombat is Spišská Sobota, a section of Poprad, Slovakia.

48. Coffee shops like Ernesztina's were legally different from the grander establishments known as coffeehouses. See András Koerner, *How They Lived: The Everyday Lives of Hungarian Jews, 1867–1940* (Central European University Press, 2017), 193.

49. GRI, AK diary, January 18, 1913.

50. Ibid., October 20, 1913.

51. Ibid., December 17, 1913.

52. Ibid., October 4, 1913.

53. AK diary, June 13, 1913, "Chronology, 1894–1985," 247.

54. GRI, Béla Ugrin, Part III: Sixty Years of Photography, in "Dialogues with Kertész," edited by Manuela Caravageli Ugrin, transcript of taped conversations between AK and Béla Ugrin, 1978–1985, 21.

55. This remark by Bismarck has been widely quoted. See, for example, Patrick Smyth, "The War to End All War," *The Irish Times*, May 4, 2014.

56. Paul Ignotus, *Hungary* (Praeger, 1972), 136.

57. Dorothy S. Gelatt, "André Kertész at 80 — How He Works — What He Feels," *Popular Photography* 75, no. 5 (November 1974): 154.

58. Nicolas Ducrot, interview by author, August 8, 2014.

59. Barbaralee Diamonstein, "André Kertész," in *Visions and Images: American Photographers on Photography* (Rizzoli, 1981), 90.

60. AK, *Hungarian Memories* (New York Graphic Society/Little, Brown, 1982), 189.

61. Robert Hayes, "Andre Kertesz," *Interview* 13, no. 4 (April 1983): 60.

62. GRI, AK diary, October 25, 1914.

63. Ibid., letter from JK and Ernesztina Kertész to AK, November 17, 1914.

64. Greenough, "A Hungarian Diary, 1894–1925," in *André Kertész*, 270n62. AK later inaccurately claimed that he invented the self-timer.

65. Salcano is today part of Nova Gorica, Slovenia. Vertjoba is now Vrtojba, Slovenia.

66. Ernest Hemingway, *A Farewell to Arms* (Charles Scribner's Sons, 1929; Scribner Classics, 1997), 12.

67. Pierluigi Lodi and Raffaella Sgubin, "L'Ultimo Inverno della Nizza Austriaca Nello Sguardo di André Kertész," in *André Kertész: Inediti a Gorizia—Dicembre 1914/Marzo 1915* (Musei Provinciali di Gorizia, 2004), 7. My thanks to Gianfranco Ellero for this catalog.

68. AK, *Kertész on Kertész: A Self-Portrait* (Abbeville Press, 1985), 22.

69. GRI, letter from JK and Ernesztina Kertész to AK, November 17, 1914.

70. Gunther E. Rothenberg, *The Army of Francis Joseph* (Purdue University Press, 1976), 141.

71. AK quoted in Kincses, "A Belated Interview with André Kertész," 102.

72. AK quoted in GRI, Ugrin, Part III: Sixty Years of Photography. For *Soldier Writing a Letter, Görz, Austria*, see Anna Fárová, *André Kertész*, edited by Robert Sagalyn (Grossman, 1966), image 7.

73. MPP, letter from JK to AK, November 17, 1914.

74. GRI, AK diary, March 28, 1915.

75. AK diary, July 8–15, 1915, translated by Bulcsú Veress, in "Chronology, 1894–1985," 247.

76. GRI, AK diary, July 8–15, 1915.

## CHAPTER TWO

1. GRI, AK diary, July 8–15, 1915.

2. See S. Ansky, *The Enemy at His Pleasure: A Journey Through the Jewish Pale of Settlement During World War I*, edited and translated by Joachim Neugroschel (Metropolitan Books, 2003), 3.

3. GRI, AK diary, July 8–15, 1915. The hut may have belonged to Poles, but Andor was not in Poland. Many people of Polish origin lived in Galicia. The Russians drove home their point of view by using the name "Poland" for Austrian-ruled Galicia. Andor's entire fighting career transpired in the Habsburg province.

4. AK diary, July 15, 1915, in László Beke, "The Hungarian Period (1894–1925): A Photographer from Birth," in Pierre Borhan, *André Kertész: His Life and Work* (Bulfinch Press Book/Little, Brown: 1994), 37.

5. Mitulin and Lonie are today known as Mytulyn and Loni.

6. János Bodnár, ed., "Talking to André Kertész," in *André Kertész: Magyarországon* (Főfoto, 1984), 91. On the Allied side, most camera-toting soldiers carried a Vest Pocket Kodak, which took 127-format roll film. Using film would have made Andor's life easier. But when he tried a few film packs with his Goerz Tenax, he found the results insufficiently sharp. See Roger Clark, "The Fall & Rise of André Kertész," *The British Journal of Photography* 132, no. 6401 (April 1985): 359. See also Jane Carmichael, *First World War Photographers* (Routledge, 1989), 10.

7. GRI, letter from JK to AK, August 17, 1915.

8. George Szirtes, "Kertész: Latrine," *Poetry* (February 2008), https://www.poetryfoundation.org/poetrymagazine/poems/50738/kertesz-latrine. *Latrine at the Frontline, Poland* can be seen at https://art.nelson-atkins.org/objects/47882/latrine-at-the-frontline-poland.

9. Unknown widow quoted by AK in Colin Ford, "Introduction," in National Museum of Photography, Film & Television, *André Kertész: A Ninetieth Birthday Celebration* (National Museum of Photography, Film & Television, 1984), 8.

10. AK diary, August 11, 1912, translated by Bulcsú Veress, "Chronology, 1894–1985," in Sarah Greenough, Robert Gurbo, and Sarah Kennel, *André Kertész* (National Gallery of Art/Princeton University Press, 2005), 248.

11. Andor initially labeled this picture "Bilinski," but there was no village called Bilinski in Galicia. Evidently, he had misunderstood "Zalishchyky," the name of the town on the Dniester River that was the birthplace of the former governor of Galicia, Leon Biliński. *The Eternal Tender Touch* appears in AK, *Hungarian Memories* (New York Graphic Society/Little, Brown, 1982), 105.

12. The first wave of Jews arrived on August 21, 1915. See MPP, letter from Frigyes Groszmann to AK, October 24(?), 1915.

13. Frigyes Groszmann, "Flashback from the Middle Ages," *Egyenlőség*, October 24, 1915. I used a translation of this article by Gergely Tóth. Groszmann was murdered in the Holocaust.

14. John Lukacs, *Budapest 1900: A Historical Portrait of a City and Its Culture* (Weidenfeld & Nicolson, 1988), 153.

15. MPP, letter from AK to JK, August 11, 1915.

16. Letter from JK to AK, August 23, 1915, in Greenough, Gurbo, and Kennel, *André Kertész*, 270n57.

17. MPP, postcard from AK to Ernesztina Kertész, IK, JK, and Lipót Hoffmann, August 23, 1915, translated into French by Katalin Szabolcs-Perry.

18. Ibid., postcard from AK to Jolán Balog, August 23, 1915, translated by Gergely Tóth.

19. "Official Reports of the Operations," *The New York Times*, September 1, 1915.

20. Ansky, *The Enemy at His Pleasure*, 176.

21. Károly Kincses, "A Belated Interview with André Kertész," *The Hungarian Quarterly* 47, no. 181 (Spring 2006): 100.

22. Sylvia Plachy, "Hungary by Heart," *Artforum International* 24 (February 1986): 90.

23. Hungarian National Museum, *André Kertész in Esztergom* (Hungarian National Museum, 2024), 24–25.

24. *André Kertész of the Cities: Budapest, Paris, New York: Portrait of André Kertész*, directed by Teri Wehn-Damisch (TF1 with support of the French Ministry of Culture, 1986; Biography Series American Masters, 1988).

25. *Young Intellectual Notables from a Small Town* appears in AK, *Hungarian Memories*, 68.

26. Ibid., 112.

27. Carol Schwalberg, "André Kertész: Unsung Pioneer," *U.S. Camera* 26, no. 1 (January 1963): 64.

28. Although this phrase has been widely quoted and attributed to General Erich Ludendorff, he probably never used exactly those words. See Mesut Uyar, review of *Austro-Hungarian War Aims in the Balkans During World War I* (review no. 1846), *Reviews in History* (January 2015), doi: 10.14296/RiH/2014/1846.

29. "Hungary in Straits for Food Supply," *The New York Times*, January 8, 1917.

30. Gábor Szilágyi, "An Album of War," translated by Erika László in László Beke, Gábor Szilágyi, and Klára Tőry, *The Hungarian Connection: The Roots of Photojournalism*, edited by Colin Ford (National Museum of Photography, Film, and Television, 1987), 10.

31. Andor may have won fifth place too, for a photograph credited to "Kertész Jenő (lieutenant), Russian front."

32. UNESCO, *Progress in Literacy in Various Countries* (Firmin-Didot, 1953),

105. See also Michael Károlyi, *Memoirs of Michael Karolyi: Faith Without Illusion*, translated by Catherine Karolyi (Jonathan Cape, 1956), 373.

33. GRI, AK quoted in Part I: Hungarian Memories, in Béla Ugrin, "Dialogues with Kertész," edited by Manuela Caravageli Ugrin, transcript of taped conversations between AK and Béla Ugrin, 1978–1985, 31.

34. GRI, AK correspondence, December 3, 9, 12, 14, and 23, 1916.

35. MPP, AK diary, April 3, 1917.

36. Ibid.

37. GRI, Part I: Hungarian Memories in Ugrin, "Dialogues with Kertész," 47.

38. *André Kertész of the Cities.*

39. Gunther E. Rothenberg, *The Army of Francis Joseph* (Purdue University Press, 1976), 211. See also "Hungary in Straits for Food Supply," *The New York Times*, January 8, 1917.

40. "Third Search for Food Ordered in Hungary," *The New York Times*, February 2, 1917.

41. AK quoted in AK, *Hungarian Memories*, 190. The photograph appears on page 56.

42. This photograph appears in *Hungarian Memories*, 58.

43. AK quoted in Agathe Gaillard, *André Kertész* (Pierre Belfond, 1980), 18.

44. This photograph appears at https://www.getty.edu/art/collection/object/109P40.

45. AK, *Kertész on Kertész: A Self-Portrait* (Abbeville Press, 1985), 24. *Underwater Swimmer* can be seen at https://collections.artsmia.org/art/37283/underwater-swimmer-andre-kertesz.

46. See Péter Bihari, "Aspects of Anti-Semitism in Hungary 1915–1918," *Quest: Issues in Contemporary Jewish History* 9 (October 2016), doi: 10.48248/issn.2037-741X/803.

47. Michael Edelson, "The Diary of André Kertész," *Camera 35* 19, no. 7 (October 1975): 50; GRI, Part I: Hungarian Memories, in Ugrin, "Dialogues with Kertész," 59; William Houseman, "André Kertész," *Infinity* 8, no. 4 (April 1959): 6.

48. GRI, letter from JK to AK, July 19, 1918; MPP, letter from JK to AK, July 29, 1918.

49. MPP, letter from JK to AK, September 25, 1918. In 1937, Jolán and Ármin Gál and their son György left Budapest for New York. Three years later, they were living in the East Bronx. Ármin was unemployed. Jolán supported the family on

the $600 monthly paycheck of a factory seamstress. Eventually, the Gáls moved to West Eighteenth Street in Manhattan, not far from the Kertézses' apartment on Washington Square. In 1981, Jolán died in Miami Beach, an eighty-six-year-old widow. See Yolan Gál death notice, *The Miami Herald*, January 11, 1981. It's not known if Andor and Jolán ever saw each other in the United States.

**50.** GRI, letter from Jóska (Józsi) Frankl to AK, n.d. (October 1918). My thanks to Eszter Wainwright-Déri for her translation.

**51.** Ibid., and Part I: Hungarian Memories in Ugrin, "Dialogues with Kertész," 50.

**52.** János Bodnár, "Talking to André Kertész," in János Bodnár, ed., *André Kertész: Magyarországon* (Főfoto, 1984), 91.

**53.** Paul Ignotus, *Hungary* (Praeger, 1972), 143.

**54.** *Otago Daily Times* (Otago, New Zealand), October 10, 1918, National Library of New Zealand, http://paperspast.natlib.govt.nz/cgi-bin/paperspast?a=d&d=ODT19181010.2.29.

## CHAPTER THREE

**1.** Kati Marton, *The Great Escape: Nine Jews Who Fled Hitler and Changed the World* (Simon & Schuster, 2006), 216. Andor made the comment to Robert Gurbo. See also Erla Zwingle, "Inspirations: Eight Photographers Talk About What Has Shaped Their Own Art," *The Connoisseur* 215 (January 1985): 87.

**2.** Endre Ady, "I Am the Son of Gog and Magog," in Zsuzsanna Ozsváth and Frederick Turner, eds., *Light Within the Shade: Eight Hundred Years of Hungarian Poetry* (Syracuse University Press, 2014), 241.

**3.** Endre Ady in Lóránt Czigány, *The Oxford History of Hungarian Literature: From the Earliest Times to the Present* (Clarendon Press, 1984), 293.

**4.** See "Recollections of a Summer Night" and "A Harvest Song." Both appear in *Poems of Endre Ady*, translated by Anton N. Nyerges (Hungarian Cultural Foundation, 1969), 406 and 424.

**5.** Zsigmond Móricz and Virág Móricz, *Apám regénye*, 102, quoted in John Lukacs, *Budapest 1900: A Historical Portrait of a City and Its Culture* (Weidenfeld & Nicolson, 1988), 165. The historian Zoltán Horváth, another age-mate of Andor's, writes in his memoir that later generations could never understand "our excitement at the publication of a new poem by Ady." See Zoltán Horváth, *Magyar századforduló: A második reformnemzedék története, 1896–1914* (Gondolat, 1961), 7,

10, cited in Judit Frigyesi, *Béla Bartók and Turn-of-the-Century Budapest* (University of California Press, 1998), 3. Ady's work also proved vital to the creative lives of the philosopher György Lukács and the composer Béla Bartók.

6. Gene Thornton, "Kertész: The Great Democrat of Modern Photography," *The New York Times*, July 22, 1984.

7. AK quoted in Avis Berman, "The 'Little Happenings' of André Kertész," *ARTnews* 83, no. 3 (March 1984): 68.

8. Károly Kincses, "A Belated Interview with André Kertész," *The Hungarian Quarterly* 47, no. 181 (Spring 2006): 104.

9. Bryn Campbell, *World Photography* (Ziff-Davis Books, 1981), 273. *The Circus, Budapest* can be seen in Anna Fárová, *André Kertész*, edited by Robert Sagalyn (Grossman, 1966), inside front cover.

10. For *Budapest 1914* (with the goat), see AK, *Hungarian Memories* (New York Graphic Society/Little, Brown, 1982), 27. *Camera in Landscape, 1918–1925* appears in Robert Gurbo, *André Kertész: The Early Years* (W. W. Norton, 2005), 27 (plate 1).

11. Raphael Patai, *The Jews of Hungary: History, Culture, Psychology* (Wayne State University, 1996), 465.

12. Ibid.

13. "Hungarian Reds Ask Armistice," *The New York Times*, April 24, 1919.

14. "Amikor a béna ember vadászni megy és kilövi a hajtója szemét" (When the disabled man goes hunting and shoots his guide's eye), *Nyírvidék*, November 18, 1923.

15. *Jenő as Icarus* (full-frame image) can be seen at https://www.nga.gov/collection/art-object-page.111395.html. The cropped version appears at https://capacenter.hu/en/kiallitasok/andre-kertesz-his-photographs-donated-to-szigetbecse/.

16. See Ana Carden-Coyne, *Reconstructing the Body: Classicism, Modernism, and the First World War* (Oxford University Press, 2009); Gabriella Vincze, "History of Hungarian Movement Art and International Parallels of Some of Its Motifs," PhD dissertation, Budapest, Eötvös Loránd University Faculty of Humanities Art History Doctoral School of Science, 2015, http://doktori.btk.elte.hu/art/vinczegabriella/thesis.pdf; and Gabriella Vincze, "André Kertész (1894–1985) és a Magyar Mozdulatművészet," *Archívum* 5 (2014): 28–35, http://www.artmagazin.hu/artmagazin_hirek/andre_kertesz_1894–1985_es_a_magyar_mozdulatmuveszet.2515.html. I used a translation of the latter by Gergely Tóth.

17. Andor and Jenő may have learned about the movement from the Hungarian

magazine *Vital Force — Mazdaznan*. See Erika Koltay, "History of Alternative Medicine in Hungary in 19th and Early 20th Century," *Communicationes de Historia Artis Medicinae* 49, no. 3 and no. 4: 65.

18. MPP, letter from JK to AK, November 13, 1926.

19. Paul Ignotus, *Hungary* (Praeger, 1972), 151.

20. Patai, *The Jews of Hungary*, 468.

21. Bryn Campbell, *World Photography* (Ziff-Davis Books, 1981), 273.

22. The uncropped and cropped versions appear in Michel Frizot and Annie-Laure Wanaverbecq, *André Kertész*, translated by Lucy Daniel Anderson, Anthony Roberts, and Willard Wood (Éditions Hazan and Éditions du Jeu de Paume, 2010), 58, 59.

23. The art historian Oliver A. I. Botar was the first to write about AK's association with the Szőnyi Circle and to explore its significance for AK's photography. Sarah Greenough addresses this connection in an essay for the catalog of the National Gallery of Art's 2005 exhibition *André Kertész*. My discussion is indebted to both and to András Zwickl, Árkádia tájain: Szőnyi István és köre, 1918–1928 (Hungarian National Gallery, 2000), 55–60.

24. Éva Forgács, "Avant-Garde and Conservatism in the Budapest Art World, 1910–1932," in Thomas Bender and Carl E. Schorske, eds., *Budapest and New York: Studies in Metropolitan Transformation, 1870–1930* (Russell Sage Foundation, 1994), 309–11, 329. Not even the avant-garde activists group of the 1910s viewed their city as a metaphor for modernity. For them, it was a stodgy backwater.

25. This rarely seen photograph appears at https://www.nga.gov/collection/art-object-page.132860.html. For Andor's later *cartes postales* (postcards) as photographic objects, see Elizabeth Siegel, "André Kertész's *Carte Postale* Period, Paris, 1925–28," in Elizabeth Siegel, ed., *André Kertész: Postcards from Paris* (Art Institute of Chicago, 2021), especially 23–26.

26. Erzsébet Salamon was born on July 6, 1902, as confirmed by Mgr. Lenka Hlaváčová of the State Archive Zvolen, Banská Bystrica, Public Administration Section, Ministry of the Interior, Slovakia. Her 1933 French marriage license gives her birth date as July 6, 1903. By the time she applied for naturalization in the United States, she had shaved another year off her age. The U.S. Social Security Death Index lists 1905 as her year of birth.

27. MPP, ten postcards from AK to EK, May 30–June 27, 1920. I used a translation by Eszter Wainwright-Déri.

**28.** Erzsébet Salamon sometimes used the name Erzsébet Saly or Erzsébet Sali. But, unlike the Kohns, the Salamons may not have legally magyarized their surname.

**29.** My thanks to György Németh for his extensive research on Fülöp and Zoltán Salamon from numerous archival sources. Regarding Pepi's work at a guest-house, see Sandra Sammataro Phillips, "The Photographic Work of André Kertész in France, 1925–1936: A Critical Essay and Catalogue," PhD dissertation, City University of New York, 1985, 15.

**30.** See, as possible inspirations, Erzsébet Korb's *May (Human Couple)* (1923) and István Szőnyi's *My Wife and I* (1924).

**31.** AK quoted in Béla Ugrin, "Kertesz's Photography in Full Bloom," *The Houston Post*, January 2, 1983.

**32.** GRI, Part I: Hungarian Memories in Béla Ugrin, "Dialogues with Kertész," edited by Manuela Caravageli Ugrin, transcript of taped conversations between AK and Béla Ugrin, 1978–1985, 20.

**33.** Ibid., AK diary, March 24, 1921.

**34.** MPP, AK diary, April 17, 1921.

**35.** Want ad, *Magyar Méh* 42, no. 3 (March 1922): 55.

**36.** My thanks to Béla Kurucz for generously providing information about his great-uncle Ede Papszt.

**37.** AK quoted in Guy Trebay, "Talking Heads: André Kertész: Magyar Emlékek," *The Village Voice* (November 16, 1982): 71.

**38.** MPP, AK diary, May 13, 1921.

**39.** Ibid., postcard from AK to Ernesztina Kertész, IK, JK, and Lipót Hoffmann, August 23, 1915, translated by Katalin Szabolcs-Perry.

**40.** Letter from Imre Pártos to Theodore von Kármán, June 27, 1925, Theodore von Kármán Papers, File 22.26, quoted in Tibor Frank, "Berlin Junction: Patterns of Hungarian Intellectual Migrations, 1919–1933," *Storicamente* 2 (2006): 16.

**41.** MPP, letter from IK to AK, January 11, 1926.

**42.** AK quoted in János Bodnár, ed., "Talking to André Kertész," in *Magyarországon* (Főfoto, 1984), 91.

**43.** Forgács, "Avant-Garde and Conservatism in the Budapest Art World, 1910–1932," in Bender and Schorske, eds., *Budapest and New York*, 310.

**44.** AK quoted in AK, *Hungarian Memories*, 190. The image is found on page 53.

45. Ibid., 194. The photograph appears on page 146.

46. The date of this photograph is uncertain, possibly 1923. It appears in Sarah Greenough, Robert Gurbo, and Sarah Kennel, *André Kertész* (National Gallery of Art/Princeton University Press, 2005), 1.

47. Ibid., image 22.

48. See J. Paul Getty Museum, *In Focus: André Kertész* (J. Paul Getty Museum, 1999), 16–17.

49. Kincses, "A Belated Interview with André Kertész," 106.

50. MPP, AK diary, June 23, 1924.

51. AK diary, July 8, 1924, in AK, *André Kertész*, 250.

52. AK quoted in Marton, *The Great Escape*, 51.

53. EK (then Erzsébet Salamon) quoted in "A kíváncsi fotográfus" (The curious photographer), *Színházi Élet*, March 30, 1924.

54. AK diary, July 10, 1924, in AK, *André Kertész*, 250.

55. MPP, AK diary, July 11, 1924.

56. Ibid., July 12, 1924.

57. "Magyar Est a Gellértben," *Az Ujság*, January 16, 1925.

58. Nicolas Ducrot, interview by author, August 8, 2014.

59. Tibor Korda, "A Pesti Rue de la Paix: A Váci-Utca Huszonnégy Órája," *Színházi Élet*, January 4, 1925.

60. MPP, letter from JK to AK, November 13, 1926.

61. Lukacs, *Budapest 1900*, 207.

62. Nicolas Ducrot, email to author, August 27, 2014.

63. "Művészet: Jaschik Álmos," *Ország-Világ*, December 13, 1925.

## CHAPTER FOUR

1. Ernő Goldfinger later moved to Britain, where he built tower blocks and unwillingly lent his name to the novelist Ian Fleming's most famous James Bond villain.

2. "Silent film footage from Hungarian National Gallery, 34′ film reel," in *Tihanyi Lajos*, an exhibition curated by Krisztina Passuth and presented at Budapest's Kogart Gallery in 2012. Much of my information about Tihanyi derives from Passuth's *Tihanyi Lajos: A Bohème Painter in Budapest, Berlin and Paris* (Kogart, 2012).

3. This photograph can be seen at https://www.getty.edu/art/collection/objects/55882/andre-kertesz-rue-vavin-paris-american-1925/.

4. MPP, letter from JK to AK, December 12, 1925.

5. *Eiffel Tower, Paris* is found at https://nasher.duke.edu/artwork/22773/. See also *The Fountain in the Place de la Concorde, Paris* at https://www.getty.edu/art/collection/object/104EM3; *Pigalle at Night* at https://www.icp.org/browse/archive/objects/pigalle-at-night; *Paris, Notre Dame* and *Fishermen Behind Notre Dame* in Sandra S. Phillips, David Travis, and Weston J. Naef, *André Kertész: Of Paris and New York* (Thames and Hudson, 1985), 129 and 130, respectively.

6. Livia Sibalin, "De *Kaleidoscope* à *Gaz*, itinéraire parisien d'un artiste hongrois, Gyula Zilzer entre 1924 et 1932," MA thesis, Université de Lille 3, 2014, 20–22; letter from Mary Zilzer to Sandra S. Phillips, December 27, 1982, cited in Sandra Sammataro Phillips, "The Photographic Work of André Kertész in France, 1925–1936: A Critical Essay and Catalogue," PhD dissertation, City University of New York, 1985, 115.

7. *Lajos Tihanyi* appears at https://www.npg.org.uk/collections/search/portrait/mw161648/Louis-Tihanyi.

8. This photograph, as André later cropped it, can be seen at https://www.getty.edu/art/collection/objects/55776/andre-kertesz-legs-paris-american-negative-1925-print-1930s/.

9. André Breton, "First Manifesto of Surrealism," in Charles Harrison and Paul Wood, eds., *Art in Theory, 1900–1990* (Blackwell, 1992), 436.

10. *Behind Notre Dame, Paris* can be viewed in in Sarah Greenough, Robert Gurbo, and Sarah Kennel, *André Kertész* (National Gallery of Art/Princeton University Press, 2005), image 34.

11. AK quoted in Sandra S. Phillips, David Travis, and Weston J. Naef, *André Kertész: Of Paris and New York* (Thames and Hudson, 1985), 259.

12. André Breton in *Manifestoes of Surrealism*, translated by Richard Seaver and Helen R. Lane (University of Michigan Press, 2010), 15, https://monoskop.org/images/2/2f/Breton_Andre_Manifestoes_of_Surrealism.pdf.

13. GRI, letter from Rózsi Klopfer to AK, December 20, 1925.

14. Ibid., letter from IK to AK, January 11, 1926.

15. Ibid., letter from JK to AK, February 7, 1926.

16. Ibid., letter from JK to AK, February ?, 1926.

17. AK quoted in Károly Kincses, "A Belated Interview with André Kertész," *The Hungarian Quarterly* 47, no. 181 (Spring 2006): 98.

18. GRI, letter from AK to IK, April 1, 1926.

**19.** Ibid., letter from JK to AK, n.d. February 1926.

**20.** *Après le Bal* can be found at images.grandpalaisrmn.fr.

**21.** Arthur Lubow, *Man Ray: The Artist and His Shadows* (Yale University Press, 2021), 152.

**22.** Françoise Denoyelle, *La lumière de Paris: Les usages de la photographie, 1919–1939, vol. II* (Harmattan, 1997), 56 and 58–59.

**23.** Michel Seuphor, "Le jeu de je. Vingt tranches de vie racontées par Seuphor," in Rik Sauwen, Germain Viatte, and Michel Seuphor, *Seuphor* (Fonds Mercator and Centre national d'art et de culture Georges Pompidou, 1976), 313. I use the translation in David Travis, *At the Edge of the Light: Thoughts on Photography & Photographers, Talent & Genius* (David R. Godine, 2006), 37–38.

**24.** Phillips, "The Photographic Work of André Kertész in France, 1925–1936," 30 and 292n2.

**25.** Seuphor, "Le jeu de je. Vingt tranches de vie racontées par Seuphor," 313.

**26.** AK quoted in Béla Ugrin, "André Kertész: Brother Seeing Eye," *Popular Photography* 93, no. 1 (January 1986): 65.

**27.** See Nancy Joslin Troy, "Piet Mondrian's Atelier," *Arts Magazine* 53, no. 4 (December 1978): 82–87, and Carel Blotkamp, *Mondrian: The Art of Destruction* (Harry N. Abrams, 1995), 245.

**28.** Alfred Roth in *Begegnungen mit Pionieren*, quoted in Frans Postma, *26, rue du Départ: Mondrian's Studio in Paris, 1921–1936* edited by Cees Boekraad (Ernst & Sohn, 1995), 33; Alexander Calder, "What Abstract Art Means to Me," *Museum of Modern Art Bulletin* 18, no. 3 (Spring 1951): 8.

**29.** Douglas Davis, "I Looked, I Saw, I Did," *Newsweek* (December 6, 1982): 142.

**30.** Michel Seuphor, *Piet Mondrian: Life and Work* (Harry N. Abrams, 1957), 86; Hans Janssen, *Piet Mondrian: A Life* (Ridinghouse, 2022), 11.

**31.** Piet Mondrian, "The Home — The Street — The City," in Postma, *26, Rue du Départ*, 74–80.

**32.** César Domela, quoted in Betty van Garrel, "César Domela, de laatste overlevende van de Stijlgroep," *Haagse Post*, 21-26-5, 1973: 57, quoted in Troy, "Piet Mondrian's Atelier," 87n17.

**33.** This photograph can be seen at https://www.artic.edu/artworks/50157/mondrian-s-glasses-and-pipe.

**34.** Much of my information about André's *cartes postales* derives from Nancy

Reinhold, "Exhibition in a Pocket: The *Cartes Postales* of André Kertész," in Mitra Abbaspour, Lee Ann Daffner, and Maria Morris Hambourg, eds., *Object: Photo: Modern Photographs—The Thomas Walther Collection, 1909–1949* (Museum of Modern Art, 2014), www.moma.org/interactives/objectphoto/assets/essays/Reinhold.pdf; and from Elizabeth Siegel, ed., *André Kertész: Postcards from Paris* (Art Institute of Chicago, 2021).

35. Sylvie Pénichon, "'It Was a Beautiful Paper': Notes on Guilleminot Cartes Postales," in Siegel, *André Kertész*, 50.

36. This photograph can be seen at https://www.artic.edu/articles/938/a-close-look-at-andre-kerteszs-quartet. In an example of even more radical cropping, André pared down one image of the cellist playing to simply the strings, bridge, tailpiece, and bow. That print, which was not a *carte postale*, measured 20.3 by 4.4 centimeters.

37. *At Zadkine's* can be viewed at https://www.moma.org/collection/works/83810.

38. For *Portrait of Mme R.*, see https://www.moma.org/collection/works/84017.

39. *Tristan Tzara* is found at https://images.grandpalaisrmn.fr/ark:/36255/12-577975; *Gunvor Berg* appears in Siegel, *André Kertész*, 50.

40. *Chairs, Luxembourg Gardens* can be seen at https://www.artic.edu/artworks/102597/chairs-luxembourg-gardens.

41. Seuphor, "Le jeu de je. Vingt tranches de vie racontées par Seuphor," 313.

42. Lajos Tihanyi quoted in Phillips, "The Photographic Work of André Kertész in France, 1925–1936: A Critical Essay and Catalogue," 292n2. Phillips interviewed both Seuphor and André about this incident. Tihanyi had died in 1938.

43. Jean Gallotti, "La photographie est-elle un art? André Kertész," *L'Art Vivant* (March 1, 1929): 211.

44. GRI, *Magyar Hírlap*, October 17, 1926, and October 28, 1926.

45. MPP, letter from IK to AK, July 2, 1926.

46. Ibid., letter from IK to AK, November 22, 1926.

47. Seuphor, "Le jeu de je. Vingt tranches de vie racontées par Seuphor," 313.

48. MPP, letter from JK to AK, November 13, 1926.

49. *Self-Portrait with Jean Jaffe and František Reichentál* can be viewed in *carte postale* format at https://www.artic.edu/artworks/216547/self-portrait-with-jean-jaffe-and-frantisek-reichental.

50. *One and Half of Actor Aguet* can be found in Anna Fárová, *André Kertész*, edited by Robert Sagalyn (Grossman, 1966) page 27.

51. MPP, letter from IK to JK, November 2, 1926.

52. One version appears at https://www.centrepompidou.fr/en/ressources/oeuvre/c9jqy4.

53. GRI, letter from JK to IK with instructions to forward to AK, February 5, 1927.

54. MPP, letter from Sándor Márai to AK, October 20, 1926.

55. Ibid., letter from IK to AK, February 15, 1927.

56. Much of my information about Éva Révai comes from Csaba Mórocz, who shared with me what he learned in his interview with the elderly Révai. Her mother, Ilka Révai, died in the Budapest ghetto. See also Gergely Barki, "Damn, Cyla, This Really Is a Cubist Csáky!," *Artmagazin Online* (June 2, 2020), https://www.artmagazin.hu/articles/in_english/damn_cyla_this_really_is_a_cubist_csaky.

57. *San Bernadino County Sun*, April 16, 1933, 15.

58. Le Corbusier (Charles-Édouard Jeanneret) and Saugnier (Amédée Ozenfant), "Des Yeux qui ne voient pas...Les Paquebots," *L'Esprit Nouveau* 8 (May 1921): 850, in Le Corbusier, *Toward an Architecture*, translated by John Goodman (Getty Research Institute, 2007), 156.

59. Guillaume Apollinaire, "Zone," in *Alcools*, translated by Donald Revell (Wesleyan University Press, 1995), 3, 7.

60. Paul Dermée, "Brother Seeing-Eye," translated by Nicolas Ducrot, in *André Kertész, Stranger to Paris* (Jane Corkin Gallery, 1992), 15. See also MPP, letter from AK to IK, January 4, 1927.

61. "Art and Artists," *Chicago Tribune*, March 13, 1927; Montpar, "Photo-Kertész," *Chantecler* 47 (March 19, 1927): 5.

62. M.S., "Frère Voyant," *Comœdia* 5184 (March 12, 1927): 2.

63. *Man at Pissoir, Latin Quarter* appears in *André Kertész, Stranger to Paris* (Jane Corkin Gallery, 1995), 59.

64. AK quoted in Danièle Boone, "Ma France," *Révolution* 540 (July 6, 1990): 33.

65. AK quoted in Béla Ugrin, "Kertész's Photography in Full Bloom," *The Houston Post*, January 2, 1983.

66. MPP, letter from IK to AK, February 17, 1927.

67. Ibid.

68. MPP, Evsa Model drawing.

## CHAPTER FIVE

1. Maria Giovanna Eisner, "Citizen Kertesz," *Minicam* 7 (June 1944): 30.

2. Jean Marèze, *Le Soir*, June 9, 1927.

3. The Art Works, *The Förstner Memorial Exhibition: Magda the Dancer, Denis the Painter* (The Art Works, 1979), n.p. André probably knew Magda's brother, the painter and caricaturist Dénes Faddi-Förstner, in Hungary. Like André, Faddi-Förstner was friendly with members of the Szőnyi Circle. He died in a gas chamber at Mauthausen on the eve of the camp's liberation.

4. "André Kertész" in H.E., "André Kertész történetei," *Magyar Nemzet*, March 20, 1984, quoted in László Beke, "The Hungarian Period (1894–1925): A Photographer from Birth" in Pierre Borhan, *André Kertész: His Life and Work* (Bulfinch Press Book/Little, Brown: 1994), 42–43.

5. My discussion is indebted to Kate Alice Hamilton, "Re-membering: The Aesthetics of Disarticulation in André Kertész's *Satiric Dancer*," MA thesis, University of Texas, 2018, http://hdl.handle.net/2152/67997.

6. My thanks to Celia Stahr for sharing her ideas about this photograph. André took at least one other photograph of Förstner in her dog-collar dress, perhaps after friends arrived at Beöthy's studio on that same occasion. The dancer perches on a table as if on a stage, chatting with Beöthy, Rózsi Klein, and a third person. In another Kertész photograph of the dancer, now in a feminized version of a man's suit, she shares the sofa with Beöthy. In yet another, she romps in a froufrou frock. The photo historian Sarah Kennel suggests that the latter may be a publicity picture commissioned and paid for by Förstner. See Sarah Kennel, "The Grotesque Dancer from Pest: Madga Förstner and the Making of *Satiric Dancer*," in Elizabeth Siegel, ed., *André Kertész: Postcards from Paris* (Art Institute of Chicago, 2021), 38.

7. Improbably, there were two Hungarian pantomime dancers named Magda in André's life. One was Magda Förstner of *Satiric Dancer*, born in 1899. The other was Magda Zahler, born in 1904. André probably met Zahler in Budapest, where Angelo took her publicity pictures. After performing and touring for almost a decade, she traveled to the Dutch East Indies. There she married a doctor, had a daughter, and became a moving spirit in the dance community. Following World War II, Zahler divorced and went to the Netherlands. In 1965, she married the American Maarten Oudegeest. The couple lived in a retirement community in Walnut Creek, California. According to Zahler's stepson, Bill Oudegeest, André visited her once in the Bay Area. She died in 2001 at age ninety-six. Förstner continued to dance professionally

until 1934, when she turned to doll-making and weaving. Later she emigrated to Canada. André visited Förstner and her husband, the biochemist George Barta, in Toronto. Chronically ill and in severe pain, Förstner died by suicide in 1977.

In June 1965, *Harper's Bazaar* published "Six Exceptional Women—A Portfolio by Kertesz." Above *Satiric Dancer* are André's words: "MAGDA ZAHLER. 'What capacity for caprice! She was Hungarian, a doctor's wife, and had studied classical dance. But when she came to Paris in 1925, she was a satiric dancer—her exuberant caricatures took us by storm." André's confusion opened a door for Magda Zahler. After Förstner died, Zahler appropriated her identity as *Satiric Dancer*. Around 1985, for instance, she visited Michael Shapiro Photographs in San Francisco and signed her name to the back of a large print of *Satiric Dancer*.

My thanks to Oliver Botar, Stephen Bulger, Meutia Chaerani, Bill Oudegeest, Michael Shapiro, Judy Stoffman, and Maia Sutnik for working with me to investigate the two Magdas.

8. Sophie Delaporte, "Mutilation and Disfiguration (France)," in *1914–1918: International Encyclopedia of the First World War*, https://encyclopedia.1914-1918-online.net/article/mutilation_and_disfiguration_france.

9. *Hôtel des Clochards* appears at https://americanhistory.si.edu/collections/object/nmah_2009491.

10. AK, *Kertész on Kertész: A Self-Portrait* (Abbeville Press, 1985), 76. This photograph appears in J. Paul Getty Museum, *In Focus: André Kertész* (J. Paul Getty Museum, 1999), 66.

11. MPP, cable from Intendente Policía, Villazón, Bolivia, to Familia Eugenio Kertész, June 24, 1927, and letter from JK to Ernesztina Kertész, IK, and AK, June 26, 1927.

12. Ibid., letter from IK to AK, September 15, 1927.

13. Ibid., letter from Lajos Tihanyi to AK, September 6, 1927.

14. Kim Deborah Sichel, "Photographs of Paris, 1928–1934: Brassaï, André Kertész, Germaine Krull, and Man Ray," PhD dissertation, Yale University, 1986, 118.

15. My information about Rózsi Klein (later Rogi André) comes chiefly from Renée Beslon, *Rogi André: Portraits* (Éditions du Regard, 1981); Jean Lattès, "Rogi André ou la vraie lumière du Bon Dieu," *Techniques Graphiques* 60 (October 1965): 388–91; Muriel Jaeger, interview by author, July 27, 2013; Jean-François Jaeger, interview by author, July 17, 2014; Andra Samelson's unpublished essay "Rogi," my conversation with Samelson, and the letters from Rogi that she generously shared

with me; my conversations with Brigitte Ollier; and Ollier's book with Elisabeth Nora, *Rogi André: Photo sensible* (Éditions du Regard, 1999).

**16.** MPP, Lajos Tihanyi letter to AK, September 6, 1927.

**17.** Sandra S. Phillips, David Travis, and Weston J. Naef, *André Kertész: Of Paris and New York* (Thames and Hudson, 1985), 264n46.

**18.** Paul Katz, telephone interview by author, December 5, 2022.

**19.** James McQuaid, phone conversation with Julia Van Haaften, July 12, 2011, cited in Julia Van Haaften, *Berenice Abbott: A Life in Photography* (W. W. Norton, 2018), 280, 558n31; Julia Van Haaften, telephone conversation with author, April 20, 2023.

**20.** Agathe Gaillard, *André Kertész* (Pierre Belfond, 1980), 42–43.

**21.** Ibid., 42; GRI, Béla Ugrin, Part III: Sixty Years of Photography, in "Dialogues with Kertész," edited by Manuela Caravageli Ugrin, transcript of taped conversations between AK and Béla Ugrin, 1978–1985, 42.

**22.** The photographers Henri Cartier-Bresson and Jacques Henri Lartigue used this same tactic. Lartigue called it setting an "eye-trap." See Clément Chéroux, "Jacques Henri Lartigue: The Memory of the Instant," in Martine d'Astier, Quentin Bajac, and Alain Sayag, eds., *Lartigue: Album of a Century* (Centre Pompidou/Éditions du Seuil, 2003), 24.

**23.** Robert Hayes, "Andre Kertesz," *Interview* 13, no. 4 (April 1983): 60.

**24.** GRI, Ugrin, Part III: Sixty Years of Photography, 38.

**25.** Károly Kincses, "A Belated Interview with André Kertész," *The Hungarian Quarterly* 47, no. 181 (Spring 2006): 105. André also used the Satz Plasmat lens for *Place Gambetta* and *Rue des Ursins* and for his Distortions series.

**26.** Hayes, "Andre Kertesz," 60. André intensified the effect of the Satz Plasmat with judicious cropping. *Stairs, Montmartre* (first version) can be seen at https://www.artic.edu/artworks/125490/stairs-montmartre. *The Stairs of Montmartre, Paris* (second version) can be seen at https://www.dia.org/art/collection/object/stairs-montmartre-paris-50876. The Detroit Institute of Arts dates it 1926.

**27.** John Colapinto, *This Is the Voice* (Simon & Schuster, 2021), 247, 248. Colapinto cites Milton Metfessel and Carl E. Seashore's study *Phonophotography in Folk Music: American Negro Songs in New Notation*.

**28.** "Eyes Which Do Not See" is the title of a section in *Toward an Architecture*, Le Corbusier's book-length manifesto originally published in 1923.

**29.** *Corner of Léger's Studio* appears in Michel Frizot and Annie-Laure

Wanaverbecq, *André Kertész*, translated by Lucy Daniel Anderson, Anthony Roberts, and Willard Wood (Éditions Hazan and Éditions du Jeu de Paume, 2010), 99.

30. AK quoted in "The World of Kertesz: A Great Photographer Has Spent a Lifetime in Pursuit of His Art," *Show* 4, no. 3 (March 1964): 56.

31. AK, interview by David Travis, Edwynn Houk, and Nicholas Pritzker, 1991, cited in Sarah Greenough, Robert Gurbo, and Sarah Kennel, *André Kertész* (National Gallery of Art/Princeton University Press, 2005), 65.

32. AK quoted in Jean Gallotti, "La photographie est-elle un art? Kertesz," *L'Art Vivant* (March 1, 1929): 211.

33. AK, interview by James Borcoman, 1971, cited in Greenough, Gurbo, and Kennel, *André Kertész*, 273n63.

34. AK, *Kertész on Kertész: A Self-Portrait* (Abbeville Press, 1985), 79. The eighteenth-century poet André Chénier lived in this building.

35. Letter from Frederic Littman to Frank Dobo, October 17, 1978. Michael Dobo and György Németh kindly shared this letter with me.

36. Sandra Sammataro Phillips, "The Photographic Work of André Kertész in France, 1925–1936: A Critical Essay and Catalogue," PhD dissertation, City University of New York, 1985, 282.

37. R.H., "La photographie est-elle un art? Le Salon Indépendant va nous l'apprendre," *Paris-Midi*, May 14, 1928.

38. Pierre Mac Orlan, "Preface to *Atget Photographe de Paris*," translated by Robert Erich Wolf, in Christopher Phillips, ed., *Photography in the Modern Era: European Documents and Critical Writings, 1913–1940* (Metropolitan Museum of Art/Aperture, 1989), 44.

39. Mac Orlan, "The Literary Art of Imagination and Photography," ibid., 29.

40. *Boy with Ball* appears in Frizot and Wanaverbecq, *André Kertész*, 137.

41. MPP, letter from JK to Lipót Hoffmann, April 4, 1928.

42. Pierre Assouline, *Henri Cartier-Bresson: A Biography* (Thames & Hudson, 2005), 65.

43. Jean Gallotti, "Les Panneaux Sacrilèges," *Vu* 25 (September 5, 1928): 571.

44. Another assignment for *Vu* led André to photograph Charles Maurras, the ultranationalist ideologue who proclaimed that foreign Jews were bringing to Paris "lice, plague, and typhus while awaiting the revolution." See Charles Maurras, October 6, 1920, in Ralph Schor, "Le Paris des libertés," in André Kaspi and Antoine Marès, eds., *Le Paris des étrangers depuis un siècle* (Imprimerie Nationale,

1989), 29. André may have been unaware of Maurras's anti-Semitism. In any case, he kept his mouth shut.

**45.** Eugen Weber, *The Hollow Years: France in the 1930s* (Norton, 1994), 162.

**46.** Nicolas Ducrot, interview by author, August 8, 2014; Nicolas Ducrot, "Hommage à André Kertész," in *André Kertész: Une importante collection française*, Artcurial auction catalog, November 14, 2014, 8.

**47.** GRI, this figure appears in André's day planner for June 1928. Regarding the film and processing equipment he may have also purchased, see Françoise Denoyelle, *La lumière de Paris: Le marché de la photographie, 1919–1939*, vol. I (Harmattan, 1997), 30–31.

**48.** At first, André used an Eastman Kodak panchromatic film with low sensitivity to light. But film would soon become faster too. By 1931, a type with an ISO rating of 100 was on the market. See Michel Frizot and Cédric de Veigy, *Vu: The Story of a Magazine* (Thames & Hudson, 2009), 306.

**49.** AK quoted in Denes Devenyi, "Kertesz: Denes Devenyi interviews the 'Father of 35mm Vision,'" *Photo Life* (January 1978): 30. Other photo reporters of that era, like Germaine Krull, who used an Icarette, did the same. André's photograph *Les Halles* can be found in Frizot and Wanaverbecq, *André Kertész*, 129.

**50.** AK, *Kertész on Kertész*, 80.

**51.** Felix H. Man quoted in "Photojournalism in the 1920s: A Conversation Between Felix H. Man and Stefan Lorant, Picture Editor," in Beaumont Newhall, ed., *Photography, Essays & Images: Illustrated Readings in the History of Photography* (Museum of Modern Art, 1980), 175.

**52.** AK, *Kertész on Kertész*, 55.

**53.** See Edmond Wellhoff, "Sous la règle de Saint-Benoît," *Vu* 109 (April 16, 1930): 340.

**54.** MPP, letter from Germaine Krull, André Kertész, and Eli Lotar to Lucien Vogel, December 17, 1928.

**55.** "Das Haus des Shweigens [The House of Silence]," *Berliner Illustrirte Zeitung* 1 (January 6, 1929): 35–37; Heinrich Siemer, "Als ich noch Frater Julian war," *Uhu* 5 (February 1929): 28–31.

**56.** MPP, letter from Edmond Wellhoff to AK, February 4, 1929.

**57.** Ibid., February 19, 1929.

**58.** Phillips, "The Photographic Work of André Kertész in France, 1925–1936," 494; Nicolas Ducrot, interview by author, August 8, 2014.

59. Jean-François Jaeger, interview by Brigitte Ollier, March 4, 1998.

60. André-Charles Gervais, "Géza Blattner: La naissance et l'évolution du théâtre de marionnettes 'Arc-en-Ciel,'" in *Marionnettes et Marionnettistes de France* (Bordas, 1947), 131–42. My thanks to Csaba Mórocz for copies of this and other key documents about Géza Blattner.

61. Ibid., 132; Program, Arc-en-Ciel. From 1928 to 1930, Blattner's puppet theater was located at 12, rue Tisserand in Boulogne-Billancourt (previously Boulogne-sur-Seine).

62. The Galerie Surréaliste at 16, rue Jacques-Callot in the Latin Quarter showed Giorgio de Chirico's work around this same time (February 15–March 1, 1928). It's not known if André saw the exhibition. In 1929, the rue des Vignes was renamed the rue du docteur Vuillième.

63. Béla Ugrin, "André Kertész: Brother Seeing Eye," *Popular Photography* 93, no. 1 (January 1986): 64.

64. Hans-Michael Koetzle, *50 Photo Icons: The Story Behind the Pictures* (Taschen, 2011), 134.

65. *Meudon* can be seen at https://www.getty.edu/art/collection/object/104EJE. The earlier version is in Michel Frizot, "Jardinier, Mine de rien," in Pierre Bonhomme et al., *André Kertész: Ma France* (La Manufacture/Ministère de la Culture, 1990), 160.

66. GRI, AK day planner, June 1928. See Marc Daubrive, "Le Pardon des Oiseaux," *Vu* 64 (June 5, 1929): 439–41.

67. Tim N. Gidal, *Modern Photojournalism: Origin and Evolution, 1910–1933* (Macmillan, 1973), 18–19. Henry Guttmann is not to be confused with Simon Guttmann, a founder of Dephot (Deutscher Photodienst).

68. U.S. Department of Labor, Bureau of Labor Statistics, *Monthly Labor Review* 29 (U.S. Department of Labor, Bureau of Labor Statistics, 1929), HathiTrust Digital Library. In July 1926, André earned 1,267 francs (about $520 in 2024 dollars).

69. MPP, letter from Lucien Vogel to AK, November 15, 1929.

70. Gallotti, "La photographie est-elle un art? Kertesz," 211.

71. Carlo Rim, "A Defense and Illustration of Photography," *Vu* 214 (April 20, 1932): 587.

72. Pierre Mac Orlan, "L'art littéraire d'imagination et la photographie," *Les Nouvelles Littéraires* (September 22, 1928), in Phillips, ed., *Photography in the Modern Era*, 24.

## CHAPTER SIX

1. GRI, Part III: Sixty Years of Photography, in Béla Ugrin, "Dialogues with Kertész," edited by Manuela Caravageli Ugrin, transcript of taped conversations between AK and Béla Ugrin, 1978–1985, 79.

2. Ibid., 81; Dorothy S. Gelatt, "André Kertész at 80 — How He Works — What He Feels," *Popular Photography* 75, no. 5 (November 1974): 155.

3. Jean d'Erleich (Brassaï's pen name), "La Tour Eiffel a quarante ans," *Vu* 63 (May 29, 1929): 431–33.

4. Florent Fels, "Dans toute sa force," *Vu* 11 (May 1928): 284.

5. AK, interview by László Lugosi Lugo, January 13, 1981, in Károly Kincses, *Measure: The History of Hungarian Photography* 43 (Association of Hungarian Photographers/Hungarian Museum of Photography, 2006), 93.

6. GRI, Part III: Sixty Years of Photography, 50. Although André took the photographs in 1928, they were not published in *Uhu* until October 1931.

7. AK quoted in Jean Vidal, "En photographiant les photographes: Kertész," *L'Intransigeant*, April 1, 1930.

8. Germaine Krull with Françoise Denoyelle, *La vie mène la danse* (Textuel, 2015), 200n145. See also Julia Van Haaften, *Berenice Abbott: A Life in Photography* (W. W. Norton, 2018), 55.

9. GRI, AK day planner, 1929.

10. AK, *Kertész on Kertész: A Self-Portrait* (Abbeville Press, 1985), 57.

11. Bruce Downes, "André Kertész: Day of Paris," *Popular Photography* 16, no. 6 (June 1945): 102.

12. Brassaï quoted in Maria Giovanna Eisner, "Brassaï," *Minicam Photography* (April 1944): 22.

13. Brassaï, "My Friend André Kertész," *Camera* 42, no. 4 (April 1963): 32.

14. See Miller's essay "The Eye of Paris" in Henry Miller, *The Wisdom of the Heart* (New Directions, 1941): 173–86. It's not uncommon for writers to assume that Brassaï was the more established photographer. The historian Pascal Ory, for one, describes the 1935 exhibition *Documents of Social Life* as follows: "A few names, already familiar in both extreme left and avant-garde circles (Brassaï, Germaine Krull, John Heartfield, Man Ray), hung alongside a majority of young unknowns: Yves Allégret, Henri Cartier (Bresson), Chim (the nickname of David Seymour), Kertez [*sic*], Eli Lotar..." See Pascal Ory, *La belle illusion: Culture et politique sous le signe du Front Populaire, 1935–1938* (Plon, 1994), 600.

15. MPP, letter from AK to Petra Burkhard, May 14, 1938.

16. Colette and AK quoted by AK in Roger Clark, "The Fall and Rise of André Kertész," *The British Journal of Photography* 132, no. 6401 (April 1985): 360; Avis Berman, "The 'Little Happenings' of André Kertész," *ARTnews* 83, no. 3 (March 1984): 70.

17. AK, *Kertész on Kertész*, 58.

18. Berman, "The 'Little Happenings' of André Kertész": 70. My thanks to Brandy Kuhl and the Council on Botanical and Horticultural Libraries at the San Francisco Botanical Garden for identifying the flowers on Colette's table. This photograph appears at https://www.sfmoma.org/artwork/93.208/.

19. MPP, AK day planner, February 7, 1930, and letter from Jeanne Fernandez to AK, May 21, 1930.

20. MPP, letter from AK to Lajos Tihanyi, March 28, 1930. Americans had shown little interest in Tihanyi's paintings. The timing of his trip was lousy. After the US economy shattered, art buyers vanished. Then Tihanyi's love affair with an American ended badly. After seventeen months, he returned to Paris financially, creatively, and emotionally drained. He got by with help from his friends, André included. See Krisztina Passuth, *Tihanyi Lajos: A Bohème Painter in Budapest, Berlin and Paris* (Kogart, 2012), 142; Brassaï, *Letters to My Parents*, translated by Peter Laki and Barna Kantor (University of Chicago Press, 1997), 182–83.

21. See Sarah Greenough, Robert Gurbo, and Sarah Kennel, *André Kertész* (National Gallery of Art/Princeton University Press, 2005), image 60.

22. Gaston Chérau, "La chasse à la palombe," *Art et Médecine* (January 1931): 24–25; Sandra Sammataro Phillips, "The Photographic Work of André Kertész in France, 1925–1936: A Critical Essay and Catalogue," PhD dissertation, City University of New York, 1985, 937.

23. Phillips, "The Photographic Work of André Kertész in France, 1925–1936," 494n43. That September, André's day planner lists what appear to be the addresses of Parisian friends' families in Hungary; its October and November pages are virtually blank.

24. Ibid., 494n43; David Travis, interview by author, January 9, 2016.

25. Hervé Guibert, "Les tendres malices d'André Kertész," *Le Monde*, October 1, 1985.

26. GRI, ad for Madame Paulin, February 1930.

27. Erzsébet's cousin, also named Erzsébet Salamon, married the Polish-born painter Eugène Chichoff in Paris in 1927. She was the daughter of the aunt and uncle of André's Erzsébet, Laura Goldberger and Samuel Salamon. Actes d'état civil, Marriages, 15th arrondissement, July 12, 1927, Archives de Paris.

28. Nicolas Ducrot, interview by author, August 8, 2014. Ducrot heard this story from Erzsébet.

29. Jean and Renée Nicolas and Pascal Lemaître, *La Savoie d'André Kertész* (La Fontaine de Siloé, 2004), 34.

30. Pierre Assouline, *Simenon: A Biography*, translated Jon Rothschild (Alfred A. Knopf, 1997), 103.

31. AK quoted in Colin Ford, *André Kertész: An Exhibition of Photographs from the Centre Georges Pompidou* (Arts Council of Great Britain, 1979), 10.

32. Lisette Model, interview by Jim McQuaid and David Tait, New York, 1977, International Museum of Photography at the George Eastman House, New York, available at https://archives.eastman.org/repositories/5/archival_objects /12295.

33. Rózsi met the Austrian-born musician-turned-painter Lisette Seybert in 1934. Seybert asked her how to use a Rolleiflex that she had borrowed. Rózsi had never used a Rolleiflex, but together they figured it out. Rózsi's instruction proved to be the sum of Seybert's training in photography. In 1937, Lisette would marry André's old friend Evsa Model and take the name Lisette Model. As Lisette Model, she was known for her unflinching close-ups of people on the street, spotlighting human foibles and flaws.

34. Jean Lattès, "Rogi André ou la vraie lumière du Bon Dieu," *Techniques Graphiques* 60 (October 1965): 389.

35. Andra Samelson, unpublished manuscript.

36. Phillips, "The Photographic Work of André Kertész in France, 1925–1936": 494n43.

37. GRI, Part III: Sixty Years of Photography, 57.

38. Eugen Weber, *The Hollow Years: France in the 1930s* (W. W. Norton, 1994), 116.

39. Albert Flament, "André Derain" in *La Revue de Paris*, c. 1931, in Romy Golan, "The 'École Française' vs. the 'Ecole de Paris': The Debate About the Status of Jewish Artists in Paris Between the Wars," in Kenneth E. Silver and Romy Golan, *The Circle of Montparnasse: Jewish Artists in Paris: 1905–1945* (Universe Books, 1985), 86.

40. Ibid., 82.

41. György Németh, emails to author, May 26, 2024, based on his communications with Báthory's step-grandson, András Szilágyi.

42. Brassaï, *Letters to My Parents*, translated by Peter Laki and Barna Kantor (University of Chicago Press, 1997), 202.

43. Document DU5 6629 (1932), Répertoire de Jugements Civils, Archives de Paris.

44. Samuel Stoljar, "A History of the French Law of Divorce–II," *International Journal of Law and the Family* 4 (1990): 4.

45. Ibid., 3 and 6. See also Lindell T. Bates, "The Divorce of Americans in France," *Law and Contemporary Problems* 322 (1935): 327.

46. DU5 6634 (1933), Répertoire de Jugements Civils, Archives de Paris. Records for 1934, 1935, and 1936 do not show that the case was reopened.

47. MPP, letter from Max Winterstein to AK, n.d. [1933].

48. Bates, "The Divorce of Americans in France": 327, http://scholarship.law.duke.edu/cgi/viewcontent.cgi?article=1760&context=lcp.

49. Neil Baldwin, *Man Ray, American Artist* (Da Capo, 2000), 107. The art dealer Csaba Mórocz offers an alternate explanation of Rogi's portmanteau name. He suggests that Rogi and André used that name to sign photographs they took together. If so, those signed photographs have disappeared.

50. Jean Lattès, "Rogi André ou la vraie lumière du Bon Dieu," *Techniques Graphiques* 60 (October 1965): 389.

51. László Beke, "The Hungarian Period (1894–1925): A Photographer from Birth" in Pierre Borhan, *André Kertész: His Life and Work* (Bulfinch Press Book/Little, Brown: 1994), 40.

52. "Six Exceptional Women — A Portfolio by Kertesz," *Harper's Bazaar* (June 1965): 67.

53. Ibid., 66–71.

54. Patrick Mahony, *Maurice Maeterlinck: Mystic and Dramatist* (Institute for the Study of Man, 1984), 111.

## CHAPTER SEVEN

1. Françoise Denoyelle, *La lumière de Paris: Les usages de la photographie, 1919–1939, vol. II* (Harmattan, 1997), 136–37.

2. AK, interview by László Lugosi Lugo, January 13, 1981, in Károly Kincses,

*Measure: The History of Hungarian Photography* 43 (Association of Hungarian Photographers, 2006): 93–94.

3. AK quoted in Avis Berman, "The 'Little Happenings' of André Kertész," *ARTnews* 83, no. 3 (March 1984): 70.

4. Brassaï, "Technique de la photographie de nuit," *Arts et Métiers Graphiques* 33 (January 15, 1933): 24–27.

5. Anne Wilkes Tucker, *Brassaï: The Eye of Paris* (Museum of Fine Arts, 1999), 150.

6. AK interview by Lugo, January 13, 1981, in Kincses, *Measure*, 94.

7. Jain Kelly, *Nude: Theory* (Lustrum, 1979), 117–18.

8. AK quoted in Agathe Gaillard, *André Kertész* (Pierre Belfond, 1980), 35–36.

9. MPP, letter from IK to AK, February 15, 1927. See also Kelly, *Nude*, 120.

10. Jain Kelly, *Nude: Theory* (Lustrum, 1979), 118.

11. AK quoted by Teri Wehn-Damisch, interview by author, August 14, 2014.

12. Pierre Borhan, "The Double of a Life" in Pierre Borhan, *André Kertész: His Life and Work* (Bulfinch Press Book/Little, Brown: 1994), 18; Todd Gustavson, email to author, November 6, 2017.

13. Kelly, *Nude*, 118; Ugrin, "André Kertész: Brother Seeing Eye," 62. André was not the first photographer to do distortions. In 1888, Louis Ducos du Hauron used special lenses to create a series of twisted self-portraits.

14. See AK, "Caricatures and Distortions," in *The Encyclopedia of Photography, Volume Three*, edited by Willard D. Morgan. (Greystone, 1963), 568–76.

15. Although negative number 200 exists, there are gaps in the numbering.

16. AK, *Kertész on Kertész: A Self-Portrait* (Abbeville Press, 1985), 55.

17. AK quoted in Agathe Gaillard, *André Kertész* (Pierre Belfond, 1980), 39.

18. See Aymé-Paul Barancy, "Fenêtre ouverte sur l'au-delà," *Le Sourire* (March 2, 1933): n.p.

19. AK, "Caricatures and Distortions," 269.

20. Bertrand Guégan, "Kertész et son miroir," *Arts et Métiers Graphiques* (September 15, 1933): 25.

21. Renée Moutard-Uldry, "André Kertész: Le Groupe des Dix," *Beaux-Arts* (April 3, 1936): 44–45.

22. This photograph has been dated both 1933 and 1931, in which case it would mark Elizabeth's arrival in Paris.

23. GRI, Part III: Sixty Years of Photography, Béla Ugrin, "Dialogues with

Kertész," edited by Manuela Caravageli Ugrin, transcript of taped conversations between AK and Béla Ugrin, 1978–1985, 3.

24. MPP, letter from Max Winterstein to AK, n.d.

25. René Morel, "The French Law of Bigamy," translated by Francis Norris, *Journal of Comparative Legislation and International Law* 3, no. 1 (1921): 92, 95–96, https:// www.jstor.org/stable/753055.

26. Sandra Sammataro Phillips, "The Photographic Work of André Kertész in France, 1925–1936: A Critical Essay and Catalogue," PhD dissertation, City University of New York, 1985, 476.

27. MPP, letter from AK to JK, June 28, 1933.

28. "Nus maudits," *Photo* (March 1972): 60–67, cited in Anne de Mondenard, *L'odyssée d'une icône: Trois photographies d'André Kertész* (Actes Sud/Maison Européenne de la Photographie, 2006), 53.

29. MPP, AK's contract with Plon/Éditions d'histoire et d'art, and letter from René Wittmann to AK, January 19, 1937.

30. Eugen Weber, *The Hollow Years: France in the 1930s* (W. W. Norton, 1994): 212 and 36.

31. See AK, *Soixante photographies d'enfants*, text by Jaboune (Plon/Éditions d'histoire et d'art, 1933). The writer, Jean Nohain, went by the name Jaboune.

32. Ibid., n.p.

33. Paul Ignotus, "Radical Writers in Hungary," *Journal of Contemporary History* 1, no. 2 (1966): 159. Five hundred copies of *Az Igazi Ady* were sold by subscription, mostly to Hungarians living abroad. The political situation precluded its open distribution in Hungary until 1947. The book's printers, two Hungarians working in France, were shot during World War II for printing tracts for the Resistance. See MPP, letter from Csaba Mórocz to Pierre Bonhomme, April 9, 1999.

34. Robert Solyom, interview by author, July 31, 2014.

35. Endre Ady, "The Ghost Got into Paris," in *The Poems of Endre Ady*, translated by Anton N. Nyerges (Hungarian Cultural Foundation, 1969), 31. The poem is also known as "Autumn Passed Through Paris."

36. Renee Winegarten, "Who Was Paul Morand?," *The New Criterion* 6, no. 3 (November 1987): 73.

37. AK quoted in Berman, "The 'Little Happenings' of André Kertész," 69.

38. This image is found at https://www.metmuseum.org/art/collection/search/265597.

39. Maria Giovanna Eisner, "Citizen Kertesz," *Minicam* 7 (June 1944): 28–29.

40. Herbert R. Lottman, *The Left Bank: Writers, Artists, and Politics from the Popular Front to the Cold War* (Houghton Mifflin, 1982), 8.

41. Hervé Le Goff, *Pierre Gassmann: La photographie à l'épreuve* (Éditions France Delory, 2000), 38.

42. Richard Whelan, *Robert Capa: A Biography* (Alfred A. Knopf, 1985), 62. See also GRI, Hiroji Kubota, "André Kertész/Personality and His Photography," translated by Misuzu Rukunaga, unpublished typescript, c. 1975.

43. Cornell Capa, "André: A Personal Reminiscence," in Susan Harder, ed., with Hiroji Kubota, *André Kertész, Diary of Light, 1912–1985* (Aperture Foundation, 1987), 8.

44. Letter from Robert Capa to Julia Berkovits Friedman, September 30, 1935, quoted in Éva Fisli, "Egy kapcsolat verzójára: André Kertész és Robert Capa" "(On the verso of a relationship: André Kertész and Robert Capa)," *Fotóművészet* 56, no. 3 (2013): 86. My thanks to Csaba Mórocz for giving me this article and to Maryll Telegdy for her translation.

45. *Parisi Futár*, March 15, 1934.

46. Simon Dell, *The Image of the Popular Front: The Masses and the Media in Interwar France* (Palgrave Macmillan, 2007), 37.

47. Carlo Rim, "Grandeur et servitude du reporter photographe," *Marianne: Grand Hebdomadaire Littéraire Illustré* (February 21, 1934): 8.

48. MPP, letter from Florent Fels to AK, November 9, 1934. See also Florent Fels, "Pour être parfait, un reporter doit être à la fois poète et photographe," *Presse-Publicité* (December 7, 1938): 3.

49. Jean Vidal, "En photographiant les photographes: Kertész," *L'Intransigeant* (April 1, 1930).

50. Pierre Mac Orlan, "L'art littéraire d'imagination et la photographie," *Les Nouvelles Littéraires* (September 22, 1928): 1.

51. Pierre Mac Orlan, "Preface" and captions in *Paris vu par André Kertész* (Plon/Éditions d'histoire et d'art, 1934), n.p.

52. MPP, letter from Marcel Natkin to AK, November 13, 1934.

53. Françoise Denoyelle, François Cuel, and Jean-Louis Vibert-Guigne, *Le Front Populaire des photographes* (Éditions Terre bleue, 2006), 39n4.

54. AK quoted in Phillips, "The Photographic Work of André Kertész in France," 464; MPP, Wick Miller, André Kertész information sheet, c. 1940.

55. Dodie Kazanjian and Calvin Tomkins, *Alex: The Life of Alexander Liberman* (Alfred A. Knopf, 1993), 53.

56. MPP, AK day planner, 1935.

57. John G. Morris, "A Gentle Vision: Photographs by André Kertész," *Quest* 1, no. 2 (January–February 1978): 51.

58. Charles Harbutt in André Kertész et al., *The Manchester Collection* (Manchester Collection, 1984), 159.

59. MPP, letter from AK to Monsieur le Caissier Principal, Banque de France, October 6, 1936.

60. Ibid., letter from AK to JK and OK, August 30, 1935.

61. Brassaï, *Letters to My Parents*, translated by Peter Laki and Barna Kantor (University of Chicago Press, 1997), 215. Brassaï's letter is dated December 5, 1935.

62. Richard Whelan, *Robert Capa: A Biography* (Alfred A. Knopf, 1985), 74.

63. Russell Miller, *Magnum: Fifty Years at the Front Line of History* (Grove Press, 1988), 26. Capa's photographs appeared in the July 8, 1936, issue of *Vu*.

64. Burt Glinn quoted in "The Concerned Capa," *American Photographer* 19, no. 6 (December 1987): 59.

65. Whelan, *Capa*, 126.

66. Eugène Dabit, "Paris, par André Kertész," *La Nouvelle Revue Française* (March 1, 1935): 474–75.

67. MPP, letter from IK to AK, April 17, 1936.

68. Ibid., letter from AK to Monsieur le Caissier Principal, Banque de France, October 6, 1936.

69. Ibid., letter from H. W. Sierichs to AK, September 4, 1936; Weston Naef, "André Kertész: The Making of an American Photographer," in Sandra S. Phillips, David Travis, and Weston J. Naef, *André Kertész: Of Paris and New York* (Thames and Hudson, 1985), 93.

70. "Incomes of Families and Single Persons, 1935–36," *Monthly Labor Review* 47, no. 4 (October 1938): 729, https://www.jstor.org/stable/41816377.

71. Sarah Greenough, Robert Gurbo, and Sarah Kennel, *André Kertész* (National Gallery of Art/Princeton University Press, 2005), 275n146; MPP, letter from GK and IK to AK, July 13, 1936, and letter from IK to AK, September 1, 1936.

72. Phillips, "The Photographic Work of André Kertész in France," 174.

73. MPP, letter from AK to Mme. Auguste Lambiotte, August 15, 1936; Paul

Hill and Thomas Cooper, eds., *Dialogue with Photography: Interviews by Paul Hill and Thomas Cooper* (Farrar, Straus and Giroux, 1979), 46.

74. AK quoted in Barbaralee Diamonstein, "André Kertész," in *Visions and Images: American Photographers on Photography* (Rizzoli, 1981), 86.

75. MPP, letter from Erney Prince to AK, August 1, 1936.

76. Ibid., August 20, 1936.

77. Eugène Dabit, quoted in Herbert R. Lottman, *The Left Bank: Writers, Artists, and Politics from the Popular Front to the Cold War* (Houghton Mifflin, 1982), 112.

78. Alan Sheridan, *André Gide: A Life in the Present* (Harvard University Press, 1999), 503.

79. MPP, AK note to Lucien Vogel to accompany his signed copy of *Soixante photographies d'enfants*, c. 1933. For Vogel's ousting, see Gisèle Freund, *Photographie et Société* (Éditions du Seuil, 1974), 122.

80. Phillips, "The Photographic Work of André Kertész in France," 1400; Greenough, Gurbo, and Kennel, *André Kertész*, 274n120.

81. AK, *Kertész on Kertész*, 46.

82. Hill and Cooper, eds., *Dialogue with Photography*, 46; Phillips, "The Photographic Work of André Kertész in France," 1296; Pascal Ory, email to author, November 4, 2017.

83. AK quoted in Robert Hayes, "Andre Kertesz," *Interview* 13, no. 4 (April 1983): 63.

84. MPP, "Diplomats Among Many Notables Returning Today on *Washington*," *New York Herald Tribune*, October 8, 1936.

## CHAPTER EIGHT

1. AK quoted in Ben Lifson, "Kertész at Eighty-Five," *Portfolio* (June/July 1979): 61.

2. This self-portrait appears in Sarah Greenough, Robert Gurbo, and Sarah Kennel, *André Kertész* (National Gallery of Art/Princeton University Press, 2005), image 75.

3. See Bruce Downes, "Photography of the Nude," *Popular Photography* (February 1947): 48. The conviction was overturned by the New York Court of Appeals, which affirmed photographers' right to photograph nudes.

4. Carol Brower, "The Handling, Presentation, and Conservation Matting of Photographs," in Henry Wilhelm with Carol Brower, *The Permanence and Care of*

*Color Photographs: Traditional and Digital Color Prints, Color Negatives, Slides, and Motion Pictures* (Preservation, 1993), 407, ebook.

5. AK, *Kertész on Kertész: A Self-Portrait* (Abbeville Press, 1985), 90.

6. AK quoted in Paul Hill and Thomas Cooper, "André Kertész," in *Dialogue with Photography* (Farrar, Straus and Giroux, 1979), 46–47.

7. AK quoted in Ben Lifson, "Kertész at Eighty-Five," *Portfolio* (June/July 1979): 61.

8. Ibid., 61.

9. AK quoted in Károly Kincses, "A Belated Interview with André Kertész," *The Hungarian Quarterly* 47, no. 181 (Spring 2006): 109.

10. Alexey Brodovitch quoted in Andy Grundberg, *Brodovitch* (Documents of American Design, 1989), 30.

11. "5:30: The Curtain Falls," *Harper's Bazaar* 70, no. 2694 (April 1937): 116.

12. "Peas in a Pod: The Children of Mr. and Mrs. Nicholas Ludington of Ardmore," *Harper's Bazaar* 70, no. 2698 (August 1937): 60–63.

13. Theodore Peterson, *Magazines in the Twentieth Century* (University of Illinois Press, 1964), 59, 62.

14. Donald Albrecht, "Scene and Be Seen," in Donald Albrecht, ed., *Cecil Beaton: The New York Years* (Museum of the City of New York/Skira Rizzoli, 2011), 18.

15. Nineteen months later, André was paging through the October 25, 1938, issue of *Look* when he spotted seven pictures of firefighters in training that he'd taken for Keystone (the *only* reportage, he claimed, that he did for the agency). *Look* credited the pictures to Erney Prince. André flew into a rage. Yet a perusal of *Look* in that era reveals that the magazine typically credited photo agencies (or gave no credit at all). The legal wrangling between André and Keystone would drag on until mid-1939 when Keystone dropped its suit. See MPP, letter from Alexander Lindey to AK, August 11, 1939.

16. *Arm and Ventilator* can be seen at https://www.getty.edu/art/collection/object/104EKF.

17. GRI, AK quoted in Part III: Sixty Years of Photography, Béla Ugrin, "Dialogues with Kertész," edited by Manuela Caravageli Ugrin, transcript of taped conversations between AK and Béla Ugrin, 1978–1985, 99.

18. For *Lost Cloud*, see https://www.moma.org/collection/works/50509.

19. *Poughkeepsie, New York* appears at https://www.metmuseum.org/art/collection/search/265553.

20. Cornell Capa, "André: A Personal Reminiscence," in Susan Harder, ed., with Hiroji Kubota, *André Kertész: Diary of Light 1912–1985* (Aperture, 1985), 8.

21. Richard Whelan, *Robert Capa* (Alfred A. Knopf, 1985), 128.

22. MPP, AK's bank statements from the National City Bank of New York, and letter from Alexander Lindey to AK, October 9, 1937.

23. Gray Strider, "Kertesz—Camera Surrealist," *Popular Photography* 2, no. 3 (March 1938): 42.

24. Alene Talmey quoted in Carol Schwalberg, "André Kertész: Unsung Pioneer," *U.S. Camera* 26, no. 1 (January 1963): 76.

25. Arnold Gingrich, *Nothing But People: The Early Days at Esquire* (Crown, 1971), 115.

26. Arnold Gingrich, "Program Notes on a Few of the Photograph Pages in This Issue," *Coronet* 2, no. 4 (August 1937): 55.

27. AK quoted in Barbaralee Diamonstein, "André Kertész," in *Visions and Images: American Photographers on Photography* (Rizzoli, 1981), 82.

28. AK quoted in Gray Strider, "Kertesz—Camera Surrealist," *Popular Photography* 2, no. 3 (March 1938): 42.

29. David Travis, "Kertész and His Contemporaries in Germany and France," in Sandra S. Phillips, David Travis, and Weston J. Naef, *André Kertész: Of Paris and New York* (Thames and Hudson, 1985), 91n72; Maria Giovanna Eisner, "Citizen Kertesz," *Minicam* 7 (June 1944): 33.

30. Gray Strider, "Kertesz—Camera Surrealist," *Popular Photography* 2, no. 3 (March 1938): 42.

31. Edward Alden Jewell, "Fantasy in Perspective: The Museum of Modern Art Opens Show of Dada and Surrealism, Old and New," *The New York Times*, December 13, 1936; "Fantastic Zanies of Painter's Brush," *The Literary Digest* (December 12, 1936): 26, http://www.oldmagazinearticles.com/article-summary/dada_exhibit_museum_of_modern_art#.YosX7C1h3NA.

32. AK quoted in Strider, "Kertesz—Camera Surrealist," 42.

33. "Links Surrealism and Ads," *The New York Times*, January 23, 1937.

34. "*Vogue*'s-Eye View of Holiday Time," *Vogue* 91, no. 10 (May 15, 1938): 53. *Vogue* later published four Daliesque distortions of unidentifiable objects by André. They illustrate a minor feature about the sensible shoes *Vogue*'s readers should purchase for their excursions to the 1939 New York World's Fair. André was attempting to convey the foot aches of one who tramps the fairgrounds in the

wrong shoes. See "Fair Views Depend on Your Feet," *Vogue* 93, no. 9 (May 1, 1939): 130–31. Taking advantage of an assignment to photograph scenes from *The Cradle Will Rock*, a play directed by Orson Welles, André also did a distorted-mirror portrait of Welles. Shots of the scenes appeared in the magazine; the distorted portrait did not.

**35.** K.G.S., "European Photography on View," *The New York Times*, February 25, 1932.

**36.** Ansel Adams to William Zorach, November 20, 1933, quoted in Nancy Newhall, *Ansel Adams: The Eloquent Light* (Aperture, 1980), 96.

**37.** Ansel Adams, unpublished article for the *Fortnightly* dated May 17, 1932, CCP/Ansel Adams Archive, cited in Erin Kathleen O'Toole, "No Democracy in Quality: Ansel Adams, Beaumont and Nancy Newhall, and the Founding of the Department of Photographs at the Museum of Modern Art," PhD dissertation, University of Arizona, 2010, 145.

**38.** John Raeburn, *A Staggering Revolution: A Cultural History of Thirties Photography* (University of Illinois Press, 2006), 96–97.

**39.** M. F. Agha, "Preface," in T. J. Maloney, ed., *U.S. Camera 1935* (William Morrow, 1935): 3, 4.

**40.** Ansel Adams, "Introduction," in T. J. Maloney, ed., *A Pageant of Photography* (S. F. Bay Exposition Company, 1940), 5.

**41.** MPP, letter from IK to AK, December 14, 1933.

**42.** Foster Tochukwu Orji, "The Influence of Psychological Factors in Meniere's Disease," *Annals of Medical and Health Science Research* 4, no. 1: 3–7: doi: 10.4103/2141-9248.

**43.** Janis Bultman, "André Kertész (1894–1985): An Up and Down Life," in *Legacies: Interviews with Masters of Photography from Darkroom Photography Magazine* (Quercus Agrifolia Press, 2018), 69.

**44.** MPP, letter from IK to AK, June 4, 1939.

**45.** Ibid., Wick Miller, AK information sheets.

**46.** Ibid., letter from IK and GK to AK and EK, April 21, 1938. On April 24, 1939, Imre reported to André and Elizabeth that he'd lost his case.

**47.** Letter from Cornell Capa to Robert Capa, October 3, 1938, Cornell Capa Archive, International Center of Photography.

**48.** MPP, letter from IK and GK to AK and EK, September 19, 1938.

**49.** Ibid., letter from IK and GK to AK and EK, April 21, 1938.

**50.** Agathe Gaillard, *André Kertész* (Pierre Belfond, 1980), 70–71.

**51.** Charles Payne, *American Ballet Theatre* (Alfred A. Knopf, 1979), 370. *Ballet* appears in Greenough, Gurbo, and Kennel, *André Kertész*, image 84.

**52.** GRI, AK quoted in Part III: Sixty Years of Photography, Béla Ugrin, "Dialogues with Kertész," edited by Manuela Caravageli Ugrin, transcript of taped conversations between AK and Béla Ugrin, 1978–1985, 103.

**53.** AK, *Kertész on Kertész* , 94.

**54.** MPP, Wick Miller, AK information sheets.

**55.** AK, *Kertész on Kertész*, 90.

**56.** Robyn Thom, Polina Teslyar, and Rohn Friedman, "Pseudologia Fantastica in the Emergency Department: A Case Report and Review of the Literature," *Case Reports in Psychiatry*, published online May 10, 2017, doi: 10.1155/2017/8961256.

**57.** Samantha D'Acunto and Anita Finkle-Guerrero, New York Botanical Garden, email to author, March 24, 2018.

**58.** Jacob Deschin, "Drooping Tulip Heralds New Business," *Popular Photography* 24, no. 2 (August 1970): 32.

**59.** Alexander King, "Are Editors Vandals?," *Minicam* (April 1939): 28.

**60.** MMP, Wick Miller, AK information sheet. For Morgan's tenure at *Life*, see Jennifer Steensma, "Willard Morgan at LIFE," in Jennifer Steensma, "The Willard D. Morgan Archive," MFA thesis, Rochester Institute of Technology, 1992, https://scholarworks.rit.edu/theses/5391/.

**61.** Letter from Mrs. Brokaw [Clare Boothe] to Condé Nast, May 9, 1931, LIFE 1935 & Before Time-Life Archive, New York Historical Society.

**62.** Ibid., letter from Natasha von Hoershelman to *Vu*, May 1, 1934.

**63.** Henry Luce, cable to the family of Lucien Vogel, 1954. Vogel had just died. See Gisèle Freund, *Photographie et Société* (Éditions du Seuil, 1974), 123.

**64.** AK quoted in Denes Devenyi, "Kertesz: Denes Devenyi Interviews the 'Father of 35mm Vision,'" *Photo Life* (January 1978): 12.

**65.** See Wilson Hicks, *Words and Pictures: An Introduction to Photojournalism* (Harper and Brothers, 1952), 47–52, and John G. Morris, *Get the Picture: A Personal History of Photojournalism* (Random House, 1998), 22.

**66.** Some of these photographs appear at https://loeildelaphotographie.com/en/andre-kertesz-tugboat-stories/.

**67.** Weston Naef, "André Kertész: The Making of an American Photographer," in Phillips, Travis, and Naef, *André Kertész*, 103.

**68.** Not until 1969 did *Life* publish two of AK's photographs in its Gallery section. See "André Kertész in Washington Square," *Life* 67, no. 20 (November 14, 1969): 2.

**69.** E. B. White, *Here Is New York* (The Little Bookroom, 1999), 19.

**70.** Hicks, *Words and Pictures*, 14–15, 47–52, 85.

**71.** Morris, *Get the Picture*, 37.

**72.** AK quoted in Bultman, "André Kertész (1894–1985): An Up and Down Life," 68.

**73.** Morris, *Get the Picture*, 36.

**74.** AK quoted in Naef, "André Kertész: The Making of an American Photographer," 104.

**75.** For AK's self-portrait, see Sarah Greenough, Robert Gurbo, and Sarah Kennel, *André Kertész* (National Gallery of Art/Princeton University Press, 2005), 155. The museum dates this work 1940.

**76.** Morris, *Get the Picture*, 36.

**77.** William A. H. Birnie, "Cleveland Takes the Stage," *The American Magazine* 130, no. 8 (August 1940): 117–24.

**78.** MPP, "Cleveland – Playhouse Job for American Magazine," memo.

**79.** "*Vogue*'s Eye-View of Photography," *Vogue* (June 15, 1941): 17.

**80.** Martin Munkácsi quoted in Susan Morgan, "Creating the Impromptu Attitude," in *Martin Munkácsi* (Aperture, 1992), 50.

**81.** Merwin Dembling, "Art in the Kitchen: Dime Store Models," *Modern Minicam Photography* 12 (November 1948): 26.

**82.** MPP, letter from Mathias F. Correa to AK, January 20, 1942.

**83.** "Regulations Concerning Travel and Other Conduct of Aliens of Enemy Nationalities," Francis Biddle, United States Department of Justice, Washington, DC, February 5, 1942, https://dp.la/item/a516f7e1b356b5163f3a8a3f16455f96. See also "Biddle Exempts 2 Alien Classes," *The New York Times*, February 10, 1942: 21; "A Plan for Loyal Aliens," *The New York Times*, April 6, 1942: 14; and "Wartime Regulations for the Photographer compiled by the editors of *Popular Photography*," September 1942, in Harvey V. Fondiller, *The Best of Popular Photography* (Ziff-Davis, 1979), 9.

**84.** AK quoted in Károly Kincses, "A Belated Interview with André Kertész," *The Hungarian Quarterly* 47, no. 181 (Spring 2006): 108–9.

**85.** AK quoted in Bultman, "André Kertész (1894–1985): An Up and Down Life," 68.

**86.** Agathe Gaillard, *André Kertész* (Pierre Belfond, 1980), 70.

**87.** André would have anticipated a change in his status when his friend Willard Morgan took a position as MoMA's director of photography in 1943. Widening the department's view of photography, Morgan organized *The American Snapshot: An Exhibition of the Folk Art of the Camera*. But his tenure at MoMA was brief. By the time the exhibition opened, Morgan had moved on.

**88.** Alfred Barr quoted in Erin Kathleen O'Toole, "No Democracy in Quality: Ansel Adams, Beaumont and Nancy Newhall, and the Founding of the Department of Photographs at the Museum of Modern Art," PhD dissertation, University of Arizona, 2010, 179. O'Toole cites page 115 of Nancy Newhall's unfinished manuscript of *Ansel Adams: The Enduring Moment*, Nancy Newhall Collection, Center for Creative Photography, University of Arizona, Tucson.

**89.** GRI, Nancy Newhall memo to Beaumont Newhall, August 27, 1942; Beaumont Newhall memo to Nancy Newhall, August 31, 1942; Beaumont and Nancy Newhall Papers.

**90.** Edna Chase quoted in Caroline Seebohm, *The Man Who Was Vogue: The Life and Times of Condé Nast* (Viking, 1982), 171. See also Dodie Kazanjian and Calvin Tomkins, *Alex: The Life of Alexander Liberman* (Alfred A. Knopf, 1993), 124–25.

**91.** MPP, letter from Ken McCormick to AK, February 27, 1942; letter from William Harlowe Briggs to AK, March 23, 1942.

**92.** Ibid., telephone company notice to R. D. Statile, November 26, 1943.

**93.** The lab's co-owner, a darkroom wizard named Leo Cohn, developed André's films himself, using deep tanks (instead of the usual reels) and inspection (instead of standard times). Leco's printers were instructed to confer with exacting clients like André after their proofs emerged from the developing trays. See Etna M. Kelly, "Photofinishing Plus," *Popular Photography* (February 1947): 84–85 and 192–94.

**94.** John Adam Knight, "Photography," *New York Post*, December 31, 1942.

**95.** MPP, letter from AK to JK and OK, August 30, 1936.

**96.** Ibid., letter from JK to AK and EK, November 21, 1936.

**97.** Ibid., letter from JK to AK and EK, January 12, 1943.

## CHAPTER NINE

**1.** "Rubber on the Rebound," *Fortune* 30, no. 1 (July 1944): 134–41, 188, 190, 192, 194, 197–98. André probably met Peter Piening, *Fortune*'s art director, when Piening worked for Condé Nast in Paris in the early 1930s.

2. “Beauty Bazaar,” *Harper’s Bazaar* 96, no. 3021 (August 1963): 151.

3. AK quoted in Janice Bultman, “André Kertész (1894–1985): An Up and Down Life,” in *Legacies: Interviews with Masters of Photography from Darkroom Photography Magazine* (Quercus Agrifolia Press, 2018), 69.

4. GRI, AK quoted in Maria Martinez Bell, “On André Kertész, 1894–1985,” in *Santa Fe Center for Photography Newsletter* 4, no. 3 (November 1985): n.p.

5. This photograph can be seen at https://www.metmuseum.org/art/collection/search/264072.

6. André dated the picture October 13, 1944, but he must have been off by a day. The weather was clear on the 13th. On the 14th, it rained off and on all morning. *Homing Ship* appears in Sarah Greenough, Robert Gurbo, and Sarah Kennel, *André Kertész* (National Gallery of Art/Princeton University Press, 2005), image 83.

7. Annette Kuhn, *Family Secrets: Acts of Memory and Imagination* (Verso, 1995), 1.

8. GRI, AK quoted in Part III: Sixty Years of Photography, Béla Ugrin, “Dialogues with Kertész,” edited by Manuela Caravageli Ugrin, transcript of taped conversations between AK and Béla Ugrin, 1978–1985, 106.

9. AK quoted in Avis Berman, “The ‘Little Happenings’ of André Kertész,” *ARTnews* 83, no, 3 (March 1984): 72. It’s possible that André’s friend Manuel Komroff suggested the title *Homing Ship*, which brings to mind the last sentence of the first episode of James Joyce’s *Ulysses*: “Moving through the air high spars of a three-master, her sails braided up on the crosstrees, homing, upstream, silently moving, a silent ship.” James Joyce, *Ulysses* (Random House, 1946), 51. Komroff corresponded with Joyce when both lived in Paris in the 1920s. In 1927, Komroff was among those who signed a letter of protest against the unauthorized and unpaid publication of *Ulysses* in a US magazine.

10. MPP, letter from A. M. Mathieu to AK, April 11, 1944.

11. Because László Moholy-Nagy’s business records were later destroyed, the extent of his involvement in *Minicam*’s editorial decisions is unknown. Email from Hattula Moholy-Nagy to author, June 8, 2018. All the same, Moholy-Nagy was aware of André’s situation. A few months earlier, he had invited André to teach at the School of Design (now the IIT Institute of Design), the school he founded after his flight from the Nazis ended in Chicago. But André could not picture himself in an academic setting and declined. MPP, letter from László Moholy-Nagy to AK, June 8, 1944.

12. Daniel T. Brigham, "Inquiry Confirms Nazi Death Camps: 1,715,000 Jews Said to Have Been Put to Death by the Germans Up to April 15," *The New York Times*, July 3, 1944.

13. M. F. Agha, "Horseless Photography: Photography 1839–1944," *Harper's Bazaar* 78, no. 2795 (November 1944): 67–71, 112, 114–17, 119–20.

14. MPP, letter from A. M. Mathieu to AK, January 18, 1945.

15. "Üzenetek Magyarországról," (Messages from Hungary), *Magyar Jövő*, October 27, 1945.

16. Kati Marton, *The Great Escape: Nine Jews Who Fled Hitler and Changed the World* (Simon & Schuster, 2006), 212; MPP, letter from IK and GK to AK and EK, January 31, 1946.

17. My thanks to György Németh for his research about the fate of André's and Elizabeth's relatives during the Holocaust.

18. "Obituary of André Kertész," *The Times*, September 30, 1985.

19. Lee Miller, "Paris is free . . . cables its joy . . . New York cheers," *Vogue* 104, no. 6 (October 1, 1944): 148–49.

20. AK, *Kertész on Kertész: A Self-Portrait* (Abbeville Press, 1985), 90.

21. Robert Gurbo, "The Circle of Confusion, 1936–1961," in Sarah Greenough, Robert Gurbo, and Sarah Kennel, *André Kertész* (National Gallery of Art/ Princeton University Press, 2005), 277n83.

22. André said more than once that almost all of his French photographs were lost to him after he moved to New York. But he did have the 35 millimeter negatives used for most of the *Day of Paris* images. As for the images from glass-plate negatives, copy prints could have been made from extant prints.

23. Elliot Paul, "A Mood from the Dim Past," *Saturday Review* (May 19, 1945): 10.

24. *The Christian-Science Monitor* (August 25, 1945); *Sunday Call-Chronicle*, October 7–13, 1945; Bruce Downes, "André Kertész: Day of Paris," *Popular Photography* 16, no. 6 (June 1945): 103. A critic for the *Twin City Sentinel* in Winston-Salem, North Carolina, touted "an introduction to Paris at its best . . . and modern photography at its best." (Annie Lee, June 10, 1945) "A wonderful book!" rhapsodized Cleveland's *Plain-Dealer*. (June 10, 1945).

25. Carl O. Schniewind quoted by David Travis, interview by author, January 9, 2016.

26. MPP, letter from Carl O. Schniewind to AK, March 4, 1946.

27. Ibid., July 24, 1946.

**28.** Ibid., Eleanor Jewett, "Art Institute Has Show of Masterpieces," *Chicago Tribune*, June 30, 1946.

**29.** AK quoted in Ugrin, "Kertész's Photography in Full Bloom," *The Houston Post*, January 2, 1983.

**30.** MPP, letter from Katharine Kuh to AK, May 8, 1946.

**31.** Peter Galassi, *Robert Frank in America* (Steidl, 2014), 19, 38n14; Richard Whelan, *Double Take: A Comparative Look at Photographs* (Clarkson N. Potter, 1981), 158–59; "Speaking of Pictures: A Photographer in Paris Finds Chairs Everywhere," *Life* (May 21, 1951): 26–28.

**32.** MPP, J. J. Augustin royalty statements.

**33.** *The New York Times Magazine*, October 9, 1955.

**34.** AK quoted in Avis Berman, "The 'Little Happenings' of André Kertész," *ARTnews* 83, no. 3 (March 1984): 72.

**35.** Ibid.

**36.** AK's friend and sometime editor Stefan Lorant, born in Budapest in 1901, also refused to label himself a Jew. See Michael Hallett, *Stefan Lorant: Godfather of Photojournalism* (Scarecrow Press, 2006), 106.

**37.** AK quoted by Teri Wehn-Damisch, interview by author, August 11, 2014.

**38.** Irving Penn, "Someone Is Always Watching You," *Vogue* 105, no. 5 (March 1, 1945): 136, 178, 181, 182; "Cecil Beaton's London House," *Vogue* 109, no. 2 (January 15, 1947), 110–11.

**39.** "Picasso and His Studio: Photographed by Brassai," *Harper's Bazaar* 80, no. 2810 (February 1946): 132–35.

**40.** "Child Life" in Shopping Bazaar, *Harper's Bazaar* 80, no. 2810 (February 1946): 112.

**41.** MPP, letter from AK to Priscilla Carden, March 25, 1946.

**42.** Ibid., note from AK to Jacob Deschin, n.d. The only real article André ever signed was a how-to piece about distorting-mirror photography for *The Complete Photographer* commissioned and probably ghostwritten by his friend Willard Morgan.

**43.** Manuel Komroff, "Circle of Confusion," unpublished handwritten document, Manuel Komroff Papers, 1897–1979, Rare Book and Manuscript Library, Columbia University Libraries, n.p.

**44.** EK quoted in Arthur Goldsmith, "The Kertész-Ugrin Tapes," *Popular Photography* 93, no. 1 (January 1986): 40.

**45.** Hunter Drohojowska-Philp, *Full Bloom: The Art and Life of Georgia O'Keeffe* (W. W. Norton, 2004), 413; Ann Thomas, *Lisette Model* (National Gallery of Canada, 1990), 62; Nina Barrett, telephone interview by author, March 29, 2022.

**46.** Julia Van Haaften, *Berenice Abbott: A Life in Photography* (W. W. Norton, 2018), 279–80.

**47.** Brendan Gill, "Outrageous Fortune – Memories of André Kertész," *Architectural Digest* 47 (September 1990): 36.

**48.** AK quoted in Agathe Gaillard, *André Kertész* (Pierre Belfond, 1980), 71.

**49.** Dodie Kazanjian and Calvin Tomkins, *Alex: The Life of Alexander Liberman* (Knopf, 1993), 115, 136.

**50.** Martha Scotford, *Cipe Pineles: A Life of Design* (W. W. Norton, 1999), 51, 54, 171.

**51.** AK quoted in teaser for "A New House That Looks Old," *House & Garden* 90, no. 5 (November 1946): 41.

**52.** Michael Augspurger, *An Economy of Abundant Beauty:* Fortune *Magazine and Depression America* (Cornell University Press, 2004), 6, 47.

**53.** Gaillard, *André Kertész*, 71.

**54.** Kazanjian and Tomkins, *Alex*, 138. Over the next fourteen years, André's work would appear in *Vogue* nearly one hundred times. Virtually all the photographs were of interiors, gardens, or art collections.

**55.** AK quoted in János Bodnár, "Talking to André Kertész," in János Bodnár, ed., *André Kertész: Magyarországon* (Főfoto, 1984), 93.

**56.** Kazanjian and Tomkins, *Alex*, 138.

**57.** AK quoted in Andy Grundberg, "At 90, André Kertész Remains a Poet of the Everyday," *The New York Times*, April 28, 1985.

**58.** Brooke Astor, *Footprints* (Doubleday, 1980), 216.

**59.** *House & Garden*'s editors launched the slogan "Live as well as you look" in 1948. See "On the Cover," *House & Garden* (October 1949): 131.

**60.** Astor, *Footprints*, 223.

**61.** Carol Schwalberg, "André Kertész: Unsung Pioneer," *U.S. Camera* 26, no. 1 (January 1963): 65.

**62.** Dorothy S. Gelatt, "André Kertész at 80 – How He Works – What He Feels," *Popular Photography* 75, no. 5 (November 1974): 171. See also MPP, letter from Pierre Guédenet to AK, August 19, 1948, and AK's Application for Priority Assistance, filed on October 2, 1944.

63. Alexander Liberman, *The Art and Technique of Color Photography* (Simon & Schuster, 1951), xi, 44.

64. Astor, *Footprints*, 219.

65. Jain Kelly, *Nude: Theory* (Lustrum, 1979), 117.

66. *Manhattan Bridge* has been dated both 1937 and 1947. By 1984, when the director Sergio Leone featured that same stretch of Washington Street in his mobster epic *Once Upon a Time in America*, the overpass had vanished. Today Washington Street is a favorite spot for selfies with the backdrop of the bridge.

67. This photograph appears in Sandra S. Phillips, David Travis, and Weston J. Naef, *André Kertész: Of Paris and New York* (Thames and Hudson, 1985), 242.

68. GRI, Part III: Sixty Years of Photography, in Béla Ugrin, "Dialogues with Kertész," edited by Manuela Caravageli Ugrin, transcript of taped conversations between AK and Béla Ugrin, 1978–1985, 102.

69. Louis Dienes, email to author, February 7, 2015.

70. MPP, letter from Patsy Swank to AK, May 16, 1949.

71. Ibid., letter from Marie Berger to AK, January 30, 1950. See "Gardens in Texas," *House & Garden* (February 1950): 94–96.

72. *Weather Vane and New York Skyline, September 19, 1952* can be found at https://www.nytimes.com/2019/03/28/lens/andre-kerteszs-photos-from-his-window.html.

73. Robert Gurbo, "The Circle of Confusion, 1936–1961," in Sarah Greenough, Robert Gurbo, and Sarah Kennel, *André Kertész* (National Gallery of Art/Princeton University Press, 2005), 161; Béla Ugrin, "André Kertész: Brother Seeing Eye," *Popular Photography* 93, no. 1 (January 1986), 98; AK, *Kertész on Kertész*, 111, 113; Ellen Odoner, interview by author, January 18, 2016.

74. Jeffrey Steinman, email to author, February 26, 2016; MPP, Agreement of Lease, August 12, 1952.

75. Michael Hallett, *Stefan Lorant: Godfather of Photojournalism* (Scarecrow Press, 2006), 113.

76. Milton Ellenbogen, interview with author, July 21, 2015. See also Franklin Riehlman, *Theodore Fried & André Kertész: An Enduring Friendship* (H. V. Allison Galleries, 1987).

77. MPP, letter from Meyer Levin to AK, February 16, 1953. André's friendship with the American writer, editor, and marionettist Meyer Levin dated to the 1920s, when Levin was a Paris-based reporter for the *Chicago Daily News*. He and André traveled together to gatherings of European marionettists.

**78.** This photograph is sometimes titled *Washington Square, January 9, 1954*. The date is incorrect. That Christmas and New Year's had been snowless. January 9, 1954, brought New York City's first dusting of snow, too slight to be measured. The next afternoon, the sky started dumping what turned out to be the biggest snowfall in years.

**79.** AK quoted in Lois Greenfield, *Changes* (April 1975), quoted in Pierre Borhan, "The Double of a Life," in Pierre Borhan, *André Kertész: His Life and Work* (Bulfinch Press Book/Little, Brown: 1994), 10.

**80.** Inge Bondi, telephone interview by author, May 9, 2020.

**81.** Letter from Robert Capa to AK, June 8, 1950, in Éva Fisli, "Egy kapcsolat verzójára: André Kertész és Robert Capa," *Fotóművészet* 56, no. 3 (2013): 88.

**82.** MPP, letter from Cornell Capa to AK and EK, n.d.

**83.** Cornell Capa, "André: A Personal Reminiscence," in Susan Harder, ed., with Hiroji Kubota, *André Kertész: Diary of Light 1912–1985* (Aperture, 1985), 8.

**84.** André and Elizabeth owned thirteen and a half acres of noncontiguous land. They had a $12,000 mortgage with the Newtown Savings Bank with a monthly payment of $80. See deeds of sale, Ernest and Gertrude Follows to André and Elizabeth Kertész, August 2, 1955, and André and Elizabeth Kertész to Mary V. Sanford, January 13, 1961; Daniel Cruson, interview by author, June 15, 2016.

**85.** This photograph is found in AK, *On Reading* (Grossman, 1971), 5.

**86.** Charles Friedman, "Going for a Walk: Many Scenic Trails Near New York Make for Pleasant Hiking," *The New York Times*, August 17, 1958. This photograph appears in J. Paul Getty Museum, *In Focus: André Kertész* (J. Paul Getty Museum, 1999), 95.

**87.** David Vestal, "André Kertész, 1894–1985," *Popular Photography* 92, no. 12 (December 1985): 80.

**88.** AK quoted in Brassaï, "My Friend Kertész," *Camera* 42, no. 4 (April 1963): 32.

**89.** Endre Ady, "Gare de l'Est" ("A Gare de l'Est-en"), in *Endre Ady: Poems*, translated by René Bonnerjea (Dr. Vajna & Bokor, 1941), 43–45.

**90.** Brassaï quoted in Agnès de Gouvion Saint-Cyr, *Brassaï in America, 1957* (Flammarion, 2011), 32.

**91.** AK quoted by Brassaï in Anne Wilkes Tucker with Richard Howard and Avis Berman, *Brassaï: The Eye of Paris* (Museum of Fine Arts, 1999), 150, 155n14.

**92.** Alexander Liberman quoted in Kazanjian and Tomkins, *Alex*, 146.

**93.** Jesse Kornbluth, "The Art of Being Alex," *New York* (October 12, 1981): 47.

**94.** "How to Put New Life in Your Living Room," *House & Garden* 120, no. 4 (October 1961): 130.

**95.** Alexander Liberman, "Steichen's Eye: A Study of the Greatest Living Photographer," *Vogue* (August 1, 1959): 95–99, 140, 142; Kazanjian and Tomkins, *Alex*, 146, 203.

**96.** "Homage to Penn, and His 'Moments Preserved,'" *Vogue* (November 1, 1960): 157.

**97.** Kazanjian and Tomkins, *Alex*, 138.

**98.** AK quoted in Gaillard, *André Kertész*, 73–74.

**99.** Kazanjian and Tomkins, *Alex*, 7.

**100.** Deirdre Carmody, "Alexander Liberman, Condé Nast's Driving Creative Force, Is Dead at 87," *The New York Times*, November 20, 1999.

**101.** AK quoted in Gaillard, *André Kertész*, 73; Bultman, *Legacies*, 70; AK quoted in Bodnár, "Talking to André Kertész," 94. See also "House-Moving Day at Cole Porter's," *Vogue* (May 1, 1957): 186–93.

**102.** Bultman, *Legacies*, 70.

**103.** Winthrop Sargeant, "A Woman Entering a Taxi in the Rain," *The New Yorker* (November 8, 1958): 54.

**104.** Margaret Kress, "André Kertész in *House and Garden*," unpublished research, 1983, cited in Weston Naef, "André Kertész: The Making of an American Photographer," in Sandra S. Phillips, David Travis, and Weston J. Naef, *André Kertész: Of Paris and New York* (Thames and Hudson, 1985), 118; Harvey V. Fondiller, "Persistence of Vision," *Popular Photography* 92, no. 8 (August 1985): 148.

**105.** AK quoted in Berman, "The 'Little Happenings' of André Kertész," 72.

**106.** Bryn Campbell, *World Photography* (Ziff-Davis Books, 1981), 275.

**107.** Kazanjian and Tomkins, *Alex*, 138.

**108.** MPP, letter from AK to GK, November or December 6, 1962.

## CHAPTER TEN

**1.** Michel Frizot and Annie-Laure Wanaverbecq, *André Kertész*, translated by Lucy Daniel Anderson, Anthony Roberts, and Willard Wood (Éditions Hazan and Éditions du Jeu de Paume, 2010), 300.

**2.** AK quoted in Dorothy S. Gelatt, "André Kertész at 80 – How He Works – What He Feels," *Popular Photography* 75, no. 5 (November 1974): 171.

3. AK quoted in Ruth Spencer, "André Kertész," *British Journal of Photography* 122, no. 5985 (April 4, 1975): 290.

4. Allain Daigle, "How the 50-mm Lens Became 'Normal,'" *The Atlantic* (May 13, 2018), https://www.theatlantic.com/technology/archive/2018/05/how-the-50-mm-lens-became-normal/560276/.

5. Anonymous, interview by author, July 29, 2016; Sylvia Plachy quoted in J. Paul Getty Museum, *In Focus: André Kertész* (J. Paul Getty Museum, 1999), 120.

6. Jimmy Fox, interview by author, July 16, 2014; Marvin Heiferman, interview by author, July 30, 2015; Teri Wehn-Damisch, interview by author, August 11, 2014.

7. Nicolas Ducrot, interview by author, August 8, 2014.

8. Laurence Miller, email to author, March 17, 2022.

9. Three of André's pictures were later featured in "The Mysterious Photograph" series in *Alfred Hitchcock's Mystery Magazine*. The magazine invited readers to invent mystery stories based on *Bocskay Square*, *The Circus*, and *Homing Ship*. See *Alfred Hitchcock's Mystery Magazine* October 1984 – February 1985 issues.

10. AK quoted in Cornell Capa, ed., *The Concerned Photographer: The Photographs of Werner Bischof, Robert Capa, David Seymour ("Chim"), André Kertész, Leonard Freed, Dan Weiner* (Grossman, 1968), n.p. *Broken Bench* can be seen at https://www.metmuseum.org/art/collection/search/260077.

11. Henri Cartier-Bresson, *The Mind's Eye: Writing on Photography and Photographers* (Aperture Foundation, 1999), 85.

12. Frizot and Wanaverbecq, *André Kertész*, 326n48.

13. MPP, letter from Romeo Martinez to EK, July 11, 1962.

14. JK quoted in Kati Marton, *The Great Escape: Nine Jews Who Fled Hitler and Changed the World* (Simon & Schuster, 2006), 213.

15. Jacob Deschin, "Careers in Review: Retrospective Exhibits by Kertesz, Ruohomaa," *The New York Times*, October 28, 1962.

16. MPP, letter from AK to GK, November 6, 1962.

17. Russell Lynes, *Good Old Modern: An Intimate Portrait of the Museum of Modern Art* (Atheneum, 1973), 324–25.

18. Joseph Bartscherer, email to author, July 18, 2016; *John Szarkowski: A Life in Photography*, produced by Richard B. Woodward, produced and directed by Sandra McLeod, 1998.

19. John Szarkowski, "The Photographs of Jacques Henri Lartigue," *Bulletin of the Museum of Modern Art* 30, no. 1 (1963): 4, https://www.jstor.org/stable/4058307.

20. John Szarkowski, "The Photographs of Jacques Henri Lartigue," 3.

21. Mihály Klopfer, want ad, *Pesti Hírlap*, January 8, 1908.

22. See Kirsten Belgum, *Popularizing the Nation: Audience, Representation, and the Production of Identity in Die Gartenlaube, 1853–1900* (University of Nebraska Press, 1998).

23. AK quoted in Krisztina Passuth, "Conversation in Paris with André Kertész," October 15, 1982, in Károly Kincses and Magdolna Kolta, *Pictures from Home: Photo Diary. André Kertész and Hungarians* (Mai Manó House, 2005), 20. Julia Michael translated for me.

24. Sarah Greenough, "A Hungarian Diary, 1894–1925," in Sarah Greenough, Robert Gurbo, and Sarah Kennel, *André Kertész* (National Gallery of Art/ Princeton University Press, 2005), 269n31.

25. Ibid., xiii.

26. Carol Schwalberg, "André Kertész: Unsung Pioneer," *U.S. Camera* 26, no. 1 (January 1963): 76.

27. Ibid.

28. Brassaï, "My Friend André Kertész," *Camera* 42, no. 4 (April 1963): 7.

29. Bertrand Girod de l'Ain, "Une biennale de la photographie à Venise, recherches Américaines et réhabilitation d'un Parisien," *Le Monde*, September 20, 1963. Throughout this section, I relied on *André Kertész: Paris Automne 1963* (Flammarion, 2013).

30. André Jammes, interview by author, June 8, 2012.

31. MPP, AK datebook, October 12, 1963.

32. Ibid., October 31, 1963.

33. Ibid., letter from EK to AK, October 23, 1963.

34. Ibid., telegram from EK to AK, November 15, 1963.

35. Ibid., letter from EK to AK, November 18, 1963.

36. Ibid., letter from EK to AK, November 21, 1963.

37. Jacqueline Martinez, interview by author, July 15, 2014.

38. Hervé Le Goff, *Pierre Gassmann: La photographie à l'épreuve* (Éditions France Delory, 2000), 144–45.

39. André reciprocated for Brassaï's "My Friend André Kertész" with six stilted paragraphs titled "My Friend, Brassaï." They appeared in the July 1966 issue of *Infinity*, the journal of the American Society of Magazine Photographers.

40. André Jammes, interview by author, June 8, 2012.

41. MPP, letter from Jacqueline Paouillac to AK, October 23, 1963.

42. Károly Kincses, "A Belated Interview with André Kertész," *The Hungarian Quarterly* 47, no. 181 (Spring 2006): 110; Patricia C. Johnson, "Focusing on His Life's Work," *Houston Chronicle*, December 11, 1983; Bill Jay, "AK: A Meeting of Friends," *Creative Camera* 63 (August 1969): 280; MPP, letter from AK to Jacqueline Paouillac, July 7, 1964.

43. Maria Eisner, "Citizen Kertesz," *Minicam* 7 (June 1944): 30.

44. MPP, letter from H. W. Sierichs to AK, September 4, 1936.

45. Jay, "AK: A Meeting of Friends," 280; Kincses, "A Belated Interview with André Kertész," 109.

46. "Jacob Deschin, "Kertész: Rebirth of an Eternal Amateur," *Popular Photography* 55, no. 6 (December 1964): 42. The photo historian Michel Frizot has made this same analogy.

47. He did make a sale to the editor and god of café society Frank Crowninshield, who first saw the Distortions at the home of the artist Sari Dienes. Crowninshield purchased fourteen prints. He also proposed a detour around the obscenity issue. Why not create a portfolio that the editor would sell privately? André leaped at the idea. Before anything came of it, however, Crowninshield died. Another time, André's friend Rudy Hoffmann showed several Distortions to Arturo Toscanini, the conductor of the NBC Symphony Orchestra. According to André, Toscanini was wild for the work. So NBC purchased a set for him as a gift. See Mary Ellen Slate, "The Magazines," *Popular Photography* 19, no. 2 (August 1946): 154; Gelatt, "André Kertész at 80," 156.

48. MPP, letter from Jacqueline Paouillac to AK, March 11, 1964.

49. John Szarkowski, *The Photographer's Eye* (Museum of Modern Art, 2007), 12.

50. The words are those of the curator William M. Ivins Jr., quoted by Szarkowski on page 11 of *The Photographer's Eye*. See William M. Ivins Jr., *Prints and Visual Communication* (Harvard University Press, 1953), 180.

51. Peter MacGill, interview by author, August 11, 2015; Irene Borger, interview by author, July 17, 2015.

52. David Vestal, "Kertész at MoMA: An Improper Review," *Contemporary Photographer* 5, no. 2 (Spring 1965): 65.

53. John Szarkowski, *André Kertész, Photographer* (Museum of Modern Art, 1964), 6, 9.

54. MPP, letter from EK to AK, November 18, 1963.

55. AK quoted in John G. Morris, "A Gentle Vision," *Quest* (January–February 1978): 48.

56. Nina Barrett, telephone interview by author, March 29, 2022.

57. André Jammes, interview by author, June 8, 2012.

58. M. H. Miller, "She Chronicled the Great Photographers of the Twentieth Century. Then, She Stopped Taking Portraits," *The New York Times Style Magazine,* August 10, 2018, https://www.nytimes.com/2018/08/10/t-magazine/lynn-davis-photographs.html; Lynn Davis, telephone interview by author, June 21, 2020.

59. Cornell Capa to Robert Capa, September 11, 1938, Robert Capa papers, International Center of Photography.

60. MPP, letter from Anna Fárová to AK, September 18, 1965.

61. Pavel Vančát, "Anna Fárová (1928–2010): Instilling Style in Photography," https://fotografmagazine.cz/en/magazine/prague/reviews/anna-farova-1928-2010/.

62. Cornell Capa archive, André Kertész file and Kertész-Hoving file, International Center of Photography; Jimmy Fox, interview by author, July 16, 2014.

63. Igor Bakhtamian, interview by author, January 20, 2016; Stuart I. Frolick, "Igor Bakhtamian: Master Printer," *Black & White* 120 (April 2017): 74.

64. AK quoted in Carol Schwalberg, "André Kertész: Unsung Pioneer," *U.S. Camera* 26, no. 1 (January 1963): 65.

65. Arthur Goldsmith, "The Kertész-Ugrin Tapes," *Popular Photography* 93, no. 1 (January 1986): 40; Sylvia Plachy, interview by author, January 16, 2014; Lajos Magasitz in conversation with author, June 19, 2012.

66. László Baki, "Soha nem látott André Kertész-képek kerültek elő egy világhírű magyar artista fiókjából," *Punkt*, February 7, 2021, https://punkt.hu/2021/02/07/soha-nem-latott-andre-kertesz-kepek-kerultek-elo-egy-vilaghiru-magyar-artista-fiokjabol/.

67. AK quoted by Nicolas von dem Bussche, telephone interview by author, August 15, 2020; GRI, Hiroji Kutoba, "André Kertész/Personality and His Photography," translated by Misuzu Rukunaga, unpublished typescript, c. 1975.

68. Duane Michals, interview by author, January 16, 2014; Duane Michals, *ABCDuane: A Duane Michals Primer* (Monacelli Press, 2014), 104; Robert Kotlowitz, "The World of Kertesz: A Great Photographer Has Spent a Lifetime in Pursuit of His Art," *Show* 4, no. 3 (March 1964): 56–61.

69. GRI, Alexey Brodovitch quoted in Kubota, "André Kertész/Personality and His Photography."

**70.** Lewis Hine quoted in Capa, ed., *The Concerned Photographer*, n.p. André's photojournalism before photojournalism existed had come to wider attention with the 1965 group show *The Photo Essay* at MoMA.

**71.** Susan Harder, interview by author, July 28, 2015; Igor Bakhtamian, interview by author, January 20, 2016.

**72.** CCP, Tennyson Schad, Memo to File, April 19, 1972, Light Gallery Archive.

**73.** Cornell Capa, "André: A Personal Reminiscence," in Susan Harder, ed., with Hiroji Kubota, *André Kertész: Diary of Light 1912–1985* (Aperture, 1985), 9; Jacob Deschin, "Japan Crowds See 'Concerned' Show," *The New York Times*, August 25, 1968.

**74.** GRI, AK quoted in Part III: Sixty Years of Photography, in Béla Ugrin, "Dialogues with Kertész," edited by Manuela Caravageli Ugrin, transcript of taped conversations between AK and Béla Ugrin, 1978–1985, 128–29. *Nara (Oct. 8, 1968)* is image no. 114 in Harder, *André Kertész*.

**75.** Agathe Gaillard, interview by author, June 9, 2012; Louis Mespla, "L'histoire de la photo perd sa galerie parisienne," *L'Obs* (January 25, 2017). Among those who purchased a *Satiric Dancer* postcard in Paris was the choreographer Remy Charlip. Remembering his promise to create a dance for an American friend, Charlip wrote a message on the back—"This is the first position of the dance"—then mailed it to her. Other postcards followed, "a whole set of positions, movements, signs." Charlip left it to the friend to connect the dots. Thus *Air Mail Dances* was born. See Joan Acocella, "Remy Charlip's 'Air Mail Dances,'" *The New Yorker* (January 12, 2015): 8; and Anna Heyward, "How to Write a Dance," *Paris Review* (February 14, 2015), www.theparisreview.org/blog/2015/02/04/how-to-write-a-dance/.

**76.** Inge Bondi, telephone interview by author, May 9, 2020. André later falsely denied that he had approved these prints or that they had been put on the market. See Jacob Deschin, "Drooping Tulip Heralds New Business," *Popular Photography* 24, no. 2 (August 1970): 32.

**77.** Avis Berman, "The 'Little Happenings' of André Kertész," *ARTnews* 83, no. 3 (March 1984): 73.

**78.** In 2006, the Museum of Contemporary Photography at Columbia College Chicago organized the exhibition *On Reading* based on André's book, then sent it on a six-year tour. It proved a hit in Carlsbad, Winter Park, Grand Rapids, Easton, Portland, Pittsburgh, and beyond. Librarians loved it. The *PBS NewsHour* aired a feature. Curators at Pittsburgh's Carnegie Museum of Art set up reading nooks in their galleries. When the show traveled to London, one teacher developed an activity called Drop Everything and Read. See Mary Thomas, "André Kertész: On Reading," *Pittsburgh Post-Gazette*, January 19, 2011; Sue Penny, "Ways to Improve Your Reading: Photographic Inspiration," *School Librarian* 63, no. 1 (Spring 2015), Gale Academic OneFile.

79. Steve McCurry, telephone interview by author, August 30, 2020.

80. Nicolas Ducrot, "Hommage à André Kertész," in Artcurial, "André Kertész: Une importante collection française," auction catalog, November 14, 2014, 8.

81. Nina Barrett, telephone interview by author, March 29, 2022.

82. GRI, Part III: Sixty Years of Photography, in Ugrin, "Dialogues with Kertész," 2.

83. Sanford Schwartz, "Still, Photography," *The New York Times*, December 3, 1972; Ainslie Ellis, "A Triumph for the Innocent Eye: The Work of André Kertész," *British Journal of Photography* 119, no. 42 (October 20, 1972): 923; A.L., "André Kertész: Soixante ans de photographie 1912–1972," *Le Monde*, December 12, 1972.

84. Nancy Stevens, "André Kertész Today," *Photo World* (December 1973): 107. Deschin's comment appears in *The Photo Reporter* 3, no. 2 (1973).

85. MPP, letter from Henri Cartier-Bresson to AK, August 1972.

86. This photograph appears at https://www.artnet.com/artists/andré-kertész/mon-ami-henri-merci-IoJ4wXBX_InBFPy0OLG5cQ2.

87. Pierre Assouline, *Henri Cartier-Bresson: A Biography* (Thames & Hudson, 2005), 87; David Travis, interview by author, January 9, 2016.

88. Dan Budnik, "A Point de Vue," *Infinity* 14, no. 3 (March 1965): 8.

89. Assouline, *Henri Cartier-Bresson*, 148.

90. Cartier-Bresson, *The Mind's Eye*, 22.

91. AK quoted in Berman, "The 'Little Happenings' of André Kertész," 73.

92. Cartier-Bresson quoted in Assouline, *Henri Cartier-Bresson*, 175.

93. AK quoted in Berman, "The 'Little Happenings' of André Kertész," 68.

94. Assouline, *Henri Cartier-Bresson*, 224.

95. Cartier-Bresson quoted in Yves Bourde, "Nul ne peut entrer ici s'il n'est pas geomètre," *Le Monde*, September 5, 1974.

96. GRI, Kubota, "André Kertész/Personality and His Photography"; Nicolas Ducrot, interview by author, August 8, 2014.

## CHAPTER ELEVEN

1. CCP, letter from Tennyson Schad to AK, April 18, 1972; and Tennyson Schad, Memo to File, April 19, 1972, both Light Gallery Archive.

2. Ibid., and GRI, letter from Tennyson Schad to AK, August 1, 1972, Light Gallery Archive.

3. CCP, letter from Tennyson Schad to AK August 23, Light Gallery Archive.

4. A. D. Coleman, "Images with a Cartoon Quality / André Kertész," *The New York Times*, January 28, 1973; A. D. Coleman, "Eight Photographers' Views of 19th-Century Egypt: Photography," *The New York Times*, September 23, 1973.

5. AK quoted by Joan Liftin, interview by author, July 30, 2015.

6. GRI, letter from EK to Inge Bondi, April 2, 1973.

7. AK quoted in Brigitte Ollier, "André Kertész Ragaillardi," *Libération*, November 12–13, 1994, 35.

8. John Szarkowski, *André Kertész, Photographer* (Museum of Modern Art, 1964), 7–8.

9. Annie Cohen-Solal, *Picasso the Foreigner: An Artist in France, 1900–1973*, translated by Sam Taylor (Farrar, Straus and Giroux, 2023), 36.

10. Szarkowski, *André Kertész, Photographer*, 7–8.

11. Vicki Goldberg, "Too Human," *Art on Paper* 9, no. 4 (March–April 2005): 72.

12. Anonymous, interview with author, January 13, 2016.

13. François-Marie Banier, interview by Michel Guerrin, "Il y a toujours eu du vacarme derrière moi," *Le Monde*, December 10, 2009.

14. CCP, Tennyson Schad, Memo to File, September 18, 1972, Light Gallery Archive; Paul Katz, telephone interview by author, December 5, 2022.

15. Duane Michals, interview by author, January 16, 2014.

16. "K is for Kertész," Tate Museum, "A–Z of Modernist Photography," http://www.tate.org.uk/art/art-terms/p/photography/a-z/.

17. Duane Michals, *ABCDuane: A Duane Michals Primer* (Monacelli Press 2014), 105; Igor Bakhtamian, interview by author, January 20, 2016; Duane Michals, interview by author, January 16, 2014.

18. AK quoted in Denes Devenyi, "Kertesz: Denes Devenyi Interviews the 'Father of 35mm Vision'," *Photo Life* (January 1978): 30.

19. Joseph Foldes, "To Become a Photographer," *Popular Photography* 68, no. 3 (March 1971): 73.

20. EK quoted in Agathe Gaillard, *André Kertész* (Pierre Belfond, 1980), 51–52.

**21.** Sylvia Plachy, interview by author, January 16, 2014; Sylvia Plachy, *Self-Portrait with Cows Going Home* (Aperture, 2004), 36; J. Paul Getty Museum, *In Focus: André Kertész* (J. Paul Getty Museum, 1999), 140; Zsusanna Ardó, *Culture Shock! Hungary: A Guide to Customs and Etiquette* (Graphic Arts Center, 2001), 25–26.

**22.** János Hock, *Virágmesék: Felnőttek Számára* (E. Prager-Verlag, 1931), quote translated by Maryll Telegdy.

**23.** *Perfidy* appears in Michel Frizot and Annie-Laure Wanaverbecq, *André Kertész*, translated by Lucy Daniel Anderson, Anthony Roberts, and Willard Wood (Éditions Hazan and Éditions du Jeu de Paume, 2010), 19. For André's comment about being murdered in Paris, see Avis Berman, "The 'Little Happenings' of André Kertész," *ARTnews* 83, no. 3 (March 1984): 72.

**24.** Pablo Picasso quoted in Renée Beslon, *Rogi André: Portraits* (Éditions du Regard, 1981), 7.

**25.** Fernand Léger quoted in ibid., 7, 10. My information about Rogi André's life after André derives from Andra Samelson, "Rogi," unpublished manuscript, 2–3; Muriel Jaeger, interview by author, July 27, 2013; "Jeanne Bucher, grande prêteresse de l'art d'avant garde," in *Supérieur Inconnu* 19 (October–December 2000): 60; Brigitte Ollier and Elisabeth Nora, *Rogi André: Photo sensible* (Éditions du Regard, 1999), 11.

**26.** Bernard Dufour, "Rogi André: Photo Sensible, Negative Work," translated by L.-S. Torgoff, *Artpress* 251 (1999): 63.

**27.** Teri Wehn-Damisch, interview by author, August 11, 2014; Nicolas Ducrot, interview by author, August 8, 2014; Peter Galassi, conversation with author, September 14, 2014.

**28.** A young New York painter named Andra Samelson befriended Rogi when Samelson was studying in Paris. After Rogi's death, she visited the Bibliothèque Nationale to view her work. There she got permission to photograph Rogi's post-mortem portrait of Wassily Kandinsky. The Russian artist is shrouded in white with one of his celestial abstractions behind him: body and ascending spirit. Back in New York, Samelson asked her neighbor, the photographer Diane Arbus, to print the negatives. Arbus, as it happened, had studied with Rogi's friend Lisette Model. Three days after giving the negatives to Arbus, Samelson returned from a trip to find a manila envelope under her door. In it were the last prints Arbus ever made—those of Rogi's photograph. Over the weekend, Arbus had committed suicide. Andra Samelson, "Rogi," unpublished manuscript, 10.

**29.** Peter MacGill, interview by author, August 11, 2015.

**30.** CCP, AK quoted in Tennyson Schad, Memo to File, May 2, 1973, Light Gallery Archive.

**31.** GRI, Light Gallery records, April 4, 1975; Andy Grundberg, *How Photography Became Contemporary Art: Inside an Artistic Revolution from Pop to the Digital Age* (Yale University Press, 2021), 91.

**32.** Irene Borger quoted in Carol Kismaric and Marvin Heiferman, *Talking Pictures: People Speak About the Photographs That Speak to Them* (Chronicle Books, 1994), 84.

**33.** Brendan Gill, "Outrageous Fortune—Memories of André Kertész," *Architectural Digest* 47 (September 1990): 44, 50; MPP, letter from Brendan Gill to AK, September 5, 1973.

**34.** Judy von dem Bussche, "Homage to André Kertész of New York: A Portfolio of Fifteen Photographs by Wolf von dem Bussche & a Personal Remembrance by Judy von dem Bussche," 1974–1976; email from Gerd Sander to author, November 29, 2015; Nicolas von dem Bussche, telephone interview by author, August 15, 2020.

**35.** Igor Bakhtamian, interview by author, January 20, 2016; J. Paul Getty Museum, *In Focus*, 115–16; Sandra Sammataro Phillips, "The Photographic Work of André Kertész in France, 1925–1936: A Critical Essay and Catalogue," PhD dissertation, City University of New York, 1985, 670.

**36.** CCP, AK quoted in Tennyson Schad, Memo to File, January 21, 1972, Light Gallery Archive. *Broken Plate* can be seen at https://www.getty.edu/art/collection/object/104EJY.

**37.** "A Sense of Manhattan as Reflected in Landscape Design and Photography," Ada Louise Huxtable, *The New York Times*, June 2, 1974.

**38.** CCP, Tennyson Schad, Memo to File, June 5, 1974, Light Gallery Archive.

**39.** Ibid.; Alden Whitman, "The Greatest People in Town," *New York* (December 31, 1973–January 7, 1974): 28–31.

**40.** CCP, Tennyson Schad, Memo to File, April 8, 1974, Light Gallery Archive.

**41.** Ibid., June 5, 1974; April 24, 1974; June 18, 1974.

**42.** Sylvia Plachy, "Hungary by Heart," *ArtForum International* 24 (February 1986): 90.

**43.** André photographed Elizabeth often enough that he later contemplated doing a book about her. But that never happened. In a will dated October 1984, he excluded unpublished negatives of Elizabeth from his bequest to the André and Elizabeth Kertész Foundation.

**44.** This photograph appears in Sarah Greenough, Robert Gurbo, and Sarah Kennel, *André Kertész* (National Gallery of Art/Princeton University Press, 2005), image 107.

**45.** AK quoted in Denes Devenyi, "Kertesz: Denes Devenyi Interviews the 'Father of 35mm Vision,'" *Photo Life* (January 1978): 11.

**46.** AK quoted in Harvey V. Fondiller, "Persistence of Vision," *Popular Photography* 92 (August 1985): 52.

**47.** AK quoted in Denes Devenyi, "Kertesz: Denes Devenyi Interviews the 'Father of 35mm Vision,'" 30.

**48.** Alan G. Artner, "An 80-year-old Master... Pitted Against Young Lions," *Chicago Tribune,* November 10, 1974.

**49.** Gill, "Outrageous Fortune," 42.

**50.** Joel Meyerowitz quoted in Michael Grieve, "Any Answers: Joel Meyerowitz," *British Journal of Photography* (August 17, 2017), https://www.1854.photography/2017/08/any-answers-joel-meyerowitz/.

**51.** Lee Friedlander in an email to Frish Brandt, forwarded to author, March 26, 2016.

**52.** CCP, Tennyson Schad, Memo to File, May 1, 1975, and June 19, 1975, Light Gallery Archive; Marvin Heiferman, interview by author, July 30, 2015.

**53.** EK to Gizella and Eugene Lux, December 23, 1975, courtesy Julie DeStefano; CCP, Tennyson Schad, Memo to File, September 22, 1975, Light Gallery Archive; CCP, Tennyson Schad letter to AK, March 28, 1975, Light Gallery Archive; Paul Katz, telephone interview by author, December 5, 2022.

**54.** GRI, letter from Ileana Sonnabend to AK, April 27, 1976; letter from AK to Ileana Sonnabend, May 4, 1976.

**55.** Such prices later seemed unbelievably low. In 2005, Sotheby's London sold a vintage print of *Chez Mondrian* for $464,000. See MPP, letter from AK to Sandy Wilder, July 26, 1977, cited in Anne de Mondenard, *L'odyssée d'une icône: Trois photographies d'André Kertész* (Actes Sud/Maison Européenne de la Photographie, 2006), 116; Sarah Kennel, "'The Grotesque Dancer from Pest': Magda Förstner and the Making of *Satiric Dancer,*" in Elizabeth Siegel, ed., *André Kertész: Postcards from Paris* (Art Institute of Chicago, 2021), 36; Brian Appel, "Fall 2005

Photography Auction Report at Sotheby's, Christie's and Phillips de Pury & Company," October 2005, Artcritical.com.

56. AK quoted in Tamás Féner, "Presence and Consistency," in János Bodnár, ed., *André Kertész: Magyarországon* (Főfoto, 1984), 98.

57. Annette and Rudolf Kicken and Simone Förster, eds., *Points of View: Masterpieces of Photography and Their Stories* (Steidl, 2007), 103.

58. Letter from AK to Gizella and Eugene Lux, April 4, 1976, courtesy Julie DeStefano.

59. AK quoted in Caroline Bernstein, "Eye View: The Mobile Living Legends," *Women's Wear Daily* 133, no. 79 (October 22, 1976): 10.

60. Letter from EK to Gizella and Eugene Lux, December 30, 1976, courtesy Julie DeStefano.

61. Laurence Miller, email to author, March 17, 2022; Paul Katz, telephone interview by author, December 5, 2022.

62. GRI, letter from Nicolas Ducrot to AK, April 12, 1976.

63. Nina Barrett, telephone interview by author, March 29, 2022.

64. See https://collections.artsmia.org/art/115702/chez-moi-andre-kertesz.

65. Joan Liftin, interview by author, July 30, 2015.

66. "André Kertész ou le don du voyage," *Le Monde*, October 30, 1980; Peter MacGill, interview by author, August 11, 2015.

67. AK quoted by Trudy Lee Cohen, telephone interview by author, January 8, 2014.

68. Letter from EK to Gizella and Eugene Lux, December 30, 1976, courtesy Julie DeStefano.

69. Carol Brower Wilhelm, interview by author, January 13, 2016; Eva Rubinstein, email to author, August 24, 2023.

70. MPP, letter from AK to Jennie Boddington, December 17, 1977.

71. AK to Krisztina Passuth, "Conversation in Paris with André Kertész," October 15, 1982. I used an unpublished translation by Maryll Telegdy.

72. CCP, AK quoted in Lee Witkin notes, September 26, 1978, Witkin Gallery Archives.

73. Hervé Guibert, "Le mouvement de la vie," *Le Monde*, January 5, 1978.

74. Susan Nash, telephone interview by author, February 17, 2014.

75. Von dem Bussche, "Homage to André Kertész of New York," 1974–1976; Peter MacGill, interview by author, August 11, 2015.

76. Paul Strand quoted in Sean O'Hagan, "Stephen Shore: 'People Would Chase Me Off Their Lawns with My Leica,'" *The Guardian*, February 29, 2020.

77. AK quoted in Ben Lifson, "A Great Photographer's Love Story," *Saturday Review* 8, no. 12 (December 1981): 23.

78. JoAnn Verburg, telephone interview with author, May 6, 2024.

79. AK quoted in Ben Lifson, "A Great Photographer's Love Story," 23.

80. AK, *Kertész on Kertész*, 114.

81. AK quoted in Ben Lifson, "Kertész at Eighty-Five," *Portfolio* (June/July 1979): 60.

82. Endre Ady, "Alone with the Sea," in *Poems of Endre Ady*, translated by Anton N. Nyerges (Hungarian Cultural Foundation, 1969), 140. The biography was *Ady Endre: Élete és Pályája* (Endre Ady: Life and Career) by the literary historian Erzsébet Vezér. In the 1960s, André sounded out Vezér about collaborating on an Ady book. Although she expressed interest, funding never materialized. See Károly Kincses and Magdolna Kolta, *Pictures from Home: Photo Diary. André Kertész and Hungarians* (Mai Manó House, 2005), 168.

## CHAPTER TWELVE

1. Ralph Gibson, interview by author, July 29, 2015.

2. Lauren Valenti, "Happy Birthday, Veruschka! The '60s Supermodel's Best Beauty Looks of All Time," *Vogue* (May 14, 2021), https://www.vogue.com/article/veruschka-60s-supermodel-best-beauty-looks-graphic-eyes-big-hair; Teri Wehn-Damisch, interview by author, August 11, 2014; GRI, "Kertesz, Veruschka, Arles et Les Autres," *Photo Journal* clipping, 1979.

3. "Romeo Martinez hommage," *Le Monde*, June 27, 1991.

4. Agathe Gaillard, *André Kertész* (Pierre Belfond, 1980), 78–79; Susan Harder, interview by author, July 28, 2015.

5. Anne de Mondenard, *L'odyssée d'une icône: Trois photographies d'André Kertész* (Actes Sud/Maison Européenne de la Photographie, 2006), 115.

6. CCP, Tennyson Schad memo to Peter MacGill, February 7, 1980; Peter MacGill memo to Tennyson Schad, February 19, 1980, both Light Gallery Archive.

7. CCP, AK Schedule of Prices, January 1, 1980, Light Gallery Archive.

8. Richard B. Woodward, "On Artificial Rarity and Fakery," *The New York Times*, April 23, 2000.

9. *Chez Mondrian* hung in a few exhibitions in the late 1920s and early 1930s.

In 1934, a French publication used it to illustrate a how-to article for shutterbugs. Then it was forgotten until 1956, when it appeared, uncredited, in Michel Seuphor's biography of the artist. Not until 1963 did the image burst into public awareness when it appeared in *Camera* and was exhibited at the Venice Photography Biennale and the Bibliothèque Nationale. See de Mondenard, *L'odyssée d'une icône*, 41, 67, 115, 125. In 2005, a boom year for the photography market, a bid of $464,000 was hammered down for a *carte postale* of *Chez Mondrian*. See Brian Appel, "Fall 2005 Photography Auction Report at Sotheby's, Christie's and Phillipe de Pury & Company," artcritical.com (October 2005), http://www.artcritical.com/appel/BAFall2005.htm.

**10.** AK quoted in Lee D. Witkin, "Salford 8 — A More Modest Extravaganza in the Midlands," *The Print Collector's Newsletter* 11, no. 4 (September–October 1980): 121–23; Joan Liftin, interview by author, July 30, 2015.

**11.** Nina Barrett, telephone interview by author, March 29, 2022.

**12.** Ducrot offers an example of André's fastidiousness about print quality. Judging the highlights in certain images in *On Reading* a tad too bright, André carried a no. 2 pencil in his jacket pocket. When asked to sign a copy, he would slip out the pencil, turn to those images, and tone down the highlights, while entertaining the buyer with an anecdote or two. Nicolas Ducrot, interview by author, August 8, 2014.

**13.** AK quoted by Katy Homans in *André Kertész: Observations, Thoughts, Reflections: Essays by Curators, Colleagues, Friends and Collectors* (Stephen Daiter Gallery, 2005), 14; Katy Homans, telephone interview by author, January 11, 2021; Floyd Yearout, telephone interview by author, February 8, 2021.

**14.** Yearout, telephone interview by author, February 8, 2021.

**15.** Sandra S. Phillips, David Travis, and Weston J. Naef, *André Kertész: Of Paris and New York* (Thames and Hudson, 1985), 13.

**16.** AK quoted in Béla Ugrin, "André Kertész: Brother Seeing Eye," *Popular Photography* 93, no. 1 (January 1986): 64–65. In emails to the author dated February 27 and November 25, 2016, the photo historian and curator Colin Ford describes a postcard version of *Meudon* that André mailed to the Fords' son. André writes: "Hier [*sic*] I send you your grandfather. Love, Uncle André."

**17.** Frederick H. Marks, "Honors Heap on Bitter André Kertész, Decries Lack of Praise," October 19, 1980, https://www.upi.com/Archives/1980/10/19/Honors-heap-on-bitter-Andre-Kertesz-Decries-lack-of-praise/3278340776000/.

**18.** AK quoted by Ben Lifson, "Kertész at Eighty-Five," *Portfolio* (June/July 1979): 61.

**19.** AK quoted by Sandra Phillips, interview by author, February 1, 2016.

**20.** David Travis, interview by author, January 9, 2016; J. Paul Getty Museum, *In Focus: André Kertész* (J. Paul Getty Museum, 1999), 120–21.

**21.** AK quoted in Avis Berman, "The 'Little Happenings' of André Kertész," *ARTnews*, 83, no. 3 (March 1984): 72.

**22.** Robert Hayes, "Andre Kertesz," *Interview* 13, no. 4 (April 1983): 59.

**23.** Charles Osgood, "Kertész," *Chicago Tribune*, May 3, 1985; AK in Jain Kelly, *Nude: Theory* (Lustrum, 1979), 120. André had additional reasons for resenting Newhall. The curator had slighted André's work during his years as a curator at MoMA and the director of the George Eastman House (today the George Eastman Museum). Moreover, André's name was long missing from Newhall's *The History of Photography: From 1839 to the Present*, the book that grew out of the 1937 exhibition and became America's master narrative of the history of photography. Not until the 1964 edition did Newhall reproduce two photographs by André and weave his work into a wider narrative.

**24.** Alan G. Artner, "Recalcitrant Photographer André Kertész: Success Came on His Own Terms," *Chicago Tribune*, October 3, 1985.

**25.** Carol Brower, "The Handling, Preservation, and Conservation Matting of Photographs," in Henry Wilhelm with Carol Brower, *The Permanence and Care of Color Photographs: Traditional and Digital Color Prints, Color Negatives, Slides, and Motion Pictures* (Preservation, 1993), 406–7, ebook.

**26.** AK quoted in Barbaralee Diamonstein, "André Kertész," in *Visions and Images: American Photographers on Photography* (Rizzoli, 1981), 88.

**27.** Liza Macrae, telephone interview by author, November 30, 2022.

**28.** Peter C. Jones in *André Kertész: Observations, Thoughts, Reflections*, 64.

**29.** AK quoted in Christian Caujolle, "Kertész: Un siècle de photo s'est arrêté à New York," *Libération*, September 30, 1985; Dorothy S. Gelatt, "André Kertész at 80 — How He Works — What He Feels," *Popular Photography* 75, no. 5 (November 1974): 155.

**30.** John Szarkowski, *Looking at Photographs: 100 Pictures from the Collection of the Museum of Modern Art* (Museum of Modern Art, 1973), 134.

**31.** AK quoted in Patricia C. Johnson, "Focusing on His Life's Work," *Houston Chronicle*, December 11, 1983.

32. Bryn Campbell, *World Photography* (Ziff-Davis 1981), dust jacket.

33. Ed Ruscha quoted in A. D. Coleman, "I'm Not Really a Photographer," *The New York Times*, September 10, 1972.

34. AK quoted in Diamonstein, "André Kertész," 90.

35. AK, *Kertész on Kertész: A Self-Portrait* (Abbeville Press, 1985), 99.

36. François Buoy, *Hervé Guibert: Le jeune homme et la mort* (Grasset & Fasquelle, 1999), 129.

37. Ralph Gibson, *Self-Exposure* (Heni, 2018), 171; Gilles Walusinski, "André," *Délibéré* (September 23, 2018), https://delibere.fr/entomologie-photographieque-andre/.

38. AK quoted in Robert Gurbo, *André Kertész: Lost in America* (Linfield College Renshaw Gallery, 1998), 15.

39. Francisco Bessière, Hôtel Esmeralda, email to author, March 8, 2021.

40. Michael Somoroff, "A Moment. Master Photographers: Portraits of André Kertész (and more)," *LensCulture*, https://www.lensculture.com/articles/michael-somoroff-a-moment-master-photographers-portraits-of-andre-kertesz-and-more; Michael Somoroff, telephone interview by author, February 5, 2021.

41. AK quoted by Agathe Gaillard, interview by author, June 9, 2012.

42. AK quoted by Agathe Gaillard, *Mémoires d'une galerie* (Gallimard, 2013), 75.

43. AK quoted by Tamás Féner, "Presence and Consistency," in János Bodnár, ed., *André Kertész: Magyarországon* (Főfotó, 1984), 97.

44. *André Kertész of the Cities: Budapest, Paris, New York*, directed by Teri Wehn-Damisch (TF1 with support of the French Ministry of Culture, 1986; Biography Series American Masters, 1988). When Brian O'Doherty of the National Endowment for the Arts urged Susan Lacy, the creator of American Masters, to include the film about André in the series, she replied: "But, Brian, how can he be an American master and not speak English?" Teri Wehn-Damisch, interview by author, August 11, 2014.

45. *André Kertész of the Cities.*

46. Ferenc Karinthy, *Napló, Kötet 3: 1974–1991* (Magyar Közlöny Lap és Könyvkiadó, 2016), Petőfi Irodalmi Múzeum, Digitális Irodalmi Akadémia, 2023, https://reader.dia.hu/document/Karinthy_Ferenc-Naplo-43583. André's seatmate, the writer Ferenc Karinthy, was the son of the writer and humorist Frigyes Karinthy, whose books André would have known from his youth. My thanks to György Németh for finding this comment in Karinthy's diary entry dated March 21, 1985.

47. In the original French, the "totalité de l'oeuvre d'André Kertész," quoted by Gilles Walusinski, "Histoire de la 'donation Kertész' à l'État et du role d'Henri Cartier-Bresson," typescript for Henri Cartier-Bresson Foundation.

48. Ibid.

49. "L'imbroglio Kertész: L'œuvre du photographe hongrois André Kertész (1894–1985) divise Français et Américains," *Le Monde*, July 5, 2008.

50. AK quoted in Gaillard, *Mémoires d'une galerie*, 75.

51. Agathe Galliard quoted by Robert Solyom, interview by author, August 8, 2013; AK quoted by Gaillard, *Mémoires d'une galerie*, 75.

52. AK, interview by László Lugosi Lugo, January 13, 1981, in Károly Kincses, *Measure: Brassai, Capa, Kertész, Munkácsi, Moholy* (Association of Hungarian Photographers/Hungarian Museum of Photography, 2006), 237. André is speaking about *A Portfolio of Ten Photographs by Brassaï* (Witkin-Berley, 1973).

53. AK, interview by Lugo, January 13, 1981, in Kincses, *Measure*, 237.

54. Stefan Lorant, interview by Károly Kincses and Magdolna Kolta, collection of the Hungarian Museum of Photography, April 1–2, 1996. I used a translation by György Németh.

55. AK, interview by Lugo, January 13, 1981, in Kincses, *Measure*, 238.

56. "Brassaï," in Paul Hill and Thomas Cooper, eds., *Dialogue with Photography: Interviews by Paul Hill and Thomas Cooper* (Farrar, Straus and Giroux, 1979), 38.

57. Brassaï quoted in Anne Wilkes Tucker, *Brassaï: The Eye of Paris* (Museum of Fine Arts, 1999), 150.

58. AK, interview by Lugo, January 13, 1981, in Kincses, *Measure*, 237.

59. AK quoted in Berman, "The 'Little Happenings' of André Kertész," 71.

60. The Last Will and Testament of André Kertesz, October 30, 1984.

61. Cornell Capa, "André: A Personal Reminiscence" in Susan Harder, ed., with Hiroji Kubota, *André Kertész: Diary of Light 1912–1985* (Aperture, 1985), 10.

62. Nina Barrett, telephone interview by author, March 29, 2022; Susan Harder, interview by author, July 28, 2015.

63. Gibson, *Self-Exposure*, 171.

64. AK quoted by Susan May Tell, telephone interview by author, August 17, 2020.

65. AK quoted in Sylvia Plachy, "André Kertész, 1894–1985," *The Village Voice* (October 8, 1985).

66. Steve McCurry, telephone interview by author, August 30, 2020; Trudy

Lee Cohen, telephone interview by author, January 8, 2014; Hal Hinson, "Little Happenings," in Harder, *André Kertész*, 205; Igor Bakhtamian, interview by author, January 20, 2016.

67. David Travis quoted in Abigail Foerstner, "On the Trail of André Kertész: Curator's Detective Moments," *Chicago Tribune*, May 10, 1985; Sandra Phillips, interview by author, February 1, 2016; David Travis, interview by author, January 9, 2016; Weston Naef, interview by author, June 21, 2016.

68. AK quoted by David Travis, interview by author, January 9, 2016.

69. AK quoted in Tamás Féner, "Presence and Consistency" in Bodnár, ed., *André Kertész*, 98.

70. Sandra Phillips, interview by author, February 1, 2016.

71. Nina Barrett, telephone interview by author, March 29, 2022.

72. AK quoted by David Travis, interview by author, January 9, 2016.

73. Carol Brower Wilhelm, interview by author, January 13, 2016.

74. Carol Brower Wilhelm in *André Kertész: Observations, Thoughts, Reflections*, 84.

75. Brendan Gill, "Outrageous Fortune — Memories of André Kertész," *Architectural Digest* 47 (September 1990): 36.

76. Berman, "The 'Little Happenings' of André Kertész," 73.

77. Sylvia Plachy in J. Paul Getty Museum, *In Focus: André Kertész*, 117; Robert Solyom, interview by author, August 8, 2013.

78. AK quoted in Hervé Guibert, "Les tendres malices d'André Kertész," *Le Monde*, October 1, 1985.

79. Gaillard, *Mémoires d'une galerie*, 79.

80. AK quoted in Plachy, "André Kertész, 1894–1985."

81. Béla Ugrin, "André Kertész: Brother Seeing Eye," *Popular Photography* 93, no. 1 (January 1986): 60.

82. Ralph Gibson, interview by author, July 29, 2015; Susan Harder, interview by author, July 28, 2015; *Libération*, September 30, 1985; Ugrin, "André Kertész: Brother Seeing Eye," 96.

83. Alexandra Anderson, "André Kertész: Of Paris and New York," *Artforum* 24, no. 4. (December 1985): https://www.artforum.com/print/198510/andre-kertesz-of-paris-and-new-york-3513.

84. Andy Grundberg, "Modern Masters and Views of War Held Center Stage," *The New York Times*, December 29, 1985.

85. "Kertész, c'était nous," *Libération*, September 30, 1985.

86. "Le devenir de l'oeuvre de Kertész," *Libération*, October 2, 1985.

87. Judd Tully, "Spring Photo Auctions," *Artnet* (1997), http://www.artnet.com/magazine_pre2000/news/tully/tully4-28-97.asp.

88. Susan Harder quoted in Jennifer Landes, "A Complex Relationship with Light," *East Hampton Star*, March 5, 2020. See also "Kertész Images in Shady Area," *New York* 24, no. 31 (August 12, 1991): 10; and Ugrin, "André Kertész: Brother Seeing Eye," 96.

89. Jose Fernandez quoted in "Kertész Images in Shady Area," 10.

90. It happened first in December 1987, when the Musée Jacquemart-André in Paris opened a Kertész retrospective. According to *Le Monde*, it comprised three hundred photographs: vintage prints made by André, prints made by others under his supervision, and—controversially—some thirty posthumous prints using negatives selected by the curators and made by a French printer. André had helped conceptualize such an exhibition but did not survive to carry it out. The Association des Amis d'André Kertész denounced the exhibition. See Patrick Roegiers, "Kertész malgré tout," *Le Monde*, February 11, 1988.

91. Walusinski, "André," https://delibere.fr/entomologie-photographieque-andre/; Claire Guillot, "Patrimoine photographique: L'état ne soigne pas son image," *Le Monde*, July 3, 2008.

92. Michelle Chomette quoted ibid.

93. Gabriel Bauret, "Rereading the Past: Interview with Pierre Bonhomme," *Aperture* 142 (Winter 1996): 75.

94. Nicolas Ducrot, interview by author, August 8, 2014.

95. Mary Price, *The Photograph: A Strange, Confined Space* (Stanford University Press, 1994), 118, 121.

96. Brigitte Ollier, "Kertész, vues d'en France," *Libération*, July 25, 1990.

97. AK, *Kertész on Kertész*, 103.

98. AK quoted in Burt Britton, *Self-Portrait: Book People Picture Themselves* (Random House, 1976), 246.

### EPILOGUE

1. Abigail Foerstner, "At the End of His Life, André Kertész Wins the Battle for Recognition," *Chicago Tribune*, October 4, 1985.

2. Jean-Claude Lemagny, "André Kertész, maître de la mesure," in *André Kertész: Ma France*, edited by Pierre Bonhomme (Ministère de la Culture, 1990), 105.

3. AK quoted in Zan Dubin, "On Photography: Kertesz Getting His Due," *Los Angeles Times*, August 11, 1985.

4. AK quoted in Cornell Capa, ed., *The Concerned Photographer: The Photographs of Werner Bischof, Robert Capa, David Seymour ("Chim"), André Kertész, Leonard Freed, Dan Weiner* (Grossman, 1968), n.p.

5. David Vestal, "Kertész at MoMA: An Improper Review," *Contemporary Photographer* 5, no. 2 (Spring 1965): 65.

# SELECT BIBLIOGRAPHY

## ARCHIVAL SOURCES

André Kertész, Selected Papers, Photocopies, 1899–1985, Getty Research Institute (GRI), Los Angeles, California

André Kertész Archive, Médiathèque du patrimoine et de la photographie (MPP), Ministry of Culture, Charenton-le-Pont, France

## PUBLISHED WORKS

Baki, Péter, Colin Ford, and George Szirtes. *Eyewitness: Hungarian Photography in the Twentieth Century: Brassaï, Capa, Kertész, Moholy-Nagy, Munkácsi.* Royal Academy of Arts, 2011.

Beslon, Renée. *Rogi André: Portraits.* Éditions du Regard, 1981.

Bodnár, János, ed. *André Kertész: Magyarországon.* Főfoto, 1984.

Bodnár, János. *André Kertész ismeretlen fotográfiái. Képek és tárgyak a Washington Square-i lakásból. / In the New York Apartment of André Kertész.* Magyar Fotográfiai Múzeum, 2001.

Bölöni, György. *Az igazi Ady.* Éditions Atelier de Paris, 1934.

Borhan, Pierre. *André Kertész: His Life and Work.* Bulfinch Press Book/Little, Brown, 1994.

Capa, Cornell, ed. *The Concerned Photographer: The Photographs of Werner Bischof, Robert Capa, David Seymour ("Chim"), André Kertész, Leonard Freed, Dan Weiner.* Grossman, 1968.

Centro di Ricerca e Archiviazione della Fotografia. *André Kertész: Inediti a Gorizia: Dicembre 1914/Marzo 1915.* Musei Provinciali di Gorizia, 2003.

Fávová, Anna. *André Kertész.* Edited by Robert Sagalyn. Grossman, 1966.

Frizot, Michel, and Cédric de Veigy. *Vu: The Story of a Magazine*. Translated by Ruth Sharman. Thames & Hudson, 2009.

Frizot, Michel, and Annie-Laure Wanaverbecq. *André Kertész*. Translated by Lucy Daniel Anderson, Anthony Roberts, and Willard Wood. Éditions Hazan and Éditions du Jeu de Paume, 2010.

Gaillard, Agathe. *André Kertész*. Belfond, 1980.

J. Paul Getty Museum. *In Focus: André Kertész*. J. Paul Getty Museum, 1999.

Greenough, Sarah, Robert Gurbo, and Sarah Kennel. *André Kertész*. National Gallery of Art/Princeton University Press, 2005.

Hill, Paul, and Thomas Cooper. *Dialogue with Photography*. Farrar, Straus and Giroux, 1979.

Kelly, Jain. *Nude: Theory*. Lustrum, 1979.

Kertész, André. *André Kertész: Diary of Light, 1912–1985*. Edited by Susan Harder with Hiroji Kubota. With a text by Hal Hinson. Aperture, 1987.

———. *André Kertész: The Early Years*. With a text by Robert Gurbo. W. W. Norton, 2005.

———. *André Kertész: A Lifetime of Perception*. Edited by Jane Corkin. With a text by Ben Lifson. Harry N. Abrams, 1982.

———. *André Kertész: The Manchester Collection*. Edited by Harold Riley. Texts by Henri Cartier-Bresson and others. Manchester Collection, 1984.

———. *André Kertész: Paris, Autumn 1963*. Introduction by Matthieu Rivallin. Translated by David Radzinowicz. Flammarion, 2013.

———. *André Kertész: The Polaroids*. Text by Robert Gurbo. W. W. Norton, 2007.

———. *André Kertész: Sixty Years of Photography, 1912–1972*. Edited by Nicolas Ducrot. Grossman, 1972.

———. *Les Cathédrales du Vin*. With a text by Pierre Hamp. Sainrapt et Brice, 1937.

———. *Day of Paris*. Edited by George Davis. J. J. Augustin, 1945.

———. *Distortions*. Edited by Nicolas Ducrot. With a text by Hilton Kramer. Knopf, 1976.

———. *From My Window*. With a text by Peter MacGill. New York Graphic Society/Little, Brown, 1981.

———. *Hungarian Memories*. With a text by Hilton Kramer. New York Graphic Society/Little, Brown, 1982.

———. *J'aime Paris: Photographs Since the Twenties*. Edited by Nicolas Ducrot. Grossman, 1974.

——. *Kertész on Kertész: A Self-Portrait*. With a text by Peter Adam. Abbeville, 1985.

——. *Of New York*. Edited by Nicolas Ducrot. Knopf, 1976.

——. *On Reading*. Grossman, 1971.

——. *Paris Vu par André Kertész*. With a text by Pierre Mac Orlan. Plon/Éditions d'histoire et d'art, 1934.

——. *Stranger to Paris: André Kertész*. With a text by Robert Enright. Jane Corkin Gallery, 1992.

——. *Washington Square*. Edited by Nicolas Ducrot. Text by Brendan Gill. Grossman Viking, 1975.

Kertész, André, Pierre Bonhomme, Sandra S. Phillips, Isabelle Jammes, Jean-Claude Lemagny, and Michel Frizot. *André Kertész: Ma France*. Paris: La Manufacture/Ministère de la Culture, 1990.

Kertész, André, and Jean Nohain (Jaboune). *Nos Amies les Bêtes*. Plon/Éditions d'histoire et d'art, 1936.

——. *Soixante Photographies d'Enfants*. Plon/Éditions d'histoire et d'art, 1933.

Kincses, Károly, and Magdolna Kolta. *Hazai Anyag: Fotónapló. André Kertész és a magyarok. / Pictures from Home: Photo Diary. André Kertész and Hungarians.* Mai Manó House, 2005.

Marton, Kati. *The Great Escape: Nine Jews Who Fled Hitler and Changed the World.* Simon & Schuster, 2006.

Mondenard, Anne de. *L'Odyssée d'une Icône: Trois Photographies d'André Kertész.* Actes Sud/Maison Européenne de la Photographie, 2006.

Nicolas, Jean, Renée Nicolas, and Pascal Lemaître. *La Savoie d'André Kertész*. La Fontaine de Siloé, 2004.

Ollier, Brigitte, and Elisabeth Nora. *Rogi André: Photo Sensible*. Éditions du Regard, 1999.

Phillips, Sandra S., David Travis, and Weston J. Naef. *André Kertész: Of Paris and New York.* Thames and Hudson, 1985.

Rogniat, Évelyne. *André Kertész: Le Photographe à l'Oeuvre.* Presses universitaires de Lyon, 1997.

Siegel, Elizabeth, ed. *André Kertész: Postcards from Paris*. Art Institute of Chicago, 2021.

Szarkowski, John. *André Kertész, Photographer.* Museum of Modern Art, 1964.

Travis, David. *At the Edge of the Light: Thoughts on Photography & Photographers, Talent & Genius*. David R. Godine, 2003.

## FILMS


Adam, Peter, producer. *André Kertész* (BBC Master Photographers Series). With photography by Ron Bleicher, Ira Brenner, David Gray, and Malcolm Kipling. BBC Television in association with Chanowski Productions and Andreas Landshoff Productions, 1983.

Musilli, John, director. *Everything Is Photograph: A Profile of André Kertész.* Written by Stephan Chodorov, with photography by Michael Livesey and Reuben Aaronson. Camera Three Productions and Creative Arts Television, 1978.

Ugrin, Béla, director. *André Kertész: A Poet with the Camera.* You Gotta Have Art series. With support from the Olympus Corporation. KUHT, 1985.

Wehn-Damisch, Teri, director. *André Kertész of the Cities: Budapest, Paris, New York.* TF1 with support of the French Ministry of Culture, 1986; Biography Series American Masters, 1988.

# CREDITS

Unless otherwise noted, all photographs by André Kertész
© The Estate of André Kertész / courtesy Stephen Bulger Gallery

## CHAPTER HEADS

| | |
|---|---|
| **Introduction, p. xiv** | André Kertész, *Self-Portrait, Paris*, 1927 |
| **One, p. 10** | André Kertész, *Sleeping Boy*, 1912 |
| **Two, p. 44** | André Kertész, *Forced March to the Front*, 1915 |
| **Three, p. 76** | André Kertész, *We Lost the War*, c. 1918 |
| **Four, p. 110** | André Kertész, *Chez Mondrian*, 1926 |
| **Five, p. 144** | André Kertész, *Satiric Dancer*, 1927 |
| **Six, p. 180** | André Kertész, *Clock of the French Academy*, 1929 |
| **Seven, p. 212** | André Kertész, *Elizabeth and I*, 1933 |
| **Eight, p. 246** | André Kertész, *Melancholic Tulip*, 1939 |
| **Nine, p. 282** | André Kertész, *Manhattan Bridge, New York*, 1947 |
| **Ten, p. 318** | André Kertész, *Martinique*, 1972 |
| **Eleven, p. 356** | André Kertész, *Flowers for Elizabeth*, 1977 |
| **Twelve, p. 392** | André Kertész, *Self-Portrait with Masks*, 1976 |

PHOTO INSERT

1 André Kertész, Untitled (Self-portrait as soldier, Gorizia, 1914)

2 André Kertész, *Dunaharaszti, June, 1919*

3 André Kertész, Untitled (Self-portrait with Elizabeth, 1921)

4 André Kertész, Untitled (André, Ernesztina, Jenő, 1922)

5 André Kertész, Untitled (André Kertész, his brother Imre, and Rózsi on the balcony of the Kertész family apartment), © GrandPalaisRmn / André Kertész / Donation André Kertész, Ministère de la Culture (France), Médiathèque de l'architecture et du patrimoine

6 André Kertész, *Party at Joseph Csáky's, 1927*

7 André Kertész, Photo on cover of *Vu*, October 3, 1928, Collection Musée Nicéphore Niépce, Ville de Chalon-sur-Saône

8 Rogi André, Untitled (Self-portrait), courtesy Bibliothèque nationale de France

9 André Kertész, *Elizabeth and I, Café in Montparnasse*, 1931

10 André Kertész, Untitled (Self-portrait working for Condé Nast, 1946), © The Estate of André Kertész / courtesy Stephen Bulger Gallery and Condé Nast

11 André Kertész, Untitled (André and Elizabeth at Newtown, Connecticut, c. 1955)

12 Photographer unknown, Untitled (André with Frank Dobo) / courtesy Michael Dobo and György Németh

13 Martine Franck, Untitled (André Kertész with portrait of Elizabeth), 1979, © Martine Franck, Magnum Photos, Inc.

14 Martine Franck, Untitled (Manual Álvarez Bravo, André Kertész, and Henri Cartier-Bresson, 1979), © Martine Franck, Magnum Photos, Inc.

15 Gilles Walusinski, Untitled (Jack Lang), 1984, courtesy Gilles Walusinski, © Gilles Walusinski, reproduced with permission

16 Sylvia Plachy, Untitled, 1984, photograph © Sylvia Plachy

# INDEX


Aba-Novák, Vilmos, 89, 90, 101, 102, 157
Abbott, Berenice, 5, 130, 153, 159, 190, 197, 294, 295, 341; scribbled self-portrait, 426
academies, 12, 63: Académie Française, 181, 182; Academy of Commerce, Budapest, 14–15, 26; *Clock of the French Academy*, 180, 182–83, 192; Hungarian Academy of Fine Arts (now the Hungarian University of Fine Arts), 89, 152
accordion, 60, 290, 408
Ács, Márta, 310, 337, 384, 415, 421
Adams, Ansel, 277, 294, 309, 337, 369, 373, 387, 421; and photography, 249–50, 260–61
Adhémar, Jean, 331–32, 333
advertising industry, 198, 229, 242, 256–57, 260, 284, 298, 322, 383, 387; advertisements, 188–89, 194, 293
Ady, Endre, 78, 79, 89, 225–27, 391, 443n5, 491n82; *Az Igazi Ady*, 225–26, 463n33; "Gare de l'Est," 152, 313
AEAR. *See* Association of Revolutionary Writers and Artists (AEAR)
Agha, M. F., 257, 260, 261, 287, 296
André, Rogi, 221, 222, 235, 293, 367, 368, 399, 459n23, 461n49; portrait of Wassily Kandinsky, 487n28. *See also* Klein, Rózsi
André and Elizabeth Kertész Foundation, the, 409, 415, 423, 430, 489n43
Angelo (Pál Vilmos Funk), 103–4, 106, 107, 113, 452n7; shades of, 123, 272
anti-Semitism, 46, 53, 72, 87, 116, 228, 455–56n44; in Hungary, 87, 98, 200, 263, 264, 281
Arbus, Diane, 5, 487n28
Arc-en-Ciel puppet theater, 174, 175, 176
Archipenko, Alexander, 116, 219
Arma, Paul, 2, 159
Art Institute of Chicago, 291, 292, 326, 401, 416–18
Association des Amis d'André Kertész, 408, 422, 423–24, 497n90
Association of Revolutionary Writers and Artists (AEAR), 234, 235
Atget, Eugène, 121, 158, 233
auction houses, 306, 368, 379, 380, 402, 423, 489n55
Austria-Hungary, 33, 36, 46, 49, 55, 73; Austro-Hungarian Dual Monarchy, 424
Avedon, Richard, 316, 378, 393, 426
awards: *Borsszem Jankó*, contest prize, 63; Chevalier of the Legion of Honor, 407; Duke of Edinburgh Award, 396; French National Grand Prize in Photography, 407; International Center of Photography, Master of Photography Lifetime Achievement Award, 415; National Association of Hungarian Amateur Photographers, certificate of honorable mention 100–101;

awards (*cont'd*):
Order of Arts and Letters Award, 381; Order of the Banner, Budapest, 410; Prix Nadar, 351

Bakht, Igor (Igor Bakhtamian), 342, 345, 346, 359, 371, 377, 395, 396, 402, 416
Balog, Jolán, 11–13, 15, 22, 30, 41, 54–55, 131; AK and, 45–46, 49, 64, 72, 79; and Ármin Gál, 73, 442n49; and Révész, 31, 32
Baumeister, Willi, 139, 176
Beaton, Cecil, 252, 257, 294, 316
Beaux-Arts apartment, New York, 247, 253, 262, 273
beekeeping, 94, 95, 97, 98
benches, 29, 32, 60, 117–18, 131, 228–29, 234; broken, 6, 323; empty, 285, 301–2, 308; park, 3, 33, 302
Beöthy, István, 138, 145, 151, 152, 452n6, 452n6; *Héros, Action Direct (Torso)*, 146–48
Bibliothèque Nationale, Paris, 331, 336, 340, 349, 368, 492n9
billboards, 3, 140, 154, 164, 228–29, 334
Bing, Ilse, 151, 214
Bismarck, Otto von, 33, 438n55
Blattner, Géza, 138, 174–75, 176, 217, 389, 457n61
Bois de Boulogne, Paris, 162, 232
Bölöni, György, 225, 226
Bondi, Inge, 348, 360
book projects: *Day of Paris*, 290–93, 474nn22, 24; *Distortions*, 278, 371; *From My Window*, 398; *Hungarian Memories*, 398, 401–2; *J'aime Paris: Photographs since the Twenties*, 382; *Kertész on Kertész: A Self-Portrait*, 414; *Landscapes, Birds, Portraits, and Americana*, 397–98; *La Route Paris Méditerranée*, with Morand, 228; *Les Cathédrales du Vin*, 242; *New York Seen by André Kertész*, 239, 253, 266, 337; *Nos Amies les Bêtes*, 242, 303; *Of New York*, 377; *On Reading*, 349, 484n78, 492n12; *On S'amuse*, 409; *Paris Automne*, 332, 337, 338; *Paris Vu par André Kertész*, 232–33, 234, 238, 239; *Report on Israel*, by Robert Capa and Irwin Shaw (layout), 308–9; *Sixty Years of Photography, 1912–1972*, 350–51, 358, 360–61, 363; *Soixante Photographies d'Enfants*, 224–25, 232, 332, 338; *Washington Square*, 370, 382. *See also* publishers
booksellers, 12, 63, 225, 236–37, 408, 426
Boothe, Clare, 268, 269
Brady, Mathew, 5, 338–39
Brandt, Bill, 4, 294
Brassaï, 4, 5, 88, 151, 235, 237–38, 312–13, 331; and AK, 208, 330, 481n39; death of, 412–13, 414, 421; in *Harper's Bazaar*, 237, 294, 313; *Paris de Nuit (Paris by Night)*, 213, 214, 215, 233; *Transmutations*, 334. *See also* Halász, Gyula
Breton, André, 117, 118, 259
Brodovitch, Alexey, 250–51, 256, 257, 290, 295, 344–45
bromoil, 99, 100, 101, 103
Brower, Carol, 385, 418
Brüll, Adél, 78, 79
Buda, 22, 31, 35, 56, 57–58, 82, 95, 154. *See also* Budapest; Pest
Budafok, 102, 103, 104
Budapest, 17–19, 24, 62, 67, 90, 93, 200, 377, 410; artists and, 445n24; assignment to photograph Hungarian thermal baths in, 235–36; Franz Joseph Bridge, 21, 437n30; and the Nazis, 287–89; parks in, 22, 33, 81; postwar, 73, 206, 302; theater in, 26–27. *See also* Buda; Jews, in Budapest; Pest

Café Bonaparte, New York, 247, 256
Café du Dôme, Paris, 2, 111, 149, 159, 206, 230, 302; AK with Rózsi at, 164, 174; blind man at, 150–51; contacts made at, 120–21, 124, 138, 143, 162–63, 187, 192, 208, 236–37, 254; friends at, 129, 165, 230, 243, 257; Hungarian table at, 2, 112, 132, 197; Soviet table at, 208
Calder, Alexander, 125, 187–88, 217, 290, 381, 389
Callahan, Harry, 294, 358

cameras: AK's first, a German-made box camera, 27; Canon FT QL, 405; Contax, 290; drawn as a self-portrait, 426; Eastman Kodak Super XX panchromatic, 299–300; Ermanox, 122; Gaumont Reporter, 122, 135, 168–69; glass-plate, 169, 192; Goerz Anschütz, 115, 135; Goerz Tenax, 2, 48, 49, 56, 69–70, 104, 108, 111, 131, 135, 440n6; Graflex Speed Graphic, 252, 270; Ica Bebe, 40; Icarette, 456n49; Leica I Model A, 166–67; Linhof, 168–69, 216, 247, 299, 427; Lorillon, 168–69; minicams, 251, 268; and motor drives, 403; Olympus, 405, 411, 412, 427; Polaroid SX-70, 386, 387, 427; Rolleiflex, 299, 460n33; SLR (single-lens reflex) cameras, 320, 405; Solyom and Minox, 412; Tri-X (ISO 400), 300; Vest Pocket Kodak, 440n6; view camera, 81, 121, 299, 427; Voigtländer Alpin, 9, 34, 82, 108, 135, 154, 155, 168–69, 193, 368; Zeiss Ideal, 168–69; Zeiss Super Ikonta, 299. *See also* Leica
Capa, Cornell, 263–64, 309, 310, 341, 342, 345, 415, 421; *Death in the Making*, 255; *The Falling Soldier*, 242; show *The Concerned Eye* at Riverside Museum, 345–46
Capa, Edie, 306, 310, 346
Capa, Robert, 4, 237–38, 263–64, 308–9, 341, 346, 352; and civil war in Spain, 241–42, 255; mentioned 5, 415. *See also* Friedman, Endre
*cartes postales* (postcards), 148, 168, 380, 388, 416, 423, 492n9; project, 61, 64, 127–29, 348
Cartier-Bresson, Henri, 4, 151, 154, 324, 334, 341, 351–52, 353, 393, 427; and Association des Amis d'André Kertész, 408–9, 422, 423–24; retrospective at Musée des Arts Décoratifs, 331
Centre Pompidou, Paris, 381, 385
Cézanne, Paul, 91, 112
Chagall, Marc, 116, 223, 399
Champs-Élysées, Paris, 157, 198, 207, 235
Circle of Confusion, 268, 294–95, 325
circus, 81, 102, 151, 213, 296, 343–44, 408; acrobats, 6, 148, 150, 187, 427; Alexander Calder and, 187–88, 217, 389; clowns, 107, 131; *The Circus, Budapest*, 81–82, 480n9
Clicquot Club Company, 194, 198
clochards, 148, 150, 167, 234, 407
Colette, 195–96, 211, 399
concentration camps, 264, 281, 286–88, 293, 366–67, 452n3; Auschwitz, 287, 288, 289, 367; prison camps, 65, 289
contact sheets, 167–68, 319, 336
copyright, 171, 409, 411–12, 423
Cosmia Laboratories, 262, 284, 310, 322, 330, 333, 340, 342, 409
Courbevoie, 113, 127, 136
cropping, 89, 128, 248, 353, 401, 427; of photos, 85, 88, 253, 256, 350, 401
Csáky, Joseph, 115–16, 128, 138, 156
Cubism, 129, 267, 427

Dabit, Eugène, 205–6, 238, 241
Dadaists, 117, 130, 139–40
Daguerre, Louis-Jacques-Mandé, 130, 178, 287
Dalí, Salvador, 259, 260
dance, 86, 93, 145, 197, 290; *Air Mail Dances*, 484n75; the bal musette, 408; companies, 264–65; halls, 120, 131
dancers, 90, 111, 112, 148, 176, 214, 216, 259; Clayton "Peg Leg" Bates, 191; marionette's shadow and, 129–30; to photograph, 209, 264–65; *Satiric Dancer*, 144, 146–48, 369, 377, 402, 452–53n7, 484n75. *See also* Förstner, Magda
darkroom, 27, 35, 54, 173, 253, 426, 472n93; costs of, 262, 279; first one in Paris, 3, 113, 136; Igor Bakhtamian and, 342, 371; in New York, 284, 286; trickery in, 122, 182–83, 249; work become impossible, 262, 279, 342; work in the, 129, 154–55, 183, 191, 192–93, 218; working without one, 60, 113, 127, 342
depth of field, 35, 103, 267, 299, 388
d'Erleich, Jean. *See* Halász, Gyula
Deschin, Jacob, 294, 351

Deutscher Werkbund, 188, 189, 190, 197
Distortions series, 8, 217–20, 222, 256, 292, 335–37, 370; a book of the, 239, 278, 371, 425; camera used for, 247, 454n25; exhibitions of, 230, 248, 307, 406; French-German edition of the, 223–24; #157, 400, 401; owned by Graham Nash, 386; sold to Frank Crowninshield, 482n47; Steiglitz and, 258–59
divorce proceedings, 208–10, 221–22, 368
Doisneau, Robert, 4, 151, 377
Ducrot, Jean, 165, 350
Ducrot, Nicolas, 370, 371, 378, 382–83, 397, 425, 492n12; and Elizabeth Kertész, 350, 381

Eiffel Tower, Paris, 103, 114, 170, 128, 137, 138–39, 236, 291; *Eiffel Tower, Paris*, 183–85, 207; *Self-Portrait, Paris*, 1, 3, 9
Eisner, Maria Giovanna, 229–30, 286, 287, 336
El, the, in Chicago, 253, 256
enlargers, 60, 88–89, 127, 284, 372
Ernst Museum, Budapest, 89, 101
estate planning, 382, 408, 409
European Picture Service, 251, 278
Evans, Walker, 5, 261, 297, 421
exhibitions, 188, 256, 340, 360, 377, 401, 408, 421, 458n14; *André Kertész: A Portrait at Ninety*, Osaka, 419; at the Art Institute of Chicago, 292, 326, 416–17; *Film und Foto* (*FiFo*), Stuttgart, 188, 189, 190, 197; at Maison Leleu, 230; at the Musée des Arts Décoratifs, Paris, 238, 248, 331; at the Pavillon des Arts, Les Halles, Paris, 423–24; at the Salon de l'Escalier, Paris, 158, 159, 160; Venice Photography Biennale, May 1963, 324–25, 492n9. *See also* Museum of Modern Art (MoMA), exhibitions at

Fárová, Anna, 6–7, 341
Fekete, Lajos, 22–23, 28, 29
Fels, Florent, 184, 232
Fifth Avenue, New York, 247, 251, 279, 310, 359, 381, 395, 415; AK's apartment at number 2, 305–6, 308, 398
flute, 12, 13, 19, 22, 37, 108, 123, 152, 160, 214, 306
Förstner, Magda, 146–48, 211, 369, 452nn6, 7; caricatures, 145
Foujita, Tsuguharu, 112, 164, 187, 458n6
Frank, Robert, 4, 5, 292, 421
French Ministry of Culture, 407, 408, 410, 411–12
Freund, Gisèle, 168, 393, 408, 422
Friedlander, Lee, 376–77
Friedman, Endre, 230–31, 237–38. *See also* Capa, Robert
Frizot, Michel, 320, 430, 482n46
Futurists, 123, 139

Gaillard, Agathe, 69, 408–9, 402, 412, 420; Galerie Agathe Gaillard, Paris, 407, 411; and Susan Harder, 394–95; and postcard project, 348
galleries, 198, 357, 368, 379, 396, 422, 485n78; Au Sacre du Printemps, Paris, 138–41, 162, 176, 185; Carleton Gallery, Ottawa, 372; Corcoran Gallery of Art, Washington, DC, 413; E. Weyhe, New York, 278; Edwynn Houk Gallery, Chicago, 416; Galerie Agathe Gaillard, Paris, 407, 411; Galerie de la Pléiade, Paris, 235; Galerie Georges Petit, Paris, 219; Galérie Surréaliste, Paris, 457n62; Gentry Galleries, New York, 307; Hallmark Gallery, New York, 359, 360, 370; Hungarian National Gallery, Budapest, 32; Hungarian National Museum, Budapest, 93; Julien Levy's, New York, 260, 357; L'Esthétique, Paris, 173–74; Limelight, Greenwich Village, 357; Marlborough Fine Art Gallery, New York, 378–79, 414; Olympus Gallery, London, 414; Pace/MacGill Gallery, New York, 406; Photography House, New York, 348; PM Galleries, New York, 256, 259; Serpentine Gallery, London, 399; Susan Harder Gallery, New York, 401–3.

*See also* gallerists; Light Gallery, New York; Museum of Modern Art (MoMA)
gallerists, 379, 385, 396; Daniel Wolf, 417; Helen Gee, 362; Ileana Sonnabend, 379; Jan Slivinsky, 138, 140; Julien Levy, 260, 357; Marjorie Neikrug, 357; Simon Lowinsky, 386
Gallotti, Jean, 164, 178
Gassmann, Peter (Pierre), 230, 334, 368
Gibson, Ralph, 393, 405, 420, 421
Gill, Brendan, 6, 370, 376, 419
Giro Bank and Transfers, 75, 83–84, 88, 92
glass plates, 34, 35, 98, 115, 130, 136, 216, 395–96; an expense, 120; at the front, 48, 49, 54, 57; for box camera, 27; for Ica Bebe, 39–40; Paouillac and, 335–36, 370; Rózsi Klein (Rogi André) and, 209, 367; for Venice Photography Biennale, 324–25. *See also* cameras, glass-plate; negatives, glass-plate
glass cutters, 38, 57
Goldfinger, Ernő, 111, 135, 159, 447n1
Goodyear Tire and Rubber, 265, 283
Greenough, Sarah, 328–29, 445n23
Greenwich Village, New York, 5, 284, 357, 376
Groszmann, Frigyes, 53, 440n13
Gruber, Fritz, 362, 377
Grundberg, Andy, 369, 421
Guggenheim Memorial Foundation, the John Simon, 370, 382
Gurbo, Robert, 78, 419, 443n1
Guttmann, Henry, 177, 209, 220, 457n67

Habsburg, House of, 16, 32, 90, 365, 424
Habsburg Empire, 23, 38, 42, 49, 62, 66, 78–79; army of the, 37, 45, 74, 439n3; loyalty to the, 52, 46
Halász, Gyula, 184, 185, 186, 192, 193; as Jean d'Erleich, 185, 193. *See also* Brassaï
Harbutt, Charles, 384, 396
Harder, Susan, 394, 401, 406, 409, 419, 421, 422
*Harper's Bazaar*, 241, 257, 273, 284, 294, 297, 344; AK portfolio in, 211; Brassaï and, 237, 313; history of photography in, 287–88; reportage for, 250–52
Hearst, William Randolph, 250, 252
Hine, Lewis, 271, 345–46, 421
Hitler, Adolf, 220, 224, 227, 228, 263, 281
Hockney, David, 362–63, 379
Hoffmann, Rudolf, 264, 482n47
Holocaust, 6, 264, 289, 366–67, 440n13. *See also* concentration camps
Hôtel Esmeralda, 407, 411
*House & Garden*, 296, 313, 314–17; postwar slogan at, 298, 476n59; scattered assignments for, 254, 256, 266
Hoyningen-Huene, George, 194, 257
Hungarian Soviet Republic, 83, 88, 89

ICP. *See* International Center of Photography (ICP)
immigrant status, 241, 336
Institut de France, 181, 182, 183
International Center of Photography (ICP), 415, 419

Jammes, André, 331–32, 334, 341
Jammes, Isabelle, 408, 422
Jaschik, Álmos, 93, 108, 236
Jews, 20–21, 25, 39, 46, 80, 87, 118–19, 220, 227, 366; AK one, 39, 95, 98, 142, 293–94, 301, 367; in Budapest, 17, 21, 24, 53, 98, 103, 112, 281, 289, 475n36; Galician, 18, 46, 52–53, 54; German, 264, 290; Hungarian, 39, 70–71, 165, 190, 287, 306, 365; in Hungary, 21, 52–53, 70–71, 238, 263, 289, 437n28, 440n12; in Paris, 206, 228, 230, 367–68, 455n44; quota for, 94–95. *See also* anti-Semitism; photographers, Jewish
Jones, Harold, 358, 378

Károlyi, Count Mihály, 24, 77–78, 83, 141
Kertész, Elizabeth, 298, 303, 311, 322–24, 337, 344, 373–74, 394, 405, 407; and Brassaï, 413; in correspondence, 360–61, 378; death of, 380–82, 384, 422; and Distortions, 371; and Grossman, 349–50, 360;

Kertész, Elizabeth (*cont'd*): in London, 330, 332; and naturalization papers, 284; in New York, 262, 264, and Rogi André, 360. *See also* Cosmia Laboratories; Salamon, Erzsébet

Kertész, Ernesztina, 15–18, 25, 46, 80, 81, 88, 95, 108, 149, 200; and AK, 104, 107, 115, 118, 133; and coffee shop, 30, 84, 438n48; death of, 222, 223; inheritance from, 237, 248; photographs of, 88, 106

Kertész, Imre, 15, 16, 17, 23, 24, 46, 88, 95, 280, 288; and AK, 40–41, 104, 207, 302; in anti-Semitic Hungary, 263, 264; in correspondence, 118–20, 133, 142, 216, 220, 222, 223, 239; death of, 310; and Goerz Anschütz camera, 135; and Jenő Kertész, 149, 280, 281; and Margit (Gréti), 207, 236; in photographs, 81, 106

Kertész, Jenő, 19, 23, 33, 35, 42, 46, 72, 84, 101, 173, 280; and AK in the army, 36, 38, 41, 47, 50; in AK's will, 415; bought AK an Ica Bebe, 40; in correspondence, 50–51, 87, 115, 119, 120, 129, 162, 237; in hospital, 420; in Latin America, 133, 136, 149, 161–62, 222, 223, 280, 325; married, 222, 406; and Mazdaznan, 86, 444n17; as model, 35, 81, 85, 89, 90, 91, 107, 128; "Öcskös" (little brother), 319; and photography, 27, 53, 54, 155, 166, 214, 337; reinvented as Eugenio Kertész, 162; son of, called Imre Kertész, 422

Kertész, Lipót (father), 12, 14, 15, 16, 17, 80

Kertész, Lipót (Uncle Poldi), 14, 15, 24, 36, 41, 45, 80, 106, 133, 162; and AK, 26, 104; death of, 114; and Ernesztina Kertész, 46, 104, 223

Kertész, Margit (Gréti), 207, 223, 236, 240, 281, 288, 317, 326

Keystone View Company of New York (Keystone Press Agency), 238–39, 240, 241, 243–44, 247, 280, 293, 325, 467n15; AK under contract to, 251–52; immigrant status thanks to, 336

King, Alexander, 267–68, 272

Klein, Rózsi, 138, 145, 164, 197, 199–200, 208, 209–10, 452n6; abandoned, 201–2, 204–5, 460n33; AK's lover and wife, 151–52, 172–75, 190–91. *See also* André, Rogi

Klopfer, Margit Grósz, 25, 34

Klopfer, Móricz Mihály (Misi), 25–26, 84–85, 95, 148, 328, 437n38

Klopfer, Rózsi, 118, 119, 289

Kodachrome transparencies, 300, 332, 387

Kodak, 300, 370, 371, 456n48

Koenig, Alexander. *See* King, Alexander

Komroff, Manuel, 257, 268, 473n9

Korb, Erzsébet, 91, 101

Kramer, Hilton, 370, 371

Krull, Germaine, 151, 197, 203, 233, 235, 237, 421, 456n49, 458n14; AK's colleague, 158, 161, 184, 190, 192; *Vu* and, 163, 170, 178, 184

Kubota, Hiroji, 4–5, 347, 353, 419, 421

Kun, Béla, regime, 83, 84, 86, 87

La Trappe, Soligny-la-Trappe, 169–72, 232, 267, 271

Lang, Jack, 408, 411

Lange, Dorothea, 342, 421

Lartigue, Jacques Henri, 5, 154, 327, 328, 329, 337, 393, 407–8

Le Corbusier (Charles-Édouard Jeanneret), 138, 140, 192

Leco lab, 279, 472n93

Lefèvre, Frédéric, 202, 203, 204

Léger, Fernand, 116, 156–57, 367; *Corner of Léger's Studio*, 156

Leica, 3–4, 168, 226, 250, 311, 332, 405, 426–27; in hand, 312, 376; *Leica Manual*, 268; negatives, 167; photographers and, 157, 192, 208, 241, 251, 268, 300, 320, 345, 352; as portrait in absence, 3, 130, 365–66; Robert Frank and, 292, 376

Lemagny, Jean-Claude, 7, 368, 427

Lenses, 100, 122, 155, 218, 268, 321, 352; Angénieux, 320; Busche, 192–93; Elmar, 166; Goerz Anschütz, 115, 135; Goerz Dagor, 48, 115, 135; Satz Plasmat lens, 155, 217, 254, 454nn25–26; Schneider, 320;

Telepeconar, 371; telephoto, 9, 301, 320, 419; Tessar, 270; Zeiss Tessar, 34, 40, 217; zoom, 320, 321, 332, 352, 371, 411
Les Halles, Paris, 154, 167, 423–24
Levin, Meyer, 307, 477n77
Liberman, Alexander, 236, 295–97, 300, 314–15, 317, 362
Liebermann, Jakab (Jaksay), 13–14, 64
*Life* magazine, 7, 168, 271, 272, 292, 297, 307, 337, 471n68; Cornell Capa and, 255, 308, 309, 341; editors at, 267, 290; RKO movie company suing, 252–53; and *Vu*, 268, 269
Liftin, Joan, 384, 396, 405
Light Gallery, New York, 357–60, 368–69, 381, 394–96, 406, 418; AK and, 372–74, 376–77, 379
light meters, 35, 40, 56, 193, 405
Littman, Frederic, 137, 159, 365, 425
Loos, Adolf, 2, 132, 135, 139
Lorant, Stefan, 177, 184, 220, 306, 413, 475n36
Lotar, Eli, 163, 169, 170, 190, 197, 235
Louvre, the, Paris, 182, 183, 192, 238, 428
Luce, Henry, 252, 269, 271. *See also* publications, *Fortune* magazine
Lurçat, André, 135, 159
Luxembourg Garden, Paris, 123, 165, 193, 197, 214, 215, 226, 292; in photos, 131–32, 214, 226

Mac Orlan, Pierre, 160–61, 178, 189, 206–7, 234
MacGill, Peter, 384, 387, 395, 406
Maeterlinck, Maurice and Renée, 210, 211, 232
Magnum photographic cooperative, 341–42, 345, 348, 352
Magyarization 17–18, 446n28
Magyars, 12, 23, 60, 79, 99; folk culture of 267, 305; identity of, 38, 258; lands of, 83, 90; *Magyar Hírlap*, 132; *Magyar Jövő*, 288
Márai, Sándor, 132, 137
marionettes, 3, 116, 129–30, 167, 197, 306, 319, 320, 477n77; Blattner and, 174–75, 217, 389
Marshall, Brooke (Brooke Astor), 298–99, 300
Martinez, Romeo, 324, 330, 331, 334, 362, 368, 393
Mazdaznan body culture, 86–87, 133, 136, 147
Mendl, Lady, 195, 211
Ménière's disease, 262, 310, 342, 382, 416
Metropolitan Museum of Art, New York, 373, 405, 416, 417–18, 421
Meyerowitz, Joel, 376, 403
Michals, Duane, 344, 362, 363
Miller, Wick, 264, 265–66, 268, 272
mirrors, 29, 96, 131, 134, 142, 162, 219, 267; barber's, 405; distorting, 216–17, 218, 253, 259, 365, 386, 468n34, 475n42; full-length, 134; funhouse, 3, 216, 253; "intelligent," 216, 411; and self-portraits, 37, 91. *See also* Distortions series
Model, Evsa, 138, 143, 173–74, 295, 460n33
Model, Lisette (Lisette Seybert), 204, 295, 298, 312, 341, 460n33, 487n28
modernism, 78–79, 89–90, 100, 188, 249; AK and, 4–5, 114, 157, 189, 312, 320, 321, 337–38
modernists, 89–90, 176, 186, 367; AK as an early one, 200, 292, 329, 336, 338, 359
Modigliani, Amedeo, 111–12, 186–87, 219
Moholy-Nagy, László, 88, 121, 188–89, 190, 261, 286, 298, 421, 473n11
Mondrian, Piet, 130, 137, 138, 141, 367; AK and, 132, 139, 154, 157, 159, 399, 427; *Chez Mondrian*, 110, 346, 377, 395–96, 489n55, 492n9; *Mondrian's Glasses and Pipe*, 126–27; his studio, 124–27, 176
Montmartre, Paris, 2, 154, 332–33; *The Stairs of Montmartre*, 155–56
Montparnasse, Paris, 2, 132, 139, 147, 185, 198; boulevard du, 173, 202, 206; train station, 124, 165, 175, 205
Morgan, Willard, 268, 472n87, 475n42
Moulin Rouge, the, 115, 191
Munkácsi, Martin, 251, 273, 297, 352
Museum of Modern Art (MoMA), 248, 313, 337; AK and, 276, 329, 343–44; Beaumont Newhall at, 277, 309, 493n23; Distortion print #157 cropped for, 248–49, 256, 400–401; Monroe Wheeler at, 320, 326; and photography as art, 249, 277, 309, 387, 400, 415; Willard Morgan at, 472n87

Museum of Modern Art (MoMA), exhibitions at, 309, 327, 472n87; *American Photographs*, 261; *André Kertész*, 339–40; *The Artist in His Studio: Photographs by Alexander Liberman*, 314; *The Family of Man*, 309; *Fantastic Art, Dada, Surrealism*, 259; *From My Window*, 398; *Image of Freedom*, 276–77; Kertész retrospective, 337, 350; *The Photographer's Eye*, 338; *Photography 1839–1937*, 249; *Picasso: 75th Anniversary*, 311–12; *Sixty Years of Photography, 1912–1972*, 350; three-person show with Aleksandr Rodchenko and László Moholy-Nagy, 373
Museums, 331, 360; André Kertész Museum, Szigetbecse, 410; Carnegie Museum of Art, Pittsburgh, 484n78; Folkwang Museum, Essen, 190; George Eastman Museum, Rochester, NY, 493n23; Hungarian National Museum, Budapest, 93; Israel Museum, Jerusalem, 390; J. Paul Getty Museum, Los Angeles, 417; Jacksonville Art Museum (now MOCA Jacksonville), 416; Musée des Arts Décoratifs, Paris, 238, 248, 331; Musée Jacquemart-André, Paris, 497n90; Museo Nacional de Bellas Artes, Buenos Aires, 419–20; Museum of Contemporary Photography, Chicago, 484n78; National Museum of Photography, Film, and Television, Bradford, UK, 414; Riverside Museum, New York, 345–46, 348; Whitney Museum, New York, 381. *See also* Museum of Modern Art (MoMA); Museum of Modern Art (MoMA), exhibitions at
musicians, 60, 97–98, 128–29, 403, 450n36

Naef, Weston, 270, 316, 405, 416, 417
Nagybánya artists, 87, 89–90, 112
Nash, Graham and Susan, 386, 387
Nast, Condé, 273, 277, 296, 313–14, 315, 340, 387; AK and, 295, 298, 302, 303–4, 316, 325, 329; publications, 194, 252, 268–69, 278, 296, 297
National Association of Hungarian Amateur Photographers, 100, 101
Nazis, 211, 231, 235, 270, 303, 306, 366, 435n4, 473n11; AK and, 293, 335; in Budapest, 287–88, 365; and Jews, 264, 289, 366; Nazification, 236, 279; in Paris, 277–78; Rogi André and, 367–38
negatives, 88, 122, 127, 136, 148, 218, 426, 462n15; in AK's estate, 406, 408, 411, 415, 422–24, 489n43; Bakht and, 342, 346, 380, 402; of *Broken Plate*, 371–72; and contact sheets, 167–68, 243, 319, 324; cropped, 85, 91, 129, 350, 353; early difficulties with, 27, 28, 34, 35; from the front, 50, 60–61, 73–74; in glassine envelopes, 148, 243; glass-plate, 109, 128, 136, 243, 334, 336–37, 370, 371, 474n22; left behind in Europe, 243, 335–37; of *Melancholic Tulip*, 348; and permissions, 304, 342, 382; and prints, 59, 70, 153, 284, 374, 379, 395, 497n90; Rózsi (Rogi) and, 173, 197, 202, 367, 487n28; 35 millimeter, 268, 325, 474n22; of *Underwater Swimmer*, 363
Népszínház Street, Budapest, 18, 19, 436n23
Newhall, Beaumont, 248–49, 277, 309, 362, 400, 401, 493n23
Newhall, Nancy, 277, 295
Noailles, Countess Anna de, 195, 196, 211
nudes, 199, 205, 215–16, 386, 402, 418, 466n3; of Jenő Kertész, 85, 90, 91, 128; MoMA and, 248, 256; by other artists, 89, 90–91, 99, 146, 197, 219, 334; semi-, 69, 86. *See also* Distortions series

Paouillac, Jacqueline, 243, 334–35, 336, 337
Papszt, Ede, 95, 96–97
Paris, 112, 228, 233–34, 287, 348, 423; AK's early days in, 1–2, 108–9, 112–14; City of Light, 148, 158, 183, 226, 233–34, 278, 291, 333; Colonial Exposition, 207; Commune, 235, 249; Mois de la Photo in, 407. *See also* Café du Dôme, Paris; Hôtel Esmeralda, Paris; and *individual place names*

Pearl Harbor, 274, 276
Peignot, Charles, 213, 238
Penn, Irving, 294, 314, 316
Pest, 18, 21–22, 24, 31, 65, 132, 177. *See also* Buda; Budapest
Phillips, Sandra, 199–200, 222, 398–99, 416, 417, 422
photo agencies, 231; Alliance Photo, Paris, 230; Black Star, New York, 278; Continental Photo, Budapest press, 113; Rapho Guillumette, Paris, 279
photo reportage, 166, 188, 197, 232; AK and 223, 236, 252, 294, 313, 328, 345, 353, 427; Keystone Agency and, 239, 250, 467n15; for *Life* magazine, 270, 271
photographers, 1, 275, 341, 396, 401, 402–3, 418, 424; art, 231, 260; fashion, 168, 231, 251, 273, 274, 297, 422; foreign, 98, 275, 278; Jewish, 171, 224, 335; magazine, 256, 332, 481n39; poet-, 161, 220; portrait, 116, 121, 188, 367, 371, 422; rights of, 168, 170, 171; staff, 99, 268, 297, 364; street, 168, 275, 320; studio, 142, 306. *See also* photojournalists
photographers by name: August Sander, 371; Cindy Sherman, 404; Douglas Faulkner, 419; Ed Ruscha, 404; Eikoh Hosoe, 393; Hiroshi Hamaya, 347; Jessie Tarbox Beals, 5; Manuel Álvarez Bravo, 393; Marianne Breslauer, 4; Maurice Tabard, 190; Max Winterstein, 209; Michael Shapiro, 453n7; Pierre Boucher, 230; Pierre De Fenoÿl, 381; Piet Zwart, 139; Richard Prince, 404; Rudolf Balogh, 99; Willy Ronis, 4. *See also individual names*
photographic film, 56, 243, 403; developed, 279, 334, 348, 375, 426; rolls of, 166–67, 265–66, 333, 375, 397, 403, 440n6; sheet, 135, 168, 182; speed, 40, 193. *See also* glass plates; Kodak
photographic paper, 90, 120, 122, 168, 372; Arches vellum, 225; gaslight, 61, 421; Ilford Galerie, 402; Ilford Multigrade Glossy, 343; R. Guilleminot, Bœspflug et Cie, 127; Scott Paper, 265; Sédar *carte postale* stock, 127
photographs: of Brăila's rail yards, 71–72; of Brassaï, 334; of Cantine La Marseillaise, 290; of Clayton "Peg Leg" Bates, 191; in Eperjes hospital, 56; of Erzsébet (Elizabeth), 94, 205, 212, 220–21, 350, 462n22, 488n43; from the front, 49–50, 51; of gatherings, 142–43; of Gunvor Berg, 133; of Gorizia, 38; of his brothers, 29, 81, 85, 86–87, 106; of his mother, 88, 106; from his youth, 101–2, 339; of the *Louise-Catherine*, 192–93; of Madame Maeterlinck, 211; of the Moulin Rouge, 115; of musicians, 60, 97–98, 128–29, 403, 450n36; of New York, 300, 321–22; of Paris, 114; of Place de la Concorde, 115; of Place Gambetta, 454n25; of Romani people, 60, 68–89; of Rue des Ursins, 454n25; of rue Vavin, 112–13; of Savoyard, 204; of tollhouse, 68
photographs by title: *Après le Bal*, 120; *Arm and Ventilator*, 253; *At Zadkine's*, 129; *Ballet*, 265; *Behind Notre Dame, Paris*, 115, 117; *Blind Violinist*, 97–98, 403; *Bocskay Square*, 480n9; *Bocskay-tér, Budapest*, 35; *Boy with Ball*, 161; *Broken Bench*, 323; *Broken Plate*, 371–72; *Cellars at Budafok*, 403; *Chairs, Luxembourg Gardens*, 131–32; *Chez Moi, Newtown*, 311, 383; *Chez Mondrian*, 110, 125–26, 346, 377, 395–96, 489n55, 492n9; *Chez Ossip Zadkine*, 130; *The Circus, Budapest*, 81–82, 480n9; *Clock of the French Academy*, 180, 182–83, 192; *Corner of Léger's Studio*, 156; *Dancing Faun*, 85; *Eiffel Tower, Paris*, 184–85, 207; *Elizabeth and I*, 212, 220–21, 350, 462n22; *The Eternal Tender Touch*, 51, 440n11; *Fairy Tale*, 63; *Flowers for Elizabeth*, 356, 383; *Forced March to the Front*, 44, 47, 48–49, 347; *Fork*, 159, 160, 189, 287; *Going for a Walk*, 311; *Hazy Day, Budapest*, 100; *Homing Ship*, 285, 428, 473nn6, 9, 480n9; *Hôtel des Clochards*, 148; *Hotel of Hope*, 148–49;

photographs by title (*cont'd*): *Hudson River Parkway*, 285; *Lajos Tihanyi*, 140, 428; *Legs, Paris*, 117, 118; *Lost Cloud*, 253–54, 287, 404; *Man at a Pissoir, Latin Quarter*, 140–41; *Manhattan Bridge, New York*, 282, 301, 477n66; *Martinique*, 318, 353–54, 377, 402; *Mauna Kea*, 374–75; *Melancholic Tulip*, 246, 266–67, 348, 402, 404, 484n76; *Meudon*, 175, 377, 399, 492n16; *A Midinette's Bedroom*, 137–38; *Mon ami Henri*, 351; *Mondrian's Glasses and Pipe*, 126–27; *Muguet Seller*, 198; *Nara (Oct. 8, 1968)*, 348; *On the Boulevards, Paris*, 229; *One and Half of Actor Aguet*, 134; *Paris Breakfast No. 30, Jan. 3, 1982*, 407; *Perfidy*, 365–67; *Poughkeepsie, New York*, 254, 339; *River Walk of Carl Schurz Park*, 301; *Satiric Dancer*, 144, 146–48, 369, 377, 402, 452–53n7, 484n75; *Shadow Painter*, 135–36, 140, 428; *Sleeping Boy*, 10, 30, 340; *The Stairs of Montmartre*, 155–56; *The Swing*, 69, 410; *Uncle Poldi*, 106; *Underwater Swimmer*, 70, 118, 292, 339, 363, 410; *Village Council*, 63; *Washington Square, Winter*, 307–8, 478n78; *We Lost the War*, 76–77; *Weather Vane and New York Skyline, September 19, 1952*, 305; *Wine Cellars at Budafok*, 102–3

photography, 4, 28, 197–98, 261, 286, 348, 377; AK's skills, 56–57; departments, 331–32, 379, 395, 417; golden age of, 231; industrial, 284; mechanics of, 34–35, 338, 376; modern, 158, 319; night, 193, 214–15; puppet, 174, 191, 223, 375; straight, 249–50, 277, 287. *See also* cameras; depth of field; glass plates; photographic film; street photography; studio photography; tripods

photojournalism, 4, 122, 342, 345, 484n70; American, 270. *See also* photo reportage

photojournalists, 169, 335, 341, 345, 347, 403; AK not one, 107, 297; gear for, 168, 300

photomontage, 189, 236, 260

Picasso, Pablo, 112, 219, 311, 313, 334, 361, 367

pictorialism, 99, 100, 101, 103, 157

picture press, 4, 99, 177, 197, 228, 387

Plachy, Sylvia, 4–5, 364, 365, 401, 419, 421

Pohorylle, Gerta, 237–38. *See also* Taro, Gerda

Polaroid, 386–88, 389–90, 397, 398, 402, 416, 427

Pont des Arts, Paris, 182, 192, 193

portraitists, 116, 121, 188, 371, 422

portraits, 130, 135, 139, 211, 298, 367, 427; in absence, 3, 130, 149, 156, 227; of Anne-Marie Merkel, 130; of Carlo Rim, 216; double, 91, 93–94, 97, 101, 105; of Ève Curie, 279; of Gyula Zilzer, 116; of his brothers, 29, 81, 85, 86–87, 106; of Joseph Csáky, 116; of the Károlyis, 142; of Lajos Tihanyi, 116–17; by Man Ray, 121; of Paprika Horváth, 68–69; by Rogi André, 368; of Sergei Eisenstein, 339. *See also* self-portraits

postcards. *See cartes postales*

press agencies, 170, 238, 342. *See also* Magnum photographic cooperative; photo agencies

Prince, Erney, 240, 241, 250, 467n15

publications, 99, 177, 198, 252; *Alfred Hitchcock's Mystery Magazine*, 323, 480n9; *American Magazine*, 272; *Aperture*, 324; *Art et Décoration*, 197; *Art et Industrie*, 121; *Art et Médecine*, 204, 206–7, 210, 223, 232, 297; *Artforum*, 379, 421; *Arts et Métiers Graphiques*, 213, 214; *Az Érdekes Újság*, 62–64, 99, 107; *Berliner Illustrierte Zeitung*, 122, 171; *Bifur*, 191; *Borsszem Jankó*, 20–21, 53, 63, 441n31; *Boys' Life*, 342; *Bride's Magazine*, 278; *British Journal of Photography*, 351; *Ce Temps-Ci*, 191; *Chicago Daily News*, 477n77; *Chicago Tribune*, 140, 197, 292, 376; *Christian Science Monitor*, 291; *Complete Photographer*, 475n42; *Coronet*, 257–58, 274; *Creative Camera*, 324; *Das Illustrierte Blatt*, 132, 197; *Der Tog*, 134; *De Telegraaf*, 182; *Die Dame*, 148, 174, 177, 197; *Die Gartenlaube*, 328, 329; *Die Weltbühne*, 177; *Esquire*, 257, 341, 419; *Fortune* magazine, 283, 297; *Gewehr Heraus!* (soldiers' newsletter), 58; *Glamour*, 278, 296; *Holiday*, 297, 312; *Infinity*,

481n39; *Izvestia*, 208; *Jardin des Modes*, 63, 193–96, 237; *Jazz*, 191, 197; *Ladies' Home Journal*, 292, 297, 307, 309; *La France à Table*, 204, 232; *L'Art Vivant*, 174; *Le Monde*, 330, 334–35, 351, 353, 385–86, 497n90; *Les Nouvelles Littéraires*, 202, 333; *Le Soir*, 145–46; *Le Sourire*, 215, 223; *Le Sport Universel Illustré*, 132; *L'Esprit Nouveau*, 138, 139; *Le Temps*, 227; *L'Illustration*, 197; *L'Intransigeant*, 189; *Literary Digest*, 260; *Look*, 252, 278, 297, 467n15; *Mademoiselle*, 290; *Magyar Hírlap*, 132; *Magyar Jövő*, 288; *Marianne*, 204, 223; *Minicam* (later *Modern Photography*), 267, 268, 286–88, 294, 336, 473n11; *Münchner Illustrierte Presse*, 165, 174, 177, 184, 191, 192; *New York Herald Tribune*, 244; *New York* magazine, 373, 423; *New York Post*, 314; *New York Review of Books*, 379; *New York Times*, 259–60, 293, 311, 350, 360, 370, 373, 421; *Parisi Futár*, 231; *Pesti Napló*, 98, 99; *Plain-Dealer, Cleveland*, 474n24; *Popular Photography*, 259, 291, 294; *Rails de France*, 223; *Regards*, 235; *Saturday Review*, 291; *Scandale*, 232; *Show*, 344; *Stage*, 272; *Sunday Call-Chronicle*, 291; *Színházi Élet*, 104, 105, 107, 272; *Times* (London), 289; *Time* magazine, 283, 284; *Town & Country*, 272, 279; *Twin City Sentinel*, 474n24; *Uhu*, 171, 187, 458n6; *U.S. Camera*, 294, 324, 328, 330, 334, 341, 492n9; *Vanity Fair*, 121, 239, 268; *Variétés*, 191; *Village Voice*, 364; *Voilà*, 232; *Women's Wear Daily*, 381. *See also Harper's Bazaar*; *House & Garden*; *Life* magazine; *Vogue*, American; *Vogue*, British, French; *Vu*
publishers, 224–25; Abbeville Press, 414; Alfred A. Knopf, 337, 338, 371, 377; E. P. Dutton, 382; Éditions d'histoire et d'art, 225; Flammarion, 409; Grossman Publishers, 341, 349–50, 360–61, 382; Ullstein Verlag, 171, 172, 177, 220, 279; Viking, 350, 382
Purist painters, 138, 156–57, 159, 160, 427
Querelle, Louis, 215, 216, 218, 219, 223, 224

Rado, Charles, 279, 306, 327
range finders, 166, 405
Ray, Man, 161, 178, 197, 231, 238, 421; and AEAR, 235; *The Enigma of Isidore Ducasse*, 117–18; Kiki Ray and, 210; in New York, 5, 243–44; in Paris, 112, 121–22, 151, 158, 334
Rencontres Internationales de la Photographie d'Arles (now Rencontres d'Arles), 377, 393
Révai, Éva, 137, 138, 153
Révai, Ilka, 137, 451n56
Rim, Carlo, 178, 197, 216, 224
Roma people, 3, 150, 154
Romani people, 12, 60, 68–69, 21–22, 60, 435n4; and music, 21–22, 60
Rosenberg, Margit. *See* Kertész, Margit (Gréti)
Roth, Feri, and Quartet, 128–29, 450n36
Rubinstein, Helena, 236, 262

Salamon, Erzsébet, 92–98, 102, 104–8, 120, 129, 137, 153, 200–201, 445n26, 446n28; a graduate of Álmos Jaschik school, 236; married, 220, 222; opinions of, 133, 157; in Paris, 202, 205, 460n28; and Rózsi, 152. *See also* Kertész, Elizabeth
Salamon, Pepi, 92–93, 95, 108, 202, 207, 289, 310
Schad, Tennyson, 357–59, 369, 372–74, 378, 382, 395
Schwalberg, Carol, 328, 329, 330, 343
sculptors, 89, 186; Anne-Marie Merkel, 130; Gunvor Berg, 130–31, 133; Henry Moore, 219; Margit Kovács, 208; Mihail Simeonov, 425; Ossip Zadkine, 129–30; Trappist monk, 169
self-portraits, 51, 66, 91, 106, 112, 207, 222, 270; birthday, 104–5, 136–37; for Britton's *Self-Portrait: Book People Picture Themselves*, 426; Louis Ducos du Hauron and, 462n13; for mother, 36–37; in New York, 247, 272, 354; *Self-Portrait, Paris*, 1, 3, 9;

self-portraits (*cont'd*): *Self-Portrait with André Kertész in the Manner of David Hockney*, 363; *Self-Portrait with Jean Jaffe and František Reichentál*, 133–34; *Self-Portrait with Masks*, 392, 425; tripods and, 1, 2, 36, 94, 199, 247, 426; in World War I, 51–52, 56. *See also* self-timers
self-timers, 36–37, 48, 51, 57, 134, 247, 439n64
Seuphor, Michel (Louis Ferdinand Berckelaers), 122–26, 131, 133, 140, 492n9, 450n42
shutter speeds, 8, 48, 103, 115, 286, 290
Siskind, Aaron, 358, 393
Snow, Carmel, 250, 313
socialites, 194, 196, 232, 244, 298–99
Solyom, Robert, 410, 411, 412
Spanish Civil War, 255, 263
Statile, D. Richard, 262, 264, 269, 272, 279
Stavisky, Alexandre, 227, 228
Steichen, Edward, 5, 239, 252, 257, 294, 309, 326
Steiner, Anna, 151, 152
Stieglitz, Alfred, 5, 258–59, 361, 362
still lifes, 2, 112, 126, 130, 267, 383, 388–89, 405, 427; in exhibitions, 139, 256, 339
Strand, Paul, 295, 369, 387
street photography, 3–4, 135, 139, 167, 168, 208, 275, 320
Strider, Gray, 259, 260
studio photography, 122–23, 130, 142, 251, 306
subject matter, 7, 34–35, 82, 161, 261, 405; around Szigetbecse, 84–85; books, 365–67; chimney pots, 6, 157, 214, 271, 320, 321; during World War I, 37, 39–40, 59–60, 66, 71–72; the *Louise-Catherine*, 192; for magazines, 299, 342, 476n54; in New York, 253, 263, 269, 270, 307; in Paris, 131, 150, 153–54, 167, 333; of Polaroids, 388–89, 390–91; unorthodox, 36, 52, 79
Sulyok, Helén, 138, 174–75
Surrealism, 117, 160, 184, 188, 201, 277, 278, 352; AK and, 118, 334, 427; in New York, 259–60, 293
Swabians, 24, 25, 80, 303, 410
Symbolism, 210–11, 427
Szarkowski, John, 153, 326–27, 341, 344, 398, 403, 415; and AK, 340, 361, 362; *The Photographer's Eye*, 338, 481n30
Szentpál, Olga, 90, 93
Szigetbecse, Hungary, 24–25, 33–34, 93, 165, 303, 328, 410
Szőnyi Circle, 91, 427, 445n23, 451n3
Szőnyi, István, 89, 90, 101
Szűts, Ervin, 94, 95

Tamás, Frank, 262, 310, 322, 323, 324
Taro, Gerda, 255, 237–38
Teleki Tér, Budapest, 18, 19, 23, 30, 74, 281; caricature "The Prophet of Teleky Square," 89
Tihanyi, Lajos, 115, 128, 129, 152, 157, 185, 236, 302, 459n20; in America, 173, 240; as companion, 117, 131, 132, 138, 450n42; and Károlyis, 141, 142; painter, 112, 138, 150, 205
Travis, David, 416, 417, 418
tripods, 40, 57, 89, 121, 133, 167, 192, 387; AK's in military service, 48, 57; and handheld camera, 82, 104, 123; and long exposures, 115, 196; as part of equipment, 135, 203, 283, 300, 367, 397, 416; pawned, 279, 284; in portraits, 146, 173, 386; in self-portraits, 1, 2, 36, 51, 94, 199, 247, 426; and self-timer, 36, 51, 247; set up ready for the right moment, 226, 229, 307, 320, 348; in Szigetbecse, 33–34; used for the Distortions, 217, 411
tritanopia (blue-yellow color blindness), 28–29, 102, 300
Tzara, Tristan, 2, 130, 139

Venice Photography Biennale, 325, 330, 492n9
Verackhatz, Najinskaya, 216, 218
Vertès, Marcel, 63, 164, 215
Vestal, David, 312, 339, 428
Vichy France, 191, 335
viewfinders, 12, 34, 35, 82, 120, 173, 218, 321, 426; ground-glass, 267; peephole, 167; in self-portrait, 426; in SLR cameras, 405; split-image screen, 166; top-down, 115

vintage prints, 325, 327, 378, 379–80, 406, 414, 422–23; prices of, 395–96, 489n55; in retrospectives, 416–17, 497n90; exhibition *Vintage Photographs of Hungary, 1912–25*, 401–2
Vogel, Lucien, 172, 184, 193–94, 236, 242, 277, 278, 295–96; and AK, 170, 177, 196; and Friedman, 231, 238; and photographers, 168, 171; and *Vu*, 162–63, 164, 470n63
*Vogue*, American, 239, 241, 251, 256–57, 272, 273, 277–78, 290; AK and, 260, 290, 297, 360, 468n34, 476n54; Alexander Liberman at, 296–97, 314, 315; and *House & Garden*, 298, 313; and other photographers, 287, 294, 314, 316, 337. *See also Vogue*, British, French
*Vogue*: British, 290; French, 163, 188, 194, 223, 232, 237, 287. *See also Vogue*, American
*Vu*, 192, 197, 209, 223, 228, 231, 236, 295, 296; and AK, 169, 192, 204, 206–7, 224, 230, 233; and Alexey Brodovitch, 250; assignments for, 164, 165, 176, 195, 197, 455n44; Brassaï and, 185, 237; Carlo Rim as editor in chief, 216; *Life* and, 268, 269; and marionettists, 174; a new picture weekly, 162–64; and photographers' rights, 170, 171, 172; and Robert Capa, 238; and the Spanish Civil War, 242

Washington Square, New York, 5, 284, 305, 307, 371, 419, 443n49; book project *Washington Square*, 370, 382; *Washington Square, Winter*, 307–8, 478n78
Wehn-Damisch, Teri, 410, 411
Weston, Edward, 249, 421
Wheeler, Monroe, 320, 326
Witkin, Lee, 357, 358, 360, 396, 397, 414
Wittmann, René, 239, 242, 332, 334, 337
World War I, 33, 52, 79, 139–40, 148, 263; AK awarded the Second Class Silver Medal for Bravery, 55; in Esztergom, 59–60, 68, 73; *The Eternal Tender Touch*, 51, 440n11; *Forced March to the Front*, 44, 47, 48–49, 347; in Gorizia, Italy, 36–38, 40; Private First-Class, 7, 54; service as escort and courier, 65, 66, 67, 71; 26th Joint Regiment, 40, 45, 48; wounded, 55, 56
World War II, 211, 452n7, 463n33

Zilzer, Gyula, 116, 123, 138, 259

**Patricia Albers** is a San Francisco Bay Area–based writer, editor, and art historian. She is the author of *Joan Mitchell, Lady Painter: A Life*, the acclaimed first biography of the abstract painter. Her previous books include *Shadows, Fire, Snow: The Life of Tina Modotti* and *Tina Modotti and the Mexican Renaissance*. Albers's essays, art reviews, and articles have appeared in numerous publications. She has taught the history of photography and has served as a panelist for the National Endowment for the Humanities and a juror for the Biographers International Organization Plutarch Award.